Microsoft® SQL Server™ 7.0 DBA Survival Guide

Mark Spenik, Orryn Sledge, Kari Fernandez,
Laura Herb, Troy D. Rackley, Kevin Viers,
Ann Yagerline, and Michael Yocca

SAMS

A Division of Macmillan Computer Publishing
201 West 103rd St., Indianapolis, Indiana, 46290 USA

MICROSOFT® SQL SERVER™ 7.0 DBA SURVIVAL GUIDE

Copyright © 1999 by Sams Publishing

International Standard Book Number: 0-672-31226-3

Library of Congress Catalog Card Number: 97-69134

Printed in the United States of America

First Printing: January, 1999

01   00   7   6   5

Trademarks

Warning and Disclaimer

Executive Editor
Rosemarie Graham

Acquisitions Editor
Rosemarie Graham

Development Editor
Rosemarie Graham

Managing Editor
Jodi Jensen

Project Editors
Susan Ross Moore
Heather Talbot

Copy Editor
Sydney Jones

Indexer
Cheryl Landes

Proofreader
Cynthia Fields

Technical Editor
Matt Larson

Software Development Specialist
Michael Hunter

Team Coordinator
Carol Ackerman

Interior and Cover Design
Ann Jones

Layout Technicians
Ayanna Lacey
Heather Miller
Amy Parker

OVERVIEW

CONTENTS

PART IV   DATABASE OPERATION   141

7   ENTERPRISE MANAGEMENT PROCESSES   143

11   USING BCP   303

PART VII   ADVANCED DBA TOPICS   657

ABOUT THE AUTHORS

LEAD AUTHORS

Orryn Sledge is a Principal Consultant with Xerox Connect in Pittsburgh, Pennsylvania. He specializes in developing Internet and client/server applications with Microsoft SQL Server, Oracle, Visual Studio, Visual Basic, PowerBuilder, and other popular development tools. He has been actively involved with SQL Server consulting since 1992 and is a Microsoft Certified Solution Developer (MCSD). Orryn is also a frequent speaker at various Microsoft conferences and presentations. He can be reached at orryn.sledge@connect.xerox.com.

Mark Spenik is the Manager of Enterprise Technologies at Keiter, Stephens Computer Services, Inc. located in Richmond, Virginia. Mark, a graduate of George Mason University in Fairfax, Virginia, entered the computer industry in 1985. He has designed and coded large-scale applications and has consulted with numerous firms in application development, implementation, and migration. He has a broad programming background, including assembly language, C, C++, HTML, Active Server Pages, and Visual Basic. Mark is a Microsoft Certified Solution Developer and charter member, and is frequently invited to speak at various developer conferences and seminars. Mark has co-authored and contributed to several books on Visual Basic and SQL Server development. Mark can be reached via the Internet at mspenik@kscsinc.com.

Contributing Authors

Kari A. Fernandez is an Enterprise Technologies consultant for Keiter, Stephens Computer Services, Inc. in Richmond, Virginia. In 1994 she graduated from Virginia Commonwealth University's School of Business with a bachelor's in Information Systems. Since graduation she has specialized in developing database-driven applications for the Web. Kari employs the use of Microsoft's Windows NT Server, Internet Information Server, and SQL Server, as well as Visual Studio software, as the Web development foundation. Kari has succeeded in rapidly developing small Internet and intranet Web applications and has participated in team development of larger-scale Web applications. She assists clients in conceptualizing and analyzing their strategies for Web site architecture and database design. Her expertise in Web site development combines this and the use of Active Server Pages, the ActiveX Data Object model, and SQL Server along with other Web technologies such as VBScript, JavaScript, HTML, and Dynamic HTML. She has also worked with clients in setting up Web development and production site security and version control as well as determining the client's development to production process. Thanks to the tireless support of her husband, Tony, and two children,

Jon Erik and Patrick, Kari has been able to fulfill a long-held goal of writing professionally.

Laura Herb is a consultant in the Richmond metro area of Virginia. She is employed with Keiter, Stephens Computer Services, Inc., which has been recently recognized as one of the top 500 fastest growing IT consulting firms in the United States. She is currently consulting full time as a SQL Server Database Administrator for a Fortune Five company.

Troy D. Rackley is a consultant with the Enterprise Technologies group of Keiter, Stephens Computer Services, Inc. Troy is a Microsoft Certified Solution Developer (MCSD) who always tries to stay one step ahead of the cutting edge. He currently specializes in n-tiered enterprise Web solutions for your local intranet. He was a contributing author of the *Web Database Developer's Guide with Visual Basic 5*. Troy lives with his wife Annette in Richmond, Virginia; he can be reached by email at `trackley@erols.com`.

Kevin Viers is the Manager of the Enterprise Technologies group at Keiter, Stephens Computer Services, Inc. and a graduate of James Madison University. He has over five years of consulting experience specializing in designing, developing, and implementing enterprise solutions. Kevin cut his programming teeth on PowerBuilder and has since developed a broad development background including SAP, Active Server Pages, and Visual Basic. Kevin lives with his wife, Pam, and his boxer, Alli, in Richmond, Virginia. He can be reached via the Internet at `kviers@kscsinc.com`.

Anne Yagerline is a senior engineer in client/server development at IKON Technology Services in McLean, Virginia. She develops Windows- and Web-based client/server applications for firms located in the Washington, DC metropolitan area. Anne is a Microsoft Certified Solution Developer (MCSD), with over three years experience with Microsoft SQL Server in particular. Anne can be reached via email at `yagerlin@erols.com`.

Michael Yocca is a SQL Server and ERwin consultant in the Pittsburgh area, specializing in quality database design. He is Microsoft certified with SQL 6.5 and is a regular contributor to the *Pinnacle SQL Professional* magazine.

DEDICATION

This book is dedicated to my two wonderful daughters, Abigail and Emma.

Orryn Sledge

To the person I admire most—my father, John Spenik.

Mark Spenik

ACKNOWLEDGMENTS

I would like to thank my wife and my two daughters for putting up with another book! I would also like to say thanks to Mark Spenik for helping make this book a reality, Gary Renzi for keeping me up to date with SQL Server material, the SQL Server development team at Microsoft for answering questions, Matt Larson for doing a great job with technical edits, Rosemarie Graham and everyone else at Macmillan for keeping the project on track, Mike Yocca for helping out at the last minute, and to everyone who provided feedback on the previous edition of the book.

Orryn Sledge

I want to thank my wife and best friend Lisa for her patience and support while enduring the rigors of writing a book, and my daughter Hope for the comic relief. To my family: Bonnie, John, Denise, David, Kim, Adam, Chris, Gary, Debbie, Lisa, David, and all my nieces and nephews (whose numbers are steadily increasing), thanks for the support! To the Meyer (Sam, Marge, and Jonathan) and the Rimes (Denise and Pat) families for all of their encouragement. To my father John and my late mother Anna Jane for being such remarkable role models.

Mark Spenik

MARK'S AND ORRYN'S ACKNOWLEDGMENTS

We would like to thank Rosemarie Graham and the entire staff at Macmillan Computer Publishing, not only for producing this edition of the *DBA Survival Guide*, but also for all the hard work they have personally put in on this edition and on the previous editions to produce a great series of books.

Special thanks to our contributing authors who have helped to make this a better book.

TELL US WHAT YOU THINK!

As the reader of this book, *you* are our most important critic and commentator. We value your opinion and want to know what we're doing right, what we could do better, what areas you'd like to see us publish in, and any other words of wisdom you're willing to pass our way.

As the Executive Editor for the Database team at Macmillan Computer Publishing, I welcome your comments. You can fax, email, or write me directly to let me know what you did or didn't like about this book—as well as what we can do to make our books stronger.

Please note that I cannot help you with technical problems related to the topic of this book, and that due to the high volume of mail I receive, I might not be able to reply to every message.

When you write, please be sure to include this book's title and author as well as your name and phone or fax number. I will carefully review your comments and share them with the author and editors who worked on the book.

Fax:	317-817-7070
Email:	databases@mcp.com
Mail:	Rosemarie Graham
	Executive Editor
	Database Team
	Macmillan Computer Publishing
	201 West 103rd Street
	Indianapolis, IN 46290 USA

INTRODUCTION

Welcome to the third edition of the *Microsoft SQL Server DBA Survival Guide*! Not only is SQL Server 7.0 the best RDBMS ever released by Microsoft, I think you'll find that this is the best and most complete edition of the *Microsoft SQL Server DBA Survival Guide*! If you have read the 6.0 or 6.5 edition, I think you'll notice many new features and improvements in the book. Many of the improvements have been ideas and suggestions given to us by our readers either via email or on-site DBA engagements. In this edition, we have added several step-by-step exercises that actually walk you through real-world DBA scenarios such as performing back up and recoveries or merge replication conflict resolution. We have also added a Frequently Asked Questions (FAQ) section at the end of each technical chapter to try to answer common questions that we have received via email or while working with the product ourselves. For those of you familiar with SQL Server 6.x, we have added a section at the front of each chapter that outlines which 6.x features are gone and what's new with SQL Server 7.0. We also decided to get some help from contributing authors on some of the new SQL Server 7.0 features, which allowed us to focus on some of the core topics while allowing others to focus on a single topic to bring you a better survival guide.

We really do appreciate the emails, feedback, and praise we have received from the previous editions. Keep them coming!

Mark Spenik and Orryn Sledge

THE GOALS OF THIS BOOK

Managing a Microsoft SQL Server 7.0 is quite different from managing previous versions of SQL Server. For starters, you have the new MMC (Microsoft Management Console) and lots and lots of new wizards. SQL Server is now capable of running on the desktop all the way up to an Enterprise Server with a Terrabyte database. The trick to becoming a good Microsoft DBA is to become familiar with the graphical front-end, to understand what happens behind the scenes (that is, what happens when you push a particular button), and to have a good understanding of the product and your job. The goals of this book are as follows:

- To provide the knowledge and know-how to administer a SQL Server database
- To appeal to all levels of DBAs: beginner, intermediate, and experienced
- To appeal to all levels of developers: beginner, intermediate, and experienced
- To offer any tips, tricks, and suggestions buried deep within the documentation

- To offer real-world insight and experience and to pass on any tips, tricks, or suggestions learned the hard way
- To provide checklists and examples for SQL Server DBA tasks
- To provide conventions and naming standards
- To provide a quick reference from 6.x to 7.0
- To provide insight into the tasks that make up a DBA's job description

THE ORGANIZATION OF THE BOOK

The book is organized into several parts that comprise the various jobs and tasks the DBA performs.

Part I, "Introduction," is an overall introductory section that includes the following chapters.

For DBAs new to the world of enterprise computing, Chapter 1, "Introduction to Client/Server Database Computing," provides an overview of general client/server concepts. It explains what client/server really means. (All vendors seem to attach the term client/server to their products, even when it really does not meet the definition of client/server.) This chapter also explains the benefits of client/server computing compared to other types of computing (such as mainframe and PC/file server). Not sure what a DBA is or what the responsibilities of a DBA are? Chapter 2, "The Role of the Database Administrator," is for you.

Part II, "The World of Microsoft's SQL Server," is a high-level overview. Chapter 3, "The Evolution of SQL Server," discusses enhancements made to SQL Server 7.0. Chapter 4, "SQL Server Overview," details how SQL Server integrates with Windows NT and also explains the benefits of SQL Server being tightly integrated with Windows NT—and how this integration helps differentiate the product from its competitors.

Part III, "Installing and Upgrading SQL Server," does just what its title suggests. Chapter 5, "Planning an Installation or Upgrade," covers the planning steps required before you attempt a SQL Server upgrade or installation. Do you have all your bases covered in the event an upgrade fails? This chapter covers this topic and many more. Chapter 6 discusses installation and upgrade.

Part IV, "Database Operation," is the largest section of the book and includes chapters about many of the functions you will perform as a DBA.

Chapter 7, "Enterprise Management Processes," provides a high-level explanation of the types of tasks that can be performed through the Enterprise Manager. Chapter 8, "Database Management," explains how to create, manage, and delete a database.

The chapter includes a discussion about transaction logs and data files. Chapter 9, "Managing SQL Server Users and Security," discusses user management and data security, which are quite different from previous versions of SQL Server.

Curious how to use your backups to recover a database? Wonder how SQL Server 7.0 has simplified the backup and recovery process? What happens if a database fails after a backup? Can you provide up-to-the-minute recovery? These are standard questions all new DBAs are faced with. See Chapter 10, "Backup and Restore."

Can't get BCP to work? You're not alone—almost every DBA hits a snag or two when trying to work with BCP. Chapter 11, "Using BCP," discusses in detail how BCP works and provides numerous tips and examples on how to make BCP work.

Wondering what distributed transactions are all about and how to administer them with SQL Server 7.0? See Chapter 12, "Distributed Transaction Coordinator."

Have you heard about Microsoft English Query? Wouldn't it be great to join an Oracle table with an Access table with a SQL Server table without exporting and importing the data? Well, with 7.0 it's called a distributed query and you can learn more in Chapter 14, "Miscellaneous Topics and New SQL Server Utilities."

Part V, "Replication," covers all the replication features of SQL Server 7.0.

Not sure what Microsoft SQL Server's replication is all about? Having trouble installing the distribution database? Not sure what an updating subscriber is? Want to learn how to create disconnected applications using 2-way merge replication? Want to know what the difference between one way and two replication is? The *DBA Survival Guide* has you covered with three chapters dedicated to SQL Server 7.0 replication—Chapters 15, "Replication," 16, "Transactional Replication," and 17, "Snapshot and Merge Replication."

What would a database book be without a section on performance and tuning? "Part VI, "Performance and Tuning," fills that role. Having performance problems with SQL Server? Look at Chapter 18, "SQL Server Internals—Changes and Enhancements." SQL Server provides numerous tools to help diagnose and isolate bottlenecks. The secret is knowing how to effectively use these tools. For example, the Performance Monitor enables you to monitor more than 40 different SQL Server counters and several hundred different operating system counters. Which counters do you look at? Chapter 18 guides you in the right direction if you are wondering which Performance Monitor counters you should analyze. The chapter also discusses how to monitor user activity, a feature that has been extensively enhanced in version 6.5.

Need to configure SQL Server? Well, not really with SQL Server 7.0, but there are still a few knobs to turn; check out Chapter 20, "Configuring and Tuning SQL Server." Chapter 21, "Database Design Issues," provides information on database design issues. Do indexes have you all tangled up? If so, don't miss Chapters 21 and 22.

Chapter 23, "Query Optimization," explains in easy-to-understand vernacular the inner workings of SQL Server's cost-based optimizer. When transactions are slow to process or you are experiencing blocking or deadlocks, you will want to refer to the tips and tricks in this chapter. Knowing how to read a showplan is a key element to diagnosing query performance problems. The hard part about reading a showplan is knowing what to look for because lots of cryptic information is generated. This chapter explains what to look for in the output generated by a showplan, what the output really means, and how to improve performance based on showplan information.

I think every DBA has seen an application that runs fine when a single user is logged in to the system, but when multiple users log on, the system bogs down. With multi-user applications, issues such as blocking and deadlocks must be addressed. Chapter 24, "Multi-User Considerations," offers solutions that can reduce the headaches associated with a multi-user system. Be sure to read up on the SQL Server 7.0 new dynamic locking feature.

Part VII, "Advanced DBA Topics," covers many advanced issues and skills required for a Microsoft DBA including special skills required for Microsoft DBA certification.

Do you want to learn more about stored procedures and cursors? Look at Chapter 26, "Using Stored Procedures and Cursors." This chapter provides a detailed discussion on these two topics and includes several examples the DBA can use to automate common tasks. Don't know SQL very well? See Chapter 25, "SQL Essentials."

What would a book be now without a chapter on the Internet? See Chapter 28, "SQL Server 7.0 and the Internet," to learn how to use Microsoft SQL Server to create Web pages for you.

Part VIII, "Automating Maintenance and Administration Tasks," discusses topics that enable you to make your job easier by automating your administrative tasks.

Chapter 29, "Developing a SQL Server Maintenance Plan," explains why maintenance should be periodically performed on SQL Server and the Windows NT operating system. In addition to explaining why you should perform maintenance, the chapter provides step-by-step instructions on how to maintain the system.

After reading Chapter 30, "Automating Database Administration Tasks," you will want to automate several of the maintenance tasks discussed in the chapter. Chapter 30 explains how to automate common DBA jobs through the use of two core components of SQL Server: Task Scheduler and Alert Manager. Graphical automation and advanced features such as email and pager notification are two examples of how these components can help simplify a DBA's life.

You already know that OLE is included with SQL Server, but what can you do with it? Chapter 27, "Using SQL-DMO (Distributed Management Objects)," walks through the construction of an application that helps simplify database administration tasks using Visual Basic.

Part IX, "Data Warehousing," introduces you to the data warehousing and the OLAP services that are part of SQL Server 7.0. New for SQL Server 7.0 is data warehousing. Not sure what data warehousing is or unfamiliar with the data warehousing terminology? See Chapter 31, "Introduction to Data Warehousing." Need to get information from other systems into your data warehouse? Check out Chapter 32, "Using Data Transformation Services (DTS)," on SQL Server 7.0 Data Transformation Services. And above all, look into Chapter 33, "Introduction to Microsoft SQL Server OLAP Services," using the Microsoft OLAP services.

The appendixes in Part X provide valuable information too. Don't overlook the helpfulness of the appendixes

CONVENTIONS USED IN THIS BOOK

The following conventions are used in this book:

The `computer font` is used for commands, parameters, statements, and text you see onscreen.

A **`boldfaced computer font`** indicates text you type.

Italics indicate new terms or items of emphasis.

NOTE

Notes provide additional information pertinent to the current subject matter.

TIP

Tips offer useful hints and information.

CAUTION

Caution boxes present warnings and describe the consequences of particular actions.

STRANGER THAN FICTION!

Some say that truth is stranger than fiction. These boxes offer fun facts to know and tell that are stranger than fiction!

The quick reference sections have the following format:

SQL SERVER 6.5 TO 7.0 QUICK REFERENCE

What's New

What's Renamed

What's Gone

The FAQs have the following format:

TOPIC FAQ

Q. Question

A. Answer

INTRODUCTION

PART

I

IN THIS PART

INTRODUCTION TO CLIENT/SERVER DATABASE COMPUTING

by Orryn Sledge

IN THIS CHAPTER

Client/server (C/S) database computing is the standard for most corporate computing. Corporations are using C/S database computing for core business applications such as H/R, accounting, and manufacturing. Corporations are also using C/S database computing for Internet/intranet applications and for custom development. As you can see, C/S database computing has become very popular in recent years. To understand the reasons behind the success of C/S database computing, it helps to understand the other common types of database computing: mainframe and PC/file server.

MAINFRAME DATABASE COMPUTING

Before the late '80s and early '90s, *mainframe computing* was about the only computer choice for organizations that required heavy-duty processing and support for a large number of users. Mainframes have been in existence for over 20 years. Their reliability has led to their longevity. The ability of mainframes to support a large number of concurrent users while maintaining a fast database retrieval time contributed to corporate acceptance of mainframes.

Mainframe computing, also called *host-based computing*, refers to all processing carried out on the mainframe computer. The mainframe computer is responsible for running the Relational Database Management System (RDBMS), managing the application that accesses the RDBMS, and handling communications between the mainframe computer and dumb terminals. A *dumb terminal* is about as intelligent as its name implies; it is limited to displaying text and accepting data from the user. The application does not run on the dumb terminal; instead, it runs on the mainframe and is echoed back to the user through the terminal (see Figure 1.1).

FIGURE 1.1
Mainframe database computing.

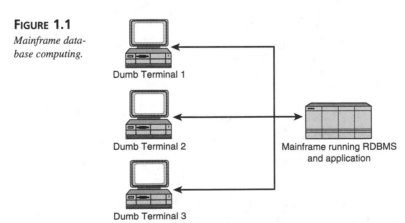

Dumb Terminal 1

Dumb Terminal 2

Mainframe running RDBMS and application

Dumb Terminal 3

The main drawback of mainframe computing is that it is very expensive. Operating a mainframe computer can run into the millions of dollars. Mainframes are expensive to operate because they require specialized operational facilities, demand extensive support, and do not use common computer components. Additionally, the idea of paying thousands of dollars to rent software that runs on the mainframe is almost inconceivable for PC users who have never used mainframe technology.

Rather than use common components, mainframes typically use hardware and software proprietary to the mainframe manufacturer. This proprietary approach can lock a customer into a limited selection of components from one vendor.

PC/FILE SERVER DATABASE COMPUTING

PC/file server-based computing became popular in the corporate environment during the mid to late '80s when business users began to turn to the PC as an alternative to the mainframe. Users liked the ease with which they could develop their own applications through the use of fourth-generation languages (4GL) such as dBASE III+. These 4GL languages provided easy-to-use report writers and user-friendly programming languages.

PC/file server computing is when the PC runs both the application and the RDBMS. Users are typically connected to the file server through a LAN. The PC is responsible for RDBMS processing, and the file server provides a centralized storage area for accessing shared data (see Figure 1.2).

FIGURE 1.2
*PC/file server
database
computing.*

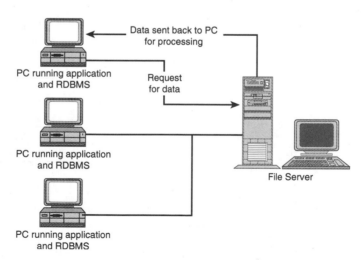

The drawback of PC-based computing is that all RDBMS processing is done on the local PC. When a query is made to the file server, the file server does not process the query. Instead, it returns the data required to process the query. For example, when a user makes a request to view all customers in the state of Virginia, the file server might return all the records in the customer table to the local PC. In turn, the local PC has to extract the customers that live in the state of Virginia. Because the RDBMS runs on the local PC and not on the server, the file server does not have the intelligence to process queries. This can result in decreased performance and increased network bottlenecks.

THE ADVENT OF CLIENT/SERVER DATABASE COMPUTING

C/S database computing evolved in response to the drawbacks of the mainframe and PC/file server computing environments. By combining the processing power of the mainframe and the flexibility and price of the PC, C/S database computing encompasses the best of both worlds (see Figure 1.3).

FIGURE 1.3
Client/server database computing.

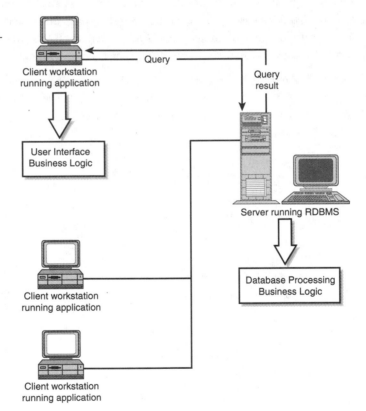

C/S database computing can be defined as the logical partitioning of the user interface, database management, and business logic between the client computer and the server computer. The network links each of these processes.

The *client computer*, also called a *workstation*, controls the user interface. The client is where text and images are displayed to the user and where the user inputs data. The user interface can be text based or graphical based.

The server computer controls database management. The server is where data is stored, manipulated, and retrieved. In the C/S database environment, all database processing occurs on the server.

Business logic can be located on the server, on the client, or mixed between the two. This type of logic governs the processing of the application.

In the typical corporate environment, the server computer is connected to multiple client computers. The server computer is a high-powered computer dedicated to running the RDBMS. The client workstations are usually PC based. The client computer and database server communicate through a common network protocol that enables them to share information.

WHY CLIENT/SERVER DATABASE COMPUTING IS THE ANSWER

Many corporations have turned to client/server database computing as their computing answer. Following are some of the underlying reasons for its popularity:

- **Affordability**: C/S database computing can be less expensive than mainframe computing. The underlying reason is simple: C/S database computing is based on an open architecture, which allows more vendors to produce competing products, which drives the cost down. This is unlike mainframe-based systems, which typically use proprietary components available only through a single vendor. Also, C/S workstations and servers are often PC based. PC prices have fallen dramatically over the years, which has led to reduced C/S computing costs.

- **Speed**: The separation of processing between the client and the server reduces network bottlenecks, and allows a C/S database system to deliver mainframe performance while exceeding PC/file server performance.

- **Adaptability**: The C/S database computing architecture is more open than the proprietary mainframe architecture. Therefore, it is possible to build an application by selecting an RDBMS from one vendor, hardware from another vendor, and development software from yet another vendor. Customers can select components that best fit their needs.

- **Simplified data access**: C/S database computing makes data available to the masses. Mainframe computing was notorious for tracking huge amounts of data that could be accessed only by developers. With C/S database computing, data access is not limited to those who understand procedural programming languages (which are difficult to learn and require specialized data access knowledge). Instead, data access is provided by common software product tools that hide the complexities of data access. Word processing, spreadsheet, and reporting software are just a few of the common packages that provide simplified access to C/S data.

N-TIER COMPUTING: THE HOME FOR BUSINESS LOGIC

A third component of the C/S database-computing environment is the placement of business logic. As previously mentioned, *business logic* is the rule that governs the processing of the application.

A recent trend in C/S computing is to encapsulate business logic as a component in a separate tier. This tier is commonly referred to as 3-tier or N-tier computing (see Figure 1.4). Conventional C/S computing is commonly referred to as 2-tier computing. N-tier computing provides the following advantages over 2-tier computing:

- centralized business logic
- improved performance (commonly referred to as scalability)
- improved security

FIGURE 1.4

N-tier architecture.

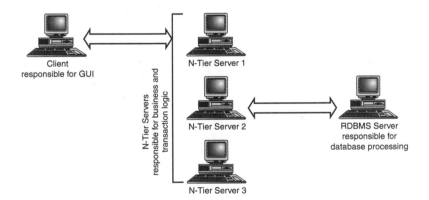

Client
responsible for GUI

N-Tier Servers responsible for business and transaction logic

N-Tier Server 1

N-Tier Server 2

N-Tier Server 3

RDBMS Server responsible for database processing

Alternatives to N-tier computing include *fat servers* or *fat clients*. A *fat server* locates business logic within the RDBMS on the server (see Figure 1.5). The client issues remote procedure calls to the server to execute the process. Fat servers are best suited for structured and consistent business logic, such as online transaction processing (OLTP). Modern RDBMS products support fat servers through stored procedures, column rules, triggers, and other methods.

FIGURE 1.5

A fat server.

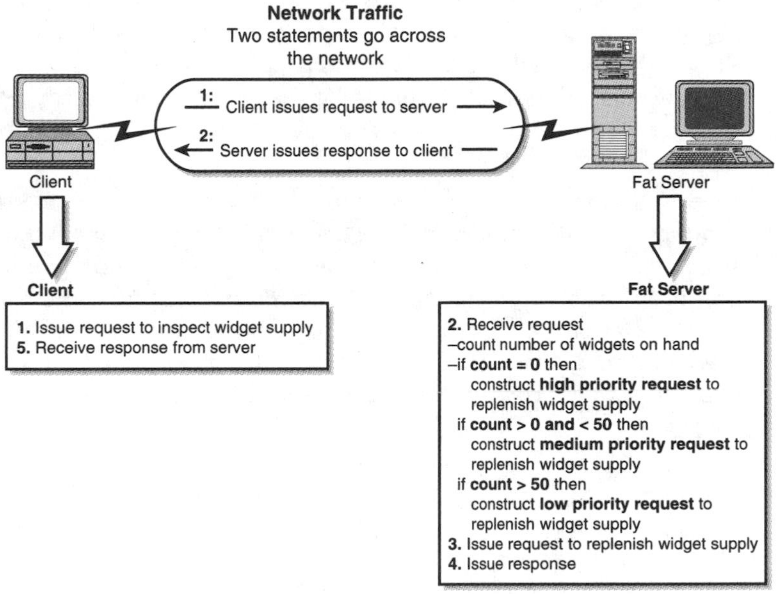

Network Traffic
Two statements go across the network

1: Client issues request to server
2: Server issues response to client

Client

Fat Server

Client
1. Issue request to inspect widget supply
5. Receive response from server

Fat Server
2. Receive request
– count number of widgets on hand
– if **count = 0** then
    construct **high priority request** to replenish widget supply
  if **count > 0 and < 50** then
    construct **medium priority request** to replenish widget supply
  if **count > 50** then
    construct **low priority request** to replenish widget supply
3. Issue request to replenish widget supply
4. Issue response

A *fat client* embeds business logic in the application at the client level (see Figure 1.6). Although a fat client is more flexible than a fat server, it increases network traffic. The fat client approach is used when business logic is loosely structured or when it is too complicated to implement at the middle-tier level. Additionally, fat client development tools, such as 4GL languages, sometimes offer more robust programming features than do middle-tier programming tools. Decision support and ad-hoc systems are often fat client based.

A *mixed environment* partitions business logic between the server, client and/or a middle tier (see Figure 1.7). For practical reasons, an application might have to implement this approach. This balancing act is a common approach with C/S database computing.

MOVING TO THE WEB AND N-TIER

Over the last couple of years, applications have been moved from a conventional 2-tier design to the Web and N-tier based design. For many systems, this is a natural extension of new technology.

An example of moving to the Web and N-tier is a mortgage banking application that I discussed in previous editions of this book. Originally, this application was mainframe based. The application was converted to Visual Basic and SQL Server during the early '90s. Recently, the application was converted to run on the Web with an N-tier architecture using the following Microsoft technology: Microsoft Transaction Server (MTS), SQL Server, Internet Information Server (IIS), and Active Server Pages (ASP).

I found that moving to the Web and N-tier computing from a 2-tier architecture requires some re-engineering. Dealing with Web programming tools, distributed logic, and a stateless environment is a different programming paradigm. This programming paradigm felt uncomfortable at first, but over time, I grew to like it. After becoming comfortable with this technology, the following benefits were obtained: improved scalability, ability to tap into data through the browser, and improved information sharing.

FIGURE **1.6**

A fat client.

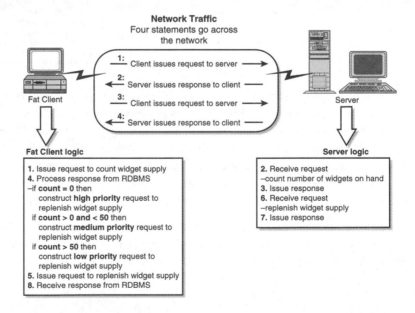

Network Traffic
Four statements go across the network

1: Client issues request to server
2: Server issues response to client
3: Client issues request to server
4: Server issues response to client

Fat Client

Server

Fat Client logic

1. Issue request to count widget supply
4. Process response from RDBMS
   –if **count = 0** then
     construct **high priority** request to replenish widget supply
   if **count > 0 and < 50** then
     construct **medium priority** request to replenish widget supply
   if **count > 50** then
     construct **low priority** request to replenish widget supply
5. Issue request to replenish widget supply
8. Receive response from RDBMS

Server logic

2. Receive request
   –count number of widgets on hand
3. Issue response
6. Receive request
   –replenish widget supply
7. Issue response

FIGURE 1.7

A mixed environment.

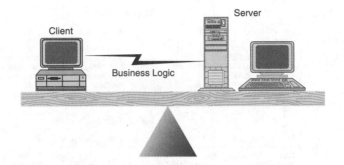

RDBMS: THE STANDARD DATABASE FOR CLIENT/SERVER COMPUTING

RDBMS (Relational Database Management System) has become the standard for C/S database computing. Database software vendors and corporate IS departments have rapidly adapted the RDBMS architecture. It is based on the relational model that originated in papers published by Dr. E.F. Codd in 1969. In an RDBMS, data is organized in a row/column manner and is stored in a table. Records are called *rows* and fields are called *columns* (see Figure 1.8).

FIGURE 1.8

Row and column layout in a relational model.

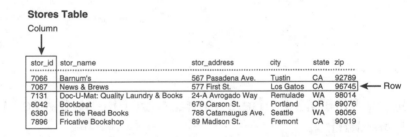

Data is structured using relationships among data items. A *relationship* is a link between tables (see Figure 1.9); relationships allow flexibility of the presentation and manipulation of data.

FIGURE **1.9**

*Relationships
among data items
in a relational
model.*

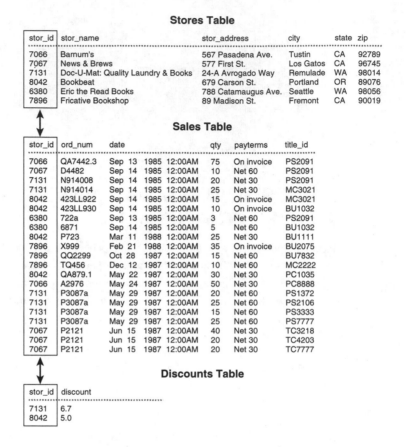

Stores Table

stor_id	stor_name	stor_address	city	state	zip
7066	Barnum's	567 Pasadena Ave.	Tustin	CA	92789
7067	News & Brews	577 First St.	Los Gatos	CA	96745
7131	Doc-U-Mat: Quality Laundry & Books	24-A Avrogado Way	Remulade	WA	98014
8042	Bookbeat	679 Carson St.	Portland	OR	89076
6380	Eric the Read Books	788 Catamaugus Ave.	Seattle	WA	98056
7896	Fricative Bookshop	89 Madison St.	Fremont	CA	90019

Sales Table

stor_id	ord_num	date	qty	payterms	title_id
7066	QA7442.3	Sep 13 1985 12:00AM	75	On invoice	PS2091
7067	D4482	Sep 14 1985 12:00AM	10	Net 60	PS2091
7131	N914008	Sep 14 1985 12:00AM	20	Net 30	PS2091
7131	N914014	Sep 14 1985 12:00AM	25	Net 30	MC3021
8042	423LL922	Sep 14 1985 12:00AM	15	On invoice	MC3021
8042	423LL930	Sep 14 1985 12:00AM	10	On invoice	BU1032
6380	722a	Sep 13 1985 12:00AM	3	Net 60	PS2091
6380	6871	Sep 14 1985 12:00AM	5	Net 60	BU1032
8042	P723	Mar 11 1988 12:00AM	25	Net 30	BU1111
7896	X999	Feb 21 1988 12:00AM	35	On invoice	BU2075
7896	QQ2299	Oct 28 1987 12:00AM	15	Net 60	BU7832
7896	TQ456	Dec 12 1987 12:00AM	10	Net 60	MC2222
8042	QA879.1	May 22 1987 12:00AM	30	Net 30	PC1035
7066	A2976	May 24 1987 12:00AM	50	Net 30	PC8888
7131	P3087a	May 29 1987 12:00AM	20	Net 60	PS1372
7131	P3087a	May 29 1987 12:00AM	25	Net 60	PS2106
7131	P3087a	May 29 1987 12:00AM	15	Net 60	PS3333
7131	P3087a	May 29 1987 12:00AM	25	Net 60	PS7777
7067	P2121	Jun 15 1987 12:00AM	40	Net 30	TC3218
7067	P2121	Jun 15 1987 12:00AM	20	Net 30	TC4203
7067	P2121	Jun 15 1987 12:00AM	20	Net 30	TC7777

Discounts Table

stor_id	discount
7131	6.7
8042	5.0

Why RDBMS Is the Standard in Client/Server Database Computing

The RDBMS has become the standard in client/server database computing for the following reasons:

- **Data integrity**: The primary goal of the relational model is *data integrity*. Data integrity prevents incorrect or invalid data from being stored. In an RDBMS, data integrity can be implemented at the server level rather than the application level. This approach offers the advantage of centralized control. When data integrity is changed at the RDBMS level, it is automatically represented at the application level, ensuring consistency and alleviating the need to modify application logic. For example, a data integrity constraint states that the `ship_to_state` for a customer's order must be a valid two-digit state code. Whenever `ship_to_state` data is entered or updated, it is checked against a list of valid state codes. If an invalid state code is entered, the RDBMS prevents the data from being saved.

- **Structured Query Language** (SQL, pronounced *sequel*): IBM developed the SQL language during the mid-1970s. The SQL language provides a common method for accessing and manipulating data in a relational database. RDBMS vendors have adapted this common language as an industry standard. The standardization of SQL enables someone to move to a new RDBMS without having to learn a new data access language.

> **NOTE**
>
> SQL is not 100 percent the same from product to product. For example, SQL Server has its own brand of SQL called Transact-SQL, and Oracle has its brand of SQL called PL/SQL. The core SQL language is similar in the two products, but each vendor has implemented SQL extensions to their products. These extensions are usually not the same between products. Fortunately, most database products are ANSI compliant, but there are different ANSI levels of compliance. The current ANSI standard is SQL-92. SQL Server 7.0 is ANSI SQL-92 compliant. This means that if you stick with ANSI style SQL, you will be able to port your SQL code and knowledge between different products.

- **Flexibility**: Modifications can be made to the structure of the database without having to recompile or shut down and restart the database. New tables can be created on the fly and existing tables can be modified without affecting the operation of the RDBMS.
- **Efficient data storage**: Through a process called *normalization* (see Chapter 21, "Database Design Issues," for more information), redundant data is reduced. Normalization is a primary concept of the relational model.
- **Security**: Data security can be implemented at the RDBMS level rather than the application level. As with data integrity, this approach offers the advantage of centralized control at the database level as opposed to the application level.

WHO ARE THE POPULAR RDBMS VENDORS?

The number of RDBMS vendors has increased over the years as C/S has grown in popularity. Although each vendor's database product stems from the relational model, vendors take different approaches to implementing it. These differences—combined with price, performance, operating systems supported, and a host of other items—make choosing the right RDBMS difficult. The following table lists popular RDBMS vendors:

Table 1.1 Listing of Popular RDBMS Vendors

Vendor	Product
IBM	DB2
Informix	Dynamic Server
Microsoft	SQL Server
Oracle	Oracle RDBMS
Sybase	Adaptive Server Enterprise

THE EVOLUTION OF THE CORPORATE SYSTEM: ENTERPRISE NETWORK

An *enterprise network* links multiple information servers so that they can be accessed and managed from a centralized source (see Figure 1.10). In the 1980s and early 1990s, distributed computing grew in popularity. Distributed computing physically moved computer systems closer to the source of the information. As a result, distributed systems are more widely dispersed geographically than are their stay-at-home mainframe counterparts.

Figure 1.10

An enterprise network.

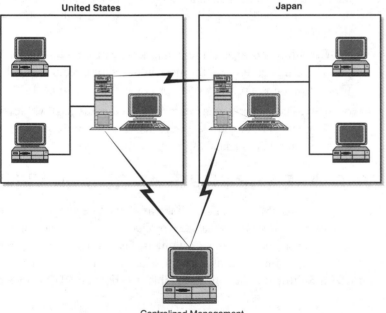

Centralized Management
of U.S. and Japanese Systems

With distributed computing comes decentralized control, and with decentralized control comes increased difficulty in managing and accessing data among distributed systems. To solve this problem, tools such as SQL Server's Enterprise Manager have been developed to manage the enterprise network.

SUMMARY

In this chapter, you learned the following:

- C/S database computing evolved as an answer to the drawbacks of the mainframe and PC/file server.

- C/S database computing partitions the user interface, database management, and business logic between the client computer and the server computer. The network links each of these processes.

- The client computer controls the user interface. The server computer controls database management. Business logic can be located on the server, on the client, or mixed between the two.

- Advantages of C/S database computing include affordability, speed, adaptability, and simplified data access.

- An RDBMS is the standard database in the C/S environment. RDBMS data is organized in a row/column manner and is stored in a table. Records are called rows and fields are called columns. Data is structured using relationships among data items.

- Advantages of an RDBMS include data integrity, SQL, flexibility, efficient data storage, and security.

- Multiple vendors offer powerful and robust RDBMS products.

- An enterprise network links multiple information servers that can be accessed and managed from a centralized source.

The next chapter discusses the role of the database administrator in RDBMS computing.

THE ROLE OF THE DATABASE ADMINISTRATOR

by Mark Spenik

IN THIS CHAPTER

In Chapter 1, "Introduction to Client/Server Database Computing," you read about the world of client/server and enterprise computing and the different RDBMS systems. In this chapter, you learn about the person who manages and maintains these RDBMS, the database administrator (DBA). Just as SQL Server has evolved from the days of 4.21 to 7.0, the role of the DBA has also evolved. SQL Server 7.0 greatly simplifies many DBA tasks, such as backups, maintenance and configuration. Because SQL Server 7.0 provides services that enable a DBA to easily set up jobs shared across multiple servers, a single DBA can handle more database servers. However, although common DBA tasks have been eliminated or simplified, the role of the SQL Server 7.0 DBA is more challenging than ever before. SQL Server 7.0 now runs on Windows 95 and Windows 98, which will surely increase the number of SQL Servers in your organization. SQL Server 7.0 adds advanced features like Heterogeneous Distributed queries, 2-way update replication (merge), Data Transformation Services, and Data Warehousing!

This is a lot of information for a single person to be responsible for. Start by looking at the traditional role of a DBA and then examine the added responsibilities of SQL Server 7.0. But first, acquaint yourself with the type of tasks and different roles required to maintain a simple client/server network shown in Figure 2.1.

FIGURE 2.1

A small client/server network.

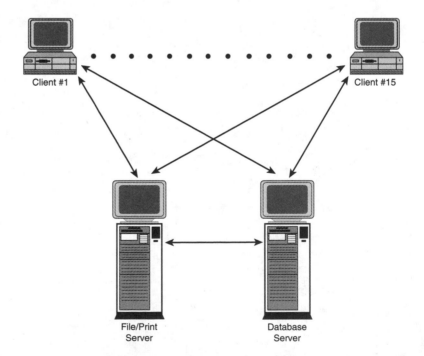

HARDWARE

Figure 2.1 shows a total of 15 client machines and 2 servers. Someone must be responsible for maintaining the physical machines to ensure that they are continually running. This person is responsible for routine maintenance and upgrades, such as adding more disk space and memory and installing or upgrading software packages.

NETWORK

The 15 client machines communicate with the 2 servers over the *network*. The network consists of the hardware and software that tie all the machines together and includes the cabling, routers, repeaters, and network protocols (TCP/IP, Named Pipes, SPX/IPX, and so on). Again, someone must make sure that the network stays up and running. If the network goes down, none of the machines can talk to each other.

OPERATING SYSTEMS

All machines—clients and servers—use some sort of *operating system*. Because this is a book about NT SQL Server, you can safely assume that the servers shown in Figure 2.1 are running Microsoft Windows NT and that the clients are running Microsoft Windows or Microsoft Windows NT Workstation. Each client and server machine must be properly configured and set up.

FILE/PRINT SERVER

The *file/print server* needs general maintenance, backups, and upgrades to protect against the loss of data. Someone must be responsible for adding user accounts, installing new applications, and maintaining the stability of the file/print servers. After all, if the file and print server go down, users cannot perform their jobs.

DATABASE SERVER

The *database server* requirements are similar to those of the file/print server. The difference is that the administration occurs with the RDBMS package. The database server must be set up and tuned correctly to produce the best performance. Database server tuning has been simplified quite a bit in SQL Server 7.0 reducing the workload of a DBA. However the most important job of a DBA, protecting the data, remains. The data in the databases must be protected; if data is lost your company could lose millions! It's the responsibility of the DBA to recover lost databases (under pressure and with peering eyes of course!). Managing database security is another chief responsibility of the DBA. The

DBA is responsible for adding users and restricting or permitting users and groups to view information in the database. SQL Server 7.0 capabilities, such as replication and data warehousing, add further responsibilities to the DBA.

WHO DOES WHAT?

You might notice that for even a small client/server network, there seem to be a lot of jobs and responsibilities behind keeping the whole network running. Imagine an Enterprise network 10 to 100 times the size of the relatively small network used in this example with thousands of internal users and Internet users! So, who is responsible for which task? The answer to who does what can become quite complex because the size of an organization and the size of the Enterprise network dictate who is responsible for each task. In some organizations, a single individual might wear many different hats. In other organizations, individuals might be more specialized. Roles and responsibilities are assigned from the company higher-ups. The following sections examine some of the general job titles and the responsibilities that accompany each position.

PC and Tech Support

The PC and tech support group is responsible for maintaining and setting up the hardware on the different client machines and sometimes on the server machines. If a new software package is installed or more disk space or memory must be added, the PC and tech support group is called in.

Network Administrator

The network administrator is responsible for maintaining the network. A network administrator makes sure that all the hardware components are working correctly and that the networking software is set up correctly. In many cases, the network administrator is also responsible for maintaining the network operating system.

System Administrator

The system administrator is responsible for maintaining the many different servers in the organization. The responsibilities include backup and recovery, maintaining user access and security, scheduling task and batch runs, and upgrading and maintaining the operating system.

Web Master

The Web master is a recent addition to the project team. Web master maintains various company Web sites (Internet or Intranet). They are responsible for Web server's maintenance and in many cases setting standards, maintaining sites and adding content produced by others to the production servers. Many Web-based applications build dynamic Web pages by pulling information from a database, so DBAs should expect to work with the Web master to provide the database access required for the Web-based applications.

Database Administrator

There is a lot more to being a DBA than just being responsible for the data; that is what you will concentrate on for the rest of the chapter!

> **NOTE**
>
> You may notice that a fine line separates job responsibilities (where one job starts and ends), such as the possible overlap of the network administrator and the system administrator. Depending on their size, most organizations divide the work realistically (that is, no one person has too many responsibilities). One of the most important things to remember is that it takes a team effort to keep a network healthy. Cooperation among the different individuals is a must.

WHAT IS A DATABASE ADMINISTRATOR?

In a very general sense, a *database administrator* is the individual responsible for maintaining the RDBMS system (in this book, Microsoft SQL Server). The DBA has many different responsibilities, but the overall goal of the DBA is to keep the server up at all times and to provide users with access to the required information when they need it. The DBA makes sure that the database is protected and that any chance of data loss is minimized.

WHO ARE THE DBAS?

Who are the DBAs and how do you become one? A DBA can be someone who, from the start, has concentrated in the area of database design and administration. A DBA can be a programmer who, by default or by volunteering, took over the responsibility of maintaining a SQL Server during project development and enjoyed the job so much that he or she switched. A DBA can be a system administrator who was given the added responsibility of maintaining a SQL Server. DBAs can even come from unrelated fields, such as accounting or the help desk and switch to Information Systems to become DBAs. To start your journey to becoming a Microsoft SQL Server DBA, you need the following:

- A good understanding of Microsoft Windows NT
- Knowledge of Structured Query Language (SQL)
- Sound database design
- General understanding of network architectures (for example, Client/Server, Internet/Intranet, Enterprise)
- Knowledge about Microsoft SQL Server

> **TIP**
>
> If you are part of a technical team looking for a Microsoft SQL Server DBA, do yourself a favor and volunteer. It is a great job and good DBAs are in demand and typically are paid more than developers.

DBA RESPONSIBILITIES

The following sections examine the responsibilities of the database administrator and how they translate to various Microsoft SQL Server tasks.

Installing and Upgrading an SQL Server

The DBA is responsible for installing SQL Server or upgrading an existing SQL Server. In the case of upgrading SQL Server, the DBA is responsible ensuring that if the upgrade is not successful, the SQL Server can be rolled back to an earlier release until the upgrade issues can be resolved. The DBA is also responsible for applying SQL Server service packs. A service pack is not a true upgrade, but an installation of the current version of software with various bug fixes and patches that have been resolved since the product's release.

Monitoring the Database Server's Health and Tuning Accordingly

Monitoring the health of the database server means making sure that the following is done:

- The server is running with optimal performance.
- The error log or event log is monitored for database errors.
- Databases have routine maintenance performed on them and that the overall system has periodic maintenance performed by the system administrator.

Using Storage Properly

SQL Server 7.0 enables you to automatically grow the size of your databases and trans-action logs or you can choose to select a fixed size for the database and transaction log. Either way, maintaining the proper use of storage means monitoring space requirements and adding new storage space (disk drives) when required.

Performing Backup and Recovery Duties

Backup and recovery are the DBA's most critical tasks; they include the following aspects:

- Establishing standards and schedules for database backups
- Developing recovery procedures for each database
- Making sure that the backup schedules meet the recovery requirements

Managing Database Users and Security

With SQL Server 7.0, the DBA works tightly with the Windows NT administrator to add user NT logins to the database. In non-NT domains, the DBA adds user logins. The DBA is also responsible for assigning users to databases and determining the proper security level for each user. Within each database, the DBA is responsible for assigning permis-sions to the various database objects such as tables, views, and stored procedures.

Working with Developers

It is important for the DBA to work closely with development teams to assist in overall database design, such as creating normalized databases, helping developers tune queries, assigning proper indexes, and aiding developers in the creation of triggers and stored procedures. In the SQL Server 7.0 environment, a good DBA will show the developers how to use and take advantage of the SQL Server Index Tuning Wizard and the SQL Server profiler.

> **TIP**
>
> I have too often seen DBAs who were content to sit back and watch developers make bad design and SQL Server decisions. I have also seen situations in which the DBA wanted to be involved in design decisions but management prevented it because it was not the DBA's job. Don't be underutilized. If you are in this sit-uation, show your management this tip! Take an active role in new project development. The entire team will benefit from your insight and knowledge!

Establishing and Enforcing Standards

The DBA should establish naming conventions and standards for the SQL Server and databases and make sure that everyone sticks to them.

Transferring Data

The DBA is responsible for importing and exporting data to and from the SQL Server. In the current trend to downsize and combine client/server systems with mainframe systems and Web technologies to create Enterprise systems, importing data from the mainframe to SQL Server is a common occurrence that is about to become more common with the SQL Server 7.0 Data Transformation Services. Good DTS DBAs will be in hot demand as companies struggle to move and translate legacy system to Enterprise systems (especially before the year 2000).

Replicating Data

SQL Server version 7.0 has added replication capabilities such as Merge replication (2-way disconnected replication). Managing and setting up replication topologies will be a big undertaking for a DBA because replication is a tremendous feature that will play a big part in many organizations.

Data Warehousing

SQL Server 7.0 has added substantial data warehousing capabilities that require the DBA to learn an additional product (the Microsoft OLAP Server) and architecture. Data warehousing provides new and interesting challenges to the DBA!

Scheduling Events

The database administrator is responsible for setting up and scheduling various events using Windows NT and SQL Server to aid in performing many tasks such as backups and replication.

Providing 24-Hour Access

The database server must stay up and the databases must always be protected and online. Be prepared to perform some maintenance and upgrades after hours. Also be prepared to carry that dreaded beeper. If the database server should go down, be ready to get the server up and running. After all, that's your job.

Learning Constantly

To be a good DBA, you must continue to study and practice your mission-critical procedures, such as testing your backups by recovering to a test database. In this business, technology changes very fast, so you must continue learning about SQL Server, available client/servers, and database design tools. It is a never-ending process.

Does It Pay to be a DBA?

Okay, here is a topic that was skipped in previous editions of the book, does it pay to be a DBA? And how much? Well, it definitely does pay to be a DBA! DBAs continue to be in demand (like all IS professionals). SQL Server 7.0 has the capability to increase Microsoft's RDBMS market share, which should mean a greater demand for SQL Server DBAs. DBAs tend to make more than your standard or great developer (but less than the gurus). Of course, this is always subject to change but it has been true for the past several years.

So what are DBAs paid? It really would not be fair to put out a dollar figure because it varies from city to city and by the time this book is published it will have already changed. Ask around in some of the Internet user groups and check various salary surveys for your region and years of experience. But DBAs make good money. DBAs that possess one or more of the following skills will be in hot demand and can require top dollar for their services:

- Data Warehousing (HOT, HOT, HOT)
- Data Transformation Services
- Replication Architect

TRICKS OF THE TRADE

Now that you understand the different responsibilities of a DBA, how can you learn the tricks of the trade? You are off to a good start by reading this book. The following sections examine some other ways to learn the tricks of the trade.

Classes and Training

Taking a Microsoft-certified SQL Server training class is very good way to get started. Find a class that gives you hands-on classroom training. The class can introduce you to many of the concepts and procedures required to maintain SQL Server. To find out about authorized Microsoft SQL Server training centers near you, call 1-800-SOL-PROV and ask for information on Microsoft Solution Provider Authorized Technical Education Centers. On the Internet, go to `http://www.microsoft.com/mcp`.

> **TIP**
>
> If you go to class, make sure that when you return, you immediately start practicing what you learned in class. Most classes last 3 to 5 days; to retain the information, you must use it immediately.

On the Job

The real DBA training occurs on the job; that is where many DBAs learned. On-the-job training can be difficult when you are the only one learning a system with which no one else is familiar. Although some people have the luxury of a seasoned DBA to teach them the ropes, ultimately, all DBAs learn on the job.

> **TIP**
>
> Practice, practice, practice. Constantly practice different procedures and tasks, such as backing up and recovering data or importing data on a nonproduction server. When the day comes to perform the task, you will be well prepared.

Microsoft TechNet, Microsoft Developers Network, and Internet News Group

Take advantage of the vast knowledge base of articles Microsoft makes available on the TechNet and Microsoft Developers Network (MSDN) CDs. Many times, you can solve a problem simply by searching the two CDs for the problem and possible resolution. You get online help by accessing the SQL Server News Group on the Internet. On the news group, you can post problems and get help from other DBAs or you can scan through the various messages posted and learn how to solve problems you have not yet encountered. The Microsoft news server is `MSNews.microsoft.com` and the newsgroup for SQL Server is `microsoft.public.sqlserver`. Microsoft's Web page for SQL Server is `http://www.Microsoft.com/SQL`. You can learn more about Microsoft TechNet by navigating the Internet to `http://www.microsoft.com/technet`. To learn more about the Microsoft Developers Network (MSDN), go to `http://www.msdn.com`.

Magazines and Books

Subscribe to various database magazines that keep you abreast of topics such as the latest database design and development tools, relational database concepts, and SQL Server.

Also search the bookstore for books on database design and SQL Server (like this book). Pinnacle publishing publishes a magazine called the *Microsoft SQL Server Professional*; it can be accessed on the Internet at 1119390@mcimail.com, or by fax at 1-206-251-5057. Another magazine that provides very good articles on SQL Server and Windows NT (including a SQL Server column managed by two SQL Server experts) is the *Windows NT Magazine*; reach the publishers at 1-800-621-1544 or on the Internet at winntmag@duke.com.

Certification

Microsoft offers product certification for SQL Server database administration and SQL Server database implementation. It is strongly recommended that you take the test to become certified. Certification does not replace experience and training but it points out possible weaknesses in your understanding of SQL Server and gives you credibility (because you understand the concepts and procedures to maintain SQL Server). To find out more about Microsoft certification, look on the Internet at http://www.Microsoft.com/mcp.

2

THE ROLE OF THE DATABASE ADMINISTRATOR

> **TIP**
>
> We are often asked, "What do I need to do to pass certification? Will this book help?" Of course this book will help! Here are some words of advice about the certification test: Before taking the test, review the test outline for SQL Server (which is part of the Certification Roadmap). The certification test asks questions on only the topics listed in the test outline. Make sure that you are familiar with each of the topics.
>
> Although managing a Microsoft SQL Server is a graphical experience, the test is likely to ask you about the command to create a database (instead of how to create a database using the Enterprise Manager). Make sure that you are familiar with the commands required to perform various administrative tasks.
>
> Last, but not least, take the practice test that comes with the Certification Roadmap. The practice test gives you a general idea of the types of questions asked on the test. Do not take the real test until you do well on the practice test.

Internet

As you can tell from the previous sections, one of the best resources for SQL Server information is the Internet. Appendix C provides you with a list of useful resources, especially Internet resources.

HOW THE DBA INTERACTS WITH OTHER TEAM MEMBERS

Now that you have decided to become a DBA, how will you interact with other team members such as the system administrator, network administrator, developers, and users? Many times, these relationships are hard to determine because each organization has people filling one or many different roles. Based on earlier job descriptions, however, the following sections quickly examine the types of interaction you can expect.

System Administrator and Network Administrator

A DBA's interaction with the network administrator is mostly concerned with the type of network protocols that can be used and the network address or port number that can be used for the server. If users are complaining about query times and SQL Server is executing the queries very fast, you and the network administrator should examine possible networking problems.

The interaction of the system administrator and the DBA is much tighter than the interaction of the network administrator and the DBA. The system administrator is responsible for tuning the Windows NT server on which your SQL Server runs. The system administrator is responsible for adding the hard drives and storage space required for your databases. If you choose to use integrated user security with SQL Server, you must work with the system administrator to set up the correct NT user accounts and groups. The different types of backup and recovery procedures for the NT Server and the SQL Server should be worked out by both parties because, in some cases, the system administrator might have to restore a system drive that contains a database or database backup.

Developers

The interaction of DBAs with developers is where the greatest differences in organizations' definitions of a DBA are found. In some organizations, the DBA works very closely with the developers; in other organizations, the DBAs work very little with the developers and are stuck maintaining the developers' systems and designs without any input. To perform most efficiently, the DBA should work closely with the developers. After all, the DBA is the one maintaining the database side of the application, and in many cases, the DBA has the most experience in relational database design and tuning. The DBA should design, aid, or review any and all database designs for the organization. The DBA should also assist developers, select proper indexes, and optimize queries and stored procedures, as well as provide a source of information to the developers.

Users

In most organizations, the DBA's interaction with the users of the system is limited to user account maintenance, security, and database recovery requirements.

SUMMARY

The role of the database administrator is very important in an organization. The job can be challenging and exciting. If you are a DBA or want to be a DBA, remember that it is important to constantly study SQL Server and database tools. Become certified and practice your backup and recovery procedures. Following is a list of the many duties and responsibilities of a DBA:

- Installing and upgrading SQL Server
- Applying SQL Server services packs
- Monitoring the database server's health and tuning it accordingly
- Using storage properly
- Backing up and recovering data
- Managing database users and security
- Establishing and enforcing standards
- Performing data transfer
- Setting up and maintaining data replication
- Data warehousing
- Setting up server scheduling
- Providing 24-hour access
- Working with development teams
- Learning!

THE WORLD OF MICROSOFT'S SQL SERVER

PART
II

IN THIS PART

THE EVOLUTION OF SQL SERVER

by Orryn Sledge

IN THIS CHAPTER

Microsoft SQL Server 7.0 has rewritten the standard for database computing. This release provides a tremendous amount of new functionality and it removes various limitations that nagged previous versions. Version 7.0 is also simpler to administer. Microsoft has taken graphical administration to a new level with version 7.0. Those administrators who are upgrading from previous versions will be very pleased with the 7.0 product.

HISTORY OF SQL SERVER

In 1988, Microsoft released its first version of SQL Server. It was designed for the OS/2 platform and was developed jointly by Microsoft and Sybase. During the early 1990s, Microsoft began to develop a new version of SQL Server for the NT platform. While it was under development, Microsoft decided that SQL Server should be tightly coupled with the NT operating system. In 1992, Microsoft assumed core responsibility for the future of SQL Server for NT. In 1993, Windows NT 3.1 and SQL Server 4.2 for NT were released. Microsoft's philosophy of combining a high-performance database with an easy-to-use interface proved to be very successful. Microsoft quickly became the second most popular vendor of high-end relational database software. In 1994, Microsoft and Sybase formally ended their partnership. In 1995, Microsoft released version 6.0 of SQL Server. This release was a major rewrite of SQL Server's core technology. Version 6.0 substantially improved performance, provided built-in replication, and delivered centralized administration. In 1996, Microsoft released version 6.5 of SQL Server. This version brought significant enhancements to the existing technology and provided several new features. In 1997, Microsoft released version 6.5 Enterprise Edition. This version included 4 GB RAM support, 8-way processor support, and Microsoft Cluster Support. In 1998, Microsoft released version 7.0 of SQL Server. SQL Server version 7.0 is Microsoft's most significant release of SQL Server to date. This version is a complete rewrite of the core engine and administration components. According to the SQL Server development team, the changes to the database engine are designed to provide an architecture that will last for the next 10 years. The remainder of this chapter is dedicated to discussing these new features found in version 7.0.

WHAT'S NEW IN VERSION 7.0

Following are several of the key features found in version 7.0:

- Architectural Enhancements
- Simplified Administration
- Data Transformation Service (DTS)
- Performance and Scalability Improvements

- Backup and Restoration Improvements
- Security Enhancements
- Replication Enhancements
- Data Warehousing Enhancements
- Distributed Queries
- Internet Enhancements

Architectural Enhancements

The biggest changes to SQL Server 7.0 are in its underlying architecture. These changes are designed to improve SQL Server's performance and simplify administration and configuration, while expanding the types of supported platforms. The following are the significant architecture enhancements found in version 7.0.

- **Elimination of devices:** 7.0 databases utilize database and transaction files at the operating system level. This is different from previous versions, in which databases utilized devices and the device resided at the operating system level. This change is significant in that it simplifies the creation and administration of databases and their corresponding logs.

- **Dynamic sizing of databases and transaction logs:** Now that devices are gone, SQL Server 7.0 has gone a step further by providing dynamic sizing for databases and transaction logs. This means that databases and transaction logs can grow and shrink without requiring any intervention by an administrator!

DYNAMIC SIZING MEANS FEWER SUPPORT CALLS FOR THE DBA

I have no doubt that DBAs will love dynamic sizing of databases and transaction logs. No longer will we get those after-hour phone calls from end-users complaining about the database running out of space!

- **8KB pages:** Version 7.0's storage format has been completely rewritten to utilize 8KB pages. (A page is SQL Server's lowest level of storage.) Previous versions utilized a 2KB page format. The increase in page size also increases the maximum row size to 8060 bytes and allows for a maximum of 1024 columns per table. Previous versions of SQL Server were limited to a maximum row size of 1962 bytes and a maximum of 250 columns per table.

- **Increased limits:** Version 7.0 has eliminated and/or significantly increased its database limits over previous versions. Table 3.1 compares version 7.0 to version 6.5 in terms of limits.

TABLE 3.1   7.0 LIMITS

Component	6.5 Maximum Value	7.0 Maximum Value
Batch size	128K	5,536*Network Packet Size
Bytes per GROUP BY or ORDER BY	900	8060
Bytes per row	1962	8060
Bytes of source text in a stored procedure	65025	Restricted by batch size or 250 MB
Columns in a GROUP BY or ORDER BY clause	16	Restricted by bytes per GROUP BY or ORDER BY (see previous entries)
Columns per table	250	1024
Columns per INSERT statement	250	1024
Database size	1 TB	1,048,516 TB
Files per database	32	32,767
File size—data	32 GB	32 TB
File size—log	32 GB	4 TB
FOREIGN KEY constraints per table	31	253
Nested subqueries	16	64
Nested trigger levels	16	32
Stored procedure parameters	255	1024
SELECT statement, max # of tables per statement	16	256

- **Dynamic Memory:** In version 7.0, the amount of RAM used by SQL Server can be automatically adjusted on an as-needed basis. No longer does the DBA have to get out his calculator and scratch pad to determine how much memory should be allocated to SQL Server, Windows NT, and any other processes running on the same server.

MEMORY CONFIGURATION

The need to manually configure the amount of memory dedicated to SQL Server is a thing of the past! It always drove me crazy that with previous versions of SQL Server, the administrator would have to go back to configure memory after installing the product.

- **Reduced configuration settings:** Version 7.0 has eliminated the maximum settings for the following:
  - User connections
  - Locks
  - Open Objects

Previous versions of SQL Server required that an administrator manually configure these settings.

FEWER PHONE CALLS FOR MICROSOFT TECH SUPPORT!

Microsoft Tech Support is probably ecstatic about version 7.0! Tech Support personnel were probably getting tired of hearing DBAs calling in with error messages about configuration issues such as running out of locks, user connections, open objects, and so on. I applaud Microsoft for finally removing the artificially low default settings for many configuration settings.

- **Dynamic Tempdb:** Tempdb no longer has to be manually sized! Version 7.0 automatically configures and manages the amount of space dedicated to Tempdb. Previous versions of SQL Server required a fixed amount of space dedicated to Tempdb. The default setting of 2 MB in previous versions was always too small. Needless to say, this is a very welcome enhancement resulting in fewer support calls for the DBA.
- **Auto-update statistics:** Version 7.0 automatically maintains index statistics. Previous versions required that the UPDATE STATISTICS command be run on a frequent basis to update an index's statistics.
- **Windows 95/98 support:** SQL Server 7.0 now runs on Windows 95 and Windows 98. This means that developers finally have a SQL Server database that does not require Windows NT. This also opens the possibilities for laptop/remote

applications. Now applications can be developed that store data in the local database running on the laptop. This data can then be submitted to the networked version of SQL Server through replication or other mechanisms of transferring data. Another great feature is that the Window 9X version of SQL Server is virtually identical to the Windows NT version. The only features not found in the Windows 9X version are SMP support, asynchronous I/O support, and integrated security.

- **SQL Server Agent (previously called SQL Executive):** SQL Server Agent is an improved scheduling engine over 6.x's SQL Executive. Improvements include the ability to schedule a single job for multiple servers (for example, the scheduling of a backup job that backs up databases on multiple servers). SQL Server Agent's jobs can be multitasking and can be scheduled to automatically run whenever the server is idle. Additionally, jobs can be extended through various scripting languages such as VBScript, JavaScript, and Windows NT script.

Simplified Administration

A key design goal of the Microsoft SQL Server development team was to reduce the amount of time required to administer SQL Server. Microsoft has achieved this goal! The following are various components of version 7.0 that help simplify administration.

- **Revised Enterprise Manager:** Enterprise Manager is now part of the Microsoft Management Console (MMC) framework (see Figure 3.1). SQL Server's Enterprise Manager is a snap-in for MMC. The MMC graphical interface is the same interface that is used for Exchange, Microsoft Transaction Server (MTS), and any other product that provides a snap-in for MMC. This means that an administrator can use the same graphical interface to manage multiple BackOffice products.

- **Wizards galore:** Version 7.0 provides wizards for just about everything associated with SQL Server. The following is a partial listing of the wizards included in version 7.0:
    - Data Transformation
    - Database Creation
    - Database Maintenance
    - Index Creation
    - Index Tuning
    - Replication Publishing and Distribution
    - Security Management
    - Scheduling Management
    - Stored Procedure Creation

FIGURE 3.1

Enterprise Manager.

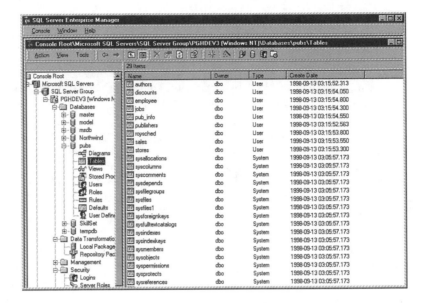

- View Creation
- Web Publishing

- **Dynamic configuration options:** As previously mentioned in the section titled "Architectural Enhancements," several of SQL Server's configuration values automatically change based on the system workload. Examples of configuration value settings that automatically change include memory, database and log size, and Tempdb.

- **ALTER Table enhancements:** No longer do you have to export your data, drop the table, re-create the table, and import your data every time your table design changes! Previous versions limited the types of changes that could be made to an existing table. (For example, you could not remove a column from a table or add a column that was NOT NULL to an existing table.) In version 7.0, tables can be modified on-the-fly.

Performance and Scalability Improvements

Version 7.0 has improved performance and scalability over previous versions of SQL Server. Changes to the database engine have enabled SQL Server to overcome limitations found in previous versions. The following are some of the improvements found in version 7.0.

- **Row level and dynamic locking:** Version 7.0 utilizes row-level and dynamic locking. Previous versions of SQL Server were limited to page-level locking. Row-level locking is designed to reduce blocking and data contention. Another new feature is dynamic locking. With dynamic locking, the lock manager automatically escalates and de-escalates locks (row, page, table) based on performance and concurrency requirements at any given moment.

> **ROW-LEVEL LOCKING**
>
> Row-level locking is finally here! Previous versions of SQL Server were always criticized for utilizing page-level locking instead of row-level locking.

- **Improved query optimizer:** Version 7.0 includes an improved query optimizer that takes advantage of parallel queries and new join formulas (hash, merge, and nested loop joins). Additionally, version 7.0's query optimizer incorporates multi-index strategies. (A query may use 1 or more indexes per table.) Previous versions were limited to single-index strategies. (A query could only utilize 1 index per table.)
- **Improved caching:** The Cache Manager has been improved to better share SQL plans across multiple users. Also the SQL statement cache has been improved to support automatic-parameterization of statements. Data access components that do not utilize stored procedures (such as ADO, RDO, DAO) benefit from this improvement.

Backup and Restoration Improvements

Version 7.0 of SQL Server simplifies the backup and restoration of databases and transaction logs. The following are the improvements made to the backup and restoration process.

- **Improved performance for online backups:** Online backups can now take place with a 95 percent throughput rate. This is a big benefit for sites that must be available around the clock.
- **Differential backups:** This is a new feature found in version 7.0, which enables administrators to implement a full backup/differential backup strategy. Differential backups run faster than full backups because they only backup the modifications to the database.

- **Simplified restoration procedures:** When restoring a database, version 7.0 automatically restores the database and associated files (data files and transaction files). In previous versions of SQL Server, the administrator had to manually back up the database and the corresponding devices (database and transaction) prior to restoring a database.

RESTORATION HEADACHES—A THING OF THE PAST

No longer does the DBA have to worry about sizing the database and the corresponding devices before performing a restoration! Version 7.0 automatically manages these settings during the restoration process. This is a great feature! In previous versions of SQL Server, it was often a guessing game as to how to size a database before performing the restoration.

- **Microsoft Tape Format:** Version 7.0 supports the Microsoft Tape Format. This allows SQL Server backups to exist on the same tape with backups from other programs such as those from the Windows NT 5.0 Backup program.

Security Enhancements

SQL Server 7.0 has a revised security model that is more tightly integrated with Windows NT than previous versions. Version 7.0 simplifies the integrated security model by doing away with the awkward SQL Security Manager that was found in previous versions. Instead, integrated security is managed directly within the Enterprise Manager. Additionally, SQL Server 7.0 has implemented the concept of roles. (The implementation is similar to Exchange's security model.) Roles are the replacement for groups, which were found in previous versions of SQL Server. Roles are more flexible than groups in that a user can belong to multiple roles in a single database, whereas previous versions limited a user to one group (not counting the public group).

Replication Enhancements

In terms of replication, version 7.0 picks up where SQL Server 6.x left off. The replication engine and the associated interfaces are more flexible and efficient than the 6.x associated components. The following are the significant enhancements to replication in version 7.0.

- **Multisite update support:** SQL Server 7.0 provides bi-directional replication through multisite update support. SQL Server 6.x replication model did not fully support bi-directional replication.

- **Merge replication:** This version supports merge replication which enables users to make data changes offline and then merge the changes back into the database. This model is intended for mobile/disconnected users that make data changes when they are disconnected from SQL Server and then upload the changes when they are reconnected.

- **Merge conflict resolution:** Version 7.0 provides merge conflict resolution through a built-in interface. The purpose of this interface is to flag and react to the conflicts that can arise from data being modified and consolidated in multiple sites. This interface can also be enhanced through user-defined business rules and priorities.

- **Anonymous pull subscriptions:** This technology enables servers to partake in replication without having to be registered with the publisher of the subscription. A benefit of this technology is that after the subscription has been synchronized, the recipient receives only the incremental changes. This technology is designed with the Internet in mind.

- **Improved replication monitoring:** Version 7.0 provides administrators with direct insight into the replication process. This information can be used to troubleshoot replication problems and monitor replication performance. The replication monitors are a vast improvement of 6.x's replication monitors.

Data Transformation Service (DTS)

DTS is a new and significant piece of technology that allows data to be imported into SQL Server and exported from SQL Server from any data source that is from OLE-DB (such as Oracle, DB2, Access), ODBC (such as Excel, FoxPro), or a text file source. You can run DTS from a graphical interface or from the command-line. DTS also includes a data transformation portion that can be used to convert values (for example, `if gender = 'M' then gender_description = 'Male', if gender = 'W' then gender_description = 'Woman'`). The transformation portion of DTS can be scripted via VBScript, JavaScript, and other languages. DTS is also integral part of Microsoft's Data Warehousing Framework.

USE DTS INSTEAD OF BCP

DBAs who are using BCP (bulk copy program) to import/export should look at using DTS. DTS is much simpler and more flexible than BCP. I'm glad Microsoft finally provided a replacement for BCP.

The only reason not to use DTS is backwards compatibility and performance. If you need maximum performance, BCP may run faster than DTS. However, BULK INSERT is faster than BCP or DTS.

Data Warehousing Enhancements

Microsoft is finally serious about data warehousing. Version 7.0 supplies the technology to deliver a serious data warehousing solution. The following are the key data warehousing enhancements found in version 7.0.

- **Online Analytically Processing (OLAP) Integration:** Version 7.0 includes Microsoft Decision Support Services (formerly known as Plato) which is Microsoft's OLAP Server product (see Figure 3.2). This product provides multidimensional database analysis. This product is a key component of Microsoft's Data Warehousing Framework (MDWF). The central goal of MDWF is to reduce the effort required to construct and manage a data warehouse.

FIGURE 3.2

OLAP Manager.

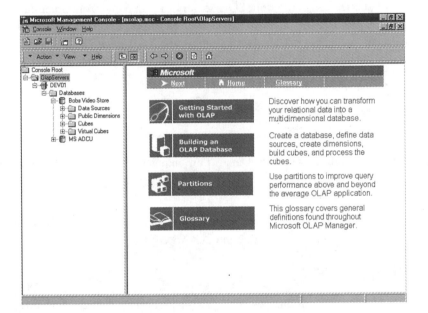

- **Data Transformation Service (DTS):** DTS is central to the import and export component of data warehousing. A useful feature of DTS, when working with data warehouses, is the ability to graphically track where and how data was transformed into SQL Server. (See the topic "Data Transformation Service (DTS)," in this chapter for more information.)

- **Very Large Database (VLDB) Support:** Version 7.0 has improved its VLDB support by significantly increasing database and table size limits (refer to Table 3.1 for more information). Additionally, version 7.0 has improved its backup and restoration process. The process is better suited to deal with the large amount of data that is often associated with a data warehouse.

- **Microsoft English Query:** Microsoft English Query enables users to type in English syntax to query the database. This is useful when users want to query a data warehouse for information. For example, a user can type in "how many blue cars did we sell in the 4th quarter of this year". English Query will translate the request into the following:

```
select count(*) from auto_sales where sales_quarter = 4 and year =
1998 and color = 'blue'
```

Distributed Queries

Version 7.0 incorporates a distributed query feature that allows a single SELECT statement to query data that resides in multiple locations or different data formats. The data being queried can come from SQL Server or it can come from other data sources that provide an OLE-DB interface (often referred to as heterogeneous data sources). Data can be relational and nonrelational. Examples of data that can participate in a distributed query include Access, Excel, Oracle, NT 5.0's Active Directory Services, and other OLE-DB sources.

Internet Integration

Version 7.0 has improved Internet integration through the following enhancements.

- **Dynamic encryption:** Data is now automatically encrypted over the Internet.
- **Proxy Server integration:** Secure transactions can be passed through Microsoft Proxy Server.
- **Microsoft Index Server integration:** Data that is stored in SQL Server 7.0 can be indexed for text searching through Microsoft's Index Server.

SUMMARY

As you can see from this chapter, 7.0 has significantly changed how a RDBMS operates. This version has simplified administration and improved performance. However, there are still several administrative and configuration tasks that must be dealt with in a production environment. The remainder of this book is designed to help you effectively deal with those tasks.

SQL SERVER OVERVIEW

by Orryn Sledge

IN THIS CHAPTER

SQL Server is a high-performance relational database system that is tightly integrated with the Windows NT and Windows 9.x operating systems. This arrangement allows SQL Server to take advantage of the features provided by the operating system. SQL Server is an excellent choice for meeting the challenging needs of today's complex client/server systems.

This chapter is designed to provide a broad overview of SQL Server's tools and features. Those new to SQL Server should use this chapter to gain a basic understanding of SQL Server's fundamental components. Those experienced with previous versions of SQL Server should review the "What's New" and "What's Gone" sections for useful information on SQL Server 7.0.

SQL SERVER 6.5 TO 7.0 QUICK REFERENCE

The following topics are a subset of changes that relate to this chapter. Review Chapter 3, "The Evolution of SQL Server," for a complete summary of what's new in version 7.0.

What's New

- **Win 9.x support:** SQL Server 7.0 supports Windows 95 and 98. The functionality that is found in the Windows 9.x version is virtually identical to the NT version.

- **Microsoft Management Console support (MMC):** SQL Server Enterprise Manager is part of the Microsoft Management Console. This console is also used to provide global management of components, via snap-ins, such as Exchange, Microsoft Transaction Server, and other products.

- **SQL Server Agent:** This service is the scheduling component of SQL Server 7.0. This product is a replacement for SQL Executive, which was found in 6.x versions.

- **Web Based Administration:** A subset of SQL Server can be managed via the Web.

- **Wizards:** Numerous wizards have been added in 7.0. If you are new to SQL Server 7.0, check out the wizards. They simplify several tasks that were time-consuming in previous versions.

- **Improved SMP support:** SQL Server 7.0 can effectively support 8-16 processors. Previous versions were effectively limited to supporting 4-6 processors.

- **SQL Version Upgrade Wizard:** This product is used to upgrade 6.x versions of SQL Server to version 7.0.

- **Distributed Transformation Service (DTS):** This new component provides import and export capability for a variety of file formats. Additionally, data can be transformed (massaged) via rules and scripts during the import and export process.

- **Full-Text Search:** Version 7.0 includes the Microsoft Search service, which enables full-text searching on SQL Server data.

What's Gone

- **ISQL/w:** SQL Server Query Analyzer has replaced this product. The SQL Server Query Analyzer enhances the functionality found in ISQL/w by offering a graphical execution plan called Showplan, color-coded query editor, and the ability to output results to a grid.

- **SQL Security Manager:** This product has been removed from SQL Server 7.0. Integrated security has been renamed to Windows NT Authentication. The management of Windows NT Authentication is controlled from within SQL Server Enterprise Manager.

- **SQL Server Web Assistant:** This product is now part of the wizards provided from within SQL Server Enterprise Manager. Previously, this product was a stand-alone product.

- **SQL Trace:** This product has been renamed to SQL Server Profiler. The SQL Server Profiler provides additional functionality such as the ability to specify trace criteria, trace events, and other trace features.

- **SQL Executive:** SQL Server Agent has replaced this product.

- **MS Query:** This product has been removed from SQL Server. Microsoft now includes the Microsoft Visual Database Tools product with the Enterprise Manager.

ARCHITECTURE

SQL Server's integration with the operating system provides the following important features:

- Symmetric multiprocessing (SMP)
- Portability
- Network independence
- Reliability

Symmetric Multiprocessing (SMP)

SMP allows SQL Server to increase performance through the use of additional processors. The Enterprise Edition of SQL Server 7.0 provides built-in support for 8-16 processors. SQL Server can automatically run a query, in parallel, on 2 or more processors. All this occurs without user interaction; it also relieves administrators from the complexities of managing multiple processors.

4

SQL SERVER OVERVIEW

> **NOTE**
>
> The Windows 9.x version of SQL Server does not provide SMP support. The Windows 9.x version of SQL Server does not provide SMP support.

Portability

SQL Server can run on different operating systems and hardware platforms. Currently, the Windows NT version of SQL Server supports the Intel platform, Digital's Alpha architecture, and other hardware platforms. SQL Server 7.0 can also run on the Windows 9.x operating systems.

> **NOTE**
>
> In case you were wondering whether you could run SQL Server 7.0 on that old 486 machine that has been lying around and collecting dust, the answer is no. The minimum processor requirement, as specified by Microsoft, is a Pentium 133 with 32MB of RAM. Maybe it's time to turn that old computer into something useful, such as a doorstop or yard-art.

Network Independence

The Windows NT and the Windows 9.x operating systems support several different types of network protocols. This level of support extends to the client-side connectivity of SQL Server. This enables you to choose the network protocol that best fits your present and future needs. TCP/IP, IPX/SPX, named pipes, AppleTalk, and Banyan Vines are currently supported.

Reliability

Windows NT and SQL Server provide crash protection, memory management, preemptive scheduling, and remote management. These types of features enable you to keep SQL Server up and running 24 hours a day, 7 days a week.

> **NOTE**
>
> Microsoft Cluster Server (MSCS, formerly known as Wolfpack) provides failover support for SQL Server 7.0. This product provides an additional level of support for those organizations that require 100% up time. MSCS is an add-on product for Windows NT and is not included with SQL Server 7.0.

OPERATING SYSTEM INTEGRATION

SQL Server is designed to take advantage of the Windows NT and Windows 9.x operating systems. This means that several common NT and Windows 9.x components provide additional functionality to SQL Server.

> **NOTE**
>
> The majority of the topics discussed in this section are specific to the Windows NT version of SQL Server. The Windows 9.x version provides similar operating system functionality.

Taskbar Integration

The status of SQL Server, SQL Server Service Manager, Microsoft DTC, and Microsoft Search are integrated with the taskbar in Windows NT and Windows 9.x. From the taskbar, you can also start and stop the services listed.

Control Panel

SQL Server (MSSQLServer), SQL Server Agent (SQLServerAgent), Distributed Transaction Coordinator (MSDTC), and Microsoft Search are defined as services in the NT Control Panel (see Figure 4.1). You use the Control Panel to start, stop, and monitor the status of SQL Server, SQL Server Agent, Distributed Transaction Coordinator, and Microsoft Search.

FIGURE 4.1
Integration with the Windows NT Control Panel.

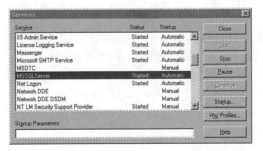

4

SQL SERVER OVERVIEW

> **NOTE**
>
> Version 7.0 of SQL Server uses a different service name for the SQLExecutive scheduling service. In version 7.0, SQLExecutive is SQLServerAgent.

Event Viewer

The *Event Viewer* allows administrators to view and track information pertaining to SQL Server (see Figure 4.2). SQL Server logs the following types of messages to the Event Viewer: information, errors, and warnings.

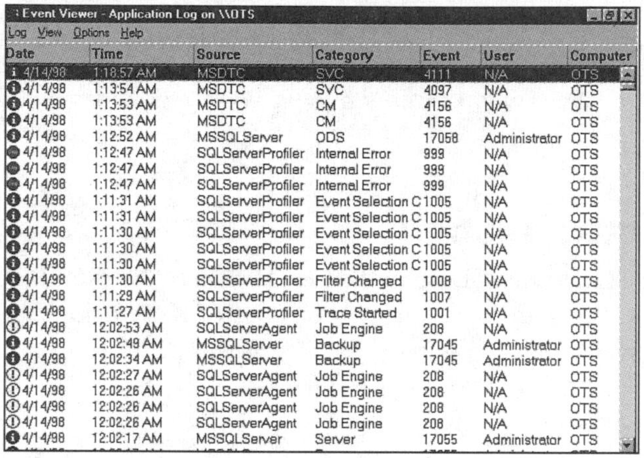

Date	Time	Source	Category	Event	User	Computer
4/14/98	1:18:57 AM	MSDTC	SVC	4111	N/A	OTS
4/14/98	1:13:54 AM	MSDTC	SVC	4097	N/A	OTS
4/14/98	1:13:53 AM	MSDTC	CM	4156	N/A	OTS
4/14/98	1:13:53 AM	MSDTC	CM	4156	N/A	OTS
4/14/98	1:12:52 AM	MSSQLServer	ODS	17058	Administrator	OTS
4/14/98	1:12:47 AM	SQLServerProfiler	Internal Error	999	N/A	OTS
4/14/98	1:12:47 AM	SQLServerProfiler	Internal Error	999	N/A	OTS
4/14/98	1:12:47 AM	SQLServerProfiler	Internal Error	999	N/A	OTS
4/14/98	1:11:31 AM	SQLServerProfiler	Event Selection C	1005	N/A	OTS
4/14/98	1:11:31 AM	SQLServerProfiler	Event Selection C	1005	N/A	OTS
4/14/98	1:11:30 AM	SQLServerProfiler	Event Selection C	1005	N/A	OTS
4/14/98	1:11:30 AM	SQLServerProfiler	Event Selection C	1005	N/A	OTS
4/14/98	1:11:30 AM	SQLServerProfiler	Event Selection C	1005	N/A	OTS
4/14/98	1:11:30 AM	SQLServerProfiler	Filter Changed	1008	N/A	OTS
4/14/98	1:11:29 AM	SQLServerProfiler	Filter Changed	1007	N/A	OTS
4/14/98	1:11:27 AM	SQLServerProfiler	Trace Started	1001	N/A	OTS
4/14/98	12:02:53 AM	SQLServerAgent	Job Engine	208	N/A	OTS
4/14/98	12:02:49 AM	MSSQLServer	Backup	17045	Administrator	OTS
4/14/98	12:02:34 AM	MSSQLServer	Backup	17045	Administrator	OTS
4/14/98	12:02:27 AM	SQLServerAgent	Job Engine	208	N/A	OTS
4/14/98	12:02:26 AM	SQLServerAgent	Job Engine	208	N/A	OTS
4/14/98	12:02:26 AM	SQLServerAgent	Job Engine	208	N/A	OTS
4/14/98	12:02:26 AM	SQLServerAgent	Job Engine	208	N/A	OTS
4/14/98	12:02:17 AM	MSSQLServer	Server	17055	Administrator	OTS

FIGURE 4.2
The Event Viewer.

> **TIP**
>
> In the Event Viewer, you can control the size of the event log. To control its size, select the Log Settings option from the Log menu. This action opens the Event Log Settings dialog box. From this dialog box, you can specify a maximum log size and the overwrite behavior.
>
> From within SQL Server, you can write your own messages to the event log. Use the extended stored procedure, as in the following syntax:

```
xp_logevent error_number, message, [severity]
```

The Registry

SQL Server configuration information is stored in a database called the *Registry*. To view and edit the Registry, run `REGEDIT.EXE` (see Figure 4.3). Normally, your software automatically maintains the Registry. You should change information in the Registry only when absolutely necessary. Otherwise, you may inadvertently introduce errors into your software and operating system.

Following is the Registry key to SQL Server 7.0:

```
HKEY_LOCAL_MACHINE
 \SOFTWARE
 \Microsoft
 \MSSQLServ70
```

FIGURE 4.3

The Registry.

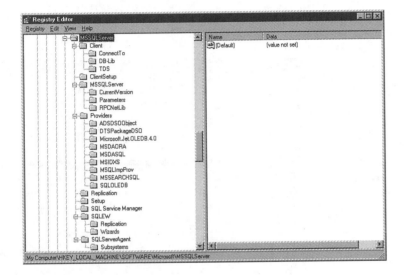

NT User Accounts

Through *Windows NT Authentication*, SQL Server can use Windows NT user accounts and passwords (see Figure 4.4). This means that a single user account can be used to control access to NT and SQL Server. This significantly reduces account maintenance, eliminates duplication, and simplifies login procedures.

For more information on user accounts and *Windows NT Authentication*, see Chapter 9, "Managing SQL Server Users and Security."

Performance Monitor

The *Performance Monitor* provides graphical statistics about the performance of SQL Server and Windows NT (see Figure 4.5). For more information about using the Performance Monitor, see Chapter 19, "Monitoring SQL Server." You also can define alerts in the Performance Monitor. *Alerts* enable you to track and monitor the frequency of an event (see Figure 4.6).

4

SQL SERVER OVERVIEW

FIGURE 4.4

NT user accounts.

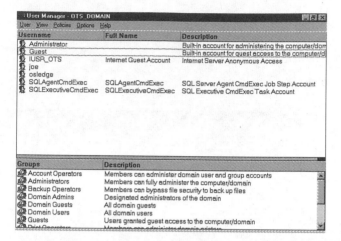

FIGURE 4.5

*Performance
Monitor.*

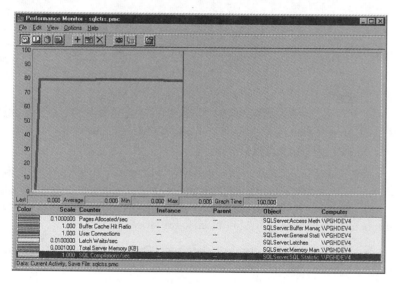

FIGURE 4.6
Alerts in the Performance Monitor.

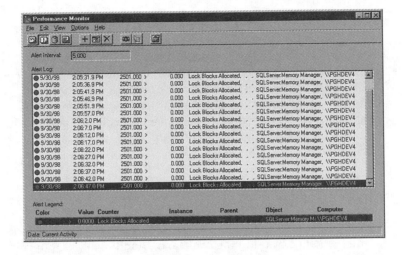

VISUAL ADMINISTRATION TOOLS

A primary goal of SQL Server 7.0 is to provide administrators with easy-to-use graphical administration tools. The ease with which someone can administer SQL Server 7.0 is a testimony to the success of Microsoft's development efforts.

The following tools enable you to easily set up, administer, and interact with SQL Server.

 ## SQL Server Service Manager

From the SQL Server Service Manager, you can start, stop, and pause SQL Server, SQL Server Agent, Microsoft Distributed Transaction Coordinator, and Microsoft Search (see Figure 4.7).

FIGURE 4.7
The SQL Server Service Manager.

4

SQL SERVER OVERVIEW

> **TIP**
>
> What is the purpose of the Pause button in the SQL Server Service Manager? This is a commonly asked question. By pausing the server, you can prevent users from logging into SQL Server while still keeping it up and running. This makes the feature useful when you want to halt users from making new connections but allow existing connections to continue processing; it also allows users a chance to log off normally before bringing down the database.

> **NOTE**
>
> The SQL Server service can also be started through the Control Panel or from the command line by using the command . Additionally, SQL Server can be started independently from the Control Panel by running from the command prompt (see Chapter 6, "Installing or Upgrading SQL Server," for more information on starting and stopping SQL Server).

SQL Server Enterprise Manager

As an administrator, you will probably spend the majority of your time interacting with SQL Server through the SQL Server Enterprise Manager. This is where you can administer multiple database servers through a single interface (see Figure 4.8).

Using the Enterprise Manager, you can perform the following functions:

- Start, configure, or shut down the following services   SQL Server, SQL Agent, SQL Mail, Distributed Transaction Coordinator, Microsoft Search
- Manage backups
- Manage databases
- Manage database maintenance tasks
- Manage logins and permissions
- Manage replication
- Manage tables, views, stored procedures, triggers, indexes, rules, defaults, and user-defined datatypes
- Schedule tasks
- Generate Web pages
- Generate SQL scripts

FIGURE 4.8

SQL Server Enterprise Manager.

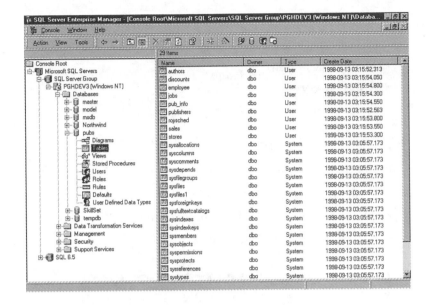

SQL Server Query Analyzer

SQL Server Query Analyzer is the Windows-based product used to execute SQL scripts (see Figure 4.9). The product also provides a color-coded query editor and a graphical execution plan. It does not provide graphical administration (use the SQL Server Enterprise Manager for graphical administration).

FIGURE 4.9

SQL Server Query Analyzer.

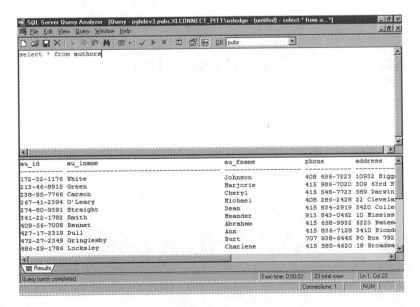

4

SQL SERVER OVERVIEW

Using SQL Server Query Analyzer, you can perform the following functions:

- Execute SQL statements
- Analyze query plans
- Display query statistics
- Perform index analysis

SQL Server Setup

Through SQL Setup, you can perform the following functions (see Figure 4.10):

- Set up SQL Server
- Configure an existing SQL Server installation
- Remove SQL Server

FIGURE 4.10
SQL Server Setup.

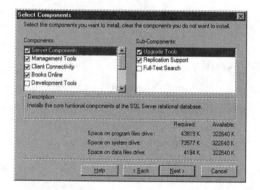

SQL Server Client Network Utility

From the SQL Server Client Network Utility, you can perform the following functions (see Figure 4.11):

- Configure client-side connections
- Determine network library version information

FIGURE 4.11
The SQL Client Network Utility.

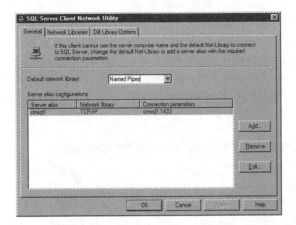

SQL Server Profiler

SQL Server Profiler is a graphical tool that displays Transact-SQL activity for a selected server (see Figure 4.12). SQL Server Profiler can be used by an administrator or developer to probe user activity and to generate audit trails. The output from SQL Server Profiler can be saved as a script or as an activity log. See Chapter 19, "Monitoring SQL Server," for more information on SQL Server Profiler.

FIGURE 4.12
SQL Server Profiler.

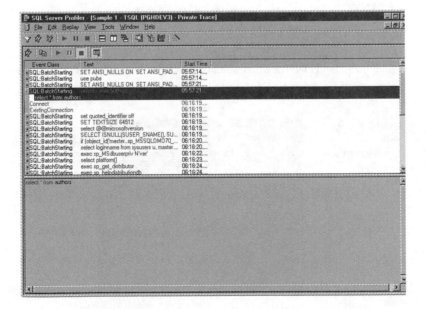

4

SQL SERVER OVERVIEW

Version Upgrade Wizard

The Version Upgrade Wizard is used to upgrade 6.x databases to SQL Server 7.0 (see Figure 4.13). This wizard exports the contents of a 6.x database and imports it into 7.x. Additionally, the wizard performs data- and object-level validation to ensure that the 6.x database is properly migrated to 7.0. See Chapter 6, "Installing or Upgrading SQL Server," for more information on the Version Upgrade Wizard.

FIGURE 4.13

Version Upgrade Wizard.

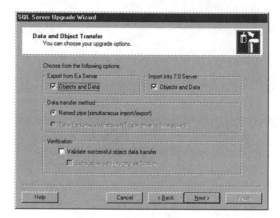

MSDTC Administrative Console

The MSDTC Administrative Console is used to manage the Microsoft Distributed Transaction Coordinator (DTC), (see Figure 4.14). Microsoft Transaction Coordinator (MTC) utilizes DTC for distributed transactions. See Chapter 12, "Distributed Transaction Coordinator," for more information on MSDTC.

FIGURE 4.14

MSDTC Administrative Console

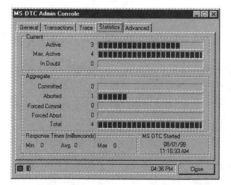

SQL SERVER COMPANION PRODUCTS

SQL Server 7.0 includes several companion products that are designed to integrate with Microsoft's goals of simplifying data access and providing an integrated data warehousing solution. The following are the companion products:

- Microsoft English Query
- OLAP Manager

Microsoft English Query

Microsoft English Query is a tool that can translate English syntax to into SQL statements (see Figure 4.15). For example, the following question can be entered by a user: "Who wrote The Gourmet Microwave?". Microsoft English Query automatically translates the English syntax into the following SQL statement:

```
select distinct dbo.authors.au_fname as "First Name",
➥ dbo.authors.au_lname as "Last Name" from dbo.titles,
➥ dbo.titleauthor, dbo.authors where
➥dbo.titles.title='The Gourmet Microwave'
➥and dbo.titles.title_id=dbo.titleauthor.title_id
➥and dbo.titleauthor.au_id=dbo.authors.au_id
```

FIGURE 4.15

Microsoft English Query.

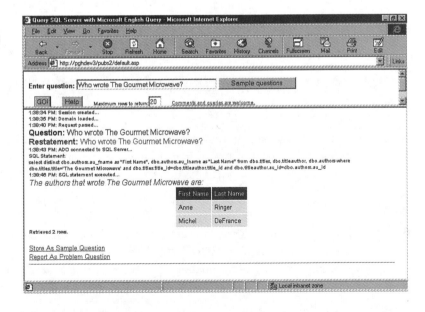

OLAP Manager

With OLAP Manager you can build and manage OLAP databases that are used to perform multidimensional database analysis (see Figure 4.16). Dimensions, cubes, and partitions are key components of this OLAP product. See Chapter 33, "Introduction to Microsoft SQL Server Olap Services," for more information on the OLAP Manager.

FIGURE 4.16
OLAP Manager.

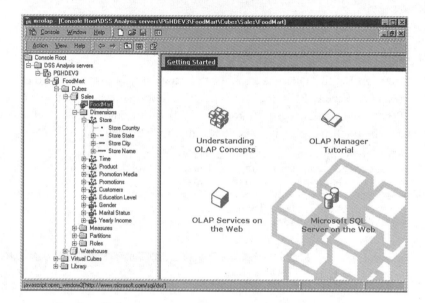

NONVISUAL ADMINISTRATION TOOLS AND COMMAND-LINE TOOLS

A DBA probably spends the majority of his or her time using the visual administration tools included with SQL Server. However, there are several nonvisual administration tools that a DBA might also use: BCP, ISQL, OSQL, TEXTCOPY, and ODBCPING.

BCP

BCP stands for *Bulk Copy Program*. It is a command-line utility that enables you to import and export data to and from SQL Server. The advantage of BCP is that it is fast. Users new to SQL Server are often amazed at how quickly it operates. The drawback of BCP is that it can be difficult to use.

By default, BCP.EXE is installed in the `mssql7\binn` directory. For more information on BCP, see Chapter 11, "Using BCP."

Following is the syntax for BCP (see Listing 4.1):

LISTING 4.1 SYNTAX FOR BCP

```
bcp dbtable {in ¦ out ¦ format} datafile
  [-m maxerrors]           [-f formatfile]        [-e errfile]
  [-F firstrow]            [-L lastrow]           [-b batchsize]
  [-n native type]         [-c character type]    [-w wide character type]
  [-N keep non-text native] [-6 6x file format]   [-q quoted identifier]
  [-C code page specifier] [-t field terminator]  [-r row terminator]
  [-i inputfile]           [-o outfile]           [-a packetsize]
  [-S server name]         [-U username]          [-P password]
  [-T trusted connection]  [-v version]
  [-k keep null values]    [-E keep identity values]
  [-h "load hints"]
```

> **NOTE**
>
> BCP switches are case sensitive.

ISQL

ISQL is a command-line utility used for executing queries. ISQL communicates with SQL Server through DB-Library. With the advent of graphical administration tools for SQL Server, the importance of ISQL has diminished. Most people prefer to perform day-to-day administration tasks from the SQL Server Enterprise Manager instead of using ISQL.

ISQL's minimal overhead, however, makes it useful for processing noninteractive routines such as nightly batch jobs.

By default, ISQL.EXE is installed in the mssql7\binn directory (see Listing 4.2).

Following is the syntax for ISQL:

LISTING 4.2 SYNTAX FOR ISQL

```
isql [-U login id] [-e echo input] [-x max text size]
  [-p print statistics] [-b On error batch abort] [-n remove numbering]
  [-c cmdend] [-h headers] [-w columnwidth] [-s colseparator]
  [-m errorlevel] [-t query timeout] [-l login timeout]
  [-L list servers] [-a packetsize]
  [-H hostname] [-P password]
  [-q "cmdline query"] [-Q "cmdline query" and exit]
  [-S server] [-d use database name]
```

continues

LISTING 4.2   CONTINUED

```
[-r msgs to stderr] [-E trusted connection]
[-i inputfile] [-o outputfile]
[-O use Old ISQL behavior disables the following]
        <EOF> batch processing
        Auto console width scaling
        Wide messages
        default errorlevel is -1 vs 1
[-? show syntax summary]
```

> **NOTE**
>
> ISQL switches are case sensitive.

OSQL

OSQL is a command-line utility used for executing queries. OSQL communicates with SQL Server through ODBC. OSQL is similar to ISQL except for the communication layer.

By default, OSQL.EXE is installed in the `mssql7\binn` directory (see the syntax in Listing 4.3).

LISTING 4.3   SYNTAX FOR OSQL

```
osql [-U login id]       [-P password]
  [-S server]            [-H hostname]          [-E trusted connection]
  [-d use database name] [-l login timeout]     [-t query timeout]
  [-h headers]           [-s colseparator]      [-w columnwidth]
  [-a packetsize]        [-e echo input]
  [-L list servers]      [-c cmdend]
  [-q "cmdline query"]   [-Q "cmdline query" and exit]
  [-n remove numbering]  [-m errorlevel]
  [-r msgs to stderr]
  [-i inputfile]         [-o outputfile]
  [-p print statistics]  [-b On error batch abort]
  [-O use Old ISQL behavior disables the following]
    <EOF> batch processing
    Auto console width scaling
    Wide messages
    default errorlevel is -1 vs 1
  [-? show syntax summary]
```

TEXTCOPY

TEXTCOPY is a command-line utility used for importing and exporting image files with SQL Server.

By default, TEXTCOPY.EXE is installed in the `mssql7\binn` directory.

Following is the syntax for TEXTCOPY:

```
TEXTCOPY [/S [sqlserver]] [/U [login]] [/P [password]]
  [/D [database]] [/T table] [/C column] [/W"where clause"]
  [/F file] [{/I | /O}] [/K chunksize] [/Z] [/?]
```

ODBCPING

ODBCPING is a command-line utility that can be used to verify an ODBC connection between the client and the server.

By default, ODBCPING.EXE is installed in the `mssql7\binn` directory.

Following is the syntax for ODBCPING:

```
odbcping [-S Server | -D DSN] [-U Login Id] [-P Password]
```

COMMON SQL SERVER OBJECTS

SQL Server uses the term *object* to describe a database component. Common database objects include tables, rules, defaults, user-defined datatypes, views, triggers, and stored procedures.

NOTE

Do not be misled by the term *object*. SQL Server is *not* an object-oriented database.

Tables

A *table* is used to store data. It is organized in a row/column manner (see Figure 4.17). You can retrieve, modify, and remove data from a table by using the SQL language.

4

SQL SERVER OVERVIEW

FIGURE 4.17

An example of a table.

stor_id	stor_name	stor_address	city	state	zip	last_update
7066	Barnum's	567 Pasadena Ave.	Tustin	CA	92789	8/1/1995 4:25 PM
7067	News & Brews	577 First St.	Los Gatos	CA	96745	8/15/1995 3:00 PM
7131	Doc-U-Mat	24-A Avrogado Way	Remulade	WA	98014	3/11/1995 1:00 PM
8042	Bookbeat	679 Carson St.	Portland	CA	89076	4/25/1995 3:00 PM

Rules

A *rule* is used to enforce a data constraint (see Figure 4.18). Rules are column specific and cannot perform table lookups. Generally, rules are used to enforce simple business constraints.

FIGURE 4.18

An example of a rule.

stor_id	stor_name	stor_address	city	state	zip	last_update
7066	Barnum's	567 Pasadena Ave.	Tustin	CA	92789	8/1/1995 4:25 PM
7067	News & Brews	577 First St.	Los Gatos	CA	96745	8/15/1995 3:00 PM
7131	Doc-U-Mat	24-A Avrogado Way	Remulade	WA	98014	3/11/1995 1:00 PM
8042	Bookbeat	679 Carson St.	Portland	CA	89076	4/25/1995 3:00 PM

Business Rule: All store ids must be between 1 and 9999.

SQL Server Translation: CREATE RULE stor_id_rule AS
@stor_id > = 1 AND @stor_id < = 9999

sp_bindrule stor_id_rule, 'stores. stor_id'

NOTE

An alternative to creating a rule is to use the constraint. Another alternative to creating a rule is to use a trigger.

Defaults

Defaults are used to populate a column with a default value when a value is not supplied (see Figure 4.19).

FIGURE 4.19

An example of defaults.

Business Rule: If store address is not known when adding a new record, enter "unknown."

SQL Server Translation: CREATE DEFAULT stor_address_default AS
'unknown'

sp_bindefault stor_address_default, 'stores, stor_address'

User-Defined Datatypes

With a *user-defined datatype*, you can create a custom, reusable datatype based on an existing SQL Server datatype (see Figure 4.20). By using user-defined datatypes, you can ensure datatype consistency.

FIGURE 4.20

An example of a user-defined datatype.

Business Rule: Store id is an integer and can not be null.

SQL Server Translation: sp_addtype stor_id_data type, 'integer,' 'not null'

    CREATE TABLE stores (stor_id stor_id_datatype, stor_name char (35).

Views

A *view* is a virtual table that looks and feels like a real table. Views limit the amount of data a user can see and modify. Views can be used to control user access to data and to simplify data presentation (see Figure 4.21).

FIGURE 4.21

An example of a view.

stor_id	stor_name	stor_address	city	state	zip	last_update
7066	Barnum's	567 Pasadena Ave.	Tustin	CA	92789	8/1/1995 4:25 PM
7067	News & Brews	577 First St.	Los Gatos	CA	96745	8/15/1995 3:00 PM
7131	Doc-U-Mat	24-A Avrogado Way	Remulade	WA	98014	3/11/1995 1:00 PM
8042	Bookbeat	679 Carson St.	Portland	CA	89076	4/25/1995 3:00 PM
8100	Johnston	unknown	Fairfax	VA	23294	

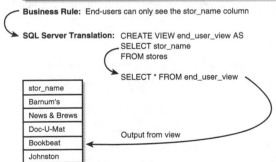

Business Rule: End-users can only see the stor_name column

SQL Server Translation: CREATE VIEW end_user_view AS
  SELECT stor_name
  FROM stores

SELECT * FROM end_user_view

stor_name
Barnum's
News & Brews
Doc-U-Mat
Bookbeat
Johnston

Output from view

4

SQL SERVER
OVERVIEW

Triggers

A *trigger* is a user-defined collection of Transact-SQL commands that is automatically executed when an INSERT, DELETE, or UPDATE is executed against a table (see Figure 4.22). Triggers are flexible and powerful, which makes them useful for enforcing business rules, referential integrity, and data integrity. Triggers can be column, row, or table specific.

FIGURE 4.22

An example of a trigger.

stor_id	stor_name	stor_address	city	state	zip	last_update
7066	Barnum's	567 Pasadena Ave.	Tustin	CA	.92789	8/1/1995 4:25 PM
7067	News & Brews	577 First St.	Los Gatos	CA	96745	8/15/1995 3:00 PM
7131	Doc-U-Mat	24-A Avrogado Way	Remulade	WA	98014	3/11/1995 1:00 PM
8042	Bookbeat	679 Carson St.	Portland	CA	89076	4/25/1995 3:00 PM
8100	Johnston	unknown	Fairfax	VA	23294	8/1/1995 1:00 PM

Application Requirement: Every time a record is modified, update the last_update column to reflect the date and time of the modification.

SQL Server Translation: CREATE TRIGGER stores_trigger ON dbo.stores
FOR INSERT, UPDATE
AS
UPDATE stores
SET last_update = GETDATE()
FROM stores, inserted
WHERE stores.stor_id = inserted.stor_id

This trigger automatically enters the date and the time of the last modification to the record.

NOTE

Older versions of SQL Server used triggers to enforce referential integrity. It is recommended that referential integrity be enforced through declarative referential integrity by using the FOREIGN KEY, PRIMARY KEY, and REFERENCE statements. Triggers must still be used to perform cascading changes such as cascading deletes or cascading updates.

Stored Procedures

A *stored procedure* is a compiled SQL program (see Figure 4.23). Within a stored procedure, you can embed conditional logic (if/else logic), declare variables, pass parameters, and perform other programming tasks.

FIGURE 4.23

An example of a stored procedure.

stor_id	stor_name	stor_address	city	state	zip	last_update
7066	Barnum's	567 Pasadena Ave.	Tustin	CA	92789	8/1/1995 4:25 PM
7067	News & Brews	577 First St.	Los Gatos	CA	96745	8/15/1995 3:00 PM
7131	Doc-U-Mat	24-A Avrogado Way	Remulade	WA	98014	3/11/1995 1:00 PM
8042	Bookbeat	679 Carson St.	Portland	CA	89076	4/25/1995 3:00 PM
8100	Johnston	unknown	Fairfax	VA	23294	8/1/1995 1:00 PM

Application Requirement: Store name can be retrieved by passing a parameter to a stored procedure.

SQL Server Translation: CREATE PROCEDURE retrieve_store_name @stor_id integer AS
SELECT stor_name
FROM stores

execute retrieve_store_name 8100

Output from
stored procedure

stor_name
Johnston

SQL SERVER FAQ

The following lists some of the common questions asked by DBAs about SQL Server:

Q. What is the difference between the NT version and the Windows 9.x version of SQL Server?

A. The two products are virtually identical. The only features not found in the Windows 9.x version are SMP support, asynchronous I/O support, and *Windows NT Authentication* security.

Q. Can I use SQL Server Enterprise Manager, version 7.0, to administer 6.x versions of SQL Server?

A. No, you cannot use Enterprise Manager, version 7.0, to administer previous versions of SQL Server. However, the 6.x version of the Enterprise Manager will automatically load when you attempt to manage a 6.x server from the 7.0 version of the Enterprise Manager (note: the 6.x version of the Enterprise Manager must be already installed on the computer).

Q. Can I use SQL Server Enterprise Manager on a Windows 9.x client to manage SQL Server running on NT?

A. Yes, SQL Server Enterprise Manager on a Windows 9.x client can be used to administer SQL Server on NT.

4

SQL SERVER OVERVIEW

SUMMARY

The following is summary information of this chapter:

- The Enterprise Manager is used to administer SQL Server. From this console, you can administer multiple database servers through a single interface. Tasks, such as starting and stopping SQL Server, managing databases, managing backups, managing permissions, and others, are performed through this interface.

- The Enterprise Manager is part of the Microsoft Management Console (MMC). This console is also used to manage products, via snap-ins, such as Exchange, Microsoft Transaction Server, and other products through a single interface.

- SQL Server Agent is the scheduling manager provided with SQL Server. It is responsible for managing jobs and alerts. Jobs are typically used to schedule and automate tasks such as database backups and database maintenance. Alerts are notifications that are executed automatically upon the occurrence of an event. An example of an alert is a notification, such as a page or email, which is automatically sent to a DBA when the database is corrupted.

- SQL Server 7.0 supports the Windows NT and Windows 9.x operating systems. The functionality in each version of SQL Server is nearly identical, and each product uses the same code base.

- SQL Server 7.0 is integrated with NT's Control Panel through the following services: SQL Server (MSSQLServer), SQL Server Agent (SQLServerAgent), Distributed Transaction Coordinator (MSDTC), and Microsoft Search.

- Information about SQL Server is stored in the following registry key:
  ```
  HKEY_LOCAL_MACHINE
   \SOFTWARE
   \Microsoft
   \MSSQLServer
  ```

- SQL Server Query Analyzer is used to perform the following functions: execute SQL statements, analyze query plans, display query statistics, perform index analysis.

- SQL Server Profiler is a tool that graphically traces activity. The information generated by the SQL Server Profiler is often used to probe user activity, troubleshoot queries, and generate audit trails.

- Microsoft English Query is a tool that can translate English syntax into SQL statements.

- Microsoft OLAP Manager provides multidimensional database analysis. This is a key component to Microsoft's data warehousing strategy.

- The Distributed Transformation Service (DTS) provides import and export capability for a variety of file formats. It also includes a data transformation component that can translate data into different formats through rules and scripts.

- A *table* is used to store data and is organized in a row/column manner.

- A *trigger* is a user-defined collection of Transact-SQL commands that is automatically executed when an INSERT, DELETE, or UPDATE is executed against a table.

- A *stored procedure* is a compiled program that contains Transact-SQL statements.

INSTALLING AND UPGRADING SQL SERVER

IN THIS PART

PLANNING AN INSTALLATION OR UPGRADE

by Mark Spenik

IN THIS CHAPTER

In this chapter, you develop plans and strategies to help you correctly install or upgrade SQL Server. Why bother with a planning stage? Why not just skip right to the installation or upgrade? SQL Server installation and upgrading is a simple process, but by planning, you can make the correct decisions that affect the performance and operation of SQL Server before the installation. When upgrading, you can never make too many plans to limit server downtime and protect your database against problems encountered during the upgrade. Additionally, the SQL Server 7.0 upgrade process is entirely different from any previous version's upgrade process. SQL Server 7.0 changed many of the database structures and formats, such as the database page size. Therefore, the data has to be transferred from 6.x databases to new 7.0 databases instead of upgrading the 6.x databases as in previous upgrades. Whether you are upgrading or planning a new installation, the first step of the process is the installation of SQL Server 7.0. Start by examining installation strategies and plans and then tackle the subject of upgrade strategies and plans.

> **NOTE**
>
> Installing SQL Server has been simplified. You can get by during the installation process by answering a few simple questions such as your name and company. However, I still think it is important to understand what happens during installation and what defaults you are accepting if you do not select custom install.

DEVELOPING AN INSTALLATION STRATEGY AND PLAN

Developing an installation plan starts with the assessment of the requirements of your business or users, includes the selection and purchase of the hardware, and finishes with making decisions for specific SQL Server options. Begin by collecting user and system requirements. After the requirements have been collected, you examine possible hardware configurations and SQL Server options. You then create a checklist to use during system installation, and finally, you install SQL Server.

Step 1: Determine System and User Requirements

How do you determine the hardware system requirements and user requirements for SQL Server? You ask questions and do some homework. Start with the user requirements or business requirements. Based on the requirements of the users or business, you can determine the size and type of hardware system you need to meet the requirements. Start with the following questions:

- What is the purpose or goal of the system?
- What are the database requirements?
- What are the user or business requirements?
- How much money will it cost?

> **NOTE**
>
> One decision you won't have to make is whether to use UNIX, NetWare, or Windows NT. Microsoft SQL Server 7.0 is supported on Windows NT Server 4.0 and later, Windows NT Workstation 4.0 and later, and Windows 95 and later. If you have decided to use Microsoft SQL Server, the operating system war is already over; it will be a Microsoft Operating System! For a database that handles multiple users, use Windows NT Server; for laptop or mobile users, use Windows 95 or Windows 98. NT workstation can be used on high-end laptops, desktops, or for developers working with their own copy of SQL Server during the development process.

The following sections expand on each of the preceding questions to help you determine the type of system you need.

What Is the Intended Use of the System?

The first questions you might ask yourself are what the system is for and how many concurrent users the system must accommodate. (For example, is the system for a single department with 10 users or for a very large database system with several thousand users?) A system supporting more users requires more memory, disk space, and processing power. Is the system a dedicated SQL Server system or does it perform other activities like file and printing services? Is the system replacing another system due to of downsizing or right-sizing? If it is replacing an existing system, you already have a lot information available to you (such as the current load on the system and the current system's shortcomings). Is the system a production system or a development/test system? You want more fault tolerance and more storage capability on a production server than you typically need on a development server.

What Are the Database Requirements?

What are the database requirements for the system? Will the SQL Server primarily support decision support systems or transaction systems? How heavy is the expected transaction load? If the system is transaction driven, try to determine the number of expected transactions per day and how the transactions will be processed. For example, is the server idle for eight hours and does it then process all the transactions during a few hours, or does it process the transactions evenly throughout the day? What is the expected size of the database? Are you moving databases from another system to SQL Server because of downsizing or right-sizing? If so, you should be able to obtain information such as the current database size, expected database size, and the transaction load of the system from the current system.

> **TIP**
>
> If you have the means, dedicate a machine for SQL Server. Then you can tune the hardware to give the best SQL Server performance.

What Are the User's Requirements and Expectations?

It is always important to understand the requirements and expectations of the individuals who use SQL Server. What type of query response time do the users expect? How many users will be logged on to SQL Server at one time? What are the backup and storage requirements of the users or business? After you understand the user's expectations, determine whether you can provide them with a system that meets their expectations. You might need to bring them back to earth to face the reality of what their system can do.

How Much Does It Cost?

Maybe this question should be listed first! In the real world, the difference between the system you need and the system you get is the amount of money you have available to spend on the system. (Enough said!) The good news is that system prices are steadily dropping, making the server you need more affordable.

Step 2: Select the Right Platform

After you obtain the answers and information to the questions described in "Step 1: Determine System and User Requirements," in the first part of this chapter, you are ready to select the hardware platform for your SQL Server. For this discussion, the hardware platform is divided into four areas:

- Hardware (including the processor or processors and peripherals)
- Memory
- Disk drives
- File system

The following sections examine each area and the type of decisions you need to make for each area.

Hardware

When determining which hardware platform to use, check the Windows NT Hardware Compatibility List to make sure that the brand and model of the machine you are considering is on the list. If the brand and model you are interested in is not on the compatibility list, download the latest list from an electronic bulletin board. If the machine is still not listed, check with the manufacturer or Microsoft. When you are purchasing the machine, it is always good to let the vendor know that you plan to use the machine as a database server. Mention that you plan to use Microsoft SQL Server as the database engine and ask if there are any known issues or problems with using the selected platform with SQL Server.

> **TIP**
>
> Save yourself a lot of problems and potential headaches by using only the machines approved for Microsoft Windows NT. Although you may get other machines to work, I have seen the difficulty involved and the potential to fail to get the machine up and running when using unapproved platforms and configurations.

At the time this book goes to press, Windows NT and Windows 9x are supported on the following microprocessors:

- Digital Alpha AXP
- Intel 32-bit x86 (Pentium 133 or greater and so on)

So, how do you determine the correct hardware platform for your business or organization? Start with cost and examine hardware platforms within your budget. There is no point wasting your time researching hardware platforms you can't afford.

Use the information you gathered earlier, such as the expected number of transactions during a given time period, and talk to the hardware manufacturers or integrators to see whether the platform you are considering can meet those goals and requirements. Check for SQL Server benchmarks on the particular platform and ask to speak to other clients currently using the platform. Consider other factors such as manufacturer reliability, service, and maintenance. These three factors are extremely important if the machine runs into a hardware problem and you are faced with downtime. Consider expandability;

5

PLANNING AN
INSTALLATION OR
UPGRADE

for example, will you require multiple processors in the future? If so, can the current platform be expanded to accept more processors?

DO I NEED SMP (SYMMETRIC MULTIPLE PROCESSORS)?

Right out of the box, Windows NT 4.0 supports up to four processors and this number will only increase in future versions of Windows NT; SQL Server can take advantage of these processors without any special add-ons or configuration changes. In theory, a perfect scaleable SMP machine would scale 100 percent; meaning that if your SQL Server performed 20 transactions per second and you added a second processor, you would increase the number of transactions to 40 per second. The scalability of systems varies widely and can range from near 100 percent to below 60 percent. Check with the manufacturer.

What does it mean to you and SQL Server? If you are performing heavy transaction database processing, you can expect your transaction performance to increase with the scalability of the system. If you perform 10 transactions per second and add a second processor on a system that provides 80 percent scalability, you can expect roughly 18 transactions per second. SMP works very well for transaction-based systems.

What if you do primarily decision support (such as database queries)? In the 6.x version of SQL Server, adding a second processor may not be the best way to improve your system performance. In decision support systems, the queries are I/O bound and not processor bound, so adding additional processors does not provide the same substantial performance gain you get with transaction-based systems. However, with SQL Server 7.0, adding additional processors in a decision support environment enables you to take advantage of SQL Server 7.0 parallel query capabilities, which can greatly decrease the time required to run long running queries. SQL Server 7.0 has many features that can take advantage of an SMP system whether it is transaction based or decision support based. That's why I would recommend starting with a SMP machine if you can fit it into your budget!

Memory

A common theme in this book is *giving SQL Server enough memory*, not because SQL Server is an inefficient memory hog, but because SQL Server uses memory very intelligently. Extra memory can provide you with some very cost-effective performance enhancements. The minimum memory requirement of SQL Server is 32MB. (See the tip later in this section for comments on the minimum amount.)

You are no longer required to configure and tune SQL Server's memory usage. SQL Server 7.0 dynamically adjusts the amount of memory it uses based on its current requirements and the requirements of the system on which it is running.

Regardless of the amount of memory you start with, after SQL Server is up and running, you can monitor SQL Server to more accurately determine your memory requirements.

TIP

The cost of memory has plummeted to the point where memory is now cheap! Do yourself a favor and get database servers that start with a fair amount of memory. A few years back I would have said start with 128MB and then tune up. With current memory prices, I now recommend starting with 256MB to 512MB, depending on your budget and user requirements. SQL Server uses memory very effectively, and giving it enough memory to cache a fair amount of data pages in memory means improved performance. If you are planning to use SQL Server for a laptop and merge replication, 32MB of memory works, but 64MB works even better.

Disk Drives

One of the most important system decisions you can make is the type of disk drives and disk controllers you select. Selecting the proper disk system has a big impact on the overall performance of the SQL Server system and the type of data fault tolerance used to protect the databases.

CAUTION

Take special care in selecting your disk system. Disk I/O is the typical bottleneck found in database systems. If the disk system you are purchasing contains a write-caching disk controller, disable the write-caching disk controller. SQL Server database recovery can be compromised along with the data integrity when a write-caching disk controller is used. The exception is if the write-caching disk controller is designed to be used with database servers like SQL Server. In this case, check with the vendor.

Before you get into the specifics, you want to select fast disk drives and smart controller cards to take advantage of Windows NT multitasking and asynchronous read-ahead features. When buying disk drives for a database server, consider using more, smaller physical drives rather than one large physical drive. Doing so enables you to spread your databases and transaction logs over several different physical devices. If you are considering buying one 12 GB hard drive, for example, reconsider and purchase three 4 GB hard drives or six 2 GB hard drives.

TIP

The Asynchronous Read-Ahead Technology in SQL Server is beneficial only with multiple disk configurations and smart disk controllers that have asynchronous capabilities.

Just as important as the speed of your hard disk system is the fault tolerance offered in modern disk drive systems. You want the best protection for your databases with optimum performance. One option available to you is the use of RAID (Redundant Array of Inexpensive Disks) disk drive configurations. RAID disk configurations use several disk drives to build a single logical striped drive. Logically, a striped drive is a single drive; physically, the logical drive spans many different disk drives. *Striping the drives* allows files and devices to span multiple physical devices. By spreading the data over several physical drives, RAID configurations offer excellent performance. Another benefit of RAID configurations is fault tolerance and recovery. A RAID 5 configuration can lose a single disk drive and recover all the data on the lost drive. When a new drive is added, the RAID configuration rebuilds the lost drive on the new drive. A RAID 5 system offers good protection and performance for your databases. RAID configurations can be hardware-based solutions or Windows NT software-based solutions. Hardware-based RAID solutions are typically faster than software-based RAID solutions. For more information on when to use RAID 5 or RAID 1 (disk mirroring) see the FAQ section of this chapter.

File System

When working with Windows NT, should you use NTFS (New Technology File System) or FAT (File Allocation Table)? From a performance standpoint, it does not really matter. (The performance difference between the two file systems is negligible.) In general, NTFS performs faster in read operations and FAT performs faster in write operations. If you use the NTFS file system, you can take advantage of Windows NT security. If you are required to have a dual boot computer, you should use a FAT partition.

> **TIP**
>
> I typically recommend NTFS on Windows NT systems, which enables you to take advantage of NT security and auditing features.

The Right Platform

The right platform for SQL Server is the best system you can afford that does the SQL Server processing you require! A good configuration for a SQL Server system is shown in Figure 5.1: a computer configured with one or many processors and starting with 256MB of memory. Use a RAID 5 stripe set disk configuration for the databases; place the transaction logs on a RAID 1 (disk mirroring)stripe set, and place the operating system and SQL Server on a nonstriped drive or a RAID 1 stripe set. What makes this a good configuration? SQL Server 7.0 is designed to take advantage of SMP systems with features like parallel queries. The RAID 5 disk configuration for the databases gives you fault tolerance and the RAID 5 configuration is very fast in performing disk read operations. RAID 5 also takes care of spreading the data across multiple drives. The RAID 1 configuration for the logs is desirable because a transaction log is used only for sequential writes and does not benefit from RAID 5's fast disk reads. RAID 5 is slower than RAID 1 when performing sequential writes due to the time required to compute and write out the parity data and the RAID 1 configuration offers you fault tolerance. How could this system be enhanced? Add additional stripe sets or more memory. Additional stripe sets can give you additional logical drives so that you can place a table on one logical drive and its index on another. For the memory requirements, monitor your SQL Server and determine the correct amount of memory for your Server. More memory enables you to cache more data without having to go to the disk to retrieve the information.

FIGURE 5.1

A typical SQL Server hardware configuration.

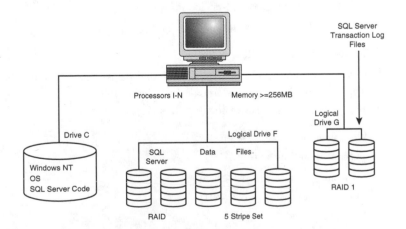

The Microsoft Recommended Software and Hardware Requirements

Now that you have decided what you would like the system to do and have begun to select your hardware configuration, take a look at the minimum SQL Server 7.0 configurations as suggested by Microsoft. Remember, these are the minimum hardware platform requirements. As you work with these products, you will learn that the minimum suggested processor and memory requirements run the software but don't give great performance. Whenever possible, use the best processor you can afford. More important than the processor is the memory. Start with more than the minimum memory requirements; after all SQL Server loves memory!

Supported Hardware Platforms

The following is a list of the SQL Server 7.0 supported hardware platforms:

- DEC Alpha
- Intel and compatible systems—minimum recommended processor—Pentium 133 MHz or higher, Pentium Pro, or Pentium II

Memory

The following is the minimum memory requirements for SQL Server 7.0:

- A minimum of 32MB of RAM

Operating Systems

SQL Server 7.0 now supports more than just Windows NT and if even you are using Windows NT, you'll need the proper service pack. The operating systems supported are as follows:

- Windows 95 or later (Includes Windows 95 OSR2 and Windows 98)
- Windows NT 4.0 Server, Service Pack 4 or later
- Windows NT 4.0 Workstation, Service Pack 4 or later,

Disk Space Requirements

SQL Server has several different installation options, such As Install Client Utilities Only, Typical Installation, and Compact Installation to name a few. The estimated disk space requirements for these various options are as follows:

- Full Installation 190MB
- Typical Installation 163MB
- Minimum Installation 74MB
- Management Tools only 73MB

As far as disk space goes, the numbers listed are the required amounts to install SQL Server and the system databases. They do not include the size required for your various user databases or for any other applications you may want to install. When you are looking at disk requirements, don't forget to add in the anticipated size of your user databases. If the server does not have a tape backup unit, add additional space (about the same amount for user databases) to allow disk backups of your databases.

> **NOTE**
>
> IE 4.01 with Service Pack 1 must be installed before you can install SQL Server 7.0. IE 4.01 and IE Service pack 1 are located on the SQL Server CD.

Step 3: Answer Required Questions and Understand Why They Are Important

When you begin a new SQL Server installation or an Upgrade from SQL Server 6.x to 7.0, you are asked several questions such as your name and company name. You should be able to answer these questions with no problem and with SQL Server 7.0 that's about all you have to answer to install the product! However, if you select a custom install, you are asked to answer other questions that affect SQL Server performance, maintenance, and behavior. If you select the typical or compact installation, you won't be asked these question but you should be familiar with them and with the defaults the defaults used by SQL Server when making these selections. Examine the following installation topics in more detail to help you make the correct choices for your SQL Server:

- Data File Location
- Character set
- Sort order
- Unicode collation
- Network
- SQL Server and SQL Server Agent Windows NT accounts

Data File Location

During installation, you are asked to give the drive and path to install the SQL Server system databases. The system databases are as follows:

- master   SQL Server's configuration database
- model   Serves as a template on which other databases are created

- `tempdb`   Temporary storage area
- `msdb`   Scheduling database and SQL Server Agent database
- NorthWind   Example database
- `pubs`   Example database

The default location used for the data files is the SQL Server root directory, \MSSQL7, sub-directory DATA. You can change the location of these files or leave them on the default. Select a drive that has enough space to allow these databases to expand. The `master`, `msdb`, `model`, and `pubs` database typically do not grow rapidly (adding several megabytes a day). However, `tempdb` is a different story. SQL Server 7.0 allows `tempdb` to automatically expand if the databases configured size is exceeded. When SQL Server is shutdown and restarted, `tempdb` automatically shrinks to its initial configured size. For this reason, it is wise to select a drive or stripe set for `tempdb` that has room for the database to expand as well as a drive or stripe set that provides you with good performance.

Character Set

The *character set* is the set of valid characters in your SQL Server database. A character set consists of 256 uppercase and lowercase numbers, symbols, and letters; the first 128 characters in a character set are the same for all the different character sets.

The following are some common character sets you can choose from at installation time:

Code page 850 (Multilingual)	Code page 850 includes all the characters for North American, South American, and European countries.
	Code page 850 is the default character set for SQL Server 4.21 installations.
(DEFAULT) Code Page 1252 (ISO, 8859-1, Latin 1 or ANSI)	This character set is compatible with the ANSI characters used by Microsoft Windows NT and Microsoft Windows.
	Code Page 1252 is the default sort order for SQL Server version 6.x and 7.0.
Code Page 437 (US English)	The common character set used in the United States. Code Page 437 also contains many graphical characters that are typically not stored in databases.

Other available character sets are as follows:

- Code Page 874   Thai
- Code Page 932   Japanese
- Code Page 936   Chinese (simplified)
- Code Page 949   Korean
- Code Page 950   Chinese (traditional)
- Code Page 1250   Central European
- Code Page 1251   Cyrillic
- Code Page 1253   Greek
- Code Page 1254   Turkish
- Code Page 1255   Hebrew
- Code Page 1256   Arabic
- Code Page 1257   Baltic

CAUTION

Deciding on the correct character set is important! *The character set cannot be changed easily!* Changing the character set requires exporting all of the data out of your databases, rebuilding the databases, and then reloading all your databases.

Sort Order

The sort order you select for your SQL Server determines how the data is presented in response to SQL queries that use the GROUP BY, ORDER BY, and DISTINCT clauses. The sort order also determines how certain queries are resolved, such as those involving WHERE clauses. For example, if you choose a sort order that is case sensitive and you have a table called MyTable, the query to select all the rows from MyTable must have the following format:

```
Select * from MyTable
```

If the sort order selected is case insensitive, the preceding query could be written in following manners:

```
Select * from MyTable
Select * from mytable
Select * from MYTABLE
```

SQL Server offers many different sort orders, each with its own set of rules. The following section briefly examines some of the possible sort order choices. Not all sort orders are available for every character set.

(DEFAULT)Dictionary Order, Case Insensitive

Dictionary order means that the characters, when sorted, appear in the order you find them in a dictionary. Dictionary Order, Case Insensitive, uses the following rules to compare characters:

- Uppercase and lowercase characters are treated as equivalents.
- Characters with diacritical marks are treated as different characters.

> **NOTE**
>
> Dictionary Order, Case Insensitive, is the default sort order for SQL Server 6.x and 7.0.

Binary Sort Order

The *binary sort* order uses numeric values to collate the data. Each charter is compared to its numeric representation of 0 to 255. Data does not always come back in dictionary order; for example, UUU returns before aaa in ascending order.

Dictionary Order, Case Sensitive

Dictionary Order, Case Sensitive, uses the following rules:

- Uppercase and lowercase characters are not treated the same.
- Characters with diacritical marks are treated as different characters.

> **TIP**
>
> If you have two servers available and you want to change the sort order or character set, use the DTS services or the BCP (Bulk Copy) utility to rebuild the database and transfer the data.

The sort order affects the speed and performance of SQL Server. Binary sort order is the fastest of the sort orders; the other sort orders are 20 to 35 percent slower than the binary sort order. The default sort order (Dictionary Order, Case Insensitive) is about 20 percent slower than the binary sort order.

CAUTION

Selecting the correct sort order is important because changing the sort order—just as changing the character set—requires exporting the data, rebuilding your databases, and then reloading the data.

TIP

If you have several SQL Servers in your organization, you should use the same character set and sort order for each of the servers, especially if you want to share databases using the BACKUP and Restore commands. You can't load a database that was backed up with a different character set and sort order unless both servers use a binary sort order; then they can have different character sets. Another reason to select the same sort order is so that users of different servers can run queries that process the data the same (for example, a lowercase b = uppercase b, and so on).

Unicode Collation

Unicode collation is the sort order of Unicode data. Unicode data is new for SQL Server 7.0. Unicode is double the size of the standard ANSI character, which is a byte; therefore Unicode is two bytes. The possible different character values that can be represented with the standard ANSI character are 256 bytes (or 2 to the eighth). Unicode characters can represent 2 to the sixteenth or 65,536 different character values. SQL Server 7.0 datatypes nchar, nvarchar, and ntext store Unicode characters. The Unicode collation consists of a locale and several comparison styles. The Unicode collation determines whether an uppercase B is equal to a lowercase b. The default value selected during installation is based on the character set and sort order. Be careful if you want to change the default so that it's not difficult for you to move non-Unicode data to Unicode and so that non-Unicode data and Unicode data sort the same.

CAUTION

Do not change the Unicode Collation setting when upgrading SQL Server; take the default. The 7.0 master database contains unicode columns that were non-Unicode in SQL Server 6.x and could present problems if a Unicode collation that sorts differently from the 6.x database is selected.

Network

Because SQL Server supports many different network options simultaneously, clients running TCP/IP can connect to SQL Server along with clients using IPX/SPX—all at the same time. SQL Server installs different network libraries during installation to handle network communication with other servers and client workstations. SQL Server 7.0 installs TCP/IP, multiprotocol and the named-pipes protocol (not available in Windows 9x installations) by default. You have the option during installation (and after) to install one or more network libraries. Keep in mind that the type of network support you select determines the security mode you can use for SQL Server. Before you examine the network libraries available to you, look at the two different security modes:

- **Windows NT Authentication:** Takes advantage of Windows NT user security and account mechanisms. Windows NT Authentication requires a trusted connection and can be implemented over the named-pipes protocol or multiprotocol network protocols. Note: Windows NT Authentication is not supported with Windows 95/98 clients.

- **Mixed:** Enables users to connect via Windows NT Authentication or SQL Server Authentication. Using SQL Server Authentication, an individual logging on to SQL Server supplies a username and a password that is validated by SQL Server against a system table. Users using trusted connections (named-pipes or multiprotocol) can log in using Windows NT Authentication; users from trusted or nontrusted connections (any network protocol supported by SQL Server) can log in using standard security.

The following sections describe the network options available for SQL Server 7.0.

Named-Pipes Protocol

The named-pipes protocol is the default protocol installed with SQL Server. Named-pipes allows for interprocess communication locally or over networks and is used in NT networks.

Multiprotocol

The multiprotocol uses Windows NT Remote Procedure Call (RPC) mechanisms for communication and requires no setup parameters. Multiprotocol currently supports NWLINK IPX/SPX, TCP/IP and named pipes. Multiprotocol enables users of IPX/SPX and TCP/IP protocols to take advantage of Windows NT Authentication.

NWLink IPX/SPX Protocol

IPX/SPX is the familiar network protocol used for Novell networks. If you select NWLink IPX/SPX during installation, you are prompted for the Novell Bindery service name to register SQL Server.

TCP/IP Protocol

TCP/IP is a popular communications protocol used in many UNIX networks. If you select TCP/IP, you are asked to provide a TCP/IP port number for SQL Server to use for client connections. The default port number and the official Internet Assigned Number Authority socket number for Microsoft SQL Server is 1433.

Banyan Vines

Banyan Vines is another popular PC-based network system. Support for Banyan Vines is included only on Intel-based SQL Server systems. If you install Banyan Vines, you are prompted for a valid street talk name that must first be created using the Vines program MSERVICE.

AppleTalk ADSP Protocol

AppleTalk ADSP enables Apple Macintosh clients to connect to SQL Server using AppleTalk. If you select AppleTalk, you are prompted for the AppleTalk service object name.

SQL Server and SQL Server Agent Windows NT User Accounts

The SQL Executive was first introduced in SQL Server 6.0; for SQL Server 7.0, the SQL Executive is now called the SQL Server Agent. The SQL Server Agent is the service responsible for managing SQL Server tasks such as replication, events, alerts, and job scheduling. During system installation and upgrade, you are required to assign an NT system user account for the SQL Server Agent and for SQL Server. You can use the local system account (in which case you do not have to create a new NT user account) but you will not be able to perform tasks with other servers like replication, backups to network drives, SQL mail, or shared heterogeneous joins because the local system account has no network access rights. SQL Server also requires a Windows NT account. It is recommended that you set up a Windows NT domain user account for SQL Server and for the SQL Server Agent. Then you can access files on other servers, such as a Novell NetWare server or NT server and perform server-to-server replication and scheduling. You can use the same Windows NT domain user for both SQL Server and the SQL Server Agent or create a separate account for each. If you are planning to upgrade your SQL Server 7.0 installation, you will need to use a domain account for SQL Server. When you or your NT administrator create the domain user account(s) for SQL Server and the SQL Server Agent make sure the following is true for the user:

- The account has Password Never Expires set
- The account is a member of the SQL Server's local Administrators group

The account must have the following advanced user rights selected:

- Log On as a Service

NOTE

If you are installing on Windows 95 or later, SQL Server does not use an NT user account for SQL Server or the SQL Server Agent. Both services use the identity of the currently logged in user to the Windows 9x machine.

Step 4: Install SQL Server

The next step is to read the next chapter and begin the installation process. Use the following worksheet to help you prepare for the installation; use the worksheet later as a reference:

```
SQL Server Installation WorkSheet
                                        Installation Date:
                                        Installed By:
Name:
Company:
Product ID:
# of Client Licenses:
SQL Server Installation Path:
Master database Path:
Master Database Size:
Character Set:
Sort Order:
Network Support
_X_ Named Pipes          ___ TCP/IP
___ NWLink IPX/SPX       ___ Banyan Vines      ___ Apple Talk ADSP
Auto Start SQL Server at Boot Time
Yes    No
Auto Start SQL Server Agent at Boot Time
Yes    No
SQL Server Agent and SQL Server Log On Account
```

DEVELOPING AN UPGRADE STRATEGY AND PLAN

The plan and strategy for an upgrade is different from the plan and strategy for a new installation. In an upgrade, you have already decided on a platform and are currently running SQL Server. You may have many large production databases and hundreds of users that depend on the databases, or you may have small development databases with a few users. In many ways, upgrading an existing SQL Server is more critical than installing a new SQL Server. The existing SQL Server contains data being used and depended on by your organization.

> **NOTE**
>
> As you begin to examine upgrade plans for SQL Server 6.x to 7.0, it should be pointed out that although the two systems can not run simultaneously on the same machine, they can exist on the same machine. Microsoft has provided a very useful utility (shown in the next chapter) that enables you to quickly point and click to toggle the server from 6.5 to 7.0 or vice versa. This makes it easier to switch between the two during the upgrade process (assuming you have enough disk space to keep a live copy of your 6.5 databases).

With your organization depending on these databases, it is easy to see why it is important to develop a plan that enables you to upgrade to the new release with the least amount of risk. If the upgrade is not successful, your plan should allow you to return the system to its pre-upgrade state.

> **MARK AND ORRYN'S FIRST RULE OF UPGRADING**
>
> Never under estimate the difficulty of an upgrade. Remember Mark and Orryn's first rule of upgrading: *Expect something to go wrong*; when it does, make sure that you can get the system back and running to its previous state. Creating an upgrade plan is essential. I was once involved with what was to be a simple upgrade for a banking organization that gave me a six-hour window to get their high powered multiprocessor SQL Server upgraded from SQL Server 4.21 to SQL Server 4.21a. No problem, right? After all, the upgrade was not even a major revision number—just a revision letter. Nothing could go wrong...NOT! Five hours later, when the SQL Server was still not working correctly and tech support was trying to resolve the problem, we opted to restore the system to the pre-upgrade state. After the SQL Server was restored, it did not work either! It appears that the problem had to do with the SQL Server registry entries. This was not a problem because our upgrade plan called for backing up the system registry. After the registry was restored, the SQL Server was up and running with no problems, and the upgrade was pushed off to another day, awaiting information from tech support.
>
> *continues*

The moral of this story is never underestimate the potential problems that might be encountered during an upgrade, and be overly cautious. It's better to have too many files backed up and ready to restore than not enough.

The Word Is Out—SQL Server 7.0 Version Upgrade Wizard

The database upgrade process for SQL Server 7.0 is unique compared to previous versions and upgrades. In previous versions, SQL Server applied whatever changes were necessary to the existing databases as well as upgraded the code and registry settings. As stated earlier, SQL Server 7.0 made many fundamental changes to the SQL Server storage engine, including increasing the size of a data page from 2KB to 8KB. The net result of all the changes (improvements) to SQL Server 7.0 prevents the previous 6.x databases from being upgraded. Instead, the upgrade process involves installing SQL Server 7.0, and then using the Version Upgrade Wizard to import the existing 6.x databases into SQL Server 7.0. Also, unlike previous releases of SQL Server, Microsoft leaked information to the public during the development cycle and held several seminars openly talking about SQL Server 7.0 and the upgrade process. The SQL Server 7.0 upgrade process via the Version Upgrade Wizard has not been very popular with some of the press (early reviews). The complaints do not stem from the difficulty of the task or from problems encountered during upgrades. The real fear seems to be that existing databases cannot be upgraded in place, but must be exported into new 7.0 databases increasing the amounts of disk space required to keep live copies of SQL Server 6.5 databases around. However, Microsoft knew that an upgrade process that did not upgrade the existing databases would immediately cause a lot of anxiety to the existing customer base. So, Microsoft needed the upgrade to be bulletproof and simple. One sure way to bulletproof the process is to test as many databases as possible with the Version Upgrade Wizard. Microsoft did just that. Microsoft set out to upgrade several hundred databases to find and correct any problems. It also encouraged many of its partners to upgrade databases in what amounted to an impressive programming and testing effort. So after all of this testing, the one drawback the Version Upgrade Wizard has is the disk space requirements if you want to keep copies of the 6.5 databases around and don't have a new box or enough disk space on your current machine. In all fairness, Microsoft has tried to do all it can to ease the pain by enabling you to use drives located on your machine, network drives, direct pipeline, or tape.

The Version Upgrade Wizard was designed for ease of use, performance, and fault tolerance. The Version Upgrade Wizard is not a souped-up version of the 6.x Transfer Manager or BCP. As a matter of fact, the data transfer is not performed with BCP but OLE DB. Upgraded databases are defaulted to 6.x compatibility mode, which is good news for those of you concerned about key words or changes in ANSI SQL. Following are some highlights of the Version Upgrade Wizard:

- Easy to use wizard
- Performs fast data transfer mechanism (NOT BCP or Transfer Manager)
- Maintains 6.x compatibility (Can be changed to 7.0 after the upgrade)
- Gets customers quickly to SQL Server 7.0
- Stop and Go capabilities
- Ensures data integrity
- Converts all databases or select individual databases for upgrading

TIP

I think the Version Upgrade Wizard opens up upgrade possibilities that were not available in previous versions. For instance, if you are in an organization that is thrifty, you may not have an available NT test server to load the latest release of SQL Server, upgrade your databases, and test your applications. Instead, you are required to upgrade the production server and hope and pray the existing applications work without a hitch. With SQL Server 7.0, if you don't have a test server, find yourself a hefty client workstation running Windows NT Workstation or NT Server and install SQL Server 7.0 on the desktop. Use the Version Upgrade Wizard to bring over your production databases and test them locally. When everything checks out, you can confidently upgrade the production server (Note: even if it works great, still execute a well-planned backup plan with a fallback strategy.) If you find a problem, you can correct it prior to upgrading the production server.

When upgrading an existing SQL Server 6.x to SQL Server 7.0, you have two options available:

- Upgrade the existing SQL Server (single computer)
- Install a new SQL Server and use the Version Upgrade Wizard to migrate the databases to the new server (two computers)

> **NOTE**
>
> Upgrades from SQL Server version 4.2x systems are not supported in SQL Server 7.0. These 4.2x systems must first be upgraded to SQL Server 6.5.

Upgrade the Existing SQL Server (Single Computer)

If you are upgrading an existing SQL Server 6.x installation to SQL Server 7.0 on the same machine, SQL Server 7.0 will be installed on the machine along with SQL Server 6.5. The two versions cannot run simultaneously; however you can easily toggle between the two systems. You use the SQL Server 7.0 Version Upgrade Wizard to export your 6.5 databases to disk, tape, or network drives and then import them into SQL Server 7.0.

Installing a New SQL Server 7.0 Computer to Migrate Existing 6.x Databases (Two Computers)

In this upgrade process, you are dealing with two machines. Because you are not installing SQL Server 7.0 on the same machine as SQL Server 6.5, you are in a good upgrade position. You can migrate all of your databases at once or a few at a time. You and your users will have access to the 7.0 server and the 6.x server after the upgrade process because the 7.0 and 6.5 servers are on different computers.

General Version Upgrade Wizard Information

If you have two computers, then you can access both databases after the upgrade process has ended. When upgrading on a single machine, the state of your SQL Server 6.5, after the SQL Server 7.0 Version Upgrade Wizard completes, depends on the method selected to transfer the databases. If you have enough disk space on your server to install SQL Server 7.0 without removing SQL Server 6.x's data devices, then you can use a direct pipeline to transfer the data. The direct pipeline approach is the best approach to take when performing an upgrade. The direct pipeline approach transfers the data and objects in memory from SQL Server 6.x to SQL Server 7.0, leaving the SQL Server 6.x intact. The direct pipeline approach also offers the best upgrade performance. If you do not have enough disk space to upgrade without removing your SQL Server 6.x databases first, then you will have to export the SQL Server 6.x data and objects to tape or a network share. The taped drive option is the faster of the two options; however, if you don't have a tape drive use the network drive option.

Version Upgrade Wizard Steps with Tape Drive and Network Drive Options

The following is a list of the steps taken by the Version Upgrade Wizard when using a tape drive or network:

1. Exports 6.x. objects
2. Shuts down SQL Server 6.x
3. Exports 6.x data
4. Backs up and deletes 6.x devices
5. Starts SQL Server 7.0
6. Imports SQL Server 6.5 objects into SQL Server 7.0
7. Imports SQL Server 6.5 data into SQL Server 7.0

Version Upgrade Wizard Steps Using the Direct Pipeline Options

The following is a list of the steps taken by the Version Upgrade Wizard when using a direct pipeline:

1. Exports SQL Server 6.x objects
2. Shuts down SQL Server 6.x
3. Starts SQL Server 7.0
4. Imports SQL Server 6.x objects
5. Exports and imports data from SQL Server 6.x to SQL Server 7.0

Behind the Scenes with the Version Upgrade Wizard

Take a close look at what the Version Upgrade Wizard is doing after you have answered all of the required questions to transfer SQL Server 6.x databases to SQL Server 7.0.

Installing SQL Server 7.0

The first thing to happen in the upgrade process is the installation of SQL Server 7.0. At this time, you will set up the server with required information such as SQL Server Agent account information and the proper sort order and character set.

1. **Validate the 6.x Databases**—The Version Upgrade Wizard examines the SQL Server 6.x database to try to detect any possible problems that might occur in the upgrade process.
2. **Export Server Settings**—After the Version Upgrade Wizard has validated the 6.x databases, the Server configuration information is exported (scripted out).

5

PLANNING AN
INSTALLATION OR
UPGRADE

3. **Export MSDB Database and Replication Information**—The msdb database in SQL Server 7.0 is quite different from the msdb found in SQL Server 6.5. Several 6.5 system tables no longer exist and new 7.0 tables have been added. In this step the Version Upgrade Wizard exports the msdb database objects and SQL Executive objects. If the server is being used in replication, then replication information is also exported out.

4. **Export Logins**—The Version Upgrade Wizard then exports the login information. The login information is exported based on default users located in databases being exported. The security model is also exported.

5. **Export the Database Objects**—The next step in the process is to export the 6.x objects. Objects are scripted per database. The Version Upgrade Wizard generates the required script to create the file/filegroups and the databases. Files are a one-to-one mapping with the 6.x devices. (You can change them during the upgrade process.) The database objects are then exported in the following order:

   - User-defined datatypes
   - Tables and clustered indexes
   - Rules and defaults
   - Stored procedures, triggers, and views

6. **Import 6.x Server Settings into 7.0**—After all database objects are exported, the 6.5 SQL Server is shut down, and the SQL Server 7.0 server is started. The 6.x Server settings exported earlier are loaded into SQL Server 7.0.

7. **Create SQL 7.0 Databases**—The SQL Server 7.0 filegroups and files are created.

8. **Converts the SQL 7.0 MSDB Database**—The msdb database in SQL Server 7.0 is quite different from the 6.x msdb. Therefore, the 6.x objects are converted to the 7.0 format.

9. **Import Logins**—The user logins are imported into SQL Server 7.0.

10. **Import 6.x Objects into 7.0 Databases**—The scripts created for the various database objects are loaded into the 7.0 server.

11. **Export/Import 6.x Data into 7.0 Database**—The data is exported from 6.x and imported into the 7.0 database, using OLE DB.

12. **Import 6.x SQL Executive Settings into 7.0**—The converted SQL Server 6.x Executive settings are imported into SQL Server 7.0.

13. **Update Statistics and Verify Object and Data Transfer**—Update statistics is performed and the objects and data transferred are verified. At a bare minimum the transfer of all objects is verified along with the number of rows for each table. The wizard can be configured to do a more extensive CRC check.

Estimating the Amount of Disk Space Required to Upgrade

Use the Version Upgrade Wizard discussed in Chapter 6, "Installing or Upgrading SQL Server," to estimate the disk space requirements. The disk space requirements estimates show the amount of space required to perform a direct pipeline (leaving SQL Server 6.x intact) or if you remove SQL Server 6.x.

The Upgrade Plan

Before you begin to upgrade an existing SQL Server installation, it is important to create an upgrade plan. The Upgrade Wizard provides different mechanisms for recovery from data loss. However, you should have the capabilities to recover the databases without relying on the Version Upgrade Wizard, in case yours is the one database in a million where the wizard does not perform correctly.

TIP

When performing an upgrade, use the direct pipeline transfer mechanism of the Version Upgrade Wizard, if possible. The direct pipeline offers the best performance and leaves your 6.x databases intact.

The following sections provide you with an example of an upgrade plan to upgrade an existing SQL Server installation to SQL Server 7.0.

1. **Determine whether you have the required disk space.**

   Make sure that you have the required amounts of disk space to upgrade your existing SQL Server. Because SQL Server 7.0 does a complete installation, you need 74MB to 190MB, depending on the type of SQL Server installation you select. As a rough estimate, you need 1.5 times your current databases size in disk space to perform a direct pipeline. If you are upgrading a SQL Server 4.2x installation, you need to upgrade to 6.5 first.

2. **Determine proper amount of tempdb space.**

   Make sure that the 6.x database Server being upgraded has tempdb set to at least 25MB.

3. **Make sure NT and SQL Server have the proper service pack installed.**

   SQL Server 7.0 requires NT Services Pack 4 or later, for Windows NT and the miniservice pack. The SQL Server 6.5 server must be on Service Pack 3 or later.

4. **Estimate downtime and schedule the upgrade with users.**

   Estimate the amount of time you expect the upgrade to take. Remember that the larger the database, the longer the upgrade takes. Don't forget to give yourself time to perform any necessary backups before the upgrade begins, time to test the upgraded server, and time to handle any possible problems—including going back to the original installation, if necessary. After you have determined the amount of time required to perform the upgrade, schedule a date with your users to perform the upgrade. If you have a Microsoft Technical Support contract, notify tech support of your upgrade plans and check for any last minute instructions or known problems.

On the day of the upgrade, follow these steps:

1. **Perform database maintenance.**

   Before backing up the databases, perform the following DBCC commands on each database: CHECKDB, NEWALLOC, and CHECKCATALOG.

2. **Check the SQL Server's open databases' configuration parameter.**

   Make sure that the SQL Server's open databases' configuration parameter is equal to or greater than the number of databases on your server (including master, pubs, model, and tempdb). If the parameter is less than the total number of databases on your system, use the SQL Enterprise Manager or the system stored procedure sp_configure to increase the value.

3. **Back up all databases.**

   Perform SQL Server backups on the databases, including the master database. If possible, shut down SQL Server and use the Windows NT backup facilities to back up the SQL Server directories, including all the SQL Server devices for possible restoration.

4. **Back up the NT Registry.**

   Back up the NT System Registry again, in case you need to restore the system to the original SQL Server installation.

5. **Turn off read-only on databases.**

   For any databases that have the read only option set to TRUE, use sp_dboption to set the read only option to FALSE. The CHKUPG utility reports any databases in read-only mode.

6. **Make sure that no SQL Server applications are executing.**

   Before upgrading the SQL Server, ensure that no one is using SQL Server.

7. **Upgrade the server.**

   Run the setup program and select the Upgrade SQL Server option.

The Fallback Plan

An SQL Server upgrade is a straightforward process, but because you are usually dealing with valuable data and systems that can be down only for a limited time, upgrades should be treated with extreme caution and care. Just as important as a good upgrade plan is a good fallback plan in case the upgrade does not go as smoothly as you hoped. Here are some suggestions on how to protect yourself. Above all, make sure that you have the backups (tapes, and so on) to return your SQL Server to its earlier state if necessary.

CAUTION

Always make sure that you have a valid backup of the Windows NT System Registry before starting any upgrade.

Suggestion 1: Complete System Backup Recovery Plan

If possible, shut down the SQL Server before the upgrade and perform a backup of the SQL Server directories and all the data devices. You must shut down SQL Server to back up files that the SQL Server is using, such as devices. If the upgrade fails for some reason, you can restore the SQL Server directories, devices, and the NT Registry, returning your system to its earlier setup.

Suggestion 2: Complete Database Backups—Reinstall Previous Version

Perform SQL Server database backups on the databases, including the master. Make sure that you have all the valid SQL Server configuration information such as the server name, character set, sort order, network configuration, and device and database layouts. If you cannot get the SQL Server 6.5 upgrade to work correctly, having the database dumps and the required SQL Server information enables you to reinstall your previous SQL Server system and reload your databases if necessary.

Suggestion 3: Complete System Backup and Database Backups

Perform suggestions 1 and 2. You can never be too careful!

The bottom line is that the information and data completely recover your system if the upgrade fails. Play it safe. Have a backup plan to use if the backup plan fails!

UPGRADE/INSTALLATION PLANNING FAQ

The following are some frequently asked questions about upgrade and installation planning:

Q. **My company typically purchases hardware RAID 5 servers for SQL Server. However, I'm bringing up an application that is purely transaction based (lots of writes, updates, and deletes). Is RAID 5 the best hardware configuration from a performance standpoint for transaction-based systems? (Note: I want fault tolerance!)**

A. When it comes to pure transaction-based systems with fault tolerance, a RAID 1 (disk mirroring) is better from a performance standpoint than RAID 5. RAID 5 is slower than RAID 1 when performing writes (because of the checksum computation and additional write), but faster than RAID 1 when performing reads, and because transaction-based systems are write intensive, RAID 1 offers better performance.

Q. **I read somewhere that if I planned not to migrate some databases or to migrate a few databases at a time, I should beware of cross database dependencies. What exactly is that?**

A. The Version Upgrade process creates user logins based on the default logins located in databases being migrated. If a login is not created because a database is not migrated, future objects owned by the login fail when other databases are migrated; this is called cross database dependency. For example, suppose you have a user login called Test1 that defaults to the pubs database, but the user owns objects in a database called Finance. If you do not migrate pubs (before Finance), when the Version Upgrade Wizard creates the objects owned by Test1, the object creation fails because Test1 does not exist.

Q. **If I have 6.5 replication setup, do I need to do anything special when upgrading?**

A. Make sure you upgrade the distribution server first to SQL Server 7.0, which supports both 7.0 and 6.5 publishers and subscribers.

Q. **Can I install SQL Server on an NT Server that is also a Primary or Backup Domain Controller?**

A. Yes, you can install SQL Server on a PDC or BDC; it is not recommended, and you are much better off if you can dedicate a machine to SQL Server. If you must use your PDC or BDC, add more memory and if possible additional processors.

SUMMARY

This chapter helps you prepare for a SQL Server upgrade or installation. In the next chapter, you walk through the installation and upgrade process.

The Upgrade Checklist

Use the following checklist to help prepare for a SQL Server upgrade. Check off each item on the list as it is completed. Perform each step in order from top to bottom.

❏   Free disk space 74MB compact install, 163MB Typical and 190MB Full.

❏   tempdb on 6.5 Database Server 25MB or greater.

❏   NT Service Pack 4 or later.

❏   SQL Server 6.5 Service Pack 3 or later.

❏   Shut down all applications or services that use SQL Server.

Estimated Downtime: _____ hours

❏   Alert users.

❏   Fallback recovery plan in place.

❏   Fallback recovery plan in place in case fallback plan fails.

❏   SQL Server DBCC maintenance commands of *all* databases.

❏   SQL Server backup of *all* databases.

❏   SQL Server backup of master database.

❏   Back Up Windows NT System Registry.

❏   Operating system backup of SQL Server directories and files (including devices).

❏   Make sure that no users are on the system.

❏   Make sure that no applications are using SQL Server.

❏   Start the SQL Server upgrade.

INSTALLING OR UPGRADING SQL SERVER

by Mark Spenik

IN THIS CHAPTER

In this chapter, you walk through the actual installation and upgrade of SQL Server as well as the installation of software for the client PCs. Take a look at what the SQL Server installation program actually loads on your computer. Following are the directories created from the SQL Server root directory (MSSQL7) during installation:

- **BACKUP:** Default backup directory
- **BINN:** SQL Server, Dynamic Link Library files (DLLs) and client executable files as well as online help files
- **BOOKS:** SQL Server Books Online
- **:** SQL Server system database files
- **HTML:** MMC and SQL Server HTML files
- **DevTools:** SQL Server 7.0 programming examples
- **INSTALL:** Installation scripts and output files
- **JOBS:** Temporary storage location for job output files
- **LOG:** Error log files
- **REPLDATA:** Replication synchronization task working directory
- **Upgrade:** Files used by the Version Upgrade Wizard to upgrade 6.x databases

The following services are installed:

- **MSDTC** (SQL Server Distributed Transaction Coordinator)
- **MSSQLServer** (SQL Server)
- **SQLServerAgent** (SQL Server Agent)

The following utilities are installed:

- **Bulk Copy Utility (BCP):** Enables you to configure some SQL Server startup parameters and network support and remove SQL Server after installation
- **SQL Service Manager:** Used to start and stop SQL Server
- **SQL Server Query Analyzer:** Utility to issue SQL queries
- **SQL Enterprise Manager:** Primary tool used to manage SQL Server and SQL Server objects
- **SQL Client Network Utility:** Used to set up SQL Server connection information and check versions of the database DB-Library installed
- **SQL Server Profiler:** Utility to monitor and record database activity
- **Version Upgrade Wizard:** Utility to upgrade SQL Server 6.x databases to 7.0
- **MS DTC:** Microsoft Distributed Transaction Coordinator

Installing or Upgrading SQL Server

CHAPTER 6

111

6

INSTALLING OR
UPGRADING SQL
SERVER

- **Server Network Utility:** Used to add additional protocols to SQL Server
- **Import and Export Utility**: Allows you to create DTS packages for importing and exporting data
- **BCP:** Bulk Copy Utility to import and export flat files with SQL Server

DIFFERENT EDITIONS OF SQL SERVER

SQL Server now comes in the following editions:

Desktop

Standard

Enterprise

All the editions of SQL Server share the majority of SQL Server 7.0 features and are built on the same code base. Installing and using each edition is the same; for example, you can manage all editions with the Enterprise Manager. The key differences are where in your enterprise each edition fits in. The desktop edition is for Windows 9x or Windows NT workstations, and can be used by developers or mobile users. The desktop edition has the majority of SQL Server 7.0 features found in the standard and enterprise editions with some limitations. For example, the desktop version will only scale across 2 processors, supports full merge and snapshot replication, but can only act as a subscriber for transactional replication. The desktop edition does not support the following SQL Server 7.0 features:

Failover clusters

Extended memory addressing

Parallel queries

Fiber mode scheduling

OLAP Server

The differences between the standard edition and the enterprise edition are the scalability and fault tolerance. The enterprise edition requires Windows NT Enterprise edition and supports failover clustering, extended memory, and more processors than the standard edition, which lacks failover clustering and extended memory support, and runs on NT Server.

INSTALLING SQL SERVER

Before installing SQL Server, make sure that you have read the documentation regarding installation that ships with SQL Server 7.0. Also, make sure that your system meets the minimum requirements. To help you with your installation, use the following worksheet.

> **NOTE**
>
> Before you can install SQL Server 7.0, you must install IE 4.01 with service pack 1. IE 4.01 is located on the SQL Server CD under the subdirectory IE4, off of ALPHA (for alpha processor based machines) or I386 for x86-based machines (Intel). On Windows NT machines, you must have the proper service packs: service pack 4 or greater and IE 4.01 service pack 1 or greater. (Both are included with the SQL Server 7.0 installation CD.)

> **TIP**
>
> The installation of SQL Server can cause problems if you try to install it with a user account that does not have the correct NT permissions to create new directories and files. If you get the error message `Can't create directory`, make sure that you are using an account with the correct privileges. Try creating the directory with File Manager. If you have the correct privileges, you will be able do so; otherwise, use a different account that has the correct permissions.

Step 1: Running Setup

Installing SQL Server requires running the setup program, located on the SQL Server 7.0 CD. The CD contains several directories, including different directories for each of the currently supported microprocessors:

- \x86 for Intel machines
- \ALPHA for Digital Alpha AXP machines

Select the correct directory for the processor you are using and run the setup program (if autorun has not already displayed the setup program shown in Figure 6.1).

Step 2: Select an Installation Option

If you have already installed IE 4.01 and any required service packs, viewed the readme file and you are ready to begin your SQL Server installation. Click the Install SQL Server 7.0 Components option shown in Figure 6.1; the Component Selection dialog box opens (see Figure 6.2).

SQL Server Installation Checklist

Check off the following items as you complete or verify them:

Hardware and PC Setup:

❑ Computer is Alpha AXP or INTEL (32-bit x86) Pentium 166 MHz or higher and is on the Windows NT Hardware Compatibility list

❑ Memory: 32M (64M Enterprise edition)

❑ Operating System: Windows NT 4.0 Server or Workstation Service pack 4 or greater, Windows 95 or later

❑ Free Disk Space depending on the installation

Minimum	65 MB
Typical	170 MB
Full	180 MB

on the hard drive to which SQL Server is to be installed. Note: For upgrades using direct pipeline, you need about 1.5 times your current database size in disk space.

File System: ❑ FAT

❑ NTFS

Computer Name:

SQL Server Options (Check or fill in)

User Name:_____Company Name:_____Product ID:_____

SQL Server Root Directory:_____

Program File Location: _____

Program Data Files Location: _____

Selected Character Set:

❑ Code Page 1252(Default)   ❑ Code Page 850 (Multilingual)

❑ Code Page 437 (US English)   ❑ Other _____

Selected Sort Order:_____

Selected Unicode Collation:_____

Network Protocols:

❏ Named-Pipes (Default-except Win 95) ❏ Multiprotocol (default)

❏ NWLink IPX/SPX ❏ TCP/IP Sockets (default Win 95 & 98)

❏ Banyan Vines ❏ AppleTalk ADSP

Books Online Installed: ❏ Yes ❏ No (Requires an additional 1M to 15M)

Auto-Start Options:

❏ SQL Server

❏ SQL Server Agent

IE 4.01 with Service pack 1 or greater Installed: _____

Windows NT User Accounts(Not Available on Windows 95 or Later):

MSSQL Server User Account: _____ (Required for SQL Server network access for features such as ODBC replication or Web page generation)

SQL Server Agent User Account: _____

Installing or Upgrading SQL Server

CHAPTER 6

115

6

INSTALLING OR
UPGRADING SQL
SERVER

FIGURE 6.1

The SQL Server Setup autorun Start window.

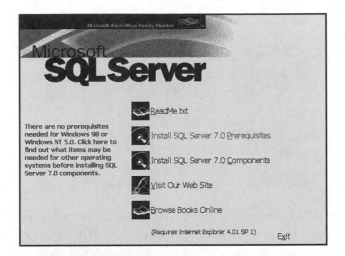

FIGURE 6.2

Install SQL Server 7.0 Components dialog box.

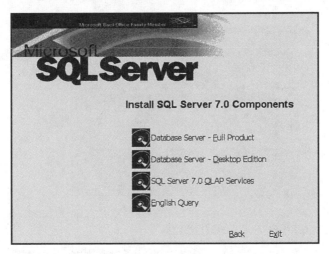

To install the standard SQL Server, select Database Server - Full Product, to install the desktop version select Database Server - Desktop Edition. To install the OLAP server, click the SQL Server 7.0 OLAP Services, and to install English Query click English query. For this walkthrough, select Database Server.

Step 3: Select Install Method

The Install Method dialog box, shown in Figure 6.3, opens.

FIGURE 6.3

The SQL Server Type dialog box.

Select the type of SQL Server installation you want, local or remote, to install: Desktop, Standard, or Enterprise edition. Click your selection; the SQL Server Welcome dialog box, shown in Figure 6.4, appears. To continue click the Next button.

FIGURE 6.4

SQL Server Setup Welcome dialog box.

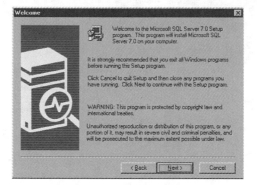

Step 4: License Agreement

The SQL Server License Agreement dialog box appears. Read through the agreement and click the Yes button (see Figure 6.5).

Step 5: User Information

Fill in your name and company, and then click the Next button (see Figure 6.6).

FIGURE 6.5

SQL Server License Agreement dialog box.

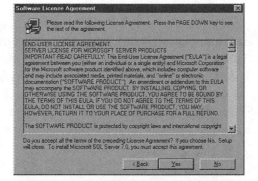

FIGURE 6.6

SQL Server User Information dialog box.

Step 6: Installation Type and File Location

Select the type of installation you want to perform. The Typical Installation installs SQL Server 7.0 with the standard defaults. The standard defaults are as follows:

- **Program Location:** C:\MSSQL7
- **Data Files:** C:\MSSQL7\DATA
- **Sort Order:** Dictionary order, case insensitive
- **Character Set:** Code Page 1252
- **Network:** TCP/IP (Windows 9x), named-pipes Windows NT
- **Books OnLine Installed**

The typical installation includes all management tools and online documentation but does not include full text search, development tools, or samples. The Minimum Installation installs only the essential SQL Server 7.0 components, which requires about 65 MB of disk space and does not include the online documentation or all of the management tools. The Custom Installation is similar to the typical installation, however, you can modify features such as the code page and network libraries and add additional components such as full text search, development tools, and samples. To change the default location of SQL Server program files or data files, click the Browse button and select a new drive or directory. The default location is C:\MSSQL7. The drive and directory you select is where SQL Server installs the initial SQL Server databases and file groups for the program files as well as the database data and log files for the data files. The Setup Type dialog box, shown in Figure 6.7, displays the required amount of disk space for the program files and data files as well as the available space on the selected drives. To continue, click the Next button. For this walk-through the custom option is selected; if you select Typical or Minimum skip to Step 10.

FIGURE 6.7

SQL Server Setup Type dialog box.

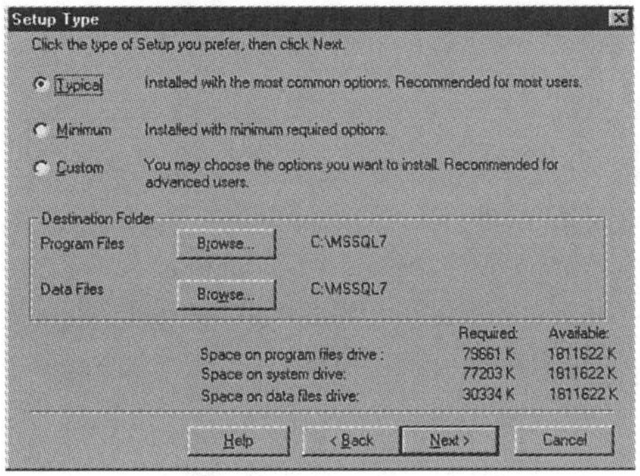

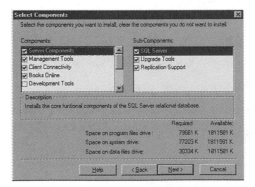

Step 7: Select Components to Install

The SQL Server Component Selection dialog box, shown in Figure 6.8, appears. Select the check boxes beside the options you want to install. To skip installation of particular option, clear the option box. When you have made all of your selections, click the Next button.

FIGURE 6.8

SQL Server Component Selection dialog box.

Step 8: Character Set, Sort Order, and Unicode Collation

The Character Set/Sort Order/Unicode Collation Selection dialog box, shown in Figure 6.9, appears. Use the drop-down boxes to select the character set and sort order. The Unicode collation will default based on your selection of character set and sort order; it is recommended that you take the default for Unicode collation. After you have made your selection, click the Next button.

FIGURE 6.9

SQL Server Character Set/Sort Order/Unicode Collation Selection dialog box.

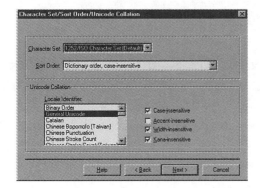

CAUTION

Refer to Chapter 5, "Planning an Installation or Upgrade," on the importance of selecting the proper character set and sort order from the start. Changing the character set or sort order requires exporting the data from the databases, rebuilding the databases, and then reloading the data.

Step 9: Network Libraries

The SQL Server Network Libraries Selection dialog box, shown in Figure 6.10, appears. To add additional network protocols, select the check box located beside the protocol. To remove a protocol, clear the check box. After you have made your selection, click the Next button.

FIGURE 6.10

*SQL Server
Network Libraries
Selection dialog
box.*

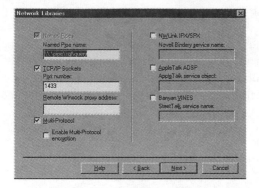

Step 9a: SQL Server, SQL Agent, MSDTC User Accounts, and Auto Start Services—Windows NT Only

If you are installing SQL Server on a Windows NT machine, you are prompted by a dialog box that enables you to assign a domain user account to SQL Server. The default is to use the system local account. If you do not assign a specific account to the SQL Server Agent and MSDTC, they use the same account as SQL Server. You are also prompted to restart SQL Server and the SQL Agent automatically if the NT server is shut down and restarted. After you have made your selections, click the Next button.

> **TIP**
>
> It is recommended that you assign SQL Server a domain user account. Without a domain user account SQL Server can not use replication, SQL mail, or the Version Upgrade Wizard. It is also recommended that you auto-start both SQL Server and SQL Agent so that if you lose power, you won't be called in the middle of the night because a application cannot connect to the database.

Step 10: Start Copying Files

The final dialog box is the SQL Server Start File Copy dialog box, shown in Figure 6.11. Click the Next button to start the SQL Server installation. Then it's wait-and-watch time as SQL Server is installed, the system databases are created, and the program group is created. When the installation is complete, you are shown a completion dialog box and told that the machine must be rebooted to complete the installation. To reboot now, click OK. Otherwise, select Reboot Later and click OK. Congratulations—you have just successfully installed SQL Server 7.0.

FIGURE 6.11

SQL Server Start File Copy dialog box.

STARTING AND STOPPING SQL SERVER

If you checked the Auto Boot options for SQL Server and the SQL Agent, the two services start automatically when the server reboots. The easiest way to start, stop, pause, or check the status of SQL Server and SQL Agent is to use the SQL Server Service Manager (see Figure 6.12).

FIGURE 6.12

The SQL Server Service Manager.

The SQL Server Service Manager is located in the Microsoft SQL Server 7.0 program group, which was created during the installation or upgrade. To start the SQL Server Service Manager, double-click its icon. If SQL Server is running, the indicator light is green. If the service is stopped, the indicator light is red. To start SQL Server, click the arrow button next to the Start/Continue label. To stop SQL Server, click the red box next to the Stop label. To pause SQL Server, click the double bar next to the Pause label. Pausing SQL Server does not halt queries in process; it prevents new users from logging in to SQL Server. When SQL Server is paused, users currently logged in to SQL Server can continue to work as normal.

Controlling the SQL Server Agent and MSDTC is the same as controlling SQL Server, except that you cannot pause the SQL Server Agent or MSDTC. To perform stop, start, and status checks on SQL Server Agent or MSDTC, use the drop-down Services list box and select SQLServerAgent or MSDTC instead of MSSQLServer.

NOTE

The service name for Microsoft SQL Server 7.0 is *MSSQLServer*.

INSTALLATION TROUBLESHOOTING

As stated earlier, the installation process for SQL Server is straightforward; however, even in the most straightforward operations, problems can and do occur. Ideally, you should be provided with error messages that pinpoint your problem. In some cases, you will have to do some debugging and observation to determine what has gone wrong. In the worst cases, you might find yourself on the telephone with tech support trying to determine the problem.

Some of the common errors encountered during an installation or upgrade are improper Windows NT permissions or insufficient disk space. If you receive an error message telling you that you can't create a directory or file, you probably have a permissions problem. Switch to an account with the correct permissions. If the installation fails, check your disk space to make sure that you have enough free space to install SQL Server.

TIP

Okay, I've done so many of these installations that I've lost count! Where have I encountered problems? Well the most common problem I've encountered is trying to install SQL Server when something is using another file that SQL Server wants to install, for instance a new ODBC driver manager. It helps to shut down other services while installing. I've also run into problems where the domain user account assigned to SQL Server was not set up correctly (for example, a local administrator, log on as service, and so on). I can say that most of the time, I have experienced no problems at all.

What can you do if you have completed an installation and your SQL Server does not work? You have to start debugging and try to determine the problem. The best place to start is the SQL Server error log.

Error Log and Windows NT Application Log

The error log, located on the SQL Server root directory in the directory \LOG, is a text file used to log audit and error information for SQL Server.

Installing or Upgrading SQL Server

CHAPTER 6

123

6

INSTALLING OR
UPGRADING SQL
SERVER

The Windows NT application log is a Windows NT system log used by applications and Windows NT to log audit and error information. The Windows NT application log contains the same information as the SQL Server error log, except that only SQL Server writes to the error log, but any Windows NT application can write to the application log. You can configure SQL Server to write to both logs (the default) or to either log.

> **TIP**
>
> When I try to read consecutive error or audit messages, I find that the SQL Server error log is easier to view than the Windows NT application log. However, one benefit of the Windows NT application log is that error messages are highlighted with a stop-sign icon and are easy to find.

Following is an example of an SQL Server error log entry during system startup:

```
98/07/27 21:35:58.29 kernel   Microsoft SQL Server  7.00 - 7.00.517
➥(Intel X86)
    Jun 19 1998 17:06:54
    Copyright (c) 1988-1998 Microsoft Corporation
    Standard version on Windows

98/07/27 21:35:58.32 kernel   Copyright (C) 1988-1997
➥Microsoft Corporation.
98/07/27 21:35:58.33 kernel   All rights reserved.
98/07/27 21:35:58.33 kernel   Logging SQL Server messages in file
➥'C:\MSSQL7\log\ERRORLOG'.
98/07/27 21:35:58.55 kernel   initconfig: Number of user connections
➥ limited to 32767.
98/07/27 21:35:58.59 kernel   SQL Server is starting at priority
➥class 'normal'(1 CPU detected).
98/07/27 21:35:58.70 kernel   User Mode Scheduler configured for
➥thread processing
98/07/27 21:36:00.05 server   Directory Size: 2559
98/07/27 21:36:00.11 spid1    Using dynamic lock allocation. [2500]
➥Lock Blocks,
                  [5000] Lock Owner Blocks
98/07/27 21:36:00.12 kernel   Attempting to initialize Distributed
➥Transaction Coordinator.

98/07/27 21:36:00.49 spid1    Failed to obtain
➥TransactionDispenserInterface:
                  XACT_E_TMNOTAVAILABLE
98/07/27 21:36:00.55 spid1    Starting up database 'master'.
98/07/27 21:36:00.55 spid1    Opening file C:\MSSQL7\data\master.mdf.
98/07/27 21:36:00.65 spid1    Opening file C:\MSSQL7\data\mastlog.ldf.
98/07/27 21:36:00.87 spid1    Loading SQL Server's  Unicode collation.
98/07/27 21:36:00.98 spid1    Loading SQL Server's  non-Unicode sort
➥order and character set.
```

```
98/07/27 21:36:01.18 spid1    4 transactions rolled forward in database
➥'master' (1).
98/07/27 21:36:01.18 spid1    0 transactions rolled back in database
➥'master' (1).

98/07/27 21:36:01.36 spid1    Starting up database 'model'.
98/07/27 21:36:01.36 spid1    Opening file C:\MSSQL7\DATA\model.mdf.
98/07/27 21:36:01.44 spid1    Opening file c:\mssql7\data\modellog.ldf.
98/07/27 21:36:01.56 spid1    Clearing tempdb database.
98/07/27 21:36:01.62 spid1    Creating file C:\MSSQL7\DATA\TEMPDB.MDF.
98/07/27 21:36:01.81 spid1    Closing file C:\MSSQL7\DATA\TEMPDB.MDF.
98/07/27 21:36:01.81 spid1    Creating file C:\MSSQL7\DATA\TEMPLOG.LDF.
98/07/27 21:36:01.81 spid1    Closing file C:\MSSQL7\DATA\TEMPLOG.LDF.
98/07/27 21:36:01.82 spid1    Opening file C:\MSSQL7\DATA\TEMPDB.MDF.
98/07/27 21:36:02.08 spid1    Opening file C:\MSSQL7\DATA\TEMPLOG.LDF.
98/07/27 21:36:02.72 spid1    Closing file C:\MSSQL7\DATA\TEMPDB.MDF.
98/07/27 21:36:02.72 spid1    Closing file C:\MSSQL7\DATA\TEMPLOG.LDF.
98/07/27 21:36:02.72 spid1    Starting up database 'tempdb'.
98/07/27 21:36:02.73 spid1    Opening file C:\MSSQL7\DATA\TEMPDB.MDF.
98/07/27 21:36:02.91 spid1    Opening file C:\MSSQL7\DATA\TEMPLOG.LDF.
98/07/27 21:36:03.14 spid1    Server name is 'WORKSTATION'.
98/07/27 21:36:03.17 kernel   Using 'SQLEVN70.DLL' version '7.00.517'.
98/07/27 21:36:03.21 kernel   Using 'OPENDS60.DLL'
              version '98/07/27 21:36:098/07/27 21:36:03.30 ods
              Using 'SSMSSH70.DLL' version '7.0.517' to listen on ''.
98/07/27 21:36:03.36 ods      Using 'SSMSSO70.DLL' version '7.0.517' to
➥listen on '1433'.

98/07/27 21:36:03.56 ods      Error: 17826, Severity: 18, State: 1
98/07/27 21:36:03.56 ods      Could not set up ListenOn connection
'1433'..
98/07/27 21:36:03.55 ods       , 98/07/27 21:36:03.69 ods
           Using 'SSMSRP70.DLL' version '7.0.517' to listen on
➥'WORKSTATION'.

98/07/27 21:36:04.48 spid6    Starting up database 'pubs'.
98/07/27 21:36:04.48 spid6    Opening file C:\MSSQL7\DATA\pubs.mdf.
98/07/27 21:36:04.61 spid6    Opening file c:\mssql7\DATA\pubs_log.ldf.
98/07/27 21:36:04.78 spid6    Starting up database 'Northwind'.
98/07/27 21:36:04.78 spid6    Opening file C:\MSSQL7\DATA\northwnd.mdf.
98/07/27 21:36:04.88 spid6    Opening file C:\MSSQL7\DATA\northwnd.ldf.
98/07/27 21:36:05.29 spid1    Recovery complete.
98/07/27 21:36:05.29 spid1    SQL Server's Unicode collation is:
98/07/27 21:36:05.29 spid1         'English' (ID = 1033).
98/07/27 21:36:05.29 spid1         comparison style = 196609.
98/07/27 21:36:05.30 spid1    SQL Server's non-Unicode sort order is:
98/07/27 21:36:05.30 spid1         'nocase_iso' (ID = 52).
98/07/27 21:36:05.30 spid1    SQL Server's non-Unicode character set is:
98/07/27 21:36:05.30 spid1         'iso_1' (ID = 1).
```

Installing or Upgrading SQL Server

CHAPTER 6

125

6

INSTALLING OR
UPGRADING SQL
SERVER

You can view the error log using any text file editor, such as Windows Notepad or SQL Server Enterprise Manager. You can view the Windows NT application log using the Windows NT Event Viewer.

Scan through the error log or application log and look for possible error messages. Every time you stop and restart SQL Server, a new error log is started. SQL Server archives the error logs by saving the previous 6 error log files, named as follows (where *X* is 1 through 6, and the current error log is ERRORLOG):

```
ERRORLOG.X
```

Another possible place to find error messages is the \INSTALL directory on the SQL Server root directory. Each installation script file writes to an output file with an OUT extension. To find the last script that was executed, enter the following on a DOS command line from the \INSTALL directory:

```
dir *.out /od
```

The last file displayed is the last script to execute. Check the OUT file for possible errors.

Start SQL Server from the Command Line

If you are having trouble starting SQL Server from the Windows NT Service Manager or the SQL Server Service Manager after an installation or upgrade, try starting SQL Server from the command line. Starting SQL Server from the command line is a great way to debug because the messages usually logged to the error log or Windows NT application log are displayed directly in the DOS command window. To start SQL Server from the command line, enter the following:

```
sqlservr <command line options>
```

Not all the command-line options are discussed here, but read on to find out about a few of the important options you can use to help get your SQL Server debugged and up and running.

-d

The -d option specifies the path and filename of the master database file.

-l

The -l option specifies the path and filename of the master transaction log file.

-e

The -e option specifies the path and filename of the error log file.

-c

The -c option starts SQL Server independent of the Windows NT Service Control Manager.

TIP

The -c option is supposed to quicken SQL Server startup time by bypassing the Windows NT Service Control Manager. If you are having problems starting SQL Server, include the -c option to help further isolate the problem. I was working with one upgraded SQL Server installation in which the NT Service Control Manager kept shutting down SQL Server every time it started. By specifying the -c option, I was able to get the server up and correct the problem. The only drawback is that you cannot stop the SQL Server with any of the conventional methods (such as the SQL Server Service Manager). SQL Server can be halted by logging off Windows NT or pressing Ctrl+C in the DOS command window running SQL Server. When you press Ctrl+C, you are prompted with a message asking if you want to shut down the server. Select Y to shut down the server.

-m

The -m option enables you to start SQL Server in single-user mode, which means that only one user can log into SQL Server. Use the -m option when restoring databases or trying to fix suspect or corrupted databases.

-T

The -T option allows you to start SQL Server with a trace flag.

-f

The -f option enables you to start SQL Server in a minimal configuration. Use the -f option only when SQL Server does not start because of a configuration parameter problem.

Following is an example of how to start SQL Server from the command line using some of the preceding options:

```
sqlservr -c -dc:\mssql7\data\master.mdf -lc:\mssql7\data\master.ldf -e
➥ dc:\mssql7\log\errorlog -f
```

UPGRADING SQL SERVER

As stated in Chapter 5, the upgrade process is done via the Version Upgrade Wizard. All of the databases can be migrated at one time or you can selectively upgrade them one at a time. Before starting the upgrade, make sure that you have performed all the items on the upgrade checklist described in Chapter 5. If you did not read the upgrade section, it is highly recommended that you go back and read the Version Upgrade Wizard section in Chapter 5. The Version Upgrade Wizard provides a very easy user interface to migrate your SQL Server 6.x databases to SQL Server 7.0. The Version Upgrade Wizard is extremely smart. At any step in the process you can pause or halt the wizard. You can then later pick up where you left off or you can restart the process all over again. If you pick up from where you left off, the wizard does not redo things that have already been completed successfully. For example, each table is treated as an individual transaction. If the wizard successfully completes the export and import of Table A but fails on Table B, halt the process and correct the problem and then restart the process. The wizard does not redo Table A because it was exported and imported successfully, instead it begins with Table B (where you left off).

As a reminder, although the Version Upgrade Wizard offers some fallback protection (when using the direct pipeline), make sure that you have done the following:

- Performed database backups
- Backed up SQL Server files, devices, and directories
- Backed up the NT Registry
- Have adequate disk space to perform the upgrade
- Set TempDB tempdb to 25MB or greater

Switching Between SQL Server 6.5 and SQL Server 7.0

SQL Server 7.0 and SQL Server 6.5 can't run simultaneously on the same machine. However, you can easily toggle back and forth from SQL Server 6.5 and SQL Server 7.0 using the switch SQL Server option. When you install SQL Server 7.0 on the same machine, as an existing SQL Server 6.5, the Windows Start Menu contains a new item called Microsoft SQL Server Switch (Common), shown in Figure 6.13.

Select the menu item and a message box appears, stating that SQL Server is restoring SQL Server 6.5 (or 7.0) information. Using the Window Start Menu option, you can switch from SQL Server 6.5 to SQL Server 7.0. This enables you to toggle back and forth between 6.5 and 7.0 during or after the upgrade process (see the following Last Minute Suggestion). As stated earlier, you should be prepared to fall back to SQL Server 6.5 without relying on the switch-over option (that is, you have full recovery capability).

FIGURE **6.13**
*Windows Start
Menu—Microsoft
SQL Server
Switch.*

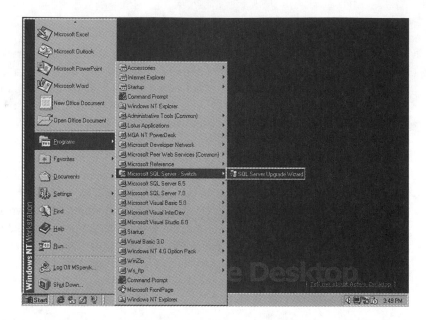

LAST MINUTE SUGGESTION

If possible, during the upgrade process, find enough disk space so you don't
have to remove your SQL Server 6.5 devices. I know that on very, very large
databases or organizations with very little cash, you will have to remove the 6.5
devices to make room for the 7.0 databases. If you can upgrade SQL Server 6.5
to 7.0 without removing the SQL Server 6.5 databases, you will be able to easily
fall back to SQL Server 6.5. Using the switch option you can switch back to 6.5 if
you find your applications are having trouble with SQL Server 7.0 or you
encounter problems during the upgrade.

Step 1: Run the Version Upgrade Wizard

NOTE

The following walkthrough of the upgrade assumes that you did not select
upgrade databases during the installation process. The example also uses the
direct pipeline for the object and data transfer.

Installing or Upgrading SQL Server

CHAPTER 6

129

6

INSTALLING OR
UPGRADING SQL
SERVER

From the Windows Start Menu select the Microsoft SQL Server Switch and then select the Version Upgrade Wizard Option (refer to Figure 6.13). The SQL Server Version Upgrade dialog box appears, as shown in Figure 6.14.

FIGURE 6.14

SQL Server Version Upgrade Wizard dialog box.

The first screen is merely a welcome screen; review the text and click the Next button.

Step 2: Select Object Transfer Options

The Object Transfer Selection dialog box, shown in Figure 6.15 appears. Using this selection dialog box, you can determine what you want to export and import into SQL Server 7.0. The default values are to export and import both objects and data, use Named pipes for data transfer (that is data pipeline). You can change any of the defaults; for example, you can transfer the data via tape or select data validation to occur—even an exhaustive data integrity check that performs checksums (CRC) to ensure the integrity of the data transferred. After you have selected your options, click the Next button.

FIGURE 6.15

Object Transfer Selection dialog box.

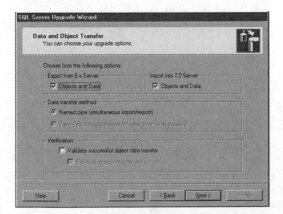

Step 3: Servers Logon

The Servers Logon dialog box appears, shown in Figure 6.16. Select the 6.x server you want to export data from the combo drop-down box. Enter in the sa password and any special command line options required to start the server. Select the 7.0 server you want to import the data into using the combo drop-down box. Enter the sa password and any special command line options required to start the 7.0 server. Click the Next button. A dialog box appears that tells you that the computer is stopping (7.0) SQL Server and restarting SQL Server (6.5) and that all users need to be off the servers. After the SQL

FIGURE 6.16

Servers Logon dialog box.

Server has restarted, the Code Page Selection dialog box, shown in Figure 6.17, appears.

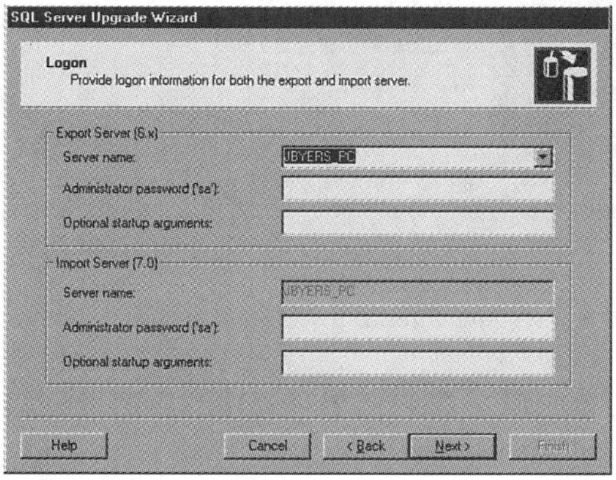

Step 4: Code Page Selection

The Code Page Selection dialog box enables you to select the code page to generate the script files used to upgrade (see Figure 6.17). It is recommended that you take the default selection. To continue, click the Next button.

FIGURE 6.17

Code Page Selection dialog box.

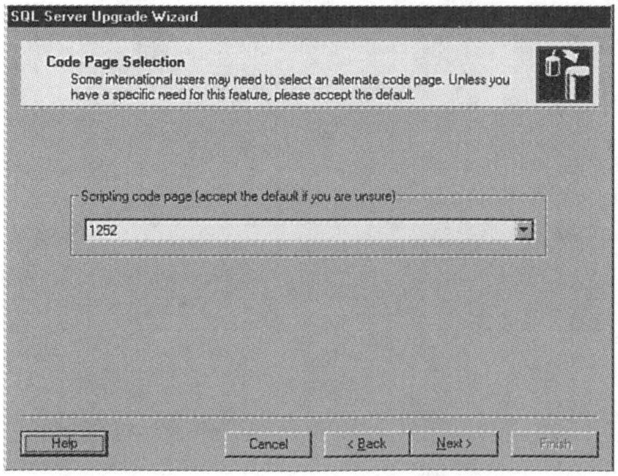

Step 5: Select Databases to Upgrade

The Database Selection dialog box appears, shown in Figure 6.18.

FIGURE 6.18

*Database
Selection dialog
box.*

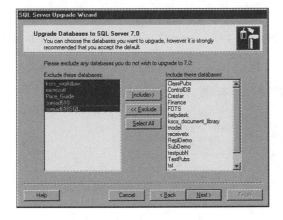

Select the databases you want to upgrade and click the Next button.

Step 6: 7.0 Database Creation

The Database Creation dialog box, shown in Figure 6.19, appears. To have your 7.0 databases created with the default options, data files located in the SQL Server 7 data directory, and a one-to-one mapping of SQL Server 6.5 devices to SQL Server 7.0 files, use the default setting. To change to the files or locations, click the Edit button. To use existing databases already created in 7.0, select the Existing Database option. To run a customized script to create the databases, select the Script option and give the path and filename of the script to execute. After you have made your selection, click the Next button.

FIGURE 6.19

*Database Creation
dialog box.*

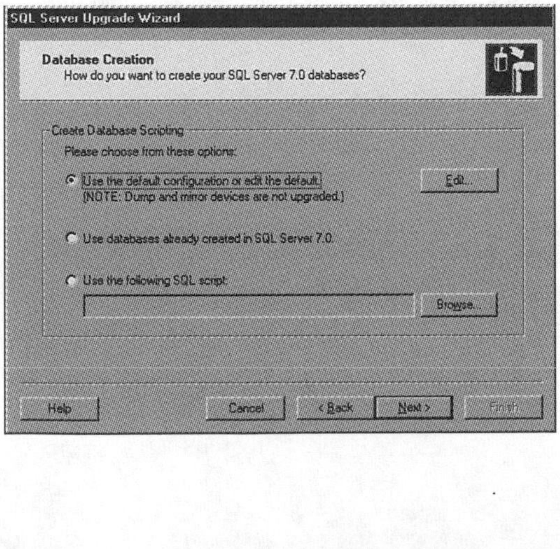

Estimating Disk Space Requirements

If you want to determine whether you have the necessary disk space to perform a direct pipeline upgrade or an upgrade without SQL Server databases, you can use the Database Creation dialog box. To estimate disk space, perform the following:

1. Click the Edit button; the SQL Server Upgrade Wizard dialog box shown in Figure 6.20 opens.

FIGURE 6.20

SQL Server Upgrade Wizard dialog box.

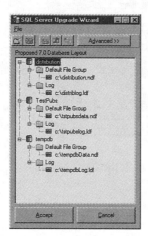

2. Click the Advanced button; the Proposed Database Layout dialog box, shown in Figure 6.21, appears.

FIGURE 6.21

Proposed Database Layout dialog box.

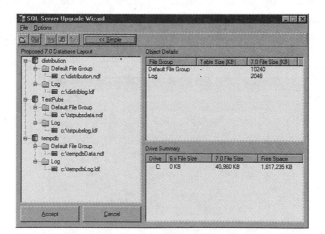

3. Click a database in the Proposed Database Layout window. The Drive Summary window displays the estimated space required by SQL Server 7.0 and the amount of free space available on the selected drive. To view the space requirements with the SQL Server 6.x files removed, click Options on the menu and select Free Space Includes 6.x files.

Step 7: System Configuration Options

The System Configuration Options dialog box, shown in Figure 6.22, appears. The default values are to transfer existing server settings and SQL Executive settings as well as turn ANSI Nulls off and mixed mode of quoted identifiers. After you have made your selection, click the Next button.

FIGURE 6.22

*System
Configuration
Options dialog
box.*

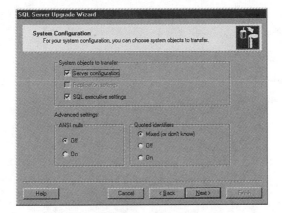

Step 8: Review Upgrade Selections

The Review Upgrade Selections dialog box, shown in Figure 6.23, appears. This dialog box gives you the opportunity to review all of your upgrade option selections and make any necessary changes before moving on to the upgrade. When you are satisfied with your upgrade selections, click the Finish button to start the upgrade.

Step 9: SQL Server 7.0 Upgrade in Progress

The Version Upgrade Status dialog box, shown in Figure 6.24, appears. This dialog box provides you with information about the current progress of the upgrade such as the tasks being executed, task status, start time, and end time. You can pause the current task by clicking the Pause button, pause between steps, close out the upgrade process, or resume a paused task.

FIGURE 6.23
Review Upgrade Selections dialog box.

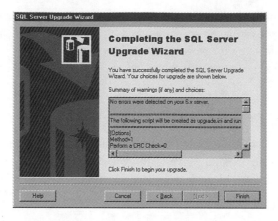

FIGURE 6.24
Version Upgrade Status dialog box.

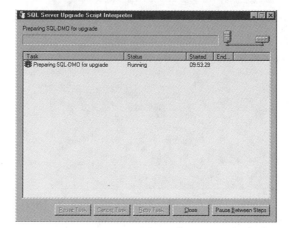

When the upgrade has completed successfully, an Upgrade Complete dialog box appears.

UPGRADE TROUBLESHOOTING

The Version Upgrade Wizard provides useful and easy-to-access information regarding errors that occur during the upgrade process. If an error does occur during the upgrade process, you will get an Informational Files Found dialog box, shown in Figure 6.25.

You can then select to view the information files to see what problem occurred with the particular object. You can then try to correct the problem and resume or redo the upgrade process.

FIGURE 6.25

Informational Files Found dialog box.

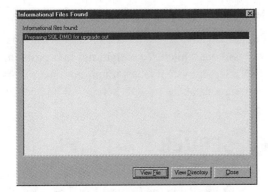

Upgrade Subdirectories and Contents

To troubleshoot the upgrade process it helps to know how the upgrade subdirectories are created and what the contents of each directory are. The main upgrade directory is the subdirectory UPGRADE located off of the main SQL Server directory.

Whenever you perform an upgrade, a subdirectory is created off of the upgrade directory that has the following format:

```
Machine name_date_time
```

For example, on the KSCSINC server, the full path is:

```
C:\MSSQL7\UPGRADE\KSCSINC_041898_125255
```

This directory contains the following:

- **.OUT files:** for each stage of the upgrade process
- **.OK files:** for all scripts run on 6.x and 7.0
- **.ERR files:** errors encountered during a stage in the upgrade process

The upgrade subdirectory created whenever you run the upgrade process also has a subdirectory for each database upgraded with the following naming convention:

```
Number Database Name
```

For example, the full path of the database Finance is as follows:

```
C:\MSSQL7\UPGRADE\KSCSINC_041898_125255\001Finance
```

This subdirectory contains the following:

- **.OK files**: for each successful object transfer
- **Script files:** for each database object with file extensions based on the type of object (for example, Table = .tab, stored procedure = .prc, and so on).

7.0 Compatibility with 6.x Applications

SQL Server 7.0 leaves an upgraded database in a 6.x compatibility mode. Therefore, your applications should run without a hitch. You might run into problems where applications or tools that used SQL Server system tables might no longer work due to system table changes in 7.0. To upgrade a database to SQL Server 7.0 compatibility use the stored procedure `sp_dbcmptlevel`.

REMOVING SQL SERVER

If you want to remove an SQL Server installation, do not delete the SQL Server directories. Run Add/Remove Programs located in the Control Panel or select the Uninstall SQL Server 7.0 option from the SQL Server 7.0 program group, shown in Figure 6.26.

FIGURE 6.26

The Uninstall SQL Server 7.0 menu option.

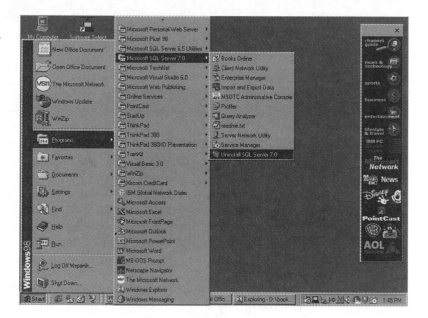

An Are You Sure dialog box, shown in Figure 6.27, appears. To continue deleting SQL Server 7.0, select Yes.

FIGURE 6.27

The Are You Sure You Want to Remove SQL Server dialog box.

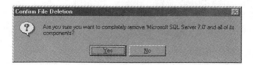

An Uninstall dialog box appears and begins the uninstall process. A progress indicator is displayed to show you the progress of the uninstall. After SQL Server is uninstalled, you must manually delete a few files like backup devices or unattached files/filegroups. Remove the leftover files by removing the SQL Server home directory, MSSQL7, which is left over after a file removal.

INSTALLING CLIENT TOOLS

SQL Server provides several different tools that allow computers acting as clients to connect to SQL Server. The following are the current 32-bit operating systems supported by the SQL Server client tools:

- Microsoft Windows NT Server version 4.0
- Microsoft Windows NT Workstation version 4.0
- Microsoft Windows NT Workstation/Server version 5.0
- Microsoft Windows 98
- Microsoft Windows 95

If you are using one of these 32-bit operating systems, you can install the following tools:

- **SQL Server Query Analyzer:** Utility to issue SQL queries
- **SQL Enterprise Manager**: Primary tool used to manage SQL Server and SQL Server objects
- **Client Network Utility**: Utility to set up SQL Server connection information and check versions of the DB-Library installed
- **Version Upgrade Wizard:** Utility to convert 6.x databases to 7.0
- **SQL Server Profiler**: Utility to monitor and record database activity
- **MS DTC**: Microsoft Distributed Transaction Coordinator client support
- **SQL Server Web Assistant**: Creates HTML files as the result of a query
- **ODBC Drivers**: Installs other ODBC drivers for replication use
- **BCP:** Bulk Copy Utility to import and export flat files with SQL Server

CONFIGURING CLIENTS

Now that you have the client utilities installed, you are ready to connect to SQL Server. SQL Server clients establish connections with SQL Server over named-pipes using dynamic server names. SQL Server clients can connect over named-pipes or any of the Microsoft-supplied protocols, including TCP/IP sockets and IPX/SPX.

Typically, you can connect to SQL Server from a client utility without any special configuration. When using ISQL/W or the SQL Enterprise Manager, click the List Servers to get a list of the active SQL Servers.

To connect to an SQL Server that is using a different network protocol or listening on an alternate named-pipe, you can set up an entry for the SQL Server using the Add button located on the General tab of the Client Network Utilities dialog box (see Figure 6.28).

FIGURE 6.28

The General tab of the SQL Server Client Network Utilities dialog box.

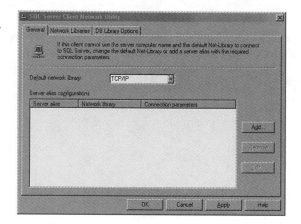

To add a new client configuration, click the Add button and enter the server name in the Server Alias text box. Select the network used to communicate with the server by checking the proper radio button. Selecting the network assigns the correct DLL to the server entry. The network DLLs for each operating system are listed in Table 6.1.

TABLE 6.1   SQL SERVER NET LIBRARIES

Network Protocol	*Windows NT/95 DLL*	*MS-DOS TSR*
Named-pipes	DBNMPNTW	DBNMPIPE.EXE
NWLink IPX/SPX	DBMSSPXN	DBMSSPX.EXE
Banyan Vines	DBMSVINN	DBMSVINE.EXE
TCP/IP Sockets	DBMSSOCN	None
Multiprotocol	DBMSRPCN	None

Click the OK button to add the new server.

> **WHAT ABOUT ODBC?**
>
> If you are trying to connect to SQL Server using the Open Database Connectivity standard (ODBC), remember that the Client Configuration Utility does not set up ODBC data sources for applications such as Microsoft Access or Powerbuilder. You must run the ODBC setup program that ships with the application or the operating system. See Chapter 15, "Replication," for examples of configuring ODBC sources. You can test ODBC connection using the DOS-based utility OSQL located in the SQL Server BINN directory.

INSTALLATION FAQ

Q. When using the SQL Server manager, what does pause do?

A. When you pause SQL Server, current users are allowed to continue to work, but any new logons are denied.

Q. SQL Server 6.5 had an option used with setup.exe that allowed you to rebuild SQL Server's registry entries. Does such a thing exist in 7.0?

A. Rebuilding SQL Server's registry entry is no longer hidden in the setup program. SQL Server comes with a utility called *regrebld* that allows you to back up the SQL Server registry and restore the registry and the SQL Server services in case it becomes corrupted.

Q. What are service packs and how do I install them?

A. After a product releases, problems or bugs might occur. These are reported to Microsoft. Microsoft tracks down the problem and fixes it. After several changes have been made, a service pack is released to correct the problem on existing SQL Servers. Service packs replace DLLs and exe files. Typically a readme file, which tells you how to install the service pack, accompanies the service pack. Service packs are cumulative as well. For example if the latest service pack is 2 and you never installed service pack 1, you have to install only service pack 2 because it contains the changes from service pack 1.

SUMMARY

You now have completed the chapters on installing and upgrading SQL Server. The remaining chapters in this book teach you how to perform database administration tasks, such as database backups, SQL Server tuning and configuration, and many other activities.

DATABASE OPERATION

PART
IV

IN THIS PART

ENTERPRISE MANAGEMENT PROCESSES

by Orryn Sledge

IN THIS CHAPTER

This chapter provides an overview of the SQL Server Enterprise Manager and how to use it to perform common tasks. It also overviews other commonly used products such as the Service Manager and the Query Analyzer.

SQL SERVER 6.X TO 7.0 QUICK REFERENCE

The What's New and What's Gone topics that follow provide a quick reference for those migrating from SQL Server 6.x to SQL Server 7.0. The following is of a summary of the changes found in SQL Server that relate to this chapter.

What's New

- **Enterprise Manager and MMC support:** The Enterprise Manager provides a graphical interface for management of SQL Server. Starting with version 7.0, the SQL Server Enterprise Manager has been rewritten to utilize the Microsoft Management Console (MMC). This provides a single console to manage multiple products and multiple servers. For example, MMC can manage the following from the same workspace: SQL Server, Microsoft Transaction Server (MTS), and Internet Information Server (IIS).
- **SQL Server Query Analyzer:** This tool executes and analyzes queries and is a separate product from the SQL Server Enterprise Manager. Previous versions of SQL Server included the tool as a part of the Enterprise Manager.
- **Wizards:** Several wizards have been added to version 7.0. Wizards, such as the Create Database Wizard, Create Index Wizard, Database Maintenance Plan Wizard, and the Security Wizard are great for performing common DBA tasks.

What's Gone

- SQL Executive   SQL Server Agent is the replacement for SQLExecutive, which was found in previous versions of SQL Server. SQL Server Agent can be managed from the MMC.

STARTING, PAUSING, AND STOPPING SQL SERVER

Before discussing the Enterprise Manager, verify that SQL Server is started. To start, pause, or stop SQL Server, double-click the Service Manager icon in the Microsoft SQL Server 7.0 (Common) group (see Figure 7.1). The SQL Server Service Manager dialog box appears (see Figure 7.2). From this dialog box, you can start, pause, or stop SQL Server.

FIGURE 7.1

The Service Manager icon.

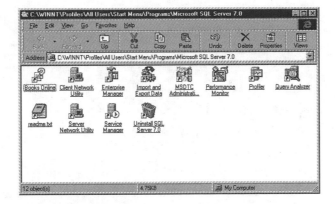

FIGURE 7.2

The SQL Server Service Manager dialog box.

TIP

SQL Server can also be started, paused, and stopped from the Task Tray icon (see Figure 7.3) in Windows NT and Windows 9.x. The following are valid actions for the task tray icon.

- Double-click the icon in the task tray to open the SQL Server Service Manager dialog box. From the SQL Server Service Manager dialog box, you can start, pause, and stop SQL Server.

- Right-click the Task Tray icon. From the right-mouse menu, select the SQL Server service to start, pause, and stop SQL Server.

FIGURE 7.3

Task tray icon.

STARTING THE SQL SERVER ENTERPRISE MANAGER

To start the SQL Server Enterprise Manager, double-click the Enterprise Manager icon in the Microsoft SQL Server 7.0 (Common) group (see Figure 7.4).

FIGURE 7.4

The Enterprise Manager icon.

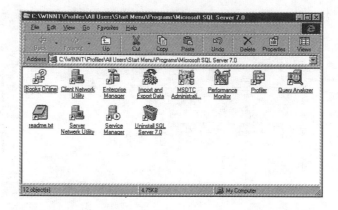

NAVIGATING THE SQL SERVER ENTERPRISE MANAGER

Because of its graphical interface, the SQL Server Enterprise Manager minimizes the number of commands required to administer a server. Following are common methods of navigation in the SQL Server Enterprise Manager:

- Menu items
- Double-click
- Right-click
- Drag and drop

REGISTERING A SERVER

When you *register a server*, you provide the SQL Server Enterprise Manager with a server name and user login with which to connect to the SQL Server database engine.

Follow these steps to register a server:

1. From the Enterprise Manager, select the Action menu bar. From the Action menu bar, select the New SQL Server Registration menu option. The Register SQL Server Wizard dialog box appears.

2. From the Register SQL Server Wizard dialog box (see Figure 7.5), click the Next button to continue.

3. From the Select a SQL Server dialog box (see Figure 7.6), select the name of a server and click the Add button to add the server to the Added Servers list. Click the Next button to continue.

FIGURE 7.5

The Register SQL Server Wizard.

FIGURE 7.6

Select a server.

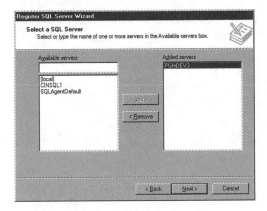

4. Select the type of authentication mode to use (see Figure 7.7): Windows NT authentication or SQL Server authentication. *Windows NT authentication* offers the advantage of having to maintain only a Windows NT login account and password. With *SQL Server authentication*, you must maintain a network account as well as a SQL Server account and password.

   If using standard security, enter the login ID and password.

   Click the Next button to continue.

5. Select a server group or create a new server group (see Figure 7.8). Click the Next button to continue.

6. Click the Finish button to register the server with the SQL Server Enterprise Manager (see Figure 7.9).

7. The Register SQL Server Messages dialog box appears (see Figure 7.10). Click the Close button to complete this operation.

FIGURE 7.7
*Select an authenti-
cation mode.*

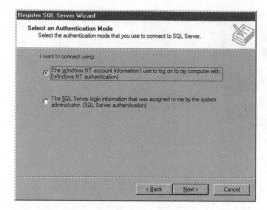

FIGURE 7.8
*Select a SQL
Server group.*

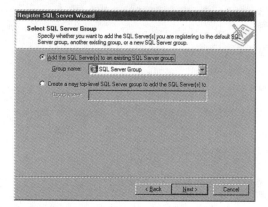

FIGURE 7.9
*Completing the
Register SQL
Server Wizard.*

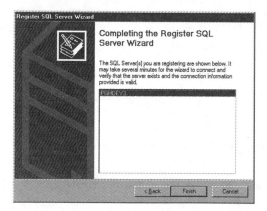

FIGURE 7.10

The Register SQL Server Messages dialog box.

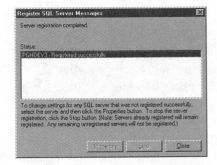

CONNECTING TO A SERVER

After you open the SQL Server Enterprise Manager and start SQL Server, perform the following to connect to a server.

1. Click the plus (+) sign next to the Microsoft SQL Servers folder.

2. Click the plus (+) sign next to the group that contains the registered server you want to connect with (usually this is the SQL Server Group).

3. Click the plus (+) sign next to the server name.

If a connection is successfully made, the connected symbol appears next to the server status icon (see Figure 7.11).

FIGURE 7.11

A successful server connection.

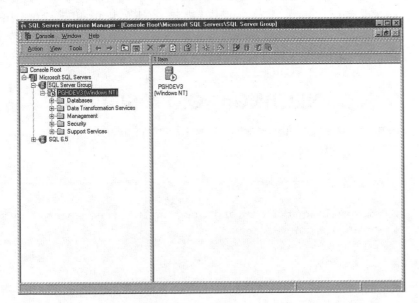

NOTE

If you are unable to establish a connection to SQL Server from the SQL Server Enterprise Manager, make sure that the MSSQLServer service is currently running. (See the topic "Starting, Pausing, and Stopping SQL Server" in this chapter for more information.)

If the MSSQLServer service is running and you are still unable to connect to SQL Server, verify the security mode, logon name, and password used to connect to SQL Server. To verify this information, right-click the server. From the right mouse menu, select the Edit SQL Server Registration menu option. The Registered SQL Server Properties dialog box appears. From this dialog box, verify the connection information.

If you are still unable to connect, verify the network protocol used to connect with SQL Server versus the network protocols in use by the server. To verify the client protocol in use, open the Client Network Utility (found in the Microsoft SQL Server 7.0 Program Group) and review the default network library and other network library settings. To verify the server protocol in use, open the Server Network Utility (found in the Microsoft SQL Server 7.0 Program Group) and review the active server network libraries. Compare the server information to the client information.

Last, if you are running TCP/IP on the client and on the server, try pinging the server from a command window by using `ping` *ipaddress*. This will tell you if you are properly networked to the server. If you are unable to ping the server, you have a networking problem. You must get the networking problem fixed before you can connect to SQL Server.

DISCONNECTING FROM A SERVER

To disconnect from a server, select the server and right-click. From the shortcut menu, select Disconnect.

NOTE

You are automatically disconnected from SQL Server when you close the SQL Server Enterprise Manager.

STARTING, STOPPING, AND CONFIGURING SQL SERVER AGENT

Follow these steps to start, stop, or configure SQL Server Agent:

1. From the SQL Server Enterprise Manager, click the plus (+) sign next to the server to manage SQL Server Agent.

2. Click the Management folder.

3. Right-click the SQL Server Agent icon (see Figure 7.12). From the right-mouse menu, select Start to start the service, select Stop to stop the service, or select Properties (see Figure 7.13) to configure the service.

FIGURE 7.12
SQL Server Agent right mouse menu.

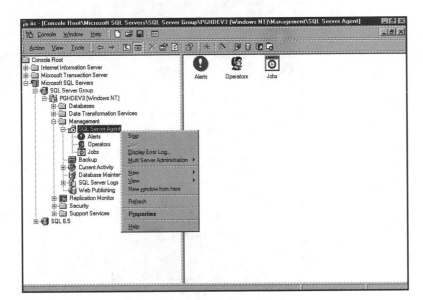

STARTING, STOPPING, AND CONFIGURING SQL MAIL

Follow these steps to start, stop, or configure SQL Mail:

1. From the SQL Server Enterprise Manager, click the plus (+) sign next to the server to manage SQL Mail.

2. Click the Support Services folder.

3. Right-click the SQL Mail icon (see Figure 7.14). From the right-mouse menu, select Start to start the service, select Stop to stop the service, or select Properties (see Figure 7.15) to configure the service.

7

ENTERPRISE
MANAGEMENT
PROCESSES

FIGURE 7.13
The SQL Server Agent Properties dialog box.

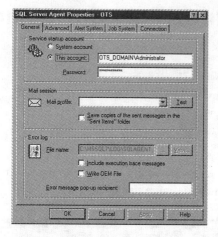

FIGURE 7.14
SQL Mail right-mouse menu.

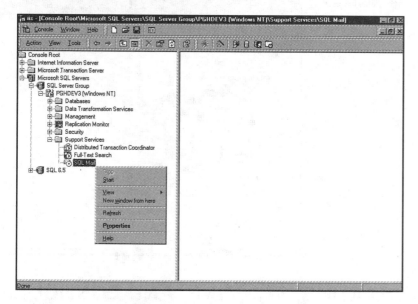

FIGURE 7.15
SQL Mail Configuration dialog box.

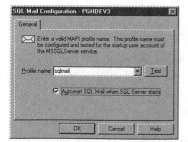

USING THE ENTERPRISE MANAGER TO PERFORM COMMON TASKS

The following sections provide brief descriptions of how to perform common administration tasks from the SQL Server Enterprise Manager. Many of these tasks are explained in greater detail in other sections of this book.

Manage Server Configurations

Follow these steps to configure a server:

1. From the SQL Server Enterprise Manager, right-click the server you want to configure.

2. From the menu, select the Properties menu option. The SQL Server Properties dialog box appears (see Figure 7.16). From this dialog box, you can configure server options by selecting the corresponding tab.

FIGURE 7.16

SQL Server Properties dialog box.

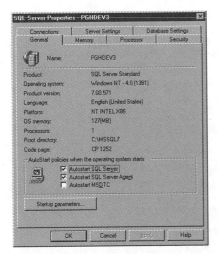

Manage Logins

Follow these steps to manage logins:

1. From the SQL Server Enterprise Manager, click the plus (+) sign next to the server to manage logins.

2. Click the Security folder.

3. Click the Logins icon. The Result pane appears with login information. Right-click in the Result pane to add, edit, and delete logins (see Figures 7.17 and 7.18).

Refer to Chapter 9, "Managing SQL Server Users and Security," for more information on managing logins.

FIGURE 7.17

The Result pane with login information.

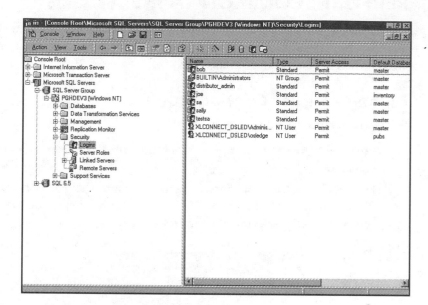

FIGURE 7.18

The Login Properties dialog box.

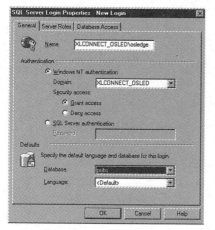

Manage Server Roles

Server roles delegate responsibility for server-wide operations. Follow these steps to manage server roles:

1. From the SQL Server Enterprise Manager, click the plus (+) sign next to the server to manage server roles.

2. Click the Security folder.

3. Click the Server Roles icon. The Result pane appears with server roles (see Figure 7.19). Double-click a server role. The corresponding Server Role Properties dialog box appears. From this dialog box, you can add, edit, and delete members of a server role (see Figure 7.20).

FIGURE 7.19

The Server Role Result pane.

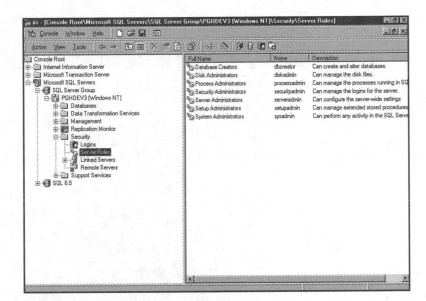

7

ENTERPRISE MANAGEMENT PROCESSES

FIGURE 7.20

The Server Role Properties dialog box.

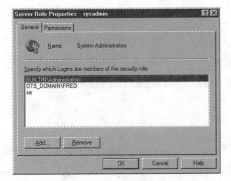

Refer to Chapter 9 for more information on server roles.

Manage Databases

Follow these steps to create, manage, and delete a database:

1. From the SQL Server Enterprise Manager, click the plus (+) sign next to the server to manage a database.

2. Open the Databases folder by clicking the plus (+) sign next to the Databases folder. From this folder, you can create a new database, edit an existing database, or delete a database by right-clicking a database (see Figures 7.21 and 7.22).

FIGURE 7.21

The Databases folder.

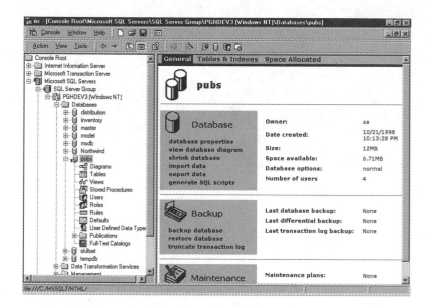

FIGURE 7.22

Database Properties dialog box.

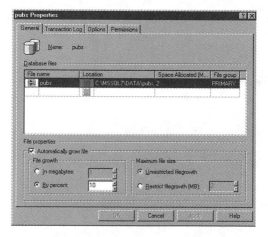

Refer to Chapter 8, "Database Management," for more information on managing databases.

Manage Database Users and Objects

Follow these steps to create, manage, and delete database objects such as database users, database roles, tables, SQL server views, stored procedures, rules, defaults, user-defined datatypes, database diagrams, and full-text catalogs.

1. From the SQL Server Enterprise Manager, click the plus (+) sign next to the server to manage database users and objects.

2. Open the Database folder by clicking the plus (+) sign next to the Databases folder. Open the database that contains the objects you want to work with by clicking the plus (+) sign next to the corresponding database.

3. From this folder (see Figure 7.23), you can manage diagrams, tables, views, stored procedures, users, roles, rules, defaults, user defined data types, and full-text catalogs. For example, to manage a table, click the Tables folder. From the Results pane, right-click a table. From the right mouse menu, select the Design Table menu option. This action opens the Design Table dialog box that can be used to create and alter table designs (see Figure 7.24).

FIGURE 7.23

Manage database users and objects.

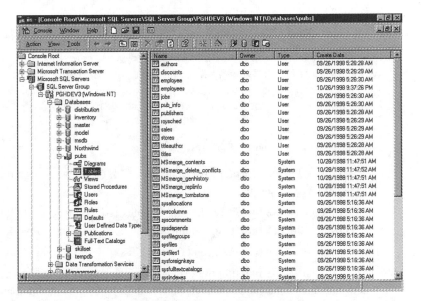

Generate SQL Scripts

From the SQL Server Enterprise Manager, you can generate SQL scripts that contain the data definition language used to create an object in a database. This enables you to reverse-engineer existing objects.

FIGURE 7.24

The Design Table dialog box.

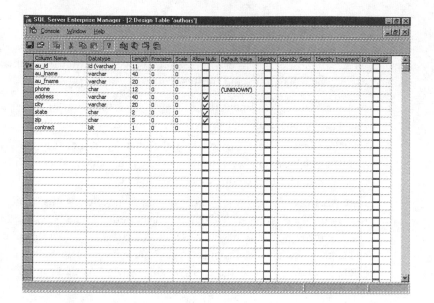

TIP

SQL Scripts are also useful for performing keyword searches. Suppose that you want to determine how many stored procedures reference the column au_id. An easy way to determine this is to generate the data definition language for all the tables in the database and then search with a text editor for au_id.

Follow these steps to generate SQL scripts:

1. From the SQL Server Enterprise Manager, click the plus (+) sign next to the server to generate SQL scripts.

2. Open the Database folder by clicking the plus (+) sign next to the Databases folder. Right-click the database that contains the objects you want to work with.

3. From the right mouse menu, select the All Tasks menu option.

4. From the All Tasks menu option, select the Generate SQL Scripts option. This action displays the Generate SQL Scripts dialog box. From this dialog box, you can generate the appropriate SQL syntax (see Figures 7.25 and 7.26). From this dialog box, you can also preview the script by clicking on the Preview command button.

FIGURE 7.25

The Generate SQL Scripts dialog box.

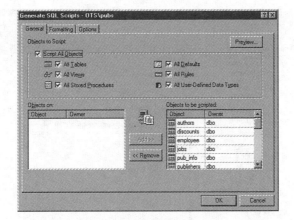

FIGURE 7.26

Sample output from the Generate SQL Scripts dialog box.

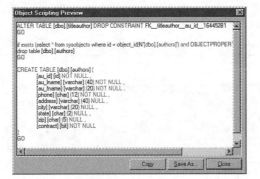

Manage Jobs

Jobs are tasks that are scheduled to automatically run at preset time intervals. The SQL Server Agent manages these jobs. Database backups, transaction log backups, and DBCC commands are just a few of types of administrative jobs that can be automated by the SQL Server Agent. To manage jobs follow these steps:

1. From the SQL Server Enterprise Manager, click the plus (+) sign next to the server to manage jobs.

2. Click the plus (+) sign next to the Management folder.

3. Click the plus (+) sign next to the SQL Server Agent icon.

4. Click the Jobs icon. The Result pane appears with job information. Right-click in the Result pane to start, stop, add, edit, and delete jobs (see Figures 7.27 and 7.28).

Refer to Chapter 30, "Automating Database Administration Tasks," for more information on jobs.

FIGURE 7.27

The Jobs Result pane.

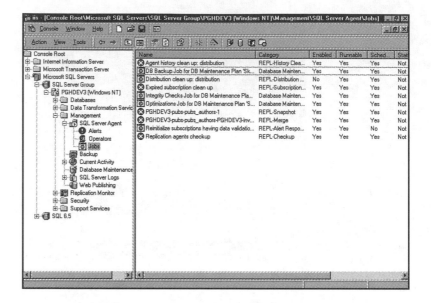

FIGURE 7.28

The Job Properties dialog box.

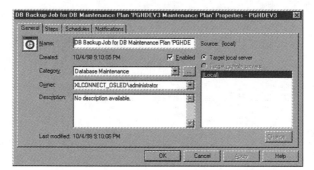

Manage Alerts

Alerts are notifications of errors and predefined conditions. Alerts can notify operators through email and pages of these conditions. The SQL Server Agent manages these alerts. Alerts are designed to provide a proactive approach to database administration. To manage alerts, follow these steps:

1. From the SQL Server Enterprise Manager, click the plus (+) sign next to the server to manage alerts.

2. Click the plus (+) sign next to the Management folder.

3. Click the plus (+) sign next to the SQL Server Agent icon.

4. Click the Alerts icon. The Result pane appears with alert information. Right-click in the Result pane to add, edit, and delete alerts (see Figures 7.29 and 7.30).

Refer to Chapter 30 for more information on alerts.

FIGURE 7.29
The Alert Result pane.

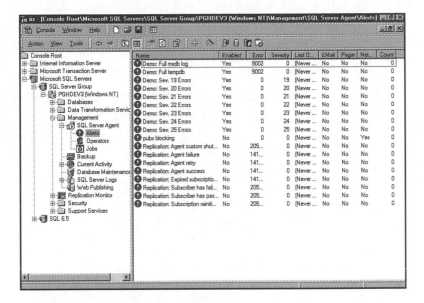

FIGURE 7.30
The Alert Properties dialog box.

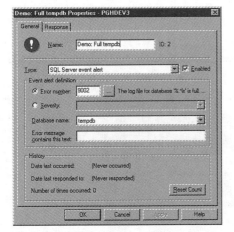

Manage Operators

Operators are recipients of alerts and notifications. The SQL Server Agent manages these operators. To manage operators, follow these steps:

1. From the SQL Server Enterprise Manager, click the plus (+) sign next to the server to manage operators.

2. Click the plus (+) sign next to the Management folder.

3. Click the plus (+) sign next to the SQL Server Agent icon.

4. Click the Operators icon. The Result pane appears with operator information. Right-click in the Result pane to add, edit, and delete operators (see Figures 7.31 and 7.32).

FIGURE 7.31

The Operator Result pane.

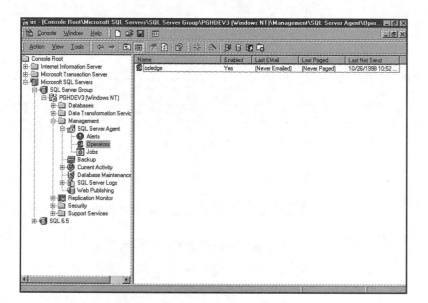

FIGURE 7.32

Operator Properties dialog box.

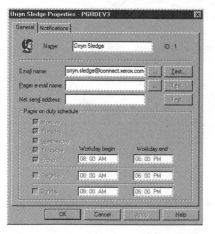

Refer to Chapter 30, "Automating Database Administration Tasks," for more information on operators.

Monitor User Activity

SQL Server provides a console within the SQL Server Enterprise Manager that monitors user activity. This information is often useful to pinpoint query problems and isolate bottlenecks.

Follow these steps to monitor user activity:

1. From the SQL Server Enterprise Manager, click the plus (+) sign next to the server to monitor user activity.

2. Click the plus (+) sign next to the Management folder.

3. Click the plus (+) sign next to the Current Activity icon.

4. Click one of the following icons: Process Info, Locks / Process ID, Locks / Object. The Result pane appears with the corresponding information. Right-click in the Result pane to send a message to the process, view detailed information about the process, or kill the process.

Refer to Chapter 24, "Multi-User Considerations," for more information on monitoring user activity.

Manage Data Transformation Packages

Data transformation packages are import and export programs. These programs transform data through OLE DB, ODBC, and user-defined validation rules.

Follow these steps to manage data transformation packages:

1. From the SQL Server Enterprise Manager, click the plus (+) sign next to the server to manage data transformation packages.

2. Click the plus (+) sign next to the Data Transformation Services folder.

3. Click the plus the Local Packages icon or the Repository Packages icon. The Result pane appears with the corresponding information. Right-click in the Result pane to add, edit, delete, and execute data transformation packages (see Figure 7.33). Double-click the package to modify its content (see Figure 7.34).

Refer to Chapter 32, "Using Data Transformation Services (DTS)," for more information on data transformation packages.

Manage Error Logs

Error logs provide detailed information about SQL Server. This information is often used to troubleshoot SQL Server errors and problems.

FIGURE 7.33

The Data Transformation Packages Result pane.

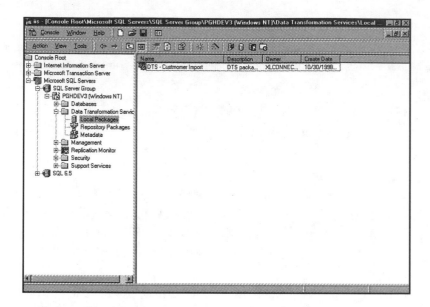

FIGURE 7.34

Sample DTS Package.

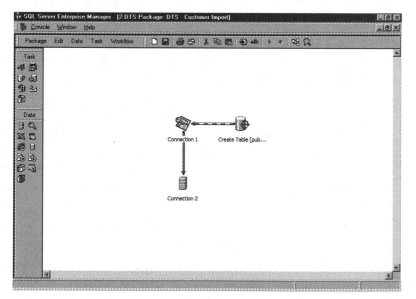

Follow these steps to manage error logs:

1. From the SQL Server Enterprise Manager, click the plus (+) sign next to the server to manage error logs.

2. Click the plus (+) sign next to the Management folder.

3. Click the SQL Server Logs folder. The Result pane appears with error log information (see Figure 7.35). Double-click an error log to display its contents (see Figure 7.36).

FIGURE 7.35

The Error Log Result pane.

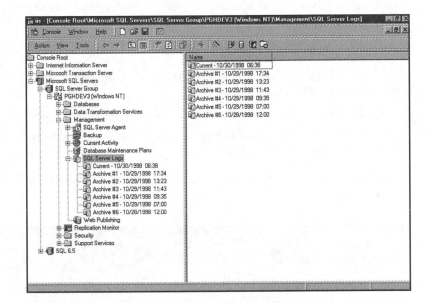

FIGURE 7.36

Error Log detail information.

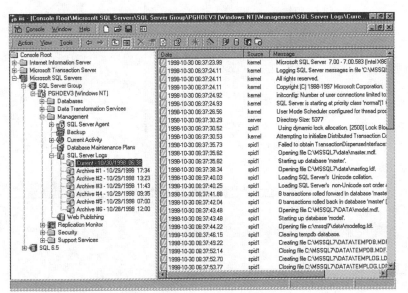

Refer to Chapters 13, "Troubleshooting SQL Server," and 29, "Developing a SQL Server Maintenance Plan," for more information on error logs.

Manage Web Assistant Jobs

Web assistant jobs turn data into HTML pages. This is a great way to publish SQL Server data to the Web.

Follow these steps to manage Web Assistant jobs:

1. From the SQL Server Enterprise Manager, click the plus (+) sign next to the server to manage Web Assistant jobs.

2. Click the plus (+) sign next to the Management folder.

3. Click the Web Publishing icon. The Result pane appears with Web Assistant jobs (see Figures 7.37 and 7.38).

Refer to Chapter 28, "SQL Server 7.0 and the Internet," for more information on Web Assistant jobs.

FIGURE 7.37

The Web Assistant Jobs Result pane.

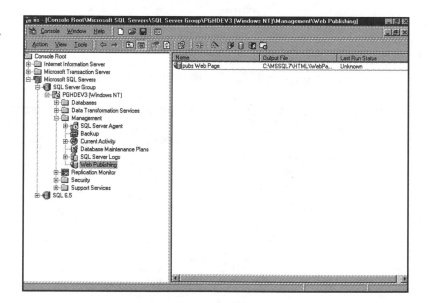

FIGURE 7.38

The Web Assistant Properties dialog box.

SQL SERVER QUERY ANALYZER

The SQL Server Query Analyzer executes and analyzes queries. To open the SQL Server Query Analyzer, double-click the Query Analyzer icon in the Microsoft SQL Server 7.0 (Common) group (see Figure 7.39). The Connect to SQL Server dialog box appears (see Figure 7.40). Select the appropriate connection mode and server and click the OK button. Upon successfully connecting to SQL Server, the Query dialog box appears (see Figure 7.41). From this dialog box, you can issue Transact SQL statements, view results, and analyze query performance and optimization plans.

FIGURE 7.39

The Query Analyzer icon.

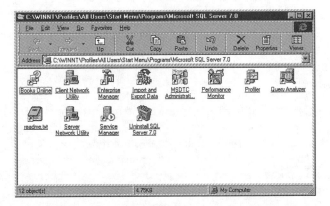

FIGURE 7.40

The Connect to SQL Server dialog box.

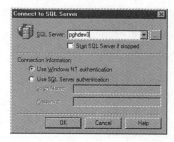

FIGURE 7.41

The Query Analyzer dialog box.

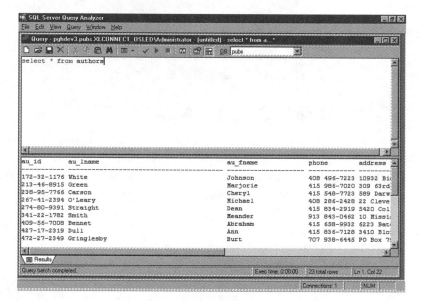

TIP

From the Query dialog box, you can concurrently run multiple SQL statements against the server. Click the New Query toolbar button in the Query dialog box. This action opens a new connection to SQL Server, which can be used to issue a new query while maintaining previous connections. This feature enables you to switch connections while queries are being processed. Because the processing takes place on the server and not on the client, your machine is free to continue with other tasks (see Figure 7.42).

Also from the Query dialog box, you can run an individual Transact SQL statement by highlighting just the text and clicking the Execute Query toolbar button (see Figure 7.43).

FIGURE 7.42

An example of multiple-query processing.

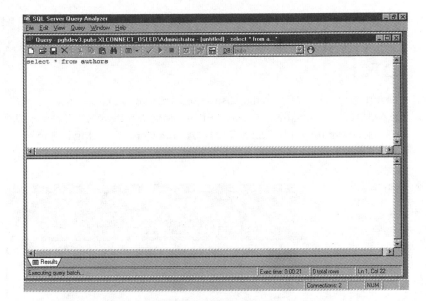

FIGURE 7.43

Executing only the highlighted text.

Only highlighted
text is executed

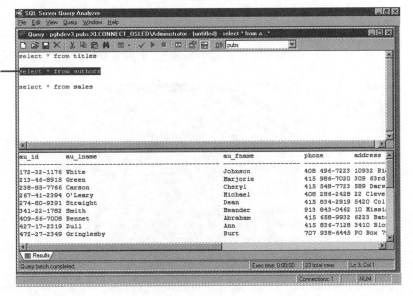

STARTING, STOPPING, AND CONFIGURING DISTRIBUTED TRANSACTION COORDINATOR (DTC)

To start, stop, or configure the Distributed Transaction Coordinator (DTC), double-click the MSDTC Administrative Console icon in the Microsoft SQL Server 7.0 (Common) group (see Figure 7.44). The MS DTC Admin Console dialog box appears (see Figure 7.45). From this dialog box, you can start, stop, and configure the DTC.

FIGURE 7.44

The MSDTC Administrative Console icon.

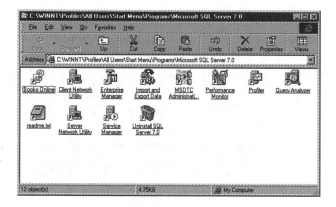

FIGURE 7.45

The MS DTC Admin Console dialog box.

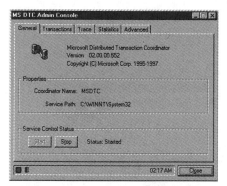

Refer to Chapter 12, "Distributed Transaction Coordinator," for more information on the DTC.

ENTERPRISE MANAGEMENT FAQ

Following are some of the common questions asked by DBAs about SQL Server Enterprise Management Process:

Q. Does deleting a registered server from the Enterprise Manager actually delete SQL Server from the machine?

A. No, when you delete SQL Server from the Enterprise Manager you are only removing Enterprise Manager's reference to SQL Server. To add the reference back, register the server with the Enterprise Manager.

Q. I'm getting the error message "Login failed for user 'username'" when I try to connect to SQL Server from the Enterprise Manager. What does this message mean?

A. Usually it means that the login/password combination is invalid. From within the Enterprise Manager, right mouse click on the server and select the Edit SQL Server Registration properties menu option. The Registered SQL Server Properties dialog box appears. From this dialog box you can change the login/password combination.

Q. Whenever I try to start or stop SQL Server from the Enterprise Manager I get the following error message: "A error 5 (Access is denied) occurred while performing this service operation on the MSSQLServer service" I'm logged in as sa. Why am I getting this message?

A. This message appears when someone is not a member of the NT Domain Admins group or the NT Administrators group. Although you are the administrator for SQL Server, you are not designated as an administrator of the NT machine that runs SQL Server. You must be a NT administrator to start or stop a service. To resolve the problem, have your account added to the NT Domain Admins group or the NT Administrators group.

Q. Can I copy the MMC settings to another machine?

A. Yes, MMC settings are portable. Select the Save As menu option from the Console menu in the Microsoft Management Console dialog box to save the current MMC settings. To open the previously saved settings, select the Open menu option from the Console menu in the Microsoft Management Console dialog box.

SUMMARY

As you can see, the graphical interface provided by the SQL Server Enterprise Manager simplifies the tasks required to manage SQL Server. However, to manage a production environment, a DBA must know more than how to right-click an object. A DBA must be knowledgeable about the various components of SQL Server and how they interact. With that in mind, the next chapter discusses one of the most fundamental components of SQL Server: databases.

DATABASE MANAGEMENT

by Orryn Sledge

IN THIS CHAPTER

It is important to understand how to manage a database in SQL Server. Every object and its corresponding data revolves around the database. If a database isn't properly managed, it can result in system downtime, countless headaches, and loss of data.

SQL SERVER 6.5 TO 7.0 QUICK REFERENCE

The What's New and What's Gone topics provide a quick reference for those migrating from SQL Server 6.x to SQL Server 7.0. The following is a summary of the changes found in SQL Server that relate to this chapter.

What's New

- **New file system for database and log files**: SQL Server 7.0 has eliminated devices and now uses the following operating system files (see Table 8.1).

TABLE 8.1 OPERATING SYSTEM FILES

Operating System File Type	Use	Default Extension
Primary	This file type is the starting point for each database and it also holds pointers to other files used by the database. Each database has one primary data file.	.MDF
Secondary	This file type contains data that does not reside that does not reside on the primary file type. Depending on the database configuration, a database may have zero, one, or more secondary data files.	.NDF
Log	This file type contains the log for the database. Every database has at least one log file. Databases can also have more than one log file.	.LDF

- **Automatic resizing of the database and transaction log**: Databases and transactions can automatically grow in size and shrink in size on an as-needed basis. In previous versions of SQL Server, database and log sizes were fixed. If they needed to be increased, an administrator had to manually increase the size of the database or log. This feature helps reduce the likelihood of a database or log running out of space.

- **New page size:** SQL Server 7.0 uses an 8KB page block to store data and index information. Previous versions of SQL Server utilized a 2KB page format. Additionally, the maximum row size has been increased to 8060 bytes, whereas previous versions were limited to 1962 bytes.

• **Filegroups**: Database files can be logically grouped together. This feature enables administrators to place specific tables, indexes, text datatypes, ntext datatypes, and image datatypes on specific filegroups. Filegroups can be placed on specific hard drives. This can help improve performance by segmenting portions of the database. Table 8.2 shows the two types of filegroups.

TABLE 8.2   FILEGROUPS

Filegroup Type	Purpose
Default	Holds the primary datafile and other datafiles that are not allocated to a user-defined filegroup. All system tables are stored on the default filegroup. Any tables and indexes that are allocated to a user-defined filegroup are stored on the default filegroup.
User-defined	Holds any datafiles that are explicitly placed in a user-defined filegroup by the FILEGROUP keyword with the CREATE DATABASE or ALTER DATABASE statement.

• **New database options**: SQL Server 7.0 includes the database options shown in Table 8.3.

TABLE 8.3   DATABASE OPTIONS

Database Option	Purpose	Notes
Autoclose	When this option is set to TRUE, the database is automatically closed when users are not in the database.	This option must be manually set with the sp_dboption command.
ANSI Null Default	If NULL or NOT NULL is not explicitly stated during column creation, SQL Server utilizes this option to determine the NULL or NOT NULL characteristic for the column. The default setting for this option is OFF.	This option was named Columns Null by Default in previous versions of SQL Server.

continues

TABLE 8.3 CONTINUED

Database Option	Purpose	Notes
Autoshrink	When this option is set to TRUE, the database and log files automatically shrink, thus reducing hard disk space. This is designed to reduce overhead.	This option must be manually set with the sp_dboption command.
Concat Null Yields Null	When this option is set to TRUE, concatenation of a null and a non-null value results in a null.	This option must be manually set with the sp_dboption command.
Cursor Close On Commit	When this option is set to TRUE, all open cursors are automatically closed when data is committed.	This option must be manually set with the sp_dboption command.
Default to Local Cursor	If this option is set to TRUE, cursors automatically default to a LOCAL scope if the cursor does not explicitly contain the GLOBAL keyword in the DECLARE statement.	This option must be manually set with the sp_dboption command.
Quoted Identifier	When this option is set to TRUE, object names within double quotes do not have to adhere to Transact-SQL Naming conventions.	This option must be manually set with the sp_dboption command.
Recursive Triggers	If this option is TRUE, a trigger can recursively call itself. The default setting for this option is OFF.	

Database Option	Purpose	Notes
Torn Page Detection	When the Torn Page Detection option is set to TRUE, SQL Server automatically detects torn pages. A torn page is a page that contains incomplete data modifications.	

- **Truncate log on checkpoint**: When this database option is TRUE, the log is automatically truncated when it is 70% full. Previously, the log was truncated whenever SQL Server issued a checkpoint command, which was approximately every minute.

- **sp_dbcmptlevel**: This option is used to set the database compatibility level (see Chapter 6, "Installing or Upgrading SQL Server," for more information).

- **Create Database Wizard**: Version 7.0 includes a Create Database Wizard to assist with the creation of a database.

- **Detach and attach database commands**: Two new system procedures have been added to support detaching and attaching of databases: sp_attach_db and sp_detach_db. These commands allow databases to be moved and copied to different servers or different directories.

What's Gone

- **Devices**: Devices are no longer supported in version 7.0. Instead, version 7.0 uses operating system files for the database and log (see Table 8.1 for more information).

- **Segments**: The usage of segments is no longer supported. Filegroups provide similar functionality.

- **DBCC SHRINKDB**: DBCC SHRINKDATABASE has replaced this command.

- **NO CHECKPOINT ON RECOVERY**: The RESTORE command WITH STANDBY option has replaced this command.

- **Log and database must reside on separate physical files:** Previous versions of SQL Server allowed the database and its log to reside on the same device. Version 7.0 requires that the database and the log reside on separate files.

8

DATABASE MANAGEMENT

A DATABASE PRIMER

The following sections discuss the fundamental terminology and concepts necessary to manage a SQL Server database.

What Is a Database?

A *database* is an organized collection of data (see Figure 8.1). This collection of data is logically structured and systematically maintained. SQL Server extends the concept of a database by allowing you to create and store other types of objects, such as stored procedures, triggers, views, and other objects that interact with your the data.

FIGURE 8.1

A database.

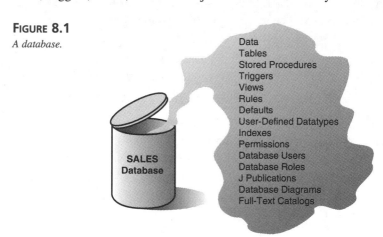

Data
Tables
Stored Procedures
Triggers
Views
Rules
Defaults
User-Defined Datatypes
Indexes
Permissions
Database Users
Database Roles
J Publications
Database Diagrams
Full-Text Catalogs

SALES Database

What Is the Transaction Log?

The *transaction log* is the history of data modifications to a database (see Figure 8.2). Whenever you create a database, SQL Server automatically creates a corresponding database transaction log. SQL Server uses the transaction log to ensure transaction completeness and to incrementally restore data changes (see Chapter 10, "Backup and Restore," for more information on restoring the transaction log).

The capability to guarantee transaction completeness helps separate SQL Server from less well-equipped RDBMS software. To SQL Server, virtually every data modification must have a starting point and an ending point. If the ending point isn't reached, SQL Server automatically reverses any changes that were made. Suppose that the power goes out to the server midway through a process that is deleting all the rows from a table. When SQL Server restarts, it automatically restores all the rows that had been deleted, thus returning the table to its original state before the delete process was run. Through the use of the transaction log, SQL Server can guarantee that all the work was done or that none of the work was done.

FIGURE 8.2

A transaction.

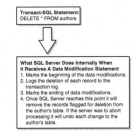

SQL Server automatically uses a *write-ahead* type of transaction log. This means that changes to the database are first written to the transaction log and then they are written to the database. Examples of database changes written to the transaction log include data modified through the UPDATE, INSERT, and DELETE SQL commands; any type of object creation; and any security changes.

SQL Server automatically marks the starting point and ending point whenever you execute a command that performs data modifications. For greater control, you can define the starting point and ending point for a group of data modifications. This is often done when more than one set of data modifications occurs within a unit of work.

For example, if a user transfers $1,000 from checking to savings, you can use a user-defined transaction to ensure that the checking account was debited and the savings account was credited. If the transaction did not complete, the checking and saving accounts return to their original states (their states before the transaction began).

To specify the beginning of a user-defined transaction, use the following statement:

BEGIN TRANsaction [transaction_name]

To specify the end of a user-defined transaction, use the following statement:

COMMIT TRANsaction [transaction_name]

To rollback any changes made within a user-defined transaction, use the following statement:

ROLLBACK TRANsaction [transaction_name ¦ savepoint_name]

The transaction log is the log operating system file (default extension of .LDF). Keep in mind that every database has at least one transaction log.

8

DATABASE MANAGEMENT

How Databases and Operating System Datafiles Interact

Every database in SQL Server must use at least one data operating system file and one log operating system file. Depending on your needs, you can create your entire database on one data operating system file and one log operating system file or on multiple data operating system files and multiple log operating system files (see Figure 8.3).

FIGURE 8.3

Database and operating system file interaction.

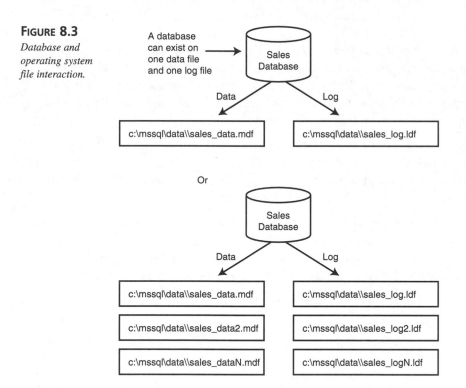

DATABASE BASICS

The following sections provide step-by-step instructions for managing a database.

Creating a Database

Before you can create tables and start to manage your data, you must create a database. Follow these steps to create a new database:

1. From the SQL Server Enterprise Manager, click the plus (+) sign next to the server that will contain the database.

2. Right-click the Databases folder. From the right mouse menu, select the New Database menu option. The Database Properties dialog box appears (see Figure 8.4).

FIGURE 8.4

Creating a database with Enterprise Manager.

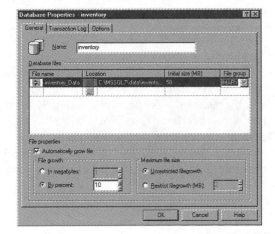

3. Select the General tab and enter a name for the database.

> **NOTE**
>
> Database names can be up to 128 characters. I recommend being consistent when naming a database such as using all uppercase or lowercase characters. Don't forget that you may often need to type the database name in a SQL statement—this may make you think twice about using all 128 characters! Try to make the name meaningful and relatively short.

4. From the Database files portion of the Database Properties dialog box, enter the filename, location, initial size, and filegroup information.

> **TIP**
>
> If you have a high-end server with separate drives and separate asynchronous disk controllers, I recommend placing the database file and log file on separate hard drives. This can dramatically improve performance.

8

DATABASE MANAGEMENT

5. Select the Automatic Grow file option if you want to have SQL Server automatically grow the database file on an as-needed basis. If this option is selected you can also enter the File Growth and Maximum File Size settings.

TIP

I recommend using the automatic grow file option so that the database does not run out of space. When using this option, I also recommend pre-sizing the database files if possible. This reduces the need for SQL Server to continuously grow the database until it reaches the proper size. Having SQL Server grow the database does introduce some overhead (approximately 5%). Although the overhead is small, the database has to work to keep up with the requests to grow the database. When SQL Server is growing the database, locks must held until the operation is complete. In a high traffic database, this delay may be noticeable.

---

6. Select the Transaction Log tab.

7. From Transaction Log files portion of the Transaction Log tab, enter the filename, location, and initial size for the transaction log.

8. Select the Automatic grow file option if you want to have SQL Server automatically grow the log file on an as-needed basis. If this option is selected, you can also enter the File Growth and Maximum File Size settings.

9. Select the Options tab of the Database Properties dialog box.

NOTE

The minimum size of a database is 1MB. The maximum size of a database is 1,048,516TB. The minimum size of a log is 1MB.

TIP

Don't worry if you allocate too little or too much space to your database. You can go back and change the size of the database after it is created.

10. From the Options tab, select or deselect the appropriate options (see the topic "Setting Database Options" later in this chapter for more information).

> **NOTE**
>
> Database options can be changed after the database is created. If an option is changed, it takes effect immediately.

11. Choose OK to create the database.

> **TIP**
>
> Always back up the `master` database after you create a new database. Doing so makes it easier to recover your database should the `master` database become damaged.

> **NOTE**
>
> The `sa` and members of the `sysadmin` (System Administrators) or `dbcreator` (Database Creators) roles are the only users that can create a database, unless the `CREATE DATABASE` statement permission is granted to other users (see Chapter 9, "Managing SQL Server Users and Security," for more information about managing statement permissions).

8

DATABASE
MANAGEMENT

Listing 8.1 shows the transact SQL command to create a database:

LISTING 8.1 CREATING A DATABASE

```
CREATE DATABASE database_name
[ ON [PRIMARY]
[ <filespec> [,...n] ]
[, <filegroup> [,...n] ]
]
[ LOG ON { <filespec> } ]
[ FOR LOAD ¦ FOR ATTACH ]
<filespec> ::=
( [ NAME = logical_file_name, ]
FILENAME = 'os_file_name'
```

continues

LISTING 8.1   CONTINUED

```
[, SIZE = size]
[, MAXSIZE = { max_size ¦ UNLIMITED } ]
[, FILEGROWTH = growth_increment] ) [,...n]
<filegroup> ::=
FILEGROUP filegroup_name <filespec> [,...n]
```

After you create a database, review the following checklist:

❑   Do you need to set any database options? See the topic "Setting Database Options" in this chapter for more information.

❑   Did you backup the master database? See Chapter 10, for more information.

❑   Did you document the configuration of the database? Use the output from sp_helpdb to document the database. Having a documented database can be useful for disaster recovery.

❑   Are you planning on backing up the database? If so, you may want to go ahead and implement your database backup strategy. See Chapter 10 for more information.

❑   Are you planning on backing up the database log? If so, you may want to go ahead and implement your log backup strategy. See Chapter 10 for more information. If you are not planning on backing up the database log, go ahead and set the database option truncate log on checkpoint to TRUE. This will prevent the database log from filling up over time.

RAID AND STRIPING DATA ACROSS DISKS

In SQL Server (or any other database server), one of the most likely bottlenecks is the disk I/O from clients reading and writing from different tables or different databases simultaneously.

Suppose that you have a PC configured as a server. It has a fast processor and a large amount of memory, but you bought a single 12GB hard drive with a single disk controller to store all your database information. Because you have only one disk drive, any database files and transaction logs you create physically reside on the single hard drive. What happens when users start inserting and retrieving data simultaneously? SQL Server has more than enough memory and the processor is fast enough to handle the request, but what about the single disk drive and disk controller?

A bottleneck will quickly form as I/O requests queue up to the single disk. An old SQL Server trick, dating back to the days of Sybase, has been to use a smart disk controller card or disk array; rather than use a single 12GB hard drive, use four 3GB hard drives. Database files and transaction logs can then be created on different physical hard drives. Although this arrangement is a better solution than a single hard drive, it still has some deficiencies. Databases are spread over multiple SQL Server data files, but the hot data everyone is after might be on a single drive causing disk I/O bottlenecks similar to those on a single drive. The NT operating system and advanced hardware systems have created a solution to address this problem: hardware or software *disk striping*.

Figure 8.5 is a conceptual diagram of disk striping for a drive labeled J. Drive J looks like a single physical drive to the SQL Server DBA who is creating data and transaction log files. Logically, a striped drive is a single drive but physically, the logical drive spans many different disk drives. A striped disk is made up of a special file system called a *striped set*. All the disks in the disk array that make up the logical drive are part of the striped set. Data on each of the drives is divided into equal blocks and is spread over all the drives. By spreading the file system over several disk drives, disk I/O performance is improved because the disk I/O is spread over multiple drives. The balancing of the I/O is transparent to the DBA, who no longer has to worry about spreading out file I/O.

Disk striping is also referred to as *RAID 0* (Redundant Array of Inexpensive Disks). RAID level 0 is the fastest RAID configuration. The level of fault tolerance is measured in levels 0 through 5, with 0 providing no fault tolerance. If a single disk fails in a RAID 0 system, none of the data in the stripe set can be accessed. Windows NT provides software-level disk striping. Disk striping can also be handled by special hardware disk arrays.

A RAID 0 system has no fault tolerance; the entire file system can be rendered useless if a single drive fails. RAID 1 is also known as *disk mirroring*. In a RAID 1 configuration, data written to a primary disk is also written to a mirrored disk. RAID 2 uses disk striping along with error correction. RAID 3 and RAID 4 also use disk striping and error correction and vary in their degrees of effectiveness and disk space requirements. A RAID 5 system has the maximum fault tolerance: a single disk can fail and the system continues to function. A backup drive can be placed in the disk array so that the lost data file or log file can be re-created on the new drive by the RAID system. RAID 5 technology can be implemented using Windows NT disk striping with parity or as a hardware-based solution.

continues

8

DATABASE
MANAGEMENT

Hardware-based disk striping (RAID configurations) outperform Windows NT software disk striping. NT's implementation is accomplished through software and requires system processor resources. The disadvantage of hardware striping solutions is cost. RAID systems can be quite expensive, depending on the level of fault tolerance you select.

FIGURE 8.5

Disk striping.

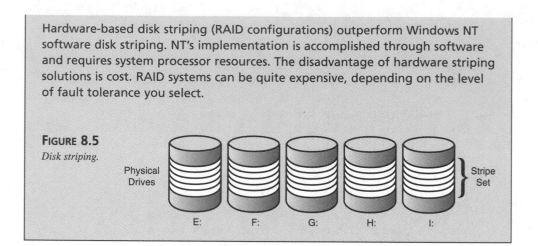

Viewing Information About a Database

After you create a database, you can view information such as general information, file space allocation and usage, log space allocation and usage, table and index space usage, and a database diagram. Follow these steps to view information about a specific database:

1. From the SQL Server Enterprise Manager, click the plus (+) sign next to the server that contains the database you want to view.

2. Click the plus (+) sign next to the Databases folder. This opens the Databases folder.

3. Left-click the database in which to view information.

4. The corresponding database information appears in the Taskpad (see Figure 8.6) portion of the SQL Server Enterprise Manager. (*Note*: the Taskpad must be active; to activate, select Taskpad from the View menu.)

You can use the following transact SQL command to view information about a database:

```
sp_helpdb [dbname]
```

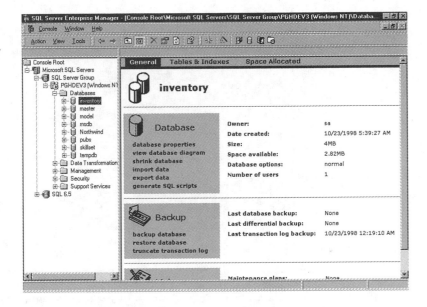

FIGURE 8.6

Database Information in the Task Pad pane of Enterprise Manager.

Setting Database Options

Each database in SQL Server has its own database options. Follow these steps to set database options:

1. From the SQL Server Enterprise Manager, click the plus (+) sign next to the server that contains the database you want to view or set options for.

2. Click the plus (+) sign next to the Databases folder. This opens the Databases folder.

3. Right-click the database in which you want to set the database option. From the right mouse menu, select the Properties menu option. The Properties dialog box appears.

4. From the Properties dialog box, select the Options tab (see Figure 8.7). From this tab, select or deselect the appropriate options.

5. Click OK to save your changes.

8

DATABASE
MANAGEMENT

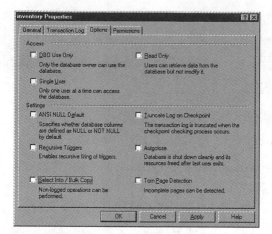

FIGURE 8.7
Setting database options on the Options tab.

TIP

When you change database options, the changes take effect immediately. You do not have to restart the server for the option to take effect.

The following sections describe each of the database options available on this tab.

DBO Use Only

Default setting: FALSE

When the DBO Use Only option is set to TRUE, only the Database Owner (DBO) can access the database. Use this option if you want to keep everyone but the database owner and sa out of the database.

Single User

Default setting: FALSE

When the Single User option is set to TRUE, only one user at a time (including the sa) can be in the database.

Read Only

Default setting: FALSE

When the Read Only option is set to TRUE, the contents of the database can be viewed but not modified.

ANSI Null Default

Default setting: FALSE

If NULL or NOT NULL is not explicitly stated during column creation, SQL Server uses this option to determine the NULL or NOT NULL characteristic for the column.

> **NOTE**
>
> The ANSI Null Default option was named Columns Null by Default in previous versions of SQL Server.

The following examples explain the impact of setting the ANSI Null Default option.

Example A:

```
ANSI Null Default = FALSE
CREATE TABLE sales (sales_id int)
```

Result: The column sales_id is defined as NOT NULL.

Example B:

```
ANSI Null Default = TRUE
CREATE TABLE sales (sales_id int)
```

Result: The column sales_id is defined as NULL.

> **NOTE**
>
> Explicitly specifying a column as NULL or NOT NULL with the CREATE TABLE command overrides the Columns Null By Default option.

Recursive Triggers

Default setting: FALSE

If this option is TRUE, a trigger can recursively call itself. An example of recursion is the following: table T1 has a trigger that modifies data in table T2; T2 modifies data in T1, which in turns fires the T1 trigger again. Another example of recursion is table T1 has a trigger that modifies data in T1. This causes the trigger in table T1 to fire again.

> **CAUTION**
>
> Look out for endless recursion! As with any programming language, recursion must be carefully controlled. If it is not properly implemented, recursion can lead to endless looping. To prevent those runaway triggers, SQL Server has limited the maximum number of recursive levels to 32.

Select Into/Bulk Copy

Default setting: FALSE

The underlying consideration for how to set the Select Into/Bulk Copy option depends on how you handle the backup of the transaction log. Use the following information to help determine how you should set this option.

Set this option to FALSE if you depend on the transaction log for recovery (see Chapter 10 for more information on database recovery). This setting should usually be FALSE for production databases. When this option is set to FALSE, you cannot perform the following operations: Select Into, fast mode BCP, Writetext, or Updatetext.

Set this option to TRUE if you do not depend on the transaction log for recovery. This setting is typical for development databases and nonmission-critical databases. By setting this option to TRUE, you can perform the following operations:

- **Select Into a destination table:** The Into portion of the SQL statement creates a copy of the source's table structure and populates the newly created table with data returned from the SQL statement.

> **NOTE**
>
> If Select Into/Bulk Copy = FALSE, you get the following error message when you use the SELECT *[column_list]* INTO *[destination_table]* statement:
>
> ```
> Server: Msg 268, Level 16, State 3
> Cannot run SELECT INTO in this database. The database
> owner must run sp_dboption to enable this option.
> ```

- **Fast mode BCP:** BCP may run significantly faster when this option is set to TRUE because the fast mode of BCP bypasses the transaction log. (Fast BCP works only on a table that does not have indexes, triggers, and is not replicated; see Chapter 11, "Using BCP," for more information.)

TIP

For those shops using the transaction log for database recovery, you can temporarily set this option to FALSE, run a nonlogged operation (such as Select[el]Into or fast-mode BCP), reset the option to TRUE, and backup the database. You must backup the database before you resume backing up the log. If you do not backup the database after performing a nonlogged operation, the next time you try to backup the transaction log, you receive an error message.

- **Writetext and Updatetext statements:** You can use these statements to perform nonlogged updating of text, ntext, or image fields.

Truncate Log on Checkpoint

Default setting: FALSE

When the Truncate Log on Checkpoint option is set to TRUE, the transaction log is automatically truncated when the log is 70% full.

Set this option to FALSE if you use the transaction log as part of your backup recovery process.

NOTE

If you try to back up the transaction log when the database option Truncate Log on Checkpoint = TRUE, you will receive an error.

Set the Truncate Log on Checkpoint option to TRUE if you are not concerned about using the transaction log as part of your backup recovery process. This option is useful for development databases or nonmission-critical databases. When you set this option to TRUE, you significantly lessen the chance of the transaction log running out of space.

CAUTION

If you do not back up your transaction log frequently, you should set Truncate Log on Checkpoint = TRUE. Failure to do so will result in a transaction log file that will continue to grow until it consumes all your available disk space or until it reaches the maximum specified log size.

Autoclose

Default setting: FALSE on Windows NT version, TRUE on Windows 9.x version.

When the Autoclose option is set to TRUE, the database is automatically closed when users are not in the database. This option is designed to reduce database resources and enables the physical database files to be copied and mailed.

The drawback of setting Autoclose to TRUE is the overhead associated with opening and closing the database. Therefore, this option is not recommended for databases that are constantly in use.

CAUTION

I do not recommend setting autoclose = TRUE for databases that are constantly in use. Setting autoclose = TRUE will create additional overhead associated with opening and closing the database files.

Torn Page Detection

Default setting: FALSE

When the Torn Page Detection option is set to TRUE, SQL Server automatically detects torn pages. A torn page is a page that contains incomplete data modifications. A torn page can occur when SQL Server has been abnormally terminated (for example during a power failure) while in the process of updating a database page. If a torn page is detected, the database must be restored from a backup.

NOTE

To prevent torn pages, configure your server with the following:

- disk cache with a battery backup
- Uninterrupted Power Supply (UPS).

Other Database Options

Several additional database options are not accessible through the Options tab of the Database Properties dialog box. You can use the following transact SQL command to set database options:

```
sp_dboption [dbname, optname, {TRUE ¦ FALSE}]
```

> **NOTE**
>
> There are other database options not discussed in this chapter (for example: merge publish, offline, published, subscribed, and so on). SQL Server typically controls these database options. Therefore, I do not recommend using `sp_dboption` to change options not discussed in this chapter.

Autoshrink

Default setting: FALSE

When the `autoshrink` option is set to TRUE, the database and log files automatically shrink, thus reducing hard disk space. For log files to automatically shrink, the database option `truncate log on checkpoint` must equal TRUE or the log files must be backed up or truncated.

> **CAUTION**
>
> `Autoshrink = TRUE` may degrade performance. The locking associated with reducing the size of the database can lead to blocking and consume server resources. Therefore, I do not recommend leaving this option on with a high-transaction database. If you need to shrink the database, I recommend temporarily turning this option on and then turning off after the database has been shrunk. An alternative to `autoshrink` is the `DBCC SHRINKDATABASE` command.

Concat Null Yields Null

Default setting: FALSE

When the `concat null yields null` option is set to TRUE, concatenation of a null and a non-null value results in a null. When this option equals FALSE, the null value is treated as an empty (zero length) string. Listing 8.2 is an example of this option.

LISTING 8.2 THE `concat null yields null` OPTION

```
/* ------------------- */
/* query with option ON */
/* ------------------- */
sp_dboption pubs,'concat null yields null',true
go
declare @x varchar(11)
select @x = null
select @x
select 'pubs' + @x

/* ------------------- */
-- result:
/* ------------------- */
NULL

/* ------------------- */
/* query with option OFF*/
/* ------------------- */
sp_dboption pubs,'concat null yields null',false
go
declare @x varchar(11)
select @x = null
select @x
select 'pubs' + @x

/* ------------------- */
-- result:
/* ------------------- */
pubs
```

Cursor Close On Commit

Default setting: FALSE

When the `cursor close on commit` option is set to TRUE, all open cursors are automatically closed when data is committed. This is in compliance with SQL-92 ANSI standards.

Default to Local Cursor

Default setting: FALSE

When the `Default to local cursor` option is set to TRUE, cursors that do not explicitly contain the GLOBAL scope keyword default to LOCAL. When the `Default to local cursor` option is set to FALSE, cursors that do not explicitly contain the LOCAL or GLOBAL scope keyword default to GLOBAL. (See Chapter 26, "Using Stored Procedures and Cursors," for more information on LOCAL and GLOBAL cursors.)

Quoted Identifier

Default setting: FALSE

When the QUOTED IDENTIFIER option is set to TRUE, object names within double quotes do not have to adhere to Transact-SQL naming conventions. For example, the following statement is valid when this option is TRUE (primary and date are SQL Server reserved words):

```
CREATE TABLE "primary" ("date" datetime)
```

Subscribed

Default setting: FALSE

When the subscribed option is set to TRUE, it permits the database to be subscribed for replication (see Chapters 15, 16, and 17 for more information on replication). It does not perform the subscription; it only allows it to be subscribed to.

When this option is set to FALSE, it prevents the database from being subscribed. Set this option to FALSE unless you want this to be a subscribed database.

Expanding the Database and Log Size

You can easily expand the size of database and its log after it has been created. SQL Server offers two approaches to increasing the size of a database. Before proceeding, you should review which approach best suits your needs.

Approach 1: Have SQL Server Automatically Expand the Database and Log

Starting with SQL Server 7.0, a database and its log can be configured to automatically expand on an as-needed basis. This eliminates the need to manually resize the database.

To have the database and log automatically expand in size, select the Automatically Grow File option (see Figures 8.8 and 8.9) from the Database Properties dialog box. File growth settings, such as Grow in Megabytes or Growth by Percentage, can also be set when the Automatically Grow File option is on.

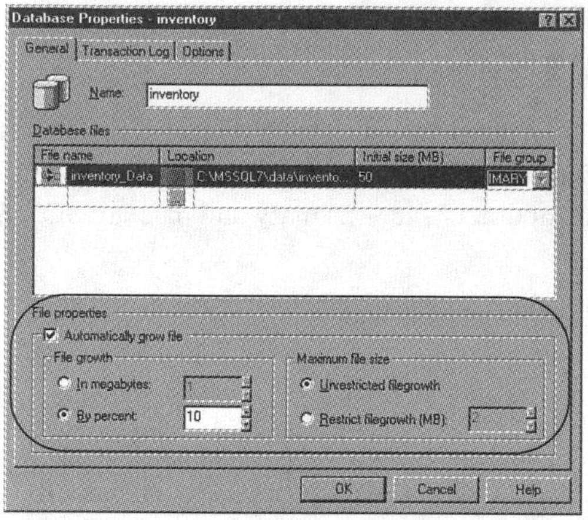

FIGURE 8.8

*Automatically
Grow File
Option—
Database.*

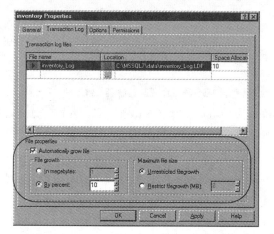

FIGURE 8.9

*Automatically
Grow File
Option—Log.*

Approach 2: Manually Expand the Database and Log

The second way you can expand the database and log is to manually increase the size of the file(s) in use. Perform the following to manually increase the size of the file(s) in use.

1. From the SQL Server Enterprise Manager, click the plus (+) sign next to the server that contains the database you want to view or set options for.

2. Click the plus (+) sign next to the Databases folder. This opens the Databases folder.

3. Right-click the database. From the right mouse menu, select the Properties menu option. The Properties dialog box appears.

4. From the Properties dialog box, select the General or Transaction Log tab. From either tab, specify the file size in the Space Allocated portion of the dialog box (see Figure 8.10).

5. Click OK to save your changes.

FIGURE 8.10

Increasing data-base size.

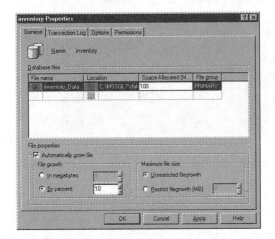

Another way to increase the size of the database or log is to assign a new file. By assigning a new file, you are supplying a new physical file for the database or log. This is useful when a database or log needs to span multiple hard drives. Perform the following to manually assign a new file.

1. From the SQL Server Enterprise Manager, click the plus (+) sign next to the server that contains the database you want to view or set options for.

2. Click the plus (+) sign next to the Databases folder. This opens the Databases folder.

3. Right-click the database in which you want to set the database option. From the right mouse menu, select the Properties menu option. The Properties dialog box appears.

4. From the Properties dialog box, select the General or Transaction Log tab. From either tab, enter one or more additional filenames (see Figure 8.11).

5. Click OK to save your changes.

8

DATABASE MANAGEMENT

FIGURE 8.11

Assigning new files to an existing database or log.

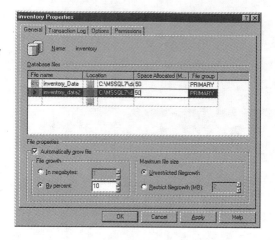

You can also use the Transact-SQL command in Listing 8.3 to expand a database or log:

LISTING 8.3   EXPANDING A DATABASE OR LOG

```
ALTER DATABASE database
{ ADD FILE <filespec> [,...n] [TO FILEGROUP filegroup_name]
¦ ADD LOG FILE <filespec> [,...n]
¦ REMOVE FILE logical_file_name
¦ ADD FILEGROUP filegroup_name
¦ REMOVE FILEGROUP filegroup_name
¦ MODIFY FILE <filespec>
¦ MODIFY FILEGROUP filegroup_name filegroup_property
}
<filespec> ::=
(NAME = 'logical_file_name'
[, FILENAME = 'os_file_name' ]
[, SIZE = size]
[, MAXSIZE = { max_size ¦ UNLIMITED } ]
[, FILEGROWTH = growth_increment] )
```

Shrinking a Database and Log

By shrinking a database and log, you decrease the amount of space allocated to the database and log. SQL Server can automatically shrink the size of a database or you can manually shrink the database.

To have SQL Server automatically shrink a database and log, set the database option `autoshrink` to `TRUE`. (See the topic "Setting Database Options," earlier in this chapter for more information on `autoshrink`.) The following is an example of setting the `autoshrink` database option for the `pubs` database.

```
sp_dboption 'pubs', 'autoshrink', TRUE
```

To manually shrink a database and log, follow these steps:

1. From the SQL Server Enterprise Manager, click the plus (+) sign next to the server that contains the database you want to view or set options for.

2. Click the plus (+) sign next to the Databases folder. This opens the Databases folder.

3. Right-click the database in which you want to shrink. From the right mouse menu, select the All Tasks menu option. From the All Tasks menu option, select Shrink Database menu option. The Shrink Database dialog box appears (see Figure 8.12).

4. From the Shrink Database dialog box, select the Shrink settings and click the OK button.

FIGURE 8.12

The Shrink Database dialog box.

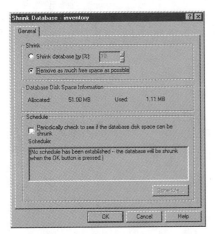

You can also use the following Transact-SQL command to shrink a database:

```
DBCC SHRINKDATABASE ( database_name [, target_percent] [, {NOTRUNCATE |
TRUNCATEONLY}])
```

> **NOTE**
>
> The log file will not immediately shrink in size. Log files shrink when the transaction log is backed up, manually truncated, or when the log is automatically truncated if the `truncate log on checkpoint = TRUE`.
>
> In addition, you cannot shrink a database to a size smaller than the `model` database.

8

DATABASE
MANAGEMENT

Renaming a Database

You can rename any database after it has been created. Only the sa or members of the sysadmin role can rename a database. Follow these steps to rename a database:

1. Set the database you are going to rename to Single-User mode. (Refer to the section "Setting Database Options" earlier in this chapter for more information about single-user mode.)

2. From the Microsoft SQL Server Query Analyzer, access the Query dialog box and enter the following syntax:

   ```
   sp_renamedb oldname, newname
   ```

3. Run the query.

4. Reset the database to multi-user mode.

The following is an example of renaming a database.

```
use master
go
sp_dboption pubs,'single user',true
go
-- change db name
sp_renamedb 'pubs','pubs_db'
go
-- change it back to its original name
sp_renamedb 'pubs_db','pubs'
go
sp_dboption pubs,'single user',false
go
```

> **CAUTION**
>
> When renaming a database, watch out for SQL statements that explicitly refer to the database name; for example, SELECT * FROM *pubs*..authors. If you rename the pubs database to pub_db, you must remember to change the statement to SELECT * FROM pubs_db..authors. Some common areas in which you should look for database references are views, stored procedures, triggers, BCP scripts, and embedded SQL commands in applications.

Deleting a Database

When you delete a database, you physically remove the database and its associated operating system files. This also destroys all objects contained within the database. Only the sa, members of the sysadmin role, and database owner can delete a database. Follow these steps to delete a database:

1. From the SQL Server Enterprise Manager, click the plus (+) sign next to the server that contains the database you want to view or set options for.

2. Click the plus (+) sign next to the Databases folder. This opens the Databases folder.

3. Right-click the database in which you want to delete. From the right mouse menu, select the Delete menu option (see Figure 8.13).

4. At the Delete Database prompt, select Yes to delete the database.

FIGURE 8.13
Deleting a database.

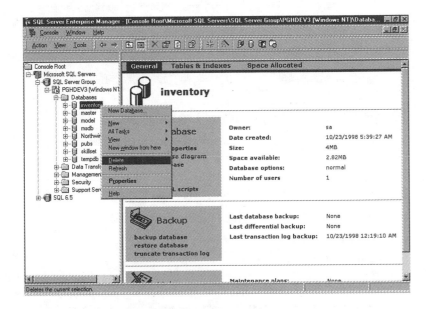

8

DATABASE
MANAGEMENT

You can use the following Transact-SQL command to delete a database:

```
DROP DATABASE database_name [ , database_name...]
```

CAUTION

You cannot delete a database if any of the following are true:

- The database is being restored
- The database is in use
- The database contains objects that are published for replication

> **NOTE**
>
> Deleting a database also removes the database files and log files associated with the database. Therefore, you do not need to manually delete these files from the operating system.

> **TIP**
>
> Always back up the `master` database after you drop a database. Doing so makes it easier to recover your database should the `master` database become damaged.

Moving and Copying a Database

Version 7.0 provides detach and attach methods to move and/or copy a database. Detaching a database removes the database from SQL Server, but does not remove the database files from the operating system. Attaching a database creates a new database that references the data stored in the existing data and log files.

Use the following Transact-SQL command to attach a database:

```
sp_attach_db [@dbname =] 'dbname',
[@filename1 = ] 'filename1'
[[, ...@filename16 = ] 'filename']
```

Use the following Transact-SQL command to detach a database:

```
sp_detach_db [@dbname =] 'dbname'
[, [@skipchecks =] 'skipchecks']
```

The following is an example of how to move the pubs database from `c:\mssql7\data` to `c:\mydatabases`. (In the real world, you probably would never move the pubs database to another directory. However, this example can be applied to situations such as moving a database to another server or to another hard drive).

1. From the Microsoft SQL Server Query Analyzer, access the Query dialog box and enter the following syntax:
   ```
   exec sp_detach_db pubs,true
   ```
2. Run the query.

3. Move the operating system files associated with the database. You can use the Cut and Paste facility found in the Microsoft Windows Explorer product. You will always have at least two files: .MDF and .LDF. Depending on the database configuration, you may have multiple .MDF and .LDF files, and you may also have .NDF files associated with the database. For this example, the pubs database was moved by cutting and pasting pubs.mdf and pubs_log.ldf to a directory named c:\mydatabases. You can also copy the files to a different directory or drive on the same computer or to another computer.

TIP

Use sp_helpdb to list the files associated with a database.

---

4. From the Microsoft SQL Server Query Analyzer, access the Query dialog box and enter the following syntax:

```
EXEC sp_attach_db @dbname = 'pubs',
@filename1 = 'c:\mydatabases\pubs.mdf',
@filename2 = 'c:\mydatabases\pubs_log.ldf'
```

5. Run the query and the pubs database now resides in the c:\mydatabases directory.

To copy the pubs database to another database named pubs2, perform the following steps:

1. Copy the operating system files associated with the database. This is similar to step 3 listed previously, except that the pubs database is copied to another directory instead of being cut and pasted.

2. Rename the operating system files so that they are not duplicates of the pubs operating system files. For this example, pubs.mdf was renamed pubs2.mdf, and pubs_log.ldf was renamed pubs2_log.ldf from within Explorer.

3. From the Microsoft SQL Server Query Analyzer, access the Query dialog box and enter the following syntax:

```
EXEC sp_attach_db @dbname = 'pubs2',
@filename1 = 'c:\mydatabases\pubs2.mdf',
@filename2 = 'c:\mydatabases\pubs2_log.ldf'
```

4. Run the query, and the pubs2 database is created with the files that reside in the c:\mydatabases directory.

8

DATABASE MANAGEMENT

> **NOTE**
>
> You can choose from several different methods to move and copy a database. In addition to using the Detach and Attach facility, you can back up and restore a database, or you can use DTS.

ADDITIONAL DATABASE INFORMATION

The following sections list tips and tricks that can help improve the management of databases. These tips can help simplify database maintenance and improve database recoverability.

Tip 1: Document the Database

Always document the configuration of the database after it has been modified. This is in addition to backing up the `master` database. The easiest way to document the configuration of a database is to use the `sp_helpdb` command. You should save the output from the command to a text file (preferably somewhere other than the server's hard drive).

Tip 2: Take Advantage of the Model Database

Use the model database to simplify object creation. The model database enables you to define a template for the creation of new databases. When you create a new database, SQL Server copies the contents of the model database into the newly created database. This makes a handy mechanism for copying frequently used database options and objects into a new database. Anything you want automatically copied into a new database should be placed in the model.

> **TIP**
>
> Perform the following steps to view the model database and other system databases from the Enterprise Manager:
>
> 1. Right-mouse click the server. From the right mouse menu, select the Edit SQL Server Registration Properties menu option. The Registered SQL Server Properties dialog box appears.
> 2. From the Registered SQL Server Properties dialog box, select the Show system databases and system objects option.
> 3. Click the OK button to save the change.

NOTE

The model database is automatically created when you install SQL Server. It cannot be deleted.

Changes to the model database do not impact existing databases. The model database is used only when creating new databases.

Following are common types of objects and settings that can be stored in the model database:

- Frequently used user-defined datatypes, rules, and defaults.

- Database options. Any database option you set in the model database is copied into a new database. For example, if you always set the SELECT INTO / BULK COPY option to TRUE, go ahead and set it in the model database.

- Any tables, views, or stored procedures that you always add to a new database can be placed in the model database.

- Database size. If you expand the model database (the default size is 1MB), that becomes the minimum size for any new database.

CAUTION

Be careful when you increase the size of the model database. It becomes the minimum size for all new databases. Whenever SQL Server creates a new database, it copies the contents of the model database into the new database. Therefore, the new database cannot be smaller than the model database.

FILEGROUPS

Filegroups allow database files and objects to be logically grouped together. Tables, indexes, text datatypes, ntext datatypes, and image datatypes can be placed on specific filegroups (see Figure 8.14). By spreading database i/o across hard-drives, filegroups provide the potential to improve database performance. Filegroups can also simplify administrative tasks such as backing up a filegroup or adding new files to new disks.

8

DATABASE
MANAGEMENT

FIGURE 8.14

Filegroups.

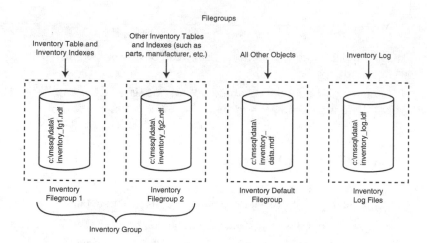

Filegroups are designed to be simpler and more powerful than segments (segments were used in previous versions of SQL Server) and provide functionality similar to Oracle's implementation of table spaces. Additionally, segments are no longer supported in version 7.0.

If you are considering implementing filegroups, you should consider implementing hardware with RAID technology. A high quality RAID system can often deliver performance gains similar to filegroups, and with fewer hassles. To successfully implement filegroups, you need detailed knowledge of table and index usage. If the knowledge used to implement filegroups changes over time, you will need to modify your filegroups. A RAID implementation does not require detailed table and index knowledge.

The following topics discuss how to implement and manage filegroups.

Implementing a Filegroup During Database Creation

To implement a filegroup during database creation, use the FILEGROUP filegroup_name <filespec> [,...n] clause of the CREATE DATABASE command.

Listing 8.4 is an example of creating a database named inventory with a filegroup named inventorygrp that contains two files: inventory_fg1 and inventory_fg2.

LISTING 8.4 CREATING A DATABASE NAMED inventory

```
CREATE DATABASE inventory
ON PRIMARY
( NAME = inventory_data,
  FILENAME = 'c:\mssql7\data\inventory_data.mdf',
  SIZE = 1MB ),
FILEGROUP inventorygrp
( NAME = inventory_fg1,
  FILENAME = 'c:\mssql7\data\inventory_fg1.ndf',
  SIZE = 1MB ),
( NAME = inventory_fg2,
  FILENAME = 'c:\mssql7\data\inventory_fg2.ndf',
  SIZE = 1MB)
LOG ON
( NAME = inventory_log,
  FILENAME = 'c:\mssql7\data\inventory_log.ldf',
  SIZE = 1MB)
```

Implementing a Filegroup for an Existing Database

To implement a filegroup for an existing database, use the ALTER DATABASE command with the ADD FILEGROUP keywords to create a filegroup:

```
ALTER DATABASE database
ADD FILEGROUP filegroup_name
```

In this statement, *database* is the name of the database you are going to use; *filegroup_name* is the name of the filegroup you are going to create. (The database must already exist. For more information, see the section "Creating a Database" earlier in this chapter.)

To create a filegroup named inventorygrp using the inventory database, use the following command:

```
ALTER DATABASE inventory
ADD FILEGROUP inventorygrp
```

Adding Secondary Data Files to the Filegroup

In Listing 8.5, the ALTER DATABASE command is used with the ADD FILE and TO FILEGROUP keywords to create the secondary data files that will be used by the filegroup.

8

DATABASE
MANAGEMENT

LISTING 8.5 CREATING SECONDARY DATA FILES

```
ALTER DATABASE database
ADD FILE <filespec>
TO FILEGROUP filegroup_name
<filespec> ::=
  (NAME = 'logical_file_name',
   FILENAME = 'os_file_name'
   [, SIZE = size]
   [, MAXSIZE = { max_size ¦ UNLIMITED } ]
   [, FILEGROWTH = growth_increment] )
```

In this statement, *database* is the name of the database you are going to use; *filespec* contains the information used to create the secondary data files; *filegroup_name* is the name of the filegroup to use. (The filegroup must already exist.)

Use the command in Listing 8.6 to add two secondary files to the inventorygrp file-group in the inventory database.

LISTING 8.6 CREATING SECONDARY DATA FILES

```
ALTER DATABASE inventory
ADD FILE
(NAME = inventory_fg1,
FILENAME = 'c:\mssql7\data\inventory_fg1.ndf',
SIZE = 1MB),
(NAME = inventory_fg2,
FILENAME = 'c:\mssql7\data\inventory_fg2.ndf',
SIZE = 1MB)
TO FILEGROUP inventorygrp
```

Place an Object on the Filegroup

The following types of objects can be placed on a filegroup.

- Table
- Index
- Text datatypes
- Ntext datatypes
- Image datatypes

Use the CREATE TABLE command with the ON filegroup_name option to create a table on a filegroup:

```
CREATE TABLE [database.[owner].]table_name
( <column_definition>
```

```
)
[ON filegroup_name¦ DEFAULT} ]
[TEXTIMAGE_ON {filegroup ¦ DEFAULT} ]
```

To create the inventory table on the inventorygrp filegroup, use the following
command:

```
CREATE TABLE inventory
(inventory_id integer primary key,
inventory_amount money,
inventory_qty integer,
inventory_location varchar(35))
ON inventorygrp
```

Creating an Index on a Filegroup

Use the CREATE INDEX command with the ON *filegroup_name* option to create an index
on a filegroup:

```
CREATE [UNIQUE] [CLUSTERED ¦ NONCLUSTERED]
INDEX index_name ON table (column [, ...n])
...
[ON filegroup_name]
```

For example, to create an index on the inventorygrp filegroup for the inventory table,
use the following command:

```
CREATE INDEX inventory_location_idx
ON inventory(inventory_location)
ON inventorygrp
```

Viewing Information about a Filegroup

To view information about a filegroup, follow these steps:

1. From the SQL Server Enterprise Manager, click the plus (+) sign next to the server
   that contains the database you want to view or set options for.

2. Click the plus (+) sign next to the Databases folder to open the Databases folder.

3. Right-click the database in which you want to view filegroup information. From
   the right mouse menu, select the Properties menu option. The database Properties
   dialog appears.

4. From the database properties dialog box, select the General Tab. The filegroup
   information is displayed (see Figure 8.15).

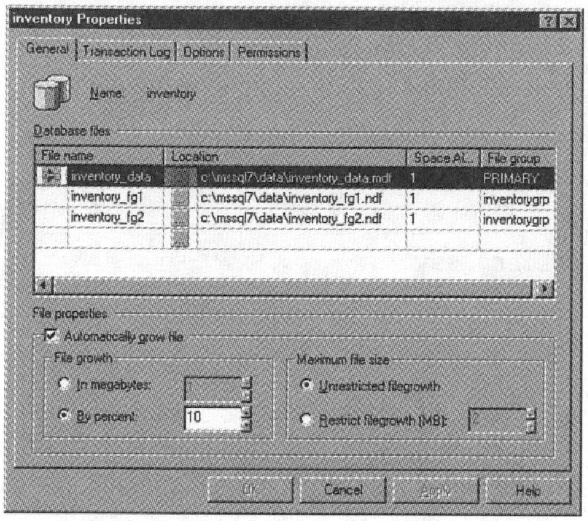

FIGURE 8.15

*Filegroup
information.*

The Transact-SQL command can also be used to view filegroup information:

```
sp_helpfilegroup [@filegroupname =] 'name'
```

Where the optional parameter `@filegroupname` specifies the filegroup name.

The following are examples.

Example 1:

```
use inventory
go
sp_helpfilegroup
```

Sample output:

```
groupname            groupid filecount
-------------------- ------- ---------
inventorygrp         2       2
PRIMARY              1       1
```

Example 2:

```
use inventory
go
sp_helpfilegroup inventorygrp
```

Sample output:

```
groupname                groupid filecount
------------------------ ------- -----------
inventorygrp             2       2
```

```
file_in_group fileid filename                      size   maxsize   growth
------------- ------ ------------------------- ------ ---------- -------
inventory_fg1 3   c:\mssql7\data\inventory_fg1.ndf 1024 KB Unlimited 10%
inventory_fg2 4   c:\mssql7\data\inventory_fg2.ndf 1024 KB Unlimited 10%
```

DATABASE FAQ

The following section lists some of the common questions asked by DBAs about SQL Server database management:

Q. Can the transaction log be disabled?

A. No, you cannot disable the transaction log. This question is commonly asked when the log is not part of someone's backup strategy. Consequently, many people would rather not periodically backup the transaction log. Unfortunately, you can't avoid having transactions written to the log. But you *can* have the transaction log truncated automatically in SQL Server; set the database option `Truncate Log On Checkpoint = TRUE` (see the section "Setting Database Options" in this chapter for more information about `Truncate Log On Checkpoint`).

Q. Can I read the transaction log or use the transaction log for auditing purposes?

A. No, you cannot read the transaction log or use it to generate audit trails. Only SQL Server can read the transaction log.

Q. What does the following error message mean?

```
Server: Msg 9002, Level 17, State 2
The log file for database 'database_name' is full.
Back up the transaction log for the database
to free up some log space.
```

A. Whenever you fill up the transaction log or run out of disk space for the transaction log, you receive the error message listed. To resolve the error you must backup the transaction log with the `no_log` option or increase free space on the hard-drive that contains the transaction log.
(*Note*: Increasing hard drive space only works if the transaction log auto-grow option is on.)

To help avoid this error, do one of the following:

- **Increase the free-space on the hard drive until the problem goes away:**
  Although this is the simplest solution, it may not be the most effective solution. If you do not properly manage your transactions, you can fill up the transaction log regardless of how space has been allocated to it.

- **Increase the frequency of the log backup:** Doing so may reduce the frequency of the error or prevent it from occurring.

- **Set the database option Truncate Log On Checkpoint to TRUE:** This option automatically truncates the inactive portion of the log when the log is 70 percent full. Only use this option if you are not backing up the transaction log; this option *is not* recommended for production databases!

- **Use a nonlogged command to perform the equivalent SQL command:** Nonlogged operations are not written to the transaction log; therefore, they will not fill-up the transaction log. You can substitute the following nonlogged commands for SQL commands:

SQL Command	Nonlogged Command Equivalent	Notes
`DELETE FROM [tablename]`	`TRUNCATE TABLE [tablename]`	Use `TRUNCATE TABLE [tablename]` to remove all rows from the table. Also, because the `TRUNCATE` command is a nonlogged operation, it runs much faster than the `DELETE` command.
`INSERT INTO [tablename]` `SELECT * FROM [tablename]`	`BCP`	Rather than using an `INSERT` statement, try using `BCP`. Use `BCP` to export the data out of a table and into another table.

Q. What does the following error message mean?

```
Server: Msg 1105, Level 17, State 2
Could not allocate space for object 'object_name'
in database 'database_name' because the 'PRIMARY'
filegroup is full.
```

A. This error message is notifying you that the data portion of the database has run out of storage space. Perform the following to resolve this error message.

- If the database auto-grow option is on, increase hard-drive free-space. If the option is off, you must manually expand the database files (see the topic "Expanding the Database and Log Size" in this chapter for more information).

- Remove unused tables.

- Remove unnecessary indexes.

SUMMARY

Basic database-management techniques combined with supplemental tips provide you with the skills to intelligently manage a database. Remember that intelligent database management is the key to keeping your database up and running. Following are some important notes to remember when managing databases:

- Use the SQL Server Enterprise Manager or Transact-SQL commands to manage databases. For ease-of-use, the Enterprise Manager is generally preferred over Transact-SQL commands.

- Every database in SQL Server has a transaction log.

- SQL Server uses the transaction log to ensure transaction completeness and to incrementally restore data changes.

- Virtually all changes to the database are first written to the transaction log and then to the database.

- Every database in SQL Server must use at least one data file and one log file.

- The `sa` and members of the `sysadmin` or `dbcreate` roles are the users that can create a database unless the statement permission is granted to another user.

- Watch out for the `Select Into/Bulk Copy` and `Truncate Log On Checkpoint` database options. When these options are set to `TRUE`, they may impact your back-up strategy.

- Use the `sp_helpdb` command to document important database information.

- Databases and logs can automatically grow and contract in size on an as-needed basis.

- Use filegroups to logically group database objects (tables, indexes, text, ntext, and image datatypes) or partition database i/o across different hard drives.

8

DATABASE MANAGEMENT

MANAGING SQL SERVER USERS AND SECURITY

by Orryn Sledge

CHAPTER

9

IN THIS CHAPTER

INTRODUCTION

This chapter discusses how to create and manage user accounts. It also discusses how to implement and manage security. I think that you will find SQL Server's account management model and security model easy to use and understand. SQL Server provides built-in security and data protection. Its security features are trustworthy and relatively easy to administer. By taking advantage of SQL Server's security features, you can create a secure database that prevents unauthorized access and allows data modification to occur in a controlled and orderly manner.

This chapter also includes a few tips and tricks that make a DBA's life easier. Veteran SQL Server DBAs will definitely want to read the "What's New" and "What's Gone" sections as well as the FAQ section near the end of the chapter.

SQL SERVER 6.5 TO 7.0 QUICK REFERENCE

The following is a quick reference to the changes that occurred between SQL Server versions 6.5 and 7.0:

What's New

- Version 7.0 adds roles to manage security. There are several types of roles: server fixed role, database fixed role, database user-defined role, and database application role. Roles are a replacement for groups, which were found in previous versions. Roles overcome the limitations of groups. In particular, roles overcome the limitation that a user could belong to only one group per database. With roles, a user can belong to multiple roles. Additionally, version 7.0 provides several predefined roles that simplify security management.

- Version 7.0 has better NT integration with NT accounts and NT groups. Integrating NT logins and NT groups in previous versions was cumbersome. Version 7.0 has simplified and streamlined the integration process.

- Version 7.0 adds the DENY Transact-SQL command. This command is different from REVOKE in that DENY allows an administrator to deny a permission, whereas REVOKE actually removes the permission.

- Several new system procedures have been added to manage NT logins and groups. The following are the new procedures:

```
sp_grantlogin [@loginame =] 'login'
sp_revokelogin {[@loginame =] 'login'}
sp_denylogin [@loginame =] 'login'
```

- Several new system procedures have been added to manage fixed server roles. The following are the new procedures:

```
sp_addsrvrolemember [@loginame =] 'login' [,[@rolename =] 'role']
sp_dropsrvrolemember [@loginame =] 'login' [,[@rolename =] 'role']
sp_helpsrvrolemember [[@srvrolename =] 'role']
sp_srvrolepermission [[@srvrolename =] 'role']
```

- Several new system procedures have been added to manage database roles and database access. The following are the new procedures:

```
sp_addrole [@rolename =] 'role' [,[@ownername =] 'owner']
sp_droprole [@rolename =] 'role']
sp_helprole [@rolename =] 'role']
sp_helprolemember [@rolename =] 'role']
sp_addrolemember [@rolename =] 'role', [@membername =]
'security_account'
sp_helpdbfixedrole [@rolename =] 'role']
sp_dbfixedrolepermission [@rolename =] 'role']
sp_grantdbaccess [@loginame =] 'login' [,[@name_in_db =] 'name_in_db'
[OUTPUT]]
sp_revokedbaccess {[@name_in_db =] 'name'}
```

- Several new system procedures have been added to manage application roles. The following are the new procedures:

```
sp_addapprole [@rolename =] 'role', [@password =] 'password'
sp_setapprole [@rolename =] 'name' , [@password =] {Encrypt N
'password'} ¦ 'password' [,[@encrypt =] 'encrypt_style']
sp_dropapprole [@rolename =] 'role'
```

- Object ownership can now be changed. Previously, the only way to change an object owner was by dropping and re-creating the object with a different owner. The following is the procedure to change an object's owner:

```
sp_changeobjectowner [@objname =] 'object' ,[@newowner =] 'owner'
```

- Several new system functions have been added to manage roles and membership. The following are the new functions:

```
IS_SRVROLEMEMBER ( 'role' [,'login'])
IS_MEMBER ({'group' ¦ 'role' })
```

- A Security Wizard has been added that helps with the creation of logins and permissions.

- The `dump database` and `dump transaction` statement permissions have been changed to `backup database` and `backup log`. However, you can still use the `dump database` and `dump transaction` syntax for backward compatibility.

9

MANAGING SQL
SERVER USERS
AND SECURITY

What's Gone

- Groups have been replaced with roles.
- Aliases have been replaced with roles.
- Standard security is now called SQL Server Authentication.
- Integrated security is now called NT Authentication.
- Mixed security is now the combination of SQL Server Authentication and NT Authentication.
- The limitation that a user could belong to only one group per database is gone. Groups have been replaced by roles, and a user can belong to multiple roles per database.
- SQL Security Manager has been eliminated. The corresponding functionality has been directly incorporated into the SQL Server Enterprise Manager.

What's Around for Backward Compatibility

The system procedures listed in Table 9.1 are retained for backward compatibility. In previous versions, these system procedures dealt with groups. The corresponding system procedures in Table 9.1 should be used instead of the 6.x system procedures. Groups no longer exist; they have been replaced with roles.

TABLE 9.1   SYSTEM PROCEDURES RETAINED FOR BACKWARD COMPATIBILITY

System Procedure in 6.5 in 7.0	*Corresponding System Procedure*
sp_addgroup	sp_addrole
sp_dropgroup	sp_droprole
sp_helpgroup	sp_helprole
sp_changegroup	sp_addrolemember

AN OVERVIEW OF SQL SERVER'S SECURITY MODEL

SQL Server's security model comprises the following components:

- SQL Server login
- Database user
- guest user

- Permissions
- Roles

SQL Server Login

The SQL Server login model supports two security modes:

- NT Authentication
- Mixed Security

> **CAUTION**
>
> By default, the sa account is not password protected! After installing SQL Server, I recommend immediately changing the sa password.

NT Authentication

NT Authentication takes advantage of Windows NT user security and account mechanisms. This security mode allows SQL Server to share the user name and password used for Windows NT and allows the user to bypass the SQL Server login process. Users with a valid Windows NT account can log in to SQL Server without supplying a user name and password.

Some benefits of NT Authentication follow.

- A user does not have to remember a separate password and user name.
- When the password changes in Windows NT, the user does not have to change the password in SQL Server.

How does NT Authentication work? When a user accesses SQL Server, SQL Server obtains the user and password information from the user's NT network security attributes. These attributes are established when the user logs in to Windows NT. If the user has been granted access to SQL Server, the user is automatically logged in to SQL Server. Using NT Authentication allows you to take advantage of Windows NT features such as password aging and login auditing.

NT Authentication requires more NT hands-on experience or working closely with the NT system administrator when setting up user accounts and groups. Setting up NT Authentication requires a few more steps than setting up SQL Server Authentication, but the benefits outweigh the additional configuration steps.

> **TIP**
>
> With NT Authentication, I recommend placing users into NT groups and adding the NT group login to SQL Server. This powerful feature allows you to group your users together at the NT Domain level and apply permissions at the SQL Server level. For example, a group named `sales` could exist in the NT Domain. A new login based on the NT `sales` group could be added to SQL Server. When a new NT account is created, the NT administrator can add the new account to the NT group named `sales`. The SQL Server DBA can apply the appropriate role(s) and permissions to the `sales` group. The new NT login automatically contains the necessary permissions to log in to SQL Server because the NT `sales` group was previously granted a login. This strategy makes it easy for new users to be added the system.

Mixed Security

In *mixed mode* security, both NT Authentication and SQL Server Authentication are enabled. When using SQL Server Authentication, an individual logging in to SQL Server must supply a user name and a password that SQL Server validates against a system table. When using NT Authentication (see the earlier section "NT Authentication" for more information), users can log in to SQL Server without being prompted for a log-id and password.

> **NOTE**
>
> Did you ever wonder where logins are stored in SQL Server? They are stored in the `master..syslogins` table.

Database User

The *database user* concept defines the database(s) an individual can access. After an individual has successfully logged in to SQL Server, either through NT Authentication or SQL Server Authentication, SQL Server determines whether the user is a valid user for the database he or she is accessing. Regardless of the security mode, a user must be permitted to access the database. If the user is not permitted in the database, SQL Server returns an error message.

The only exception to the database user concept is the `guest` user. See the next topic for more information on the `guest` user.

guest User

A special user name, guest, can be added to a database to allow anyone with a valid SQL Server login to access the database. The guest user name is a member of the public role. After the guest user has been added to a database, any individual with a valid SQL Server login—regardless of security mode—can access the database as the guest user. A guest user works as follows:

1. SQL Server checks to see whether the login ID has a valid user name or alias assigned. If so, SQL Server grants the user access to the database as the user name or aliases. If not, go to step 2.

2. SQL Server checks to see whether a guest user name exists. If so, the login ID is granted access to the database as guest. If the guest account does not exist, SQL Server denies access to the database.

> **NOTE**
>
> The guest user always has a uid of 2.
>
> A guest user is added to the master database and the pubs database when the system is installed. SQL Server prevents you from dropping the guest user from the master database so that you cannot accidentally do so. If you removed guest from the master database, only the sa user could log in to SQL Server! When users log in to SQL Server, they have access to the master database as the guest user. (Don't worry, the guest user has very few permissions in the master database.)
>
> To prevent guest access in any database other than master, drop the guest account from the corresponding database.

Permissions

A *permission* allows someone to do something within a database. There are two types of permissions: *object* and *statement*. Object permissions control who can access and manipulate data in tables and views and who can run stored procedures. Statement permissions control who can drop and create objects within a database.

SQL Server uses the commands GRANT, REVOKE, and DENY to manage permissions.

- GRANT—When you GRANT a permission to an object, you allow someone to perform an action against the object (for example, SELECT, UPDATE, INSERT, DELETE, EXECUTE). When you GRANT permission to a statement, you allow someone to run the statement (for example, CREATE TABLE).

- REVOKE—When you REVOKE a permission from an object, you prevent someone from performing an action against the object (for example, SELECT, UPDATE, INSERT, DELETE, EXECUTE). When you REVOKE permission from a statement, you take away a user's capability to run the statement (for example, CREATE TABLE).
- DENY—When you DENY a permission from an object, you explicitly prevent someone from using the permission (for example, SELECT, UPDATE, INSERT, DELETE, EXECUTE), whereas REVOKE actually removes the permission.

Object Permissions

Object permissions control access to objects within SQL Server. You can grant and revoke permissions to tables, table columns, views, and stored procedures through the Enterprise Manager or through system procedures. A user who wants to perform an action against an object must have the appropriate permission. For example, when a user wants to SELECT * FROM table1, he or she must have SELECT permission for the table. Table 9.2 summarizes the types of object permissions.

TABLE 9.2 SUMMARY OF OBJECT PERMISSIONS

Object Type	Possible Actions
table	SELECT, UPDATE, DELETE, INSERT, REFERENCE
column	SELECT, UPDATE
view	SELECT, UPDATE, INSERT, DELETE
stored procedure	EXECUTE

Statement Permissions

Statement permissions control who can perform administrative actions such as creating or backing up a database. Only the sa, members of the sysadmin role, or database owner can administer statement permissions. I advise prudence in granting access to statement permissions such as CREATE DATABASE, BACKUP DATABASE, and BACKUP LOG. Usually, the best approach is to let the sa or a member of the sysadmin role or the database owner manage these statements. Following is a list of statement permissions that can be granted or revoked:

- CREATE DATABASE—Creates a database. This permission can be granted only by the sa and only to users in the master database.
- CREATE DEFAULT—Creates a default value for a table column.
- CREATE PROCEDURE—Creates a stored procedure.
- CREATE RULE—Creates a table column rule.

- `CREATE TABLE`—Creates a table.
- `CREATE VIEW`—Creates a view.
- `BACKUP DATABASE`—Backs up the database.
- `BACKUP TRANSACTION`—Backs up the transaction log.

Roles

Roles are new with SQL Server 7.0. They provide a way to logical group users with permissions. The following are the types of roles found in version 7.0:

- Server roles
- Database roles

Server Roles

Server roles provide levels of access to server operations and tasks. If an individual is placed in a certain role, he or she can perform the function permitted by the role. For example, an individual who is member of the `sysadmin` role can perform any type of action in SQL Server.

Server roles are predefined and are serverwide. These roles are not database specific and cannot be customized.

Table 9.3 provides a listing and explanation for each type of server role.

TABLE 9.3 SERVER ROLES

Server Role	Description
sysadmin	Able to do anything in SQL Server
serveradmin	Able to modify SQL Server settings and shut down SQL Server
setupadmin	Able to install replication and control extended stored procedures
securityadmin	Able to control server logins and create database permissions
processadmin	Able to control SQL Server processes
dbcreator	Able to create and modify databases
diskadmin	Able to manage disk files

9

MANAGING SQL SERVER USERS AND SECURITY

Database Roles

Database roles provide the assignment of a set of database-specific permissions to an individual or a group of users. Database roles can be assigned to NT Authenticated logins or SQL Server Authenticated logins. Roles that are assigned to NT Authenticated logins can be assigned to NT users and NT groups. Roles can also be nested so that a hierarchical group of permissions can be assigned to logins.

Database roles are database specific. SQL Server provides three types of roles.

* Predefined database roles
* User-defined database roles
* Implicit roles

Predefined Database Roles

Predefined database roles are standard SQL Server database roles. Each database in SQL Server has these roles. Predefined database roles make it easy to delegate responsibility. For example, a developer may be assigned the db_ddladmin role in a development database. This role would allow a developer to create and drop objects (tables, stored procedures, views, and so on) on an as-needed basis.

Predefined database roles are database specific and cannot be customized. Table 9.4 provides a description of each predefined database role.

TABLE 9.4   PREDEFINED DATABASE ROLES

Database Role	Description
db_owner	Has complete access to all objects within the database, can drop and re-create objects, and has the capability to assign object permissions to other users. It can modify database settings and perform database maintenance tasks. This role encompasses all functionality listed in the other predefined database roles.
db_accessadmin	Controls access to the database by adding or removing NT Authentication users and SQL Server users.
db_datareader	Has complete access to SELECT data from any table in the database. This role does not grant INSERT, DELETE, or UPDATE permissions on any table in the database.
db_datawriter	Can perform INSERT, DELETE, UDPATE statements on any table in the database. This role does not grant SELECT permission on any table in the database.

`db_ddladmin`	Has the ability to create, modify, and drop objects in the database.
`db_securityadmin`	Performs security management within the database. This role manages statement and object permissions and roles within the database.
`db_backupoperator`	Has the capability to back up the database.
`db_denydatareader`	Denies SELECT permission on all tables in the database. However, this role does allow users to modify existing table schemas. It does not allow them to create or drop existing tables.
`db_denydatawriter`	Denies data modification statements (INSERT, DELETE, UPDATE) from being performed against any tables in the databases.
`public`	Every database user is a member of the public role. A user automatically becomes part of the public role when he or she is permitted access to the database.

NOTE

When everyone in a database needs the same permission to the same object, use the `public` role. When you grant or revoke a permission to the `public` role, everyone feels the effect. Using the `public` role is often an easy way to stream-line security administration.

User-Defined Roles

User-defined roles allow the grouping of users to a particular security function. User-defined roles are database specific, whereas server roles are server specific.

Listed below are several features of user-defined roles.

- Role security is user-defined so that flexible security models can be implemented.
- Users can participate in multiple user-defined roles in the same database, whereas in previous versions users could only belong to one group other than the public group.
- NT Authenticated logins and SQL Server Authenticated logins can participate in user-defined roles.
- Roles can be nested, thus creating a hierarchy of security relationships.

9

MANAGING SQL SERVER USERS AND SECURITY

> **NOTE**
>
> Role members must be already known to the database. Therefore, NT Authenticated logins or SQL Server Authenticated logins must be permitted in the database prior to assigning the login to a database specific role.

The following are types of user-defined database roles:

- Standard role
- Application role

Standard Role

The standard role provides a database-specific method for creating user-defined roles that are used to enforce and manage security. The standard role is conceptually similar to database groups, which were found in previous versions of SQL Server, but provides additional functionality.

A common use of a standard role is to logically group users according to their security level. For example, most applications have several types of security levels. The following security levels apply to this example:

- Power user—Can doing anything within the database. This group of users is typically granted SELECT/INSERT/DELETE/UPDATE to all the tables in the database.
- Normal user—Can modify certain types of data. This group of users is typically granted SELECT/INSERT/DELETE/UPDATE permissions to various tables and only SELECT permission to several other tables.
- Bonehead user—Is not allowed to modifying anything. These users are boneheads, and the DBA is worried that they are going to mess things up! This group of users is typically granted only SELECT access to the data.

Applying the preceding scenario to SQL Server's implementation of roles could result in the mapping of users to roles shown in Table 9.5.

TABLE 9.5   SAMPLE ROLE MAPPING

Sample User Type	*Sample Role*
Power user	db_datareader and db_datawriter; these predefined database roles allow users to query and modify all tables in the database.

Sample User Type	Sample Role
Standard user	`standard_user` role; this user-defined database role is created by the DBA. It typically contains a mix of `SELECT/INSERT/DELETE/UPDATE` permissions.
Bonehead user	`db_datareader role`; this predefined database role allows users to perform only SELECT queries in the database.

Application Role

The application role is a special type of role that allows a user to take on the characteristics of a role. When a user takes on an application role, he or she takes on a new role and temporarily forgoes all other assigned database-specific permissions. You are probably asking, Why would I want a user to take on a new role? The answer is that when an application role is active, the user can perform database querying and processing in a very controlled manner. When the role is not active, the user is limited to his or her standard database permissions.

The following points define the difference between application roles and standard roles.

- Application roles can be password protected, whereas user-defined standard roles are not. If the application role is password protected, a password must be supplied to activate the role.

- Both application roles and standard roles are user defined and database specific.

- Users are not directly assigned to application roles. Instead, users activate the role within a specific database.

A good use of the application role is whenever you have an environment in which users query and modify data through a controlled interface and ad hoc querying. A typically example would be a HR module that allows users to manage employee information. Users of the HR module probably need `SELECT/INSERT/DELETE/UPDATE` permissions to view and change employee information. But what happens when a user begins to use Microsoft Access to perform ad hoc querying and reporting? A great feature of Microsoft Access is the capability to directly modify data from within its grids. This great feature can be a big headache for DBAs because a user can make a data modification directly from Microsoft Access. This change could potentially bypass any logic and controls that are built into the application to manage the employee data.

Here's where application roles fit in. Instead of granting `SELECT/INSERT/DELETE/UPDATE` permissions directly to the users of the application, grant the `SELECT/INSERT/DELETE/UPDATE` permissions to an application role. Next, add logic to the application to activate the application role through the `sp_setapprole` system procedure. When the role is active, the users will be able to perform data modification and query operations on the employee table. When the role is not active, the users will not be able

9

MANAGING SQL
SERVER USERS
AND SECURITY

to query or modify data through Microsoft Access because the application role is not active. If the users do not know of the application role and do not know the application role's password, they will not be able to activate the role when performing ad hoc reporting.

TIP

I recommend taking advantage of application roles. Please stop writing custom security routines such as shadow logins! Application roles solve the problem of users needing permissions to modify data through an application and DBAs wanting to prevent data modifications through external tools such as Microsoft Access and Microsoft Query.

NOTE

The following are notes about application roles. The database that contains the role must be in use prior to activating the role. To activate a database from a query window, specify USE *databasename*.

To deactivate an application role, the connection to SQL Server must be broken. There is not a facility to reset an active application role.

You cannot activate an application role within a user-defined transaction or from a stored procedure.

The following is the Transact-SQL command to activate an application role:

```
sp_setapprole [@rolename =] 'name' , [@password =] {Encrypt N 'password'}
¦ 'password'
[,[@encrypt =] 'encrypt_style']
```

MANAGING LOGINS

Perform the following steps to manage SQL Server logins.

1. From the SQL Server Enterprise Manager, click the plus (+) sign next to the server that will contain the login.

2. Click the plus (+) sign next to the Security folder.

3. Right-click the Logins icon. From the right mouse menu, select the New Login menu option. The SQL Server Login Properties - New Login dialog box appears.

4. Enter the login name (see Figure 9.1).

> **NOTE**
>
> If you plan to use NT Authentication, the NT user or NT group must exist prior to adding the NT user or NT group to SQL Server. Use NT's User Manager to create NT users and NT groups.
>
> If you plan to use SQL Server Authentication, SQL Server's authentication mode must be configured to SQL Server and Windows NT (the default setting). If you plan to use only NT Authentication and you want to prevent users from using SQL Server Authentication, SQL Server's authentication mode must be configured to Windows NT Only.
>
> To change the authentication mode setting, use the SQL Server Enterprise Manager. Right-click the server and select Properties from the right mouse menu to open the SQL Server Properties dialog box. From the dialog box, select the Security tab; then select the appropriate authentication mode.

> **NOTE**
>
> If you are using NT Authentication, the login name must be the same name as the login name in the Windows NT Domain. Otherwise, an error occurs when the login is created.

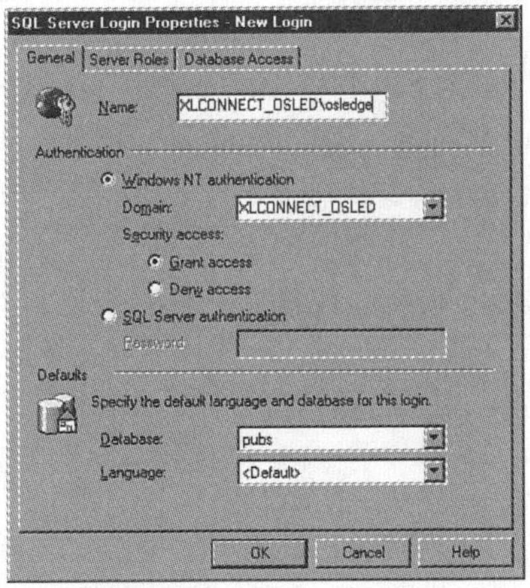

FIGURE 9.1

SQL Server Login Properties—New Login dialog box.

9

MANAGING SQL
SERVER USERS
AND SECURITY

5. Select the authentication mode. If you are using NT Authentication, select the Windows NT authentication radio button and the Domain name. If you are using SQL Server Authentication, select the SQL Server authentication radio button and enter a password for the login.

NOTE

A password is optional with SQL Server Authentication. If the optional password issue concerns you, use Windows NT Authentication, which is integrated with Windows NT Security. Through Windows NT Security, you can specify a minimum password length and force password aging.

6. Specify the default database and default language for the login.

NOTE

I recommend specifying a default database that is not the `master` database. This approach can help prevent users from accidentally creating tables or other objects in the `master` database. Additionally, it automatically places the user in the proper database when he or she uses the SQL Server Query Analyzer or another similar tool to log in to SQL Server.

7. Click the OK button to create the login.

The following are the corresponding Transact-SQL commands to manage logins:

```
sp_grantlogin [@loginame =] 'login'
sp_revokelogin [@loginame =] 'login'
sp_denylogin [@loginame =] 'login'
sp_addlogin [@loginame =] 'login' [,[@passwd =] 'password'] [,[@defdb =]
'database'] [,[@deflanguage =] 'language'] [,[@sid =] 'sid']
[,[@encryptopt =] 'encryption_option']
sp_helplogins [[@LoginNamePattern =] 'login']
```

> **NOTE**
>
> SQL Server 7.0 provides a Security Wizard that walks the user through login creation and permissions assignment. However, the wizard does not provide the following:
>
> - Modifications to existing logins and permissions
> - The ability to set the default database for a login
>
> I find the wizard to be useful for the initial creation of the account. After I create the account, I go back and set the default database setting.

MANAGING SERVER ROLES

Perform the following steps to grant a server role.

1. From the SQL Server Enterprise Manager, click the plus (+) sign next to the server that contains the login.

2. Click the plus (+) sign next to the Security folder.

3. Left-click the Logins icon. A list of logins appears in the results pane.

4. Right-click the name in the results pane. From the right mouse menu, select the Properties menu option. The SQL Server Login Properties dialog box appears.

5. From the SQL Server Login Properties dialog box, click the Server Roles tab (see Figure 9.2).

6. Left-click the corresponding server role (see Table 9.3 for a detailed explanation of each server role).

> **NOTE**
>
> Clicking the Properties button displays the Server Role Properties dialog box, which contains a list of users currently assigned to the selected Server Role (see Figure 9.3). Clicking the Permissions tab displays the commands associated with the corresponding Server Role (see Figure 9.4).

7. Click the OK button to grant the server role.

FIGURE 9.2

SQL Server Login Properties dialog box, Server Roles tab.

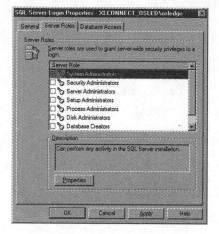

FIGURE 9.3

Server Role Properties dialog box, General tab.

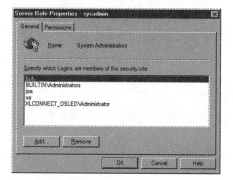

FIGURE 9.4

Server Role Properties dialog box, Permissions tab.

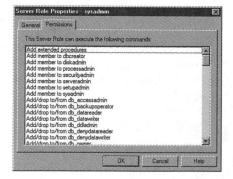

The following are the corresponding Transact-SQL commands to manage server roles.

```
sp_addsrvrolemember [@loginame =] 'login' [,[@rolename =] 'role']
sp_dropsrvrolemember [@loginame =] 'login' [,[@rolename =] 'role']
sp_helpsrvrolemember [[@srvrolename =] 'role']
sp_srvrolepermission [[@srvrolename =] 'role']
```

MANAGING DATABASE ACCESS AND DATABASE ROLES

Perform the following steps to grant database access and database roles.

1. From the SQL Server Enterprise Manager, click the plus (+) sign next to the server that contains the login.
2. Click the plus (+) sign next to the Security folder.
3. Left-click the Logins icon. A list of logins appears in the results pane.
4. Right-click the name in the results pane. From the right mouse menu, select the Properties menu option. The SQL Server Login Properties dialog box appears.
5. From the SQL Server Login Properties dialog box, click the Database Access tab (see Figure 9.5).
6. Left-click the Permit checkbox. This permits the login to access the database.

> **NOTE**
>
> If a login is not permitted access to a database, the login will not be able to perform any type of operation in the database. Logins are an effective security tool to keep users out of selected databases. The only exception to this rule is the guest user (see the section titled "guest User" for more information).

7. Left-click the Permit in Database Role check box to add the login to a database role (see Table 9.4 for a detailed explanation of each database role).

> **NOTE**
>
> Clicking the Properties button displays the Database Role Properties dialog box, which contains a list of users currently assigned to the selected Database Role (see Figure 9.6). If you are viewing a user-defined role or the public role, the Permissions button is enabled. Clicking the Permissions button displays the permissions associated with the corresponding database role (see Figure 9.7).

8. Click the OK button to grant the database role.

FIGURE 9.5

SQL Server Login Properties dialog box, Database Access tab.

FIGURE 9.6

Database Role Properties dialog box.

FIGURE 9.7

Database Role Properties, Permissions tab.

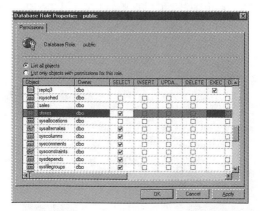

The following are the corresponding Transact-SQL commands to manage database access and database roles.

```
sp_grantdbaccess [@loginame =] 'login' [,[@name_in_db =] 'name_in_db'
[OUTPUT]]
sp_revokedbaccess {[@name_in_db =] 'name'}
sp_helpuser [[@name_in_db =] 'security_account']

sp_addrole [@rolename =] 'role' [,[@ownername =] 'owner']
sp_droprole [@rolename =] 'role'
sp_helprole  [[@rolename =] 'role']

sp_addapprole [@rolename =] 'role', [@password =] 'password'
sp_dropapprole [@rolename =] 'role'
sp_setapprole [@rolename =] 'name' ,
[@password =] {Encrypt N 'password'} ¦ 'password'
[,[@encrypt =] 'encrypt_style']

sp_helprolemember [[@rolename =] 'role']
sp_addrolemember [@rolename =] 'role', [@membername =] 'security_account'
sp_helpdbfixedrole [[@rolename =] 'role']
sp_dbfixedrolepermission  [[@rolename =] 'role']
```

VIEWING AND MODIFYING LOGIN INFORMATION

Perform the following steps to view login information.

1. From the SQL Server Enterprise Manager, click the plus (+) sign next to the server that contains the login.

2. Click the plus (+) sign next to the Security folder.

3. Left-click the Logins icon. A list of logins appears in the results pane.

4. Right-click the name in the results pane. From the right mouse menu, select the Properties menu option. The SQL Server Login Properties dialog box appears. From this dialog box you can view and modify login information.

The following are the corresponding Transact-SQL commands to view login information.

```
sp_helplogins [[@LoginNamePattern =] 'login']
sp_helpprotect  [[@name =] 'object_statement']
[,[@username =] 'security_account']
[,[@grantorname =] 'grantor'] [,[@permissionarea =] 'type']
```

9

MANAGING SQL
SERVER USERS
AND SECURITY

REMOVING LOGINS

Perform the following steps to modify login information.

1. From the SQL Server Enterprise Manager, click the plus (+) sign next to the server that contains the login.

2. Click the plus (+) sign next to the Security folder.

3. Left-click the Logins icon. A list of logins appears in the results pane.

4. Right-click the name in the results pane. From the right mouse menu, select the Delete menu option.

5. Select Yes from the delete confirmation dialog box. This step deletes the user from SQL Server.

NOTE

You cannot delete a login that is an object owner. You must drop the object(s) owned by the login or change the owner of the object(s). To change an object's owner, use the sp_changeobjectowner system procedure. The following is the sp_changeobjectowner syntax.

```
sp_changeobjectowner [@objname =] 'object', [@newowner =] 'owner'
```

Use the following query to generate a list of logins and the objects they own.

```
select 'login name' = b.name, 'object name ' = a.name
from sysobjects a, master..syslogins b
where a.uid = b.suid
order by 1,2
```

The following is the corresponding Transact-SQL command to remove a login.

```
sp_droplogin [@loginame =] 'login'
```

CHANGING PASSWORD

Perform the following steps to change a login password.

NOTE

This topic on changing passwords is relevant only to logins that use SQL Server Authentication. If the login uses NT Authentication, the password must be changed through Windows NT.

---

1. From the SQL Server Enterprise Manager, click the plus (+) sign next to the server that contains the login.

2. Click the plus (+) sign next to the Security folder.

3. Left-click the Logins icon. A list of logins appears in the results pane.

4. Right-click the name in the results pane. From the right mouse menu, select the Properties menu option. The SQL Server Login Properties dialog box appears.

5. Enter the new password.

6. Click the OK button to save the password. The Confirm Password dialog box appears.   .

7. At the Confirm Password dialog box, enter the password again to confirm the change.

8. Click the OK button to save the password.

The following is the corresponding Transact-SQL command to change a password.

```
sp_password  [[@old =] 'old_password',] {[@new =] 'new_password'}
[,[@loginame =] 'login']
```

LOGIN GOTCHAS

The following information can help you avoid login headaches!

- Removing an NT user or NT group from an NT Domain does not drop the corresponding SQL Server login. Whenever you are using NT Authentication and you remove a user or group from an NT Domain, the corresponding SQL Server login becomes orphaned (see the next paragraph for more information on orphaned logins). A record remains in the master..syslogins table after the NT user or NT group has been removed from the NT Domain. I recommend removing the login from SQL Server prior to removing the NT login. An alternative to removing the NT login is to disable the account in the NT Domain. This approach is useful if an employee quits and then gets rehired.

- An orphaned login may prevent a login from being re-created. If a login is orphaned and you try to re-create a login with the same name, you will receive an error message because the login still exists in the master.. syslogins table. To remove the login, use the Enterprise Manager. Follow the instructions discussed in the "Removing Logins" section. After the login has been removed from SQL Server, the login can be re-created.

- You cannot restore permissions to a removed user by adding the login or group back to the NT Domain: The reason is that the new login or group contains a security access identifier (SID) that is different from the login that was deleted. SQL Server uses the SID to track permissions. If this scenario occurs, you must manually re-create the corresponding permissions.

9

MANAGING SQL
SERVER USERS
AND SECURITY

MANAGING SQL SERVER SECURITY

SQL Server provides built-in security and data protection. Its security features are trustworthy and relatively easy to administer. By taking advantage of SQL Server's security features, you can create a secure database that prevents unauthorized access and allows data modification to occur in a controlled and orderly manner.

Levels of Security

The term *security* is a broad term that carries different meanings depending on how it is applied. It can be applied to the following levels (see Figure 9.8):

- Operating system—To connect to the server, a user typically must go through some type of operating system login routine that validates system access.
- SQL server—To connect to SQL Server, the user must have a valid SQL server user login.
- Database—To access a database within SQL Server, the user must have been granted permission to the database.
- Object (table, view, or stored procedure)—To access an object within a database, the user must be granted permission to the object.

When dealing with security, you spend most of your time working at the database and object level. Therefore, the remainder of this chapter concentrates on database and object security.

FIGURE 9.8

The four levels of security.

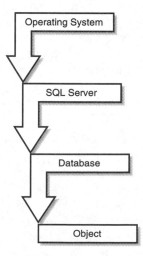

Security Hierarchy

SQL Server's security mechanism is hierarchical. Four types of users exist within the hierarchy: the system administrator, database owners, database object owners, and other users of the database (see Figure 9.9).

FIGURE 9.9

Security hierarchy.

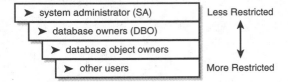

System administrator (SA) → Less Restricted
database owners (DBO)
database object owners
other users → More Restricted

System Administrator

The system administrator (login ID `sa`) and members of the `sysadmin` role are considered the "the almighty ones" who have unrestricted access to SQL Server. Any SQL Server statement or command can be executed by the `sa` or members of the `sysadmin` role. The `sa` and members of the `sysadmin` role can also grant permissions to other users.

Database Owners (DBO)

The database owner (DBO) is the user who created the database or has had ownership assigned to him or her. The DBO has complete access to all objects within his or her database and can assign object permissions to other users.

> **TIP**
>
> To determine the owner of a database, issue the following command from the Query Analyzer: `sp_helpdb [database name]`.

Database Object Owners

The person who creates the database object is considered the owner of the object and is called the *database object owner*. SQL Server assumes that if you have the necessary permission to create the object, you are automatically given all permissions to that object (`SELECT`, `UPDATE`, `INSERT`, `DELETE`, `REFERENCE`, and `EXECUTE`).

9

MANAGING SQL
SERVER USERS
AND SECURITY

> **TIP**
>
> To determine the owner of an object within a database, issue the following command from the Query Analyzer: sp_help [*object name*].
>
> To simplify object access, the DBO or system administrator should create all objects within the database. This approach automatically makes the DBO the database object owner.

Other Users

Other users must be granted object permissions (SELECT, UPDATE, INSERT, DELETE, REFERENCE, and EXECUTE) to operate within the database. The system administrator can also grant statement permissions to other users so that they can create and drop objects within the database.

Granting and Revoking Object Permissions

Perform the following steps to grant and revoke object permissions (see the "Object Permissions" section earlier in the chapter for more information).

1. From the SQL Server Enterprise Manager, click the plus (+) sign next to the server that contains the database objects.

2. Left-click the Databases folder.

3. Left-click the corresponding database.

4. Left-click the icon of the object to grant a permission: Tables, Views, or Stored Procedures. This populates the results pane with the corresponding objects.

5. Right-click the object in the results pane to grant a permission. From the right mouse menu, select the All Tasks menu option. From the All Tasks menu option, select Manage Permissions. The Object Properties dialog box appears (see Figure 9.10).

6. From the Object Properties dialog box, select the appropriate checkbox to grant SELECT, INSERT, UPDATE, DELETE, EXEC, or DRI object permissions. A check appears if the permission is granted. Deselect the appropriate checkbox to revoke object permissions. To deny a permission, click the appropriate checkbox until a red "X" appears.

7. Click the OK button to commit any changes that have been made.

> **TIP**
>
> Perform the following to grant permissions to multiple objects at once.
>
> 1. From the SQL Server Enterprise Manager, click the plus (+) sign next to the server that contains the database objects.
>
> 2. Left-click the Databases folder.
>
> 3. Left-click the corresponding database.
>
> 4. Left-click the Users or Roles icon. This populates the results pane with the corresponding information.
>
> 5. Right-click a name in the results pane. From the right mouse menu, select the Properties option. The corresponding Database User Properties or Database Role Properties dialog box appears.
>
> 6. Click the Permissions button. A second Database User Properties or Database Role Properties dialog box appears. From this dialog box, you can assign permissions to multiple objects.

FIGURE 9.10

Granting and revoking object permissions.

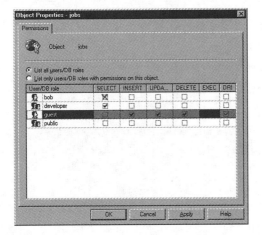

The following are the corresponding Transact-SQL commands to manage object permissions.

```
GRANT {ALL [PRIVILEGES] ¦ permission[,…n]}
{[(column[,…n])] ON {table ¦ view}
¦ ON {table ¦ view}[(column[,…n])]
¦ ON {stored_procedure ¦ extended_procedure}}
TO security_account[,…n]
[WITH GRANT OPTION]
[AS {group ¦ role}]
```

9

MANAGING SQL SERVER USERS AND SECURITY

```
REVOKE [GRANT OPTION FOR]
{ALL [PRIVILEGES] ¦ permission[,…n]}
{[(column[,…n])] ON {table ¦ view}
¦ ON {table ¦ view}[(column[,…n])]
¦ {stored_procedure ¦ extended_procedure}}
{TO ¦ FROM}
security_account[,…n]
[CASCADE]
[AS {group ¦ role}]
```

> **NOTE**
>
> For some strange reason, you cannot use the Enterprise Manager to manage column level permissions. You must use the GRANT syntax listed above to implement column level permissions. The following is an example of granting column level permissions.
>
> ```
> grant select on authors (au_lname, au_fname) to bob
> ```
>
> When bob tries to query the authors table, he will be limited to the au_lname and au_fname columns. If he tries to query other columns in the table, he will receive an error message.

> **CAUTION**
>
> Be careful when granting a permission to a user with the WITH GRANT OPTION. This option allows the user to grant the permission to another user. Therefore, a user can assign permissions without the DBA's knowledge.
>
> For example, the following statement grants the SELECT permission for the authors table to mary:
>
> ```
> GRANT SELECT ON authors to mary WITH GRANT OPTION
> ```
>
> User mary can, in turn, grant the SELECT permission to user sam:
>
> ```
> GRANT SELECT ON authors to sam
> ```
>
> User sam is now granted the SELECT permission for the authors table.

Tips for Managing Object Permissions

Use the following tips to help manage object permissions:

- Object and statement permissions take effect immediately. A user does not have to log out and log back in to SQL Server for the change to take effect.

- Permissions are object specific; therefore, each object (table, view, or stored procedure) must be assigned the appropriate permission.

- By default, the sa and members of the sysadmin role automatically have all permissions for all objects; therefore, you do not need to assign permissions to the sa or sysadmin role.

- If you are logged in as sa or a member of the sysadmin role or the database owner, you can use SETUSER to impersonate another user within the system. Using SETUSER is an easy way to test changes without having to log out and log back in. Also, you do not have to know the password of the user you are trying to impersonate. Look at the following syntax:

```
SETUSER ['username' [WITH NORESET]]
```

This command works with SQL Server Authentication and NT Authentication. The following are examples.

```
—SQL Server Authentication
setuser 'osledge'
—NT Authentication
setuser 'xlconnect_osled\osledge'
```

If the WITH NORESET parameter *was not* specified, you can issue the SETUSER statement without any parameters to revert to the profile of the logged-in user. If the WITH NORESET parameter *was* specified, you can reopen the database (USE *database_name*) to revert to the profile of the logged-in user.

If you forget who you are impersonating, you can use the user_name() function to determine the active user profile, as in the following syntax:

```
SELECT user_name()
```

> **NOTE**
>
> Microsoft has stated that future versions of SQL Server might not support the SETUSER statement. I'm not sure why Microsoft is planning on dropping the statement, but I do not recommend using the statement in stored procedures or inside applications. It is still okay to use the SETUSER statement in the Query Analyzer to test permissions.

- Be sure to save an object's permissions before you drop and re-create a table, view, or stored procedure. All permissions to the object are removed when it is dropped, and SQL Server does not prompt you to save permissions to the object. An easy way to save the permissions of an object is to use the Generate SQL Scripts feature of SQL Server. To generate SQL scripts, right-click the object in the results pane of the Enterprise Manager; from the right mouse menu, select the All Tasks menu option and then select the Generate SQL Scripts menu option. From the Generate SQL Scripts dialog box, select the Options tab. From the Options tab, select the Script Object-Level Permissions check box and generate the script. After you re-create the object, you can apply the script to restore permissions.

Granting and Revoking Statement Permissions

Perform the following steps to grant and revoke statement permissions (see the "Statement Permissions" section earlier in this chapter for more information).

1. From the SQL Server Enterprise Manager, click the plus (+) sign next to the server that contains the database.

2. Left-click the Databases folder.

3. Right-click the database in which you want to grant a statement permission. From the right mouse menu, select the Properties menu option. The Properties dialog box appears.

4. From the Properties dialog box, select the Permissions tab (see Figure 9.11).

5. From the Permissions tab, select the appropriate check box to grant CREATE TABLE, CREATE VIEW, CREATE PROCEDURE, CREATE DEFAULT, CREATE RULE, BACKUP DATA-BASE, or BACKUP LOG statement permissions. A check will appear if the permission is granted. Deselect the appropriate check box to revoke the permission. To deny a permission, click the appropriate check box until a red X appears.

6. Click the OK button to commit any changes that you made.

FIGURE 9.11

Granting and revoking statement permissions.

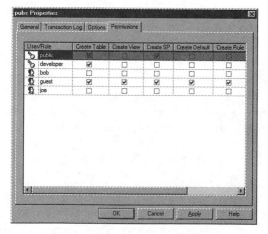

> **NOTE**
>
> The CREATE DB permission can be granted only by the sa or by a member of the sysadmin role and only to users in the master database.

The following are the corresponding Transact-SQL commands to manage statement permissions.

```
GRANT {ALL ¦ statement[,…n]}
TO security_account[,…n]

REVOKE {ALL ¦ statement[,…n]}
FROM security_account[,…n]

sp_helprotect [[@name =] 'object_statement']
[,[@username =] 'security_account'] [,[@grantorname =] 'grantor']
[,[@permissionarea =] 'type']
```

BEYOND SECURITY BASICS: SUGGESTED STRATEGIES

In addition to object and statement permissions, you can combine various components within SQL Server to facilitate administration and provide improved security. Following is a list of suggested security strategies:

- Role-based security management
- Views for data security
- Stored procedures for data security
- Triggers for audit trails

Role-Based Security Management

In the corporate environment, users often work in groups. People in these groups require similar permissions to the database. Whenever multiple users require similar permissions, you should use role-based security. With role-based security, you reduce the number of GRANT, REVOKE, and DENY statements that must be maintained.

Before diving headfirst into role-based security management, you should keep in mind the following points:

- When everyone in a database needs the same permission to the same object, use the public role. When you grant or revoke a permission to the public role, everyone feels the effect. The public role provides an easy way to streamline security administration.

- Try to avoid deep nesting of roles. Nesting of roles is a nice feature in that it allows a role to be a member of another role. However, when using deep nesting this feature may result in a performance decrease.

Views for Data Security

Views help control data security for the following reasons:

- A view can limit the amount of data a user can see and modify. To the user, a view looks and acts like a real table, even though he or she may be working with a subset of the data. Behind the scenes, a view is a virtual table that defines the presentation and manipulation of the actual table(s).

- A user only needs permissions to the view, not to the table(s) that make up the view.

Using Views for Column-Level Security

Often you use a view when a user needs access to a table but, for security reasons, you want to restrict access to certain columns (such as salary data) within the table. By using a view, you can easily restrict access to sensitive data.

Syntax:

```
CREATE VIEW view_name [(column [,...n])] [WITH ENCRYPTION]
AS select_statement [WITH CHECK OPTION]
```

For example, to prohibit access to the employee_ssn, salary, last_updated_by, and last_update_datetime columns in the employee table, use the following syntax:

```
CREATE VIEW  employee_view AS
SELECT name, address, city, state, zip
FROM employee
```

The following listing shows the schema for the employee table:

```
employee_ssn char (9)
name char (35)
address char (35)
city char (35)
state char (35)
zip char (35)
salary money
last_updated_by char (50)
last_update_datetime datetime
```

When the user issues SELECT * FROM employee_view, he or she gets back only the following columns:

```
name
address
```

```
city
state
zip
```

To users, the view looks like a real table except that they never see the `employee_ssn`, `salary`, `last_updated_by`, and `last_update_datetime` columns. Users can't modify what they can't see.

Using Views for Row-Level and Column-Level Security

A simple way to implement row-level security is to add a `WHERE` clause to the `CREATE VIEW` statement. For example, use the following syntax to create a view that limits column and row access:

```
CREATE VIEW employee_view_by_state AS
SELECT name, address, city, state, zip
FROM employee
WHERE state = 'VA' OR state = 'MA'
```

When users issue this statement, they see only the employees with a state code of VA or MA:

```
SELECT * FROM employee_view_by_state
```

TIP

To further ensure data security and to prevent typing errors, you can add the `WITH CHECK OPTION` to the `CREATE VIEW` statement.

The `WITH CHECK OPTION` prevents users from inserting rows or updating columns that do not conform to the `WHERE` clause, as in the following example:

```
CREATE VIEW  employee_view_by_state AS
SELECT name, address, city, state, zip
FROM employee
WHERE state = 'VA' OR state = 'MA'
WITH CHECK OPTION
```

With this view, users can only add rows with a VA or MA state code; they can only update a state code to MA or VA. If users try to change the state code to something other than VA or MA, they receive the following message:

```
Msg 550, Level 16, State 2
The attempted insert or update failed because the target
view either specifies WITH CHECK OPTION or spans a view
which specifies WITH CHECK OPTION and one or more rows
resulting from the operation did not qualify under the
CHECK OPTION constraint.
Command has been aborted.
```

9

MANAGING SQL
SERVER USERS
AND SECURITY

How Views and Permissions Work Together

When you grant object permissions to a view, you do not have to grant permissions to the underlying tables in the view. Therefore, users can SELECT employee data from the employee view, even though they do not have SELECT permission for the employee table. This feature can simplify administration when the view consists of multiple tables.

TIP

You may be wondering, Why not use column-level permissions to prevent access to the employee_ssn, salary, last_updated_by, and last_update_date-time columns? Good question! Both views and column-level permissions can prevent users from accessing restricted columns.

The reason for using a view rather than column-level security is that the view allows a user to issue the SELECT * statement without receiving error messages while still providing column-level security. Consider the following examples:

Example A

John's SELECT permission has been revoked from the employee_ssn column in the employee table. When John issues SELECT * FROM employee, he receives the following error message:

```
Msg 230, Level 14, State 1
SELECT permission denied on column employee_ssn of object
        employee, database xxx, owner dbo
```

To avoid the error message, John must explicitly name each column in the SELECT statement.

Example B

A view has been developed for John to use. The view does not include the employee_ssn column. John can issue a SELECT * statement against the view, and he will see only the columns specified in the view. He does not receive any error messages.

Stored Procedures for Data Security

The advantage of using stored procedures to access and modify data is that users need only EXECUTE permission to run a stored procedure; they do not need access to the tables and views that make up the stored procedure. This approach alleviates the headache of assigning permissions to all underlying tables and views referenced within a stored procedure. The following syntax is an example of a stored procedure that returns all rows in the employee table:

```
CREATE PROCEDURE usp_employee AS
SELECT * FROM employee
```

To run the procedure, the user needs only the EXECUTE permission for usp_employee. The user does *not* need the SELECT permission for the employee table.

GOING TO EXTREMES (BUT IT MAY BE WORTH IT!)

You can really clamp down on end-user data modifications by implementing stored procedures to handle *all* data modifications. To implement this strategy, you must design your applications to use only stored procedures and not embedded SQL to handle data modifications. Next, you must revoke all UPDATE, DELETE, and INSERT (and maybe even SELECT) privileges to *all* tables and views in the database. End users are now denied access whenever they try to modify data. This approach requires extensive use of stored procedures, careful planning, and tight coordination between the application developers and the DBA.

Triggers for Audit Trails

Triggers are made up of Transact-SQL statements that automatically execute when a table is modified through INSERT, UPDATE, or DELETE statements. Because a trigger is automatically executed, it can be a useful facility for auditing data changes. Additionally, you do not have to grant a user the privilege to execute a trigger.

An often-used type of trigger is one that tracks who made the last change to a table and when the change occurred. To track this information, use the following syntax:

```
CREATE TRIGGER iutrg_employee ON dbo.employee
FOR INSERT,UPDATE
AS
UPDATE employee
SET employee.last_updated_by = USER_NAME(),
employee.last_update_datetime = GETDATE()
FROM inserted,employee
WHERE inserted.employee_ssn = employee.employee_ssn
```

Whenever an INSERT or UPDATE statement is run against the employee table in this example, the column last_updated_by is set to the name of the user who made the change and the column last_update_datetime is set to the time the change was made.

MANAGING SQL SERVER USERS AND SECURITY FAQS

This section responds to some of the common questions DBAs ask about SQL Server users and security.

When should NT Authentication be used? When should SQL Server Authentication be used?

NT Authentication should be used when you do not want users going through a separate login process with SQL Server. NT Authentication does not require users to maintain separate passwords for SQL Server. Additionally, NT Authentication can map NT groups to SQL Server and force minimum password lengths and aging.

SQL Server Authentication should be used when users are connecting from clients that do not provide NT Authentication (such as Web clients or UNIX clients). SQL Server Authentication is also simpler to implement and troubleshoot than NT Authentication and is appropriate for applications that automatically log the user into the system or that always use the same login.

When an NT login or NT group is removed from the NT Domain does the corresponding login in SQL Server also get removed?

No! When a NT login or NT group is removed from Windows NT, the corresponding login is not deleted from SQL Server. This creates orphaned logins. See the sidebar titled "Login Gotchas" in this chapter for more information on orphaned logins.

Does NT Authentication require a trusted protocol (such as named pipes or multiprotocol) as in previous versions of SQL Server?

No. SQL Server's protocols—named pipes, multiprotocol, and TCP/IP—automatically support trusted connections. Therefore, you usually do not have to change any client settings (as in previous versions) to implement NT Authentication.

How can I generate a security audit trail with SQL Server?

You can use SQL Server Profiler to generate a detailed log of all activity that is taking place on the server. Keep in mind that the SQL Server Profiler can generate a lot of information, and it must be running to generate an audit trail. Therefore, I recommend using the SQL Server Profiler on an as-needed basis, rather than on a full-time basis, to generate audit trails.

Triggers can be implemented to generate audit trails on a table-by-table basis. The advantage of using a trigger is that you can record the before and after image of the data and track who made the modification and when it was made. The disadvantage of using a trigger is that you must hand-code this functionality.

Are statement permissions considered a thing of the past?

No, statement permissions are still available in 7.0. However, server roles and database roles can provide similar functionality and may be easier to implement.

Are NT administrators automatically administrators of SQL Server?

Yes. NT administrators, users of the NT administrators group, and Domain Administrators are automatically SQL Server administrators.

I forgot the sa password. Is there any way to retrieve it?

You cannot retrieve a lost password. However, you can reset the sa password by logging in to SQL Server with the NT Administrator account (Windows NT administrators are automatically SQL Server administrators).

Perform the following to reset the sa password.

1. Log in to Windows NT with an account that contains Windows NT administrative privileges.
2. Use the SQL Server Query Analyzer to connect to SQL Server. When connecting to SQL Server, select NT Authentication at the login prompt.
3. Execute the following command to reset the sa password:

```
sp_password null, 'newpassword', 'sa'
```

9

MANAGING SQL
SERVER USERS
AND SECURITY

If I add a login to SQL Server and do not permit the login access to a database (let's say pubs), the new login can query information in the database from the Query Analyzer. Why?

The answer resides in the guest account (see the section "guest User" in this chapter for more information). If the guest account exists in the database and the login is not mapped to the database, SQL Server automatically uses the guest account. Therefore the logged in user inherits the permissions assigned to the guest user. You can delete the guest account from all databases except master. Keep in mind that when you create a new database, the guest account is automatically added to the new database (this is true even after the guest account has been deleted from the model database).

Aliases are not part of 7.0, so how does 7.0 handle them? What happens when a 6.x machine with aliases is upgraded to 7.0?

Aliases are supported in an upgraded database. However, they do not work exactly the same. If you were aliased to DBO in 6.x and created a table, it was created as dbo.table. In 7.0, if you are logged in as osledge, the table is created as osledge.table, even if you are aliased to DBO (via an upgrade). I recommend implementing roles as a replacement for aliases.

SUMMARY

The following are the key points on managing SQL Server logins and security.

- SQL Server supports two authentication models: NT Authentication and SQL Server Authentication. NT Authentication is directly integrated with Windows NT.

- The guest user may exist in a database. SQL Server uses the guest login when a login is not mapped to a database. The guest user is a member of the public database role.

- SQL Server 7.0 supports several types of roles: server roles, database roles, and application roles.

- Server roles are serverwide and cannot be customized.

- SQL Server provides two types of database roles: predefined roles and user-defined roles.

- Predefined database roles are database specific and cannot be customized.

- Every database user is automatically a member of the `public` database role.

- SQL Server provides two types of user-defined roles: standard roles and application roles.

- User-defined database roles are database specific and can be customized.

- Application roles are database specific, customizable, and can be password protected. Application roles must be activated and do not contain users.

- `GRANT`, `REVOKE`, and `DENY` are Transact-SQL commands used to manage object and statement permissions.

- Views, triggers, and stored procedures can be used as additional security measures.

BACKUP AND RESTORE

by Mark Spenik

IN THIS CHAPTER

Backups are copies of SQL Server databases or transaction logs used to restore a database if the database becomes corrupt or is lost in a catastrophic event. The task of backing up and protecting the data is probably the number one job responsibility of the DBA. In many organizations, the sole responsibilities of the DBA are backup and database maintenance.

Restore is the process of recovering a damaged, corrupted, or missing database. Being able to restore a database when several disk drives crash or a table or database becomes corrupted is when good DBAs earns their keep. Remember that your ability to restore a database depends on proper planning and testing.

SQL Server 7.0 has made many improvements and enhancements to the backup and restore processes. In this chapter, you learn about the different methods available for backing up SQL Server databases and transaction logs and you learn how to use those methods to restore databases. Even more important, you learn how to create a backup and restore strategy.

NOTE

In previous versions of SQL Server, a database backup was also referred to as a database dump. SQL Server 7.0 has simplified the terminology used in backup and restore by removing the DUMP command and replacing it with the BACKUP and RESTORE commands. By the way, removing the DUMP command from SQL Server also removes the SQL Server Certification Test trick question for SQL Enterprise Manager pilots not familiar with SQL Server Transact-SQL commands. What command is used to back up a SQL Server database? I'm sure the rookies picked BACKUP or COPY instead of DUMP.

BETTER SAFE THAN SORRY!

Okay, if you have read the two previous editions of the SQL Server DBA survival guide, you're probably thinking, "hey I've read this story before." And, of course, you are right! During the 3 years since the first edition of the DBA Survival Guide was published, I have run into many corrupted databases and rescued many organizations. But, I still think this story goes a long way towards enlightening you on how it does not take a disk drive crash or database corruption to require a complete database restore. By the way, I still talk to Don from time to time and yes he still is "The Man" when it comes to SQL Server development.

I learned the value of having a good set of database backups the hard way. Several years ago, while working on a Sybase 4.2 UNIX system, I was hired as a contractor to help out an organization with several large Sybase databases. They had recently lost several key MIS employees and were shorthanded.

I was working with a gentleman I'll refer to as Don "The Man," one of the few really good jack-of-all-trades (UNIX system administrator, Sybase DBA, and Client/Server developer) individuals I have met. I had been at the organization for only two days; Don and I were busy trying to get a clean set of backups for the database and the UNIX system. The nightly UNIX backup had failed for the last two days, and the database backups were going slowly because several databases were flagged with errors during DBCC (database consistency check).

We were working with Sybase tech support to correct the database problems. Don was preparing one of the larger databases for a backup when I heard him exclaim, "Oh no! I can't believe I did that. I can't believe what I just did. We are doomed!"

It turned out that Don had entered an SQL statement incorrectly, which had started one large transaction that was deleting all the rows of a table with about four million rows! I said, "No problem. We'll just restore from a database backup." It was then that Don informed me that the only database backup was 30 days old and outdated! What to do?

Because Don had blocked the delete within a single transaction, we killed the server before it could complete the operation and commit the transaction. The server took a while to come back up as several thousand transactions were rolled back. We then verified the table row count from some numbers taken earlier that day to verify that no data had been lost (information was always added to the table, but never updated).

At this point, Don and I realized that we needed backups—*now*. We stayed late that night verifying previous backup tapes that we found could not be read because of media problems. We continued to work early into the morning and created a whole new set of UNIX system backups and database backups.

The moral of the story is "backups are serious business!" Too often, I have heard someone say, "The nightly backup did not run; not sure why, but I'll run it again tonight." Big mistake. Remember that you don't know the hour, day, or minute when the disk drive will give up, the building will be hit by a natural disaster, or someone like Don will issue a SQL command that will ruin the production database! If you don't have a good backup, you will find yourself trying to explain to your boss how you lost a day's worth of data because the nightly backup did not work and you did nothing about it that morning.

SQL SERVER 6.5 TO 7.0 QUICK REFERENCE

The following is a quick reference guide to changes from SQL Server 6.5 to 7.0.

What's New

The following are new to SQL Server 7.0 backup and recovery:

- Backup and restore process has fundamentally changed behind the scenes
- Transact-SQL BACKUP DATABASE command
- Transact-SQL BACKUP LOG command
- Transact-SQL RESTORE command
- Ability to start and restart backups
- Differential and filegroup backups
- Media sets
- Requirements for a transaction log backup with NO_TRUNCATE option are different than in SQL Server 6.5, the log file and primary data file must be intact
- The ability to detach and attach databases

What's Gone

The following is a list of SQL Server 6.5 features no longer found in SQL Server 7.0:

- DUMP command
- LOAD command
- Individual table backup and restore
- sp_help_revdatabase and the need to re-create a database for restoring with the proper segments

SQL SERVER 7.0 BACKUPS—A CHANGE IN PHILOSOPHY? FUNCTIONALITY?

For those of you who have used SQL Server 6.x and are curious about how your current backup and restore plans will change with SQL Server 7.0, you will be happy to hear that you might not have to change any of your current backup and restore plans! SQL Server 7.0 database restore still consists of database backups associated with transaction log backups. But the backup and restore philosophy of SQL Server 7.0 makes it easier for non-DBAs to successfully restore databases. Not only is it easier to backup and restore databases, SQL Server 7.0 provides new functionality and capabilities, such as a differential database backups and file/filegroup backups. SQL Server 6.x DBAs will want to re-examine their current procedures and determine if the new functionality can be used to speed up their backup and restore time or reduce the potential loss of data. SQL Server 7.0 has the following backup types:

- Database
- Differential
- Transaction Log
- File/Filegroups

What Is a Database Backup?

Think of a database backup as a full backup of a database. When you perform a database backup, SQL Server copies all user-defined objects, system tables, and data. When a database BACKUP DATABASE command is issued, SQL Server writes all completed transactions to disk and then begins to copy the database. Any incomplete transactions or transactions that occur after the database backup process is started, are *not* backed up. To back up changes that occurred while the backup process was running, you must back up the transaction log after the backup completes.

TIP

You can back up a database or transaction log while the database is in use, with a few exceptions. You cannot back up a database while a non-logged operation is occurring, an index is being created, database files are being created or deleted or the database is being shrunk (manual or automatic) Depending on the device(s) and the server being used you may notice a decrease in performance during a backup process, so consider performing backups during nonpeak hours.

What Is a Differential Backup?

A differential database backup is a new SQL Server 7.0 backup that is an incremental database backup. It is an incremental database backup because only data that has changed since the last database backup is copied, resulting in a smaller and faster backup compared to a full database backup. Like a full database backup, incomplete transactions or transactions that occur after the differential database-backup process is started are *not* backed up. A differential backup does not provide up to the point of failure recovery but the ability to recover the database up to the time the differential database was created.

10

What Is a Transaction Log Backup?

In previous editions of this book, a transaction log backup was described as an SQL Server incremental backup. But SQL Server 7.0 truly has an incremental database backup, the differential backup that copies any data changed since the last backup. You can still think of a transaction log backup as an incremental database backup that provides up to the point of failure recovery. The transaction log backup contains all of the completed transactions performed since the last database, differential or transaction log backup. (As stated in Chapter 8, "Database Management," a transaction log contains all the various transactions that have occurred on a database before the last backup.) However, unlike a differential database backup, which picks up all changes to the database, a transaction log backup contains only logged operations and does not include unlogged operations such as fast BCP.

A transaction log backup performs the following operations:

- Copies the inactive part of the transaction log to the backup device
- Truncates (clears and frees up space) the inactive part of the transaction log

The inactive part of the transaction log contains all the completed transactions up to but on the same page as the earliest outstanding transaction or the earliest transaction that has not been moved to the distribution database and is marked for replication.

> **TIP**
>
> Performing a full database backup does not clear out the inactive part of the transaction log. If you perform only database backups, eventually your transaction log fills up and you are unable to perform any transactions in the database (no INSERT, UPDATE, or DELETE actions) until you back up the transaction log. You have to perform transaction log backups to clear out the inactive part of the transaction log, even if you rely on full database backups. If you don't plan to use the transaction log for restore purposes, you can set the database option, trunc. log on chkpt, which clears out the transaction log at each checkpoint. trunc. log on chkpt keeps the transaction log clear and prohibits you from performing a BACKUP LOG command with the database or using the transaction log for restore purposes.

WHAT IS A FILE/FILEGROUP BACKUP?

If you have limited time in which to perform a database backup and you cannot perform the backup using a full database backup, differential backup, or transaction log backup, SQL Server 7.0 offers the option of performing a File/Filegroup backup. Files or filegroups can be backed up individually or together. Restoring a complete database from a File/Filegroup backup is a little trickier than a regular SQL Server backup/restore. Tables or indexes that span multiple filegroups need to have the files and filegroups with spanning objects backed up together. Fortunately, if you attempt to back up an object with spanning file/filegroups, SQL Server tells you that the missing file/filegroups must also be backed up. To properly restore using file/filegroups requires the use of transaction log backups. Although other forms of database backups and restore are simpler and easier to restore from, having the file/filegroup option definitely helps some IS shops with large databases and limited backup times. File/Filegroups recovery can be useful when only one drive goes down and you only need to recover the file/filegroups located on that drive. A file/filgroup recovery can be performed using file/filegroup backups or full database backups and in both cases the transaction logs since the backup (if data has changed). Additionally, the file/filegroup option might be more comfortable for NT administrators acting as DBAs to use. If you feel like you need to use this type of backup, here is an example of how file and filegroup backups are done. Suppose you have a very large database spread across three different filegroups. Because of time constraints, you decide that you cannot perform a complete or differential backup. Instead, you decide to back up one filegroup a day and perform a transaction log backup daily. One filegroup is backed up daily. (Each filegroup is backed up once every three days.) A transaction log backup is performed daily. To properly restore the database if you lose all of the filegroups requires a backup of each filegroup as well as transaction log backups from the oldest filegroup backup to the most recent.

> **NOTE**
>
> File and Filegroups can be restored from a full database backup as well as a File/Filegroup backup. If SQL Server detects that no modifications were made while the file/filegroup was backed up, you do not need to use a transaction log backup.

CREATING A BACKUP DEVICE

Before backing up a database, you need to create a backup device to copy the database, transaction log, or file/filegroup. The Backup devices can be tapes, disk files, or a network drive. When a disk backup device is allocated, no storage space is allocated until the database backup is performed. Tape drives must be connected to the machine running SQL Server. SQL Server cannot use a tape drive on a remote machine.

> **NOTE**
>
> Network drives use the Universal Naming Convention (UNC), which is `\\Servername\Sharename\Path\File`, or a locally mapped network drive can be used. Make sure that the user account used by SQL Server has the proper permissions to access the backup file and directory.

To create a backup device using the Enterprise Manager, select the server you want to add the backup device from and then perform the following steps:

1. Select the Management folder and then select the Backup icon. Right-click the icon. A shortcut menu appears.

2. Select New Backup Device from the shortcut menu to display the Backup Device Properties—New Device dialog box (see Figure 10.1).

    The following list describes the different parameters in the New Backup Device dialog box (see Figure 10.1):

    Name: The SQL Server logical name for the backup device. The rules and limitations for a backup device name are the same as those for database devices.

    File name: This parameter applies only if the backup device being created is a hard disk file. The location is the path and filename of the hard disk. *Tip:* The location for a backup device can be on a network drive.

    Tape Drive name: This parameter applies only if the backup device being created is a tape drive that is installed on the database server.

3. Enter the required information, described in the following options, and click the OK button to create the backup device.

FIGURE 10.1

Backup Device Properties—New Device dialog box.

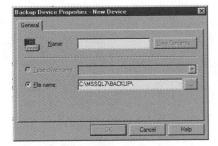

Adding a backup device with SQL Server Manager is the same as executing the stored procedure `sp_addumpdevice`, which has the following parameters:

```
sp_addumpdevice Type, 'Logical_Name',
'Physical_Name'
[,controller_type ¦ devstatus = {noskip ¦ skip}]
```

The `Type` parameter specifies the type of device and can be `'disk'`, `'tape'`, or `'pipe'`. `Logical Name` is the logical name of the dump device. `Physical Name` is the physical path and name of the dump device.

Use the `controller_type` parameter or the `devstatus` parameter although neither is required. The `controller_type` parameter can be set to 2 for a disk, 5 for tape, and a 6 for a pipe. Set `devstatus` to `skip` or `noskip`. These parameters determine whether SQL Server tries to read ANSI labels before performing a backup.

When a backup device is added, SQL Server makes an entry in the `sysdevices` table.

PERFORMING DATABASE, TRANSACTION LOG, DIFFERENTIAL, AND FILE/FILEGROUP BACKUPS

SQL Server 7.0 eases the pain of the backup process by providing a common interface for backups. Whether you are performing a database backup, differential backup, File/Filegroup backup, or transaction log backup, the same steps are followed. Examine the steps required to perform a database backup or transaction log backup using the SQL Server Enterprise Manager.

10

BACKUP AND RESTORE

> **TIP**
>
> Due to many different storage and engine changes made in SQL Server 7.0, it is not necessary to run DBCC's commands before performing a database backup; however, if you are a DBA from the SQL Server 6.x school, you can still execute the commands for peace of mind. For SQL Server 7.0, the only command required is the DBCC commands CHECKDB. CHECKDB performs all the necessary database consistency checks. If you use CHECKDB, you no longer have to perform the other DBCC commands required in previous versions: NEWALLOC (or CHECKALLOC) and CHECKCATALOG. Personally, I still think I'll use the DBCC command CHECKDB at least once a week before doing backups. A database backed up with errors has the same errors on a restored database and, in some severe cases, could prevent a successful restoration of the database.

From the SQL Enterprise Manager, select Tools and then select Backup Database. The Database Backup dialog box appears (see Figure 10.2).

FIGURE 10.2

The Database Backup dialog box—General tab.

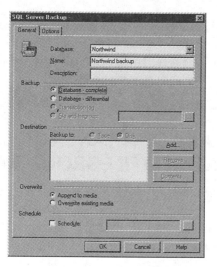

The Steps to Perform a Backup

To back up a database, transaction log, or file/filegroup follow these steps:

1. From the Database Backup dialog box—General tab, select a database to back up by selecting the database name in the combo box.

2. Enter the name for the database backup in the Name text box and a description of the database backup in the Description text box, shown in Figure 10.2. This information can be viewed later using the SQL Enterprise Manager or Transact-SQL.

3. Select the type of backup to perform by selecting the radio button in the backup section on the Database Backup dialog box—General tab (refer to Figure 10.2). The options available are as follows:

Database—Complete

Database—Differential

Transaction Log

File and Filegroup

4. Select the backup device or backup devices by clicking the Add button. The Choose Backup Destination dialog box, shown in Figure 10.3, appears. Select a current backup device by selecting the backup device radio button and then selecting the backup device from the combo box. To back up to a file, select the filename radio button and provide a file path and name. After you have selected the backup device, click the OK button.

FIGURE 10.3

The Choose Backup Destination dialog box.

5. To write over an existing backup on the selected device, select the Overwrite Existing Media option. To append to the current media, check the Append to Media option.

6. To schedule the backup for later use, check the Schedule box. Checking the Schedule box executes the backup on the default date, which is every week on Sundays at 12:00 am. To change the schedule time of the backup, click the button to the right of the default time, the Edit Schedule dialog box, shown in Figure 10.4, appears.

7. Enter a name for the scheduled job in the Name text box or accept the default name `Schedule1`.

TIP

Use a descriptive name for the scheduled backup. Using a descriptive name makes it easier to identify the backup later in the NT event log or in the SQL Server Scheduled job history log.

10

BACKUP AND RESTORE

FIGURE 10.4

The Edit Schedule dialog box.

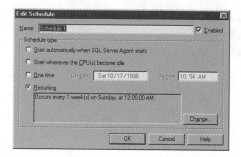

8. Select when you want the scheduled backup to occur. For the backup to occur when the SQL Server Agents starts up, select Start Automatically when SQL Server Agent Starts. To execute during a CPU idle cycle, select Start Whenever the CPU(s) Become Idle. For the job to occur one time only, select the One Time radio button, and then set the date and time you want the backup to occur. To set up a recurring backup, select the Recurring radio button. To schedule the recurring backup, click the Change button; the Edit Recurring Job dialog box appears (see Figure 10.5).

Using the Edit Recurring Job dialog box, you can easily schedule the backup to occur daily, weekly, or monthly on a given day or time. (The Task Schedule dialog box is covered in detail in Chapter 30, "Automating Database Administration Tasks.")

FIGURE 10.5

The Edit Recurring Job dialog box.

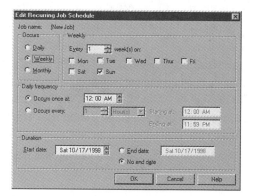

> **NOTE**
>
> Be careful about scheduling backup jobs that append to a disk device every day or weekly. I recently had a client ask me what had happened to the 40 giga-bytes of free disk space they had on their database server. I checked the server and it turned out that their DBA had scheduled 20+ database backup jobs and all 20 jobs appended backups to the backup device files. They had about 5 months worth of backups appended to the devices, which were consuming over 36 gigabytes!

9. After you choose when you want the backup to occur, click OK to schedule the backup.

   The success or failure of the scheduled job can be viewed from the SQL Server Agent—Jobs using the SQL Enterprise (see Chapter 30).

10. To set additional options, select the Options tab in the Database Backup dialog box. The Options tab is shown in Figure 10.6.

FIGURE 10.6

The Database Backup dialog box—Options tab.

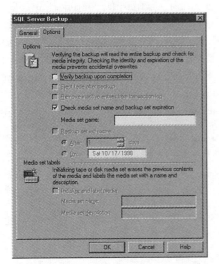

11. To check integrity of the backup media (so that SQL Server reads entire backup to verify the media can be read) check the Verify Backup upon Completion check box. To Eject a tape upon completion of the backup, check the Eject Tape after Backup check box. To check the selected media set and backup set for expiration (that is, if device can be overwritten) check the Check Media Set Name and Backup Set Expiration check box. If you select the Backup Set Will Expire check box, set one of the following check boxes to determine at what time an existing backup device tape or file can be over written with new information:

•**Expires after**: Sets the number of days before the tape or file can be overwritten

•**Expires on**: Sets the date on which the tape or file can be overwritten

---

TIP

Use the Expires On or the Expires After options to protect your backups from being accidentally overwritten.

---

12. To start the database, transaction log, or file/filegroup backup, click the OK button in the Database Backup dialog box. The Backup Progress dialog box is displayed. The Backup Progress dialog box uses a progress indicator to display the progression of the backup. To cancel a backup in progress, click the Cancel button. When the backup is complete, the Backup Progress Completion dialog box is displayed. If you selected Verify Backup Upon Completion Option, a dialog box is displayed letting you know that the backup media has been verified.

The Transact-SQL command used to back up the database is the BACKUP DATABASE command, which has the following format for a database:

```
BACKUP DATABASE {database_name ¦ @database_name_var}
TO <backup_device> [, ...n]
[WITH
[BLOCKSIZE = {blocksize ¦ @blocksize_variable}]
[[,] DESCRIPTION = {text ¦ @text_variable}]
[[,] DIFFERENTIAL]
[[,] EXPIREDATE = {date ¦ @date_var}
¦ RETAINDAYS = {days ¦ @days_var}]
[[,] FORMAT ¦ NOFORMAT]
[[,] {INIT ¦ NOINIT}]
[[,] MEDIADESCRIPTION = {text ¦ @text_variable}]
[[,] MEDIANAME = {media_name ¦ @media_name_variable}]
[[,] [NAME = {backup_set_name ¦ @backup_set_name_var}]
[[,] {NOSKIP ¦ SKIP}]
```

```
[[,] {NOUNLOAD ¦ UNLOAD}]
[[,] [RESTART]
[[,] STATS [= percentage]]
```

To back up a transaction log, use the following Transact:

```
BACKUP LOG {database_name ¦ @database_name_var}
[WITH
{ NO_LOG ¦ TRUNCATE_ONLY }]
TO <backup_device> [, ...n]
[WITH
[BLOCKSIZE = {blocksize ¦ @blocksize_variable}]
[[,] DESCRIPTION = {text ¦ @text_variable}]
[[,] EXPIREDATE = {date ¦ @date_var}
¦ RETAINDAYS = {days ¦ @days_var}]
[[,] FORMAT ¦ NOFORMAT]
[[,] {INIT ¦ NOINIT}]
[[,] MEDIADESCRIPTION = {text ¦ @text_variable}]
[[,] MEDIANAME = {media_name ¦ @media_name_variable}]
[[,] [NAME = {backup_set_name ¦ @backup_set_name_var}]
[[,] NO_TRUNCATE]
[[,] {NOSKIP ¦ SKIP}]
[[,] {NOUNLOAD ¦ UNLOAD}]
[[,] [RESTART]
[[,] STATS [= percentage]]]}
```

To back up a file/filegroup, use the Transact-SQL:

```
BACKUP DATABASE {database_name ¦ @database_name_var}
<file_or_filegroup> [, ...m]
TO <backup_device> [, ...n]
[WITH
[BLOCKSIZE = {blocksize ¦ @blocksize_variable}]
[[,] DESCRIPTION = {text ¦ @text_variable}]
[[,] EXPIREDATE = {date ¦ @date_var}
¦ RETAINDAYS = {days ¦ @days_var}]
[[,] FORMAT ¦ NOFORMAT]
[[,] {INIT ¦ NOINIT}]
[[,] MEDIADESCRIPTION = {text ¦ @text_variable}]
[[,] MEDIANAME = {media_name ¦ @media_name_variable}]
[[,] [NAME = {backup_set_name ¦ @backup_set_name_var}]
[[,] {NOSKIP ¦ SKIP}]
[[,] {NOUNLOAD ¦ UNLOAD}]
[[,] [RESTART]
[[, ] STATS [= percentage]]
]
```

And file or filegroup has the following format:

```
<file_or_filegroup> :: =
{
FILE = {logical_file_name ¦ @logical_file_name_var}
¦
FILEGROUP = {logical_filegroup_name ¦ @logical_filegroup_name_var}
}
```

For all three backup commands, backup_device has the following format:

```
{backup_device_name ¦ @backup_device_namevar}
¦ {DISK ¦ TAPE ¦ PIPE} =
{'temp_dump_device' ¦ @temp_dump_device_var}}
[VOLUME = {volid ¦ @volid_var}]
```

The optional parameters INIT and NOINIT, available with tape devices are available for other backup devices. Use the INIT option to overwrite the information stored on the dump device. Use NOINIT to append the information. Remember that the capability to overwrite a device also depends on the expiration and retention dates set for the backup device.

TEMPORARY BACKUP DEVICES

SQL Server 7.0 enables you to create and use temporary backup devices when backing up databases or transaction logs. A *temporary backup device* is a backup device that is created at the time of the BACKUP command and that has not been added to the system table sysdevices with the system stored procedure sp_adddumpdevice. To back up a database to a temporary backup device, you must specify the type of media the backup device is on (use the options DISK, TAPE, or PIPE) and then specify the complete path and filename. In the case of PIPE, you must specify the name of the named-pipe used in the client application. You can also use variables to create a temporary backup device. Look at some examples using temporary devices.

Example: Dump the master database to a temporary disk backup device called tdump_master.dat, located in the directory C:\MSSQL\BACKUP.

Using the path and filename as follows:

```
BACKUP DATABASE master
to DISK='C:\MSSQL7\BACKUP\tdump_master.dat'
```

Using a variable as follows:

```
Declare @temp_dump varchar(255)
Select @temp_dump = 'C:\MSSQL7\BACKUP\tdump_master.dat'
BACKUP DATABASE master
to DISK = @temp_dump
```

UNDERSTANDING LOG TRUNCATION OPTIONS

The different backup log truncation options are often overlooked by new DBAs. Quite frequently new DBAs do not know the options exist or if they know about them, how or when to use them. The following sections explain each of the options in detail and when to use them.

TRUNCATE_ONLY

The TRUNCATE_ONLY option removes the inactive part of the transaction log (truncates) without backing up (copying) the log to a backup device. You do not have to specify a backup device when using TRUNCATE_ONLY because the log is not copied. For example, the syntax to backup the master database transaction log with the TRUNCATE_ONLY option is as follows:

```
Backup Log master
WITH TRUNCATE_ONLY
```

Use the TRUNCATE_ONLY option in the following case:

- If you do not use the transaction log for restore purposes and rely on full database backups, use TRUNCATE_ONLY immediately after a full database backup has been performed to clear out the inactive part of the transaction log. (Note: in this scenario you are better off setting the database option trunc. log on chkpt discussed in detail later in this chapter.)

> **CAUTION**
>
> Always perform a database backup (complete or differential) before using the TRUNCATE_ONLY option. If you use the TRUNCATE_ONLY option without a database backup, you cannot restore the completed transactions in the inactive part of the transaction log at the time the BACKUP LOG with TRUNCATE_ONLY command was issued.

NO_LOG

When a BACKUP LOG command is issued with the NO_LOG option, SQL Server truncates the inactive part of the transaction log without logging the BACKUP LOG command.

10

CAUTION

After using the NO_LOG option, always perform a full database backup; otherwise, the changes that had been in the transaction log at the time the log was truncated with the NO_LOG option aren't restorable.

Use the NO_LOG option only when the transaction log is completely full. When the log fills up completely you cannot truncate the transaction log by executing a normal BACKUP LOG command. This occurs because SQL Server attempts to log the BACKUP LOG command and no room is left in the transaction log. Like the TRUNCATE_ONLY option, the NO_LOG option does not require a backup device because the log is not copied to a device.

TIP

Microsoft SQL Server 7.0 now enables you to grow the transaction log without having to specify a maximum size. This capability should go a long way in preventing the problems a full transaction log caused previous users. Automatically growing the transaction log also takes the burden of estimating the correct size of the transaction log. In previous versions, if you overestimated, you wasted disk space. If you underestimated, you were busy running commands to truncate a full log and constantly resizing the log.

NO_TRUNCATE

Use the NO_TRUNCATE option when the database you are trying to access is corrupted and you are about to restore the database. To use NO_TRUNCATE, the following must be true:

- The transaction log must reside on a separate device from the database.
- The master database must not be corrupted.

CAUTION

The requirements for NO_TRUNCATE are different in SQL Server 7.0 than in SQL Server 6.5. In 6.5 as long as the transaction log file was intact, you could use the NO_TRUNCATE option. In SQL Server 7.0, the log file AND the primary data file (file with database system tables) must be intact to use NO_TRUNCATE. For a better understanding, walk through the hands on backup and recovery example at the end of this chapter.

The NO_TRUNCATE option writes all the transaction log entries from the time of the last transaction backup to the point of the database corruption. You can then restore the transaction log backup as the last backup in the restore process for up-to-the-millisecond data restore.

> **TIP**
>
> Become familiar with the NO_TRUNCATE option. I have met many DBAs who were unfamiliar with the option or were not sure when to use it.

BACKUP WIZARD

SQL Server 7.0 goes a long way in enabling a casual user to perform standard DBA tasks successfully using wizards. Of course, there is a wizard that enables you to perform a backup. To use the Backup Wizard, perform the following:

1. From the SQL Enterprise Manager main menu select Tools and the option Wizards.

2. The Select Wizard dialog box appears. Click the + sign next to Management to expand the list of management wizards. Select the Backup Wizard and click OK. The Welcome Backup Wizard dialog box, shown in Figure 10.7, appears.

FIGURE 10.7

The Welcome Backup Wizard dialog box.

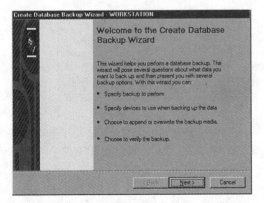

3. Click the Next button; the Select Database to Backup dialog box, shown in Figure 10.8, appears. Select the database to back up in the combo box and click the Next button.

10

FIGURE 10.8

Select Database to Backup— Backup Wizard dialog box.

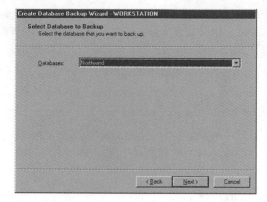

4. The Name and Description dialog box, shown in Figure 10.9, appears. Enter the name you want to use to refer to the backup. You can also enter a description to provide more information. Click the Next button.

FIGURE 10.9

The Name and Description— Backup Wizard dialog box.

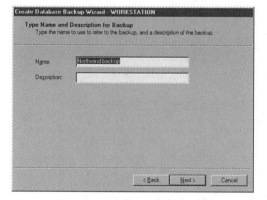

5. The Backup Type dialog box, shown in Figure 10.10, appears. Select the type of backup you want to perform by clicking the appropriate radio button. Click the Next button to continue.

6. The Destination and Action dialog box, shown in Figure 10.11, appears. Select the backup device to which you want to back up the selected database. Check one of the radio buttons to either append to the selected device or overwrite the selected device. Click the Next button to continue.

FIGURE 10.10

*The Backup
Type—Backup
Wizard dialog
box.*

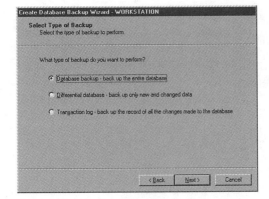

If you choose to overwrite the existing media, upon clicking the Next button
you will be prompted with a dialog box that allows you initialize the media set
as well which erases all previous content on the media set.

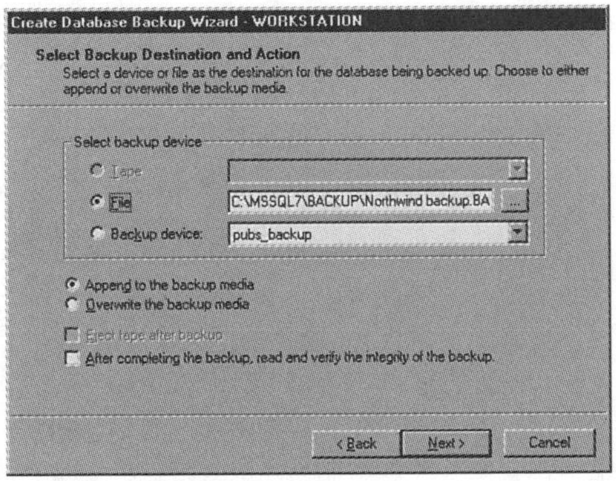

FIGURE 10.11

*The Destination
and Action—
Backup Wizard
dialog box.*

7. The Backup Verification dialog box, shown in Figure 10.12, appears. This dialog
   box enables you to check to make sure the device selected for the backup has
   expired and can be overwritten. Also you can have the media verified after the
   backup completes as well as assign a media set name to the backup as well as
   schedule the backup. After you have made your selections, click the Next button
   to continue.

10

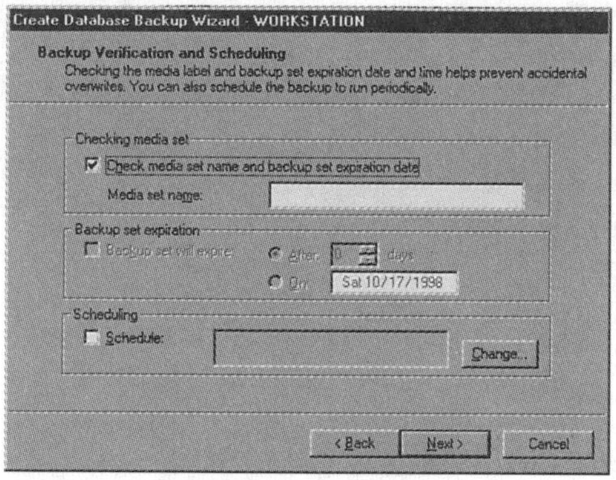

FIGURE 10.12

The Backup Verification— Backup Wizard dialog box.

FIGURE 10.13

The Display Selected Options—Backup Wizard dialog box.

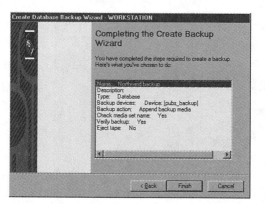

8. The Display Selected Options dialog box, shown in Figure 10.13, appears. This dialog box displays the current selections you have made. If you want to make changes, click the Back button to walk backwards through the wizard and make modifications. To perform the backup, click the Finish button. The Backup Progress dialog box appears as well as a Verification dialog box if the Verify Backup option was selected.

USING MULTIPLE BACKUP DEVICES (STRIPED BACKUPS) AND MEDIA SETS

SQL Server 6.x added the capability to perform backups to multiple backup devices called *parallel striped backups*. SQL Server 7.0 continues and enhances the capability, but now refers to it as using multiple backup devices. Using multiple backup devices lessens the amount of time required to back up a database, filegroup, or transaction log by reading/writing to backup devices simultaneously. For example if it takes you three hours to perform a database backup on a single tape drive, you can add two more tape drives and cut the backup time to about an hour. An example of a multiple device backup is shown in Figure 10.14.

FIGURE 10.14

An example of using multiple devices in a media set.

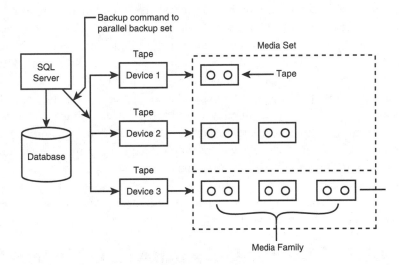

The database, file/filegroup, or transaction log can be backed up to multiple devices of the same media (tape or disk) called the *media set*. The media participating in the media set has to be the same type (that is, disk or tape) but can be of different size, speed, and storage space. In the case of tapes, if one tape runs out, the backup continues on the remaining tapes until the tape can be removed and a new tape added. Throughout the backup process, synchronization is performed across all media and requires that all media be operational. If a tape should run out during the synchronization process, the backup halts on the other tapes until the tape is replaced and the synchronization can be performed. If a database or transaction log is backed up to multiple backup devices, it must also be restored from multiple devices. SQL Server 7.0 can use from 2 to 32 backup devices in a multiple device backup. You can perform a multiple device backup with SQL Server Enterprise Manager using the Backup dialog box or the Backup Wizard by selecting more than one backup device to copy the database. To perform a multiple device backup to multiple devices using the BACKUP DATABASE command, list the backup devices separated by commas. For example, to back up the master database to three backup disk devices called backup1, backup2, and backup3, the syntax is as follows:

```
Backup DATABASE master
to backup1, backup2, backup3
```

10

BACKUP AND RESTORE

When restoring a database, using multiple devices requires that all the devices be used to restore the database in the case of disk files. If you used tapes, you can restore the database using fewer tape drives and loading the tapes as prompted.

Earlier, it was mentioned that the multiple devices used in a backup were called a media set. The term media set is new to SQL Server 7.0. A media set is all of the media used in a single backup. A media set could consists of a single disk file or 100 backup tapes. A media family is all of the media used during a backup on a specific backup device. For example, suppose you back up a database to two backup devices (that is, tape drives) Tape0 and Tape1. The backup requires a total of 20 tapes. Because Tape0 uses larger capacity tapes, six tapes are used on Tape0 and 14 tapes on Tape1. The six tapes used on Tape0 are a media family. The first tape used is referred to as the initial media, and the remaining tapes are called the continuation media. (Note: only tape media can have continuation media.) The initial media is stamped with a sequence number of 1, the next tape 2 and so on. So in our example, the media set consists of two backup devices, which translates to two media families and a total of 20 tapes. The media families break down as six tapes in the Tape0 media family and 14 tapes in the Tape1 media family.

UNDERSTANDING DATABASE OPTIONS AND THE TRANSACTION LOG

The following database options affect your capability to perform transaction log backups on a database:

- **The trunc. log on chkpt. option.** If the `trunc. log on chkpt.` option is set on a database, SQL Server performs the equivalent of a `BACKUP TRANSACTION` with `TRUNCATE_ONLY` command when SQL Server's checkpoint handler or a user performs a checkpoint on the database. How often a checkpoint is performed on a database by the checkpoint handler depends on the SQL Server configuration parameter restore interval. If the `trunc. log on chkpt.` option is set, you get an error message if you attempt to perform a transaction log dump. If the `trunc. log on chkpt.` option is set, you must rely on full database dumps for backups. Use the `trunc. log on chkpt.` option in a development environment when you are not concerned about the potential loss of data.

- **The select into/bulkcopy option.** The `select into/bulkcopy` option enables you to perform operations, such as `select into` or `bulk copy`, using `BCP`. Operations such as `select into` and fast `BCP` are nonlogged operations (that is, the changes to the database are not logged in the transaction log). If a nonlogged operation is performed on a database, you cannot perform a transaction log backup on the database. To use the `BACKUP LOG` command, you must use the `BACKUP` command to back up the database with the nonlogged operations. After you have successfully performed a full database backup, you can then use the BACKUP LOG command until a nonlogged operation is performed in the database.

USING DATABASE COMPLETE BACKUPS AND TRANSACTION LOG BACKUPS TO RESTORE A DATABASE

Before you learn how to create a backup database schedule, it is important to understand how to use database backups and transaction log backups to restore a database with up-to-the millisecond information. Let's walk through a database restore using the following example (see Figure 10.15).

FIGURE 10.15

An example of database and transaction log backups.

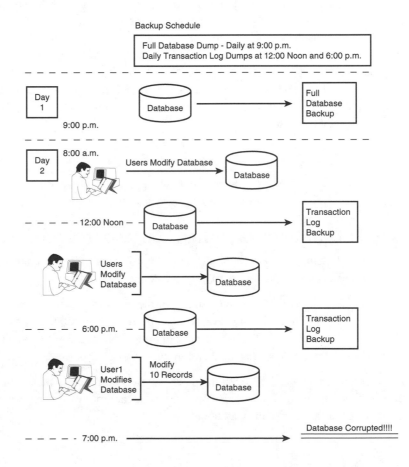

> **TIP**
>
> For those of you familiar with SQL Server 6.x backups and restore procedures, I highly recommend that you read the next section. Although the database backup and failure will sound very familiar, the restore process and error tracking are quite different!

Using the example in Figure 10.15, the backup schedule for a database is as follows:

- Full database backup performed daily at 9:00 p.m.
- Transaction log backups performed daily at 12:00 (noon) and 6:00 p.m.

The backup schedule was set up this way because the majority of the people working on the database go to lunch at noon and go home for the evening before 6:00 p.m., so the backups occur during nonpeak hours. Of course, this not a requirement. SQL Server 7.0 can perform database backups and transaction log backups while people are working with the database. SQL Server 7.0 backups are more efficient than 6.x. Therefore, the performance hit of backups is not as great as it is with 6.x. The two incremental backups and the daily full database backups meet the user's restore needs. Follow through Figure 10.15 starting with Day 1.

Day 1: Full Database Backup Occurs

Day 1 is the starting point for this example. All you are concerned about is that at 9:00 p.m. on Day 1, SQL Server successfully performs a full database backup.

Day 2: Database Modified, Database Corrupted

Between 8:00 a.m. and 11:59 a.m., the database users log on to the database and make minor modifications and changes to the data stored in the database.

Between 12:00 noon and 12:59 p.m., many of the database users are at lunch, although some continue to work. The SQL Agent kicks off the scheduled transaction log backup. The transaction log of the database is backed up to a backup device, saving all the changes made to the data since the last full backup at 9:00 p.m. the previous evening.

Between 1:00 p.m. and 5:59 p.m., the database users continue to make minor modifications to the data in the database. By 6:00 p.m., the majority of the users have logged off the database and are on their way home.

Between 6:00 p.m. and 6:59 p.m., the SQL Agent starts the evening transaction log backup, saving all the committed transactions made to the database before the previous transaction log backup at noon. Shortly after the transaction log backup completes, User 1 modifies ten records on the database.

At 7:00 p.m., the database becomes corrupted and users are no longer able to access the database. The DBA is called in to remedy the problem. Now what?

Using the Backups to Restore the Database

Later in this chapter, the commands and detailed requirements to restore a corrupted database are discussed in detail. But the basic restore process of using a complete database backup and transaction logs is part of this example. So getting back to the example, the database has become corrupted, where do you start the restore process?

Problem Resolution

The first thing to do is to evaluate the situation. What is wrong with database? Well, there are a couple things you should do to try and determine what is wrong with the database. A good starting point is to look at the error log and see what types of error messages appear when SQL Server tries to activate the database during startup or when users actually began to get database error messages. After you have viewed the error log and evaluated the situation, if any error numbers are displayed, you can search for the error number on SQL Server Books Online for possible resolution. You can also use a new SQL Server 7.0 function called `databaseproperty`. The `databseproperty` function returns `True` (1) or `False` (0) about a database and particular database property. For example, one such property is `IsShutDown`, which is set if SQL Server is unable to open a database's files during startup. To check if the `IsShutDown` status has been set on a database called Finance you would enter the following in a query window:

```
Select databaseproperty('Finance','IsShutDown')
```

If a 1 is returned, the database is in Shutdown mode and the problem can be resolved by fixing the database files and log files and then restarting the computer. Some of the property names are as follows:

- `IsEmergencyMode`
- `IsShutDown`
- `IsSuspect`
- `IsInLoad`
- `IsInRecovery`

10

For a complete list of possible properties with the `databaseproperty` function, look up the `databaseproperty` function on SQL Server Books Online. Now back to the example.

Using the Backups to Restore the Database

After evaluating the situation, it is determined that the database is unable to load because the disk drive the secondary data file is located on has burned up. You have the drive swapped out and replace it with a new drive. Now it's time to begin the restore process.

Because the log file and primary data file is intact, the first thing to do is to back up the transaction log with the `NO_TRUNCATE` option to restore the modifications made by user 1 after the last transaction log backup was performed. Unlike previous versions of SQL Server, you do not need to delete the log and data files. If the database is marked suspect, use the `DROP DATABASE` command. The syntax for the `DROP DATABASE` command is as follows:

```
DROP DATABASE dbname[,dbname1,dbname2,...,N]
```

For example, to drop the database Finance, enter the following:

```
DROP DATABASE Finance
```

> **NOTE**
>
> The `DROP DATABASE` command works differently in SQL Server 7.0 than in previous versions. `DROP DATABASE` can be used to remove a database that is marked suspect (or anything else except `OFFLINE`). The `DROP DATABASE` command in SQL Server 7.0 also removes the files used to create the database (three cheers!!!!).

For this example, you do not need to drop the database, so it's time to start restoring the database from your backups. To re-create the database, you must load a full database backup. So you load the database backup performed on Day 1 at 9:00 p.m. The database now exists in the exact same state as the corrupted database on Day 1 at 9:00 p.m. How do you get back the work that was done on Day 2? =. You use the incremental database backups (that is, the transaction log backups).

Transaction log backups are sequenced and must be loaded in the correct order. You load the first transaction log backup that was made at 12:00 noon on Day 2. Loading a transaction log (also referred to as *applying the transaction log*) causes the transactions in the transaction log to re-execute. When the transaction log has completed, the database is now in the exact state the database was in as of 12:00 noon on Day 2.

To regain the 12:00 noon until 6:00 p.m. transactions, you load the second transaction log backup performed at 6:00 p.m. on Day 2. After the second transaction log successfully loads, the database is in the same state as the original database at 6:00 p.m. on Day 2. But what about the ten records modified by User 1 after the transaction log backup completed but before the database was corrupted? If the database and transaction log were on the same device or you forgot to run the BACKUP LOG with NO_TRUNCATE command, those modified records are lost because you do not have a transaction log backup or a full database backup with the modifications in them. User 1 would have to manually go back and update the records. However, because you had the database and transaction log on separate devices and you executed the BACKUP LOG with the NO_TRUNCATE command, you load the transaction log backup produced by the NO_TRUNCATE backup command. The database is back in the same state (including the ten modified records) as the original database just before it became corrupted. You now know how transaction logs and database backups are used to restore a database.

Restore Example—Reality Check

In the previous example, the database backup and transaction log backups were loaded one at a time and in the exact order from oldest to newest. Obviously, this would be a lot of work in a production environment with a weekly full database backup and transaction logs backed up every half-hour. Don't worry. The step-by-step process used in the previous example was done to help you understand the relationships between complete backups and transaction log backups in the database restore process. In the real world, if you are using the SQL Enterprise Manager, you would only have to perform the restore operation once. SQL Server would then automatically apply all of the transaction logs associated with the complete database backup; this is demonstrated in the next section.

Using Differential Backups to Speed Up the Restore Time

The previous example of a database backup and restore scenario followed the SQL Server 6.5 pattern of full database backups with transaction log backups as the incremental backups. You can speed up your restore time by using full database backups, differential backups, and transaction log backups. Using the new SQL Server 7.0 backup capabilities, you would plan your full backups on a regular basis, maybe weekly, every three days, and so on. You would then plan differential backups in between (for example, daily). Transaction log backups would then be performed frequently (based on your requirements) just as they are in the SQL Server 6.5 backup and restore scenario. The difference is that the transaction log backups would be associated with the differential backups performed. Instead of three days worth of transactions logs being applied during

10

the restore process (if the log was backed up hourly, it would around 72 logs), you have at most a single day's worth of transaction logs.

PERFORMING A DATABASE RESTORE

In the previous section, you learned how to use database backups and transaction logs to get up to the point of disaster restore. This section covers the necessary steps and commands to restore a SQL Server database using SQL Server backups.

> **NOTE**
>
> The database being restored cannot be in use while you are trying to restore it.

To restore a corrupted, suspect, damaged, missing, or moving database, perform the following:

1. From the SQL Enterprise Manager, select Tools and then select Restore Database. The Restore Database dialog box appears (see Figure 10.16).

FIGURE 10.16

The Restore Database Backup dialog box— General tab.

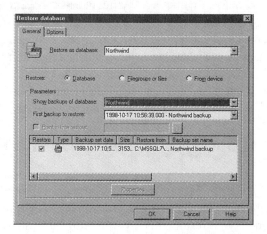

2. Use the Restore as Database combo box to select the database to restore to

3. To select the type of database backup to perform, select the appropriate backup type radio button in the Restore group shown in Figure 10.16.

4. In the Parameters frame, shown in Figure 10.16, select Point In Time Restore to select a particular point and time on the select backup to halt the restore process. Point In Time Restore is useful for situations when a user might have executed a

SQL command that wipes out lots of data and you need to restore to the time prior to them executing the command. To display recent backups of the database, use the Show Backups of Database drop-down combo box to select a database. If backups have been performed on the selected database, backup history is displayed in the grid at the bottom of the dialog box shown in Figure 10.16. If more than one complete backup has been performed on the selected database, use the First Backup to Restore combo box to select the proper backup. The default is the Most Recent Backup. The grid shown in Figure 10.16, displays the type of backups (Complete, Differential, Transaction Logs) associated with the backup selected in the combo box. Each database backup type is reflected with a different icon, and differential database backups and transaction log backups have a line that connects them with their associated complete database backup. To select the backups to load, check the Restore check box in the grid.

5. To set additional restore options click the Options tab, shown in Figure 10.17.

FIGURE 10.17

The Restore Database Backup dialog box— Options tab.

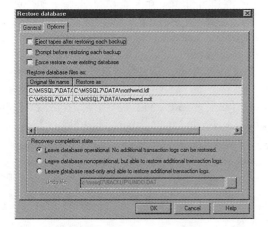

6. The Options tab enables you to set the following options:

Eject Tapes After Restoring Each Backup: Automatically ejects the tape from the tape drive when the selected backup completes.

Prompt Before Restoring Each Backup: Select this option to have SQL Server prompt you after a backup is successfully loaded and prior to loading the next backup. For example, if you select to load a complete database backup, a differential database backup, and a transaction log backup, you receive a prompt after the full backup completes and after the differential backup completes. You can press Cancel at any of the prompts to halt the restore.

10

Force Restore over Existing Database: Automatically writes over the existing database files when selected.

Restore Database Files as: The grid shown in Figure 10.17 shows the backup file physical name in the *Backup Physical Name* column. You can change the path and location of the file during the restore process by editing the *Restore As* column shown in the grid.

Recovery Completion State Frame: Contains several options that enable you to leave the database in certain states after the restore process completes. The default, *Leave Database Operational*, completes the entire restore process, including applying any transactions in the transaction logs loaded and rolling back all incomplete transactions. With this option selected, the restore is complete, and the database is ready for use. The Leave Database Non-operational, But Able To Restore Additional Transaction Logs option leaves the database in an unusable state and does not process transactions logs loaded. Use this option when you are restoring a database and are unable to load all the logs at once or with the database backup. In this scenario, when the last transaction log is loaded, check the Leave Databases Operational option. The Leave Database Read-Only and Able To Restore Additional Transaction Logs option is used for standby servers. It can also be used to enable you to check the status of a database. For example, suppose a user deleted or changed some records but is not exactly sure at what time. You could query after each transaction log loads and find out when the problem occurred and then restore the database again and not apply the last log.

7. After you have selected the backup and set any options, click the OK button shown in Figure 10.17 to restore the database. A Completion dialog box is displayed when the database is successfully restored.

The Transact-SQL command used to restore a database, the RESTORE command, has the following format for a database:

```
RESTORE DATABASE {database_name ¦ @database_name_var}
[FROM <backup_device> [, ... n]]
[WITH
[DBO_ONLY]
[[,] FILE = file_number]
[[,] MEDIANAME = {media_name ¦ @media_name_variable}]
[[,] MOVE 'logical_file_name' TO 'operating_system_file_name']
[,...p]
[[,] {NORECOVERY¦ RECOVERY ¦ STANDBY = undo_file_name}]
[[,] {NOUNLOAD ¦ UNLOAD}]
[[,] REPLACE]
[[,] RESTART]
[[,] STATS [= percentage]]]
```

To restore a transaction log, use the following Transact-SQL:

```
RESTORE LOG {database_name ¦ @database_name_var}
[FROM <backup_device> [, ...n]]
[WITH
[DBO_ONLY]
[[,] FILE = file_number]
[[,] MEDIANAME = {media_name ¦ @media_name_variable}]
[[,] {NORECOVERY ¦ RECOVERY ¦ STANDBY = undo_file_name}]
[[,] {NOUNLOAD ¦ UNLOAD}]
[[,] RESTART]
[[,] STATS [= percentage]]
[[,] STOPAT = {date_time ¦ @date_time_var}]]
```

To restore a file/filegroup, use the following Transact-SQL:

```
RESTORE DATABASE {database_name ¦ @database_name_var}
<file_or_filegroup> [, ...m]
[FROM <backup_device> [, ...n]]
[WITH
[DBO_ONLY]
[[,] FILE = file_number]
[[,] MEDIANAME = {media_name ¦ @media_name_variable}]
[[,] NORECOVERY]
[[,] {NOUNLOAD ¦ UNLOAD}]
[[,] REPLACE]
[[,] RESTART]
[[,] STATS [= percentage]]]
```

RESTORING THE master DATABASE

You have probably guessed by now that the master database is definitely not just another database and is required to allow SQL Server to execute. Restoring the master database can be performed one of two ways. If you are able to start SQL Server and you find out that the master database is damaged, you can restore the database from a previous back-up just like you would with a regular user database. If you have performed any operations that made modifications to the master database after the backup was performed; you might have to perform the operations again, for example in the case of adding or deleting logins. If you have added a database since the backup was made, you can attach the database files or load from a backup.

If SQL Server does not start, you need to execute the Rebuild Master Utility to restore the master database.

10

> **NOTE**
>
> The procedure to restore the master database has steadily improved over the last few releases. The SQL Server 7.0 version has greatly simplified the process.

To rebuild the master database, use the Rebuild Master Database Utility, rebuildm.EXE located in the BINN directory of the SQL Server 7.0-root directory (see Figure 10.18). To rebuild the master database, perform the following steps:

1. Before you can execute the Rebuild Master Utility, you must shut down SQL Server. Use the SQL Service Manager to shut down SQL Server.

2. Execute the rebuildm.EXE located in the BINN directory of the SQL Server 7.0 root directory.

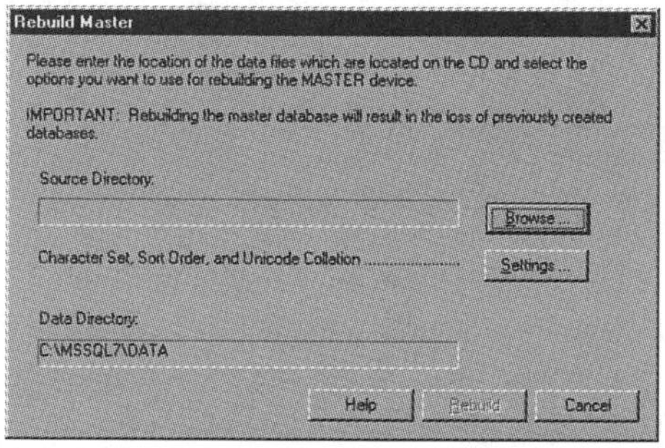

FIGURE 10.18

The Rebuild Master Database Utility.

3. Use the Browse button to select the source directory from which SQL Server was installed. The source directory is the DATA directory on the SQL Server CD or a network path for network installations.

4. Click the Settings button, shown in Figure 10.18, to modify the character set, sort order, and unicode collation.

5. Click the Restore button to rebuild the master database.

After you have rebuilt the master database, you need to load your most recent backup of the master database. If all the other databases are still available and are not lost or damaged due to drive failure, then you will be up and running. If you lost other databases, you need to restore them from backups. If you added databases since you made your current backup, you can perform an SQL Server 7.0 function that reattaches the files to re-create the database.

Reattaching Database Files

SQL Server 7.0 enables you to detach the database data and log files from a server and reattach them to the same server or another server. When database files are detached, the database is dropped from the SQL Server, but the files themselves remain intact, enabling you to move them to another machine or reattach them on the same server later. This is an awesome feature that makes moving databases or rebuilding the master database less traumatic than it previously was and saves time in both processes. To detach a database, issue the following Transact-SQL command:

```
sp_detach_db [@dbname =] 'dbname'
[, [@skipchecks =] 'skipchecks']
```

Where dbname is the database name and skipchecks, when set to True, performs and updates statistics on all of the tables in the database before reattaching the files. For example

```
sp_detach_db TestRestore, True
```

To reattach the database using Transact-SQL, use the following command:

```
sp_attach_db [@dbname =] 'dbname',
[@filename1 = ] 'filename1'
[[, ...@filename16 = ] 'filename']
```

The following example reattaches the database TestRestore:

```
sp_attach_db TestRestore,'e:\MSSQL7\data\testrestore_data.mdf',
➥'e:\\MSSQL7\data\testrestore_log.ldf'
```

INTERACTIVE EXAMPLE OF LOSING AND RESTORING A DATABASE

Database backup and restore are the most important tasks performed by a DBA. As such, it is important to be prepared for the day that you must perform your first real-world backup and restore procedure to restore critical user data. To help you along, walk through an actual backup and restore of a database. This exercise is similar to the restore process described in the previous section and simulates an actual backup and restore that you might perform some day!

10

BACKUP AND RESTORE

> **CAUTION**
>
> The following exercise is one I have been doing for several years in various DBA workshops and training sessions performed at Keiter, Stephens Computer Services, Inc. The exercise is meant to be interactive so it requires access to SQL Server. Parts of the exercise require shutting down SQL Server and deleting a file. *DO NOT PERFORM THIS EXERCISE ON A PRODUCTION SQL SERVER.* Your best bet is to perform this exercise on your workstation (Windows 9x or NT Workstation) using your own personal copy of SQL Server. Shutting down a production server and deleting files can cost you your job as well as cause your company to lose valuable information! *DO NOT PERFORM THIS EXERCISE ON A SQL SERVER WITH USERS OR INFORMATION BEING USED BY YOU OR OTHERS.*

This exercise is designed to help you understand how to properly perform a SQL Server backup/restore and the relationship of database backups with transaction log backups during the restore process. For this exercise, you will perform the following:

1. Create a database.
2. Create a table.
3. Create a backup device.
4. Add rows to the table (perform transactions).
5. Back up the database.
6. Add more rows to the table.
7. Back up the transaction log.
8. Add more rows to the table.
9. Shut down SQL Server.
10. Delete the database data file.
11. Restart SQL Server.
12. Restore and test the database.

Start the Enterprise Manager, bring up a query window and perform the following:

Step 1: Create a Database

Bring up a SQL Server Query Analyzer by selecting Tools and SQL Server Query Analyzer from the SQL Enterprise Manager. In the query window enter the following text:

```
Create Database TestRestore
go
sp_dboption 'TestRestore','trunc. log on chkpt.',false
```

Press CTRL+E to execute the script. You have now created a database called TestRestore. The files used by the database are located in the SQL Server default directory. The standard default directory is drive:\MSSQL7\DATA. To set up the database to be able to perform point of failure transaction log recovery, we need to add a new filegroup to create user tables. The primary filegroup will store the system tables and in the real world would be on a separate hard drive than the user table filegroup. Using the query analyzer, enter the following (Note: the filename parameter should reflect your setup, which may differ):

```
ALTER DATABASE TestRestore
ADD FILEGROUP tableseg
GO
ALTER DATABASE TestRestore
ADD FILE
( NAME = 'removeme',
  FILENAME = 'c:\mssql7\data\removeme.mdf',
  SIZE = 1MB,
  MAXSIZE = 10MB,
  FILEGROWTH = 5MB)
TO FILEGROUP tableseg
go
ALTER DATABASE TestRestore
MODIFY FILEGROUP tableseg DEFAULT
GO
```

Also, if using the SQL Server Query Analyzer, select Refresh from the database combo drop-down box to refresh the list of databases. If using the SQL Enterprise Manager, perform a refresh by right-clicking the databases folder and selecting Refresh to show the new database you created.

Step 2: Create a Table

Create a table called *test* that will be used to check the success of your restore process. Change the current database in the SQL Server Query Analyzer window by selecting TestRestore in the database combo box. Enter the following syntax in the Query Analyzer window and press CTRL+E to execute the script.

```
create table test(id int NOT NULL,
   date_entered datetime NOT NULL)
```

10

Step 3: Create a Backup Device

Add a backup device to back up the TestRestore database. The backup device will be named TestRestore_BackUp.

> **NOTE**
>
> Make sure the selected database in the combo box in the Query Analyzer window is TestRestore through Step 8.

Enter the following syntax in the Query Analyzer window, and press CTRL+E to execute the script. Note: For the third parameter, use the root directory of your SQL Server installation with a file name of TstRBack.dat

```
sp_addumpdevice 'disk','TestRestore_Backup','C:\MSSQL7\BACKUP\
➡TstRBack.dat'
```

Step 4: Add Rows to the Table

In this step, you add several rows into the Test table. Each row will be sequentially numbered and date and time stamped so that you can validate the information after the restore process is completed. Enter the following syntax in the Query Analyzer window and press CTRL+E to execute the script.

```
Insert Test
Values(1,getdate())
Insert Test
Values(2,getdate())
Insert Test
Values(3,getdate())
Insert Test
Values(4,getdate())
```

To verify that the information is in the table, execute the following SQL statement in the Query Analyzer window:

```
Select * from test
```

The query should return information similar to Listing 10.1. However, the dates returned will be different. (They will reflect the date and time the Insert statements were executed.)

LISTING 10.1 TEST TABLE QUERY RESULTS

```
id          date_entered
----------- ------------------------
1           1998-07-13 21:10:41.487
2           1998-07-13 21:10:41.520
3           1998-07-13 21:10:41.520
4           1998-07-13 21:10:41.523
```

Step 5: Back Up the `TestRestore` Database

Back up the database TestRestore to the backup device `TestRestore_Backup`. To back up the database, use the Enterprise Manager, the Backup Database Wizard described earlier in the chapter, or execute the following command with the Query Analyzer:

```
backup database TestRestore to TestRestore_Backup
```

Step 6: Add More Rows to the Table

Insert two more rows in the table test by executing the following script in the Query Analyzer window:

```
Insert Test
Values(5,getdate())
Insert Test
Values(6,getdate())
```

Step 7: Back Up the Transaction Log

Back up the TestRestore transaction log to the backup device `TestRestore_Backup`. To back up the transaction log, use the Enterprise Manager, the Backup Database Wizard described earlier in the chapter, or execute the following command with the Query Analyzer:

```
BACKUP LOG TestRestore to TestRestore_Backup
```

Step 8: Add More Rows to the Table

Insert two more rows in the table test by executing the following script in the Query Analyzer window:

```
Insert Test
Values(7,getdate())
Insert Test
Values(8,getdate())
```

10

BACKUP AND RESTORE

Checkpoint: Back Up Part of Exercise Completed

You have now completed the first part of the exercise! So, recap what you have accomplished so far and what will be accomplished in the remaining steps. First, you created a new database called TestRestore. You created a filegroup to store user tables and added a single table called Test. You inserted four rows of data into to the table, IDs 1-4 and backed them up using a SQL Server full database backup. You then inserted two rows with IDs 5 and 6 and performed a transaction log backup to back them up. Finally, two additional rows were inserted, IDs 7 and 8, and not backed up. So what we have created is a scenario found frequently in the real world. The DBA has a database backup and one or more transaction log backups and users have added information since the last transaction log backup was performed. Now take this one step further, by causing a media failure and then using the backups to restore the database.

Step 9: Shut Down SQL Server

Using the SQL Service Manager, click the red light to stop SQL Server. Make sure that others are not using the Server!

CAUTION

This step requires you to delete a database file. Make sure that you delete the proper file. *DO NOT PERFORM THIS EXERCISE ON A PRODUCTION SQL SERVER.* Your best bet is to perform this exercise on your workstation (Windows 9x or NT Workstation) using your own personal copy of SQL Server. Deleting the wrong file can cost you your job as well as cause your company to lose valuable information! *DO NOT PERFORM THIS EXERCISE ON A SQL SERVER WITH USERS OR INFORMATION BEING USED BY YOU OR OTHERS.*

Step 10: Delete the Database Data File

Delete the secondary data file for the TestRestore database, removeme.mdf. The data file is located off of the SQL Server root directory in the subdirectory data.

Step 11: Restart SQL Server

Using the SQL Service Manager, click the green light to start SQL Server. Log on to SQL Server using the Enterprise Manager.

Step 12: Restore the Database TestRestore

Of course, you know that the database TestRestore has a problem; after all, you deleted the data file! However, look at some of the different SQL Server facilities available to you to detect a problem with a database. First, if the database status is unknown or suspect, it appears gray in the database folder of the SQL Server Enterprise Manager. View the current error log; notice that several error messages exist when SQL Server tries to open the TestRestore database. Try the following databaseproperty function in a query window:

```
Select databaseproperty('TestRestore','IsShutDown')
```

The function returns a 1, indicating that database is in a Shutdown mode, which means that the database had problems during startup.

Now begin the restore process.

12-a Restore Transactions in the Transaction Log

When you are having problems with a database and the transaction log is intact, you don't have Truncate Log on Checkpoint set, and have not performed any unlogged operations, the first thing you should do is back up the completed transactions in the transaction log. In this example, backing up the transactions in the log since the last backup gives us rows seven and eight that were added after the last transaction log backup. To back up completed transactions in the log, enter the following:

```
BACKUP LOG TestRestore
to TestRestore_Backup
With NO_TRUNCATE
```

12-b1 Restore the Database and Transaction Logs

Use the Enterprise Manager to restore the database (for detailed steps see the Database Restore Section earlier in this chapter). Select the TestRestore database in the Database combo box on the General tab of the Restore Database dialog box. Select the Restore Database radio button on the General tab of the Restore Database dialog box. Go the Options tab of the Restore Database dialog box and check the Force Restore Over Existing Database option; this will overwrite the exiting transaction log file. Click the OK button to restore the database and transaction logs. From a query window, execute the following SQL statement in the TestRestore database:

```
Select * from Test
```

Rows one through eight appear. Congratulations, you have successfully restored a database!

10

12-b2 Restore Database and Transaction Logs: Option 2

This option is more academic than real-world. In this option, you restore the database first without the transactions logs by unchecking the Transaction Logs Restore check boxes in the list of recent backups on the General tab of the Restore Database dialog box. Execute the following query:

```
Select * from Test
```

This validates that rows one through four appear. You then restore each transaction log (the database is automatically selected each time), one at a time. Note that in order to do this you must specify the Leave Database Read-Only and Able To Restore Additional Transactions Logs option. Also, when using the SQL Enterprise Manager, you are forced to include the full backup when loading the transaction logs (as well as previous logs). After doing the first log, execute the `Select * from Test` query and rows one through six appear. When you select the final transaction log (a full restore) rows one through eight appear. Selecting one at a time and then viewing the information after each restore helps many beginners understand the relationship between database backups and transaction log backups.

CREATING A BACKUP SCHEDULE

You know *how* to schedule backups of transaction logs and databases, but *when* should you back them up? To answer that question, you are going to create two separate categories: Category 1 consists of actions performed in a database that warrant an immediate database backup. Category 2 consists of scheduling backups that meet your restore needs.

Category 1: Actions That Warrant Dumping a Database

In general, you are aware that you should perform database backups on a timely schedule. Backups should also be performed after certain actions occur in a database to ensure full and easy restores.

User Databases

After you perform certain actions on a user database, you should back up the database as soon as possible to guarantee the restore of your changes. For example, perform a database backup in the following cases:

- After the database is created.
- After performing nonlogged operations such as fast BCP, SELECT INTO, or BACKUP LOG with NO_LOG or TRUNCATE_ONLY.

- After you make substantial database modifications (new triggers, stored procedures, tables, and so on).
- After you create a large index (doing so can speed up the restore process because SQL Server does not have to rebuild the index during restore).

The `master` Database

Of course, the `master` database has its own set of rules for when it should be backed up. Remember that keeping a healthy `master` database is a high priority. Therefore, backing up the `master` database regularly is a must. The `master` database should be backed up when changes are made to system tables. A list of the commands that modify the system tables can be found in the SQL Server documentation. Here is a short list of some of those commands:

- `ALTER DATABASE`
- `CREATE DATABASE`
- `sp_addlogin`
- `sp_droplogin`

Because many of you use the SQL Enterprise Manager to perform your database administrative tasks, you might be unaware of the SQL Server commands and system stored procedures being executed. In SQL Enterprise Manager lingo, back up the `master` database after you have done the following:

- Added/removed databases
- Altered the size of a database
- Added system login IDs
- Modified system configuration parameters

msdb

Because the msdb database stores all of the information about jobs and schedules, you should back up the database after creating jobs or schedules to prevent having to re-create them in the event of a lost database.

Category 2: Scheduled Database Backups

Unfortunately, there is no exact formula to tell you when you should back up your databases. Why? Because each database has its own backup requirements. For example, in the backup and restore example you stepped through earlier in this chapter, transaction log backups were performed twice a day. In the example, it was acceptable to lose a half a day's work if the example SQL Server suddenly lost the databases transaction log.

10

Many organizations cannot afford to lose any data and require up-to-the point of disaster restore.

As another example, maybe you are in a development environment in which a bimonthly database backup is all that is required.

Your backup strategy should enable you to restore any of your databases within an acceptable amount of time and for an acceptable data loss limit for each database. Before further discussion of backup strategies, remember that it is just as important to perform routine database and table maintenance as it is to properly back up your databases. (Database maintenance plans are discussed in more detail in Chapter 29, "Developing a SQL Server Maintenance Plan.")

In general, you can find more information on setting up appropriate backup schedules in the documentation that ships with SQL Server or the white papers found on Microsoft's Web site. Review a few questions and suggestions you can use to help you setup a proper backup plan.

> **NOTE**
>
> In my opinion, a backup plan and a restore plan are the same. To test and verify your backup plan, you must use the database backups to restore your SQL Server databases; thus, the two go hand in hand.

System Databases

Having up-to-date, valid database backups can save you a lot of time, especially if you need to restore a system database (such as the `master` database). You need to back up the model database only if and when you make changes to it. Take special care with the `master` database; consider mirroring the `master` device for added protection. It is recommended that you back up the following system databases (at the minimum) daily:

- `master`
- `msdb`
- `model`
- distribution database (for distribution replication servers)

How Often Should I Back Up the Transaction Log and Database?

If the database and the transaction log both became corrupted, how many transactions can you afford to lose? How many transactions are performed in an hour? A day? You must ask and answer these questions and more to determine how often you should dump the transaction log and database. Try to perform your database and transaction log dumps during nonpeak hours.

Also, keep in mind what is required to restore a database using full database dumps and transaction logs. For example, if you perform transaction log dumps (incremental backups) six times a day and a full database backup every five days, what do you have to do to restore the database? Depending on when the database became corrupted, you stand the possibility of having to load a full database backup and 0 to 30 transaction log dumps. Is this acceptable? Get the picture? If you have a database that is not updated very often, performing a biweekly transaction log dump and a weekly database dump might meet your requirements.

How Do I Manage the Backups?

How are you going to manage the various database and transaction log dumps on tapes or dump files and how long are you going to keep your backups? Believe me, this is a problem in organizations with several databases. Organization is the key here. Come up with consistent naming conventions and a filing system for your backups. You will want to keep old backups around for several weeks or months. Organization makes it easy to find dumps that are several weeks or months old.

How Long Will It Take to Restore the Database?

If your database becomes corrupted, how long will it take to restore the database? Is the restore time acceptable? If you find that the restore time is not acceptable, you might have to consider hot backups. A *hot backup* is a term given to a system that uses specialized hardware to mirror the main database server; the hot backup can be used immediately if the main database server goes down. SQL Server 7.0 provides a mechanism to support fallback restore when two computers share the same hard drive. If one computer fails, the other computer takes over. The bottom line is that by using a hot backup or fallback restore configuration, you decrease the chance of experiencing downtime. SQL Server also allows you to create standby servers; see the FAQ at the end of this chapter.

In What Other Ways Is the Database Protected?

It never hurts to have more than one level of data protection for very sensitive data. For example, is the database on a device that is mirrored or resides on a RAID 5 drive configuration? It's always a good idea to mirror you transaction logs and master database. Is

10

the SQL Server shut down weekly and are the SQL Server directory and database devices backed up to tape by a system administrator? Always know what other restore options are available to you, just in case your well-constructed backup and restore plan fails.

BACKUP AND RESTORE FAQ

Q. Can I load a 6.x database backup into SQL Server 7.0?

A. You cannot load SQL Server 6.x databases using backup and restore. You must use the SQL Server 7.0 upgrade utility.

Q. Can I create my databases to be more fault tolerant?

A. For starters, you should always create a secondary filegroup for your database to put user objects and data on. Use the primary filegroup for the system tables (automatically placed there at the time of database creation). Also, do not put the primary data filegroup on the same drive system as the secondary filegroup; this will allow you better recovery options if media failure occurs. If possible, mirror your transaction logs and primary data files (again no user objects should be on the primary data file). Use disk storage like RAID 5 or RAID 10 that has built-in redundancy.

Q. What are nonlogged operations?

A. Nonlogged operations are operations that do not write to the transaction log and prevent you from backing up or using a transaction log backup. Nonlogged operations are as follows:

Bulk Load Operations

Select INTO

UPDATETEXT

WRITETEXT

Q. I have a single tape drive and I need to back up SQL Server and the NT box using an automated process. How can I do this?

A. Without purchasing a third-party product that backs up both SQL Server and Windows NT, you can back up a database to a disk file backup device and then copy the backup device to tape, just like a regular NT file. When you need to restore the database, copy the file from tape back to disk and then use SQL Server Enterprise Manager to restore the database.

Q. How can I move a database?

A. You can use database backups to move a database or you can copy and reattach the files that make up the database. Make sure that the two servers share the same character set, sort order, and Unicode locale.

Q. How can I see what's on a backup device (disk or tape)?

A. You can graphically view what backups are on a current backup device by double-clicking the backup device in the Enterprise Manager and then clicking the View Contents button on the Backup Device Properties page. You can also use the Transact-SQL command RESTORE HEADERONLY and specify the backup device you want to view.

Q. Can I load a backup from an Alpha machine to an Intel machine (different processors)?

A. Yes! With a SQL Server 7.0 database backup, you can load databases from an Intel processor machine to an Alpha machine assuming they meet the standard requirements of moving databases (same sort order, character set, Unicode collation and locale.)

Q. Can I create a standby server using SQL Server backup and restore?

A. Creating a standby server using backup and restore is simple. On the standby server load, use full database backups with the RESTORE STANDBY clause. Load transaction logs from the primary server to the standby server using the RESTORE STANDBY clause. If the primary server fails, use the BACKUP LOG with the NO_TRUNCATE clause on the primary server database. Load the transaction log on the standby server with the RESTORE STANDBY clause. Then execute the RESTORE DATABASE with the RECOVERY clause. The standby server can be used in read-only mode whereas the primary server is fully functional, and of course, you have to keep the standby server up-to-date with backups from the primary server.

Q. What's the best advice you can give a new DBA for backup and restore?

A. After you have created a backup plan, don't stop there. Test your backup plan by actually restoring the databases. When you are done testing, test your restore plan again. When the day comes and a database fails, you should feel very comfortable and confident in your ability to restore the database. The bottom line is: test and practice your backup and restore plans. With SQL Server 7.0 running on Windows 9x as well as NT Server, you should have no problem finding a machine to practice on.

SUMMARY

Maintaining a good set of database backups and knowing how to use them to recover a database is one of the most important responsibilities of a DBA. Use the ideas and suggestions in this chapter to help build your own backup and recovery plan.

- Database backups can be complete backups, which are full backups of the data and database objects, or differential database backups, which are just the data that has changed.

- Transaction log dumps are incremental backups that reflect the changes in the database since the previous transaction log backup or database backup.

- Users can still use the database during backups.

- Use the header information on backup devices or the Enterprise Manager to display important information about the currently stored backups.

- You can append backups to disk backup devices as well as tape backup devices.

- Review the section in this chapter about the BACKUP LOG options: TRUNCATE_ONLY, NO_LOG, and NO_TRUNCATE.

- To decrease the amount of time required for database backups, use a media set with multiple devices.

- Backups can be reliably and easily scheduled from the SQL Enterprise Manager.

- Create a backup and restore plan to protect your databases. Make sure that you test and practice the plan.

- Use filegroups for data storage. The primary filegroup should contain the system tables. Create a secondary filegroup and make it the default filegroup for the database to store use objects and data (tables, stored procedures, and so forth).

- Back up the master database daily.

USING BCP

by Orryn Sledge

IN THIS CHAPTER

You can use various methods to import and export SQL Server data. Almost all systems require some type of data transfer. BCP is the utility provided by SQL Server to transfer data. BULK INSERT is new with version 7.0. It provides an import-only Transact-SQL statement that is the fastest way to load data into SQL Server. This chapter discusses in detail the BCP utility and provides an overview of the BULK INSERT statement.

IMPORTANT NOTE

With version 7.0, you no longer have to use BCP to import and export SQL Server data. Version 7.0 provides Data Transformation Services (DTS) that simplify the process of importing and exporting data.

I recommend using DTS for the majority of import and export operations associated with version 7.0 (see Chapter 32, "Using Data Transformation Services (DTS)," for more information). Features of DTS include a graphical interface, import and export support for a variety of data sources, and the ability to transform data via rules and scripts.

The main reasons to continue running BCP are as follows:

- Backwards compatibility
- Performance   BCP with its optimization hints enabled (TABLOCK, ORDER, and so on) runs faster than DTS.
- It's hard to teach an old dog new tricks; several DBAs (including myself) spent years mastering BCP's quirks and frustrating syntax!

You will find that BCP has not radically changed in version 7.0. However, several small changes to BCP improve its performance and functionality. To those DBAs already familiar with BCP, I recommend that you browse the remainder of the chapter for notes and tips on BCP version 7.0.

SQL SERVER 6.5 TO 7.0 QUICK REFERENCE

The following is a quick reference to the changes that occurred between SQL Server version 6.5 and 7.0.

What's New

- **New switches:** The following switches have been added to the BCP utility.

    queryout   Specifies a query as the data source. This option is used when exporting the output from a query.

    -w   Unicode export.

-N   Native export for noncharacter data and Unicode character export for character data, provides better performance than the -w option.

-6   Use 6.x default datatypes.

-C   Code page {ACP, OEM, RAW, <value>}.

-k   Keep null values.

-h   Load hints, such as {ORDER, ROWS_PER_BATCH, KILOBYTES_PER_BATCH, TABLOCK, CHECK_CONSTRAINTS}, are used to improve performance and/or enforce check constraints.

- **Improved performance:** Version 7.0 of BCP runs approximately 2 times faster than previous versions. Version 7.0 also supports parallel bulk loading of data. Parallel loading is accomplished by running several instances of BCP currently on multiple computers. Near linear scalability can be achieved through parallel loading of data.

- **Unicode support:** Version 7.0 of BCP provides Unicode support.

- **Query optimizer support:** The query optimizer is now an integral part of the BCP process. This reduces the need to run UPDATE STATISTICS after running BCP. Additionally, load hints work in conjunction with the query optimizer.

- **BULK INSERT:** This is a new Transact-SQL command that provides high speed loading of data from character, native, or Unicode files. BULK INSERT is the fastest way to load data into SQL Server. Its syntax is similar to BCP and it supports the same features found in BCP such as hints and parallel loading of data.

What's Gone

- **DB-Library support:** Version 7.0 of BCP no longer uses DB-Library to communicate with SQL Server. DB-Library has been replaced with OLE-DB and ODBC. This change means that datetime, smalldatetime, and money datatypes are treated differently than previous versions.

CAUTION

Be careful when using BCP to import data from 6.x to 7.0. In particular, if the table uses date (datetime or smalldatetime) or money datatypes you must use the -6 option or use the 6.x version of BCP. Version 7.0 of BCP uses ODBC, whereas previous versions used DB-Library. ODBC treats date and money datatypes differently than DB-Library.

continues

I also recommend reviewing any BCP export routines that were upgraded from 6.x to 7.0. Again, the date and money datatypes are formatted differently upon export. If left untouched, you will find date information will appear in the ODBC format (yyyy-mm-dd hh:mm:ss) which is significantly different than the DB-Library format (mmm dd yyyy hh:mm(AM/PM)). You will also find that money data appears in the ODBC format (no commas, and 4 digits after the decimal) which is also significantly different than the DB-Library format (commas and 2 digits after the decimal). Routines that read fixed-length exports will probably choke on the new format. To avoid the export problem, use the -6 option or use the 6.x version of BCP.

BCP

BCP stands for *Bulk Copy Program*. It is a tool SQL Server provides to import and export data. Data can be either *native mode* (SQL Server specific), *character mode* (ASCII text), or unicode. ASCII text data is commonly used to share data between SQL Server and other systems.

IS IT LOVE OR HATE?

As a DBA, you will probably have a love/hate relationship with BCP. BCP is limited in scope and lacks common file formats, but it does provide excellent performance.

For those new to SQL Server, the following list provides some insight into BCP. These are the reasons why I like BCP:

- **Performance**: BCP is one the fastest raw data loaders around. I have seen BCP turn in impressive performance numbers compared to other import/export products.
- **Minimal overhead**: Because BCP is command-line based, it requires a nominal amount of memory to run compared to today's memory-intensive GUI applications. This leaves memory for other tasks.

Now for the drawbacks of BCP. These are the reasons why I hate BCP:

- **Unforgiving syntax**: BCP's switches are case and order sensitive. This is because BCP's origins stem from Sybase and the UNIX world, where commands are case sensitive.

- **Minimal file support:** Basically, the choices are ASCII text, native SQL Server format, unicode, or nothing at all. Do not try to load an Excel spreadsheet or an Access database directly into SQL Server; it will never work. (*Note*: You can now use DTS to perform this function, see Chapter 32 for more information)

- **Inadequate error messages:** BCP's error messages are minimal and too generic. It would be nice if Microsoft would enhance BCP's error messages to be more informative and specific.

As you can see, BCP is far from perfect, but it does provide some valuable import/export functionality. With this in mind, the remainder of this chapter will provide you with some useful tips and tricks to make your life easier when you use BCP.

BCP SYNTAX

Use the following syntax to perform BCP operations:

```
bcp [[database_name.]owner.]table_name ¦ "query" {in ¦ out ¦ format ¦
queryout} datafile
[switch1 parameter1] [switch2]
...
[switch10 parameter10]
...
```

where the following are the parameters:

`database_name`	Name of the database being accessed.
	Database name is optional; if the database name is omitted, the user's default database is used.
`owner`	Owner of the table or view being accessed.
	Tip: Use the `..` symbol to specify ownership. The `..` syntax is more generic than specifying an owner (for example: `pubs..authors` instead of `pubs.dbo.authors`).
`table_name`	Name of the table or view being accessed.
	Tip: Use the `#` or `##` symbol to copy a temporary table.

query	SQL statement that generates a result set. Enclose the query within double quotation marks. `queryout` must also be specified.
in ¦ out ¦ format queryout	Direction of data transfer where `in` means import and `out` means export. `queryout` is used when exporting the output from a SQL query or stored procedure. `format` specifies the creation of a format file based on the `-n`, `-c`, `-w`, or `-6` switches. The format setting also requires the use of the `-f` switch.
datafile	The name of the data file for an import or the name of the file to be created during an export. A path can be included with this statement, such as c:\mssql\binn\authors.txt.
switch1, parameter1	Choose the switch and its parameter (if and so onone is required from Table 11.1.

TABLE 11.1 BCP SWITCHES AND THEIR PARAMETERS

Parameter	*Explanation*
-m *maxerrors*	Maximum number of errors that can occur before the BCP operation is terminated. Each failed insert counts as one error. Default value is 10.
-f *formatfile*	The name of the format file used to import or export data. A path can be included with this statement, such as c:\mssql\binn\authors.fmt.
-e *errfile*	The name of the error file to store BCP error messages and unsuccessfully transferred rows. A path can be included with this statement, such as c:\mssql\binn\authors.err.
	Tip: Error files are useful for pinpointing BCP errors during unattended operations such as nightly data imports.
-F *firstrow*	The number of the first row to copy.

Parameter	Explanation
-L *lastrow*	The number of the last row to copy.
	Tip: The -F and -L switches are useful when copying portions of data. For example, to export the first 1,000 records from a table, use the following syntax: -F 1 -L 1000.
-b *batchsize*	The number of rows transferred in a batch. The default setting is the number of rows in the data file.
	Tip: Microsoft recommends against using the -b option in conjunction with the -h "ROWS_PER_BATCH = *bb*" option.
-n	Native data mode. Native data is SQL Server specific. Native data mode does not prompt the user for field information.
-c	Character data mode. Character data (ASCII) can be transferred to and from SQL Server tables and other non-SQL Server products. Character mode does not prompt the user for field information. By default, fields are tab delimited and rows are newline delimited.
	Tip: Character data mode is usually easier to work with than native data mode.
-w	Unicode data mode is new with version 7.0.
-N	Native export for noncharacter data and unicode character export for character data provides better performance than the -w option.
-6	Uses 6.x default datatypes when working with character or native mode, new with version 7.0.
	Tip: Use this option when using BCP to import files generated from SQL Server 6.x. This switch is necessary when transferring date (datetime or smalldatetime) and money datatypes between 7.0 and previous versions of SQL Server.
-q	Uses quoted identifiers.
-C *code page*	Code page in use by the file being imported. Code page needs to be specified only if the file contains char, varchar, or text datatypes and the data contains values greater than 127 or less than 32. The following is a list of valid code pages.

continues

TABLE 11.1   CONTINUED

Parameter	Explanation
	ACP—ANSI/Microsoft Windows.
	OEM—Default code page.
	RAW—No conversion between code pages.
	`<value>`—Specific code page number, such as 850.
-t `field_term`	Field terminator. See Table 11.2 for BCP terminators.
-r `row_term`	Row terminator. See Table 11.2 for BCP terminators.
-i `inputfile`	File to redirect input. This switch is not generally used.
-o `outputfile`	File to redirect BCP output.
	Tip: Use the -o switch to log BCP output during unattended BCP operation. This creates a useful trail of BCP output that can be used to monitor and diagnose BCP performance and execution.
-a `packet_size`	The number of bytes contained in a network packet. The default value for Windows NT Server and Windows NT clients is 4096; the default value for MS-DOS clients is 512. Valid sizes are 512 to 65535 bytes.
	Tip: Depending on your network architecture, you might be able to improve BCP performance by increasing the packet size. Try setting the packet size between 4096 and 8192 bytes. Use the statistics returned by BCP (the clock time and rows per second) to help tailor this setting.
-E	Used when importing data into a table that contains an `identity` datatype and you want to populate the column with values from the data file. If this switch is omitted, SQL Server automatically populates the `identity` column and ignores the field's corresponding data values in the import file. The following example shows how the -E switch impacts data imports:

```
Sample table structure:
id int identity(1,1)
descr char(15)
Sample data file:
5    xxx
6    yyy
```

Parameter	Explanation
| | ```
7       zzz
BCP syntax WITHOUT the -E switch:
bcp sales..table2 in
table2.txt -c -U sa -P
Results:
id          descr
---------- ----------------------------
1           xxx
2           yyy
3           zzz
``` |

Notice the values in the id column. SQL Server populated the id column with an automatically incremented data value. It ignored the values 5,6,7 in the data file.

The following is BCP syntax with the -E switch:

```
bcp sales..table2 in
table2.txt -c -E -U sa -P
Results:
id          descr
---------- -------------
5           xxx
6           yyy
7           zzz
```

With the -E switch, the values in the text file were observed and SQL Server did *not* automatically generate a set of data values for the id column.

Tip: Use the -E switch to preserve data values when you are unloading and reloading data in a table that contains an identity datatype. Otherwise, SQL Server automatically populates the identity column with its own set of values.

Parameter	Explanation
-U *login_id*	SQL Server login ID.
-P *password*	SQL Server password. If the *password* is omitted, BCP prompts you for a password.

Note: If you are using integrated security or your SQL Server login does not have a password, BCP still prompts you for a password. To bypass BCP's prompt, use the -P switch without a password, as in the following example:

```
BCP pubs..authors in authors.txt -U sa -P
```

continues
```

TABLE 11.1   CONTINUED

Parameter	Explanation
-S *servername*	The name of the server that contains the database and table you are working with. The -S *servername* switch is required if you are using BCP from a remote client on a network.
-v	Displays the version of BCP in use.
-T	Uses a trusted connection to connect to SQL Server.
-k	Preserves null values found in the data file. If this switch is omitted, SQL Server will apply default values if they exist. This option is new with 7.0.

-h *load hints*	Notifies SQL Server to use hints to help improve import performance. The following is a list of valid hints:
	
	ORDER (*column_list*)where *column_list* = {*column* [ASC ¦ DESC] [,*n*]}—Use this option if your data is presorted and the sort column(s) match the clustered index in the corresponding table. By presorting the data, the clustered index can be updated more quickly.
	
	ROWS_PER_BATCH = *value*, number of rows per batch. Higher values may result in faster load times.
	
	KILOBYTES_PER_BATCH = *value*, number of kilobytes per batch. Higher values may result in faster load times.
	
	TABLOCK—Specifies that a table lock is used when loading data.
	
	Tip: This option can significantly improve import performance.
	
	CHECK_CONSTRAINTS—Specifies that table constraints are observed when importing data. This can decrease import performance. This option is off by default.
	
	The following is an example of BCP hints:
	
	`bcp customer..customer in customer.n -n`
	`-T -hTABLOCK,ORDER(customer_id),`
	`➥ROWS_PER_BATCH=67000`

> **NOTE**
>
> With BCP, you can use - or / to preface a switch. For example, the following
> two statements are equivalent:
>
> ```
> bcp pubs..sales out sales.out /c /Usa /P
>
> bcp pubs..sales out sales.out -c -Usa -P
> ```

TABLE 11.2 VALID BCP TERMINATORS

Terminator Type	Syntax
Tab	\t
New line	\n
Carriage return	\r
Backslash	\\
NULL terminator	\0
User-defined terminator	character (^, %, *, and so on)

PERMISSIONS REQUIRED TO RUN BCP

No permissions are required to run the BCP command-line utility. However, to use BCP
to copy data into a table, the user must be granted INSERT permission to the target table.
To export data from a table, the user must be granted SELECT permission for the source
table.

CHARACTER MODE VERSUS NATIVE MODE

BCP can import or export data in a character file format or native file format. *Character
mode* is plain old ASCII text. Use the -c switch or a format file to specify character
mode. *Native mode* uses special formatting characters internal to SQL Server to represent
data. Use native mode only when you are transferring data between SQL Server tables.
Use the -n switch to specify native mode. Following is sample output from character
mode BCP:

```
bcp pubs..jobs out jobs.txt -c -U sa -P

1       New Hire - Job not specified    10      10
2       Chief Executive Officer         200     250
3       Business Operations Manager     175     225
```

> **TIP**
>
> Character mode is usually easier to work with than native mode because you can view the contents of a character mode data file with a standard text editor.

INTERACTIVE BCP

Interactive BCP is used to selectively import or export data. Interactive mode is automatically activated when the following switches are *not* included in the BCP statement:

> -n (native format)
>
> -N (native format for non-character data and Unicode native format for character data)
>
> -c (character format)
>
> -f (format file)
>
> -w (Unicode native format)

Through the use of interactive prompts, you can tailor BCP to your import and export specifications. Interactive BCP prompts you for four pieces of information:

- File storage type
- Prefix length
- Field length
- Field and row terminator

The following are sample interactive BCP prompts:

```
Enter the file storage type of field discounttype [char]:
Enter prefix-length of field discounttype [0]:
Enter length of field discounttype [40]:
Enter field terminator [none]:
```

> **TIP**
>
> When importing data, you can skip a column by entering 0 for prefix length, 0 for length, and no terminator. You cannot skip a column when exporting data.

At the end of an interactive BCP session, you receive the following prompt:

```
Do you want to save this format information in a file? [Y/n]
Host filename [bcp.fmt]:
```

If you answer *yes* at this prompt, your interactive responses are saved to a format file. This enables you to later specify the `-f` switch (format file) to automatically reuse the information from your interactive BCP session.

File Storage Type

The *file storage type* specifies the datatypes used to read from and write to data files. Table 11.3 lists valid file storage types.

> **TIP**
>
> When working with ASCII files, set all file storage types to `char`, regardless of the table's datatypes. This is the only way you can load ASCII data into SQL Server using BCP.

TABLE 11.3 FILE STORAGE TYPES

char	image	smallint
varchar	datetime	tinyint
nchar	smalldatetime	money
nvarchar	decimal	smallmoney
text	numeric	bit
ntext	float	uniqueidentifier
binary	real	timestamp
varbinary	int	

Prefix Length

SQL Server uses the *prefix length* to store compacted data. When working in native mode, accept the default values whenever possible.

> **TIP**
>
> When working with fixed-width ASCII data, set the prefix length to 0.

Field Length

The *field length* specifies the number of bytes required to store a SQL Server datatype. Use default field lengths whenever possible, otherwise data truncation or overflow errors can occur. Table 11.4 lists default field lengths.

TABLE 11.4 DEFAULT FIELD LENGTHS

Datatype	Length in Bytes
binary	column length + 1
bit	1
char	column length
datetime	24
decimal	41
float	30
image	0
int	12
money	30
nchar	2 times column length
ntext	0
numeric	41
nvarchar	2 times column length
real	30
smalldatetime	24
smallint	7
smallmoney	30
text	0
timestamp	17
tinyint	5
uniqueidentifier	37
varbinary	2 times column length + 1
varchar	column length

TIP

When importing and exporting ASCII fixed-width data files, you may need to modify the field length to match your import/export specification. For example, to export a `char(15)` column as a 25-byte piece of data, specify a field length of 25. This pads the data length to 25 bytes.

Field Terminator

The *field terminator* prompt controls how field data is delimited (separated). The default delimiter is no terminator. See Table 11.5 for valid field terminators.

TIP

The last field in a table acts as a row terminator. To separate rows with a new-line delimiter, specify \n at the field terminator prompt.

NOTE

At the BCP command line, you can also use the -t (field terminator) and -r (row terminator) switches to specify terminators.

TABLE 11.5 VALID FIELD TERMINATORS

Terminator Type	Syntax
Tab	\t
Newline	\n
Carriage return	\r
Backslash	\\
NULL terminator	\0
User-defined terminator	character (^, %, *, and so on)

Format Files

A *format file* is a template for BCP to use when you import or export data. With this template, you can define how BCP should transfer your data.

The easiest way to create a format file is to initiate an interactive BCP session. Interactive mode is initiated when you do *not* specify one of the following switches:

- -n (native format)
- -N (native format for non-character data and Unicode native format for character data)
- -c (character format)
- -f (format file)
- -w (Unicode native format)

At the end of your interactive session, you see the following prompt:

```
Do you want to save this format information in a file? [Y/n] y
Host filename [bcp.fmt]:sample.fmt
```

At this prompt, enter a filename to save the format information. SQL Server then creates a format file, which is really an ASCII text file (see Figure 11.1). You can make modifications to an existing format file by using a standard text editor.

TIP

Use the FMT extension when saving format files to simplify file identification.

FIGURE 11.1
A sample format file.

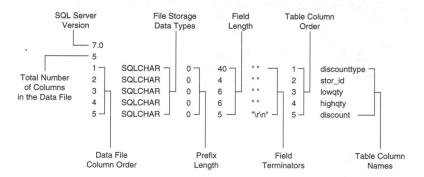

After you have saved the format file, you can reuse it by specifying the -f (format file) switch, as in the following example:

```
bcp sales..discounts in discount.txt -f sample.fmt -U sa -P
```

> **NOTE**
>
> If a table has a corresponding format file, any column modification to the table must be reflected in the format file. For example, if you drop a column from a table, you must also remove the column from the format file.

SAMPLE BCP SCRIPTS

This section describes how to use BCP to perform typical import and export routines. The examples discussed in this section use the `pubs..discounts` table.

The following is the structure of the `discounts` table:

```
discounttype varchar (40)
stor_id varchar
lowqty smallint
highqty smallint
discount decimal(4, 2)
```

The following is `discounts` table data:

discounttype	stor_id	lowqty	highqty	discount
Initial Customer	(null)	(null)	(null)	10.50
Volume Discount	(null)	100	1000	6.70
Customer Discount	8042	(null)	(null)	5.00

Simple Import

This example uses the `-c` switch to load a data file that contains tab-delimited fields and newline-delimited rows. For this example, the import data is contained in a file named `disc.txt`. Following are the contents of the sample import file:

```
Preferred Customer 6380 200 800  5.5
Valued Customer    7896 100 1000 8.5
```

The following syntax shows how to import the contents of the `disc.txt` file into the `discounts` table:

```
bcp pubs..discounts in disc.txt -c -U sa -P
```

Simple Export

This example uses the `-c` switch to export data to a file with tab-delimited fields and newline-delimited rows. The following syntax shows how to export the contents of the `discounts` table to the `discount.out` file:

```
bcp pubs..discounts out discount.out -c -U sa -P
```

Following is the output:

```
Initial Customer                                        10.50
Volume Discount                100    1000   6.70
Customer Discount              8042                5.00
```

Comma-Delimited Import

This example imports a data file that contains comma-delimited fields and newline-delimited rows. The -t switch specifies a comma delimiter; the -r\n switch specifies a newline row delimiter. For this example, the import data is contained in a file named disc2.txt. Following are the contents of the sample import file:

```
Preferred Customer,6380,200,800,5.5
Valued Customer,7896,100,1000,8.5
```

The following syntax shows how to import the contents of the disc2.txt file into the discounts table:

```
bcp pubs..discounts in disc2.txt -c -t, -r\n -U sa -P
```

Comma-Delimited Export

This example exports the discounts table to a file with comma-delimited fields and newline row delimiters. The following syntax shows how to export the contents of the discounts table to the disc3.txt file:

```
bcp pubs..discounts out disc3.txt -c -t, -r\n -U sa -P
```

Following is the output:

```
Initial Customer,,,,10.50
Volume Discount,,100,1000,6.70
Customer Discount,8042,,,5.00
```

Fixed-Length Import

This example uses a fixed-length ASCII text file named disc4.txt. Table 11.6 shows the layout of the text file.

Table 11.6 File Layout of DISC4.TXT

Column Name	File Length	File Position
discounttype	40	1-39
stor_id	4	40-43
lowqty	6	44-49
highqty	6	50-55
discount	5	56-60

The following is sample data from `disc4.txt`:

```
12345678901234567890123456789012345678901234567890
Preferred Customer                6380200   800   5.5
Valued Customer                   7896100  1000   8.5
```

For fixed-length data transfers, SQL Server needs to know the field positions in the data file. An easy way to do this is to use interactive BCP. To begin interactive BCP, use the following command.

```
bcp pubs..discounts in disc4.txt -U sa -P
```

For the first two prompts, you can accept the default values because they match the layout in the data file. For the third, fourth, and fifth prompts (see the highlighted text in Figure 11.2), you have to override the default prompts.

> **NOTE**
>
> When importing fixed-length ASCII data, *always* use char for the file storage type and 0 for the prefix length.

FIGURE 11.2
Interactive BCP responses.

```
Enter the file storage type of field discounttype [char]:
Enter prefix-length of field discounttype [0]:
Enter length of field discounttype [40]:
Enter field terminator [none]:

Enter the file storage type of field stor_id [char]:
Enter prefix-length of field stor_id [0]:
Enter length of field stor_id [4]:
Enter field terminator [none]:

Enter the file storage type of field lowqty [smallint]: char
Enter prefix-length of field lowqty [0]:
Enter length of field lowqty [6]:
Enter field terminator [none]:

Enter the file storage type of field highqty [smallint]: char
Enter prefix-length of field highqty [0]:
Enter length of field highqty [6]:
Enter field terminator [none]:

Enter the file storage type of field discount [decimal]: char
Enter prefix-length of field discount [1]: 0
Enter length of field discount [47]: 5
Enter field terminator [none]: \n

Do you want to save this format information in a file?  [Y/N] Y
Host filename [bcp.fmt]: disc4.fmt
```

Always use char when working with fixed length ASCII files.

Always use 0 for prefix length when working with fixed length ASCII files.

In the disc4.txt file, the discount column has a file length of 5 bytes. Therefore, 5 is used for the field length.

The last field terminator is actually the row delimeter. \n = new line row delimeter.

Fixed-Length Export

Suppose that you need to export the discounts table in a fixed-length file format and the format must follow the specification used in the previous example. No problem; you can reuse the format file you created in the previous example (see Figure 11.3).

The following syntax shows how to export the contents of the discounts table to the disc4.out file:

```
bcp pubs..discounts out disc4.out -c -f disc4.fmt -U sa -P
```

FIGURE 11.3

The disc4.fmt format file.

7.0						
5						
1	SQLCHAR	0	40	" "	1	discounttype
2	SQLCHAR	0	4	" "	2	stor_id
3	SQLCHAR	0	6	" "	3	lowqty
4	SQLCHAR	0	6	" "	4	highqty
5	SQLCHAR	0	5	"\r\n"	5	discount

Skipped Fields on Import

Suppose that you want to skip the columns stor_id, lowqty, and highqty when you load the disc4.txt ASCII file. To do this, you must modify the format file. To skip a column, enter **0** for the table column order (see Figure 11.4).

FIGURE 11.4

The format file used to skip columns.

7.0						
5						
1	SQLCHAR	0	40	" "	1	discounttype
2	SQLCHAR	0	4	" "	0	stor_id
3	SQLCHAR	0	6	" "	0	lowqty
4	SQLCHAR	0	6	" "	0	highqty
5	SQLCHAR	0	5	"\r\n"	5	discount

A 0 indicates
that the column
should be skipped

After you modify your format file, you can use the following BCP syntax to load the data:

```
bcp pubs..discounts in disc4.txt -c -f disc4.fmt -U sa -P
```

Skipped Fields on Export

BCP does not allow you to skip a column in a table during an export. However, you can trick BCP into skipping a column by creating a view that only references the columns you want to export, thus skipping unwanted columns. Then use BCP to export the data from the view.

The following syntax shows how to export only the `discounttype` and `discount` columns from the `discounts` table:

```
create view discounts_view as
select output = convert(char(40),discounttype) + convert(char(5),discount)
from discounts
```

Next, create a format file that contains one column (see Figure 11.5). Only one column is listed in the format file because the view concatenates the `discounttype` and `discount` columns.

FIGURE 11.5

The format file used to export data from a view.

```
7.0
1
1    SQLCHAR    0    45    "\r\n"    1    output
```

Finally, use BCP to export the data from the view:

```
bcp pubs..discounts_view out discview.txt -f discview.fmt -U sa -P
```

The following is sample output:

```
Initial Customer                              10.50
Volume Discount                                6.70
Customer Discount                              5.00
```

MODES OF OPERATION

When importing data, BCP has two modes of operation: fast mode and slow mode. As you probably guessed, the fast mode runs faster than the slow mode. The performance difference is caused by the logging of transactions. Fast mode bypasses the transaction log; slow mode posts all data inserts to the transaction log.

> **NOTE**
>
> You need to be concerned with fast and slow mode BCP only when you import data. BCP does not use a fast or slow mode when you export data.
>
> When you run BCP, SQL Server automatically decides which BCP mode to run. There is no BCP switch that enables you to toggle between fast and slow modes.

Achieving Fast Mode BCP

In SQL Server 7.0, several factors determine whether BCP can run in fast mode: SELECT INTO/BULKCOPY and indexes. For BCP to run in fast mode, the following four conditions must be true:

- The database option SELECT INTO/BULKCOPY must equal TRUE.
- Indexes must not exist on the target table.
- Triggers must not exist on the target table.
- The target table must not be replicated.

If any of these conditions are FALSE, BCP runs in slow mode (see Figure 11.6).

FIGURE 11.6

How SQL Server determines which BCP mode to run.

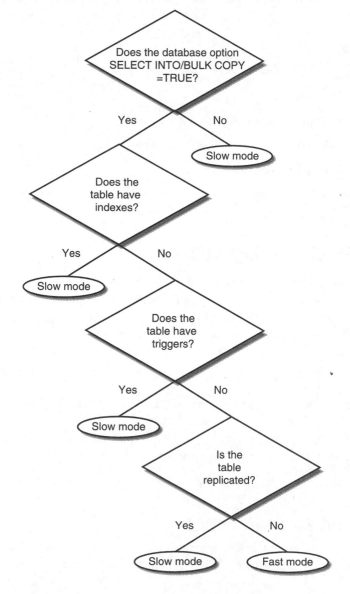

Why You Should Be Concerned with Which BCP Mode Is Running

You might be asking yourself, "Why not always run the BCP in fast mode?" The answer is based on the following two factors:

- Backup strategy
- Window of opportunity

Backup Strategy

To run the fast mode of BCP, you must have the SELECT INTO/BULKCOPY option set to TRUE. By setting this option to TRUE, you might be sacrificing data recovery for BCP performance. When SELECT INTO/BULKCOPY is set to TRUE, you cannot back up the transaction log for a database. Instead, you can only back up the entire database. This means that you will be unable to use the transaction log to provide up-to-the-minute data recovery.

Window of Opportunity

Fast mode BCP requires that the target table not contain any indexes. This means that you must consider the downtime involved with dropping the indexes and/or triggers, loading the data, and re-creating the indexes and/or triggers. For a table that requires 24-hour data access, it is not feasible to drop and re-create indexes.

TIP

To significantly reduce the time required to create a clustered index, have your import data presorted on the fields that make up your clustered index. Then use the WITH SORTED_DATA option to create the clustered index, as in the following example:

```
CREATE CLUSTERED INDEX pk_idx ON table1 (id) WITH SORTED_DATA
```

The WITH SORTED_DATA option bypasses the physical data sort step normally used to create a clustered index.

Table 11.7 helps clarify the differences between the two modes.

TABLE 11.7 FAST BCP VERSUS SLOW BCP

	Fast Mode	*Slow Mode*
PROS	Fast! Operations are not logged.	Maximum recoverability.
	Don't have to worry about filling up the transaction log.	
CONS	Zero recoverability.	Slow! Every insert is written to the transaction log.
	Must back up the database after using BCP. Cannot back up the transaction log.	Can easily fill up the transaction log during large data imports, thus complicating the import process.
	Indexes must be rebuilt after loading the data.	

NOTE

BCP does not display the mode that is in use (fast or slow). To get BCP to run in fast mode, you need to know the rules of fast mode BCP!

BCP AND ENFORCEMENT OF TRIGGERS, RULES, DEFAULTS, CONSTRAINTS, AND UNIQUE INDEXES

When using BCP to import data into a SQL Server table, it is important that you understand how triggers, rules, defaults, constraints, and unique indexes are enforced. Many people forget that certain types of objects are bypassed when using BCP to import data. Table 11.8 summarizes which objects are enforced when BCP is used to import data.

TABLE 11.8 ENFORCEMENT OF OBJECTS

Object	*Enforced?*
Default	Yes
Unique index/unique constraints	Yes
Primary key and foreign key constraints	Yes
Check constraint	No*

Object	Enforced?
Rule	No
Trigger	No

*By default, constraints are not enforced. However, in version 7.0, you can enable constraint checking by using the CHECK_CONTRAINTS hint.

CAUTION

Do not forget that triggers, check constraints (unless the CHECK_CONSTRAINTS hint is enabled), and rules are not enforced when using BCP. To prevent data integrity problems, load your data into a work table and run it through a validation routine similar to the validation defined in your triggers, constraints, and table rules. When you are satisfied that the data meets your integrity requirements, transfer the data to your target table.

NOTE

Defaults are not enforced if the -k option is specified when importing data.

COMMON BCP TRAPS

Be on the lookout for the following traps. They always seem to be lurking out there.

- **Invalid dates**: When importing data, a data file that contains dates represented as 00/00/00 and 000000 will fail. These are invalid SQL Server date formats. This problem often arises when data is transferred from a mainframe system to SQL Server. You must adhere to SQL Server date formats when importing date information into datetime columns.

- **Space-filled dates**: When importing spaces into a datetime column, SQL Server defaults the column to 1/1/1900. This is probably not what you want! To avoid this problem, do not pad the column with any data; just follow the column with a delimiter. SQL Server sets the data column to NULL, which is presumably more in line with what you expected.

- **Improper delimiter**: Do not use a delimiter that exists in your data or you will have problems. For example, if the first and last names are stored as one field and a user enters **Smith, Mike**, do not use a comma delimiter. For this example, use a tab or another type of delimiter.

BCP TIPS

Use the following tips to help simplify data imports and exports:

- **Use BCP hints to improve performance.** The following hints can significantly improve BCP performance.

Hint	Purpose
TABLOCK	Implements a table level lock for the duration of the import. During informal testing of this option, BCP load times have decreased as much as 400 percent!
ORDER (`column_list`) where `column_list` = {column [ASC ¦ DESC] [,*n*]}	Use this option if your data is presorted and the sort column(s) match the clustered index in the corresponding table. By presorting the data, the clustered index can be updated more quickly.

- **Load from local files.** BCP runs faster when importing a file on the local machine, as opposed to importing a file over the network. Loading locally can improve BCP performance by a magnitude of 2-3 times.

- **Use parallel loading to improve performance.** By running BCP in parallel on multiple machines, you can greatly decrease the time required to import data files.

- **Use views to export data.** Views allow increased flexibility to filter and physically arrange your data. For example, to export only the date portion of a datetime column, use a view and the CONVERT function.

- **Sample table**:
```
emp_id char(3)
hire_date datetime
```

- **Sample view**:
```
CREATE VIEW date_example_view AS
SELECT emp_id,convert(char(12),hire_date,1)
FROM sample_table
```

- **Sample BCP statement**:
```
bcp sales..date_example_view out sample.out -c -Usa -P
```

> **NOTE**
>
> Refer to the CONVERT function in SQL Server's Books Online for other date formats.

- **Echo BCP output and errors to a text file.** To capture BCP's output, use the -o switch. To capture BCP's error messages, use the -e switch.
- **Automate data imports and exports.** An easy way to automate this process is to create a stored procedure that calls BCP and then runs any additional processes. The advantage of creating a single stored procedure to run your import process is that you can schedule it through SQL Server Agent. The following syntax is an example of a stored procedure that calls BCP to load data into the system and then executes summary procedures against the data:

```
CREATE PROCEDURE usp_load_example AS
/* flush out work table */
truncate table table1

/* BCP in data */
exec master..xp_cmdshell "bcp sales..table1 in
➥C:\mssql7\binn\table1.txt -c -Usa -P"

/* run summary procedures */
exec usp_summary1
exec usp_summaryN
```

> **CAUTION**
>
> Do not use xp_cmdshell to call BCP from within a user-defined transaction in a stored procedure. Doing so can lead to endless blocking!

> **TIP**
>
> Do you ever have to export or import data for all the tables in a database? To perform this task, you could manually create BCP scripts, but that can be tedious and time consuming, especially if you must use BCP to copy data from numerous tables in the database. An alternative to manually creating the scripts is building a SQL statement that automatically generates the BCP syntax. Suppose that you need to export data from all the tables in the pubs
>
> *continues*

database. To generate the BCP syntax, create a query that references the sysobjects table (each database in SQL Server has a sysobjects table and a corresponding record for each object in the database). In the WHERE clause of the query, specify type = 'U' (this clause only returns user tables). The following is a sample query used to generate the BCP syntax (the -c switch is used in this example to export the data in a tab-delimited character format):

```
select 'bcp pubs..' + name + ' out ' + name + '.txt' + ' -c -Usa -
Ppassword -Stfnserver'
            from pubs..sysobjects
            where type ='U'
            order by name
```

Following is the output from the query:

```
bcp pubs..authors out authors.txt -c -Usa -Ppassword -Stfnserver
bcp pubs..discounts out discounts.txt -c -Usa -Ppassword -Stfnserver
bcp pubs..employee out employee.txt -c -Usa -Ppassword -Stfnserver
bcp pubs..jobs out jobs.txt -c -Usa -Ppassword -Stfnserver
bcp pubs..pub_info out pub_info.txt -c -Usa -Ppassword -Stfnserver
bcp pubs..publishers out publishers.txt -c -Usa -Ppassword -
Stfnserver
bcp pubs..roysched out roysched.txt -c -Usa -Ppassword -Stfnserver
bcp pubs..sales out sales.txt -c -Usa -Ppassword -Stfnserver
bcp pubs..stores out stores.txt -c -Usa -Ppassword -Stfnserver
bcp pubs..titleauthor out titleauthor.txt -c -Usa -Ppassword -
Stfnserver
bcp pubs..titles out titles.txt -c -Usa -Ppassword -Stfnserver
```

Now that you have the proper BCP syntax, you can save the output from the query to a .BAT file and automatically run the file from the command line. As you see, the combination of SQL Server syntax with information from the system tables can simplify common DBA chores.

BULK INSERT

BULK INSERT is an import-only Transact-SQL statement that is similar in syntax and operation to BCP. BULK INSERT is faster than BCP and DTS, thus making it very appealing for those operations that require maximum performance.

Use the following syntax to perform BULK INSERT operations.

```
BULK INSERT [['database_name'.]['owner'.]{'table_name' FROM data_file}
[WITH
([switch1 parameter1] [switch2]
...
[switch10 parameter10]
...)
```

where the following are the parameters:

database_name	Name of the database being accessed.
	Database name is optional; if the database name is omitted, the user's default database is used.
owner	Owner of the table or view being accessed.
table_name	Name of the table or view being accessed.
datafile	The name of the data file for an import or the name of the file to be created during an export. A path can be included with this statement, such as c:\mssql\binn\authors.txt.
switch1, parameter1	Choose the switch and its parameter (if and so on one is required from Table 11.9.

TABLE 11.9   BULK INSERT SWITCHES AND THEIR PARAMETERS

Parameter	*Explanation*
BATCHSIZE = *batch size*	The number of rows transferred in a batch. The default setting is the number of rows in the data file.
CHECK_CONSTRAINTS	Specifies that table constraints are observed when importing data. This can decrease import performance. By default, this option is off.
CODEPAGE = *code page*	Code page in use by the file being imported. Code page only needs to be specified if the file contains char, varchar, or text datatypes and the data contains values greater than 127 or less than 32. The following is a list of valid code pages: ACP—ANSI/Microsoft Window0s. OEM—Default code page. RAW—No conversion between code pages. <value>—specific code page number, such as 850.
DATAFILETYPE = '*filetype*'	The type of file to import. The following is a list of valid file types.

continues

TABLE 11.9   CONTINUED

Parameter	Explanation
	char—Character data mode. By default, fields are tab delimited and rows are newline delimited. This is the default DATAFILETYPE.
	native—Native data mode. Use this option when importing data that was exporting via BCP and the -n switch (native mode export).
	widechar—Unicode data mode.
	widenative—Native import for noncharacter data and Unicode import for character data, provides better performance than the widechar option.
FIELDTERMINATOR = 'field_terminator'	Field terminator. See Table 11.2 for terminators.
FIRSTROW = first_row	The number of the first row to copy.
FORMATFILE = 'format_file'	The name of the format file used to import or export data. A path can be included with this statement, such as c:\mssql\binn\authors.fmt.
KEEPIDENTITY	Used when importing data into a table that contains an identity datatype and you want to populate the column with values from the data file. If this switch is omitted, SQL Server automatically populates the identity column and ignores the field's corresponding data values in the import file. If this switch is included, the values from the data file are observed.
KILOBYTES_PER_BATCH = kilobytes_per_batch	Number of kilobytes per batch. Higher values may result in faster load times.
KEEPNULLS	Preserves null values found in the data file. If this switch is omitted, SQL Server applies default values if they exist.
LASTROW = last_row	The number of the last row to copy.
MAXERRORS = max_errors	Maximum number of errors that can occur before the operation is terminated. Each failed insert counts as one error. Default value is 10.
ORDER (column_list) where column_list = {column [ASC ¦ DESC] [,n]}	Use this option if your data is presorted and the sort column(s) match the clustered index in the corresponding table. By presorting the data, the clustered index can be updated quicker.

Parameter	Explanation
`ROWS_PER_BATCH =U` `rows_per_batch`	Number of rows per batch. Higher values may result in faster load times.
`ROWTERMINATOR =` `'row_terminator'`	Row terminator (see Table 11.2 for terminators).
`TABLOCK`	Specifies that a table lock is used when loading data. *Tip:* This option can significantly improve import performance.

TIP

As I previously mentioned, `BULK INSERT` is very similar to BCP. Therefore, the BCP examples discussed in this chapter (format files, field terminators, row terminators, tips, and so on) can be directly applied to `BULK INSERT`.

The following are `BULK INSERT` examples:

```
/* simple character data import */
bulk insert customer from  'c:\temp\bcptest\customer.txt'
/* simple native data import */
bulk insert customer from  'c:\temp\bcptest\customer.n'  with
(DATAFILETYPE = 'native')

/* high performance character data import
   with ORDER and TABLOCK options */
bulk insert customer from  'c:\temp\bcptest\customer.txt'  with
(ORDER(customer_id),TABLOCK)
```

BCP FAQ

The following section lists some of the common questions asked by DBAs about BCP:

Q. How can I use BCP to import data from a 6.x version of SQL Server? Whenever I use BCP to import the data, I get various ODBC errors.

A. Use the 6 option when importing data from a 6.x version of SQL Server. Version 7.0 of BCP uses ODBC to interface with SQL Server, whereas previous versions used DB-Library. ODBC treats datatypes differently than DB-Library.

Q. When should I use BCP instead of DTS?

A. The main reason to use BCP is performance. BCP can import and export data faster than DTS. If performance is not an issue, I recommend using DTS. DTS is easier to use and is more flexible than BCP.

Q. Which file formats are supported by BCP?

A. BCP supports the following formats: ASCII text, native, and Unicode. Use DTS to import and export other file formats.

Q. Can BCP export the result returned by a query? What about exporting the contents of a stored procedure?

A. Yes, instead of specifying a table name, specify a query and use the `queryout` option. The following is an example of using BCP to export the output from a query to a text file.

```
bcp "select * from pubs..authors order by au_lname" queryout
authors.txt -c -Usa -P -Spghdev3
```

The following is an example of using BCP to export the output from a stored procedure to a text file.

```
bcp "exec sp_who" queryout sp_who.txt -c -Usa -P -Spghdev3
```

SUMMARY

The following is BCP and `BULK INSERT` summary information:

- BCP and `BULK INSERT` use three file types to transfer data: character mode, native mode, and unicode. Character mode is ASCII text and native mode is a SQL Server file type. Character mode is usually easier to work with.

- When working with fixed-length ASCII files, always use the `char` datatype and `0` prefix length.

- To skip a column in interactive BCP, enter `0` for prefix length, `0` length, and no terminator.

- When importing data, BCP has two modes of operation: fast and slow. Fast mode bypasses the transaction log; slow mode posts all data inserts to the transaction log.

- To achieve fast mode BCP, set the database option `SELECT INTO/BULKCOPY` to `TRUE`, drop the indexes on the target table, drop any triggers on the table, and do not have the table participate in replication.

- Your ability to continuously run fast mode BCP depends on the backup and data access requirements in your production environment.

- Check constraints, rules, and triggers are not enforced when using BCP and `BULK INSERT`, unless the `CHECK_CONSTRAINTS` hint is enabled. The `CHECK_CONSTRAINTS` hint specifies that table constraints are enforced when running BCP and `BULK INSERT`.

- When importing data into a date column, spaces in a data file convert to `1/1/1900`.

- The `TABLOCK` and `ORDER` hints can significantly improve BCP and `BULK INSERT` performance.

DISTRIBUTED TRANSACTION COORDINATOR

by Mark Spenik

IN THIS CHAPTER

SQL Server 7.0 includes a distributed transaction coordinator, the Microsoft Distributed Transaction Coordinator (DTC). DTC provides an easy-to-use distributed transaction capability for the Windows NT and Windows 95/98 environments. The DTC uses OLE transaction objects to provide complete transaction management in a distributed environment. This technology allows applications to modify data in multiple SQL Server databases through a single transaction object. By using the distributed transactions through the MS DTC, you can guarantee that each data modification completes in its entirety; in the event of an aborted transaction, the modified data retains its original state (before the transaction was initiated).

> **NOTE**
>
> The DTC was introduced in SQL Server 6.5. MS DTC is now included with other Microsoft products such as the Microsoft Transaction Server (MTS).

SQL SERVER 6.5 TO 7.0 QUICK REFERENCE

The following is a quick reference to the changes that occurred between SQL Server version 6.5 and 7.0:

What's New

- Windows 9x support
- MS DTC used in SQL Server 7.0 Updating Subscriber Replication
- Separate DTC configuration program

What's Gone

- Integrated DTC configuration program with the SQL Server Enterprise Manager (although you can still stop and start DTC from the Enterprise manager)

KEY COMPONENTS OF A DISTRIBUTED TRANSACTION

The MS DTC can be easily started or stopped from the SQL Enterprise Manager and is easily configured using the MSDTC Administrative Console program. Before you look at the Microsoft DTC, you should understand the different components involved in distributed transactions. The following sections explain the key components involved in a distributed transaction and the role played by SQL Server and the Distributed Transaction Coordinator.

Transaction Manager

The Transaction Manager is responsible for the coordination and management of a transaction. The MS DTC serves as the transaction manager. The MS DTC creates transaction objects on behalf of the calling application. Resource Managers participating in the transaction enlist with the Transaction Manager. The Transaction Manager is then responsible for initiating and coordinating the two-phase commit protocol for the participants. The Transaction Manager is also responsible for keeping a log of transaction events. For the MS DTC, this log is the sequential file MSDTC.LOG. The log is used in case Transaction Manager should fail, so that the Transaction Manager can reconstruct the transaction by reading the log.

Resource Manager

The Resource Manager is responsible for performing the request of the transaction. In the case of an SQL Server acting as a Resource Manager, this request could be an INSERT, UPDATE, or DELETE statement. Resource Managers are responsible for keeping enough information so that they can commit or roll back the transaction. Currently, any Transaction Manager that supports the X/Open XA specification for distributed transactions can act as a Resource Manager.

Two-Phase Commit

The MS DTC uses a two-phase commit algorithm to guarantee that a distributed data modification runs in its entirety or that the modified data returns to its original state (the state it was in before the transaction was initiated). The two-phase commit algorithm is based on the following logic.

When a commit statement is issued, the Transaction Manager (in the case of SQL Server, the MS DTC) asks the resources involved in the transaction if they are ready to commit the transaction. This step is known as *preparing to commit*. If every resource is ready to commit the transaction, the Transaction Manager broadcasts a message to commit the transaction. Each resource sends back a message stating that the transaction is committed. If each resource successfully commits the transaction, the Transaction Manager marks the transaction as successfully committed. If a resource fails to commit a transaction, the Transaction Manager continues to hold the transaction in a pending state. This state must be resolved before the transaction is considered complete; otherwise the transaction is rolled back.

WALKING THROUGH A DISTRIBUTED TRANSACTION PROCESS

Refer to Figure 12.1 as you walk through a simple example of a distributed transaction. The transaction begins with the application, which issues a BEGIN DISTRIBUTED TRANS-ACTION command, causing the Transaction Manager (MS DTC) to create a transaction object for the transaction. When the application begins to perform an SQL statement as part of the transaction (for example, an INSERT statement), the Resource Manager (in this case, SQL Server) calls the Transaction Manager to enlist in the transaction. Keeping track of enlisted Transaction Managers is part of the responsibility of the Transaction Manager.

During the life of the transaction, the Transaction Manager (MS DTC) records file events in the MSDTC.LOG, such as transaction starts, enlistments, and commits or aborts. By keeping the log file up to date, the Transaction Manager ensures that it can reconstruct a transaction in case the Transaction Manager should go down. When the application commits or aborts the transaction, the Transaction Manager begins the two-phase commit with all the enlisted Resource Managers. (The example in Figure 12.1 involves only a single computer with a single Transaction Manager and Resource Manager.)

FIGURE 12.1

Walking through a distributed transaction process.

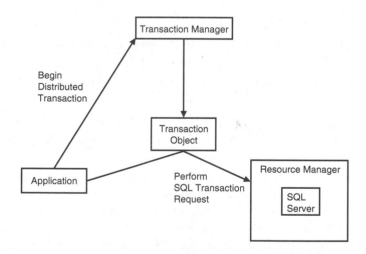

The real power behind the DTC is that you can use it in a distributed environment for transactions that span multiple computers and Transaction Managers. In a distributed environment, each system has a local Transaction Manager. The Transaction Manager for each system works with the other Transaction Managers in the distributed environment to manage transactions that span multiple systems. The Transaction Manager that

Distributed Transaction Coordinator

CHAPTER 12

339

12

DISTRIBUTED
TRANSACTION
COORDINATOR

initiates a distributed transaction is referred to as the *global commit coordinator* (or the *root Transaction Manager*). When a transaction crosses to other systems, the Transaction Managers from each system establish relationships. The system making the request is said to have an *outgoing relationship* to the Transaction Managers on the other systems. Transaction Managers receiving the request establish an *incoming relationship* with the root Transaction Manager. The relationship between the different Transaction Managers is called a *commit tree*. The general idea is that, when a distributed transaction is committed or aborted, the request flows outward. Any Transaction Manager in the commit tree can abort the transaction before it agrees to prepare to commit or abort the transaction.

DEVELOPING AN APPLICATION WITH DISTRIBUTED TRANSACTIONS

By using Transact-SQL stored procedures, C/C++ functions, or the Microsoft Transaction Server, you can develop an application that incorporates distributed transactions. The following sections explain each method.

Using Stored Procedures

By using SQL Server's stored procedures, you can implement distributed transaction logic. To implement distributed transaction logic, use the following syntax: `begin distributed tran`, `commit tran`, `rollback tran`. You can also use stored procedures to make remote procedure calls (RPC) to stored procedures located on servers. These RPC calls enable you to modify data located on another server.

Using C/C++ Functions

You can also implement distributed transaction logic by using C or C++ functions with DB-Library or ODBC. If you use C or C++ functions, you can directly initiate a DTC transaction within an application through an OLE transaction-compliant Resource Manager.

Microsoft Transaction Server

The Microsoft Transaction Server (MTS) greatly simplifies building distributed transaction applications. With MTS, you do not concentrate on building in the logic to start, commit, or rollback a distributed transaction. Instead you concentrate on building COM based components that incorporate the MTS APIs. Your component simply indicates whether the operation it was performing completed successfully or has an error. If the component is participating in a single transaction or a distributed transaction, MTS manages the commit or rollback of the overall transaction. If you plan to do distributed applications, MTS will make your life much easier!

SQL Server 7.0 Immediate Updating Subscriber Replication

SQL Server 7.0 enables you to build an application that uses distributed transactions without writing a single line of code. With SQL Server 7.0, snapshot and transactional replication can be configured to use an immediate updating subscriber. An immediate updating subscriber means that a subscribing site can edit published data and the changes made at the subscriber are also made at the publisher using a two-phase commit and the MS DTC. To read more about this type of replication see Chapter 16, "Transactional Replication."

CONFIGURING THE DTC SERVER COMPONENT

Preparing to use the DTC service on the server where SQL Server resides is relatively straightforward. By default, the DTC service is automatically installed when you install SQL Server 7.0, and the MSDTC service is automatically added to the operating system.

THE MS DTC uses remote procedure calls (RPC) to make modifications to other servers. When you use remote procedure calls (RPC) to modify data on another server, the remote server must be added to the list of available remote servers. Follow these steps to add a remote server:

1. From the Enterprise Manager, select the server that will act as the DTC coordinator. Select the Remote Server icon from the Security folder tree list. Right-click and select New Remote Server from the pop-up menu. The Manage Remote Servers dialog box opens.

2. In the Manage Remote Servers dialog box, enter the remote server's name. Select the RPC option (which allows the remote server to execute stored procedures on the local server using Remote Procedure Calls, RPC) and enter Remote Login information (see Figure 12.2). You can use this tab to set up trusted connections between the servers as well map local and remote users. Click the OK button to save the information.

FIGURE 12.2

The Manage Remote Server dialog box.

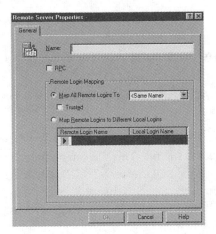

CONFIGURING THE DTC CLIENT COMPONENT

If you want a client to initiate a DTC transaction, the MS DTC client utility must be installed and configured on a client machine.

> **NOTE**
>
> The DTC client utility is required only when a client initiates a DTC transaction. It is not required when a client calls a stored procedure in SQL Server and the stored procedure initiates the DTC transaction. Therefore, if you code the begin distributed tran, commit tran, and rollback tran logic using stored procedures, you do not have to install the DTC client utility.
>
> You can also avoid the MS DTC client installation and configuration by using Microsoft Transaction Server components.
>
> The DTC client must be installed on a 32-bit client and is installed as part of the SQL Server client tools. It does not work with Windows for Workgroups or Windows 3.1.

Before you can install the Microsoft DTC client component, you must first install the Microsoft Remote Registry Service. To determine whether the Microsoft Remote Registry Service is installed on your computer, double-click the Network icon in the Control Panel. If you do not see Microsoft Remote Registry listed as an installed component (see Figure 12.3), you must install it by performing the following steps:

1. Double-click the Network icon in the Control Panel. The Network dialog box appears.

2. Click the Add button in the Network dialog box. The Select Network Component Type dialog box opens.

3. Select Service and click the Add button. The Select Network Service dialog box opens.

4. Click the Have Disk button. The Install From Disk dialog box opens.

5. Enter the location of the REGSRV.INF file. This file can be found in the \i386\remotereg directory on the SQL Server v7.0 CD. Click the OK button to install the service. You return to the Select Network Service dialog box. At this point, you are ready to install the Microsoft Remote Registry Service. Click the OK button to continue the installation.

6. The Microsoft Remote Registry Service begins to install. Depending on your Windows 9x configuration, you might be prompted for additional files that reside on the Windows 9x installation CD or disks. When the installation is complete, you see Microsoft Remote Registry listed as an installed component.

FIGURE 12.3

The Microsoft Remote Registry service.

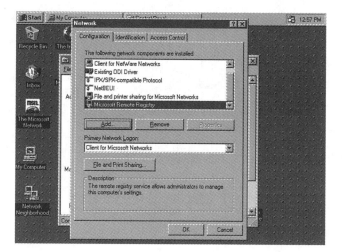

7. In addition to installing the Microsoft Remote Registry service, you must also enable user-level access control. To enable user-level access control, select the Access Control tab in the Network dialog box. Click the User-Level Access Control option and enter the source for user information (see Figure 12.4).

FIGURE 12.4

Enabling user-level access control.

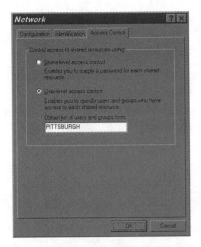

After you successfully complete the installation of the Microsoft Remote Registry Service, you must run the DTCCFG.CPL control panel extension to configure the default commit coordinator. Follow these steps to configure the DTCCFG.CPL control panel extension:

To configure the MS DTC client perform the following:

1. Click the MS DTC icon located in the system control panel or find the installed location of DTCCFG.CPL and double-click the file. The MS DTC Client Configuration dialog box opens.

2. From the MS DTC Client Configuration dialog box, enter a default MS DTC server and a network protocol (see Figure 12.5). Click the OK button to save the information.

FIGURE 12.5

Configuring the MS DTC client.

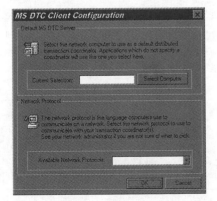

STARTING THE DTC

Follow these steps to start the DTC from the Enterprise Manager:

1. To manually start the DTC from the Enterprise Manager, select the server that will be running the DTC service and right-click the Distributed Transaction Coordinator icon located under the support services folder. From the shortcut menu that appears, select the Start option (see Figure 12.6).

2. After the Distributed Transaction Coordinator has started, the DTC icon appears with a green arrow, which indicates that the DTC is currently running.

FIGURE 12.6

Starting the Distributed Transaction Coordinator from the Enterprise Manager.

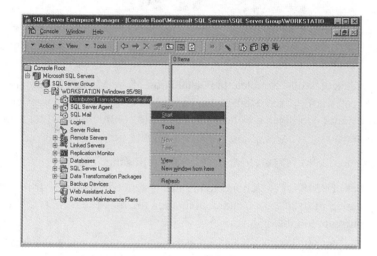

NOTE

You can also start the DTC from the Services icon in the Control Panel or by typing net start msdtc. To manually start the DTC from Windows 9.x, type msdtc –ns.

TIP

If you plan to use the DTC on a regular basis, you should configure it to start automatically whenever the NT Server starts. To automatically start the DTC service, double-click the Services icon in the Windows NT Control Panel. The Services dialog box opens. In the Services dialog box, double-click the MSDTC service. A dialog box containing information about the MSDTC service opens. From this dialog box, select Automatic as the Startup Type (see Figure 12.7). Click the OK button to save the changes.

FIGURE 12.7
Configuring the DTC service to start autom atically.

TESTING THE DTC

Follow these steps to verify that the DTC is properly configured:

1. From the NT/Windows 9.x start menu, select the DTC Administration Console. The MSDTC Administration Console dialog box appears. Select the Statistics tab. Keep this tab open for the remainder of the test.

2. From the Enterprise Manager, open a Query dialog box by selecting Tools and the option SQL Server Query Analyzer.

3. In the Query Analyzer dialog box, type **begin distributed transaction** and click the Execute Query button to execute the query. Keep this dialog box open for the remainder of the test.

4. Return to the MS DTC Statistics tab. If the DTC is properly configured, you should see one active transaction in the Current/Active counter section of the dialog box (see Figure 12.8).

5. Return to the Query Analyzer dialog box. Type **rollback transaction** and click the Execute Query button to execute the query.

6. Return to the MS DTC Statistics tab. If the DTC is properly configured, you should see no active transactions in the Current/Active counter section of the dialog box.

FIGURE 12.8

The MS DTC Statistics dialog box, showing one active transaction.

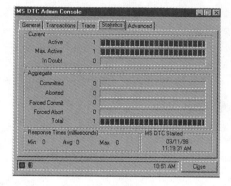

ADMINISTERING THE DTC

Although DTC sounds complex, Microsoft supplies a graphical tool to simplify the administration of DTC, the DTC Administration console. To start the DTC Administration console, from the NT/Windows 9.x start menu, select the DTC Administration Console. The MS DTC Administration Console dialog box, shown in Figure 12.9, appears.

FIGURE 12.9

The DTC Administration Console dialog box.

The DTC Administration console is a tabbed dialog box with the following tabs:

- **General tab** (shown in Figure 12.9). Shows the current version of the Microsoft DTC. You can also use the General tab to start and stop the service as well as view the service properties such as the name and service path.
- **Advanced tab.** Enables you to set advanced MS DTC options.
- **Trace tab.** Enables you to monitor trace messages issued by the MS DTC.
- **Transactions tab.** Provides a graphical view of transaction states and enables you to manually resolve a transaction.
- **Statistics tab.** Provides a graphical view of transaction statistical information.

Let's drill down on several of the tabs to see how they are used to monitor and configure the DTC.

Advanced Tab

You can use the Advanced tab to set advanced parameters such as the MS DTC display parameters or the MS DTC log and timers. The Advanced tab is shown in Figure 12.10.

FIGURE 12.10

The Microsoft DTC Administration Console — Advanced tab.

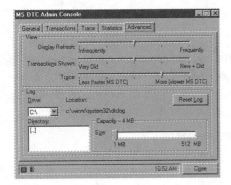

The following sections examine the MS DTC Administration, Advanced tab in more detail.

View Frame

The View frame shown in Figure 12.10 is used to control how often the MS DTC updates information. To adjust any values in the View frame, move the slider bars.

The **Display Refresh slider bar** determines how often the statistical, transaction list, and trace information is sent to the various graphical interfaces. The more frequently the information is updated, the more accurate the information. However, updating frequently increases the administrative overhead required. The Display Refresh slider bar starts at `Infrequently` and goes to `Frequently`. Following are the display update intervals for each value:

- Every 20 seconds (Infrequently)
- Every 10 seconds
- Every 5 seconds (Default value)
- Every 3 seconds
- Every 1 second (Frequently)

The **Transactions Shown slider bar** determines how long a transaction must be active before it appears on the graphical interfaces. The Transactions Shown slider bar goes (from left to right) from Very Old to New + Old; the associated values are as follows:

- Transactions 5 minutes old (Very Old)
- Transactions 1 minute old
- Transactions 30 seconds old
- Transactions 10 seconds old
- Transactions 1 second old (New + Old)

The **Trace slider bar** controls the amount of trace information sent to the graphical interface. The Trace slider bar goes from Less (faster MS DTC) to More (slower MS DTC). The more trace statements you send back to the graphical interface, the slower MS DTC performs. The values for the Trace slider bar are as follows:

- Send no traces (Less; faster MS DTC)
- Send only error traces
- Send error and warning traces
- Send error, warning, and informational traces (default)
- Send all traces (More; slower MS DTC)

TIP

So how should you configure the different settings in the Advanced tab? If you want the best possible performance, set the display refresh to infrequently, and transactions shown Very Old and Trace to Less. This reduces the amount of time the MS DTC is collecting statistics and refreshing the display; however it's not great for debugging. If you are in a development environment or experiencing problems and not concerned about performance, you should take the middle-road defaults and even consider setting values to the max for display refresh (frequently, transactions shown (Old + New) and trace (more). You can change the parameters in the View frame dynamically while the MS DTC is running.

Log Frame

The Log frame enables you to adjust the size of the MS DTC log. The MS DTC log file is called MSDTC.LOG.

> **CAUTION**
>
> Do not modify the size of the MS DTC log while an MS DTC has unresolved transactions.

To modify the size of the MS DTC log, follow these steps:

1. Make sure that the MS DTC has no unresolved transactions by viewing the MS DTC Transaction tab (discussed later in this chapter). If no unresolved transactions exist, click the Stop button located on the MS DTC Administration Console — Advanced tab, to stop the MS DTC.

2. After the MS DTC has stopped, the Status indicator at the bottom of the MS DTC Administration Console status bar changes from green to red (refer to Figure 12.10). Then you can change the size of the log by using the slider bar. You can also change the location of the file by using the Drive and Directory boxes.

3. After you have modified the MS DTC log (either the size or the location or both), click the Reset Log button.

4. Click the Start button, located on the General tab, to restart the MS DTC.

Trace Tab

1. The MS DTC Administration Console — Trace tab, enables you to view the trace messages issued by MS DTC. Use this information to track or debug problems or potential problems. The type of information displayed in the Trace window depends on the message trace level set with the MS DTC Advanced tab, which includes errors, warnings, or informational messages. The MS DTC Administration Console, Trace tab is shown in Figure 12.11.

FIGURE 12.11

The Microsoft DTC Administration Console — Trace tab.

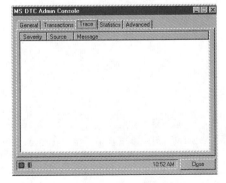

Transactions Tab

The MS DTC Administration Console — Transactions tab enables you to quickly view current transactions and resolve the transaction manually if required. The following sections explain how to accomplish both of these tasks.

Viewing Current Transactions

The MS DTC Transactions tab enables you to quickly view current transactions that might require a DBA's intervention or attention. Because a single MS DTC can have many concurrent transactions, the MS DTC Transactions tab displays only those transactions that have remained in the same state for an extended time or whose status is in doubt. You can configure the time interval for which transactions must remain in the same state before they appear in the MS DTC Transactions tab by using the MS DTC Advanced tab discussed earlier in this chapter. The MS DTC Administration Console — Transactions tab is shown in Figure 12.12.

FIGURE 12.12

*The Microsoft
DTC
Administration
Console —
Transactions tab.*

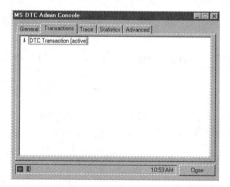

Figure 12.12 shows the Transactions List view of current transaction. You can change the tab to view the transactions in the following views:

- Large Icon
- Small Icon
- Details
- List

To change the view of the MS DTC Transactions tab, follow these steps:

1. Right-click anywhere in the MS DTC Transactions tab window. The pop-up menu shown in Figure 12.13 appears.

FIGURE 12.13
*The MS DTC
Transactions
tab—pop-up
menu.*

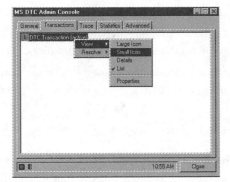

2. Select View, and then select the type of view you want to see; the Large Icon view is shown in Figure 12.14.

FIGURE 12.14
*The MS DTC
Administration
Console —
Transactions tab
(Large Icons).*

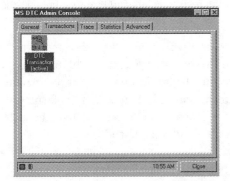

The transactions displayed in the MS DTC window will be in one of the following states:

- **Active.** The transaction has been started and the Resource Manager has done work on it.

- **Aborting.** The transaction is aborting.

- **Aborted.** Subordinate Transaction Coordinators and Resource Managers have been notified or are currently unavailable.

- **Preparing.** The application has issued a commit request.

- **Prepared.** All enlisted Resource Managers and MS DTC have agreed to prepare.

- **In-Doubt.** The transaction is prepared and initiated by a different server; the MS DTC coordinating the transaction is unavailable.

- **Forced Commit.** An In-Doubt transaction has been manually committed.

- **Forced Abort.** An In-Doubt transaction has been manually aborted.
- **Notifying Committed.** The transaction has prepared and MS DTC is notifying all enlisted Resource Managers that the transaction has committed.
- **Only Fail Remain to Notify.** All connected Resource Managers and subordinates have been notified of the transaction commit; the only ones left to notify are not connected.
- **Committed.** The transaction has been successfully committed.

Manually Resolving Transactions

From time to time, you may be required to resolve a distributed transaction manually because of a break in the commit tree (for example, one caused by a break in the communications link). Transactions that remain in the In-Doubt state can prove to be a problem because they might cause the Resource Manager to hold all the locks on the various resources, which makes the resources unavailable to others so that they must be manually resolved.

To determine the proper action to take when manually resolving an In-Doubt transaction, use the MS DTC Administration Console — Transactions tab to locate the transaction's immediate parent. You can determine the transaction's parent by selecting a transaction and right-clicking. The pop-up menu shown in Figure 12.14 is displayed. Select properties from the pop-up menu and the Transaction Properties dialog box, shown in Figure 12.15, appears, displaying the transaction's parent and ID.

FIGURE 12.15

*MS DTC
Transaction
Properties dialog
box.*

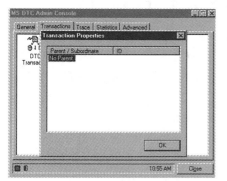

Examine the parent node using the MS DTC Administration Console — Transactions tab to determine the fate of the transaction. If the transaction does not appear in the MS DTC Transactions tab, the transaction has been aborted. If the transaction shows up with the Only Failed To Notify state, the transaction has been committed and you can manually commit the transaction. If the status reads In-Doubt, you must look at the next parent node in the chain. Continue to search the nodes until you can determine whether the transaction has been aborted or committed. When you know the status of the transaction, commit or abort the transaction on the child node and forget the transaction with the Failed To Notify status on the parent node.

To manually resolve a transaction, follow these steps:

1. From the MS DTC Transactions tab, select the transaction you want to resolve.

2. Right-click the transaction and select Resolve; the shortcut menu shown in Figure 12.16 opens.

FIGURE 12.16

The MS DTC Administration Console — Transactions tab—Resolve shortcut menu.

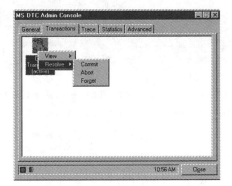

3. Select the proper option: Commit, Abort, or Forget.

Statistics Tab

The MS DTC Statistics window provides cumulative and current information about the transaction in which a server has participated (see Figure 12.17). The DBA can use this information to monitor the performance of MS DTC and make adjustments if required. If possible, you should leave the MS DTC running at all times to get the most out of the cumulative statistics. The cumulative statistics displayed in the MS DTC Statistics window are reset to zero when the MS DTC is stopped and restarted.

The MS DTC Statistics tab has several frames, each of which is described following.

The **Current frame** displays the following information:

- **Active.** The current number of transactions yet to complete in the two-phase commit protocol.

- **Max Active.** The peak number of transactions reached at any time while the MS DTC is running.

FIGURE 12.17

*The MS DTC
Administration
Console —
Statistics tab.*

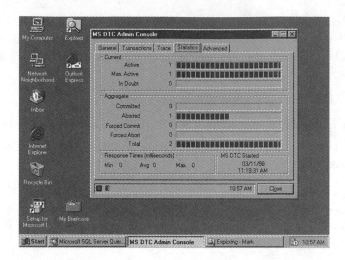

- **In-Doubt.** The current number of transactions that are unable to commit because of communication problems between the commit coordinator and the local SQL Server.

The **Aggregate frame** displays the following information:

- **Committed.** The cumulative total of committed transactions (excluding those committed manually).

- **Aborted.** The cumulative total of aborted transactions (excluding those aborted manually).

- **Forced Commit.** The cumulative total of manually committed transactions.

- **Forced Abort.** The cumulative total of manually aborted transactions.

- **Total.** The cumulative total of all transactions.

The **Response Time frame** displays the average, minimum, and maximum response times in milliseconds. The *response time* is the time between when the transaction was started and when the commit coordinator committed it.

The MS DTC Started frame displays the date and time on which the current MS DTC was started.

DTC FAQ

The following are some frequently asked questions about the Microsoft DTC.

Does the DTC Require Any Performance Tuning?

Like SQL Server, MS DTC comes out of the box ready to use without requiring any special configuration. However, if you want to try to achieve the best possible performance, use the MS DTC Administrative Console Advanced tab to reduce the amount of statistics being gathered by turning down the Display Refresh (set to Infrequently), Transaction Shown (set to Very Old), and Trace (Less). By collecting fewer statistics, you can enhance the performance of MS DTC.

Can MS DTC Be Used with SQL Server Distributed Queries to Make Changes in Other Data Sources (For Example Oracle)?

If the OLE DB provider supports the ItransactionJoin interface, the MS DTC will commit or roll back any changes in an update being performed via distributed queries.

SUMMARY

With the Microsoft Distributed Transaction Coordinator, the process of distributed transactions and two-phase commits has been greatly simplified. Read through this chapter—as well as the Microsoft documentation—and experiment with setting up and administering a Distributed Transaction Coordinator. Here is a list of the important points to review when using the Microsoft Distributed Transaction Coordinator:

- The Transaction Manager is responsible for the coordination and management of a transaction.
- The Resource Manager is responsible for performing the request of the transaction.
- Any transaction manager that supports the X/Open XA specification for distributed transaction processing can serve as a Resource Manager.
- The DTC uses a two-phase commit algorithm to guarantee that a distributed data modification runs in its entirety or that the modified data returns to its original state (that is, the state it was in before the transaction was initiated).
- SQL Server Updating Subscriber replication as well as the Microsoft Transaction Server use MS DTC.
- The MS DTC Administration Console is used to monitor and tune the MS DTC.

TROUBLESHOOTING SQL SERVER

by Mark Spenik

IN THIS CHAPTER

So far, each chapter in this book has covered common problems and resolutions. This chapter steps back and focuses on how SQL Server alerts you to possible problems with databases, objects, or the server; how to find more information about the problem; how to fix the problem; and how to get help in determining and fixing your problem. You also learn about several tools that ship with SQL Server to help you track and debug problems, as well as other resources readily available to aid in problem resolution. Start by taking a look at SQL Server error messages.

SQL ERROR MESSAGES

If you run a query and accidentally make a mistake by entering a table that does not exist in the database, what happens? SQL Server returns an error message. Actually, SQL Server reacts to all errors in the same manner, whether those errors are generated by users, databases, objects, or the system. SQL Server returns a formatted error message or writes the error message to the error log or event log. Here is a quick example that executes a SQL statement to update a nonexistence table in the pubs database. The SQL statement for the example is as follows:

```
UPDATE new_authors
Set author1 = "Spenik",
author2 = "Sledge",
title="Microsoft SQL Server DBA Survival Guide"
```

When the statement is executed, the following error message is returned:

```
Server: Msg 208, Level 16, State 1
Invalid object name 'new_authors'.
```

The preceding error message demonstrates the standard message format for error messages returned by SQL Server.

> **TIP**
>
> The first thing presented in the error message is the message number, severity level, and the state. To most users, these numbers are just garbage to be ignored, so they skip down to the message and try to resolve the problem. In reality, the error message number is very useful for obtaining more error information. You can use the severity levels to help find errors that need to be handled. When tracking a problem, always write down all the error information, including the message number, severity level, and state. In many cases, these will be of more assistance than the actual message.

Examine the format of a standard SQL Server error message.

Error Message Number

Each error message displayed by SQL Server has an associated error message number that uniquely identifies the type of error.

> **TIP**
>
> You can define your own error messages. User-defined error message numbers must be greater than 50,000 and less than 2,147,483,647. You can use the system stored procedure `sp_addmessage` to add the error message to the system table, `sysmessages`. From a trigger or stored procedure, you can use the `RAISERROR` statement to report a user-defined error message to the client and SQL Server. You can also use the Transact-SQL function `FormatMessage` to construct an error message to send to a client from an existing error message in the `sysmessages` table.

Error Severity

The error severity levels provide a quick reference for you about the nature of the error. The severity levels range from 0 to 25.

0 to 10	Messages with a severity level of 0 to 10 are informational messages and not actual errors.
11 to 16	Severity levels 11 to 16 are generated as a result of user problems and can be fixed by the user. For example, the error message returned in the invalid update query, used earlier, had a severity level of 16.
17	Severity level 17 indicates that SQL Server has run out of a configurable resource, such as user connections or locks. Severity error 17 can be corrected by the DBA, and in some cases, by the database owner.
18	Severity level 18 messages indicate nonfatal internal software problems.
19	Severity level 19 indicates that a nonconfigurable resource limit has been exceeded.

> **NOTE**
>
> Severity errors 20 through 25 are fatal errors and can only be used via RAISERROR by members of the fixed database role sysadmin with the with log option required. Severity 0–18 can be used by all users, 19 can only be used by a sysadmin databse role. When a fatal error occurs (20–25), the running process that generated the error is terminated (nonfatal errors continue processing). For error severity levels 20 and greater, the client connection to SQL Server is terminated.

20	Severity level 20 indicates a problem with a statement issued by the current process.
21	Severity level 21 indicates that SQL Server has encountered a problem that affects all the processes in a database.
22	Severity level 22 means a table or index has been damaged. To try to determine the extent of the problem, stop and restart SQL Server. If the problem is in the cache and not on the disk, the restart corrects the problem. Otherwise, use DBCC to determine the extent of the damage and the required action to take.
23	Severity level 23 indicates a suspect database. To determine the extent of the damage and the proper action to take, use the DBCC commands.
24	Severity level 24 indicates a hardware problem.
25	Severity level 25 indicates some type of system error.

State Number

The error state number is an integer value between 1 and 127; it represents information about the source that issued the error (such as the error can be called from more then one place).

Error Message

The error message is a description of the error that occurred. The error messages are stored in the sysmessages system table. Figure 13.1 shows a query result of the sysmessages table.

FIGURE 13.1

Query results of sysmessage using the Query Analyzer.

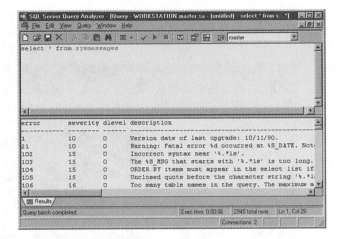

TIP

To use the SQL Enterprise Manager to view error messages or search for error messages, select a server and right-click. Select All Tasks and Manage SQL Server Messages, the SQL Server Message dialog box appears. Using the dialog box, you can search for error messages by error number or key words.

USING THE ERROR MESSAGE NUMBER TO RESOLVE THE ERROR

Earlier in this chapter, you learned that, by using the error message number, you could quickly retrieve detailed information about the error and possible ways to resolve the error. How, you may ask? Books Online!

INFORMATION AT YOUR FINGERTIPS

Isn't technology great! I believe that to really appreciate Microsoft's Books Online, you have to have been a Sybase DBA from the 4.2 UNIX days. When an error would occur that displayed the error number, you jotted down the error number and then tried to locate the error messages and the troubleshooting guide. Of course, the book was never in the same place. And if you had my luck, when you found the book, the error number was never in the book—it always fell within the "reserved" section or something similar. Microsoft first gave us Books Online in SQL Server 6.0 and they continue to improve the overall content and usefulness of the product. New DBAs, who start with SQL Server 7.0, will truly be spoiled by Microsoft's Books Online. By the way, always, always install the Books Online to your hard drive; it's well worth the 10MB or so of disk space.

When you installed SQL Server, you should have included the Books Online utility shown in Figure 13.2.

FIGURE 13.2

The SQL Server Books Online dialog box.

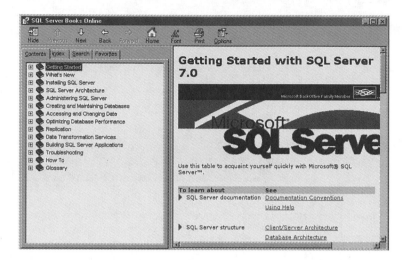

To see how to use Books Online to find more information on the error message number displayed during the invalid query example (error message number 208), follow these steps:

1. From the Windows NT or Windows 9x start menu, select the SQL Server 7.0 program group and select Books Online. The SQL Server Books Online dialog box, shown in Figure 13.2 appears. From the SQL Server Books Online dialog box, click the Search tab, shown in Figure 13.3.

FIGURE 13.3

The Search tab.

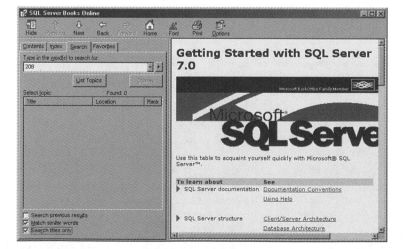

2. The Search tab enables you to quickly search Books Online for specific information. In the Query combo box, type the error message number: 208. In the Topic Area To Search frame, select the Title Only checkbox.

3. To run the search, click the List Topics button. The query runs, searching for 208 in the title of any of the book topics. If one or more items are found, they are displayed in a Query Results frame in the SQL Server Books Online dialog box (see Figure 13.4).

FIGURE 13.4

Query Results frame in the SQL Server Books Online dialog box.

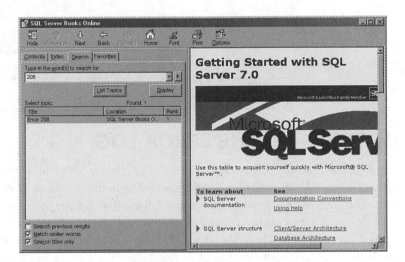

4. To view the document(s) found in the search, double-click the item or select the item and click the Display button. The detailed information for the error message number, including a detailed explanation and the action to take, is displayed in the document. You can even print the document! Just think, no more trying to locate a troubleshooting or error message book! No more flipping through pages searching for error messages; if the error number is not in the book, you know immediately! When getting multiple documents back for an error message query, select the document title Error Error_Number. For example the document title Error 208 displays detailed information on error 208. The detailed information found for error number 208 is displayed in Figure 13.5. Once you have displayed the error number document, read through the document for an explanation of the error and then follow the directions in the Action section of the document to correct the error.

FIGURE 13.5

The Books Online description of error message 208.

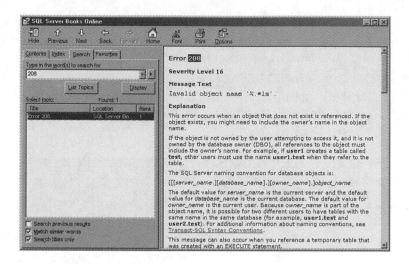

DECIPHERING THE ERROR LOG

The error log is a standard text file that holds SQL Server information and error messages. The error log is used both in Windows NT systems as well as Windows 9x systems. The error log can provide meaningful information to help you track down problems or to alert you to potential or existing problems. SQL Server maintains the current error log and the six previous error log files. The current error log filename is ERRORLOG; the previous error log files, referred to as *archived error logs*, are named ERRORLOG.1 (most recent) to ERRORLOG.6 (the oldest). The default location of the error log file is in the \LOG directory off the SQL Server home directory. The following is an example of a SQL Server error log:

```
998-10-08 09:23:12.79 kernel   Microsoft SQL Server  7.00 - 7.00.571
(Intel X86)
    Sep 13 1998 02:20:00
    Copyright  1988-1998 Microsoft Corporation
    Desktop Edition on Windows 4.0 (Build 1111:  B)

1998-10-08 09:23:12.80 kernel   Copyright  1988-1997 Microsoft
Corporation.
1998-10-08 09:23:12.80 kernel   All rights reserved.
1998-10-08 09:23:12.80 kernel   Logging SQL Server messages in
    ➥file 'C:\MSSQL7\log\ERRORLOG'.
1998-10-08 09:23:13.05 kernel   initconfig: Number of user connections
    ➥limited to 32767.
1998-10-08 09:23:13.08 kernel   SQL Server is starting at priority
    ➥class 'normal'(1 CPU detected).
1998-10-08 09:23:13.23 kernel   User Mode Scheduler configured for thread
processing
```

```
1998-10-08 09:23:14.73 server    Directory Size: 2559
1998-10-08 09:23:14.79 spid1     Using dynamic lock allocation. [500]
    ➥Lock Blocks, [1000] Lock Owner Blocks
1998-10-08 09:23:14.83 spid1     failed to get sqlservr image range
1998-10-08 09:23:14.90 spid1     Starting up database 'master'.
1998-10-08 09:23:14.90 spid1     Opening file C:\MSSQL7\data\master.mdf.
1998-10-08 09:23:15.06 spid1     Opening file C:\MSSQL7\data\mastlog.ldf.
1998-10-08 09:23:15.27 spid1     Loading SQL Server's  Unicode collation.
1998-10-08 09:23:15.39 spid1     Loading SQL Server's  non-Unicode sort
    ➥order and character set.
1998-10-08 09:23:15.69 spid1     3 transactions rolled forward in
    ➥database 'master' (1).
1998-10-08 09:23:15.74 spid1     0 transactions rolled back in
    ➥database 'master' (1).
1998-10-08 09:23:15.93 spid1     Starting up database 'model'.
1998-10-08 09:23:15.94 spid1     Opening file C:\MSSQL7\DATA\model.mdf.
1998-10-08 09:23:16.02 spid1     Opening file c:\mssql7\data\modellog.ldf.
1998-10-08 09:23:16.22 spid1     Clearing tempdb database.
1998-10-08 09:23:16.33 spid1     Creating file C:\MSSQL7\DATA\TEMPDB.MDF.
1998-10-08 09:23:16.50 spid1     Closing file C:\MSSQL7\DATA\TEMPDB.MDF.
1998-10-08 09:23:16.50 spid1     Creating file C:\MSSQL7\DATA\TEMPLOG.LDF.
1998-10-08 09:23:16.50 spid1     Closing file C:\MSSQL7\DATA\TEMPLOG.LDF.
1998-10-08 09:23:16.51 spid1     Opening file C:\MSSQL7\DATA\TEMPDB.MDF.
1998-10-08 09:23:16.74 spid1     Opening file C:\MSSQL7\DATA\TEMPLOG.LDF.
1998-10-08 09:23:17.76 spid1     Closing file C:\MSSQL7\DATA\TEMPDB.MDF.
1998-10-08 09:23:17.88 spid1     Closing file C:\MSSQL7\DATA\TEMPLOG.LDF.
1998-10-08 09:23:17.93 spid1     Starting up database 'tempdb'.
1998-10-08 09:23:17.96 spid1     Opening file C:\MSSQL7\DATA\TEMPDB.MDF.
1998-10-08 09:23:18.12 spid1     Opening file C:\MSSQL7\DATA\TEMPLOG.LDF.
1998-10-08 09:23:18.97 spid1     Server name is 'WORKSTATION'.
1998-10-08 09:23:19.01 kernel    Using 'SQLEVN70.DLL' version '7.00.571'.
1998-10-08 09:23:19.04 kernel    Using 'OPENDS60.DLL' version
'7.00.00.0571'.
1998-10-08 09:23:19.07 spid6     Starting up database 'msdb'.
1998-10-08 09:23:19.13 ods       Using 'SSMSSH70.DLL'
    ➥version '7.0.571' to listen on ''.
1998-10-08 09:23:19.23 ods       Using 'SSMSSO70.DLL'
    ➥version '7.0.571' to listen on '1433'.
1998-10-08 09:23:19.35 ods       Using 'SSMSRP70.DLL'
    ➥version '7.0.571' to listen on 'WORKSTATION'.
1998-10-08 09:23:19.37 spid6     Opening file c:\mssql7\DATA\msdblog.ldf.
1998-10-08 09:23:20.05 spid6     Starting up database 'pubs'.
1998-10-08 09:23:20.12 spid6     Opening file C:\MSSQL7\DATA\pubs.mdf.
1998-10-08 09:23:20.31 spid6     Opening file c:\mssql7\DATA\pubs_log.ldf.
1998-10-08 09:23:20.84 spid6     Starting up database 'Northwind'.
1998-10-08 09:23:20.91 spid6     Opening file C:\MSSQL7\DATA\northwnd.mdf.
1998-10-08 09:23:21.24 spid6     Opening file C:\MSSQL7\DATA\northwnd.ldf.
1998-10-08 09:23:22.15 spid1     Recovery complete.
1998-10-08 09:23:22.15 spid1     SQL Server's Unicode collation is:
1998-10-08 09:23:22.15 spid1               'English' (ID = 1033).
1998-10-08 09:23:22.15 spid1               comparison style = 196609.
```

13

TROUBLESHOOTING
SQL SERVER

```
1998-10-08 09:23:22.15 spid1    SQL Server's non-Unicode sort order is:
1998-10-08 09:23:22.15 spid1            'nocase_iso' (ID = 52).
1998-10-08 09:23:22.15 spid1    SQL Server's non-Unicode character set is:
1998-10-08 09:23:22.15 spid1            'iso_1' (ID = 1).
1998-10-08 09:23:22.34 kernel   Warning: override, autoexec procedures
skipped.
1998-10-08 09:23:45.54 spid7    Using 'xpstar.dll' version '1998.09.12'
➥to execute extended stored procedure 'xp_regread'.
```

The error log output includes the time and date the message was logged, the source of the message, and the description of the error message. If an error occurs, the log contains the error message number and description.

> **TIP**
>
> Spend some time looking at and understanding the messages in the error log, especially the proper startup sequence messages. When and if your SQL Server begins to have problems, you will be able to quickly decipher abnormal events or messages in your error log. The archive files come in handy here as well because you can use them as a reference for when things were running fine.

You can view the error log using the SQL Server Enterprise Manager. To use the Enterprise Manager, simply expand the error log tree located in the management folder on the server you want to view, and then select the error log you want to see. The error log is loaded into the right-hand frame of the SQL Enterprise Manager as shown in Figure 13.6.

FIGURE 13.6

The Server Error Log displayed in the Enterprise Manager.

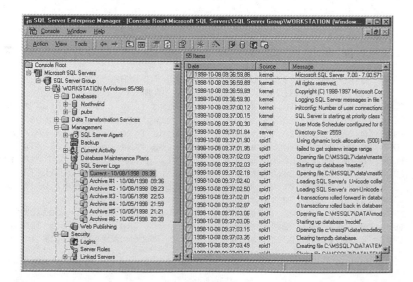

The error log can be a useful source of information in certain problems. For example, if SQL Server immediately shuts down after start up or when clients lose network connections, the error log provides you with valuable information to debug the problem. If you are unable to connect to SQL Server with the Enterprise Manager, you can use the Windows Notepad application to open and view the error log.

USING THE EVENT VIEWER

SQL Server also logs information and error messages to the Windows NT event log. NT uses the event log NT as a repository for the operating system and applications to log informational and error messages. The Event Viewer is located in the Windows NT Administrative Tools group. The advantage of using the Event Viewer over the error log is that errors are easy to spot because NT highlights all error messages with a red stop sign; it highlights information messages with a blue exclamation mark (see Figure 13.7).

FIGURE 13.7

The Windows NT Event Viewer, showing the application event log.

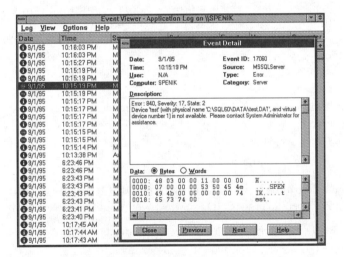

13

TROUBLESHOOTING SQL SERVER

To view the detailed error message description, severity level, and state, double-click the line item. An Event Details dialog box appears. The Event Viewer also provides a search utility that enables you to search for specific types of events in the event log. For example, you can search for all the error messages in the event log.

NOTE

Of course the Windows NT Event log is only available with SQL Server 7.0 running on NT platforms and is not available with Windows 9x.

KILLING A PROCESS

An SQL Server *user process* is a task or request made to SQL Server by a user. Occasionally, you might be required to halt (stop) a user process before it completes. Perhaps the user has incorrectly formatted a query or launched a massive transaction that will take hours to complete and that has blocked out other users from necessary table information. Whatever the case may be, you can bet that sooner or later someone will ask you to stop his or her process or someone else will complain about not getting any information back. The proper terminology for halting a process is called *killing a process*, which sounds much more severe than just halting or stopping the process. When you kill a process, you completely remove the process from SQL Server.

> **TIP**
>
> The number one reason to kill a process is interference with other users' processing (that is, the rogue process prevents them from getting to the required information by "blocking" them out, as in exclusive table locks, for a lengthy transaction).

SQL Server assigns each task a unique identity number called a spid (system process ID). To view the currently running processes and their spids, issue the system stored procedure sp_who, which has the following format:

```
sp_who [login id ¦ 'spid']
```

In this syntax, *login_id* is the specific user login ID for which you want to report activity and *spid* is a specific process ID for which you want to report activity.

Issuing the sp_who command with no parameters displays a report on all the current processes on SQL Server, as in the following example:

```
spid   status      loginame    hostname    blk   dbname      cmd
-----  ---------   ---------   ---------   ----- ---------   ---------------
1      sleeping    sa                      0     master      MIRROR HANDLER
2      sleeping    sa                      0     master      LAZY WRITER
3      sleeping    sa                      0     master      CHECKPOINT SLEEP
4      runnable    sa                      0     master      RA MANAGER
10     sleeping    sa          SPENIK      0     master      AWAITING COMMAND
11     runnable    sa          SPENIK      0     master      SELECT
```

To kill a process, use the KILL command, which has the following syntax:

```
KILL spid
```

In this syntax, *spid* is the system process ID of the process you want to terminate.

You can kill only one spid at a time and the statement cannot be reversed. After you have issued the command, the process *will* be killed. If the command being killed has a lot of work to rollback, it may take some time for the process to shut down. To kill spid number 11 shown in the previous sample, you issue the following command:

```
kill 11
```

> **NOTE**
>
> In pre-system 10 versions of Sybase and pre-Windows NT versions of Microsoft SQL Server, the KILL command did not always work. If the spid was a sleeping process, the only way to kill the process was to shut down the server. The inability to kill a process with the KILL statement was a kind of joke among DBAs; the processes were nicknamed *zombies*. A zombie process was a serious problem when a process really did need to be shut down and the KILL command was ineffective. Microsoft corrected the problem in SQL Server for Windows NT 4.21. In some cases with Microsoft SQL Server, you may be unable to kill a process or should not attempt to kill the process; in such cases, you must shut down the server. For instance you can not kill your own process, system processes or processing that are executing an extended stored procedure. You should also avoid killing the following processes:
>
> Awaiting Command
>
> Select
>
> Signal Handler
>
> Checkpoint Sleep
>
> Lazy Writer
>
> Lock Monitor

You also can kill a process using the SQL Server Enterprise Manager by performing the following steps:

1. After you select a server, expand the Management folder and expand the Current Activity icon with a single click. Select the Process Info icon. All the current processes running on SQL Server as well as the spids of the processes are displayed in the right-hand frame of the Enterprise Manager, shown in Figure 13.8.

FIGURE 13.8

*The Current
Activity dialog
box.*

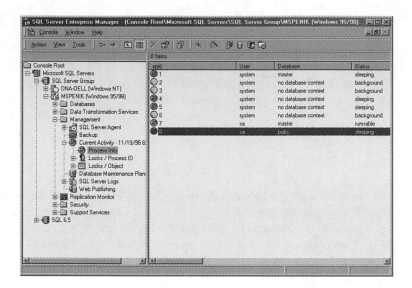

2. To kill a process, select the process you want to terminate with a single mouse click, and then right mouse-click and select the Kill Process option. A dialog box appears asking if you want to terminate the process; click Yes to terminate the selected process.

VIEWING DETAILED PROCESS ACTIVITY

The day will come when your phone is ringing off the hook because suddenly the system is slow or a user has been waiting a very long time for a report to complete. With SQL Server 7.0, you can easily view the current activity of the system using the Current Activity dialog box (refer to Figure 13.8). To view detailed information on an executing process, select the process you wish to view the information from the current activity view (refer to Figure 13.8) with a single mouse-click, and then right mouse-click and select the Properties option. The Process Information dialog box of the Current Activity dialog box appears (see Figure 13.9).

The process information dialog box allows you to view the last command executed by a process or the resource usage of the process (CPU and disk usage).

FIGURE 13.9

The Process Information dialog box.

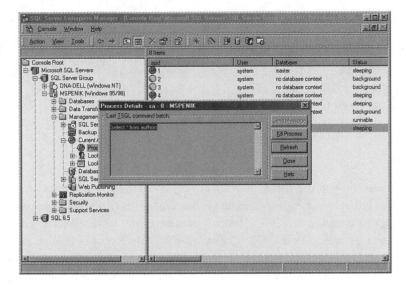

USING DBCC AND TRACE STATEMENTS TO TROUBLESHOOT

DBCC stands for *Database Consistency Checker*. DBCC consists of a series of commands that perform a variety of functions on databases and database objects. DBCC commands are used to perform database and database object maintenance but also can be used to find errors—and in some cases, fix them. SQL Server also provides a series of trace flags that can be used to provide additional information about SQL Server such as the estimated and actual cost of a sort (trace flag 326). To turn a trace flag on for a single user connection use the following syntax:

```
DBCC TRACEON(FLAG_NUMBER)
```

For example, the following syntax would turn on trace flag 326:

```
DBCC TRACEON(326)
```

To turn off a trace flag, use the following syntax:

```
DBCC TRACEOFF(FLAG_NUMBER)
```

To turn off trace flag 326, you would issue the following command:

```
DBCC TRACEOFF(326)
```

To turn a trace flag on for all connections, use the SQL Server startup commandline option –T followed by the trace flag number. You can add startup commandline options using the Enterprise Manager or by starting the server from the command line. For useful trace flag settings, see the FAQ later in this chapter.

13

TROUBLESHOOTING SQL SERVER

NOTE

DBCC commands are detailed in Appendix B. It is highly recommended that you read and reread Appendix B. Understanding when and how to use DBCC can save you a lot of headaches. In previous versions of SQL Server, DBCC was required for maintenance as well. In SQL Server 7.0 the maintenance aspect of DBCC has diminished but it is still useful for troubleshooting and in some cases correcting database problems.

So how do you use DBCC to track errors? For starters, you can examine the output of your DBCC maintenance commands for standard SQL Server error messages. If you find an error message in a DBCC output, treat the error message like any other SQL Server error message and use Books Online or technical support to resolve the error. When you call technical support or find the error number in Books Online, one or many of the resolution steps may be to execute DBCC command(s) to resolve the problem.

Become familiar with DBCC commands. Use the correct DBCC options (if any) to fix a problem in your database when instructed to do so.

FOLLOW THE CLUES

The following story is a story I have used in the previous editions, but I still think it rings true. It also brings to light a frustration many readers have expressed about the lack of documentation, articles, or information about problems encountered at your sites. As the story shows, a lot can happen, especially unexpected things that are hard to document.

One night, while working late to help a group fix an SQL Server problem, I was reminded of a very important tip when troubleshooting SQL Server problems: *Follow the clues. Do not speculate first.* The reason I was reminded of this tip is that, when I arrived on the scene, everyone involved was ready to blame the problem on the new release of SQL Server that they had upgraded to two weeks earlier (the upgrade was from release 4.21 to release 6.0—and I performed the upgrade). When I looked over the error log and the general state of the system, I quickly ruled out the upgrade.

The problem they were having was running a new stored procedure that pulled information in from a mainframe flat file and massaged and reformatted the data to be output to another flat file to feed the mainframe. Whenever the stored procedure ran, the transaction log filled up before the process could complete. They had expanded the log several times and still the stored procedure could not run to completion. One important fact to mention is that the procedure had been tested with 500 rows on versions 4.21 and 6.0 but now they were attempting to run 16,000 rows.

One problem I spotted and fixed immediately with DBCC commands was that the transaction log's size was invalid and would not respond correctly to `TRANACTION WITH NO_LOG` command. After the transaction log problem was corrected, I set up a threshold to back up the log when it was 80 percent full. Still the procedure would not run. When I examined the stored procedure, I found nothing unusual. A transaction was started and then the 16,000 rows were copied to four tables. This organization had several stored procedures that performed the same operation and nothing looked unusual with the stored procedure. Again the cry of "maybe it's version 6.0—let's try 4.21" was echoed.

Because there was no evidence to suggest that it was a version 6.0 problem, we tried the procedure again. This time, we monitored the server from the version 4.21 Object Manager using `sp_who`, `sp_lock`, and `DBCC SQLPERF(LOGSPACE)` to track what was going on. It was not long before we noticed that the `spid` executing the stored procedure seemed to be stuck on an `UPDATE` statement. That seemed odd because the only `UPDATE` occurred outside of the transaction and had already occurred. Again moans about the upgrade or the corrupted transaction log rose across the room. Except for the developer, who quietly stated, "I bet there is an update trigger on the table I'm inserting into." Well, she was right. Not only was there an update trigger but the SQL statement was incorrectly copying 16,000 rows into a table with an update trigger when only 39 rows should have been copied. The problem was quickly solved.

The moral of this story is that troubleshooting can be difficult and often consists of more then one clue (such as an upgrade, a corrupted transaction log, and a new process). Try not to jump to conclusions. Solve each problem, one at a time, and if something does not make sense, keep searching for the real reason the process fails so that you can fix it. It is very easy to go down the wrong road. Oh, by the way, beware of triggers on tables when troubleshooting a developer process. They are easy to forget and, in some cases, may be the unexpected root of the problem!

Table/Index Fragmentation

Table/Index fragmentation occurs on tables that have a lot of insert/update/delete activity. Because the table is modified over time, pages begin to fill, possibly causing page splits on clustered indexes. As pages split, the newly added pages may use disk space that is not contiguous; this hurts performance because contiguous pages are a form of sequential I/O which is faster (about twice as fast) than non-sequential I/O. The fullness of each data page can also vary (that is, pages are not full) under heavy data modifications. You can defragment the table by executing DBCC DBREINDEX on the tables clustered index, which packs each page with the fill factor amount of data and reorders the information on contiguous data pages. You can also drop and recreate the index, however, using the DBREINDEX command is faster then dropping and re-creating the index(es). Not only does rebuilding an index improve performance when you read the table, it also can increase the available database space. Rebuilding a clustered index on a very large table can take a fair amount of time. SQL Server 6.x and 7.x provide the DBCC SHOWCONTIG command, which enables you to determine how fragmented a table or index is (that is, whether or not you need to rebuild it). The SHOWCONTIG option has the following format:

```
DBCC SHOWCONTIG (table id, [index id])
```

In this syntax, `table id` and `index id` are the IDs of the object found in the `sysobjects` table of the database. For example, the following is the command line and output from a DBCC SHOWCONTIG command performed on the `authors` table in the `pubs` database:

```
DBCC SHOWCONTIG scanning 'authors' table...
Table: 'authors' (117575457); index ID: 1, database ID: 5
TABLE level scan performed.
- Pages Scanned................................: 1
- Extents Scanned..............................: 1
- Extent Switches..............................: 0
- Avg. Pages per Extent........................: 1.0
- Scan Density [Best Count:Actual Count].......: 100.00% [1:1]
- Logical Scan Fragmentation ..................: 0.00%
- Extent Scan Fragmentation ...................: 0.00%
- Avg. Bytes Free per Page.....................: 6008.0
- Avg. Page Density (full).....................: 25.77%- DBCC execution
completed.
If DBCC printed error messages, see your System Administrator.
```

To determine whether you need to rebuild the index because of excessive index page splits, look at the Scan Density value displayed by DBCC SHOWCONTIG. The Scan Density value should be at or near 100%. If it is significantly below 100%, rebuild the index.

> **TIP**
>
> For those of you wondering how to find the table ID using sysobjects, the query used for the authors table is shown here. Remember: To get a table ID for a specific table, you must be in the database when you query sysobjects or make a direct reference to the database such as database..sysobjects. The query (executed from the master database) is as follows:
>
> ```
> select id from pubs..sysobjects where name = "authors"
> ```
>
> Better yet, use the Transact-SQL function, object_id as follows:
>
> ```
> Select object_id('authors')
> ```

TROUBLESHOOTING APPLICATIONS

SQL Server 7.0 comes with many different utilities to help you debug your applications and get the best performance. The SQL Server Profiler (previously SQL Trace) enables you to monitor SQL Server while your applications are executing in a production or test environment. You can use the SQL Server Profiler to look at different events, objects, Transact-SQL statements, locking, and errors. You can save the traces to a file to replay on the server (or a different server). This ability is useful when tuning a server and application or in situations where an event occurs that causes your server or application to behave in an undesirable manner. You can read more about the SQL Server Profiler in Chapter 19, "Monitoring SQL Server."

The ISQL/W tool has also been improved and is now called the SQL Server Query Analyzer. The SQL Server Query Analyzer provides more SHOWPLAN detail about the query being executed, allowing you to make better decisions about tuning the query. Another new feature to help you tune applications is the SQL Server Index Tuning Wizard, which can read a trace from the SQL Server Profiler as well as a query from the SQL Server Query Analyzer, and make recommendations on how to index the tables to get better performance. You can learn more about these utilities in Chapter 22, "Understanding Indexes," and Chapter 23, "Query Optimization."

OTHER SOURCES OF HELP AND INFORMATION

In SQL Server 7.0, Microsoft has done a good job of providing useful and valuable information in Books Online. However as a DBA, it is important for you to know that there are many other good sources of information for Microsoft SQL Server (such as this book). What happens when the problem is beyond the scope of published resources? The following sections discuss some of the options available to you.

Technical Support

When you run across a problem not covered in this book or one of a very critical and urgent nature, it's time to get in touch with your tech support company. If you have purchased SQL Server, you have also (hopefully) purchased a support agreement with Microsoft or with a Microsoft Solution Provider to help you in an emergency. If not, Microsoft can still provide help (for per-incident charge). In general, Microsoft's support contracts and agreements are less expensive than those of some of the other RDBMS companies. A Microsoft Solution Provider is an independent organization that provides consulting and integration services for Microsoft products and also can provide support. Before calling tech support, be sure to have all the information required to start an incident report. You should have the following information:

- Hardware platform
- Version of Windows NT
- Version of SQL Server (you can get this from the error log or by using the @@Version global variable)
- Complete error message (number, level, state, and description)
- Type of environment (production/development)
- Urgency of problem resolution
- Description and scenario of the problem and the cause

SQL Server 7.0 provides a utility called sqldiag that will collect the above information for you besides lots and lots of additional information to supply to tech support. For more information see the Troubleshooting FAQ in this chapter.

TIP

If the problem is one that can be reproduced using SQL commands or a sequence of events, have this information written down so that the tech support person can duplicate the results. Even better than writing it down, you can use the SQL Server 7.0 extended stored procedure xp_trace_setqueryhistory to create a trace file of the last 100 queries executed. You can also use xp_trace_flushqueryhistory to include exceptions that occur as well as SQL.

Microsoft TechNet and Microsoft Developer Network

Before there was SQL Server Books Online, there was Microsoft TechNet. Microsoft TechNet is a monthly CD subscription that provides a wealth of information about Microsoft products. TechNet provides product white papers, release notes, current patches and drivers, and a knowledge base of product information and problem resolution. TechNet is fairly inexpensive for a yearly subscription of 12 monthly CDs packed with information. To find out more about TechNet, visit its Web site at `http://www.microsoft.com/technet`.

TIP

TechNet is my second line of defense. If I can't resolve the problem based on my knowledge and Books Online, I check TechNet for information on the problem. Do yourself a favor and subscribe!

The advantage of TechNet is that it is a monthly CD, so problem resolution not available when SQL Server 7.0 shipped can be placed in the TechNet knowledge base for your immediate use. TechNet's search facility is similar to the Books Online search facility (or vice-versa, because TechNet was here first), as shown in Figure 13.10. As you can with Books Online, you can perform searches on error numbers or keywords and get a list of articles that contain the keyword or error number.

13

TROUBLESHOOTING SQL SERVER

FIGURE 13.10
Microsoft TechNet.

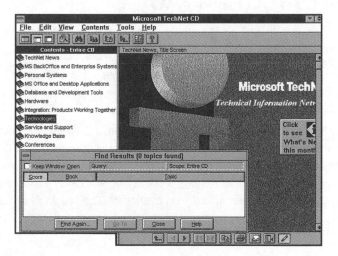

Microsoft Developer Network is also a very useful source of highly technical information on SQL Server. You can subscribe to MSDN like TechNet, and you can also view MSDN online at `http://www.microsoft.com/MSDN`.

The Internet

To obtain interactive support without using tech support, try one of the many Internet sites or news group offered by Microsoft for SQL Server. The Microsoft news server is `MSNews.microsoft.com` and the newsgroup for SQL Server is `microsoft.public.sqlserver`. Microsoft's Web page for SQL Server is `http://www.Microsoft.com/SQL`. Using the online services, you can search for existing messages that deal with problems you are experiencing or you can post messages asking for help from your peers. The online services have proven to be very useful. Many individuals have their problems resolved on the online services, but most of these problems are of a noncritical nature because turnaround time for a posted question is an unknown. You can also check out the Keiter, Stephens Computer Services Developer Corner at `http://www.kscsinc.com/devcorner`.

User Groups

SQL Server user groups can provide a forum in which you can discuss problems or issues with your local peers. They also tend to enlighten you on current products and future releases.

TROUBLESHOOTING FAQ

The following section lists some commonly asked questions and answers about SQL Server 7.0 troubleshooting.

Q. I have heard that an open transaction can block a user from a table due to an exclusive lock and prevent the transaction log from truncating completely. How can I check SQL Server for an open transaction?

A. An open transaction can be a problem when a user is running an exteremly long process that starts one large transaction, thus locking users out of the system until the transaction is committed, rolled back, or someone has issued a Begin Transaction statement, with issuing a `COMMIT` or `ROLLBACK`. To find an open transaction, use the DBCC command with `OPENTRAN`. The syntax is as follows:

```
DBCC OPENTRAN [('database_name' or 'database_id')]
[With TABLERESULTS or NO_INFOMSGS]
```

Q. What are some useful trace statements to find out additional dead locking information?

A. To find out what types of locks are being acquired and released during a session, use trace flag 1200. To track down additional locking information for deadlocks, set trace flags 1204 and 1205. Using these trace flags provides you with information about the types of locks and the commands being executed at the time of the deadlock.

Q. How can I send trace information to the error log?

A. Use the trace flag 3605.

Q. How can I send trace information to my screen?

A. Use trace flag 3604.

Q. I'm having trouble starting my SQL Server because of a startup stored procedure I added. How can I disable the startup stored procedure from executing so I can start SQL Server?

A. You can disable startup stored procedures from executing by using trace flag 4022. Set the flag by adding it to the SQL Server startup parameters (or command line) using the –T option.

Q. I'm having trouble installing SQL Server; what do I do?

A. Look in Chapters 5, "Planning an Installation or Upgrade," and 6, "Installing or Upgrading SQL Server," for additional information on installing and upgrading SQL Server. Additionally look in the SQL Server Install directory at the files with an extension of .OUT. These are output files for the installation process and contain success and error messages that can be used to help you troubleshoot an installation problem.

Q. I need to call tech support. Is there any easy way to gather all the information they may need about my server and my SQL Server?

A. SQL Server provides a utility called `sqldiag` which captures information about SQL Server and the environment like registry information, Diagnostic Reports (System report, Drivers report, Memory report, and so forth), output from several system stored procedures (`sp_who`, `sp_lock`, `sp_configure`, `sp_helpdb`, `xp_msver`, `sp_helpextendedproc` and `sysprocesses`) and lots of other information.

Q. Are there any good monthly publications that are helpful for troubleshooting SQL Server problems?

A. A column of useful SQL Server information, be it troubleshooting, tips, or tricks is found in the monthly magazine, "Windows NT Magazine" by Duke Publishing (`http://www.winntmag.com`). The column is the "SQL Server Source" by Karen Watterson and Brian Moran.

13

TROUBLESHOOTING SQL SERVER

SUMMARY

You should now know where to search for SQL Server error messages as well as understand the format and meaning of SQL Server error messages. This chapter provided the foundation for your understanding how to interpret and research the error messages you receive during routine maintenance. Another important point in this chapter is that to be a good DBA, you need to stay informed. You can get involved in your local SQL Server user group or spend a few hours a week on the Web, or interacting with your peers and learning more about SQL Server. In Chapter 29, "Developing a SQL Server Maintenance Plan," and Chapter 30, "Automating Database Administration Tasks," you learn how to perform preventive maintenance on your SQL Server to limit the amount of time you spend troubleshooting. Here are some of the important points to review when you troubleshoot SQL Server:

- SQL Server displays error messages in the following format: `Msg #`, `Level #`, `State #`, `Description`.
- If an error occurs, write down the entire message, not just a part of it.
- Use Books Online and the Microsoft TechNet search facilities to help resolve problems.
- Make it a point to understand the SQL Server error log.
- Check the Windows NT event log for errors by using the Event Viewer search facility.
- Stop user processes with the `KILL` command.
- Use DBCC and trace flags to help troubleshoot problems.
- For application troubleshooting, take advantage of SQL Server 7.0's index tuning wizard the SQL Server Profiler.
- Stay informed by taking advantage of user groups and online services on the Internet.

MISCELLANEOUS TOPICS AND NEW SQL SERVER UTILITIES

by Kevin Viers

IN THIS CHAPTER

This chapter is a catchall chapter; it covers several topics that are not all related to each other, including both new functionality that has been added to SQL Server and new utilities that ship with the product. The following topics are covered in this chapter:

- SQL Mail
- Distributed queries
- Microsoft English Query

After reading this chapter, you should have a working knowledge of each of these topics.

SQL MAIL

SQL Mail is a service that enables the SQL Server to utilize email functionality via any MAPI-compliant email host. SQL Mail enables you to automatically send email notifications on alerts, when performance monitor thresholds are exceeded, and when scheduled tasks succeed or fail. Additionally, you can use system stored procedures to send email within a trigger or user-defined stored procedure. You can include an object within a Data Transformation Services (DTS) package to send email notifications as packages are executed. In fact, SQL Server can even receive email and respond to those email requests with a query resultset.

As you can see, SQL Server provides a rich set of functionality that enables you to integrate your SQL Server and your email functionality in the way most beneficial to your particular needs. SQL Mail is relatively easy to configure and even easier to use. The remainder of this section illustrates how you configure SQL Mail to run with your SQL Server and provides various scenarios in which you might want to use SQL Mail.

Setting Up Your SQL Server as a Mail Client

As mentioned previously, SQL Mail can utilize any MAPI-compliant email service. In order to keep this chapter manageable, however, we will only discuss SQL Mail in the context of Microsoft Exchange Server. SQL Mail works equally well with Microsoft Mail or any other MAPI-compliant software.

Before you can use SQL Mail, your SQL Server machine must be set up as a valid MAPI mail client. If you are running Microsoft Exchange, this means that you must have the Microsoft Exchange client software installed on your SQL Server and you must have a valid mailbox established for the SQL Server user on the Exchange Server. Because this chapter is about SQL Mail and not Microsoft Exchange, it does not cover setting up a Microsoft Exchange client other than to mention a couple important points:

- Your Exchange Server must have a valid mailbox for the user who is configured to run the MSSQLServer service. By default, the SQL Mail service runs under the same security context as the MSSQLServer service. To see the account under which the MSSQLServer service is running, use the Services applet under Control Panel.

- You must set up a mail profile using the Mail and Fax applet under Control Panel. This profile should be configured to point to the appropriate Microsoft Exchange Server and mailbox.

The exact details of setting up your SQL Server machine as a MAPI mail client vary depending on your email software.

> **TIP**
>
> You should test that your SQL Server machine is set up correctly as a mail client before going any further with SQL Mail configuration. To test this, log on to the machine under the same account that MSSQLServer will use and try to send an email message using your email client (Outlook, MS Mail, Exchange, and so on). If you cannot send an email message, then SQL Server certainly won't be able to.

Configuring SQL Mail

After your SQL Server machine has been successfully configured with a MAPI mail client, you are ready to configure SQL Mail. To do this, follow these steps:

1. Open the SQL Server Enterprise Manager. Expand the appropriate Server group, and then expand the appropriate Server and open the Support Services Folder. Right-click the SQL Mail icon and click Properties. You will see the dialog box shown in Figure 14.1.

FIGURE 14.1
The SQL Mail Configuration dialog box.

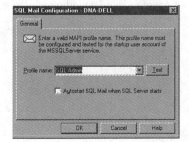

2. Use the drop-down list to choose the mail profile you created when you set up your mail client. Click Test. You should see the dialog box shown in Figure 14.2.

   If your mail profile were incorrectly configured, you would receive a similar dialog box that reads "Unable to start a mail session on the server with this dialog."

FIGURE 14.2
*The SQL Mail
Configuration
dialog box.*

> **NOTE**
>
> By default, SQL Mail must be started manually. You can do this by right-clicking the SQL Mail icon in the SQL Server Enterprise Manager and choosing Start. If you would like for SQL Server to automatically start SQL Mail every time SQL Server is started, simply check the Auto-Start check box on the SQL Mail Configuration dialog box as shown in Figure 14.1. This is highly recommended if you would like to use SQL Mail for any automated notification scenarios.

That is really all there is to configuring SQL Mail itself.

Using SQL Mail

Now that you have configured SQL Mail, it would be nice to use it. SQL Mail allows you to integrate email functionality into your SQL Server installation by enabling SQL Server to send, receive, and process email messages. The bulk of the SQL Mail functionality is implemented via a system stored procedure called `sp_processmail`. In addition to `sp_processmail`, several extended stored procedures are shipped with SQL Server that will enable you to customize SQL Mail within your databases and applications. The extended stored procedures are included in `SQLMAP70.dll`, a dynamic link library that is installed with SQL Server. A summary of these stored procedures follows:

- `xp_startmail`—Used to manually start an SQL Mail session. Remember that you can configure SQL Mail to start automatically.

- `xp_stopmail`—Used to manually stop an SQL Mail session.

- `xp_sendmail`—Used to manually send an email message to any recipient or group of recipients. This email message can contain a plain-text message, the results of a query, or even a file attachment.

- `xp_findnextmsg`—Used to find the message ID of the next message waiting in the SQL Server inbox. Remember that SQL Server can receive email messages as well as send them.

- `xp_readmail`—Used to manually read a mail message that is in the SQL Server inbox by using the message ID returned from the `xp_findnextmsg` stored procedure. Alternatively, `xp_readmail` can be used to return the entire inbox as a result-set to the client.

- `xp_deletemail`—Used to delete a mail message after it has been processed.

- `sp_processmail`—Used to process mail in the SQL Server inbox. This stored procedure uses all of the extended stored procedures mentioned previously.

For a more complete explanation of these stored procedures, including all available parameters, you can refer to the Transact-SQL help.

The following sections describe how to use these stored procedures to add email functionality to your SQL Server implementation.

Sending Email from SQL Server

There are many scenarios in which you might want to use SQL Server to send email messages. Probably, the most common scenario is when system operators are automatically notified of certain database conditions. This functionality is implemented through the SQL Agent, and is discussed in detail in Chapter 7. However, the SQL Agent email functionality is limited to sending email based on events and conditions. If you want a more robust use of email, you must use the SQL Mail stored procedures.

Suppose you want to embed an email notification in a trigger so that SQL Server would automatically send an email message when a certain table is updated. For example, you might want to allow users to update information about themselves via a corporate intranet. After the user has updated his or her employee record, you want to send an email notification to an HR representative. This functionality could be implemented by using the SQL Mail extended stored procedures within a trigger.

To do this, simply create an UPDATE TRIGGER on the desired table that contains the following syntax:

```
CREATE TRIGGER notify ON employee
FOR INSERT, UPDATE
AS

declare @msgtext varchar(256), @employee varchar(10)

--populate message text
select @employee = inserted.emp_id
```

14

NEW SQL SERVER UTILITIES

```
from inserted

select @msgtext = 'Please verify records for employee number: ' +
@employee

--send email notification to HR Representative
EXEC xp_sendmail @recipient = 'kviers', @message = @msgtext,
@subject = 'Employee Update'
```

In this trigger, we specify that an email notification will be sent to a specific recipient any time an employee record is updated or inserted. This email notification will include the employee id of the record that has been affected.

The preceding code sample illustrates how you can use the extended SQL Mail stored procedures within a trigger to automatically send email notifications. You could just as easily use the extended stored procedures within user-defined stored procedures to accomplish the same goal.

> **NOTE**
>
> A SQL Mail session must be started before you can run the xp_sendmail stored procedure. If you are going to use these stored procedures as part of a trigger it is probably wise to have SQL Mail auto-start when SQL Server starts. If you do not have a SQL Mail session started you can use the xp_startmail and xp_stopmail stored procedures to dynamically start and stop a SQL Mail session from within your trigger or stored procedure.

Processing Incoming Email

SQL Mail can not only send email messages, but also can receive and respond to them. A user can actually send an email message to SQL Server with a query embedded in the message text and SQL Server can read that email and return the result set of the query to the user.

> **NOTE**
>
> An incoming email message must contain a single SQL query statement in the message text of the email. The sp_processmail stored procedure will read the email message, process the query, and then return the result set to the user as an attached file with a filename of SQLxxx.yyy, where xxx is a random number generated by SQL Server and yyy is the file type specified in the sp_processmail stored procedure.

Any time a user sends an email message to the mailbox that is assigned in the SQL Mail configuration, that email is stored in a SQL Server inbox. The SQL Server inbox is really just a table that stores certain information about the email message such as the sender, subject, CC list, and message text. The sp_processmail stored procedure is used to read and respond to all messages in the SQL Server inbox. The following are the parameters used to modify the behavior of the sp_processmail stored procedure:

- @subject—This parameter is used to determine which email messages to process. If this parameter is supplied sp_processmail will only process those email messages that have a subject equal to that specified. If this parameter is not specified, sp_processmail will process all email messages in the inbox.

- @filetype—This parameter is used to specify the filetype that will be returned to the recipient(s). All query results are returned as an attached file. If this parameter is not specified, all result sets are returned as txt files.

- @set_user—This parameter is used to specify the user context under which to run the queries that are being processed. If this parameter is not specified, all queries will be processed using the Guest user account.

- @dbuse—This parameter is used to specify in which database to process the query. If this parameter is not specified, all queries will be processed in the master database.

The sp_processmail stored procedure can be run manually at any time by executing the stored procedure in a SQL Query Analyzer session.

> **TIP**
>
> You can use SQL Agent to set up the sp_processmail stored procedure as a scheduled task that runs at set intervals to process the inbox. You can also create multiple sp_processmail tasks that each provide different parameters. This would allow you to process email differently, depending on the subject provided.

With the sp_processmail stored procedure and the extended stored procedures, there are virtually limitless ways to use SQL Mail to implement email functionality in your SQL Server scenario. The options are only limited by the imagination of the DBA.

DISTRIBUTED QUERIES

Wouldn't it be nice if all the data in the world were kept in a set of replicated SQL Server databases? Many of us have had that thought at one time or another. The reality, however, is that most of our mission-critical information is scattered across many different, or heterogeneous, data sources.

14

NEW SQL SERVER UTILITIES

For many years, one of the biggest challenges facing information technology (IT) has been how to get to all the organizational data, regardless of its source, and present that data to users as one homogenous entity. Typical users couldn't care less that one set of data is in Oracle, another is in SQL Server, a third is in DB2, and yet other set of data is in an Excel spreadsheet. They want to see data as it should be seen, as one interrelated grouping of information.

This section covers how SQL Server is dealing with the challenge of pulling data from many disparate data sources by using heterogeneous or distributed queries.

Distributed Queries Explained

A *distributed query* within SQL Server enables you to access data from multiple data sources within the context of a single Transact-SQL statement. In other words, a distributed query enables you to issue a single SELECT statement that pulls data from not only SQL Server, but from Oracle, Access, DB2 and other data sources. Distributed queries allow objects from other data sources (on the same or remote machines) to appear as any other table or view within SQL Server; Figure 14.3 illustrates this concept.

FIGURE 14.3

Illustration of a distributed query scenario.

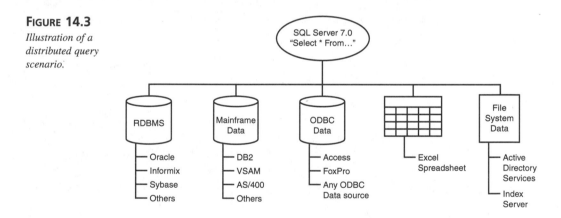

Now that you understand what a distributed query is, let's look at how they work. Implementing a distributed query in SQL Server is actually quite easy because OLE DB has already taken care of the underlying complexity of the problem. As you are probably aware, OLE DB is Microsoft's universal data access standard. It is a published Component Object Model (COM) programming specification that allow any third-party vendor to write custom providers to expose their data. As long as a data source can expose its data via an OLE DB provider, SQL Server can execute a distributed query against that data source. A full discussion of the OLE DB specification is beyond the scope of this text. All you need to understand for now is that distributed queries in SQL Server only work against a data source for which you have an OLE DB provider.

> **NOTE**
>
> The OLE DB provider for your data source must be installed and registered on the SQL Server machine from which you intend to execute distributed queries.

Adding a Linked Server

In order to execute a distributed query, you must *link* all the heterogeneous data sources that you will want to query. When you create a linked server, you are providing SQL Server with all the information it needs to connect to the data source via the appropriate OLE DB provider. To add a linked server, follow these steps:

1. Open the SQL Server Enterprise Manager.

2. Expand the appropriate Server group.

3. Expand the appropriate Server.

4. Expand the Security folder.

5. Right-click the Linked Servers icon and click New Linked Server. The Linked Server Properties—New Linked Server dialog box, shown in Figure 14.4, appears.

FIGURE 14.4

The General tab of the Linked Server Properties— New Linked Server dialog box.

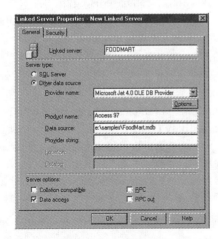

Providing Connection Information

To provide connection information, follow these steps:

1. Enter a name for your linked server in the Linked Server text box. This will be the server name you use when you reference the linked server in any Transact-SQL statements.

2. Click the Provider Name drop-down list; you will see a list of all available OLE DB providers for your installation. Remember, the OLE DB provider must be installed and registered on the SQL Server. Choose the OLE DB provider you want to use for the linked server.

3. Fill out the appropriate connection parameters. The required parameters will vary depending on the OLE DB provider you have chosen. The following is a summary of the parameters that may be required in this section.

   - *Provider Name*—The name of the OLE DB provider you want to use to connect to your data source. The drop-down list displays all available OLE DB providers.

   - *Product Name*—The product name of the OLE DB data source, such as Access 97 or Oracle. This parameter is generally optional. You should refer to your OLE DB provider documentation to determine the appropriate entry.

   - *Data Source*—The data source required by the OLE DB provider. Again, this parameter varies, depending on the OLE DB provider you are using. For example, setting up an Access 97 database using the Microsoft.Jet.OLEDB.4.0 OLE DB provider requires the full pathname of the .MDB file. Setting up an Oracle data source using the MSDAORA OLE DB provider, however, requires a valid SQL Net alias. You should refer to your OLE DB provider documentation to determine the appropriate data source entry.

   - *Provider String*—An optional parameter that can be used when connecting to an Open Database Connectivity (ODBC) data source by using the MSDASQL OLE DB provider. The provider string is a typical ODBC connect string. Alternatively, you can set up a system Data Source Name (DSN) and enter that as the Data Source parameter without entering a provider string.

   - *Location*—An optional parameter that may be required by some OLE DB providers.

   - *Catalog*—If your OLE DB data source supports multiple catalogs, enter the appropriate catalog name in this text box. Many OLE DB data sources, such as Access 97 and Oracle, do not use a catalog name. In these instances, you should leave this parameter blank.

> **NOTE**
>
> Although OLE DB is a standard, each OLE DB provider has some variations in the way connections are made to the data source. You must reference your OLE DB provider documentation to determine the exact parameters required to establish a successful connection.It is beyond the scope of this text to go into detail about every possible OLE DB provider and how to connect to each.

Providing Security Information

After you have provided the appropriate connection information for your linked server, you probably want to set up security information. In many cases, the SQL Server login account under which your user is logged in will not have access to the linked server data source. SQL Server allows you to map local SQL Server login accounts to remote login accounts.

To add security information to the linked server, click the Security tab of the New Linked Server—Linked Server Properties dialog box. You will see the dialog box as shown in Figure 14.5.

FIGURE 14.5

The Security tab of the Linked Server Properties - New Linked Server dialog box.

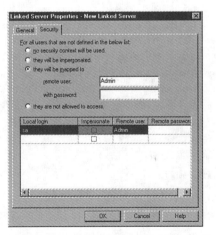

This tab allows you to map local SQL Server logins to remote logins on the linked server. For example, if you are connecting to an unsecured Access 97 database, you must map any local SQL Server login to the remote login Admin with a NULL password. If you do not provide the correct login mappings, SQL Server will be unable to process any queries against the linked server.

To map a local login to a remote login, enter the local login account name in the grid at the bottom of the dialog box as seen in Figure 14.5. You can then choose to provide a remote login and password or to have SQL Server impersonate the local login. If you check the Impersonate check box, SQL Server will use the local login account information to connect to the linked server data source. You should check this option only if you are certain that the linked server data source login account exactly matches the local login. If you do not check the Impersonate check box, SQL Server will use the remote login and password to access the linked server.

TIP

In addition to using the graphical user interface (GUI) within SQL Server Enterprise Manager to add linked servers, you can use the sp_addlinkedserver and sp_addlinkedsrvlogin system stored procedures. These stored procedures can be executed from within any Transact-SQL statement and allow you to dynamically link to remote servers.

NOTE

SQL Server distributed queries can be run against SQL Server 6.5 using the SQL Server 7.0 OLE DB provider. If you are going to do this, you need to update the catalog stored procedures on the SQL Server 6.5 machine before it can be referenced by an SQL Server 7.0 distributed query. (This upgrade will not affect the operation of the 6.5 database.) To update the catalog stored procedures, the administrator of the SQL Server 6.5 machine must run the Mssql7\Install\Inscat.sql file that is installed with SQL Server 7.0.

Executing a Distributed Query

After you have established your linked servers, you can refer to them in any Transact-SQL statement by using a logical name. In this way they are like any other table or view.

To reference a linked server within a Transact-SQL statement, you must use a four-part naming convention: *linked_server.catalog.schema.object_name*. The following explains each component.

- *linked_server*—The name of the linked server that references the OLE DB data source. This is the name you define in the Linked Server Properties—New Linked Server dialog box (refer to Figure 14.4).

- *catalog*—The name of the catalog in the OLE DB data source that contains the object. The use of this will differ depending on OLE DB Providers.

- *schema*—The name of the schema in the catalog that contains the object. The use of this will differ depending on the OLE DB provider.

- *object_name*—The name of the data object in the schema.

As mentioned previously, not all OLE DB providers are implemented in the same way. Therefore, some OLE DB providers require catalog and schema names and others do not. You should refer to the OLE DB provider documentation for exact implementation details.

Figure 14.6 shows an example of a distributed query that is referencing data in an Access 97 database. In this example, a linked server called FoodMart uses the OLE DB provider for Jet. The query is a simple select statement that returns data from the Access database.

FIGURE 14.6

An example of a distributed query.

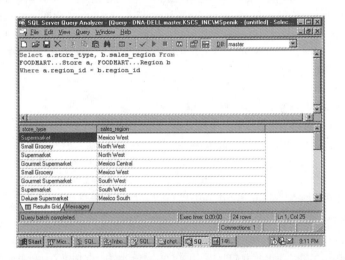

NOTE

When you reference a linked server in a Transact-SQL statement, you *must* use the four-part naming convention. In some cases, the OLE DB provider does not require either catalog or schema information. In that case, simply leave out the element that is not required and supply all the rest. For example, Oracle does not require a catalog; however, you must supply the table owner as the schema name. So for an Oracle linked server, you would reference the table as *linked_server..table_owner.table_name*. You must supply all periods, even if the element is missing.

As you have seen, setting up and using distributed queries within SQL Server is quite easy. The real power of using distributed queries is that you can actually execute queries that join tables from many different data sources in the same SQL statement. This enables you to pull data from Oracle, SQL Server, Access, and even DB2 within the context of a single SQL statement executed on a single SQL Server.

MICROSOFT ENGLISH QUERY

If you are reading this book, you are probably very familiar with SQL and would have no problem firing off a SELECT statement with all the appropriate joins and where clauses to return a resultset to a user. What happens, however, when you want to provide your users with a robust ad hoc querying application that allows them to query data from your database while shielding them from the complexity of writing SQL statements? In years past, this type of application was extremely difficult to create, requiring a tremendous amount of custom programming. Microsoft has introduced a tool to assist with this problem: Microsoft English Query.

English Query Explained

Microsoft English Query is a tool that ships with SQL Server; it enables you to create applications that translate English questions into appropriate SQL commands and retrieve a resultset. For example, an application written using the English Query engine would enable a user to type How many cars did Auto City sell last year? English Query would then translate that question into an appropriate SQL command.

An English Query application can be deployed within a Microsoft Visual Basic or C++ application or as a Web application by using Internet Information Server and Active Server Pages. In fact, English Query applications can be deployed with any development environment that supports ActiveX controls. It is important to note that the client application is responsible for all user interface issues and all database connectivity and SQL execution. In other words, English Query is only responsible for parsing the English question and returning a valid SQL command. The client application must do the rest of the work.

Now that you understand what English Query is, let's take a look at how you use the tool. Like the OLAP services, English Query is a feature-rich product in its own right and this one chapter can't possibly cover all aspects of the application. It does, however, provide you with a basic understanding of the tool so that you can begin using its functionality.

English Query includes two components: the English Query Domain Editor and the English Query Engine. The Domain Editor is an interface that enables you to design and build your English Query applications. The English Query Engine is the component that actually processes user requests and returns SQL statements. We will look at each of these components in greater detail in the following sections.

Creating an English Query Application

Before you can use English Query in your client applications, you must create an English Query application (an `*.eqd` file). This application contains all the information about your database that is required to turn an English question into an appropriate SQL command. Just as you had to learn English before you could effectively communicate, English Query must learn about your database in the context of English definitions of entities and relationships. This body of knowledge about your database is known as the English Query domain.

The English Query domain comprises two types of information:

- *Physical database information*—This is the metadata about your database, including table names, field names, keys, and table join information.

- *Semantic information*—This is the information you provide about entities and relationships, along with all appropriate English phrasing information.

To create an English Query domain, open the Microsoft English Query Domain Editor. You will be prompted to open a project (see Figure 14.7).

FIGURE 14.7

The New Project dialog box.

If you are creating a new project, you can choose to load physical database information from an existing data source. Alternatively, you can create an empty English Query project and manually insert physical database information from a data source. If this is a new project, you probably want to allow English Query to automatically load the physical database information by choosing a data source. To do this, choose the Structure Loaded from Database option. After you click OK, you will be prompted with a standard ODBC data source dialog box. Choose the data source for which you want to create an English Query application.

> **NOTE**
>
> At the time this book went to press, English Query would only support SQL Server 6.5 or later datasources. Microsoft does, however, plan to provide connectivity to other datasources in future releases of the product.

Adding Physical Database Information

After you choose a data source, the English Query domain editor will load all of the physical database information and open into the dialog box shown in Figure 14.8.

FIGURE 14.8

The Database tab of the English Query Domain Editor.

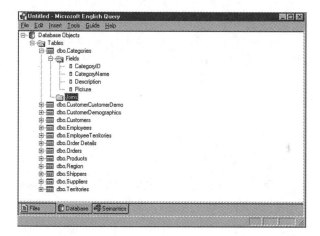

From this screen, you can also import new tables into English Query by choosing File, Import New Tables. Additionally, you can define joins between tables. English Query attempts to create joins based on the foreign key relationships that exist within your database schema. After all your database schema information has been loaded into English Query, you need to define your semantic information.

Adding Semantic Information

Semantic information is really the heart of the English Query application. The semantic information is what provides definition and adds context to the entities and relationships that are present within your database. Adding semantic information is how you teach your English Query application to interpret the questions that it receives from users. The English Query Domain Editor allows you to define semantic information for your database by clicking the Semantics tab. The screen shown in Figure 14.9 will appear.

FIGURE 14.9

The Semantics tab of the English Query Domain Editor.

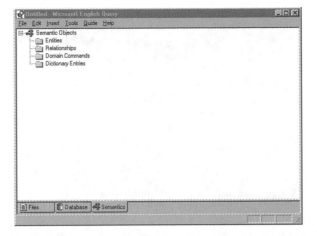

CAUTION

Don't underestimate the importance (or difficulty) of defining a complete and useful set of semantics for your database. If you neglect to include an entity or you do not define all appropriate relationships with the correct phrasing, your application may not understand many of the questions asked by users. The up-front work involved in creating an effective English Query application can be significant, but the payoff is in the end product.

Four primary types of semantic information are used by English Query: entities, relationships, domain commands, and dictionary entries. Each of these types of semantic information is covered in more depth in the following sections.

Entities

Entities are the real-world objects that add meaning to your database. Typically these objects are described by nouns (for example, people, places, things). In the context of a database, most entities are represented by at least one table. These types of entities are called *major entities*. Additionally, most entities have traits that are generally represented by fields within a table and are called *minor entities*.

Let's say we want to create an entity to represent an author. We need to do this to allow English Query to interpret user questions about authors. To create this entity in the English Query Domain Editor, right-click the Entities folder on the Semantics tab shown in Figure 14.9 and choose Insert Entity. The dialog box shown in Figure 14.10 will appear.

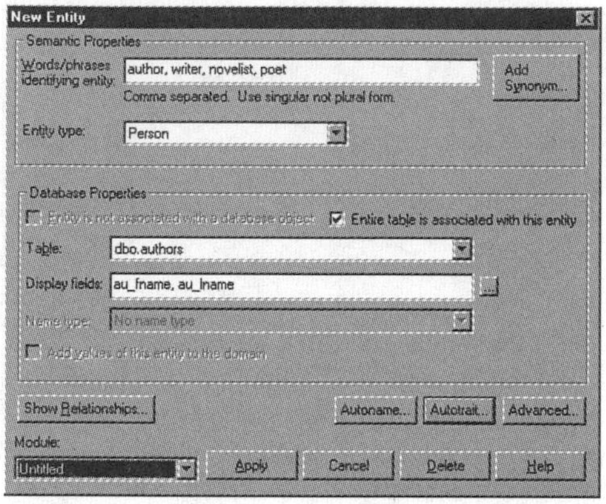

FIGURE 14.10
*The New Entity
dialog box.*

The New Entity dialog box provides a number of options to help you create your entity. The following is a summary of the parameters and options available:

- *Words/Phrases Identifying Entities*—Enter any word or phrase that you want to identify your entity. You can enter multiple words in a comma-separated list. English Query uses these words to help identify which tables and fields are part of the SQL statement to be built. For example, in creating the author entity, we may want to associate the words author, writer, novelist, and poet to this entity. These will be words which users may use in their questions to refer to an author.

- *Entity Type*—Choose the type of entity you are creating. Choices include Person, Geographic Location, Animate Object, Physical Object, Date, and Time. The entity types help English Query to interpret user questions. If you identify your entity as a Person, English Query will allow that entity to be referred to as "Who" in a question. For the author entity, choose Person.

- *Entity Is Not Associated with a Database Object*—Check this option to specify that the entity you are defining is not represented by any table or field in the database.

- *Entire Table Is Associated with This Entity*—Check this option to indicate that the entity is represented by each row in the table and not by a specific field's contents. For example, each record in the author table represents a different author. Choosing this option will enable English Query to recognize each author as an author entity.

- *Table*—Choose the table that you want to associate the entity. You can associate an entity with only one table. For the author entity, choose the authors table.

- *Fields/Display Fields*—If you check the Entire table Is Associated with This Entity option, this option is labeled Display Field. When creating the author entity, you would want to choose those fields that will be displayed to represent the author, such as `first_name` and `last_name`.

- *Add Values of This Entity to the Domain*—Check this option to indicate that you want English Query to load all the data values of the selected table or field to your domain. This option allows users to ask questions about specific data elements. You should be forewarned that loading this data could take anywhere from several minutes to several hours, depending on the size of the underlying data option.

> ## CAUTION
>
> The words or phrases you use to describe your entity are case sensitive. If you enter the word Writer as a word describing an entity, you must be sure to also enter the word writer. If you do not enter both versions of the word, English Query may not be able to correctly interpret the user's question.

Relationships

Creating the entities is the first step in creating your domain. Next, English Query needs to know how these entities are related to one another. The relationships that you define in your English Query domain are what give meaning to the entities. If a user asks a question such as "How many authors sold books in Utah?" English Query needs to understand the relationships that exist between entities. To answer this question, English Query needs to know that "authors write books" and that "books are sold in states" and that "Utah is a state." In order for English Query to understand these relationships, you must define them.

To define a relationship, right-click the Relationships folder on the Semantics tab as shown in Figure 14.9 and choose Insert Relationship. The dialog box shown in Figure 14.11 will appear.

FIGURE 14.11
The Entities tab of the New Relationship dialog box.

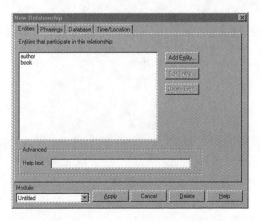

The first thing you must do is to choose the entities you want to have participate in the relationship. For example, to help answer the question "How many authors sold books in Utah?" you need to create a relationship between authors and books. To do this, you would choose the author and book entities. After you have decided which entities will participate in the relationship, you need to define the phrasings that will represent this relationship. To do this, click the Phrasings tab as shown in Figure 14.11 and click Add. The dialog box shown in Figure 14.12 will appear.

FIGURE 14.12

A new relationship in the Select Phrasing dialog box.

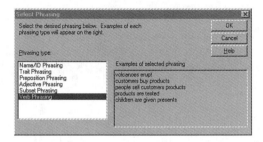

You can choose which type of phrasing you would like to create based on the relationship you are creating. The phrasings are basic English sentence constructs. Based on your choice, English query will assist you in building an appropriate phrase. To create the relationship "Authors write Books," we would choose a verb phrasing.

As you can see in Figure 14.13, English Query helps you build your phrasing with prompts. This is a relatively simple phrasing example. It is possible, however, to create extremely complex phrasings, but English Query always prompts you for information.

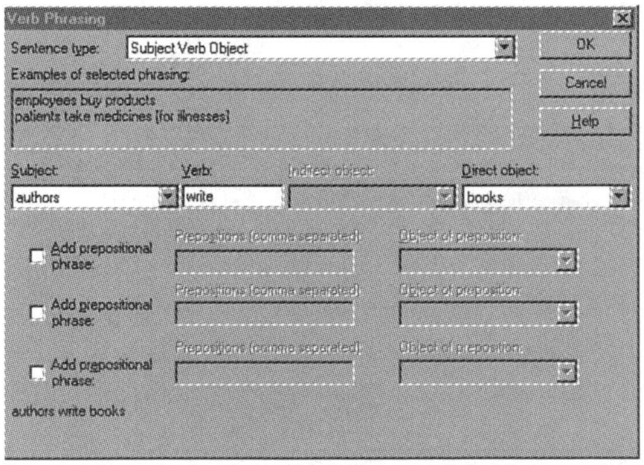

FIGURE 14.13

A new relationship in the Trait Phrasing dialog box.

The Trait Phrasing dialog box prompts you for most of the required information to create the relationship phrasing. In our example, the subject entity is authors and the object entity is books. We can enter any verb to indicate a relationship between authors and books. For example, we could have said "authors own books" or "authors sell books."

Additionally, you can add prepositional phrases to help describe your relationship. For example, you could add a prepositional phrase that says "authors write books at home." Does any of this remind you of English class?

You will find that building the relationships is the most complex, time-consuming, and important aspect of creating your English Query domain. As a developer of an English Query application, you must consider all possible ways you think users may want to phrase their questions and make sure all appropriate relationships exist between entities.

Domain Commands

You may want your English Query application to do more than simply interpret a command as an instruction to display a set of data. You can extend the functionality of your English Query application by creating domain commands that pass instructions back to the client along with data.

For example, let's say you wanted to use an English Query application as part of an online bookstore. You might want to allow users to enter a statement such as "Buy the latest book by Tom Clancy." You could create a domain command which would instruct the client application to execute a sales order for the appropriate book based on information from your database. In this instance, the English Query application is doing more than just returning the data about the book, rather it is returning an instruction to the client application.

You create a domain command in much the same way that you create a relationship. To create a domain command, right-click the Domain Commands folder on the Semantics tab as shown in Figure 14.9 and choose Insert Domain Command. You will notice that the dialog box looks exactly the same as Figure 14.11, with the exception of a command.

You must choose the entities that you want to participate in the command. For example, we want the book entity to participate in the command "buy books." After you have chosen the entities, you need to set up the phrasing. Again, this is very similar to setting up a relationship. After you choose the Phrasings tab, you will notice in Figure 14.14 that you now have an additional phrasing option: 'Command Phrasing.'

FIGURE 14.14

A new domain command in the Trait Phrasing dialog box.

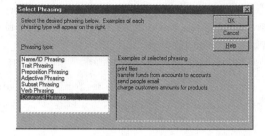

Choose this phrasing type to create a command phrasing. This allows you to create a command phrase such as "buy books" as shown in Figure 14.15.

FIGURE 14.15

A new domain command in the Trait Phrasing dialog box.

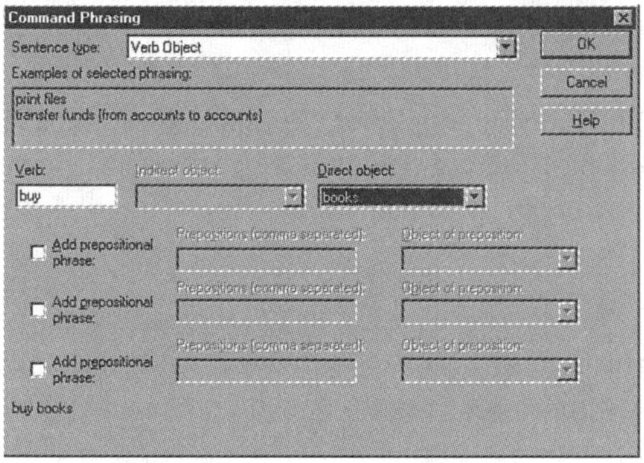

Finally, by choosing the Command tab in the New Domain Command dialog box, you can create a name for the command and specify the command parameters (see Figure 14.16).

FIGURE 14.16

The Command tab of the New Domain Command dialog box.

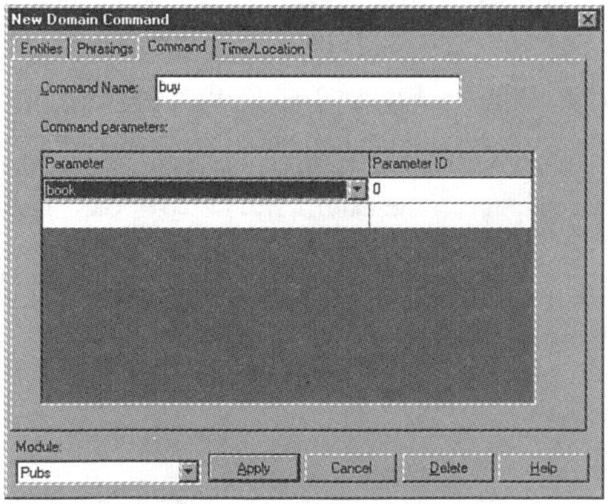

The command parameters identify what is returned to the client application when the command is requested. The parameter must be an entity that has been chosen as part of your command. For example, you could specify that the book entity is the parameter for the "buy books" command. When the client application tells English query to "Buy the latest book by Tom Clancy," English query will return the command along with the book id of the book that the user asked for. The client application can then use that information to process the request into a sales order.

Dictionary Entries

English Query maintains a dictionary of thousands of English words. Generally, the entities and relationships you define should provide English Query with sufficient dictionary entries. However, your application may require a custom word that might not be associated with a defined entity or relationship. In this case, you can define the word as a dictionary entry.

Dictionary entries can also be used to set up read and write synonyms. For example, you could set a read synonym to indicate that "VA:" should always be read as "Virginia." Likewise, you could establish a write synonym to indicate that "Virginia" should always be written back as "VA."

Testing Your English Query Application

After you have defined all the physical database information and all appropriate semantic information, you can test your application by choosing Tools, Test Application. This utility, as seen in Figure 14.17 allows you to fine-tune your English Query domain.

FIGURE 14.17

The Test Application dialog box.

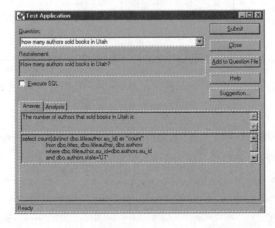

Essentially, you enter sample questions into the Test Application dialog box, and English Query shows you the SQL statement it creates based on your current domain definition. If you ask a question that English Query cannot answer, the utility shows that it did not have enough information in your domain to formulate an SQL statement. This may be because you did not define a necessary entity or relationship. If you click on Suggestions, English Query helps you refine your domain by assisting you with adding the appropriate entity or relationship.

Building Your English Query Application

When you are satisfied that your English Query domain contains sufficient physical database and semantic information to answer the user's questions, you need to build the English Query application. To do this, choose Tools, Build Application from the menu to create the `*.eqd` file that will be used from your client applications.

Deploying Your English Query Application

The English Query engine is a COM automation server and, as such, has an object model that is exposed to any programming or scripting language that supports ActiveX controls. The English Query application file (that is, the `*.eqd` file) is used by the English Query engine to process questions and return valid SQL statements. The client application is responsible for all user interaction and execution of all SQL statements returned by the English Query engine.

An English Query application can be leveraged in a straight client/server application environment, as a middle tier component or business object, and in a Web-based scenario. Typical client applications can be written in Visual Basic, Visual C++, or as an Active Server Pages application running on Internet Information Server.

THE NEW SQL SERVER UTILITIES FAQ

This section lists some commonly asked questions and answers about SQL Server 7.0 utilities.

Why might I want to customize the `sp_processmail` stored procedure and how would I do it?

Yes, it is very possible that you would want `sp_processmail` to behave differently in your particular SQL Server installation. For example, you might want to return query results in the body of the message instead of as an attached file. You may also want to prevent `sp_processmail` from deleting email messages once they have been processed. All of this behavior can be customized by using the parameters of the extended stored procedures (`xp_readmail`, `xp_sendmail`, and so on).

To customize the sp_processmail stored procedure, you can use the sp_helptext stored procedure to retrieve the created syntax of the sp_processmail stored procedure. You can then modify any of the parameters used by the extended stored procedures to alter the stored procedure behavior and then use that syntax to create a custom stored procedure.

Do SQL Agent and SQL Mail have to use the same mail profile?

No, the SQL Agent and SQL Mail services operate independently of one another. In other words, you do not even need to start the SQL Mail service for the SQL Agent to send email notifications to operators on alerts. They can each use their own mail profiles.

Can I execute a distributed query from SQL Server that accesses a saved query in an Access database?

Yes; as far as SQL Server is concerned, the query that is saved in Access is just another table. As such, you can execute a Transact-SQL query against an Access query just like you would any other table.

Can you write an English Query application that allows users to explore the domain themselves?

Yes, English Query provides a Question Builder object model. The Question Builder object model is a set of properties and methods that can be used to allow users to explore the domain that has been created. For example, you can provide users with a list of all major and minor entities that exist in the domain and all relationships that those entities participate in. Additionally, the question builder can provide sample questions and can maintain a collection of previously asked questions. This allows users to better understand how to formulate questions to receive the desired results.

SUMMARY

This chapter provides information on how to leverage some of the utilities that are available to you as part of SQL Server. SQL Mail is a vital component for any DBA notification and alert mechanism; it is easy to configure and even easier to use. Distributed queries are a very exciting addition to the SQL Server product; they give you the capability to execute a single SQL statement that retrieves data from SQL Server, Access, and Excel at the same time! Microsoft English Query helps you to develop some fun and interesting applications. Your users can type in questions in the forms that make the most sense to them and get appropriate answers.

14

NEW SQL
SERVER UTILITIES

REPLICATION

PART

V

IN THIS PART

REPLICATION

by Mark Spenik

IN THIS CHAPTER

One of the most exciting features that ships with SQL Server 7.0 and that has been greatly enhanced from previous versions is *data replication*.

> **NOTE**
>
> I throw in the fact that it ships with the standard product because several other RDBMS vendors treat replication as a separate product for which you pay extra.

In a nutshell, *replication* is the capability to reliably duplicate data from a source database to one or more destination databases. Using Microsoft SQL Server replication, you can automatically distribute data from one SQL Server to many different SQL Servers through ODBC (Open Database Connectivity) or OLE DB. SQL Server 7.0 enables you to replicate to nonSQL Server subscribers (heterogeneous subscribers), such as Microsoft Access or Oracle, using ODBC or OLE DB and enables support for Internet anonymous subscribers. SQL Server 7.0 replication capabilities have been greatly enhanced by adding update replication capabilities like Immediate Updating Subscribers and merge replication. With all of the new enhancements to SQL Server replication, the number of possible applications and business scenarios are mind-boggling. In later chapters (16 and 17), you examine the different types of replication in detail as well as appropriate and inappropriate applications for each type. However, for starters here are some examples of applications or scenarios in which SQL Server replication can be used:

- To distribute the workload across servers (such as moving ad-hoc query and reporting capability from a source server).
- To move specific subsets of data (such as a company department or one month's worth of data) from a main central server.
- When you have a central database that is updated and the updates must be moved out to other databases (such as a department store changing prices for an item).
- Account management/tracking applications used by salesmen or field reps using laptops in a disconnected mode that later replicate changes to a central internal server.
- A Web-based user group or subscription application that can periodically pull down database changes via the Web.
- Environments in which servers are importing flat-file information. Use a central database to import the flat file and replicate the information to the other sites.

> **NOTE**
>
> Some of the screens in this chapter will differ, depending on the platform and edition of SQL Server. The screens for this chapter were captured on a Windows NT Server using the standard version of SQL Server. You will find that on the Desktop version some buttons or functionality may be missing. The Desktop version of SQL Server 7.0 can be a subscriber for all forms of replication, but can only be a publisher for merge and snapshot replication.

SQL SERVER 6.5 TO 7.0 QUICK REFERENCE

The following is a quick reference to the changes that occurred between SQL Server version 6.5 and 7.0:

What's New

- Support for multisite updates (merge and Immediate Updating Subscribers)
- Increased scalability
- Major changes to replication system tables and procedures
- Open interfaces to allow third-party support for nonSQL server (heterogeneous) publishers
- Distributor process that can execute at subscriber
- Multiple distribution databases possible
- Replication of stored procedures
- Better built-in monitoring and troubleshooting
- More flexible network support (includes replicating via Internet)
- Support for OLE DB
- Ability to script replication publications and topology
- Enhanced security model
- Wizards to make replication task simple
- Major changes to graphical administration
- New replication agents
- ActiveX control for merge and distributor agents
- Bi-directional replication to Microsoft Access (Office 2000)
- Anonymous Pull Subscribers

15

REPLICATION

What's Been Renamed

- Synch task is replaced by Snapshot Agent
- SQL Server 6.x replication is referred to as transactional replication

What's Gone

- Trusted connection requirement between servers
- Restrictions on datatypes (example: identity and text columns can be replicated)

REPLICATION OVERVIEW AND TERMINOLOGY

As stated earlier, SQL Server 7.0 has added many new capabilities and functions to data replication. In previous editions of the DBA Survival Guide, replication was covered in a single chapter, which is no longer possible. This chapter focuses on introducing you to SQL Server replication terminology and the different types of replication. Additionally it shows you how to perform standard administrative tasks like creating a distribution database. To become familiar with replication terminology, consider a replication scenario common to SQL Server 6.x and SQL Server 7.0 (transactional replication), shown in Figure 15.1. With transactional-based replication, the publication is modified at the publisher's site and the changes are replicated to the subscribers of the publication. Transactional-based replication was part of SQL server 6.x replication.

FIGURE 15.1

Overview of replication (Transactional).

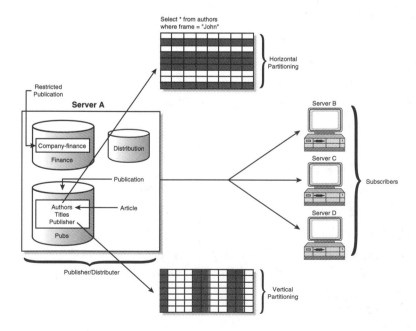

Publish and Subscribe

SQL Server replication uses a *publish and subscribe* metaphor. Servers publish publications to which other servers can subscribe. A SQL Server that makes data available to other servers for subscribing purposes is called a publisher. For example, Server A in Figure 15.1 is a publisher. A SQL Server that subscribes to a publication published by another SQL Server is said to be a subscriber. (An example of a subscription server is Server B in Figure 15.1.) A SQL Server that contains the distribution database is said to be a distributor. (The distribution server is Server A in Figure 15.1.)

Publication and Articles

A publisher publishes a collection of one or more articles called a *publication*. The publication shown in Figure 15.1 contains the authors, titles, and publishers table found in the SQL Server example database, pubs. An *article* is the basic unit of replication and can be a table, a subset of the table or stored procedures.

NOTE

Articles are always associated with a publication and cannot be published by themselves. SQL Server 6.5 allowed subscriptions to a single article. SQL Server 7.0 still supports this feature for compatibility reasons via Transact-SQL. However, it is recommended that you only subscribe to publications, which is much easier to administer than a subscription to a single article.

Publications can contain one or more of the following:

- Tables
- Vertically partitioned tables
- Stored procedures (New for SQL Server 7.0)
- Horizontally partitioned tables
- Horizontally and vertically partitioned tables

A *vertical partitioned table* (refer to Figure 15.1) is an article that uses a filter to select only certain columns of a table. A *horizontal partitioned table* (refer to Figure 15.1) is an article that uses a filter to select only specific rows in the table.

The following cannot be published:

- The model, tempdb, and msdb databases
- The system tables in the master database

Subscriptions Types (Push and Pull)

Changes made at the publisher can be replicated to the subscribers via a push subscription or a pull subscription. With a *push subscription*, the publication server is responsible for replicating all changes to the subscribers without the subscribers asking for the changes. A push subscription is typically used when the subscribing databases want the changes as soon as they are made or a high level of security is required. With a *pull subscription*, the subscriber initiates the replication instead of the publisher. Pull subscriptions require lower overhead than push subscriptions and are better suited for situations with a large number of subscribers or lower security requirements.

Server Roles

SQL Server can play one or more of the following roles during the replication process:

- **Publisher.** A publisher server is responsible for maintaining its source databases, making the data available for replication, and sending the data to the distribution database to be replicated to subscribing servers.

- **Subscriber.** A subscriber server is a server that receives and maintains published data. Subscribers can also make changes to publications. In cases where a subscriber changes the publication, the subscriber is still a subscriber and not a publisher. (The information still has only a single publisher.)

- **Distributor.** The distribution server maintains the distribution database, which is responsible for the store and forward capabilities of SQL Server snapshot and transactional replication. The job of the distribution server is to replicate data from the distribution database to the appropriate subscribing servers.

SQL Server can participate in one or more replication roles. For example, in many cases, a publication server also serves as a distribution server and can also subscribe to other publications from other publishers (in which case, the same server that was acting as a publisher and distributor is also acting as a subscriber). It is not uncommon for a subscriber also to be a publisher. However, in all SQL Server replication cases, for a publication there exists only a single master copy of the database, which is maintained by the publisher (regardless of how many different subscribers are allowed to update the publication). For example, in a merge replication publication scenario, server A publishes the pubs database. Server B and server C are subscribers and make modifications to the database. The master copy of the database that is receiving the changes is the publisher's database, server A. Server B receives server C's changes when server B replicates with server A.

Out of the box, nonSQL Server systems, such as Oracle and Microsoft Access, can be subscribers of all types of replication (except Immediate Updating Subscribers). However, Microsoft has created an open interface to SQL Server's transaction-based replication services so that third parties can create products that allow nonSQL Server systems (that is, heterogeneous data sources) to become publishers.

Replication Types

SQL Server 7.0 has several different types of replication that can be used for a variety of business applications. The next few chapters look at each different type of replication in detail and when and how to use it. The SQL Server 7.0-supported replication types are as follows:

- Transactional
- Snapshot
- Merge
- Immediate Updating Subscribers

Transactional

In Transactional-based replication, the publication is modified at the publisher's site and the changes are replicated to the subscribers of the publication. Transactional-based replication was part of SQL server 6.x replication. In essence, subscribers of the publication do not modify the publication but treat the information as read-only. This does not mean that all updates to an underlying table must happen at one site. Using vertical and horizontal partitioning, you can create solutions that allow for multiple sites editing information in the same table. The key, however, to partitioning is that each site owns a particular partition of data that can only be modified by the publishing site. SQL Server 7.0 makes it possible to use bi-directional transactional replication without partitioning by using custom stored procedures and loopback detection. But essentially because the majority of transaction replication is used by subscribers that treat the publications as read-only or use partitioning, there is no need for conflict resolution or lost updates; such problems are avoided by the transactional-replication model and data partitioning. Examples of good transactional-based applications/scenarios are a database of rollup information, data marts, databases with regional or divisional information, and a central sales or inventory database that is updated and replicated to different sites.

Snapshot

Snapshot replication takes a snapshot of the schema and data at a certain point in time and replicates this information to subscribing databases. Snapshot replication was also included in SQL Server 6.x and is the simplest type of replication to implement. Because

15

REPLICATION

the data is provided as a snapshot of information at some point and time, there is no need to worry about conflicts or loss of transactions. Examples of good Snapshot-based applications/scenarios are lookup tables that do not change frequently, anonymous subscribers, static information, or information that is infrequently updated.

Merge

Merge replication is new to SQL Server 7.0 and is categorized as a form of update replication. Essentially, Merge replication enables users to subscribe to a publication and edit the same articles (tables) in the publication without any partitioning or custom procedures. When a subscriber edits the publication, the change is replicated back to the publisher. If a conflict occurs (for example, different users modify the same row at different sites after the databases are synched), the conflict is resolved either by priority-based rules or first one to change the row wins. A good merge application or scenario is a sales tracking/call application where a salesman uses a laptop computer in a disconnected mode to add a new customer or record a sales call. Later when the salesman is back in the office and connects the laptop to the network, the SQL Server database on the laptop merges the changes made to the central SQL Server database.

Immediate Updating Subscribers

Immediate Updating Subscribers is another form of SQL Server 7.0 update replication. The Immediate Updating Subscriber is transactional-based replication (available with Snapshot and Transaction replication)that enables the subscriber to modify articles in the publication. The modification is then made at the publisher using the two phase-commit protocol (discussed in detail in Chapter 12, "Distributed Transaction Coordinator") and replicated to the other subscribers using the standard transaction-based replication mode. The two-phase commit protocol requires that the change occur immediately on all servers participating in the transaction or the transaction is rolled back. Therefore, all servers participating in the transaction must have a reliable connection to one another. Immediate Updating Subscribers removes the complexity of having to have all sites participate in a two-phase commit (which requires that all sites are connected) and yet still maintain transaction integrity. Good applications/scenarios for Immediate Updating Subscribers are applications with good network connections, applications that do not have high levels of OLTP (on-line transaction processing), and applications that need the same number at the remote site as well as a central site.

Transactional Consistency

Transactional consistency in the context of replication means that the data will be identical across all sites with a result that could have been achieved had all transactions been performed at a single site. Replication also adds the caveat of eventually or at some point in time because there may be a time delay from the time the change is made to the time the data is replicated to the subscribers. SQL Server 7.0 replication falls into two modes of transaction consistency: *guaranteed loose consistency* and *guaranteed no consistency*.

Guaranteed loose consistency means that the data synchronization between the source and destination server does not occur simultaneously. Before going into more detail, look at another distributed data model: *guaranteed tight consistency*. A Guaranteed tight consistency distributed data model can be accomplished with SQL Server using two phase commits. In a tight consistency model, all transactions are committed or rolled back on all the servers so that the data is in synch 100 percent of the time. In a loose consistency model, transactions are committed or rolled back on a source server. The transactions on the source server are then replicated asynchronously to subscribing servers. The big difference between the guaranteed tight consistency model and the guaranteed loose consistency model is that, with the guaranteed loose consistency model, there is some lag time between when changes are made to the source server and when they are replicated to the destination servers (that is, the databases are temporarily out of synch). Transactional-based replication and snapshot replication are all examples of the guaranteed loose consistency model. The transactional-based Immediate Updating Subscriber model lies somewhere between guaranteed loose consistency and guaranteed tight consistency. With an Immediate Updating Subscriber, a two-phase commit (tight consistency) is used between two sites (the publisher and a subscriber) and then the standard transactional-based replication (loose consistency) is used to replicate the change to all other subscribers.

Merge replication falls into the guaranteed no consistency model. With no consistency the data will be identical across all sites with a result that might not have been achieved had all transactions been performed at a single site (see Chapter 17, "Snapshot and Merge Replication," for an actual example). Because Merge replication is for sites that are regularly disconnected, site autonomy is more important than transaction consistency. All of the sites end up with the same value; however it might be a value that would not have been achieved had all of the changes been made at a single site.

The Problem SQL Server 7.0 Replication Cannot Solve

As stated through out this book, the SQL Server 7.0 beta was unlike any Microsoft beta. Not only did Microsoft tout key SQL Server features to the press, they held different technical briefings and conferences for key partners and developers to help get DBAs and developers up to speed on the product. During one of these conferences, a program manager at Microsoft discussed the one situation which SQL Server replication could not address and (nor could any of the competition despite their "update anywhere claims). It is having multiple sites without reliable connections update data at any time with any frequency and maintain transactional integrity. The problem is that as sites become disconnected (through

15

REPLICATION

for example, unreliable connections), transaction integrity is rapidly lost. A disconnected site could make a change to a record that is deleted by another site. When the site reconnects a problem occurs as the update fails because the record no longer exist on the master database. As you read the details about the different types of replication in the next few chapters, you will see further reasons why the problem can't be solved.

Distribution Database

The distribution database stores all of the transactions to be replicated to subscribing servers (transactional replication) and acts as the store-and-forward database for replicated transactions. Transactions stay in the distribution database until all subscribers have successfully received the transaction. The distribution database is used to store publication and subscriber synchronization information as well. The following are some of the system tables that make up the distribution database:

- MSmerge_history   contains history information about previous subscriber updates.
- MSmerge_agents   contains information about merge agents.
- MSdistribution_agents   contains information about distribution agents.
- MSdistribution_history   contains historical information for distribution agents.
- MSlogreader_agents   contains information about log reader agents at the local distributor.
- MSlogreader_history   contains historical information for log reader agents.
- MSrepl_commands   contains replicated commands.
- MSrepl_errors   contains information about failed replication.
- MSrepl_transactions   contains a row for each replicated transaction.
- MSrepl_version   contains a single row with the current version of replication installed.

An Overview of the SQL Server Replication Agents

To effectively administer SQL Server 7.0 replication, you need to make yourself familiar with the different agents that are used for replication. Chapters 16, "Transactional Replication," and 17, "Snapshot and Merge Replication," cover each of the agent's roles in detail. The agents are as follows:

- **Log reader agent.** The *log reader* agent searches the transaction log of published databases for transaction log entries marked for replication. The log reader agent moves the marked transactions to the distribution database. All transactional-based publications have a log reader agent.

- **Merge Agent.** The *merge agent* is responsible for merging incremental changes as well as applying the initial snapshot created by the snapshot agent. Each merge publication has a merge agent.

- **Snapshot Agent.** The *snapshot agent* creates the snapshot files on the distributor and tracks the synchronization status in the distribution database between the published database and the subscribing databases. All publications have a snapshot agent.

- **Distribution Agent.** The *distribution agent* distributes the transactions stored in the distribution database to the subscribing servers. Transactional and snapshot publications have a distribution agent for each subscriber.

In previous versions of SQL Server, the agents (called tasks in SQL Server 6.x) could only execute on SQL Server. However, in SQL Server 7.0, the merge agent and distribution agent can be run from other applications using the ActiveX controls provided. Additional functionality can be added using SQL-DMO and third-party agents. Figure 15.2 shows an overview of the different interfaces and agents possible in SQL Server 7.0.

Figure 15.2

Overview of SQL Server replication interfaces and agents.

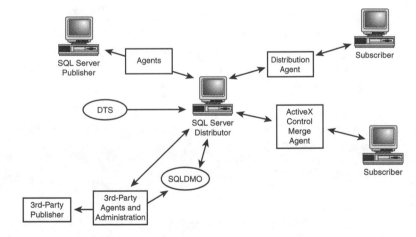

Synchronization Modes

Synchronization is the process of the publisher and the subscriber acknowledging that the databases are in the same exact state and replication can begin. SQL Server supports the following synchronization modes:

- Automatic
- Manual
- No Synchronization

15

REPLICATION

The default synchronization mode is automatic, which means that SQL Server performs the synchronization process automatically at a scheduled interval. Manual synchronization requires you to synchronize the databases; however, the initial snapshot is created for you, but you must apply it to the databases.

> **TIP**
>
> Use manual synchronization when dealing with very large tables or a slow communications line. The files required for synchronization can be copied to a tape or other media and applied to the destination server or servers.

With the No Synchronization option, SQL Server assumes that the articles in the source are already in synch with articles in the destination. SQL Server does nothing to verify that the databases are synchronized; that task is up to you.

Walking Through Automatic Synchronization

For this example, assume that server B selects Automatic synchronization during the subscription process. The distribution server creates two files referred to as a *synchronization set* in the replication working directory (the default is \REPLDATA off the SQL Server home directory). The synchronization set consists of a BCP data file with the actual data of the subscribed articles and the article's table schema file.

> **TIP**
>
> Schema files created for replication have a .SCH extension; the data files have a BCP file extension.

After the synchronization set is created, a synchronization job is added to the distribution database. The distribution process reads the distribution database and applies the synchronization file set to the subscribing server (in this example, server B). First the schema file is applied to create the table schema. The table information is then copied to the subscribing server using BCP. The distribution server is notified that synchronization has completed, and server A can begin to replicate the publication MyPubs to server B.

> **NOTE**
>
> After all other subscriptions have acknowledged successful synchronization, the BCP files are removed from the replication working directory.

Any transactions that occurred to the published articles after the subscribing server first sub-scribed but before the synchronization process occurred are then replicated to the subscriber.

CREATING/ASSIGNING THE DISTRIBUTION DATABASE

Now that you have an overview of SQL Server replication, examine how to set up repli-cation. First, examine how to create or specify the distribution database.

To create a distribution database, follow these steps using the SQL Enterprise Manager:

1. Select the server on which you want to install the distribution database.

2. From the SQL Enterprise Manager menu, select Tools and then select Replication. A drop-down menu appears (see Figure 15.3). Select the Configure Publishing and Subscribers option. The Configure Publishing and Distribution Wizard dialog box appears (see Figure 15.4).

FIGURE 15.3

The Replication Configuration menu and option list.

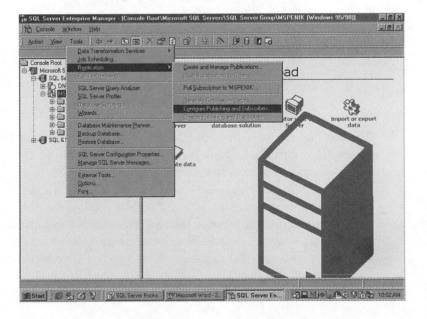

15

REPLICATION

FIGURE 15.4

The Configure Publishing and Distribution Wizard dialog box.

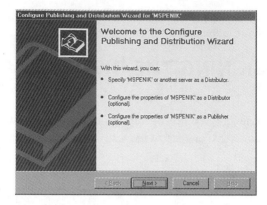

3. The Configure Publishing and Distribution Wizard walks you through the process of creating a distribution database or a publication. To continue the process, click the Next button.

4. The Choose Distributor dialog box, shown in Figure 15.5 appears.

FIGURE 15.5

The Choose Distributor dialog box.

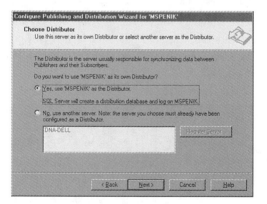

To make the selected server a distributor and create a distribution database on the server, select the default option, Yes, Use Server_Name as the Distributor. This action creates a distribution database on the selected server. To use another server with an existing distribution database, select the No, Use Another Server option, and select the server you want to use. To use this option, the selected server must already be setup as a distribution server and have an existing distribution database. For this example, you create a new distribution database on the selected server. Click the Next button. The Configure Publishing and Distribution dialog box appears (see Figure 15.6).

FIGURE 15.6

The Configure Publishing and Distribution dialog box.

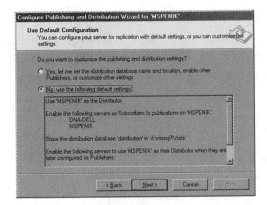

The Configure Publishing and Distribution dialog box enables you to take the default or use a custom configuration. The custom configuration lets you configure the following options:

- Distribution database (name and location)
- Enable Publishers
- Enable Databases for publishing
- Enable Subscribers

If you take the default, the distribution database is called distribution (unless there is more than one distribution database). The files for the data and log are located in the *\MSSQL7\Data* directory. All registered servers are selected as eligible subscribers. No databases are published and the server, the distribution database is being installed on, is enabled for publishing. After you have made your selections, custom or default, (in the case of the custom install, fill in the required parameters), click the Finish button.

A progress dialog box appears as the distribution database is created, publishers and subscribers are added, followed by a successful creation dialog box. The distribution database has been created. The distribution database contains the system tables described and system stored procedures used by the Distributor during replication.

CONFIGURING REPLICATION DISTRIBUTION OPTIONS

Using the SQL Enterprise Manager, you can configure the distribution database agent logon information, amount of time to hold replicated transactions, and holding time of replication performance information. Additionally you can view all of the publishers using the distribution database. To set distribution database options, perform the following:

15

REPLICATION

Select the server on which you want to configure the distribution database options.

From the SQL Enterprise Manager menu, select Tools and then select Replication. A drop-down menu appears; select the Configure Publishing, Subscribers and Distribution option. The Publisher and Distributor Properties dialog box appears, with the Distributor tab, shown in Figure 15.7.

FIGURE 15.7

The Publisher and Distributor Properties dialog box—Distributor tab.

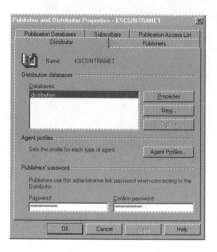

By using the Agent Profiles button of the Publisher and Distributor Properties dialog box, you can set the user account used by replication agents when they log into the distribution database. The default option is to impersonate the SQL Server Agent account used on the distribution computer. The Publishers password text box in the Publisher and Distributor Properties dialog box allows you to set up a password to be used by non-trusted Publishers to connect to the distribution database. This is not required for trusted publishers.

Click the Properties button, to display the Properties of the selected distribution database, the Distribution Database dialog box, shown in Figure 15.8, appears.

The Distribution Database properties dialog box shows the current publishers using the distribution database. Also you can use the Distribution Database properties dialog box to set the minimum and maximum number of hours/days to store transaction records that have already been replicated before purging them (see Figure 15.8). This parameter is very important when creating a backup and recovery plan for the distribution server (see Chapter 10, "Backup and Restore"). You can also set the amount of time replication performance history is maintained (in hours or days). The Publishers tab (not shown) displays a list of publishers using the distribution database.

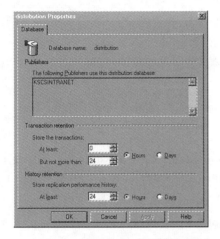

FIGURE 15.8

The Properties of Distribution Database dialog box.

DELETING A DISTRIBUTION DATABASE

SQL Server 7.0 enables you to create multiple distribution databases on the same server. You can delete a distribution database without disabling the server as a distributor. However, when you remove a distribution database, any publications using the database are removed. To delete a distribution database perform the following:

1. Select the server on which you want to delete the distribution database.

2. From the SQL Enterprise Manager menu, select Tools and then select Replication. A drop-down menu appears. Select the Configure Publishing, Subscribers and Distribution option. The Publisher and Distributor Properties dialog box appears, shown in Figure 15.9.

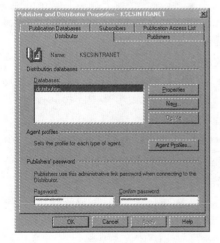

FIGURE 15.9

The Publisher and Distributor Properties dialog box.

15

REPLICATION

3. Select the distribution database you want to remove and click the Delete button.

NOTE

Before you can delete a distribution database, you must remove all publications and disable all the publishers using the distribution database.

The Transact-SQL command used to remove a distribution database is *sp_dropdistributiondb*, which has the following syntax:

```
sp_dropdistributiondb 'database'
```

where database is the name of the distribution database to drop. The following example drops the distribution database `distribution1`:

```
sp_dropdistributiondb 'distribution1'
```

`sp_dropdistributiondb` removes the database from SQL Server and the data and log file if they are not being used by other databases.

CONFIGURING REPLICATION PUBLISHING

After the distribution database has been successfully installed, or you have been given permission to publish to a remote distribution server, you can then configure a server to be a publisher.

NOTE

To set up SQL Server as a publisher, you must have one of the following:

- A local distribution database
- Access to a remote distribution database

If you have a local distribution database on your server (that is, your server is acting as a distribution server), you can perform the following:

- Set distribution working directory
- Allow other servers access to your distribution database for publishing

Both distribution servers and publisher servers can control which servers allow access to published articles and which databases on your local server can publish articles.

Adding a Publisher to a Distribution Database

To allow a remote server to use a local server's distribution database perform the following:

1. Select the server on which you want to add publishers to the distribution database.

2. From the SQL Enterprise Manager menu, select Tools, and then select Replication. A drop-down menu appears. Select the Configure Publishing, Subscribers and Distribution option. The Publisher and Distributor Properties dialog box appears. Select the Publishers tab, shown in Figure 15.10.

FIGURE 15.10

The Publisher and Distributor Properties dialog box—Publishers tab.

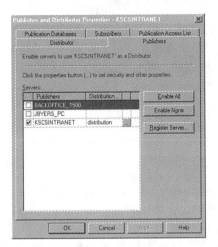

Check the box by the server to which you want to grant access. Select the distribution database to which you are granting the server publication access by clicking the square to the right of the selected server. To enable all remote servers, click the Enable All button. To remove a server from a distribution database and server, uncheck the server. Click the Enable None button to remove all remote servers from publishing to the server's distribution databases. To select a distribution database for the selected publisher, click the square to the right of the selected server. The Publisher's Distribution Database Properties dialog box, shown in Figure 15.11, appears.

If the server has more then one distribution database, use the Distribution database combo box, shown in Figure 15.11, to select the distribution database for the publisher to use. Use the Snapshot folder text box to set the path where snapshot information for publications is to be stored. The Replication agents on the Distributor Log into the Publisher area, in Figure 15.11, allow you to set up security and accounts used by the distributor's replication agents to log in to the publisher. The default setting is to impersonate the SQL Server Agent on the publisher, which requires a trusted connection. You can also use a regular SQL Server account. The Administrative link area allows you to determine how a publisher logs into the distributor. You can setup a trusted connection or require a password.

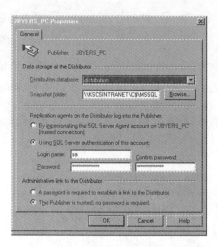

FIGURE 15.11

The Publisher's Distribution Database Properties dialog box

The Transact-SQL command to add a publisher to a distribution database is *sp_adddistpublisher*, which has the following syntax:

```
sp_adddistpublisher 'publisher','distribution database'
➥[,security_mode[,logon[,password']]],
'working directory'
```

where *publisher* is the server name to add as a publisher, *distribution database* is the distribution database to add the publisher to, *security_mode* determines how the server is being administered—0 uses SQL Server authentication, a 1 uses Windows NT authentication, *logon* is the user logon name (sa if security_mode = 0), *password* is the logon password and *working directory* is the path of the working directory.

Enabling a Database for Publishing and Removing a Database from Publishing

Before you can create a publication that subscribers can subscribe to, you must first enable the database for publication. Enabling a database for publication allows publications to be created within the database for replication. You can also remove a database from having publication capabilities. To enable or disable a database for publishing, perform the following steps:

1. Select the server on which you want to add a publication.

2. From the SQL Enterprise Manager menu, select Tools and then select Replication. A drop-down menu appears. Select the Configure Publishing, Subscribers and Distribution option. The Publisher and Distributor Properties dialog box appears. Select the Publication Databases tab, shown in Figure 15.12.

FIGURE 15.12

The Publisher and Distributor Properties dialog box—Publication Databases tab.

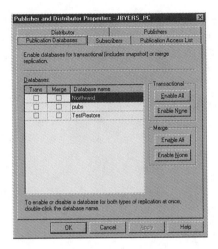

3. To enable a database for transactional or merge publication, select the check box next to the appropriate database.

4. To remove a database from publishing, deselect the server's check box beside name of the database you want to remove. All existing publications in the database are removed.

5. The Enable All or Enable None buttons enable you to select all the databases or deselect all the databases for transactional or merge replication.

ENABLING REPLICATION SUBSCRIBERS

To allow remote servers to receive data from your server, you must enable permissions for the remote servers using the SQL Enterprise Manager.

To enable subscribers, follow these steps:

1. Select the server on which you want to add a publication.

2. From the SQL Enterprise Manager menu, select Tools and then select Replication. A drop-down menu appears. Select the Configure Publishing, Subscribers and Distribution option. The Publisher and Distributor Properties dialog box appears. Select the Subscribers tab, shown in Figure 15.13.

   To enable a server to subscribe, select the check box next to the server's name. To disable a server from subscribing, deselect the check box next to the server's name. To add a new server as a subscriber, click the New Subscriber button. The Enable New Subscriber dialog box, shown in Figure 15.14, appears.

15

REPLICATION

FIGURE 15.13

The Publisher and Distributor Properties dialog box—Subscribers tab.

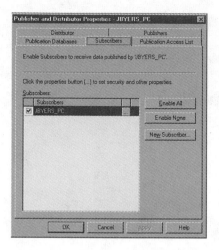

FIGURE 15.14

The Enable New Subscriber dialog box.

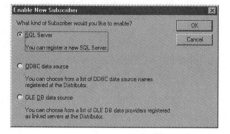

This dialog box allows you to add new subscribers. It is discussed in more detail in the section on Adding NonSQL Server Subscribers.

USING THE DISABLE PUBLISHING AND DISTRIBUTION WIZARD

To quickly remove all of the distribution servers on a specific server, drop all publishers and publications using the distribution database and remove all subscriptions to the deleted publication—use the SQL Server 7.0 *Disable Publishing and Distribution Wizard*. This wizard is a great example of the SQL Server team paying attention to problems encountered by DBAs in real-world situations with SQL Server 6.5. Previously, DBAs often had to manually drop all the publications and subscriptions to a distribution database and then manually re-create them! The wizard solves the first problem of removing publishers, subscribers, and distribution databases. The capability to script a replication topology solves the second problem. The Disable Publishing and Distribution Wizard disables all the publishers using the Distributor and, if possible, logs on to the publishing servers to drop the publications. The wizard also disables all the subscribers using the publications and drops the distribution databases. Of course, the wizard lets you selectively decide if you want to remove the distribution databases or leave the distribution databases and drop all the publications. To use the wizard, perform the following steps:

1. Select the server on which you want to add a publication.

2. From the SQL Enterprise Manager menu, select Tools and then select Replication. A drop-down menu appears. Select the Disable Publishing option. The Disable Publishing and Distribution Wizard Startup dialog box, shown in Figure 15.15, appears. Read over the dialog box and click the Next button.

FIGURE 15.15

The Disable Publishing and Distribution Wizard Startup dialog box.

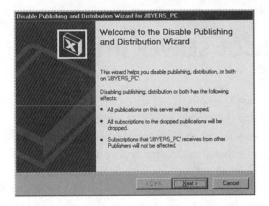

3. The Disable Distribution dialog box appears (see Figure 15.16). If you want to drop all the distribution databases and disable all the publishers using the distributor, select the Yes, Disable Distribution (and Publishing) on Server_Name option. Selecting this option disables the publishers. If possible, drop the publications on the publishing servers and remove the distribution databases. If this is the option you want to perform, click the Next button. The wizard begins the process just described. If you select No, then you are finished and the Wizard completes without performing any task.

4. Select your option and click the Next button. The process of disabling the publisher begins, or, if you selected no or clicked the Cancel button, the wizard stops without dropping the distribution database or removing any publications.

15

REPLICATION

FIGURE 15.16

*The Disable
Distribution
dialog box.*

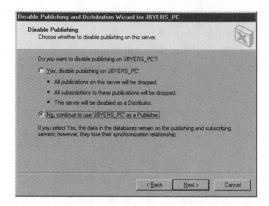

ADDING NONSQL SERVER (HETEROGENEOUS) SUBSCRIBERS

SQL Server 7.0 can replicate to nonSQL Server ODBC or OLE DB subscribers such as Microsoft Access and Oracle databases. As stated earlier in this chapter, nonSQL Server ODBC sources can only be subscribers. You can use transactional and snapshot replication with all heterogeneous subscribers, merge replication with Microsoft Access subscribers, and immediately update subscribers with SQL Server 7.0. However, Microsoft has opened up the interface to SQL Server replication so that ODBC or OLE DB subscribers can be publishers using third-party software (which may or may not be available for your particular data source).

NOTE

Because nonSQL Server subscribers use ODBC or OLE DB, the list of possible nonSQL Server subscribers will increase. For an updated list of supported heterogeneous subscribers, refer to your Microsoft documentation or check the SQL Server forums on the Internet. Microsoft provides and supports ODBC/OLE DB drivers for Microsoft Access, Oracle, and DRDA. All other systems must have ODBC drivers that are thread-safe, ODBC Level-1–compliant, transaction-capable, and able to support DDL. From this point on in this chapter, the discussion *ODBC and OLE DB subscribers* means *nonSQL Server data sources.*

Heterogeneous subscribers must be set up by the publishing server using the push subscription method (see Chapters 16 and 17 for setting up push subscriptions). Each Heterogeneous subscriber participating in SQL Server replication has its own individual requirements and restrictions. For example, when creating the ODBC Data Source Name

DSN with Oracle, you must include a username; with Microsoft Access DSN, some datatypes are not supported. Check out the Microsoft SQL Server documentation for the various restrictions that apply between Microsoft SQL Server and the selected ODBC subscriber.

Here are a few known restrictions that apply to all ODBC subscribers:

- ODBC DSN must follow SQL Server naming conventions.
- The character bulk copy method must be selected for synchronization.
- The publication option Truncate Before Synchronization is not supported.
- Target server's quoted identifier, reported by the ODBC driver, is used.
- Batch statements are not supported.

The following sections describe how to set up an ODBC subscriber using Microsoft Access 7.0.

Step 1: Create an ODBC Data Source Name (DSN)

The first step in setting up replication to an ODBC subscriber is to create a system (DSN) for the subscribing server. The ODBC DSN must be created on the distribution server. To create a system ODBC DSN, follow these steps:

1. Double-click the ODBC icon located in the Control Panel to start the ODBC Administrator. The ODBC Administrator dialog box appears. Click the System DSN tab, shown in Figure 15.17.

FIGURE 15.17
The ODBC Administrator dialog box—System DSN tab.

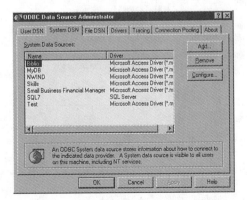

2. Click the Add button to add a new system DSN. The Create New Data Sources dialog box appears (see Figure 15.18).

3. A list of installed ODBC drivers appears. Select the correct ODBC driver for your subscribing server (for this example, select Microsoft Access). After you select the correct ODBC driver, click Finish. The ODBC Microsoft Access 98 Setup dialog box appears (see Figure 15.19).

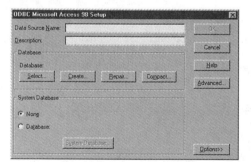

> **NOTE**
>
> The look of the ODBC Setup dialog box varies for different data sources. For this example, Microsoft Access is used. Compare the Microsoft Access Setup dialog box in Figure 15.19 to the ODBC Setup screen for SQL Server (shown in Figure 15.20).

Figure 15.20

The ODBC SQL Server Setup dialog box.

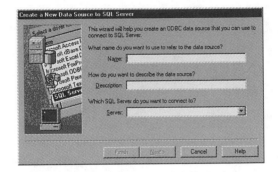

4. Enter the Data Source Name for the Microsoft Access database. The Data Source Name is how SQL Server references the ODBC subscriber. Select the Access database to push the replicated data to, and click the Advanced button. If you register an Access database that resides on a remote server, use the UNC name (\\ServerName\directory\database.mdb). After you enter the correct information, click the OK button to add the ODBC data source.

> **Note**
>
> To replicate to Microsoft Access subscribers requires that the MSSQLServer service use the domain user account used by the SQL Agent, which must have the necessary permissions to connect to Access databases over the network.

Step 2: Register the ODBC Source as a Subscribing Server

The next step is to add the ODBC DSN to SQL Server's list of subscribing servers. To add an ODBC DSN to the list of subscribing servers, follow these steps:

1. Select the server on which you want to add a publication.

2. From the SQL Enterprise Manager menu, select Tools and then select Replication. A drop-down menu appears, select the Configure Publishing, Subscribers and Distribution option. The Publisher and Distributor properties dialog box appears. Select the Subscribers tab (refer to Figure 15.13). Click the New Subscribers button. The Enable New Subscriber dialog box, shown in Figure 15.21, appears.

FIGURE 15.21

The Enable New Subscriber dialog box.

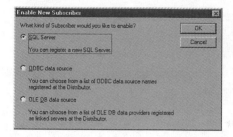

3. Select the ODBC data source option. For OLE DB sources, select the OLE DB data source and SQL Server for SQL Servers. Once you have made your selection, (in this example ODBC data source) click the OK button. The Register Non-SQL Server Subscriber dialog box appears (see Figure 15.22).

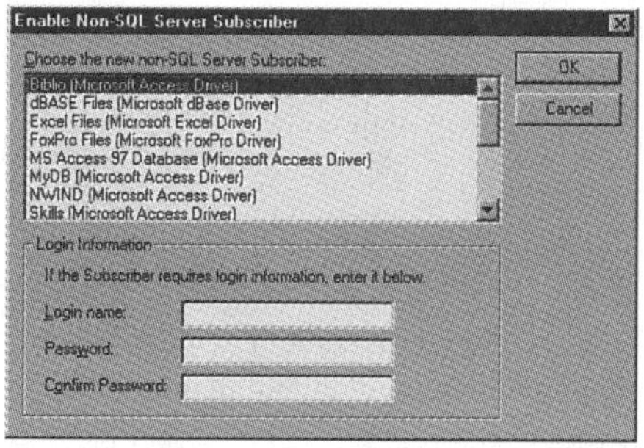

FIGURE 15.22

The Register NonSQL Server Subscriber dialog box.

4. Use the combo box to select the correct ODBC DSN. Enter the login ID and password if required. The login ID and password are optional because they may not be needed. In the case of Microsoft Access, unless you have added security, leave the login and password fields blank. To register the ODBC subscriber, click the OK button. *Note:* This action adds the DSN to the SQL Server system table `sysservers`.

After you register a nonSQL Server subscribe, you can add the subscriber to push subscriptions (see Chapters 16 and 17). The system-stored procedures that deal with ODBC subscribers are `sp_dsinfo`, which retrieves information about the ODBC DSNs installed on a distribution server, and `sp_enumdsn`, which shows all of the ODBC DSNs defined for a specific Windows NT account of a server.

REPLICATION FAQ

Following are some of the common questions asked by DBAs about SQL Server replication:

Q. **If I need to perform multiple updates at many sites, why not always use Merge replication instead of transaction replication and partitioning?**

A. Merge replication is good in cases where your sites are disconnected or the data does not partition well. If your application can be partitioned between updating sites, updates can be made without worrying about conflict resolution and loose transactional consistency can be obtained instead of no consistency. (See Chapters 16 and 17 for more details.)

Q. **Does the ODBC DSN for a nonSQL Server subscriber belong on the Distributor or the Publisher?**

A. The ODBC DSN for a nonMicrosoft SQL Server subscriber belongs on the distribution server.

SUMMARY

Replication is an exciting technology that will play an important part in many real-world solutions. As a Microsoft SQL Server DBA, you must fully understand how to correctly set up and administer replication and how to correctly use replication to benefit your company or organization.

Following are some of the important things to remember for SQL Server replication:

- SQL Server replication is transaction-based and follows a loose consistency data distribution model to a no consistency data model.
- Replication uses a publisher/subscriber metaphor.
- Subscribing databases can perform updates when using merge replication or Immediate Updating Subscribers.
- SQL Server uses ODBC or OLE DB for replication.
- A server can play multiple roles and be a subscriber, publisher, or distributor.
- To set up replication to a nonSQL Server ODBC source, add the ODBC DSN using the ODBC administrator on the distribution server.
- NonSQL Server ODBC sources can only be subscribers (without third-party software).
- The merge and distribution agents do not have to be executed via SQL Server. You can write applications that run these agents using ActiveX controls that ship with SQL Server.
- You can have multiple distribution databases on a single server.

TRANSACTIONAL REPLICATION

by Laura Herb

IN THIS CHAPTER

Transaction replication is one of the methods provided by SQL Server for distributing data from one database to each subscribing database. SQL Server monitors changes made in the publishing database and passes those changes (inserts, updates, deletes) to the subscribers of the data. The distribution of data can take place within seconds, providing a near-real time environment.

This chapter will cover the different replication topology scenarios and appropriate applications for them. It also covers various components that make transactional replication work. You will be guided through the steps of creating a publication and learn how to partition the data.

> **NOTE**
>
> Publications can be created for transactional replication only in the standard or enterprise editions of SQL Server 7.0. The desktop edition does not support this feature.

APPLICABLE USES FOR TRANSACTIONAL REPLICATION

Different types of applications are complimented by transactional replication. In an environment where data needs to be distributed with little latency, transaction replication is well suited for the task.

In a manufacturing scenario, different sections within a factory could collect production data. Each division within the factory could distribute that data to a central collection point for reporting. Taking that scenario one step further, the collection of data from multiple factories could be distributed to a centralized location for further analysis and reporting.

A bank with branch offices would be a perfect candidate for transactional replication. Each branch keeps track of its own records within a database. The main office subscribes to the branches to collect all the data for the organization.

SQL SERVER 6.5 TO 7.0 QUICK REFERENCE

The following is a quick reference to the changes that occurred between SQL Server version 6.5 and 7.0:

What's New

There are many changes to Transactional Replication in version 7.0 just as there are many changes to SQL Server itself. Following are the major changes:

- The user interface used for setting up publications and subscriptions is completely different from previous versions of SQL Server. Most of the functionality is the same, but you will have to go to different places to do the same things.

- Version 7.0 includes a publication wizard to help you through the process of creating a new publication.

- There are agents for distribution, log reader, and synchronization functions.

- A replication monitoring tool is included with SQL 7.0 to aid you in troubleshooting and monitoring replication.

- Stored Procedures can now be included in publications to decrease the number of commands issued to the distribution database and to the subscribers.

- Immediate updating subscriptions provide two-phase commits. Scripting is now provided for replication.

REPLICATION AGENTS

Following are three major components in transaction replication used to carry out the process of distributing data from the publisher to each subscriber:

- **Snapshot Agent**: Prepares schema and data files to be used to synchronize new subscribers to a publication.

- **Log Reader Agent**: Reads transactions marked for replication in the publisher's transaction log and inserts them into the distribution database.

- **Distribution Agent**: Moves the replicated transactions from the distribution database to all subscribers of the publication.

Here is how these agents work together to move the data. A publication is created specifying all data to be replicated to a subscribing database. The Snapshot Agent creates a schema file to create the table structure on a subscribing database. The Snapshot Agent also creates files containing the data in each of the articles and updates the Distribution database to reflect the synchronization task.

Flags are placed in the publisher's transaction log to distinguish all transactions being replicated to one or more subscribing databases. The Log Reader Agent reads the flagged INSERT, UPDATE, and DELETE statements in the transaction log. The agent monitors the replicated transactions on the publisher for each publication and copies them to the distribution database. The Distribution Agent will then disburse the replicated commands to all the subscribers of that publication.

After the subscribers are initially synchronized with the publisher, actual data is no longer distributed to them. Subscribers are kept up-to-date by the Distribution Agent, which relays all INSERT, UPDATE, and DELETE commands that were performed on the publication. It is important to understand the flow when changes made on a publisher are distributed to the subscribers. This can be very useful when it is time to troubleshoot problems with replication.

REPLICATION TOPOLOGY

Publishers, distributors, and subscribers each play a role in the distribution of data. The method of connecting all these pieces together and their relationship to one another establishes your topology. In a simple topology, the publisher and distributor are located on a single server and there can be one or more subscribers. Specific requirements for distributing data might call for a more complicated topology. If there are hundreds of subscribers to a publication, a single publisher or distributor might not have the resources necessary to manage the heavy processor load and disk I/O. By carefully arranging your publishers and distributors, you could alleviate some of the burden on a server that contains the primary source of data for distribution.

SQL Server 7.0 supports only a hub-and-spoke topology. A data flows from the publisher/distributor (hub) to each subscriber (spoke). Data cannot move directly from subscriber to subscriber. If a subscriber becomes disabled, the hub and the other subscribers are not affected. If the hub becomes disabled, all data flow will cease until the problem is resolved.

The Hub-and-Spoke topology can be configured to accommodate different scenarios as follows:

- Central Publisher
- Central Publisher with remote Distributor
- Publishing Subscriber
- Central Subscriber

Central Publisher

In this scenario, the publisher and the distributor coexist on the same physical SQL Server. The subscriber resides on a different server. This is the simplest form of replication topology. Keep in mind, with this topology, the burden of transaction processing, the synchronization of the subscribers, the LogReader, and the distribution to the subscribers are all performed by the same server. If the amount of transactions or subscribers is substantial, it is recommended that you separate the distributor from the publisher. Figure 16.1 represents the central publisher scenario:

FIGURE 16.1
Central Publisher.

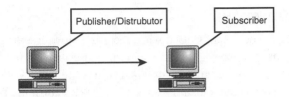

Central Publisher with Remote Distributor

As the level of replication increases, the burden of the publisher and distributor also increases. Server resources become labored and efficiency decreases. Now is the time to separate the distributor from the publisher. If low latency is a requirement, make sure the connection between the publisher and the distributor is reliable and fast.

The LogReader will scan the flagged transactions in the publishing database from across the network and copy those transactions into the distribution database. The major tasks of the LogReader—distributor, and synchronization—will be performed by the distribution server, freeing resources on the publisher.

The tradeoff for this scenario is increased traffic over the network. Using Performance Monitor will help determine whether a server can bear the burden of a combined publisher/distributor scenario or whether it is necessary to separate those components. Figure 16.2 depicts the central publisher with remote distributor scenario.

FIGURE 16.2
Central Publisher with Remote Distributor.

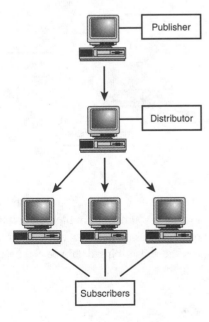

Publishing Subscriber

A publishing subscriber model can be used when there is a slow or expensive network link between the original publisher of the data and the subscribers. A publisher could distribute data to a subscriber with a reliable communications link. That subscriber could then publish the same data to the remaining subscribers. The publishing subscriber would be in a better position to distribute the data than the original publisher would be. This scenario is useful when crossing continents, spanning states, or any other situation where unfavorable network conditions exist.

It is not difficult to create this type of replication model. The original publisher and the publishing subscriber act as their own distributors. The publishing subscriber is the only subscriber to the original publication and has the same publication defined on that server. The remaining subscribers are subscribed to the publishing subscriber. Figure 16.3 is a graphic depiction of a publishing subscriber model.

FIGURE 16.3
Publishing subscriber.

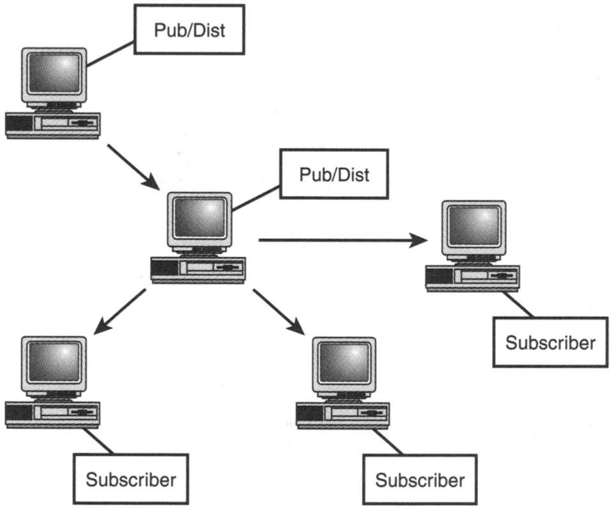

Central Subscriber

If data comes from multiple sources to populate a single, central database then you have a central subscriber scenario. This is relatively simple to implement when setting up replication. Each source of data is configured as a publisher. All publishers distribute the data to a single subscriber. In this case, the subscribing database can be used as a central reporting point.

Suppose a company has a headquarters site as well as individual branches. Specific data corresponding to each branch is populated by the branch and then distributed to headquarters. The data collected at the central point would be readily available for reports on any branch or totals accumulated by all.

If a DBA has the ability to administer the databases for all branches, it might be prudent to use a single SQL Server as the distributor. This enables the DBA to monitor all distribution agents for all the publishers from a central location. If each branch is charged with maintaining its own data, distribution could reside on the same servers as the publishers. Figure 16.4 shows a central subscriber where the publishers and distributors reside on single servers.

FIGURE 16.4
*Central
subscriber.*

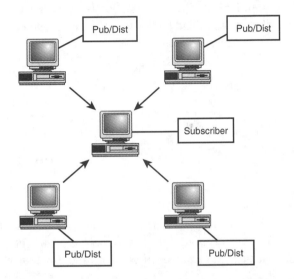

IMMEDIATE UPDATING SUBSCRIBERS

When a publication is created, the creator has the option of allowing a subscriber to update the copy of its local data. The updates the subscriber makes will be propagated back to the publisher, and then to the remaining subscribers of the data. The two-phase commit protocol provides assurance that the publisher has received the data and there are no conflicts. If the publisher is unable to receive the data, the transaction made by the subscriber will not be committed on the subscriber's database. The following components are used when immediate updating subscribers is enabled:

- Triggers
- Stored procedures
- Microsoft Distributed Transaction Coordinator
- Conflict detection
- Loopback detection

Triggers

Triggers are located on the subscriber. The triggers ensure that any transaction beginning on the subscriber is committed on the publisher before being committed by the subscriber. The protocol utilized for this type of transaction is called a two-phase commit (2PC). If the transaction is not committed by the publisher, it is rolled back on the subscriber and both databases remain synchronized.

> **NOTE**
>
> If the subscription is dropped and data will be modified at the subscriber, the triggers that were created for 2PC need to be manually dropped on those tables.

Stored Procedures

Stored procedures are located on the publisher. They ensure that any transactions being replicated are applied only if there are no conflicts. If there is a conflict, the transaction will be rolled back at both sites. Stored procedures are created for INSERT, UPDATE, and DELETE transactions.

> **NOTE**
>
> The logic within the stored procedures can vary depending on the method of conflict detection.

Microsoft Distributed Transaction Coordinator

Microsoft Distributed Transaction Coordinator (MS DTC) is the component that manages the two-phase commit execution between the publisher and the subscriber. A remote stored procedure call initiates MS DTC using the Begin Distributed Tran statement.

16

Conflict Detection

There are two methods used to detect conflicts with updating subscribers: timestamp and row compare.

Timestamp Conflict Detection

If there is a timestamp column on the publishing table, SQL Server automatically uses this method to detect conflicts. SQL Server uses this column to determine whether the value has changed since it was replicated to the subscriber. When the subscriber requests a synchronous transaction, it passes the timestamp and other column values of the row to the publisher. If the timestamp values are the same, the publisher accepts the transaction. This method of conflict detection works in conjunction with loopback detection.

> **NOTE**
>
> This method of conflict detection does not work when the publisher and the subscriber are located on the same server.

Row Compare Conflict Detection

There is no timestamp column on the published table using this method of conflict detection. SQL Server verifies the value of the row in question from the deleted table on the subscriber and checks it against the values of those columns in the corresponding row in the publishing table. If the values match, the transaction is applied.

Loopback Detection

SQL Server determines if a transaction has already been applied to a server by using the loopback detection mechanism. When a subscriber initiates a change and it is propagated to the publisher, loopback detection prevents the change from being reapplied to the subscriber. If Subscriber A inserts a row, the insert is reflected on the publisher. The publisher then sends the insert command to all its subscribers. If loopback detection were not enabled, the Insert statement would be passed along back to Subscriber A, causing a constraint violation. This violation could stop the distribution agent to that server and replication will stop. If you are not using loopback detection and problems occur, add a timestamp to the published tables and re-create publication and subscriptions.

RECOMMENDED TOPOLOGY FOR UPDATING SUBSCRIBERS

An effective model to use for immediate updating subscribers would be a central publisher with remote distributor. Not all subscribers have to be updating subscribers.

CREATING A TRANSACTION-BASED PUBLICATION

The new interface for SQL Server 7.0 provides a Create Publication Wizard to guide you when you create a publication. There are many ways you can configure replication to fine-tune it to your needs. The wizard provides options and you make your choices. Following are the steps to use to create a typical transactional replication publication.

> **TIP**
>
> The creation of your publication will probably progress more smoothly if you have already started your SQL Server Agent and the MS DTC Agent before creating the publication.

1. In Enterprise Manager, make sure you have the correct server selected. There may be several SQL Servers registered in Enterprise Manager. From the Tools menu, point to Replication, and then click Create and Manage Publications. When the dialog box appears, click the database that you want to publish; then click the Create Publication button. If you have already created a publication for the same database, SQL Server gives you the option of using it as a template for your new one. This section assumes you have not already created a publication in the pubs database.

> **NOTE**
>
> You must have already enabled publishing for this database to create your publication. A hand appears under each database that is enabled for publishing.

2. The Create Publication Wizard dialog box appears. Click the Next button (see Figure 16.5).

FIGURE 16.5

*The Create
Publication
Wizard dialog
box.*

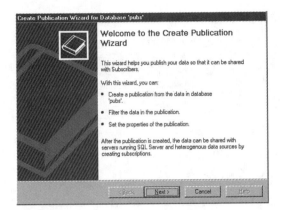

3. Now it's time to choose the type of publication you are creating. Because this chapter is on transactional replication, you should choose Transactional publication. Click the radio button next to the appropriate option: then click the Next button (see Figure 16.6).

FIGURE 16.6

*The Choose
Publication Type
dialog box.*

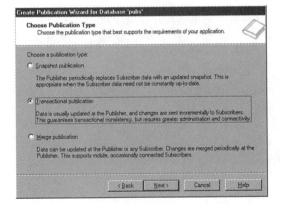

4. The next dialog box that appears permits you to choose to allow updatable subscriptions. Based on analysis of your needs, you may have already decided whether to allow subscribers to update the articles that will be defined in your publication. If you choose to allow updating subscribers, make sure you have timestamp columns in your tables if loopback detection is a requirement (see Figure 16.7).

FIGURE 16.7

Specify Allow Immediate-Updating Subscriptions types.

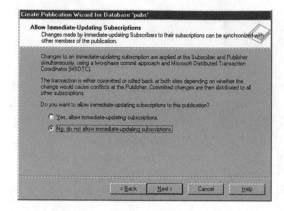

5. Choose whether all the subscribers will be SQL Server databases or if some can be non-SQL Server (see Figure 16.8).

FIGURE 16.8

The Specify Subscriber Types dialog box.

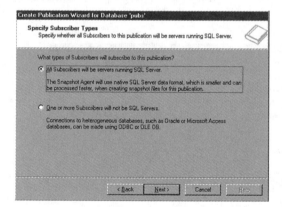

6. The next window enables you to choose which tables and stored procedures you want to include as articles in your publication. Click the corresponding check boxes to include the articles. Notice the tables that do not contain primary keys cannot be selected (see Figure 16.9).

FIGURE 16.9

The Specify Articles dialog box.

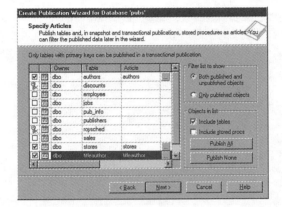

7. Type an appropriate name and description for your publication and click the Next button (see Figure 16.10).

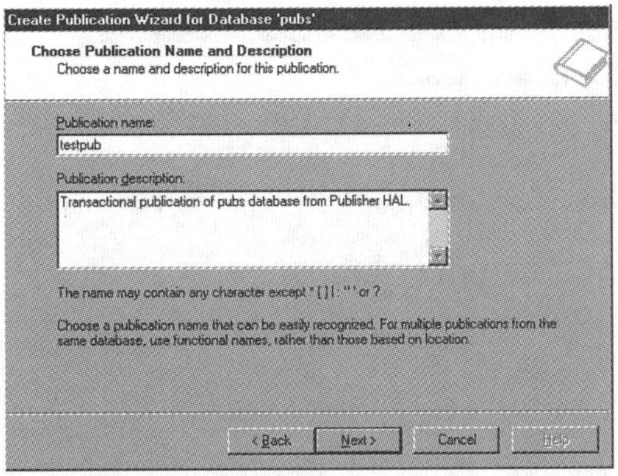

FIGURE 16.10

The Choose Publication Name and Description dialog box.

8. If you want to change default settings such as filtering columns, rows, or anonymous subscribers, check the Yes box. If you check No, your publication will be completed. If you check Yes, you will be able to further define your publication (see Figure 16.11).

FIGURE 16.11

The Use Default Properties of the Publication dialog box.

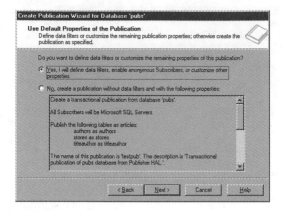

9. Here is where you select columns or rows to be filtered from your publication. If you click Yes, the following dialog box appears (see Figure 16.12).

FIGURE 16.12

The Filter Data dialog box.

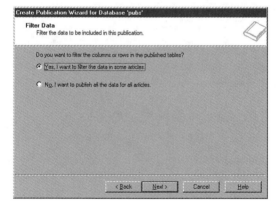

10. Specify any columns you do not want to be in your publication. In the following example, the boxes beside the phone and zip column names have been unchecked. When the publication is created, those columns will not be included (see Figure 16.13).

FIGURE 16.13
The Filter Table Columns dialog box.

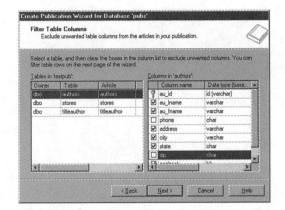

11. Click the ellipse (…) next to the appropriate columns to filter records from your tables you do not want to publish (see Figure 16.14).

FIGURE 16.14
The Filter Table Rows dialog box.

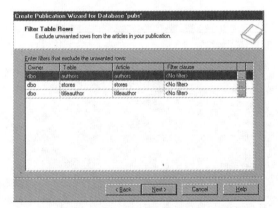

12. If you click to create a filter on table rows, the Specify Filter dialog box (see Figure 16.15) gives you the opportunity to type a select statement to filter your rows. After you have entered your statement, click OK and then click the Next button.

FIGURE **16.15**

*The Specify Filter
dialog box.*

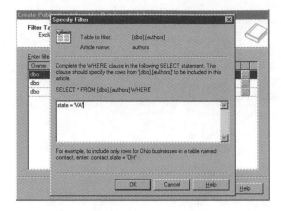

13. If your publication will be published to the Internet or open to everyone, choose the option to allow anonymous subscribers. Otherwise, choose No (see Figure 16.16).

FIGURE **16.16**

*The Allow
Anonymous
Subscribers
dialog box.*

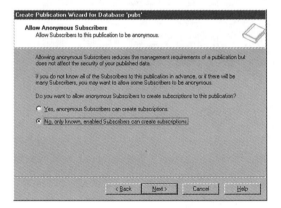

14. Customize your schedule for the Snapshot Agent to run. If you are running database maintenance or backups during the default time, you can choose another schedule for your Snapshot Agent (see Figure 16.17).

FIGURE 16.17

*The Set Snapshot
Agent Schedule
dialog box.*

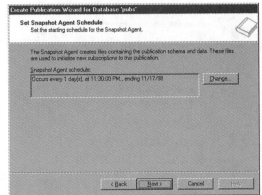

15. The login of the pull-subscribing server determines whether SQL Server allows the
subscription to initiate. You can leave the default settings from SQL Server, or you
can alter them to your needs (see Figure 16.18).

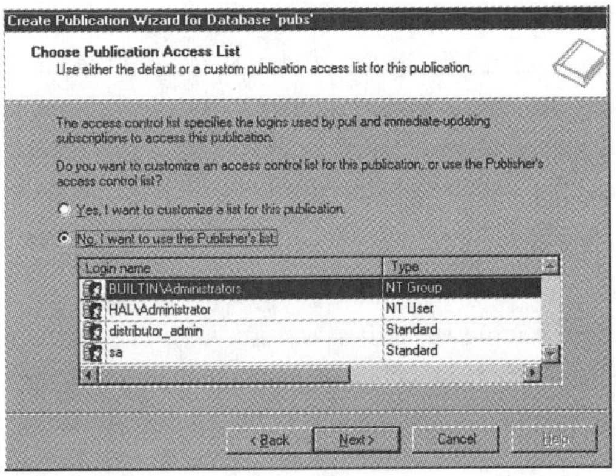

FIGURE 16.18

*Choose
Publication
Access List
dialog box.*

16. All the questions have been answered, and now SQL Server will create your publication for you (see Figure 16.19). Click the Finish button and you are done!

FIGURE 16.19

*Completing the
Create
Publication
Wizard dialog
box.*

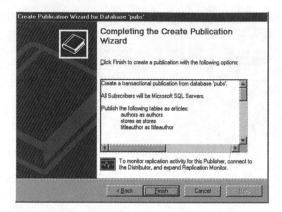

CUSTOM STORED PROCEDURES

Why use stored procedures during replication? Let's start with the obvious: Use stored procedures to improve the performance of the replication process. Stored procedures improve performance by using precompiled SQL statements during replication. Stored procedures also reduce network traffic because you pass only the stored procedure name and parameters rather than the entire SQL statement. You can also use stored procedures to perform custom processing on the subscribing server such as reformatting the data to simplify end-user queries. The customer-stored procedures might be as simple as translating an integer status field to a character field that reports "SUCCESS" or "ERROR".

Here's an example of using custom replication stored procedures to reduce the number of joins (that is, denormalizing a table for a data warehouse). Suppose that you are replicating to a database that is to be used by several end users. The primary table the end users are concerned with, My_Customer, consists of several ID columns that reference description values in other tables. You want to prevent the end users from having to join the My_Customer table to any other tables to retrieve the descriptions associated with the ID columns (that is, you want to flatten the table). Here are the steps required to perform this operation using replication:

1. Create an article on the publishing server for the table My_Customer.

2. From the Specify Articles dialog box (refer to Figure 16.9), click the (...) beside the article name, and click the Commands tab. Specify the stored procedure names for the data modification statements you plan to support (for example, INSERT, UPDATE, and DELETE).

3. Subscribe the end-user database server to the article set up on the publishing server for the My_Customer table. Select No, the Subscriber(s) Already Has the Schema and Data for the Initialize Subscription option.

4. On the subscribing server, create the `My_Customer` table with a different table schema than the one found on the publishing server (that is, replace the datatypes for the ID columns with the datatypes for the description columns).

5. Create stored procedures for all the data modifications you plan to support (for example, `INSERT`, `UPDATE`, and `DELETE`) on the subscribing server that. For example, the `INSERT` stored procedure uses the ID columns of the `My_Customer` table passed in during replication to retrieve the description columns from the other tables in the database and inserts them (along with the other associated information for a row) into the subscriber's `My_Customer` table.

6. After everything is in place, you must synchronize the data between the two tables so they are identical. The easiest and safest way to sync the data is to copy all the data from the publisher server's `My_Customer` table to a holding table on the subscribing server. Create a cursor that reads each row in the holding table and executes the replication `INSERT` stored procedure to place the information in the correct format in the subscriber's `My_Customer` table.

When the two tables are synchronized and the data is the same, you are ready to go. When data is changed on the publisher, the changes are replicated to the subscribing server. The stored procedure is executed on the subscribing server, retrieving the correct columns and inserting them in the subscribing server's copy of the `My_Customer` table. You have created a more user-friendly table on the subscribing server by using custom stored procedures.

One more thing, if you use stored procedures for replication, all subscribing servers must have the stored procedures in the subscribing database. The stored procedures do not have to exist on the publishing server.

> **NOTE**
>
> In the SQL Server Books OnLine, another way of implementing Custom Stored Procedures is documented. Look in the Building SQL Server Applications book. Then go to Replication Programming, Replication Programming Samples. The article name is "Using a Custom Resolver."

REPLICATING STORED PROCEDURES

Here is another new feature in SQL Server 7.0. Stored procedures can be replicated instead of Individual `INSERT`, `UPDATE`, and `DELETE` statements. Suppose there is a large update on a table that is being published. The update involves 5,000 rows. The optimizer within SQL Server will change those update statements into 5,000 deletes and 5,000 inserts. These 10,000 SQL statements then travel through the network to populate 10,000 rows in the Distribution database. This can dramatically affect network bandwidth due to the large amount of transactional traffic. These transactions could also fill the Distribution database up if you aren't careful about sizing it.

If you want to optimize performance on the network and you would rather not clutter up your distribution database with a tremendous amount of SQL commands, you might want to replicate stored procedures to reduce your load. If the changes to the data are made on a one-time basis, replicating a stored procedure might not be applicable. If the changes are made on a fairly regular basis, a stored procedure can be very beneficial.

> **NOTE**
>
> Data stored in the publishing and subscribing tables should be identical when using stored procedures for replication. There will be a lot less troubleshooting in your future if you are dealing with the same data on both sides!

To define a stored procedure as an article, follow these steps:

1. Create your publication up to step 5 in the preceding section, which describes how to add a publication.
2. Select the Include Stored Procedures check box, if it is not already checked. Make sure the radio button for Both Published and Unpublished Objects is selected.
3. Select the appropriate stored procedure and then click Next.
4. Follow the remaining steps in the preceding section to complete the creation of your publication.

SUBSCRIPTIONS

After the publication is created, subscriptions to the data need to be performed. The subscription can either be pulled from the subscriber or pushed by the publisher.

- **Push Subscriptions** To initiate a push subscription, select the Tools menu option; then click Replication. Click Push Subscriptions to Others. Expand the database that contains the publication, and click the publication. Click the Push New Subscription button. The Push Subscription Wizard appears. Follow the instructions to select the subscription server, database, and distribution options.

- **Pull Subscriptions**: To initiate a pull subscription, select the Tools menu option: then click Replication. Click Pull Subscription to '%'. Click the Pull New Subscription button. The Pull New Subscription Wizard appears. Follow the instructions to select the publication server, publication, and destination database.

REPLICATION MONITOR

You have defined a publication and are ready to push data to a subscriber. What if something goes wrong? SQL Server 7.0 provides a new tool to aid DBAs with troubleshooting replication problems. The Replication Monitor has been developed to help pinpoint problems with replication.

When the server functions as a Distributor and the user is in the Sysadmin role, replication monitoring is enabled. The Replication Monitor can be used for viewing publishers, publications, and all subscriptions. The following replication objects can be monitored by the Replication Monitor:

- Subscriptions to the publication
- Snapshot Agent
- LogReader Agent
- Distribution Agent Merge Agent
- Miscellaneous Agents (cleanup)
- Replication Alerts

If you create a publication and synchronization fails, you can use Replication Monitor to determine where the failure occurred and the problem can be corrected. Existing tables on the subscribers may not be dropped and re-created due to foreign key constraints, or the server being unavailable at the time of synchronization. The error messages supplied by Replication Monitor provide invaluable aid in solving replication mysteries. Look at the following scenario.

If an agent fails to complete a job (see preceding list), a big red "X" will appear on the Replication Monitor icon in the SQL Enterprise Manager (see Figure 16.20). If you look at Figure 16.20, you will see an error in the publication and in the Distribution Agent. The agent in trouble has a red "x" beside it when the Distribution Agents folder is double-clicked.

When the agent is double-clicked, the Distribution Agent Error Details dialog box will contain the error that caused the agent to stop functioning (see Figure 16.21). In this case, the subscribing database has the Read only option enabled and the Distribution Agent is unable to update the database.

FIGURE 16.20

The Enterprise Manager with Replication Monitor errors.

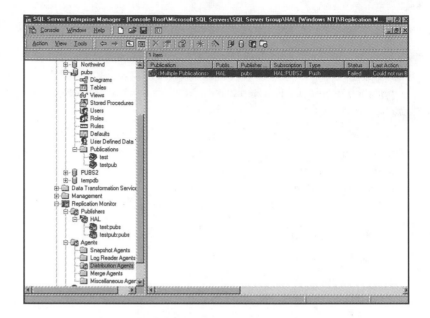

FIGURE 16.21

The Distribution Agent Error Details dialog box.

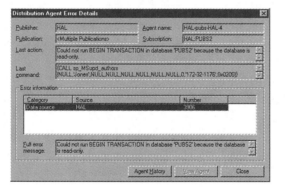

After the Read-only option is removed from the database, right-click the Distribution Agent and click Start on the shortcut menu. All the red "x"s will go away and everything will be back to normal (see Figure 16.22).

The preceding scenario was a simple problem to solve with the Replication Monitor. There will be more complicated replication issues you will encounter. Make use of the monitor and rely on it heavily.

FIGURE 16.22

The Enterprise Manager showing no replication problems.

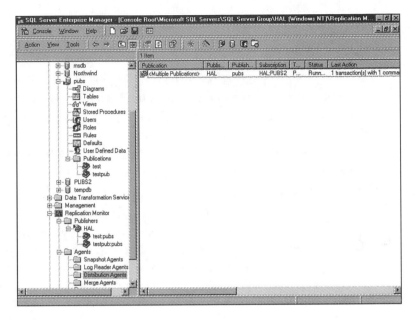

TRANSACTION REPLICATION FAQ

Following are some of the common questions asked by DBAs about SQL Server transaction replication:

Q. In SQL 6.5, I set my Distribution options within the Distribution Task. I don't see the option to do that now. Where do I go to configure my options?

A. In the Replication Monitor, you have the option to configure options on all the replication agents. Double-click an agent folder (LogReader, Snapshot, Distribution, Miscellaneous). When the current agents populate the right pane of the Management Console, right-click the one you want to configure. Choose Agent Properties from the shortcut menu.

Q. How do I unsubscribe from a publication?

A. The publisher may delete a push or pull subscription from a publication. Expand the database in the topic tree of the Enterprise Manager. Expand the Publications folder and right-click the name of the publication you want to modify. When the shortcut menu appears, click Properties. A dialog box pops up to warn you about modifying a publication with existing subscribers. Click OK to acknowledge the warning. In the Properties dialog box, click the Subscriptions tab. Click the subscription you want to unsubscribe, and click the Delete button.

If you are pulling a subscription from another SQL Server, select the Tools menu option in SQL Server Enterprise Manager. Click Replication, then click Pull Subscription to "?". In the Pull Subscription dialog box, select the publication you want to unsubscribe, and then click the Delete Subscription button.

Q. How do I view transactions that have not been delivered to the distributor?

A. The `sp_replshowcmds` stored procedure gives you a view of transactions remaining in the transaction log of the publisher. You can view the actual commands of the transactions in the log. See SQL Server books online for further details about this stored procedure.

Q. How do I modify a publication after I have already created it?

A. To modify a publication, make sure no other databases subscribe to it. Follow the steps stated above to remove existing subscriptions on your publication. Expand the database. Expand the Publications folder and right-click the name of the publication you want to modify. The Properties dialog box contains tabs with all the options available during the creation of a publication when using the Create Publication Wizard. Click the tabs to make the appropriate modifications to your publication.

SUMMARY

In this chapter, you learned about the various topologies of transactional replication. You saw how the replication agents act to move data from publisher to subscriber. You now have many more options for configuring replication such as updating subscribers and making use of stored procedures. The Replication Monitor is a centralized tool that enables you to view all aspects of replication and determine the cause of problems if they occur.

SNAPSHOT AND MERGE REPLICATION

by Mark Spenik

IN THIS CHAPTER

This chapter examines the simplest form of replication, Snapshot replication. Snapshot replication was available in SQL Server 6.x; however, SQL Server 7.0 adds the capabilities to use updating subscribers and anonymous subscribers with Snapshot replication. This chapter also includes one of the more exciting SQL Server replication modes, merge replication. You learn which types of applications work well with merge replication and which types of applications do not. Configuring, managing, and monitoring merge and snapshot publications are covered, as is troubleshooting. This chapter also discusses using the Internet to replicate changes or snapshots.

> **NOTE**
>
> This chapter builds on previous chapters and focuses on using Snapshot and Merge replication. Snapshot replication has many capabilities common to standard transactional replication, such as horizontal and vertical filtering, anonymous subscribers, and immediate updating subscribers. Implementation of these features is the same as in transactional replication. If you skipped Chapters 15, "Replication," and 16, "Transactional Replication," you may want to refer to them to learn about
>
> - Setting up publishers and subscribers (Chapter 15)
> - Setting up a distribution database (Chapter 15)
> - Creating publications (Chapter 16)
> - Configuring articles (Chapter 16)

WHAT IS SNAPSHOT REPLICATION?

Snapshot replication takes a picture of the data (that is, copies all the data in the table as defined by the article) at a certain point in time and replicates the "snapshot" of data to subscribers. Snapshot replication can be thought of as a "table refresh" because all the information for the article is exported and loaded into the subscriber's table. With Snapshot replication, no transactional information is kept or required. SQL Server 7.0 gives you the flexibility to determine how the subscriber's tables are refreshed. Tables can be dropped and re-created, tables can be truncated (that is, all the rows deleted) and the data refreshed, or the data can be added to an existing table without dropping the table or deleting all the records. Like transactional-based replication, Snapshot replication can also use "immediate updating subscribers." *Immediate updating subscribers* means that a subscriber can update the information in the article via a two-phase commit with the publisher. The change then replicates to the other subscribers at the scheduled synchronization time, using standard Snapshot replication.

Snapshot Applications

Before going into the details of Snapshot replication, take a minute to examine appropriate and inappropriate uses of Snapshot replication. In general, Snapshot replication is a good solution when performing a table refresh meets the business requirements and the lag time between data modifications and the table refresh is acceptable. Snapshot replication is not an appropriate solution when subscribers want to stay current with information from a publication that is being modified constantly or even several times a day. Such a scenario would require moving entire tables back and forth to reflect a single transaction! Some appropriate uses of Snapshot replication are as follows:

- Static lookup tables
- Tables that change infrequently
- Information that is rolled up or summarized and then distributed on a scheduled basis (daily, weekly, monthly, and so on) to subscribers for reporting
- Subscriptions that are not transaction based (such as very limited updating) whose users may be disconnected for long periods of time
- Internet applications that want to receive information for viewing purposes
- Company information such as an employee list, a store list, a price list, or a product list that is updated at a central site and then distributed on a scheduled basis (daily, weekly, monthly, and so on) to subscribers

Inappropriate uses of Snapshot replication are as follows:

- Contact management or sales force automation databases that are updated frequently offline and at multiple sites
- High transaction based applications that require real-time replication to subscribers
- Multisite data entry applications
- Financial applications and other applications that require all information be up-to-date with all database changes
- Applications in which the data is changed frequently at a single site and replicated to other sites
- Applications that use data partitioning

Snapshot Replication: Step by Step

Snapshot replication is one of the simpler modes of replication to administer and maintain because the entire content of the article is replicated, and you don't have to worry about applying transactions or resolving merge conflicts. As such, a Log Reader Agent or Merge Agent is not required. Snapshot replication uses the Snapshot Agent and the

Distribution Agent. Figure 17.1 shows an example of Snapshot replication. In Figure 17.1, Server A is the publisher and distributor (you can also use a remote server as a distributor), and Server B is the subscriber. The pubs database contains a publication called *Pubs*MyPubs with a single article, the authors table. You can use Figure 17.1 to walk through the Snapshot replication process; assume that a publication has been created and that the publisher is pushing the publication to a subscriber.

> **NOTE**
>
> When you create a Snapshot publication, a Snapshot Agent and a Distribution Agent are created for the publication. The Snapshot Agent typically executes at the distributor. For push subscriptions, the Distribution Agent executes at the distributor. For a pull subscription, the Distribututution Agent executes on the subscriber server. Both the Snapshot Agent and the Distribution Agent can be embedded in other applications and run outside of the SQL Server environment, using ActiveX controls provided with SQL Server 7.0.

FIGURE 17.1

Snapshot replication—step by step.

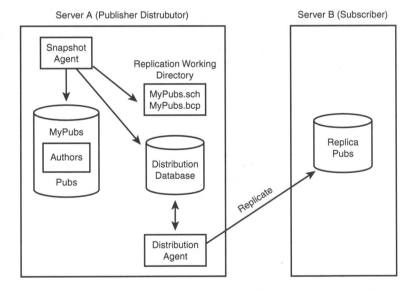

Step 1—Snapshot Agent Executes: Synchronization Set Created

When a Snapshot publication is created and a subscriber subscribes to the publication, the Snapshot Agent executes as either part of a scheduled job or when information in the article(s) is changed. When the Snapshot Agent executes, the first thing the agent does is to put a read lock on all tables that make up the publication. Using Figure 17.1, a read lock would be placed on the single article, the authors table in the publication MyPubs.

The Snapshot Agent then generates a schema file (that is, Data Definition Language [DDL]) for each table (article) in the publication. The agent then uses BCP (Bulk Copy) to copy the data out of each table. Both the schema file and the data file are written to the replication working directory of the distributor, shown in Figure 17.1. The schema file has a .sch extension, and the data file has a .bcp extension for articles distributed to SQL Servers only (that is, native). Articles replicated to SQL Server and other data sources are copied out in text format and have the extension .txt. The schema file and the data file are called the *synchronization set* for the article (table). Each article in the publication contains a synchronization set.

> **CAUTION**
>
> Be careful when scheduling the update frequency of a Snapshot publication. While the snapshot synchronization set is being created, read locks are placed on all the tables in the publication (that is, articles) for the entire time that schema files and data files are being created. The read locks prevent any application from obtaining an exclusive table lock on one of the articles, which could cause your application to block (wait until the synchronization set[s] are built). Also, the process of building a large number of synchronization sets or creating large data files for replication adds overhead to your system and can affect the performance of the distribution server (push) or subscription server (pull). You should try to schedule Snapshot updates (refresh) during off-peak hours or days.

Step 2—Snapshot Agent Updates Distribution Database

After the synchronization set(s) are built, the Snapshot Agent inserts new rows in the distribution database's MSRepl_commands table and MSRepl_transactions table, shown in Figure 17.1. MSRepl_commands table contains information about the publisher, the article, and the location of the schema and data files. MSRepl_transactions contains commands that reference the Subscribers synchronization task.

Step 3—Snapshot Agent Releases Read Locks on Articles

After the synchronization set(s) have been created and the distribution database updated, the read lock(s) are removed from the article(s). In the case of Figure 17.1, they are removed from the authors table.

Step 4—Distribution Agent Checks the Distribution Table

The Distribution Agent, shown in Figure 17.1, checks the MSrepl_transactions and MSrepl_commands tables in the distribution database for a synchronization set for the subscriber.

Step 5—Distribution Agent Copies Data to Subscriber

When a synchronization set is found for a subscriber, the Distribution Agent copies the data and schema to the subscriber server. The Distribution Agent then places a read lock on the table(s) and applies the commands found in the distribution database, which includes importing the data. The read lock is held on the table(s) until all synchronization sets and commands are applied for the entire publication to ensure that referential integrity is maintained.

PLANNING AND SPECIAL DESIGN CONSIDERATIONS FOR SNAPSHOT REPLICATION

As stated earlier, snapshot replication is one of the simplest and easiest forms of replication to set up and administer; however, planning and design considerations are still important to ensure smooth operation and the best performance.

Unlike other forms of replication, Snapshot replication (without an updating subscriber) does not require the tables being published to have a primary key.

As a publisher and/or distributor, you should pay special attention to the timing of the creation of synchronization sets, which add additional overhead to your server while they are being generated. If at all possible, the synchronization sets should be generated during off-peak hours. Keep in mind that while the synchronization set is being generated, the tables that make up the publication will have read locks placed on them for the duration of the synchronization set build, preventing other applications from obtaining exclusive locks.

If your publication is going to have numerous subscribers, you should consider using a pull subscription, as opposed to a push subscription. A pull subscription is more scalable and can handle a larger number of subscribers compared to a push subscription. With a pull subscription, the Distribution Agent executes on the subscriber server instead of the distribution server, which greatly reduces the amount of resources required on the distribution server to handle the publication/subscribers. Remember, with a push subscription, a distribution task exists on the distribution server for each subscriber.

As with all other forms of update replication, avoid using identity columns, which can produce conflicts when replicating between sites. Instead, use the unique identifier data type.

Keep in mind that snapshot replication copies entire tables over the network. So be realistic about the amount of data you want to send to each site with Snapshot replication. For example, you would not want to try to replicate 100MB of data using Snapshot replication between two sites with a 56KB RAS connection; however with a T1, the time required may be acceptable.

SETTING UP A SNAPSHOT PUBLICATION

In Chapter 16, you learned how to use the Publication and Subscription Wizard to create a transactional-based publication.

> **TIP**
>
> SQL Server 7.0 allows you to use any existing publication as a template for a new publication. This feature can come in handy for configuring different sites that use vertical or horizontal filters or very large publications. After you create the publication as a template, you can modify or remove the articles as required.

You create a Snapshot publication in the same manner, using the Publication and Subscription Wizard. Instead of walking through the wizard again, you can examine the screens that differ in transactional-based replication and Snapshot replication.

> **NOTE**
>
> Some of the following screens may appear slightly different depending on the edition of SQL Server you are using. These are screens from the Desktop edition. Items disabled in the Desktop edition are enabled in the Standard and Enterprise editions.

The first screen to examine, the Publication Type screen, is shown in Figure 17.2.

FIGURE 17.2
The Choose Publication Type dialog box.

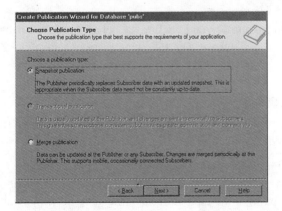

For a Snapshot publication, select the Snapshot radio button shown in Figure 17.2.

17

SNAPSHOT AND MERGE REPLICATION

> **NOTE**
>
> Obviously, to create a Merge replication (discussed later in this chapter), select the Merge radio button.

As you walk through the wizard, you reach the Specify Articles dialog box that allows you to select the tables and stored procedures that make up the publication. To set Snapshot-specific options for each article, click the square box located to the right of the selected article in the Specify Article dialog box. The article properties dialog box appears. Click on the Snapshot Option tab, shown in Figure 17.3.

FIGURE 17.3

The Snapshot Option tab of the Article Properties dialog box.

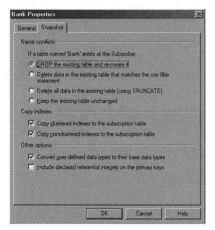

The Snapshot Option tab allows you to define the behavior of the Snapshot when it is loaded into the subscriber database. The following sections take a close look at each part of the dialog box.

Name Conflicts

The Name Conflicts section allows you to define what to do at the subscriber database with the Snapshots synchronization set. The options are as follows:

- Drop the Existing Tables and Re-create It—Select this option if you want to drop and re-create the tables as well as refresh the data at the subscriber server. Select this option if you want the table refreshed; the table may then undergo column changes periodically.

- Delete Data in the Existing Table That Matches the Row Filter Statement—If you are using vertical partitioning in defining the article, select this option so that only data that is being published by the article is removed from the subscriber table.

- Delete All Data in the Existing Table (Using TRUNCATE)—Select this option to clean out the data in the table and reload the data using the synchronization set. Select this option to perform a "table refresh."

- Keep the Existing Table Unchanged—To add new data to a subscriber table but leave the existing data alone, select this option.

Copy Indexes

This section allows you to specify whether to create clustered and nonclustered indexes when the publication is distributed to subscribers.

Other Options

This section allows you to set the following options:

- Convert User-Defined Data Types to Their Base Data Types—Selecting this option ensures that tables that use user-defined datatypes can be re-created without requiring the user-defined datatype to be present in the subscribing database.

- Include Declarative Referential Integrity on the Primary Keys—Check this option if you want to maintain referential integrity between tables within the publication.

WHAT IS MERGE REPLICATION?

Merge replication is the capability for multiple sites to make changes in a database (that is, publication), track the changes, and then merge the changes back into a destination database. With merge replication, each site works by itself without having to be connected to any other site(s), and users can update, add, or delete any information in the published articles without using data partitioning or a two-phase commit. At some point, the site connects to another site (that is, destination database) and merges the changes to the destination database. If both sites update the same information, a conflict occurs. In this case, merge replication performs conflict resolution and accepts one of the changes based on the rules set up for conflict resolution.

Merge replication applications and solutions differ from the transactional-based solutions previously examined. Transactional solutions require that sites are connected and transaction consistency maintained. The whole idea behind merge replication is to have disconnected sites, the downside being that transactional consistency is not maintained. When I say transactional consistency is not maintained, I mean that eventually all sites will have the same results in the database, but the results in the database may include results that could not have been achieved had all the changes been made at a single location. A demonstration of how transactional consistency is lost appears later in this section. In the meantime, don't panic! Merge replication is a great solution for many applications, and it allows full site autonomy. Eventually, all databases will end up with the same result, but unlike transactional replication, the result could be one that could not have been achieved had all transactions been performed at a single site (that is, transactional consistency).

Merge Applications

Before going into the details of merge replication, here's a summary of appropriate and inappropriate uses of merge replication. In general, merge replication is a good solution for applications that require sites to be disconnected (that is, site autonomy) and require the capability to modify and make changes to the data in the database. Merge replication is not an appropriate solution when transactional consistency is required. Some appropriate uses of merge replication are as follows:

- Contact management or call-tracking databases that are frequently updated offline and at multiple sites
- Company timesheet database
- Road-warrior database solutions: salespeople, district managers, and so on who spend a lot of time out of the office (often at company or client sites) and update database applications from the field to merge back to the "main" company database at a later time
- Company information such as an employee list, a store list, a price list, or a product list that is updated at satellite sites and replicated to a central database

Inappropriate uses of merge replication are as follows:

- Static lookup tables
- High transaction-based applications that require real-time replication to subscribers and have a high likelihood of collisions
- Financial applications and other applications that require transactional consistency
- Applications that require transactional consistency and use data partitioning with frequent updates and changes replicated ASAP to other sites (note: all sites are connected)

Merge Replication: Step by Step

Unlike snapshot replication, merge replication is not a simple form of replication. Fortunately, SQL Server hides the complexities of merge replication from the DBA and the programmers and makes it as simple to set up and administer as any other form of replication. Before walking through the merge replication process, though, you need to know what happens when you create a merge publication.

When you create a merge publication, SQL Server makes modifications to your database and the tables that make up the articles. SQL Server makes sure that all published tables have a unique column for each row in the table. SQL Server looks for and uses unique identifier columns with the ROWGUIDCOL property set. If one is not found, SQL Server adds one. SQL Server then adds triggers to track the changes made to the data in the tables and adds to the database several system tables that are used to track changes and perform conflict detection and resolution.

Because merge replication tracks when a row changes and only its final state is replicated, a Log Reader Agent is not required (that is, one row could change 100 times, but the row would only be reconciled once). Merge replication uses the Snapshot Agent and the Merge Agent. The following sections describe the steps that occur with merge replication.

Step 1—Snapshot Agent Executes

Before the merge replication process can begin between the publisher and the subscriber, the databases must be synchronized (that is, identical). The synchronization process is performed by the Snapshot Agent, which copies synchronization sets from the publisher to the subscriber and applies them to the subscriber database. The process of synchronization is similar to the step-by-step Snapshot replication described earlier in this chapter. For very large databases or very slow networks, you don't have to rely on the snapshot agent for the initial synchronization; the database can be synchronized manually as well. You can perform a manual synchronization of the database by using the Backup and Recovery utility.

Step 2—Subscriber Updates a Row in an Article

When a subscriber makes a change to a row in an article (table), a trigger on the table fires and sets the generation column for the modified row to zero.

Step 3—Merge Agent Executes

The Merge Agent executes and retrieves all the rows where the generation column has been set to zero and sends them to the destination database.

17

SNAPSHOT AND
MERGE
REPLICATION

Step 4—Merge Agent Merges Data at the Destination Database

The Merge Agent examines the data changes arriving at the destination database with the existing rows in the destination database. If no conflicts are found, the change is made to the destination database. A *conflict* is a row that has been modified by more then one site since the last synchronization. Conflicts can be determined by column changes or row changes. The default conflict-tracking mode is column-based changes. If a conflict occurs, the conflict is resolved using a priority-based system. In the priority-based system, each site participating in replication is assigned a priority with 100 being the highest priority and 0 the lowest. The default is for the highest priority to win; however, the default conflict resolution system can be overridden with a custom resolution system. In the case of two sites with equal priority updating the same row, the tie goes to the change that is already at the destination database.

Step 5—Subscribers Receive Changes at Synchronization

Other subscribers receive the changes made to the article when the subscriber synchronizes with the publication, which can be performed at any time.

Merge Replication and Transactional Consistency

Earlier in the book, the statement was made several times that merge replication did not maintain transactional consistency, but that each site's database would converge to the same result over time. So what does all this mean? The easiest way to help you understand merge replication and transactional consistency is to walk through a simple example. For simplicity, this example uses a table called "test" that has two columns and two rows, as shown in Table 17.1.

TABLE 17.1 TEST—INITIAL PUBLISHERS DATABASE

Name	State
Mark	Va
Orryn	Pa

Now assume two different users execute the following transactions:

User1:

```
BEGIN TRANSACTION
Update Test
Set State = "Tx" where Name = "Mark" and State = "Va"
Update Test
Set State = "NC" where Name = "Orryn" and State = "Pa"
COMMIT TRANSACTION
```

User2:

```
BEGIN TRANSACTION
Update Test
Set State = "NY" where Name = "Orryn" and State = "Pa"
COMMIT TRANSACTION
```

Now if all of the changes were made at the same site (that is, transactional consistency), the following outcomes would be possible:

TABLE 17.2   TEST—BOTH TRANSACTIONS FAILED

Name	State
Mark	VA
Orryn	PA

TABLE 17.3   TEST—USER1 TRANSACTION SUCCEEDS

Name	State
Mark	TX
Orryn	NC

TABLE 17.4   TEST—USER2 TRANSACTION SUCCEEDS

Name	State
Mark	VA
Orryn	NY

With merge replication, all the above outcomes (refer to Tables 17.2 and 17.3) are possible; however, one other outcome is possible, shown in Table 17.5, that could not have been achieved had all the changes been made at a single site (that is, transactional consistency is lost). In the case of Table 17.5, both transactions succeed at disconnected sites. When the data is merged back to the destination database, User 2 has a higher priority than User 1. Therefore, User 2's change to row 2 is applied, and because User 2 did not change row 1, the row 1 change made by User 1 also applies.

TABLE 17.5   TEST—DATABASE AFTER TRANSACTIONS MERGED

Name	State
Mark	TX
Orryn	NY

Planning and Special Design Considerations for Merge Replication

When planning a successful merge replication application, remember to think about the amount of data that will be modified and required to travel over the network or a modem during the merge process and the frequency and ramifications of replication conflicts. Your goal should be to limit the amount of data traveling over the wire and to reduce the number of conflicts. This discussion starts with the recommended topology for merge replication, a spoke-and-hub topology as shown in Figure 17.4.

FIGURE 17.4

Recommended Merge Replication Topology—Spoke and Hub.

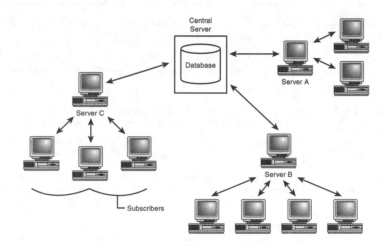

Currently, the SQL Server Enterprise Manager supports the spoke-and-hub topology only when setting up merge replication. You can use other topologies, but use them with caution and good planning. The two examples in Figure 17.4 show a simple spoke-and-hub topology and a more complex example of a spoke-and-hub topology.

Merge replication also places several restrictions on your table design. For starters, all timestamp columns must be removed from tables that are articles in a Merge publication.

NOTE

This situation is a Catch-22 for client/server developers. Typically, timestamp columns are added to improve update performance to SQL Server tables when using tools like Visual Basic and Microsoft Access via RDO, ODBC, DAO, and ADO.

The identity column, which is a sequential number, must be used with caution because identity columns are generated as unique sequential values for each database. It is very likely that users adding the same article in disconnected sites that use identity columns will end up with unique identifier conflicts when the results are merged into the destination database. You are better off modifying the table to use a uniqueidentifier datatype, which avoids such conflicts, instead of an identity column. If you must use identity columns, you may want to assign different starting values for each autonomous site and the central site to avoid the sequential number conflicts and lost transactions.

To ensure data integrity and maintain referential integrity, all lookup and reference tables must be part of the subscriber's database. One way to meet this requirement is to include them as part of the publication.

Text and image columns can be used only if the UPDATE statement is used to modify the text or image column. The WriteText or UPDATEXT statement do not work here.

SETTING UP A MERGE PUBLICATION

When creating a merge publication, you use the Publication and Subscription Wizard described in detail in Chapter 16 and select Merge as the type of publication. As stated in the Snapshot overview, instead of walking you through the wizard again, this chapter examines the screen that differs in transactional-based replication and merge replication. The Article Option dialog box is shown in Figure 17.5.

FIGURE 17.5

The Article Option dialog box—Resolver tab.

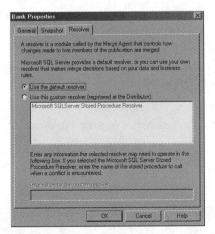

The Article Option dialog box can be displayed when choosing which tables to include in the publication. You place a check beside the table you want to include in the publication and then click the box to the far right of the selected table to bring up the Article Option dialog box. The Resolver tab, shown in Figure 17.5, allows you to assign a custom resolver to resolve conflicts that occur during merge replication. Custom resolvers can be written using Transact-SQL and stored procedures.

MERGE REPLICATION AND RESOLVING CONFLICTS—HANDS-ON EXAMPLE

The following section walks you through creating a merge publication, subscribing to the merge publication, and using the conflict resolution manager. The following prerequisites apply to the exercise:

- Your SQL Server is configured to use a distribution database (local or remote; for details on adding a distribution database see Chapter 15).
- The pubs database is enabled for Merge Replication publication.

In this exercise, you perform the following steps:

1. Create a database called DBA_pubs.
2. Create a Merge publication called test_authors.
3. Push the publication.
4. Make changes to the information in one of the articles.
5. Replicate the changes.
6. Deal with conflicts.

Step 1—Create a Database

In a SQL Query Analyzer Tool window, enter the following script and click the Execute Query button (green arrow) or use the Enterprise Manager to create the database DBA_Pubs:

```
Create Database DBA_Pubs
```

NOTE

The size and location of the database files are not specified so they will default to the same size (data and log) of the model database with autogrow on.

In the Enterprise Manager, select the database folder and right mouse click to refresh the databases on the server.

Step 2—Create a Merge Publication Called test_authors

In this step, you use the Merge Publication Wizard to create a simple merge publication. The wizard greatly simplifies the process, and each step here details which selections to make on the dialog boxes.

1. Select the server to create the publications. From the Tools menu, select Replication and then select Replication Create and Manage Publications; the Create Manage Publications dialog box appears.

2. Select the pubs database and click the Create Publication button. The Create Publication Wizard Introduction dialog box appears. Click the Next button.

3. The Publication Type dialog box appears; Select the Merge publication option (which creates a Merge publication) and click the Next button.

4. The Subscriber Type dialog box appears; select the All Subscribers Will Be SQL Server Subscribers radio button and click the Next button.

5. The Specify Articles dialog box appears. For this exercise, the publication contains a single article. Select the authors table by checking the check box next to the table name; then click the Next button. A dialog box appears stating that a new column with the uniqueidentifier data type needs to be added to the authors table for merge replication, click the OK button.

6. The Publication Name dialog box appears. Enter **test_authors** in the Publication Name text box and click the Next button.

7. The Use Default Publication Properties dialog box appears. For this exercise, take the defaults (the No, Create a Publication Without Data Filters and With the Following Properties radio button is already checked) by clicking the Next button.

8. To create the publication, click the Finish button.

The publication test_authors is created.

Step 3—Push the Publication

In the following step, you use the SQL Enterprise Manager to push the publication to the database DBA_Pubs.

1. In the Enterprise Manager, select Tools, then Replication and then the Push Subscription to Others option; the Create and Manage Publication dialog box appears.

2. Expand the pubs database publication folder and select the test_authors publication.

3. Click the Push New Subscription button. The Push Subscription Wizard dialog box appears, as shown in Figure 17.6. Click the Next button.

FIGURE 17.6

Push Subscription Wizard dialog box.

4. The Choose Subscribers dialog box, shown in Figure 17.7, appears. Select the server to push the subscription; for this exercise, select your server (the one that is also the publisher) and click the Next button.

FIGURE 17.7

The Choose Subscribers dialog box.

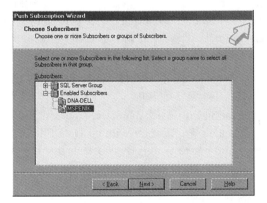

5. The Choose Destination Database dialog box, shown in Figure 17.8, appears. Select the DBA_Pubs database created earlier and click the Next button.

FIGURE 17.8

*The Choose
Destination
Database dialog
box.*

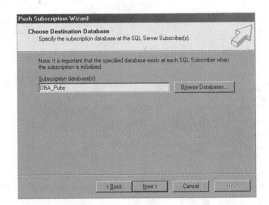

6. The Set Merge Agent Schedule dialog box, shown in Figure 17.9, appears. Click the next button to take the default schedule (the default is to execute daily every hour) and click the Next button.

NOTE

This dialog box allows you to determine whether the Snapshot of the publication should be constantly maintained on the distributor or maintained only as needed. If you select to maintain a Snapshot on the distributor, you can have the synchronization set created immediately or later at a scheduled time. If you choose to maintain a snapshot only as needed, the Snapshot files will be randomly generated. Scheduling the creation of the synchronization set allows you to determine the times of day the set is created (for example, off-peak hours).

FIGURE 17.9

*The Set Merge
Agent Schedule
dialog box.*

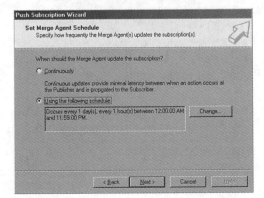

7. The Initialize Subscription dialog box, shown in Figure 17.10, appears. Select the Yes, Start the Initialization Process Immediately so I Can Start Using My Subscription as Soon as Possible radio button. Click the Next button.

FIGURE **17.10**

Initialize Subscription dialog box.

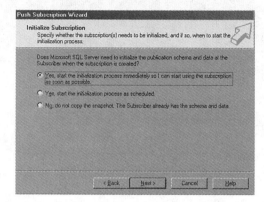

8. The Set Subscription Priority dialog box appears, as shown in Figure 17.11. This dialog box allows you to set the priority of the subscription to be used in conflict resolution. Take the default by clicking the Next button.

FIGURE **17.11**

Set Subscription Priority dialog box.

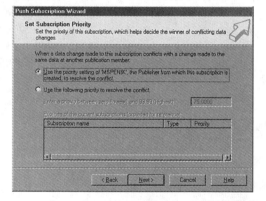

9. The Start Required Service dialog box, shown in Figure 17.12, opens. Check the Agent check box to make sure the agent is executing, and click the Next button.

FIGURE 17.12

Start Required Service dialog box.

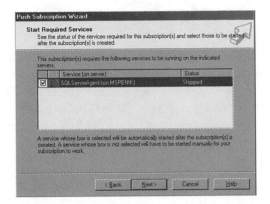

10. The Push Subscription Wizard Finish dialog box is displayed. Click the Finish button to push the publication to the DBA_Pubs database. The Merge Publication Wizard executes the required steps to push the publication to the subscriber.

Before beginning the next step, make sure that the replication Snapshot Agent has created the snapshot and that the push has succeeded. You can check the status of the agents by selecting the test_authors publication, located under your server name in the Publishers folder of the Replication Monitor icon of the SQL Enterprise Manager. By selecting the test_authors publication, the agents and their status will appear in the right-hand dialog box of the Enterprise Manager. If the test_authors Snapshot Agent does not show a status of Succeeded, select the SnapShot Agent by clicking it, right mouse click, and select Start to run the agent. The process of debugging replication tasks is covered in Chapter 15, but as a refresher you can read the history by double-clicking the agent to bring up the Agent History dialog box. For detailed information of the steps performed by the agent, select a history item and click the Session Details button located on the Agent History dialog box. The Session Details dialog box, shown in Figure 17.13, appears.

FIGURE 17.13

Replication Agent Session Details dialog box.

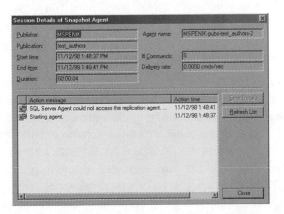

Step 4—Make Changes to the Information in One of the Articles

This step modifies two records in the pubs database and one record in the DBA_Pubs database. One of the modifications is replicated to the DBA_Pubs database without incident to show you that merge replication can copy the changes to the new database. The other change causes a conflict, which replicates and uses the default conflict rule to apply the change. In this section, you examine ways to view the conflicts and change the outcome if you so desire.

1. In the Enterprise Manager, select Tools, SQL Server Query Analyzer; the SQL Server Query Analyzer dialog box appears.

2. Using the database combo selection box (located in the right hand corner), select the DBA_Pubs database.

3. Enter the following SQL statement in the query window:
```
UPDATE authors
Set State = 'VA'
Where au_id = '172-32-1176'

Update authors
Set au_lname = 'AAAAA'
Where au_id = 213-46-8915'
```

4. Click the green arrow to execute the SQL statements. You have now modified two records in the DBA_Pubs database.

5. Using the database combo selection box (located in the right hand corner), select the pubs database.

6. Enter the following SQL statement in the query window:
```
UPDATE authors
Set State = 'PA'
Where au_id = '172-32-1176'
```

7. Click the green arrow to execute the SQL statements. You have now modified one record in the pubs database.

Step 5—Replicate the Changes

In the previous step, you modified two records in the DBA_Pubs database and one record in the pubs database. When the two databases replicate, each database should receive a copy of the changed information from the other database. However, you also produced a conflict by updating the same record and column in both databases (that is, the column state was set to Va. in DBA_Pubs and PA in pubs). Using the default rule for the publication, the publisher's update carries a higher weight than the subscriber's, so PA overrides Va. In the next section, you learn how to view these conflicts and override the conflict resolution rules if desired. To replicate the changes, follows these steps:

1. Click the Replication Monitor.
2. Expand the Agents folder (by clicking the folder).
3. Select the Merge Agents folder (by clicking the folder).
4. The available Merge agents appear in the right-hand frame.
5. Select the test_authors agent.
6. Right mouse click and select Start.

The changes made to the DBA_Pubs database and the pubs database are replicated. You can verify the replication by using the SQL Query Analyzer and executing the following query in both the pubs database and the DBA_Pubs database:

```
Select au_id,state, au_lname from authors
```

Notice that the state for the record 172-32-1176 is PA and that the last name of record 213-46-8915 has been changed to AAAAA. You can also right mouse click the test_authors merge agent and view the history to see that the merge occurred successfully.

Step 6—Deal with Conflicts

Conflicts occur when two sites make modifications to the same information. You can define a conflict to occur whenever the same record has been modified or only if the same column has been modified. When a conflict occurs, the conflict rule is applied. By default, the rule uses a weighted system with each site carrying a certain priority value to help the conflict manager determine which changes win when a conflict occurs. You can also create your own conflict handlers. If you want to view and possibly override conflicts manually, perform the following:

1. Click the Replication Monitor.
2. Expand the Publishers folder (by clicking the folder).
3. Select your computer's publication folder.
4. Select the test_authors publication.
5. Right mouse click and select View Conflicts. The Microsoft Replication Conflict Viewer, shown in Figure 17.14, appears.
6. Select the test_authors publication in the Publication drop-down box and select the authors table in the Tables list box (shown in Figure 17.14).
7. Click the View button; the Conflict Resolution dialog box appears.

FIGURE 17.14

Microsoft Replication Conflict Viewer dialog box.

You can use the Conflict Resolution dialog box to see what changes produced the conflict. Then you can leave the existing change alone, override the conflict with the change from the lower priority site by selecting the Overwrite with Conflicting Data radio button, or apply your own changes by selecting the Keep Revised Data or Overwrite with Revised Data radio button. After you make your selection, click the Resolve button to resolve the conflict. If you are happy with the default, you can select the Keep Existing Data radio button to remove the conflict from the conflict table; alternatively, you can decide to resolve the conflict later by clicking the Postpone button.

TROUBLESHOOTING MERGE AND SNAPSHOT REPLICATION

The best way to troubleshoot Snapshot and Merge replication is to use the Replication monitor discussed in detail in Chapter 16. The replication monitor visually alerts you when replication fails and provides detailed success and error messages.

NOTE

You can set up the agent to alert you via email, pager, or network message when something goes wrong. To add such capabilities to a publication agent, use the Agent's property dialog box. You can bring up an Agent's property dialog box by selecting the agent, right-mouse clicking, and selecting Agent Properties. Figure 17.15 shows the Agent Job Properties dialog box with the Notifications tab selected. Use the Notifications tab to have the agent alert you via email or pager.

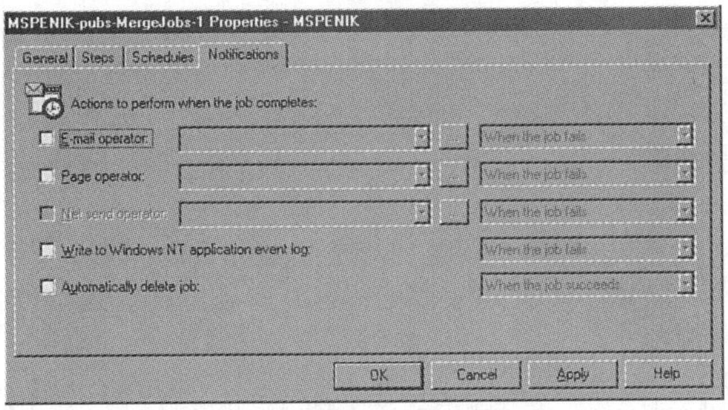

FIGURE 17.15

Agent Job Properties dialog box—Notifications tab.

Typical failure points for snapshot and merge replication are loss of connectivity and security. The Replication Monitor should give you some error messages that can help you detect whether you are having connectivity problems. You can test connectivity and security by executing a remote stored procedure in the subscriber's database.

Snapshot and Merge Agents execute in the security context of the SQL Server Agent. As such, the SQL Security Agent requires the proper permissions on the working directory of the distribution server to be able to create new schema and data files. The SQL Server agent also requires the proper permission to the databases involved in the snapshot replication.

ADDITIONAL PUBLICATION OPTIONS

Now that you have covered the different types of replication, it's time to examine some available options and features of a publication that were not covered in previous chapters. To view publication properties, select a published database and the publication folder within the database. Select a publication, right mouse click, and select Properties; the Properties of Publication dialog box, shown in Figure 17.16, appears.

FIGURE 17.16

The Properties of Publication dialog box—General tab.

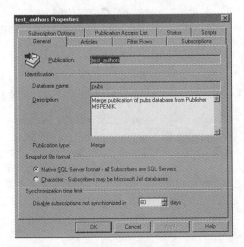

17

SNAPSHOT AND MERGE REPLICATION

The Properties of Publication dialog box is a tabbed dialog box that allows you to view specific information relating to the publication, such as the subscribers to the publication.

> **NOTE**
>
> The Articles, Filter Columns, Filter Rows, Subscription, and Subscription Options tabs are covered in Chapter 16.

The following sections examine some of the tabs on the Properties of Publication dialog box not covered earlier.

General Tab

The General tab, shown in Figure 17.16, displays high-level information about the publication, such as the database the publication belongs to, the type of publication (for example, Snapshot, merge), and an editable description of the publication. The General tab also allows you to view and modify how publication data is exported/imported for replication. You can select native SQL Server format or, for publications with non-SQL Server subscribers, character format.

> **NOTE**
>
> For those of you not sure of the difference between native and character format, character format is a text file format that you can view with NotePad. For example, numeric datatypes are converted to character strings that you can view in any text editor. When SQL Server creates a native format file, the file closely resembles a binary format file that cannot be viewed with NotePad. With native format, numeric datatypes are not converted to string types, but are exported as the actual SQL Server datatype. For example, an integer would be exported as 4 bytes with a binary value that represents the data, as opposed to an n-byte character string that represents the data. Because native format does not require data conversion during exports or imports, it is much faster when replicating between SQL Servers and should always be selected for SQL Server to SQL Server replication.

Status

The Status tab, shown in Figure 17.17, displays the current status of the snapshot agent for the publication. The tab displays the last time the agent executed and the next scheduled time the agent is to execute. You can manually run the agent by clicking the Run Agent Now button, shown in Figure 17.17. To set the agent scheduling properties, click the Agent Properties button. To start the SQL Server Agent if it is not running, click the Start Service button.

FIGURE 17.17

The Properties of Publication dialog box—Status tab.

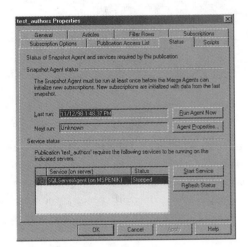

Scripts

For anyone who has used Replication with SQL Server 6.x, the Scripts tab will be a welcome sight. The Scripts tab, shown in Figure 17.18, allows you to generate a script that re-creates the entire publication (including articles, subscribers, filters, and so on). You can also generate a script that allows you to delete the publication as well as append the script to an existing file. Using the script, you could create a single file that drops all of your publications and then re-creates them. The capability to generate scripts to re-create publications is a welcome enhancement. It's hard to tell you how useful this functionality is. You may never have to re-create a publication (many of you will), but you may be required to move the publication from a test environment to a production environment. Prior to SQL Server 7.0, you either had to perform the publication re-creation manually or take the time to create your own scripts using the replication stored procedures. I can recall working with a client and SQL Server 6.5 replication and having to manually drop and re-create a publication with about 90 articles several times while the sites and infrastructure were being stabilized. To make matters worse, each article used custom replication! Ultimately, I ended up creating a script, but now it's part of SQL Server 7.0—kudos to the replication team and thanks!

FIGURE 17.18
*The Properties of
Publication dialog
box—Scripts tab.*

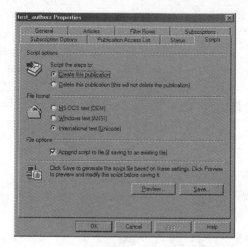

REPLICATING VIA THE WEB (INTERNET)

SQL Server 7.0 replication can be performed over the Internet using push, pull, and anonymous subscriptions for snapshot, merge, and transactional replication. For Web-based replication, you use the same wizards and Transact-SQL statements used to create standard publications and subscriptions. The only difference is the topology and the setup at the subscriber for pull and anonymous subscribers. The basic requirements for all types of subscribers are

- The publisher and distributor need a direct connection (that is, cannot be connected via the Internet).
- If a firewall is in place, the publisher and distributor need to be on the same side of the firewall.
- The TCP/IP protocol is enabled on all servers with distribution and merge agents.

Additional requirements for pull and anonymous subscribers are as follows:

- The distributor and Internet Information Server (IIS) need to be installed on the same server.
- The IIS ftp home directory is set to the distributor's working folder, which defaults to MSSQL7\repldata\ftp.
- Configure the subscriber merge and distribution agents with the proper distributor ftp information, which includes the file, transfer type, ftp address, ftp port, ftp username, and ftp password.

> **NOTE**
>
> You can set the FTP properties for a distribution agent using the Distribution Agent Utility, `distrib`, from the DOS command prompt.

Using the Web to replicate changes really is quite simple. You can also create custom applications, using the Merge ActiveX control, that allow your applications to replicate via the Web by simply setting a few properties (for example, ftp user and password).

REPLICATION FAQS

DBAs frequently ask the following questions when working with Merge and Snapshot replication.

Can I script an entire replication setup for a server?

Yes, you can script an entire replication setup for a server but to do so requires scripting each publication and appending it to a single file.

Can I replicate via a RAS connection?

A common way for merge replication users to synchronize and merge their databases is RAS. To use RAS, make sure you have RAS installed on both machines and that you have the proper security setup between the two servers. The two SQL Servers need to be in the same domain or in a trusted domain. For network selection, use the mulitprotocol or named pipes. Remember, with SQL Server 7.0 you can replicate using the Internet as well.

Can SQL Server use merge replication with an Access 98 database?

SQL Server and Access merge replication are very similar, and Access 98 replication works with SQL Server merge replication. Using Access, as opposed to SQL Server 7.0, makes sense for existing Access applications or applications using older computers that may not have the hard drive space or the processing power to run SQL Server 7.0 on Windows 9.x.

Can I write an application that runs a Merge or Distribution agent via user request or when the application is started?

Microsoft provides two ActiveX controls, a Distribution control and a Merge control with SQL Server 7.0. The ActiveX controls allow you to create applications from many sources—Visual Basic, VB Script, Visual J++, and so on; you can easily create applications that have no dependency on SQL Server agents and can control when replication takes place.

SUMMARY

Following are some of the important things to remember for SQL Server snapshot and merge replication:

- Snapshot replication takes a picture of the data at a certain point in time and replicates the "snapshot" of data to subscribers.

- Snapshot replication is a good solution when performing a table refresh meets the business requirements and the lag time between data modifications and the table refresh is acceptable.

- Snapshot replication is not an appropriate solution when subscribers want to stay current with information from a publication that is being modified constantly or even several times a day.

- Merge replication is the capability to make changes in a database, track the changes, and then merge the changes back into a destination database.

- Merge replication is a good solution for applications that require sites to be disconnected (that is, site autonomy) and require the capability to modify and make changes to the data in the database.

- Merge replication is not an appropriate solution when transactional consistency is required.

- The Snapshot, Merge, and Distribution Agents can be executed outside of SQL Server, using the provided ActiveX controls.

PERFORMANCE AND TUNING

PART VI

IN THIS PART

SQL SERVER INTERNALS— CHANGES AND ENHANCEMENTS

by Mark Spenik

IN THIS CHAPTER

As stated throughout this book, SQL Server 7.0 is a major rewrite of previous versions of SQL Server. This chapter focuses on some of the internal changes to SQL Server that have not been discussed in detail. The changes discussed in this chapter focus on how the differences between SQL Server 6.5 and SQL Server 7.0 affect the performance and scalability of SQL Server 7.0. Why bother learning about what SQL Server does behind the scenes? In addition making you look good at technical interviews, it provides you with insight into improving database performance during database design (such as page layout and effective use of filegroups), as well as determining the proper hardware server configuration. This chapter examines the following areas:

- Thread Scheduling
- Cache Manager
- Disk Storage Changes
- Locking Enhancements
- Read Ahead Improvements

IS SQL SERVER 7.0 FASTER THAN SQL SERVER 6.5?

For many of you, the new ways in which SQL Server 7.0 handles memory and disk space is good trivia. But what you are most concerned with is whether SQL Server 7.0 is really faster than previous versions. By the time you are reading this, you can easily go to Microsoft's Web site and see that 7.0 TPC benchmarks are much faster then 6.5. But faster TPC marks don't always mean noticeable performance gains for every application.

I want to share the results of some of my own testing, with this disclaimer: Your results will vary from what I report depending on your applications and hardware platform. This means that you may or may not see the same results. So what do I think of SQL Server 7.0 versus SQL Server 6.5? In a nutshell, 7.0 is faster than 6.5—*noticeably* faster!

Time after time, SQL Server 7.0 has trounced performance numbers from my 6.5 database applications. I run one query that takes 30 seconds to complete with 6.5. That same query finishes in about 12 seconds in 7.0.

One of the best performance gains I have witnessed is a stored procedure that searches a table with a large amount of data—greater than 1 million rows—and writes about 50,000 rows to a table. The 50,000 rows are then run through several stored-procedure–based business rules that update various fields in the table. In SQL Server 6.5 this process took about 4 minutes to complete; in SQL Server 7.0 the process finishes in about 1.5 minutes. My testing has been performed on SMP machines (two processors) with 512MB of memory and a RAID 5 configuration.

SQL SERVER THREAD SCHEDULING

One of the improvements made in SQL Server 7.0 is how SQL Server threads are managed and scheduled. Before you learn about the changes made to thread scheduling, the following sections cover some basic terms used when talking about threads and thread scheduling.

What Is a Thread?

When working with Windows NT and Windows 9x, the term *thread* comes up quite frequently. So what exactly is a thread? Simply put, a thread is executing code, and each Windows application has at least a single thread of execution. A multithreaded application, such as SQL Server, has the capability to have more than one thread of execution.

The term *executing code* does not mean much in the real world, so let's look at an example of using threads in SQL Server. Suppose you start a long running query—one thread—and then you start another query—a second thread. The second query executes without waiting for the first query to complete. This is an example of multithreading and multitasking.

Operating systems such as Windows NT and Windows 9x are multithreaded and multitasking systems because they provide the system services required to allow multiple threads and tasks to execute. With a single CPU system, two threads cannot truly run simultaneously on the same processor. So Windows NT and Windows 9x allow the second thread to execute while the first thread is executing an action that does not use the CPU—such as a disk read or write.

In a preemptive multitasking operating system, a thread yields the processor to another thread when it is waiting for a system resource or for a non-CPU event (such as a disk operation). The operating system can also preempt the process if an interrupt occurs such as a higher priority thread requesting CPU time. This gives the appearance of simultaneous execution because the threads execute without waiting for the other threads to complete.

Threads can execute with different privileges or modes. A Windows NT thread executes in Kernel mode, which grants the thread access to system hardware and memory. A thread that executes in User mode (such as an application) can gain access to system hardware and services by calling the operating system.

What Is a Context Switch?

Windows NT and Windows 9x are preemptive multithreaded operating systems. The term *preemptive* means that the operating system can stop the current executing thread to

18

allow another thread to execute if the current thread does not yield the processor in a certain amount of time. This time period is called a *time quantum*. Preemptive operating systems do not require the application to yield the CPU. Preempting an executing thread prevents an application from hogging the processor and allows other threads to execute.

The process of halting an executing thread and saving all the context information of a thread so that another thread can execute is called a *context switch*. A context switch can occur by way of an interrupt or a time quantum expiration. When the context switch occurs, the operating system saves information about the executing thread (such as stack pointer and register values). The saved information allows the operating system to restart the thread at its execution point prior to the context switch during the next time quantum.

What Is SMP?

SMP stands for *symmetric multiprocessor* and refers to servers with more than one processor. Windows NT and SQL Server support SMP systems. An SMP system allows Windows NT to execute threads on more than one processor so that threads can truly execute simultaneously. SQL Server can perform special operations on SMP systems. One such special operation is a *parallel query*, which is a complex query broken up into parts and executed across multiple processors.

SQL Server 6.5 Thread Scheduling

To understand how SQL Server 7.0 thread scheduling has improved, take a quick look at how SQL Server 6.5 performed thread scheduling. SQL Server 6.5 did not have a separate thread scheduler. Instead, 6.5 took advantage of Windows NT thread scheduling services by allowing NT to schedule and synchronize the threads across processors. SQL Server 6.5 maintains a pool of worker threads that translate to one thread per user until the max worker thread pool size is met. This approach works well but is not as scalable on SMP systems because excessive context-switches can become expensive (in time), and SQL Server 6.5 has very little control over when its threads are preempted (switched out).

SQL Server 7.0 Thread Scheduling

SQL Server 7.0 thread scheduling no longer relies on Windows NT thread scheduling. Instead 7.0 uses a User Mode Scheduler (UMS) and Windows NT fibers. Fibers are lightweight user-mode threads added in NT 4.0 via a service pack. Fibers run on top of Windows NT threads but cannot be preempted. By default, SQL Server uses NT threads. Fibers can be used by setting the system configuration parameter lightweight pooling to 1 (see Chapter 20, "Configuring and Tuning SQL Server," for more information).

The UMS controls the scheduling of SQL Server threads, as well as when the threads are switched out. SQL Server 7.0 still uses a pool of worker threads. One worker thread is used per CPU, and each user connection is assigned a thread up to the maximum number of worker threads. By allowing the UMS to schedule threads and to use fibers instead of native threads, SQL Server 7.0 reduces the number of context switches, reduces the amount of system resources used, and controls preemption. This translates to better scalability and performance—especially with SMP systems.

SQL SERVER CACHE MANAGER

Another change made to SQL Server 7.0 is the Cache Manager. The term *cache* refers to memory. SQL Server uses the cache to place such things as stored procedures or data pages in memory to improve performance. For example, if you execute a query and all the information required for your query resides in memory, no disk I/O is required and the query execution is extremely fast. If SQL Server is required to read every data page from the disk drive to satisfy your query, the performance is much slower. After all, memory access speeds are thousands times faster than disk drive access speeds.

SQL Server 6.5 Cache Manager

In SQL Server 6.5, the Cache Manager uses a static buffer pool that is created when SQL Server starts. The SQL Server 6.5 memory-configuration parameter determines how much memory SQL Server requires at startup. What is not used by SQL Server 6.5 internals and configuration parameters—is used for the cache. SQL Server 6.5 breaks the cache into two separate areas, a data cache for data pages and a procedure cache for stored procedures and query plans. The SQL Server 6.5 cache manager uses Memory Recently Used and Least Recently Used (MRU/LRU) lists to determine which buffers stay in the cache and which buffers are placed on the free list.

So why redo the Cache Manager in SQL Server 7.0? For starters, server memory is not utilized efficiently. If a server has 256MB of RAM and you allocated 200MB to SQL Server, those 200MB are gone and can't be used by other applications. So even if your SQL Server applications don't require that much memory, the amount of memory in the SQL Server configuration is automatically allocated during startup. Having a separate procedure cache and data cache also wastes memory. Memory not being used by the procedure cache cannot be used by the data cache without a user manually changing configuration parameters. In very large SQL Server memory allocations, DBAs who did not change the procedure cache size (which defaults to 30%) wasted lots and lots of memory that could have been used by the data cache. The MRU/LRU algorithm used by the Cache Manager is complex and produces a lot of buffer contention (that is a hotspot).

SQL Server 7.0 Cache Manager

So how is the SQL Server 7.0 Cache Manager superior to the SQL Server 6.5 Cache Manager? For starters, the SQL Server 7.0 Cache Manager is much smarter when it comes to memory allocation and usage. The 7.0 Cache Manager uses a dynamic buffer pool that can automatically shrink or grow as required by SQL Server and the systems that SQL Server executes. If SQL Server needs more memory, the buffer pool can be expanded. Likewise, if the operating system needs more memory or another application starts up and needs memory, the Cache Manager can dynamically reduce the amount of memory being used by SQL Server. This process makes memory available to NT or other applications. The Cache Manager monitors the system page/faults to determine whether to shrink or increase SQL Server's buffer pool and attempts to keep at least 5MB of physical memory free to prevent paging from occurring.

The SQL Server 6.5 data and procedure cache have been replaced in SQL Server 7.0 with a single cache. The unified cache holds data pages, stored procedures, and query plans. New for SQL Server 7.0 is the addition of storing SQL statements in the cache for reuse. The unified cache ensures that no memory is wasted and requires no manual tuning.

> **NOTE**
>
> SQL Statements stored in the cache are dynamic queries being executed from applications or users. The statements are stored so that if they are re-executed, the query plans and resolutions have already been performed, which results in faster execution times.

The MRU/LRU algorithm is gone and has been replaced with a clock algorithm shown in Figure 18.1.

FIGURE 18.1
SQL Server Cache Manager—clock algorithm.

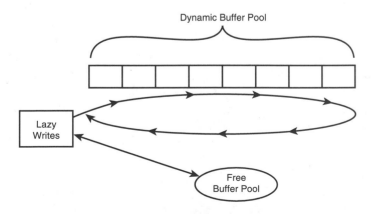

The clock algorithm is much simpler than the MRU/LRU algorithm used in previous versions of SQL Server. With the clock algorithm, the SQL Server lazy writer sweeps through the buffer pool. Buffers that have not been used since the last time around are returned to the free buffer list.

The bottom line is that thanks to the new Cache Manager, SQLServer 7.0 memory use is much more efficient than in previous versions.

DISK I/O AND DATA MANAGEMENT

SQL Server 7.0 has made several improvements to support very large databases. Several of these improvements involved changes to the underlying data storage structures, including data page size and the use of files and filegroups instead of devices. Take a closer look at some of these changes and how the changes help improve large database support.

Page Size

SQL Server 6.5 uses a 2KB data page or a 16KB extent (8 pages in an extent). The maximum width of a single row of data in SQL Server 6.5 is 1962 bytes and the maximum size of a varchar column is 255 bytes. The limitation of 1962 bytes per row and the 255-byte limit to varchars have personally caused me much grief over the years. SQL Server 7.0 introduces a new data page with a size of 8KB or a 64KB extent. Microsoft decided to change the data page size to read in larger amounts of data as well as to take advantage of modern-day disk controllers. The larger data page has increased the maximum row width of a single row of data to 8060 bytes and the maximum size of a varchar column to 8,000 bytes!

Concurrency issues (locking and blocking) due to a larger page size are no longer a problem because SQL Server 7.0 supports row-level locking on all types of data modifications (for example insert, update, and delete). SQL Server 7.0 also improves how Text and Image datatypes are retrieved and stored. In SQL Server 6.5, Text and Image datatypes use a linked list data structure, which is costly in CPU time for data retrieval. SQL Server 7.0 uses a b-tree structure that is simpler and requires less I/O.

> **NOTE**
>
> The increased page size also offers better performance for the SQL Server cache and Cache Manager.

18

SQL SERVER INTERNALS

Filegroups

With SQL Server 6.5, as drive systems become more sophisticated with RAID configurations that use disk striping (like RAID 5), the use of segments by a DBA become less and less important for your average database. The RAID disk striping is used to spread the disk I/O across several physical drives. However, for very large tables or databases, the SQL Server 6.5 segment is used to pull a table or index to a specific logical or physical drive in an attempt to improve performance. Segments have the following shortcomings:

- They are difficult to manage.
- Tables and indexes are mapped to the segment, not to databases.
- DBAs are limited to 32 segments per database.

Another problem with segments is shown in Figure 18.2.

FIGURE 18.2

SQL Server 6.5 segment fill.

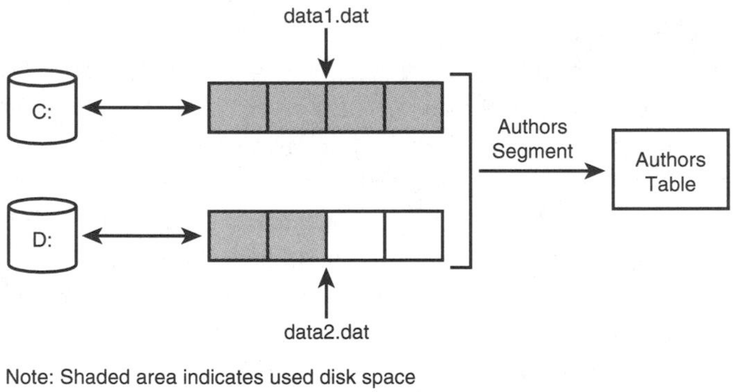

Note: Shaded area indicates used disk space

In Figure 18.2, the authors table is placed on four different segments. Each segment represents a physical hard drive or a different RAID set. With SQL Server 6.5, only one drive or set is used at a time. When the drive or set fills up, the data is stored on the next drive. In this type of environment, you cannot take advantage of the multiple segments (drives or stripe sets) assigned to the object.

SQL Server 7.0 has replaced both devices and segments with the file and filegroup concept (discussed in detail in Chapter 8, "Database Management). Files and filegroups simplify the management of databases and disk management as well as provide you the flexibility to move specific objects to a select drive or drives. Figure 18.3 shows how SQL Server 7.0 filegroups give you the flexibility of segments to place objects as well as to evenly partition the data across the multiple files (drives or RAID sets) in a filegroup. As you can see in Figure 18.3, unlike Figure 18.2, the drives are used evenly throughout the storage of the object and are not filled one at a time.

18

SQL SERVER
INTERNALS

FIGURE 18.3

SQL Server 7.0
filegroup fill.

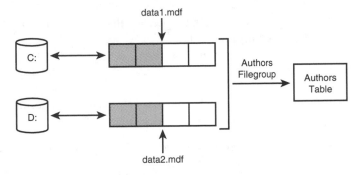

Note: Shaded area indicates used disk space

OTHER ENHANCEMENTS

SQL Server 7.0 has several changes and modifications to 6.5 read aheads and locking management. These changes improve the overall performance and concurrency of 7.0.

Read-Ahead Logic

Read-ahead logic was introduced in SQL Server 6.5. The purpose of read aheads is to read data pages from the hard drive into memory (cache) before an executing query requests the data page. Read aheads tend to benefit queries that are retrieving sequential type or range information. The 6.5 read-ahead logic does the page retrieval job quite well, retrieving 16KB extents into memory prior to a query requesting them. In 6.5, read aheads are triggered using several configuration parameters that track the number of cache hit misses. When the cache hit miss threshold is reached, read-ahead threads are invoked to retrieve the pages. The problem with 6.5 read-ahead logic is that it's difficult to tune, and the read-ahead logic doesn't work with the query processor. SQL Server 7.0 read-ahead logic requires no tuning and works hand in hand with the query processor to retrieve only data pages required by the query processor.

Locking Enhancements

SQL Server 6.5 introduced dynamic locking strategy for data inserts. The dynamic locking strategy allows SQL Server to determine whether to use a page, table, or row-level lock for data modifications. SQL Server 7.0 supports the dynamic locking strategy for all forms of data modifications (inserts, updates, and deletes). The dynamic locking strategy uses the fastest possible locking strategy while providing concurrency. The query processor determines whether to use a page lock, table lock, or row-level lock. When possible, page or table level locks are used, which are faster and more efficient than row-level locks. However, if row-level locking is required, the lock manager uses row-level locks.

The lock manager can even de-escalate page locks to row-level locks. The best thing about the SQL Server dynamic locking strategy is that it does not require any tuning! SQL Server manages and maintains all the locking for you!

SUMMARY

SQL Server 7.0 has many internal changes that help boost its performance and scalability beyond SQL Server 6.5. Some of the key changes are as follows:

- SQL Server 7.0 no longer uses Windows NT thread scheduler. Threads are scheduled using the UMS (user mode scheduler).
- SQL Server 7.0 can use NT threads or lightweight threads called fibers.
- SQL Server 7.0 uses a dynamic memory allocation scheme.
- SQL Server 7.0 uses an 8KB data page and a 64KB extent (8 pages).
- SQL Server 7.0 supports row-level locking for data modification operations.

MONITORING SQL SERVER

by Michael Yocca

IN THIS CHAPTER

SQL Server provides several utilities that enable you to easily monitor SQL Server and its interaction with the operating system. These utilities can help a DBA isolate bottlenecks and determine hardware deficiencies.

SQL SERVER 6.5 TO 7.0 QUICK REFERENCE

The following is a quick reference to the changes that occurred between SQL Server version 6.5 and 7.0:

What's New

- SQL Server Profiler is an enhanced version of SQL Trace (SQL Trace was found in SQL Server 6.5). Enhancements include the ability to replay previously created traces, capture data to SQL Server tables, and trace virtually any type of event that occurs in SQL Server.

- Performance Monitor has twice as many objects and counters. The following new terms are introduced:

  Latch: Locking synchronization object that helps transaction concurrency.

  Buffer Manager: This is the cache that manages algorithms.

  Auto parameterization (auto params): A method for generalizing query plans to increase reuse of similar query plans.

What's Gone

- Performance Monitor has lost several counters, for example the SQL Server Net counters. Being able to match the old counters to the new counters is a serious challenge due to a number of terminology changes. For the most part, the new terminology is easier to navigate.

TOOLS FOR MONITORING SQL SERVER

The following tools are used to monitor SQL Server.

- Performance Monitor
- SQL Server Enterprise Manager
- SQL Server Profiler

Performance Monitor

The *Performance Monitor* is an excellent tool for monitoring SQL Server and the Windows NT operating system. The advantage of the Performance Monitor is that it is tightly integrated with the operating system. This enables you to track real-time statistics about SQL Server and Windows NT. Together, these statistics can be used to isolate bottlenecks and track performance.

> **NOTE**
>
> The Performance Monitor might slightly degrade system performance on older machines. The overhead incurred from the Performance Monitor has been found to be 5 percent or less on single processor machines and insignificant on multiple processor machines.

Using the Performance Monitor

Use one of the following methods to access the Performance Monitor:

- Choose the SQL Performance Monitor icon in the Microsoft SQL Server 7.0 program group. The Performance Monitor dialog box appears (see Figure 19.1).
- Choose the Performance Monitor icon in the Administrative Tools (Common) program group.
- Choose the Performance Monitor icon from the toolbar of the Profiler (see Figure 19.2).

FIGURE 19.1

The Performance Monitor choice in the Microsoft SQL Server 7.0 program group.

19

MONITORING SQL SERVER

FIGURE 19.2

The Performance Monitor icon (next to last) on the Profiler tool-bar.

By default, the Performance Monitor for SQL Server tracks the following six predefined counters:

- Buffer Cache Hit Ratio
- User Connections
- Total Server Memory (KB)
- SQL Compilations/sec
- Page Reads
- Page Writes

The following five counters were predefined in SQL 6.5:

- Cache Hit Ratio
- I/O—Transactions/sec
- I/O—Page Reads/sec
- I/O—Single Page Writes/sec
- User Connections

> **NOTE**
>
> The default counters are useful but do not give a complete picture of SQL Server or Windows NT. Therefore, you will probably want to add more counters to get a clearer understanding of system performance. Further details in this chapter will help you determine which counters to choose.

Adding Counters

Follow these steps to add more counters to the Performance Monitor:

1. From the Performance Monitor dialog box, select Add To Chart from the Edit menu. The plus icon on the toolbar is a handy alternative to this step.

2. Select the object type and counter type. Click the Add button to add the counter to the chart (see Figure 19.3).

3. You might need to choose the appropriate instance of a counter (see Figure 19.4). With SQL 6.5 there were some instances that were primarily database specific. In SQL 7.0, there are three objects that have a total of 22 counters that have 70 instances not including the database-specific instances.

FIGURE 19.3

Performance Monitor dialog box for adding counters to a chart.

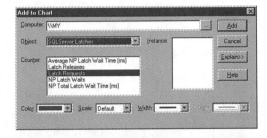

FIGURE 19.4

Performance Monitor dialog box for adding counters to a chart with instances.

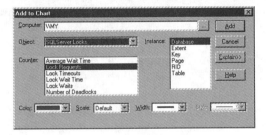

NOTE

Chart settings are valid only for the life of the chart. You must manually save the chart if you want to save your chart settings. From the File menu, select Save or Save As to save the current chart to disk.

TIP

Pressing Ctrl+H or Backspace highlights the selected counter on the chart. This is useful when the Performance Monitor is tracking several counters.

Monitoring Key Areas

The Performance Monitor can be overwhelming because it provides so much information. You can track 156 different counters (including instances) for SQL Server 7.0 and hundreds of counters for Windows NT. Trying to track this much information can drive you crazy!

19

MONITORING SQL SERVER

Instead of trying to track everything at once, you should monitor the following six key areas:

- Disk I/O
- Processor
- Memory
- User connections
- Network

> **TIP**
>
> One of the first things you should do after opening Performance Monitor is to adjust the update frequency because by the time one notices a trend, it is overwritten by the next cycle of data. To slow down the update frequency, choose Chart from the Options menu and change the interval to 10. If you are closely monitoring something, you may prefer 5, and if you are watching something over a period of time, you may prefer 15.

These six key indicators will quickly clue you in to performance bottlenecks. After you determine the general bottleneck source, you should look into the other types of counters not mentioned in this chapter (use the SQL Server Books OnLine).

> **NOTE**
>
> When using the Performance Monitor, it is important to monitor key counters over time and establish patterns before making rash decisions. Be sure that you understand the types of operations being performed by SQL Server before you add a new processor or additional memory. A hardware improvement based on incomplete data might not yield the desired improvement in performance.

Disk I/O

You always want to minimize disk I/O when working with SQL Server. However, when SQL Server does read and write to the hard disk, you want to ensure adequate disk performance. If you are not achieving adequate disk I/O, transaction throughput suffers.

To help detect disk I/O bottlenecks, you should monitor the following two counters:

- PhysicalDisk: % Disk Time
- PhysicalDisk: Current Disk Queue Length (choose the total instance if more than one disk is present)

NOTE

You must run the `diskperf` command before you can monitor disk performance statistics. To enable `diskperf`, go to the command prompt and type the following:

```
diskperf -y,
```

You can also control `diskperf` through Control Panel, Devices. If you try to start the device here, it will warn you that the system can become unstable. If you ignore this warning, it will report that it has started, but performance monitor will still not be able to get feedback until the computer is restarted.

At that point, shut down and restart the computer.

CAUTION

Disk I/O values vary from one type of disk system to another. You should contact your disk manufacturer to determine acceptable counter values.

The PhysicalDisk: % Disk Time Counter

The PhysicalDisk: % Disk Time counter monitors the percentage of elapsed time that the disk is busy with read/write activity.

A consistently high value (above 2) might indicate that your disk system is a bottleneck.

The PhysicalDisk: Current Disk Queue Length Counter

The PhysicalDisk: Current Disk Queue Length counter monitors the number of outstanding requests on disk.

Sustained queue lengths greater than 3 might indicate a disk-related bottleneck. Additionally, a consistently high value for one physical disk combined with a consistently low value for your other physical disks indicates that redistributing your data might improve performance. Examine your device and segment configuration.

19

MONITORING SQL
SERVER

> **TIP**
>
> Pressing Enter while Performance Monitor has focus causes the title to disappear to give the screen more space for displaying the chart.

Processor

SQL Server is CPU intensive. Continuously high utilization rates might indicate that your CPU is the bottleneck. The best way to determine if your CPU is the bottleneck is to use the % Processor Time Counter.

The Processor: % Processor Time Counter

The Processor: % Processor Time counter monitors the amount of time the CPU spends processing a thread.

A steady state value above 80 to 90 percent indicates that a CPU upgrade or additional processors might improve performance.

> **NOTE**
>
> Processor scalability (the capability to gain performance through additional processors) has been greatly improved with SQL Server version 7.0. Previous versions of SQL Server did not scale well beyond four processors. Benchmark tests have shown that in an online transaction processing (OLTP) environment, SQL Server 6.x scales in a relatively linear fashion up to four processors with an out-of-the-box NT Server configuration. SQL 7.0 can scale up to 32 processors running the Enterprise Edition of SQL and NT.

Memory

SQL Server likes memory. It uses memory to hold data and frequently accessed objects. An increase in memory can enable SQL Server to place more data into the memory cache, which can result in better performance.

When diagnosing memory bottlenecks, the following counters are useful to monitor (see "Adding Counters," earlier in this chapter for information on adding counters):

- SQLServer: BufferManager: Cache Hit Ratio
- Memory: Page Faults/sec
- Paging File: % Usage
- SQLServer: BufferManager: Lazy writes

The SQLServer: Cache Hit Ratio Counter

The SQLServer: BufferManager: Cache Hit Ratio counter monitors the hit rate in which data was found in the data cache. If the data is not in the data cache, the server has to read the data from disk. This counter generally provides an accurate indication of memory allocation that can be used to determine whether you have sufficient memory.

In SQL 6.x this counter was cumulative since the server was started. Therefore, it was valuable only right after the server was started. The DBCC Command to reset this counter in SQL 6.5 was `dbcc sqlperf(clear)`, but it did not always work. The equivalent statement in SQL 7.0 is not clear. A number consistently less than 85 percent might indicate that you have insufficient memory. Performance can suffer because SQL Server has to read the data from physical disk. Reading data from the physical disk is an expensive operation. When evaluating this counter, it is important to base it on the type of operation being performed on the machine and the time at which the operation occurs. In a transaction-processing environment, you can probably improve the cache hit ratio by adding more memory. In a batch environment that uses very large databases, the cache hit ratio might neveer go above 85 percent. Under this scenario, additional memory might not substantially improve performance.

If there are many stored procedures on your server, the procedure cache counters might be more relevant to you than the data cache counters.

> **TIP**
>
> The default scale choice that Performance Monitor makes is not always appropriate. It is sometimes necessary to change this because the line is either above 100 or too close to zero to see significant changes. To change this line, simply double-click the Instance or Counter and choose a more appropriate Divisor or Multiplier in the scale drop-down box. If any counter is mostly below the 10 mark, it should be increased. If it is always at or above 100, it should be decreased.

19

MONITORING SQL SERVER

The Memory: Page Faults/sec Counter

The Memory: Page Faults/sec counter monitors the number of times an operating system virtual page was not found in memory. When a page is not found in memory, the operating system must retrieve the page from disk. The time it takes to retrieve a page from disk is always longer than the time required to retrieve the page from memory.

After SQL Server has stabilized, this number should remain at or near zero. If the number is consistently greater than zero, this indicates that too much memory is allocated to SQL Server and not enough memory is allocated to Windows NT. Therefore, you should reduce the amount of memory allocated to SQL Server. SQL 7.0 does a great job of managing this balance automatically. As other applications require memory, NT will successfully request SQL to relinquish memory.

The Paging File: % Usage Counter

The Paging File: % Usage counter monitors the percent of NT's paging file currently in use. If you find that a large percentage of the page file is in use, you might want to increase the size of the paging file to prevent an out-of-virtual-memory error. An alternative to increasing the page file is to add more memory to your server. Doing so will probably reduce page file utilization. With additional memory, you can improve performance because it is always faster to read data from memory than from the paging file.

Another point to consider when analyzing the paging file counter is a growing page file. A growing page file occurs when you specify an initial page file size smaller than the specified maximum size. From the NT operating system perspective, a growing page file is considered an expensive operation. It is better to set your initial page file size the same as your maximum page file size, which eliminates the need for the operating system to grow the page file.

The SQLServer:Buffer Manager: Lazy Writes/sec Counter

The SQLServer: Buffer Manager: Lazy Writes/sec counter monitors the number of flushed pages per second by the Lazy Writer.

A number constantly greater than zero indicates that the Lazy Writer is constantly working to flush buffers to disk. This means that the data cache is too small, which indicates that you have insufficient memory.

User Connections

How many times have you been hit with the following problem? System performance crawls during peak business hours. These are the hours when everyone in the company is banging away on the system. Transactions are being processed at a snail's pace and your phone is ringing off the hook with irate users.

Every DBA, at one time or another, has experienced this problem. It is no secret that as the number of active users increases, the likelihood of performance degradation also increases.

The following counters are helpful to help track why and when user connection bottlenecks occur:

- Processor: %Process Time: CPU Utilization
- SQLServer: General Statistics: Logins/sec
- SQLServer: General Statistics: User Connections
- SQLServer: MemoryManager: Connection Memory (KB)
- SQLServer: MemoryManager: Granted Workspace Memory (KB)

The SQLServer: User Connections Counter

The SQLServer: User connections counter monitors the number of active user connections.

Use this counter to help determine when the number of active users exceeds the capabilities of your system.

TIP

In SQL 7.0, the User Connections setting defaults to zero. The zero setting permits the maximum of 32,767 connections. Unless you have a good reason, it is not necessary to adjust this to have a maximum. However, monitoring the number of user connections has merit because it provides a better understanding of server load. For example, when seeing a spike in CPU utilization, is it accompanied by an increase in user connections? The follow-up question is "why?" Executing DBCC memusage in a query window will give you clues to be able to answer this question.

Network

Another source of a potential bottleneck includes the network card.

NBT Connection: Bytes Total/sec Counter

The NBT Connection: Bytes Total/sec counter monitors the number of bytes read from and written to the network.

This statistic can help you if you are currently not using stored procedures and you find that this counter is high and your transaction rate is low, you might be able to improve performance by implementing stored procedures. Stored procedures can help reduce the amount of network traffic. If this counter is extremely high for an extended time, you might be able to improve performance by using faster network interface cards (NICs).

User-Defined Counters

SQL Server Books On Line has a good example of how to use the user-defined counters for monitoring the size of the database. This method can be used for monitoring any number of custom needs. For example, the number of logins using MS Access can be monitored by returning the count of times this name appears in program name reported by the sp_who2 stored procedure.

How to Manage PMC Files

The file extension assigned to a saved set of Performance Monitor settings is PMC. After you settle on a baseline of counters, here are a few considerations for managing the performance monitor settings.

- Unfortunately, the PMC file cannot be saved and simply applied to another SQL Server from a centralized workstation. This means that for each server you are monitoring, you need to setup your favorite counters manually.

- If the preferred choice of counters or instances to monitor changes, this choice must be manually performed on each of the PMC files for each server monitored. For this reason, it is good to work with a single server and get comfortable with the choice of Performance Monitor counters before setting up too many of them.

- The icon in the SQL Server program group can be modified to point to your PMC file. It is not a good practice to store your PMC files in the SQL Server Binn directory. A better choice would be to create a directory for your PMC files. For simplicity, you may choose to put this right on your desktop. The disadvantage to this is the need to minimize everything to get to the icons.

- Another option is to create a subdirectory where you can get these icons from the Start menu. This can be accomplished by using Explorer and adding a folder to c:\winnt\profiles\All Users\Start Menu\Programs\Microsoft SQL Server 7.0\. The folders can be named something like _Servers. The underscore in front of the folder name causes the folder to be listed at the top of the choices (see Figure 19.5).

- Some prefer to have a data directory for these settings along with procedures or other documentation. In this case, you can create shortcuts into the same directory structure mentioned previously to each server setting.

- Another option is to create a shortcut to the directory on the network with these PMC files so that they can be shared.

FIGURE 19.5

The Start menu showing quick access to multiple server Performance Monitor Settings.

Advanced Use of Performance Monitor

The data can be saved into a log file for later analysis. Follow these steps to use this feature:

1. Choose the View Output Log Status icon on the toolbar (see Figure 19.6).

2. Choose the Plus icon to add the object to log (see Figure 19.7).

3. Choose the last icon to specify the filename for saving the log and choose the Start Log button (see Figure 19.8).

FIGURE 19.6

The toolbar in the Performance Monitor application.

FIGURE 19.7

The choice of counters for Add to Log dialog box.

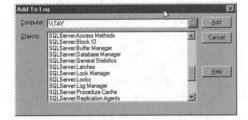

FIGURE 19.8

The Log Options dialog box for saving Performance Monitor data to a file.

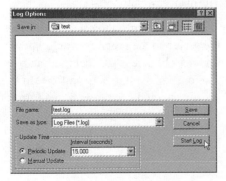

19

MONITORING SQL SERVER

Reading these values back from the log involves the following steps:

1. Choose Data From from the Options menu and choose the log file created previously.

2. Choose the Plus icon from the toolbar. You will notice that the only objects you can choose are the ones that you specified when you began to log.

Imagining Just a Moment

It requires experience and persistence to be able to effectively troubleshoot and locate bottlenecks with Performance Monitor. With over 156 instances of the counters, one quickly and inevitably faces information overload much the same way that end users face this problem with large databases. One of the objectives with decision support and OLAP systems is to enable the user to see the bigger picture and find trends. Performance Monitor does provide the charting as well as slice and dice functionality, but what it is missing is a top 10 feature. Decision support systems are frequently asked who the top 10 customers for such and such a product are.

While imagining, let's draw a parallel with another SQL 7.0 feature: Graphical Showplan. When pointing to an icon that represents one of the steps, the data about that step displays. Wouldn't it be nice if Performance Monitor had scheme such as one icon per major object (for example server, network, and database)? Each of these icons can have a vertical progress bar indicating total load. Perhaps as you double-click each icon, it can open up another more detailed set of icons with performance bars. For example, the network icon would open into basically two icons: one for read, and one for write. Wouldn't this be a great step forward in locating bottlenecks?

On a footnote to this subject, Performance Monitor is an NT application. This means that Microsoft will need to put together a development effort that extends past the boundaries of SQL Server development. With their past success with integration, this sounds like a possible future direction for Performance Monitor.

One obstacle to this vision coming true is the need to establish a baseline for each non-percentage counter specific to the server so the program would know how close to bottleneck the counter has become. Another obstacle is the fact that many counters bounce and the bottleneck can be in more than one area within a given time. In this case, an average is not very meaningful; therefore, there would need to be some form of high watermark feature.

SQL Server Enterprise Manager

In addition to monitoring SQL Server activity, it may be useful to monitor individual user activity. By using the Current Activity Monitor in the Enterprise Manager, you can view user connections, locks, process numbers, and user commands. With SQL Server Profiler you can monitor and record transact SQL activity and other statistics.

The Current Activity Monitor

One of the best features of the Current Activity Monitor is its capability to view more information about a process. This is a major plus for DBAs; it gives you all the information you need to know about a process. You can use this information to help kill a process or to pinpoint a query that is a burden to the system.

> **TIP**
>
> In many cases, you might find it easier simply to use the stored procedures named sp_who and sp_lock. There is also a procedure named sp_who2 that is more user friendly than sp_who. Unfortunately, they got rid of the sp_lock2 from SQL 6.5 that was friendly enough to tell you the name of the object. To know the name of the object in question from the output of sp_lock, you need to execute select object_name([objID]) where objID is the number found in the third column of the output.

Follow these steps to use the Current Activity Monitor:

1. Open the Management branch of Enterprise Manager.
2. Open the Current Activity branch of the Enterprise Manager. Here you can view three types of information: Server Activity, Detail Activity, and Objects Locks. Click the corresponding tab in the Current Activity dialog box to view each type of information (see Figure 19.9).

> **TIP**
>
> Be on the lookout for blocking when users are complaining that their transactions are hung. Select the Locks/Process ID in the Current Activity branch to view blocked processes (see Figure 19.10). Another quick way of finding this information is to look at the blk column of the output from sp_who2.

19

MONITORING SQL SERVER

FIGURE 19.9

The Current Activity branch showing Process, Locks, and Objects.

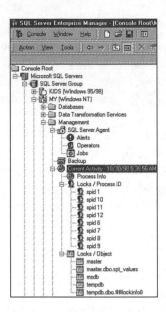

3. From the Current Activity branch, click a process to view more information about the process. The Process Details dialog box appears. From this view, you can see the last statement issued by the user, kill a process, and send a message to the user with a right-mouse click and choose properties.

FIGURE 19.10

The Current Activity branch showing a blocked and blocking process.

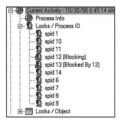

NOTE

The Send Message feature is available only for Microsoft networks.

> **TIP**
>
> The Transact-SQL commands sp_who, sp_lock, KILL, DBCC INPUT-
> BUFFER, and OUTPUTBUFFER can be used to perform functions
> similar to those found in the User Activity Monitor.

SQL Server Profiler

SQL Server Profiler is a utility included with SQL Server version 7.0 that monitors
Transact-SQL commands, object usage, locking, and other events. Using this utility, you
can perform routines such as investigating user activity, pinpointing slow queries, and
generating audit trails.

This utility is also useful for observing SQL statements generated by applications and
end users. In turn, this information can be used to pinpoint poorly constructed queries or
security problems. Another feature of SQL Server Profiler is its capability to save the
trace information to file or a SQL Server table. This feature allows an administrator or
developer to replay the queries from the trace session. Additionally, the Graphical
Showplan or the Index Tuning Wizard can analyze this information. As you can see, this
information can be beneficial when trying to tune queries and stored procedures.

Follow these steps to use SQL Server Profiler:

1. Double-click the SQL Server Profiler icon in the Microsoft SQL Server 7.0
   (Common) program group. This starts the SQL Server Profiler utility.
2. Choose the first icon on the toolbar to get the Trace Properties for a new trace (see
   Figure 19.11).
3. From the Trace Properties dialog box, specify the types of information to trace
   such as General Information, Events, Trace Criteria, Capture Data, View and so on.
   After entering the trace information in the Trace Properties dialog box, click the
   OK button to save the filter. Clicking the OK button also activates the trace you
   just created (see Figure 19.12).

19

**MONITORING SQL
SERVER**

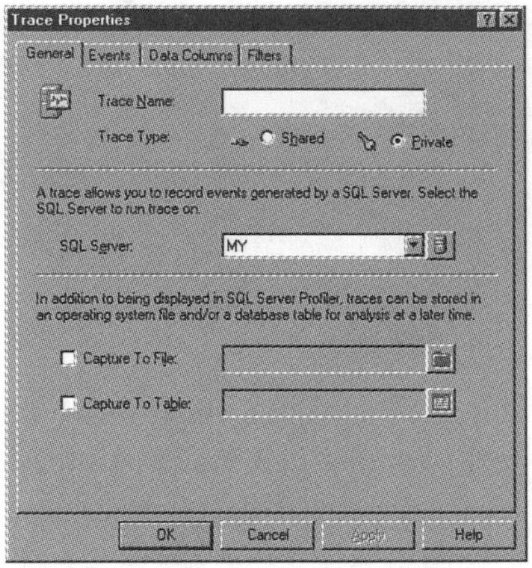

FIGURE 19.11

The Trace Properties dialog box.

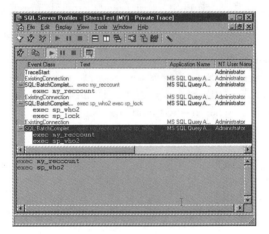

FIGURE 19.12

An active trace example.

4. When the trace is active, it displays the information that matches your trace criteria. As you can see, the ability to trace SQL statements provides a wealth of information that can be used to analyze SQL activity.

TIP

The best method I've found for tracing activity is to create a trace that tightly defines the type of information you are looking for. This eliminates a lot of extraneous information that may not be of interest to you.

To include or exclude items, separate them with a semicolon (;). For example, to exclude SQL Server Profiler and MS SQL Query Analyzer use `SQL Server Profiler%;MS SQL Query Analyzer` (see Figure 19.13).

I also recommend using the wildcard character % when tracing a variety of products or when you do not know the full name of the criteria. For example, to trace only Microsoft Access and Microsoft Query, you could set the Application Name to Microsoft% (see Figure 19.14). This works because Microsoft Access's application name is Microsoft® Access and Microsoft Query's application name is Microsoft® Query.

FIGURE 19.13

Dialog box displaying example of how to enter include syntax.

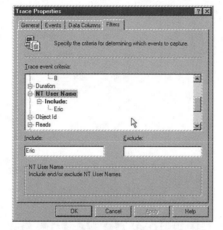

FIGURE 19.14

Dialog box displaying example of how to enter exclude syntax.

19

MONITORING SQL SERVER

MONITORING SQL SERVER FAQ

Following are some of the common questions asked by DBAs about monitoring SQL Server:

SQL Server Profiler shows only the object id and not the object name. How can I determine the object's name?

To determine an object's name use the object_name() function. For example, if SQL Server Profiler is displaying an object id = 114099447 and a database = pubs you can use the following query to determine that the object is the authors table.

Query:

```
use pubs
go
select object_name(114099447)
go
```

Output:

```
authors
```

Does SQL Server Profiler slow down the server?

The answer to this question depends on the complexity of the trace and the number of traces running concurrently. When running several complex traces, you might notice a slowdown. Therefore, you might want to limit the amount of information being traced or run individual traces instead of running multiple traces simultaneously.

How can I monitor the performance of a specific stored procedure without the information overload of a trace?

There is a session level setting that can be used that will limit the feedback to scan counts and server execution times. The server execution times are new to SQL 7.0. In SQL 6.5, the scan counts were the only things returned. The syntax appears as follows:

```
set statistics io on
```

How do I know if the bottlenecks I'm seeing in Performance Monitor are reasonable?

Experience will help here. It is important to monitor the server during normal performance to know what the range of expected values are so that when performance begins to become abnormal, you know which counters are responsible for the change.

Can I automatically start a trace whenever SQL Server is started?

The tool is not built to function in this way. It is built for user interaction and not a command line.

SUMMARY

Following is a summary of notes for monitoring SQL Server:

- The Performance Monitor is an excellent tool for monitoring SQL Server and the Windows NT operating system.

- Don't let the Performance Monitor drive you crazy! Instead of trying to track a multitude of counters, track five to eight key performance indicators. Anything over eight or ten different counters makes it difficult to determine what is happening.

- Following are some useful counters to track:

    - SQLServer: BufferManager: Cache Hit Ratio

    - Processor: % Processor Time

    - PhysicalDisk: % Disk Time

    - SQLServer: General Statistics: User Connections

    - NBT Connections: Bytes Total/sec

    - SQLServer-Locks: Total Blocking Locks

- You must run `diskperf` before you can monitor disk performance statistics.

- Use the Current Activity Monitor to track user connections, locks, and process numbers. The Current Activity Monitor can also be used view the SQL commands issued from each user.

- Use the SQL Server Profiler utility to trace SQL activity. This tool can monitor SQL activity and save trace information. It also can be used with the Graphical Showplan or Index Tuning Wizard.

19

MONITORING SQL SERVER

CONFIGURING AND TUNING SQL SERVER

by Mark Spenik

IN THIS CHAPTER

You now have SQL Server installed and running. Maybe you are about to roll out your first production database and your boss is breathing down your neck asking, "Mister (or Madam) DBA, have you tuned and optimized the server?" You tell your boss, no, but tuning and optimizing SQL Server was next on your list. You bring up the SQL Enterprise Manager. You begin to stare at the Enterprise Manager configuration screen and ask yourself, "So, which knobs do I turn?" How about very few (maybe none), which in many organizations will be the case! Remember the goal of SQL Server 7.0 is to be a self-tuning database that requires very little tuning or tweaking to get the best performance from the database engine. SQL Server 7.0 removes the server tuning requirements required by the DBA and puts the tuning back into the application developer's hands. The tuning required is minimal!

This chapter covers how to modify SQL Server's configuration parameters. Each configuration parameter is examined for functionality and its effect on SQL Server performance and tuning. With SQL Server 7.0, many of the key performance-oriented configuration parameters used in previous versions of SQL Server, like memory and read-aheads, are now dynamic and self-tuning, requiring no DBA intervention. Microsoft has excelled in SQL Server 7.0 at producing a RDBMS that is much simpler to configure and maintain.

SQL SERVER TUNING OR APPLICATION TUNING?

As you start to tune SQL Server, keep in mind that other factors, such as the hardware configuration chosen for the database, the network the database clients and SQL Server belong to, and the overall size and structure of your databases also affect the performance of the database server.

I have a friend who used to work for a Fortune 500 company that was bringing several SQL Servers online. He had spent some time tuning SQL Server and everything was up and running quite smoothly. As the days went on, the organization started to experience problems with a particular application running progressively slower. Upper management thought the problem must be a SQL Server configuration problem. My friend tried to explain to them that the problem was not a SQL Server tuning issue but an application issue. He explained how they had done everything right: researched and purchased a very fast RAID 5 machine, tuned Windows NT Server, and then used SQL Server tools to properly configure SQL Server.

Management didn't buy it, so they brought in another consulting firm with a highly certified and expensive specialist. The specialist examined the SQL Server and did not change any configurations parameters because they were all reasonably set. So the hired guns left without fixing anything and upper management was left scratching their heads. I stopped by to see if I could help them out, and as it turned out, their problem was a failure to issue a simple command that needed to be executed on three of their tables. (UPDATE STATISTICS, what else?)

The moral of the story is that many things affect the overall performance of SQL Server. Performance issues start from square one when you research and purchase the machine and set up Windows NT Server. Too often, the real problems are not understood, so people think tuning SQL Server is the answer. SQL Server 7.0 has all but eliminated the need for tuning and configuring the database server. The auto-tuning features of SQL Server 7.0 enable the server to use the available resources on the machine optimally but do not prevent problems resulting from poor database and application design or a poor hardware platform selection. It is important to understand the value and limitations of tuning SQL Server. Oh yeah, SQL Server 7.0 now automatically executes the UPDATE STATISTICS command!

SQL SERVER 6.5 TO 7.0 QUICK REFERENCE

What's New

The following configuration parameters are new to SQL Server 7.0:

- Cost threshold for parallelism
- Unicode locale id
- Index create memory
- Lightweight pooling
- Max server memory
- Max degree of parallelism
- Min server memory
- Query governor cost limit
- Resource timeout
- Scan for startup procs
- Unicode comparison style
- Query wait

What's Replaced

Min memory per query replaces the 6.x Sort Pages configuration parameter.

What's Gone

The following configuration options have been removed from SQL Server 7.0:

- Backup buffer size
- Backup threads
- Free buffers
- Hash buckets
- LE threshold maximum
- LE threshold minimum
- LE threshold percent
- Logwrite sleep
- Max lazywrite IO
- Open database
- Procedure cache
- RA cache hit limit
- RA cache miss limit
- RA delay
- RA pre-fetches
- RA worker threads
- RA slots per thread
- RA worker threads
- Recovery flags
- Remote conn timeout
- SMP concurrency

The option to place tempdb in RAM is no longer available.

CONFIGURING SQL SERVER

Before understanding the many different configuration parameters, you must learn how to modify SQL Server parameters using the Enterprise Manager. Start up the Enterprise Manager and perform the following steps:

1. From the Enterprise Manager, select an SQL Server by clicking it. Right-click and from the pop-out menu, select Properties; the Server Properties dialog appears (see Figure 20.1).

FIGURE 20.1

The Server Properties dialog box.

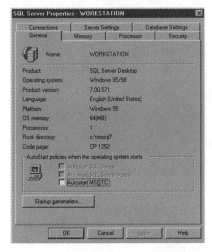

The General tab of the Server Properties dialog box displays information about the machine, the operating system, and the SQL Server version. You can also set SQL Server startup parameters as well as the Auto-start option for SQL Server, MSDTC and the SQL agent.

2. Click the Memory tab in Server Properties dialog box (see Figure 20.2).

   The Memory tab enables you to set the SQL Server memory configuration parameter. The default memory configuration is to dynamically configure memory. However, you can fix the amount of memory used by SQL Server by selecting the Use Fixed memory Setting radio button and using the slider control to adjust the memory setting. The configuration parameter Min memory per query can be set by changing the value displayed in the Minimum Query Memory text box.

3. Click the Processor tab in Server Properties dialog box (see Figure 20.3).

   The Processor tab enables you to configure several options relating to SMP systems such as which processors can execute SQL Server. The Processor tab can be used to configure the following SQL Server configuration parameters: max worker threads, priority boost, and cost threshold for parallelism (note: the SMP options are not available on a Windows 9x machine).

20

CONFIGURING
AND TUNING
SQL SERVER

FIGURE 20.2

The Memory tab in the Server Properties dialog box.

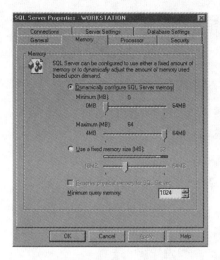

FIGURE 20.3

The Processor tab in the Server Properties dialog box.

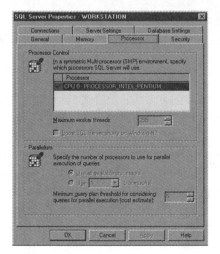

4. Click the Connections tab in Server Properties dialog box (see Figure 20.4).

   The Connections tab enables you to configure options relating to user connections such as the number of concurrent connections. The Connections tab can be used to configure the following SQL Server configuration parameters: `remote access`, `remote query timeout`, `remote proc trans`, `user connections`, and `user options`.

FIGURE 20.4

The Connections tab in the Server Properties dialog box.

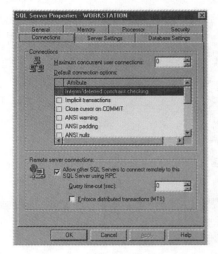

5. Click the Server Settings tab in Server Properties dialog box (see Figure 20.5).

   The Settings tab enables you to configure the following SQL Server configuration parameters: `allow updates`, `default language`, `query governor cost limit`, and `nested triggers`.

FIGURE 20.5

The Server Settings tab in the Server Properties dialog box.

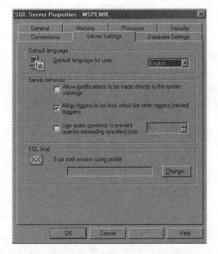

6. Click the Database Settings tab in Server Properties dialog box (see Figure 20.6).

   The Database Settings tab enables you to configure the following SQL Server configuration parameters: `fill factor` and `recovery interval`.

CONFIGURING AND TUNING SQL SERVER

FIGURE 20.6

*The Database
Settings tab in the
Server Properties
dialog box.*

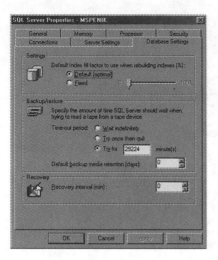

You can also change system configuration parameters using the system stored procedure
sp_configure, which has the following syntax:

sp_configure [*configuration_name* [, *configuration_value*]]

In this syntax, *configuration_name* is the configuration parameter name you want to
change and *configuration_value* is the new value for the configuration parameter.

> **NOTE**
>
> Using sp_configure with no parameters displays the current SQL Server config-
> uration.

SQL Server configuration values are stored in the system table sysconfigures. If you
use sp_configure to modify an option, you must use the RECONFIGURE command to
make the change take effect. RECONFIGURE has the following syntax:

RECONFIGURE [WITH OVERRIDE]

The WITH OVERIDE parameter is required only when you set the allow updates configuration parameter to 1. This provides an added security check to make sure that you really
want to modify allow updates. The output of sp_configure is shown in Listing 20.1.

LISTING 20.1   `sp_configure` OUTPUT WITH SHOW ADVANCED OPTIONS

Name	minimum	maximum	config_value	run_value
affinity mask	0	2147483647	0	0
allow updates	0	1	0	0
cost threshold for parallelism	0	32767	5	5
cursor threshold	-1	2147483647	-1	-1
default language	0	9999	0	0
default sortorder id	0	255	52	52
extended memory size (MB)	0	2147483647	0	0
fill factor (%)	0	100	0	0
index create memory (KB)	704	1600000	0	0
language in cache	3	100	3	3
lightweight pooling	0	1	0	0
locks	5000	2147483647	0	0
max async IO	1	255	32	32
max degree of parallelism	0	32	0	0
query wait (s)	0	2147483647	600	600
max server memory (MB)	4	2147483647	2147483647	2147483647
max text repl size (B)	0	2147483647	65536	65536
max worker threads	10	1024	255	255
media retention	0	365	0	0
min memory per query (KB)	512	2147483647	1024	1024
min server memory (MB)	0	2147483647	0	0
nested triggers	0	1	1	1
network packet size (B)	512	65535	4096	4096
open objects	0	2147483647	0	0
priority boost	0	1	0	0
query governor cost limit	0	2147483647	0	0
recovery interval (min)	0	32767	0	0
remote access	0	1	1	1
remote login timeout (s)	0	2147483647	30	30
remote proc trans	0	1	0	0
remote query timeout (s)	0	2147483647	0	0
resource timeout (s)	5	2147483647	10	10
scan for startup procs	0	1	1	1
set working set size	0	1	0	0
show advanced options	0	1	1	1
spin counter	1	2147483647	10000	0
time slice (ms)	50	1000	100	100
Unicode comparison style	0	2147483647	196609	196609
Unicode locale id	0	2147483647	1033	1033
user connections	0	32767	0	0
user options	0	4095	0	0

20

CONFIGURING
AND TUNING
SQL SERVER

> **NOTE**
>
> What is the difference between the Running column and the Current column? Most of the time, the two values are the same. As you start to change and modify SQL Server configurations, however, the Current column reflects the changes you have made. These changes do not become the running value until you execute the `Reconfigure` command. For some configuration variables, you have to shut down and restart the server before the parameter changes take effect.

Certain configuration parameters can take effect without restarting SQL Server. These configuration parameters are referred to as *dynamic configuration variables* and are as follows:

- `allow updates`
- `cursor threshold`
- `cost threshold for parallelism`
- `default language`
- `index create memory`
- `max degree of parallelism`
- `max server memory`
- `max text repl size`
- `min server memory`
- `nested triggers`
- `max worker threads`
- `network packet size`
- `query governor cost limit`
- `query wait`
- `recovery interval`
- `remote login timeout`
- `remote proc trans`
- `remote query timeout`
- `resource timeout`
- `show advanced options`

- spin counter
- min memory per query
- user_option

MAJOR TUNING CONFIGURATION CHANGES FROM SQL SERVER 6.5 TO 7.0

One goal of the Microsoft SQL Server team was to create a product that for the majority of installations would be self tuning and require very limited changes to SQL Server configuration parameters to obtain optimum performance. In the previous version of SQL Server 6.5, two key DBA tuning areas to obtain the optimum performance were in memory configuration and the read ahead parameter settings. In SQL Server 7.0, both features are dynamic and no longer require DBA intervention. Both of these features are discussed in more detail in the next section. One other key area that has changed is locking; it is discussed in more detail in Chapter 24 "Multi-User Considerations." SQL Server 7.0 now uses a hands-off dynamic locking scheme that does not require extensive configuration so previous configuration parameters dealing with locking escalation are gone.

Memory

In general, SQL Server loves memory; that is, adding more memory can enhance the performance of your SQL Server system by keeping data pages loaded in memory. SQL Server 7.0 has an auto-tuning memory feature, which allows SQL Server to dynamically increase or decrease memory utilization based on the overall system memory requirements. SQL Server 7.0 is also much smarter about how memory is used and is able to use more memory for queries than in previous versions. So how does SQL Server use memory?

First, a certain amount of memory is allocated for SQL Server overhead, which includes the size of the SQL Server executable. The amount of SQL Server static overhead is not affected in any way by configuration parameters.

SQL Server then allocates memory for various configuration options, such as user connections and open databases. For example, each user connection configured in SQL Server requires 24KB of memory up front. Other sub-systems like the Log Manager request memory for its log cache. The remaining memory is then used for a single buffer cache, which is new to SQL Server 7.0. Previous versions of SQL Server divided the remaining area into the data cache and the procedure cache. SQL Server still uses a procedure cache and data cache; however they share the same memory buffer pool. The procedure cache stores the most recently used stored procedures and query trees, and the

20

data cache stores the most recently used data and index pages. As you increase the amount of SQL Server memory, the sizes of the buffer cache increase, boosting performance because SQL Server can retrieve more information from memory without performing disk I/O to retrieve the information. SQL Server 7.0 attempts to keep 5MB or more of free memory in the system. The good thing is that with SQL Server 7.0, the auto-tuning memory feature uses as much memory as required by SQL Server. If another application, such as Microsoft Exchange, is started up and the amount of page/faults increases or the free memory falls below 5MB, SQL Server automatically decreases the amount of memory on the NT system it uses, thus freeing up memory for the new application. If SQL Server begins a query that requires additional memory and the free memory in the system exceeds 5MB, SQL Server adds the additional memory to the buffer cache. SQL Server requires some event or task to occur to have it add memory to the buffer cache; when the server is idle, it will not add memory to the buffer cache.

NOTE

The tempdb in Ram option is no longer available with SQL Server 7.0.

It is highly recommended that you use the dynamic memory allocation feature provide by SQL Server 7.0 to ensure that the memory on your system is being used effectively. However, if you want to set the amount of memory required by SQL Server, thus preallocating the full amount of memory regardless of the server load, you can set the SQL Server 7.0 memory configuration parameters `min server memory` and `max server memory`.

TIP

Is it possible to have too much memory? The answer is *yes*! If you are not using the dynamic memory allocation feature of SQL Server 7.0 and allocate too much memory to SQL Server and not enough to Windows NT, the performance of your SQL Server can decrease because of excessive paging. To determine whether you have allocated too much memory to SQL Server and not enough to Windows NT, use the Performance Monitor and watch the `Page Faults/sec` counter. If page faults are being continuously generated (after system and SQL Server startup,) you are running SQL Server with too much memory. Reduce the configuration amount and check again. Be careful about allocating more memory to SQL Server and Windows NT than is physically available (that is, relying on Virtual Memory). Configuring SQL Server so that it uses virtual memory exceeding a ratio of 1:1 can hurt SQL Server performance and shows up as excessive paging in the Performance Monitor.

Monitoring Memory

This section offers some tips to help you monitor memory use for your SQL Server. The primary tools are the SQL Performance Monitor and the DBCC MEMUSAGE command. To determine whether you have enough memory or too much memory, use the Performance Monitor and watch the counters listed in Table 20.1. Of course if you are using the dynamic memory allocation feature, you can still use these techniques to determine if the server you are using has enough memory to work with SQL Server and any other services.

TABLE 20.1 PERFORMANCE MONITOR COUNTER FOR TUNING SQL SERVER MEMORY

Performance Monitor Object	*Counter*
Memory	Page Faults/sec
SQLServer:Buffer Manager	Cache Hit Ratio

The first step—and one of the most important steps when trying to tune SQL Server for memory—is to make sure that you are running your typical processes and work loads on SQL Server while you are using the Performance Monitor. The idea behind tuning SQL Server for memory is to keep a high cache-hit ratio (that is, data being retrieved is in the cache), low physical I/O (disk I/O is low because data pages are in memory), and no page faults (a page fault occurs when not enough memory has been allocated to Windows NT, causing Windows NT to rely heavily on virtual memory). If your cache-hit ratio is below 85 to 90 percent, your SQL Server may benefit from increased memory. If you are continuously experiencing page faults, you have allocated too much memory to SQL Server and not enough to Windows NT. The problem can be corrected by reducing the amount of memory allocated to SQL Server or by adding more physical memory to be used by Windows NT. Before tuning for memory, configure your procedure cache and data cache first and then use the Performance Monitor to determine the correct amount of memory.

To determine what is currently loaded in the buffer cache, use the DBCC MEMUSAGE command to get the exact sizes stored procedures cached objects. The listing in Listing 20.2 is actual output from a DBCC MEMUSAGE command. The DBCC MEMUSAGE command prints out the top 20 objects in the buffer cache.

20

CONFIGURING
AND TUNING
SQL SERVER

LISTING 20.2   DBCC MEMUSAGE OUTPUT

```
Buffer Cache, Top 20:


dbid    objectid      indexid buffers
------  ------------  ------- -----------
1       1             2       5
1       6             0       5
1       1             0       4
2       485576768     0       4
4       2             0       4
1       2             255     3
1       3             2       3
2       99            0       3
5       3             0       3
5       3             2       3
1       2             0       2
1       6             1       2
2       -572164999    0       2
2       3             2       2
2       6             0       2
5       2             0       2
5       2             255     2
5       6             0       2
6       2             0       2
8       2             0       2
```

Asynchronous Read Ahead

SQL Server 6.x shipped with a feature called *Parallel Data Scan*, also referred to as
Asynchronous Read Ahead. The read-ahead technology (RA for short) decreases the time
required to perform logical sequential data reads, which translates to improved performance for table scans, index creation, DBCC commands, UPDATE STATISTICS, and covered queries. The idea behind the parallel data scan is simple. Using separate threads,
SQL Server reads extents (8 data pages or 64KB) into memory before the thread running
the query needs the extent. When the extent is needed to satisfy the query, the data pages
are already in the memory cache, thanks to the read-ahead. The Read Ahead features of
SQL Server 6.5 could be finely tuned with several configuration parameters and a good
DBA. In SQL Server 7.0, Asynchronous Read Ahead (RA) has been greatly improved.
For example, Read Ahead no longer needs to be configured and has been tightly integrated with the query processor. The query processor tells the RA exactly what it needs. RA
now understands logical page I/O versus physical I/O and now works on heaps as well as
clustered indexes.

CONFIGURATION PARAMETERS

The following sections examine each of the SQL Server configuration parameters. The configuration parameters are in alphabetical order, except in special cases when the parameters have already been discussed such as the memory configuration parameters. Additionally, the advanced options are reviewed separately from the standard options.

> **NOTE**
>
> For each SQL Server 7.0 configuration parameter, the Minimum, Maximum, and Default values are listed in table format as well as the dynamic variable status.

New VB `allow updates`

If the value of `allow updates` is set to 1, the SQL Server system tables can be modified. But *do not set this configuration value to 1* unless told to do so by Microsoft Technical Support.

> **CAUTION**
>
> Directly updating system tables is risky business and could prevent your SQL Server from running.

If you need to update system tables, use the system stored procedures, after all that is what they are for. If you need to turn on this option, start SQL Server in single-user mode (command-line option –m) to prevent any other users from accidentally modifying the system tables.

> **Minimum:** 0
> **Maximum:** 1
> **Default:** 0
> **Dynamic Variable:** Yes

> **NOTE**
>
> Stored procedures created to modify system tables while the `allow updates` option is on can always modify the system tables, even after the `allow updates` option is turned off.

default language

The `default language` option determines the number of the language used to display system messages.

> **Minimum:** 0
> **Maximum:** 9999
> **Default:** Varies (US_English = 0)
> **Dynamic Variable:** Yes

language in cache

The `language in cache` option determines the number of languages that can be held simultaneously in the language cache.

> **Minimum:** 3
> **Maximum:** 100
> **Default:** 3
> **Dynamic Variable:** No

max text repl size

This option specifies the maximum amount of data that can be written to a replicated text or image column.

> **Minimum:** 0
> **Maximum:** 2147483647
> **Default:** 65536
> **Dynamic Variable:** Yes

nested triggers

When the `nested triggers` option is set to 1, a trigger can call another trigger (that is, triggers can be nested). When this option is set to 0, calling a trigger from another trigger is prohibited.

> **Minimum:** 0
> **Maximum:** 1
> **Default:** 1
> **Dynamic Variable:** Yes

NOTE

You can have up to 16 levels of nesting.

remote access

The `remote access` option controls the logins from remote SQL Servers. When set to 1, users from remote SQL Servers have access to the server.

> **Minimum:** 0
>
> **Maximum:** 1
>
> **Default:** 1
>
> **Dynamic Variable:** No

remote login timeout

The `remote login timeout` option specifies the number of seconds to wait before returning from a remote login attempt. The default of `0` specifies an infinite time-out value. This parameter effects connection's made to linked servers using distributed queries.

> **Minimum:** 0
>
> **Maximum:** 2147483647
>
> **Default:** 5
>
> **Dynamic Variable:** Yes

remote query timeout

The `remote query timeout` option specifies the number of seconds to wait before timing out as a result of a remote query (be it a remote stored procedure or distributed query). The default of `0` specifies an infinite time-out value.

> **Minimum:** 0
>
> **Maximum:** 2147483647
>
> **Default:** 0
>
> **Dynamic Variable:** Yes

20

CONFIGURING
AND TUNING
SQL SERVER

remote proc trans

When set to 1, the `remote proc trans` option provides a DTC distributed transaction that protects the ACID properties of transactions.

> **Minimum:** 0
>
> **Maximum:** 1
>
> **Default:** 0
>
> **Dynamic Variable:** Yes

show advanced options

The `show advanced options` option displays the advanced configuration options when using the SQL Server Enterprise Manager or the `sp_configure` system stored procedure. Set this value to 1 to display the advanced options.

> **Minimum:** 0
>
> **Maximum:** 1
>
> **Default:** 1
>
> **Dynamic Variable:** Yes

user_option

The `user_option` option enables you to set global default options for all users. Using this parameter, you can control implicit transactions, ANSI warnings, ANSI NULLs, ANSI defaults, the distinction between a single quote and a double quote, and several other options. The options set take effect during the user's login session; the user can override them by using the SET statement.

> **Minimum:** 0
>
> **Maximum:** 4095
>
> **Default:** 0
>
> **Dynamic Variable:** Yes

ADVANCED CONFIGURATION PARAMETERS

> **CAUTION**
>
> The following configuration parameters are considered to be advanced configuration parameters and can be seen only by turning on the show advanced options configuration option. I highly suggest leaving them alone. Microsoft has done a good job setting the default values, and you can easily hinder the performance of your SQL Server by incorrectly setting one of the advanced configuration options. If you do modify them, make sure that you fully understand the option and the overall impact of your changes!

affinity mask

The affinity mask option enables you to associate a thread to a processor and specify which processors SQL Server can use.

> **Minimum:** 0
>
> **Maximum:** 2147483647
>
> **Default:** 0
>
> **Dynamic Variable:** No

cost threshold for parallelism

The cost threshold for parallelism option is used only on systems with multiple processors. The option enables you to set the threshold for which a parallel plan is created and executed by SQL Server. The cost is the estimated amount of time in seconds required to complete the plan in a serial fashion. If the query exceeds the parameter setting a parallel plan will be used. In general, longer queries benefit from the execution of a parallel plan and shorter queries benefit from a serial plan, so don't set the parameter too low.

> **Minimum:** 0
>
> **Maximum:** 32767
>
> **Default:** 5
>
> **Dynamic Variable:** yes

cursor threshold

The cursor threshold option determines how the keyset for a cursor is generated. If the option is set to –1, all cursor keysets are generated synchronously (good for small cursor sets). If the option is set to 0, all cursor keysets are generated asynchronously.

Otherwise, the query optimizer compares the number of expected rows in the cursor set; if the number of expected rows exceeds the `cursor threshold` configuration variable, the keyset is built asynchronously.

> **Minimum:** −1
> **Maximum:** 2147483647
> **Default:** −1
> **Dynamic Variable:** Yes

default sortorder id

The `default sortorder id` option shows the current sort order ID installed on SQL Server. Do *not* use `sp_configure` or the SQL Enterprise Manager Configuration dialog box to change the sort order! Changing the sort order is done through the SQL Setup program and is a major change to your SQL Server.

> **Minimum:** 0
> **Maximum:** 255
> **Default:** 52
> **Dynamic Variable:** No

fill factor

The `fill factor` option specifies how densely packed you want your index and data pages while creating an index. The default is `0`, which leaves room on the nonleaf pages but makes the leaf pages 100 percent full. Use a low `fill factor` value to spread data over more pages. For more information on using `fill factor`, see Chapter 22, "Understanding Indexes."

> **Minimum:** 0
> **Maximum:** 100
> **Default:** 0
> **Dynamic Variable:** No

> **NOTE**
>
> The `fill factor` option is not maintained by SQL Server after index creation and is only maintained when the index is built.

index create memory

The index create memory controls the amount of memory (in kilobytes) used by creating an index to sort the data during the index creation.

> **Minimum:** 704
>
> **Maximum:** 1,600,000
>
> **Default:** 1216
>
> **Dynamic Variable:** Yes

lightweight pooling

The lightweight pooling configuration parameter is primarily for SMP environments. By setting the option to 1, SQL Server thread scheduling switches to fiber mode scheduling, which can reduce excessive context switches that sometimes occur in an SMP environment. (See Chapter 18, "SQL Server Internals—Changes and Enhancements," for more information.)

> **Minimum:** 0
>
> **Maximum:** 1
>
> **Default:** 0
>
> **Dynamic Variable:** Yes

locks

The locks configuration variable sets the number of available locks. By default, SQL Server uses dynamic lock allocation (a setting of zero). Initially 2 percent of the memory allocated to SQL Server is used for locks using the dynamic setting. Each lock consumes about 96 bytes of memory. The dynamic locking allocation is the recommended configuration. However, you can override dynamic lock allocation by presetting the number of locks. If you preset the number of locks and run out of locks, increase the value.

> **Minimum:** 5000
>
> **Maximum:** 214748364
>
> **Default:** 0
>
> **Dynamic Variable:** No

max async IO

The max async IO option is the number of outstanding asynchronous I/Os that can be issued. Modify this option only if you have databases that span multiple physical drives or are using disk striping and your database server has separate disk controllers or a smart disk controller (such as a Compaq smart array) that supports asynchronous I/O. If you meet these requirements, you may be able to increase your system throughput by modifying the `max async IO` parameter. The procedure for modifying this parameter is to use Microsoft's TPC-B Benchmark kit (or your own benchmarks) and execute the benchmark recording the time. Slowly increase the setting using your benchmark after each change to verify that performance has increased. If performance does not increase you have found the proper value. Be careful when increasing this parameter. A value that is too high can cause performance degradation by causing excessive overhead.

> **Minimum:** 1
>
> **Maximum:** 255
>
> **Default:** 32
>
> **Dynamic Variable:** No

max degree of parallelism

The `max degree of parallelism` option is only valid for systems with multiple processors. This parameter enables you to determine the number of threads used to execute a parallel plan, the default of `0` uses the number of CPUs.

> **Minimum:** 0
>
> **Maximum:** 32
>
> **Default:** 0
>
> **Dynamic Variable:** Yes

max server memory

Use the `max server memory` configuration parameter to prevent SQL Server from using more than a certain amount of memory. You can also use this parameter with the `min server memory` parameter to disable dynamic memory allocation and force SQL Server to use a specified amount of memory. To use a fixed amount of memory set the `max server memory` parameter to the same value as the `min server memory` parameter.

> **Minimum:** 0
>
> **Maximum:** 2147483647
>
> **Default:** 2147483647
>
> **Dynamic Variable:** Yes

max worker threads

Worker threads are used by SQL Server for things such as checkpoints, users, and network support. The `max worker threads` configuration parameter sets the maximum number of worker threads SQL Server can use. If the configured value is greater than the number of concurrent user connections, each user connection has its own thread; otherwise, the user shares a pool of worker threads.

> **Minimum:** 10
> **Maximum:** 1024
> **Default:** 255
> **Dynamic Variable:** Yes

media retention

The `media retention` option sets the number of days you want to retain backup media before overwriting it with a new backup. If you attempt to overwrite the media before the number of retention days has expired, you get a warning message.

> **Minimum:** 0
> **Maximum:** 365
> **Default:** 0
> **Dynamic Variable:** No

min memory per query

This parameter enables you to specify the minimum amount of memory used to execute a query. Increasing this value can boost the performance of queries that have sorting or hashing operations.

> **Minimum:** 0
> **Maximum:** 2147483647
> **Default:** 1024
> **Dynamic Variable:** Yes

min server memory

Use the `min server memory` configuration parameter to force SQL Server to use at least a certain amount of memory. You can also use this parameter with the `max server memory` parameter to disable dynamic memory allocation and force SQL Server to use a specified amount of memory. To use a fixed amount of memory, set the `max server memory` parameter to the same value as the `min server memory` parameter.

> **Minimum:** 0
> **Maximum:** 2147483647
> **Default:** 0
> **Dynamic Variable:** Yes

20

CONFIGURING
AND TUNING
SQL SERVER

network packet size

If you have a network that supports a large packet size, you can increase the network performance with SQL Server by increasing the packet size. The default of 4096 bytes is a welcome change to the anemic 512-byte packet size used in versions prior to version 6.5. For most applications, the default packet size of 4096 is sufficient, so be careful when changing this parameter and verify that you actually do get the performance gain expected.

> **Minimum:** 512
>
> **Maximum:** 32767
>
> **Default:** 4096
>
> **Dynamic Variable:** Yes

open objects

The open objects option specifies the maximum number of database objects that can be open at one time on SQL Server. Database objects are stored procedures, views, tables, rules, defaults, and triggers. In SQL Server 7.0, open objects is dynamically configured. However, if you receive a warning stating that the number of open objects is too low, you can manually set the value to solve the problem. Each open object consumes about 276 bytes of memory.

> **Minimum:** 100
>
> **Maximum:** 2147483647
>
> **Default:** 0
>
> **Dynamic Variable:** No

priority boost

If the priority boost configuration value is set to 1, SQL Server runs at a higher priority on the Windows NT server.

> **Minimum:** 0
>
> **Maximum:** 1
>
> **Default:** 0
>
> **Dynamic Variable:** No

> **CAUTION**
>
> Even if you have a dedicated machine for SQL Server, do not boost the priority of SQL Server. It runs fine as a regular Windows NT Service; boosting the priority can cause some unexpected problems when you try to bring down SQL Server or when you try to use other NT tools on the server. This parameter should only be set for SMP machines dedicated to SQL Server.

query governor cost limit

The query governor cost limit enables you to specify the maximum amount of time a query can run in seconds on the current server. The default value of 0 turns the governor off.

> **Minimum:** 0
> **Maximum:** 2147483647
> **Default:** 0
> **Dynamic Variable:** No

query wait

The query wait option sets the amount of time in seconds SQL Server will wait before timing out a long running query (that is, if the query does not complete in this amount of time, SQL Server will halt the query due to a time-out). A value of -1 the time-out value is computed at 25 times the estimated cost of the query.

> **Minimum:** 0
> **Maximum:** 2147483647
> **Default:** 600 Seconds (that is, 10 minutes)
> **Dynamic Variable:** Yes

recovery interval

SQL Server uses the recovery interval option, the database truncate log on checkpoint setting, and the amount of database activity to determine when a checkpoint should be performed to write the "dirty pages" (modified pages not yet flushed to disk). The recovery interval specified is not the amount of time between SQL Server checkpoints; it is the maximum amount of time per database that SQL Server needs to recover the database in the event of a system failure. SQL Server 7.0 automatically configures this parameter and attempts to require less than a minute for an automatic recovery per database and a checkpoint process every minute.

Minimum: 0

Maximum: 32767

Default: 0

Dynamic Variable: Yes

resource timeout

The `resource timeout` option specifies the number of seconds to wait for a resource to be released.

Minimum: 5

Maximum: 2147483647

Default: 10

Dynamic Variable: Yes

scan for startup procs

The `scan for startup procs` parameter determines whether or not SQL Server scans for stored procedures to execute when starting up the server. The default value of `0` is not to scan and execute startup stored procedures.

Minimum: 0

Maximum: 1

Default: 0

Dynamic Variable: No

set working set size

If the value of the `set working set size` option is set to 1 when SQL Server starts, Windows NT locks all the memory in the memory configuration parameters `min server memory` and `max server memory`. By locking the memory Windows NT does not swap SQL Server pages out of memory even if the server is idle and another process needs the memory. Setting this option can potentially provide an increase in performance but must be used with caution because it could also have the reverse effect. You can disable the creation of the memory working set by setting the option to 0. When this option is disabled, SQL Server asks the Cache Manager for memory as needed up to the value in the memory configuration parameters if they are set. If you are using dynamic memory, do not turn on this option.

Minimum: 0

Maximum: 1

Default: 0

Dynamic Variable: No

spin counter

The spin counter option specifies the maximum number attempts a process makes to obtain a resource.

Minimum: 1

Maximum: 2147483647

Default: 10000

Dynamic Variable: Yes

time slice

The time slice option specifies the amount of time a user process can pass a yield point without yielding.

Minimum: 50

Maximum: 1000

Default: 100

Dynamic Variable: No

Unicode comparison style

The Unicode comparison style option is used to determine the sorting options for Unicode characters within the locale (example: case-insensitive).

Minimum: 0

Maximum: 2147483647

Default: Varies

Dynamic Variable: No

Unicode locale id

The Unicode locale id option enables you to specify the locale used for Unicode characters.

Minimum: 0
Maximum: 2147483647
Default: 1033
Dynamic Variable: No

user connections

The user connections option specifies the maximum number of simultaneous user connections allowed on SQL Server. In SQL Server 7.0, user connections are automatically and dynamically configured. If you have 50 users logged into the system, you have 50 user connections; if someone else logs in you automatically get another connection up to the maximum number of connections allowed (Select @@max_connections). If the maximum number is exceeded, you get an error and are unable to establish the new connection until one becomes available. Be careful about setting this parameter too high because each user connection takes up approximately 40KB of memory overhead, regardless of whether the connection is used.

Minimum: 5
Maximum: 32767
Default: 0
Dynamic Variable: No

extended memory size (Alpha Machines Only Enterprise Edition)

extended memory size enables you to create a separate disk cache in memory outside of the standard buffer pool. This configuration parameter should only be used for systems with large amounts of memory. For example, for a machine with 6GB of memory, you could create a separate disk cache of 3GB to 4GB.

Minimum: 0
Maximum: 2147483647
Default: 0
Dynamic Variable: No

CONFIGURATION FAQ

The following are some frequently asked questions for configuring SQL Server:

Q. I'm running a batch operation that consists of lots of queries and transactions. I'm trying to improve the performance and I'm thinking about changing several configuration parameters. Is this a good starting point?

A. As stated earlier, SQL Server 7.0 comes out of the box tuned and ready to go. (Although SMP machines may want to modify some parameters after installing.) The best place to start tuning is to look at the application and examine the query plans being used. If you are confident that the application is in good order, use the performance monitor while the batch executes to determine if you have a bottleneck in the processor, memory, or disk I/O; then modify SQL Server configuration parameters or add additional hardware.

Q. I was messing around and set several SQL Server configuration parameters. Now I'm unable to start SQL Server. What do I do?

A. You have probably over-allocated a resource (for example memory) that prevents SQL Server from starting. To restart SQL Server with a minimum configuration add –f to the SQLServr.EXE start up command line. Then use `sp_configure` or the Enterprise Manager to reset your default configuration.

SUMMARY

The answer to the question, "Which knobs do I turn?" is "Not many!" The nice thing about SQL Server 7.0 is that it provides optimal SQL Server performance for most database installations right out of the box. The majority of possible tuning parameters deal with machines that have multiple processors and the ability to run a parallel query. SQL Server 7.0 limits the amount of tuning required by the DBA. Keep in mind that for the best possible performance, tuning is a many-phase process. It includes the hardware, the installation of the operating system, the installation and tuning of SQL Server, and the overall design of the databases and applications.

This chapter examined all the SQL Server configuration parameters. Following are some of the more important points to remember about tuning and configuring SQL Server:

- Let SQL Server manage the memory configuration for you by using the dynamic memory allocation feature of SQL Server 7.0.
- When you tune SQL Server using the Performance Monitor, make sure that the SQL Server is running against the expected real-world workload.
- Understand the impact of changing configuration parameters before modifying them.

20

DATABASE DESIGN ISSUES

by Orryn Sledge

IN THIS CHAPTER

A properly designed database can increase data integrity and simplify data maintenance. To help you better understand how to design a database, the following concepts are discussed in this chapter:

- Problems that can arise from an improperly designed database
- How to correctly design a database
- How to take a properly designed database a step backward in order to improve performance

PROBLEMS THAT CAN ARISE FROM AN IMPROPERLY DESIGNED DATABASE

The following problems can occur because of an improperly designed database:

- Redundant data
- Limited data tracking
- Inconsistent data
- Update anomalies
- Delete anomalies
- Insert anomalies

Redundant Data

As you can see in the sample table in Figure 21.1, several names and descriptions are continuously repeated. This increases the amount of physical storage required to track training data.

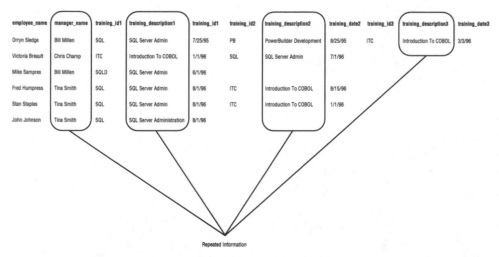

employee_name	manager_name	training_id1	training_description1	training_id1	training_id2	training_description2	training_date2	training_id3	training_description3	training_date3
Orryn Sledge	Bill Millen	SQL	SQL Server Admin	7/25/95	PB	PowerBuilder Development	8/25/95	ITC	Introduction To COBOL	3/3/96
Victoria Breault	Chris Champ	ITC	Introduction To COBOL	1/1/96	SQL	SQL Server Admin	7/1/96			
Mike Sampres	Bill Millen	SQLD	SQL Server Admin	6/1/96						
Fred Humpress	Tina Smith	SQL	SQL Server Admin	8/1/96	ITC	Introduction To COBOL	8/15/96			
Stan Staples	Tina Smith	SQL	SQL Server Admin	8/1/96	ITC	Introduction To COBOL	1/1/96			
John Johnson	Tina Smith	SQL	SQL Server Administration	8/1/96						

Repeated Information

FIGURE 21.1 *Redundant data.*

Limited Data Tracking

The table design in Figure 21.2 is limited to tracking three training courses per employee. Additional columns must be added to the table if you want to track more than three classes.

				This table allows a maximum of 3 training courses to be tracked.						
employee_name	manager_name	training_id1	training_description1	training_data 1	training_id2	training_description2	training_date2	training_id3	training_description3	training_date3
Orryn Sledge	Bill Millen	SQL	SQL Server Admin	7/25/95	PB	PowerBuilder Development	8/25/95	ITC	Introduction To COBOL	3/3/96
Victoria Breault	Chris Champ	ITC	Introduction To COBOL	1/1/96	SQL	SQL Server Admin	7/1/96			
Mike Sampres	Bill Millen	SQLD	SQL Server Admin	6/1/96						
Fred Humpress	Tina Smith	SQL	SQL Server Admin	8/1/96	ITC	Introduction To COBOL	8/15/96			
Stan Staples	Tina Smith	SQL	SQL Server Admin	8/1/96	ITC	Introduction To COBOL	1/1/96			
John Johnson	Tina Smith	SQL	SQL Server Administration	8/1/96						

FIGURE 21.2   *Limited data tracking.*

Inconsistent Data

Consider the likelihood of a training class being misspelled when a new record is added to the employee_training table (see Figure 21.3). As more records are added to the table, the potential for inconsistent data from typing errors increases.

employee_name	manager_name	training_id1	training_description1	training_date1	training_id2	training_description2	training_date2	training_id3	training_description3	training_date3
Orryn Sledge	Bill Millen	SQL	SQL Server Admin	7/25/95	PB	PowerBuilder Development	8/25/95	ITC	Introduction To COBOL	3/3/96
Victoria Breault	Chris Champ	ITC	Introduction To COBOL	1/1/96	SQL	SQL Server Admin	7/1/96			
Mike Sampres	Bill Millen	SQLD	SQL Server Admin	6/1/96						
Fred Humpress	Tina Smith	SQL	SQL Server Admin	8/1/96	ITC	Introduction To COBOL	8/15/96			
Stan Staples	Tina Smith	SQL	SQL Server Admin	8/1/96	ITC	Introduction To COBOL	1/1/96			
John Johnson	Tina Smith	SQL	SQL Server Administration	8/1/96						

Are these two different training classes or is this a data entry error?

FIGURE 21.3   *Inconsistent data.*

Update Anomalies

Suppose that you just realized that the *SQL Server Admin* class should be named *SQL Server Administration* (see Figure 21.4). To change the class name, you must update it in five different places. Wouldn't it be easier if you could change the name in one place and have it automatically reflected throughout the application?

employee_name	manager_name	training_id1	training_description1	training_date1	training_id2	training_description2	training_date2	training_id3	training_description3	training_date3
Orryn Sledge	Bill Millen	SQL ①	SQL Server Admin incorrect	7/25/95	PB	PowerBuilder Development	8/25/95	ITC	Introduction To COBOL	3/3/96
Victoria Breault	Chris Champ	ITC	Introduction To COBOL	1/1/96	SQL ⑤	SQL Server Admin incorrect	7/1/96			
Mike Sampres	Bill Millen	SQLD ②	SQL Server Admin incorrect	6/1/96						
Fred Humpress	Tina Smith	SQL ③	SQL Server Admin incorrect	8/1/96	ITC	Introduction To COBOL	8/15/96			
Stan Staples	Tina Smith	SQL ④	SQL Server Admin incorrect	8/1/96	ITC	Introduction To COBOL	1/1/96			
John Johnson	Tina Smith	SQL	SQL Server Administration correct	8/1/96						

You just realized that "SQL Server Admin" should be "SQL Server Administration."
To change the class name you will need to update it in 5 different places.

FIGURE 21.4   *Update anomalies.*

Delete Anomalies

Suppose that you are no longer interested in tracking the *Introduction to COBOL* training class, so you delete matching records (see Figure 21.5). But wait…you just realized that you deleted other important information. The removal of more than one type of information from a table is considered a *delete anomaly*.

employee_name	manager_name	training_id1	training_description1	training_date1	training_id2	training_description2	training_date2	training_id3	training_description3	training_date3
Orryn Sledge	Bill Millen	SQL	SQL Server Admin	7/25/95	PB	PowerBuilder Development	8/25/95	ITC	Introduction To COBOL	3/3/96
~~Victoria Breault~~	~~Chris Champ~~	~~ITC~~	~~Introduction To COBOL~~	~~1/1/96~~	~~SQL~~	~~SQL Server Admin~~	~~7/1/96~~			
Mike Sampres	Bill Millen	SQLD	SQL Server Admin	6/1/96						
~~Fred Humpress~~	~~Tina Smith~~	~~SQL~~	~~SQL Server Admin~~	~~8/1/96~~	~~ITC~~	~~Introduction To COBOL~~	~~8/15/96~~			
~~Stan Staples~~	~~Tina Smith~~	~~SQL~~	~~SQL Server Admin~~	~~8/1/96~~	~~ITC~~	~~Introduction To COBOL~~	~~1/1/96~~			
John Johnson	Tina Smith	SQL	SQL Server Administration	8/1/96						

You are no longer interested in tracking the "Introduction To COBOL" training class so you delete
matching records. But wait . . . you just realized that you deleted other important information.

FIGURE 21.5   *Delete anomalies.*

Insert Anomalies

Suppose that you want to track a new training course titled *Database Design* and you designate the code DD for training_id1. What values will you use for employee_name and manager_name when you insert the record into the sample table (see Figure 21.6)? Do you leave the values blank? Do you insert a special code such as unknown for employee_name and manager_name?

employee_name	manager_name	training_id1	training_description1	training_date1	training_id2	training_description2	training_date2	training_id3	training_description3	training_date3
Orryn Sledge	Bill Millen	SQL	SQL Server Admin	7/25/95	PB	PowerBuilder Development	8/25/95	ITC	Introduction To COBOL	3/3/96
Victoria Breault	Chris Champ	ITC	Introduction To COBOL	1/1/96	SQL	SQL Server Admin	7/1/96			
Mike Sampres	Bill Millen	SQLD	SQL Server Admin	6/1/96						
Fred Humpress	Tina Smith	SQL	SQL Server Admin	8/1/96	ITC	Introduction To COBOL	8/15/96			
Stan Staples	Tina Smith	SQL	SQL Server Admin	8/1/96	ITC	Introduction To COBOL	1/1/96			
John Johnson	Tina Smith	SQL	SQL Server Administration	8/1/96						
??	??	DD	Database Design							

You want to track a new training course called "Database Design." Where do you insert the record?

FIGURE 21.6 *Insert anomalies.*

NORMALIZATION

Normalization is a set of standard rules that test the soundness of database design. It can help prevent the problems described in the first part of this chapter. By applying these standard rules, you can pinpoint design flaws that may jeopardize data integrity and complicate data maintenance.

How to Normalize a Database

There are three standard normalization rules. After a design successfully passes a rule, it is said to be in # normal form (where the # represents *1st*, *2nd*, or *3rd*). Rules are cumulative. For example, for a design to be in 3rd normal form, it must satisfy the requirements of the 3rd normal form as well as the requirements for 2nd and 1st normal forms.

Technically speaking, there are other types of normalization rules beyond 3rd normal form. However, for most database designs, the first three normal forms are sufficient. You will seldom need to apply the other types of normalization. Therefore, this section concentrates only on the 1st, 2nd, and 3rd normal forms of database design.

- **1st normal form**: No repeating groups.
- **2nd normal form**: No nonkey attributes depend on a portion of the primary key.
- **3rd normal form**: No attributes depend on other nonkey attributes.

Now that you know the rules regarding normalization, apply them to a sample application.

For this application example, suppose that you are tracking training classes taken by each employee. Figure 21.7 contains a denormalized listing of the data tracked by this application. Each employee may have taken *0* or *N* (zero or many) classes.

FIGURE 21.7

A denormalized database design.

employee_id	char(5)
employee_name	char(35)
employee_address	char(35)
employee_city	char(35)
employee_state	char(2)
employee_zip	char(11)
manager_id	char(5)
manager_name	char(35)
training_id1	char(5)
training_description1	char(25)
training_date1	datetime
training_id2	char(5)
training_description2	char(25)
training_date2	datetime
training_id3	char(5)
training_description3	char(25)
training_date3	datetime

1st Normal Form

Look at the `training_id`, `training_description`, and `training_date` attributes in Figure 21.8. See how they are repeated? This violates the concept of 1st normal form: no repeating groups.

FIGURE 21.8

Repeating groups.

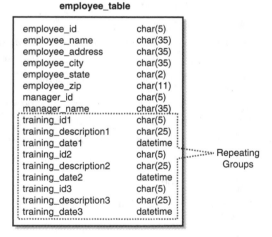

employee_table

employee_id	char(5)
employee_name	char(35)
employee_address	char(35)
employee_city	char(35)
employee_state	char(2)
employee_zip	char(11)
manager_id	char(5)
manager_name	char(35)
training_id1	char(5)
training_description1	char(25)
training_date1	datetime
training_id2	char(5)
training_description2	char(25)
training_date2	datetime
training_id3	char(5)
training_description3	char(25)
training_date3	datetime

Repeating Groups

Move the training information into a separate table called `employee_training` and create a relationship between the `employee` table and the `employee_training` table. Now the table design meets the requirements of 1st normal form (see Figure 21.9).

FIGURE 21.9

*Tables that meet
1st normal form
requirements.*

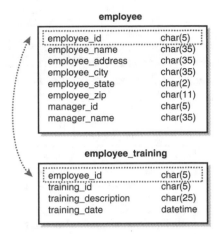

employee

employee_id	char(5)
employee_name	char(35)
employee_address	char(35)
employee_city	char(35)
employee_state	char(2)
employee_zip	char(11)
manager_id	char(5)
manager_name	char(35)

employee_training

employee_id	char(5)
training_id	char(5)
training_description	char(25)
training_date	datetime

2nd Normal Form

In Figure 21.10, notice how the `training_description` attribute depends only on the
`training_id` attribute and not on the `employee_id` attribute in the `employee_training`
table. This violates 2nd normal form: no nonkey attributes depend on a portion of the
primary key. (The primary key for this table is `employee_id` + `training_id`.) This rule
is applied only to entities that have compound primary keys (a primary key consisting of
more than one attribute).

FIGURE 21.10

*A nonkey attribute
depends on a por-
tion of the primary
key.*

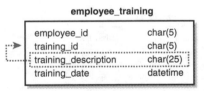

employee_training

employee_id	char(5)
training_id	char(5)
training_description	char(25)
training_date	datetime

training_description is dependent upon
training_id *not* employee_id

Move the `training_description` attribute into a separate table called `training`. Relate
the `training` table to the `employee_training` table through the `training_id` attribute.
Now the design satisfies 2nd normal form (see Figure 21.11).

FIGURE 21.11

*Tables that meet
2nd normal form
requirements.*

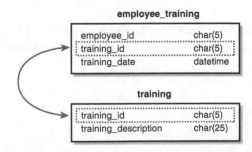

employee_training

employee_id	char(5)
training_id	char(5)
training_date	datetime

training

training_id	char(5)
training_description	char(25)

3rd Normal Form

Look at the manager_name attribute for the employee table in Figure 21.12. The primary key for the employee table is the employee_id attribute. Does the manager_name attribute depend on the employee_id attribute? No! This violates 3rd normal form: No attributes can depend on other nonkey attributes.

FIGURE 21.12

An attribute depends on a non-key attribute.

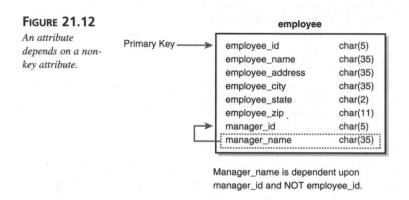

Manager_name is dependent upon
manager_id and NOT employee_id.

Move the manager_name attribute into a separate table called manager. The manager table can be related to the employee table through the manager_id attribute. By making this change, the design meets the requirements of 3rd normal form (see Figure 21.13).

FIGURE 21.13

Tables that meet 3rd normal form.

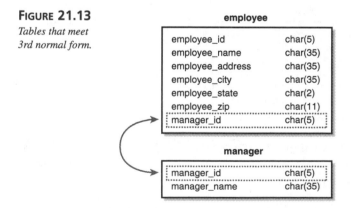

Now you have completed the normalization process (see Figure 21.14). This process helped isolate design flaws that would have led to an awkward and inefficient database design.

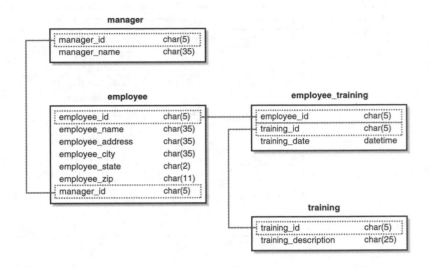

FIGURE 21.14
*A normalized
database design.*

DENORMALIZATION

Denormalization means that you are purposely designing your database so that it is *not* in 3rd normal form. This is done to maximize performance or to simplify end-user reporting. Whenever you denormalize a database, you must be willing to forego the benefits gained from the 3rd normal form.

> **NOTE**
>
> I recommend that you start your initial database design in 3rd normal form. If you find that performance problems exist, selectively step back to 2nd or 1st normal form. Keep in mind that when you denormalize a database, you do so for a specific set of application requirements. Future requirements may not need or benefit from past denormalization decisions. Only denormalize when you have to.

Performance

A database design in 3rd normal form may require more table joins to process a query than a design in 2nd or 1st normal form. These additional table joins can be expensive in terms of CPU and disk I/O.

Suppose that you need a report that lists the training classes taken by each employee (see Figure 21.15).

FIGURE 21.15

A sample report.

employee name	manager name	training description	training date
Orryn Sledge	Bill Millen	SQL Server Admin	7/25/95
		PowerBuilder Development	8/25/95
		Introduction To COBOL	3/3/96
Victoria Breault	Chris Champ	Introduction To COBOL	1/1/96
		SQL Server Admin	7/1/96
Mike Sampres	Bill Millen	SQL Server Admin	6/1/96
Fred Humpress	Tina Smith	SQL Server Admin	8/1/96
		Introduction To COBOL	8/15/96
Stan Staples	Tina Smith	SQL Server Admin	8/1/96
		Introduction To COBOL	1/1/96
John Johnson	Tina Smith	SQL Server Admin	8/1/96

NOTE

The examples used in this section are overly simplistic; however, they *do* explain how multitable joins can complicate data processing.

To retrieve the data from your fully normalized database, you create the following query, which is a sample query for a fully normalized database:

```
SELECT a.employee_name, d.manager_name,
c.training_description,b.training_date
FROM employee a, employee_training b, training c, manager d
WHERE a.emp_id = b.emp_id
 AND b.training_id = c. training_id
 AND a.manager_id = d.manager_id
```

As you can see, this simple report requires four tables to be joined. Assume that each table contains one million rows. Can you imagine the work involved to join four tables, each containing one million rows? You can be assured that performance will suffer.

To maximize performance, you sometimes have to step back to 2nd or 1st normal form. If you denormalized your data into a single table, you could use the following query, which is a sample query for a denormalized database:

```
SELECT employee_name, manager_name, training_description, training_date
FROM training_summary
```

Ad-Hoc Reporting

Another reason to denormalize a database is to simplify ad-hoc reporting. Ad-hoc reporting is the unstructured reporting and querying performed by end users. End users are often confused when they have to join a significant number of tables. To avoid the confusion, DBAs can create a special set of tables designed for ad-hoc reporting. If the data is used for reporting and not online processing, you can avoid some of the problems associated with a denormalized design.

> **TIP**
>
> Views can sometimes be used as an alternative to denormalization. Views can present your data in a denormalized manner, which can simplify ad-hoc reporting.

Denormalization Techniques

Following is brief summary of the various techniques you can use to denormalize a database:

- **Duplicate data**: Duplicate data can reduce the number of joins required to process a query, thus reducing CPU and disk I/O usage.

- **Summary data**: Summary data can provide improved query performance by reducing or eliminating the steps required to summarize your data.

- **Horizontal partitioning**: Horizontal partitioning is the splitting of a table into two separate tables at the record level, thus reducing the number of rows per table (see Figure 21.16).

- **Vertical partitioning**: Vertical partitioning is the splitting of a table into two separate tables at the column level, thus reducing the number of columns per table (see Figure 21.17).

FIGURE 21.16

Horizontal partitioning.

id	name	favorite_food	favorite_color	shoe_size
111-11-1111	Orryn Sledge	Pizza	Blue	9.5
222-22-2222	Victoria Breault	Ice Cream	Peach	6.0
333-33-3333	Mike Sampres	Pizza	Silver	9.0
444-44-4444	Fred Humpress	Fish	Red	10.0
555-55-5555	Stan Staples	Meat	Red	8.0
666-66-6666	John Johnson	Poultry	Black	9.0
777-77-7777	Mary Douglous	Pizza	White	6.0
888-88-8888	Jack Johnson	Pizza	Blue	10.0
999-99-9999	Jan Smithe	Pizza	Blue	10.0

With horizontal partitioning, a table is split into two tables at the row level. Usually, the split occurs at a predefined key value.

id	name	favorite_food	favorite_color	shoe_size
111-11-1111	Orryn Sledge	Pizza	Blue	9.5
222-22-2222	Victoria Breault	Ice Cream	Peach	6.0
333-33-3333	Mike Sampres	Pizza	Silver	9.0
444-44-4444	Fred Humpress	Fish	Red	10.0
555-55-5555	Stan Staples	Meat	Red	8.0

id	name	favorite_food	favorite_color	shoe_size
666-66-6666	John Johnson	Poultry	Black	9.0
777-77-7777	Mary Douglous	Pizza	White	6.0
888-88-8888	Jack Johnson	Pizza	Blue	10.0
999-99-9999	Jan Smithe	Pizza	Blue	10.0

FIGURE 21.17
Vertical partitioning.

id	name	favorite_food	favorite_color	shoe size
111-11-1111	Orryn Sledge	Pizza	Blue	9.5
222-22-2222	Victoria Breault	Ice Cream	Peach	6.0
333-33-3333	Mike Sampres	Pizza	Silver	9.0
444-44-4444	Fred Humpress	Fish	Red	10.0
555-55-5555	Stan Staples	Meat	Red	8.0
666-66-6666	John Johnson	Poultry	Black	9.0
777-77-7777	Mary Douglous	Pizza	White	6.0
888-88-8888	Jack Johnson	Pizza	Blue	10.0
999-99-9999	Jan Smithe	Pizza	Blue	10.0

With vertical partitioning, a table is split into two separate tables and joined by a common key.

id	name
111-11-1111	Orryn Sledge
222-22-2222	Victoria Breault
333-33-3333	Mike Sampres
444-44-4444	Fred Humpress
555-55-5555	Stan Staples
666-66-6666	John Johnson
777-77-7777	Mary Douglous
888-88-8888	Jack Johnson
999-99-9999	Jan Smithe

id	favorite_food	favorite_color	shoe size
111-11-1111	Pizza	Blue	9.5
222-22-2222	Ice Cream	Peach	6.0
333-33-3333	Pizza	Silver	9.0
444-44-4444	Fish	Red	10.0
555-55-5555	Meat	Red	8.0
666-66-6666	Poultry	Black	9.0
777-77-7777	Pizza	White	6.0
888-88-8888	Pizza	Blue	10.0
999-99-9999	Pizza	Blue	10.0

DESIGN DATABASE FAQ

Listed below are some of the common questions asked by DBAs about database design:

Q. Should an identity column be used as a primary key?

A. As a general rule, use an identity column (an identity is an auto-incrementing number) as the primary key of a table. The following are the benefits from using an identity as the primary key.

- **Guaranteed to be unique:** SQL Server automatically generates the identity value and it is guaranteed to be unique in a multi-user environment. A person's social security number is often used as the primary key of a table. Did you know that social security numbers are not truly unique? In the past, the U.S. government has issued duplicated social security numbers!! Instead of using a social security number as the primary key, you may want to consider using an identity.

- **Avoids compound keys:** An identity column removes the need to create compound keys. (A compound key is a primary key that contains 2 or more columns.) This simplifies joins between tables and creates a more compact index. Both of these factors can provide improved performance over compound keys.

Q. Does SQL Server 7.0 provide any datamodeling tools?

A. SQL Server 7.0 provides database diagrams for datamodeling. The database diagrams are somewhat limited in functionality when compared to 3rd party tools such as DataArchitect and ErWin.

SUMMARY

Following are important notes to remember when designing databases:

- The following are the 3 forms of normalization.
    - **1st normal form:** No repeating groups.
    - **2nd normal form:** No nonkey attributes depend on a portion of the primary key.
    - **3rd normal form:** No attributes depend on other nonkey attributes.

- Strive for 3rd normal form to maximize data consistency and minimize update anomalies.

- When a significant number of tables must be joined to process a query, you may want to selectively denormalize the database to improve performance.

UNDERSTANDING INDEXES

by Mark Spenik

IN THIS CHAPTER

You may wonder what a chapter on indexes and index selection is doing in a book about database administration. It is important to understand how SQL Server uses indexes and how they can be used to enhance performance. For example, developers always come to the DBA seeking words of wisdom and advice for slow applications or queries. Not only will index tuning knowledge elevate you in their eyes, but a working knowledge of indexes will help you with space management. Also, every DBA should be aware of another SQL Server 7.0 index bonus—using a clustered index to move a frequently used table to a specific file or filegroup located on a separate physical disk drive to increase application performance.

This chapter gives you a very basic understanding of an index, the type of structures used by indexes, and how to use the various utilities provided by SQL Server to help you select the proper indexes for your company's applications.

To get started, you need to know what an index is. An *index* is a separate, physical database structure created on a table that facilitates faster data retrieval when you search on an indexed column. SQL Server also uses indexes to enforce uniqueness on a row or column in a table, to order the data or to spread out the table on a separate file or filegroup to boost performance. Before moving on, take a quick glance at changes in indexes from SQL Server 6.5 to SQL Server 7.0

SQL SERVER 6.5 TO 7.0 QUICK REFERENCE

The following quick reference outlines the key differences between SQL Server Version 6.5 and Version 7.0.

What's New

- Data page and index page size has changed from 2KB to 8KB.
- Storage of nonclustered index leaf level pages on tables with clustered indexes has changed to greatly improve performance and eliminate updating nonclustered index pages when a page splits on a clustered index.
- Heap storage for tables without a non-clustered index has changed to prevent hot spots.
- The ability to gather statistical information on columns that have not been indexed.
- Index Tuning Wizard to help you take the guesswork out of creating proper indexes to improve performance.
- Automatic updating of statistical information for indexes.
- Stored procedure (sp_updatestats) to issue an Update Statistics command on all tables with indexes or columns that have been marked for statistic gathering in a database.

- The ability of SQL Server to effectively use more than one index to retrieve data.
- The ability to move a table to a filegroup or file by using a clustered index.

What's Gone

- Segments are no longer supported so you can't move a table using a clustered index with segments; instead use a file or filegroup.
- The SORTED_DATA option is no longer supported.

GENERAL PRINCIPLE BEHIND INDEXES

Take a high-level look at how indexing can help speed up data retrieval. Figure 22.1 shows a single table called School Employee that lists the name and occupation of each employee in the school.

FIGURE 22.1

The School Employee *table.*

School Employee

row	name	occupation
1	John	Janitor
2	David	Principal
3	Adam	Bus Driver
4	Gary	Teacher
5	Lisa	Janitor
6	Chris	Teacher
7	Debbie	Guidance Counselor
8	Denise	Assistant Principal
9	Bryan	Janitor

Using the table shown in Figure 22.1, what would you do if you wanted to select the names of all the people in the School Employee table who were janitors? You would have to read every row in the table and display only the names where the occupation in the row is Janitor. The process of reading every row or record in a table to satisfy a query is called a *table scan*. Now add an index to the Occupation column. Figure 22.2 shows the index on the Occupation column of the School Employee table.

The type of index shown in Figure 22.2 contains a pointer to the data. Using the index shown in Figure 22.2, walk through the same query to find the names of all employees who are janitors. Rather than performing a table scan on the School Employee table, you read the first row of the index and check the occupation until you find Janitor. When a row contains Janitor, you use the value in the row pointer column to find the exact row number in the School Employee table of a Janitor. You continue to read the index as long as the occupation is Janitor. When the occupation is no longer Janitor, you stop reading the index. Pretty simple, right?

FIGURE 22.2

An index on the Occupation column of the School Employee table.

occupation	row pointer
Assistant Principal	8
Bus Driver	3
Guidance Counselor	7
Janitor	1
Janitor	5
Janitor	9
Principal	2
Teacher	4
Teacher	6

Apply to SQL Server this little bit of knowledge of tables and indexes just described. For starters, SQL Server stores data and index information on a page (see Figure 22.3).

FIGURE 22.3

The SQL Server page format.

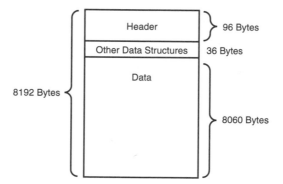

A page is 8192 bytes (8KB) in size with a 96-byte header. Additional space is used for other data structures, such as row offset information, but the majority of the page, 8060 bytes, can be used to store data (that is, table or index information). So, in SQL Server 7.0, the maximum width of a single row (not including text and image data) is 8060 bytes. Previous versions of SQL Server could store only 1962 bytes per row.

TIP

SQL Server allocates space for tables and indexes eight pages at a time—a grouping called an *extent*. When the extent is filled, another extent (eight pages) is allocated. Remember this tip if you take the Microsoft SQL Server certification test. The odds are that you will be asked a question on index and table space allocation and the name of the allocation unit.

Suppose that the `School Employee` table, used earlier, contained other information, such as the employee's home address, phone number, spouse's name, education, and number of years of service. The size of a single row of information for the `School Employee` table would be around 2000 bytes; the maximum size of the Occupation column is 25 bytes. Using these row and column sizes and placing the `School Employee` table (shown in Figure 22.1) and the index (shown in Figure 22.2) on SQL Server data pages produces Figure 22.4.

> **NOTE**
>
> The layouts of the table information and index information on the SQL Server pages shown in Figure 22.4 are not the actual index and table layouts used by SQL Server. They are used here to help you understand the general idea behind SQL Server pages, table scans, and indexes.

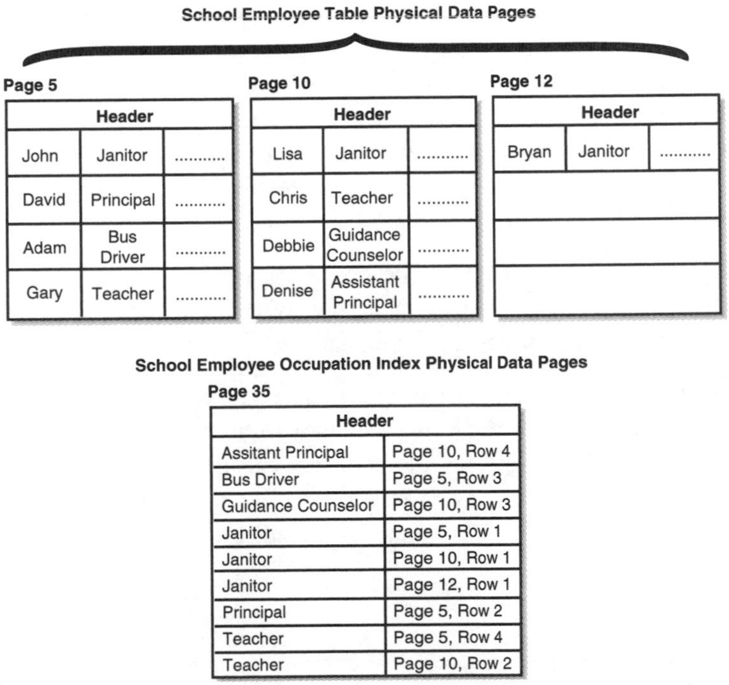

22

UNDERSTANDING INDEXES

FIGURE 22.4

The School Employee *table and index on SQL Server data pages.*

School Employee Table Physical Data Pages

Page 5

Header		
John	Janitor	....
David	Principal	....
Adam	Bus Driver	....
Gary	Teacher	....

Page 10

Header		
Lisa	Janitor	....
Chris	Teacher	....
Debbie	Guidance Counselor	....
Denise	Assistant Principal	....

Page 12

Header		
Bryan	Janitor	....

School Employee Occupation Index Physical Data Pages

Page 35

Header	
Assitant Principal	Page 10, Row 4
Bus Driver	Page 5, Row 3
Guidance Counselor	Page 10, Row 3
Janitor	Page 5, Row 1
Janitor	Page 10, Row 1
Janitor	Page 12, Row 1
Principal	Page 5, Row 2
Teacher	Page 5, Row 4
Teacher	Page 10, Row 2

Using the diagram shown in Figure 22.4, how would SQL Server find all the employee names whose occupation is `Assistant Principal` without the index? First, SQL Server would read data page five and search each record for an employee with an occupation equal to `Assistant Principal`. No records are found on the first page. SQL Server reads the second data page (page 10), searches each record, and displays the fourth record. Because SQL Server has no way of knowing how many records there are with the occupation of `Assistant Principal`, SQL Server reads and searches the third and final page, page 12.

What happened? SQL Server performed a table scan, reading all the data pages. In this example, a table scan did not seem all that bad because SQL Server only had to read three data pages. But what if the `School Employee` table had 1,000 times more records for a total of 9,000 records (a small amount for SQL Server)? SQL Server would have to read 3,000 data pages to find all the `Assistant Principals`, even if there was only one employee who was an `Assistant Principal`; and that record was located on the first data page.

Walk through the same query using the index. First, SQL Server reads the index page and begins to search for `Assistant Principal`. The first row read is `Assistant Principal`. SQL Server then checks the pointer, which tells SQL Server that the record is located on data page 10, row 4. SQL Server reads data page 10, goes to the fourth row, and displays the name. The row number of the page is called a `RID`, which stands for Row Identifier. `RID`s do not change unless the row is deleted and then reinserted. If a row is deleted, the `RID` can be reused.

The next row in the index page is checked; because the occupation is not `Assistant Principal`, SQL Server stops. The number of pages read using the index is two pages as opposed to the three pages read in the table scan example.

What about the `Janitor` query used earlier? Performing a table scan requires SQL Server to read all three data pages. Using the index requires SQL Server to read all three data pages plus the index page, for a total of four data pages—one more than a table scan! In some cases, a table scan may be faster than using the index. It's the job of the SQL Server query optimizer to determine which index to select and when to perform a table scan.

TIP

You will read recommendations in this book about keeping indexes small and the row width of a table small for maximum performance. All too often, the reasoning behind small row and index width is left out. It boils down to data pages and how many data pages SQL Server has to read to fulfill a query.

Suppose that you have a table with 5,000,000 rows; the size of a row (with overhead bytes) is 1250 bytes or maximum row width (8060 bytes) / 1250 bytes = 6) six records per data page. The number of data pages required for all 5,000,000 records is (5,000,000 / 6 = 833,333) 833,333 SQL Server pages or 104,166 extents (eight pages in an extent).

Suppose that you look at your overall table design and decide that you can shrink the size of the maximum row width just over 10 percent so that seven rather than six records fit on a data page. The number of data pages is reduced by almost 120,000 pages (or 15,000 extents)! A SQL Server page used for an index is the same. Indexing a 20-character field (with overhead) and a 6-byte field (with overhead), for example, is the difference between 100 keys per page versus 336 keys per page.

The larger index requires SQL Server to read three times as many pages to access the same number of keys. (This does not take into account the added B-Tree levels caused by a larger index key!) Select the proper data types and sizes when creating your tables. One last bit of advice, normalize your tables and select smart indexes.

STRUCTURE OF SQL SERVER INDEXES

SQL Server maintains indexes with a B-Tree structure (see Figure 22.5). B-Trees are multilevel, self-maintaining structures.

A B-Tree structure consists of a top level, called the *root*; a bottom level, called the *leaf* (always level 0); and zero to many intermediate levels (the B-Tree in Figure 22.5 has one intermediate level). In SQL Server terms, each square shown in Figure 22.5 represents an index page (or data page). The greater the number of levels in your index, the more index pages you must read to retrieve the records you are searching for. (That is, performance degrades as the number of levels increases.) SQL Server maintains two different types of indexes: a clustered index and a nonclustered index.

TIP

The levels of the B-Tree can point to possible performance problems or poor index selection. A B-Tree with a large number of levels requires more time to find rows because each level adds more data pages that must be read to get to the leaf pages.

You can reduce the number of B-Tree levels by reducing the width of the indexed columns, which increases the number of index keys per page.

FIGURE 22.5

The B-Tree struc-ture.

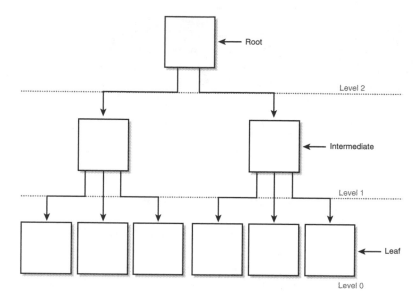

Clustered Index

A *clustered index* is a B-Tree structure where level 0, the leaf, contains the actual data pages of the table and the data is physically stored in the logical order of the index.

> **NOTE**
>
> When a clustered index is created, a lot of disk I/O occurs, the data pages are ordered, the index pages are created, and the nonordered data pages are deleted. Creating a clustered index requires you to have free space in the database that amounts to approximately 1.2 times the amount of data in the table.

Figure 22.6 shows a clustered index on the Name column in the School Employee table. Notice that the data pages are the leaf pages of the clustered index and that the data is stored in logical order on the data pages.

> **NOTE**
>
> Because data is physically ordered on the data pages, you can have only one clustered index per table. Select the clustered index wisely.

FIGURE 22.6
A clustered index on the Name column of the School Employee *table.*

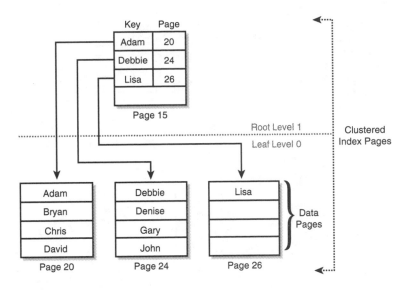

SQL Server index pages contain a page header followed by index rows. The index rows contain the key value and a pointer to an index page or the data row (leaf level of a clustered index). Index pages are further linked together using a doubly linked list.

Nonclustered Index

With a nonclustered index, the leaf-level pages contain row locators to the data pages and rows, not the actual data (as does the clustered index). A nonclustered index does not reorder the physical data pages of the table. Therefore, creating a nonclustered index does not require the large amounts of free disk space associated with creating a clustered index. Figure 22.7 shows a nonclustered index on the School Employee table. Notice that the data in the data pages is in the order in which the data was inserted, not in the order of the index key, but a random order since it uses heap storage. In SQL Server 6.5, heap storage was always at the end of the data page and could cause hot spots on tables without clustered indexes. SQL Server 7.0 changed the way heap storage works and no longer stores at the bottom of the data page, thus removing a potential hot spot for tables without clustered indexes. Also, note that the nonclustered index adds one more level by always arriving at the leaf and then having to read the data page. If the table has a clustered index on the table, the row indicator is the clustered index of the table. If the table does not contain a clustered index, the row locator is a Row ID, or RID, which is built using the file ID, page number, and row number on the page.

FIGURE 22.7

A nonclustered index on the Name column of the School Employee *table.*

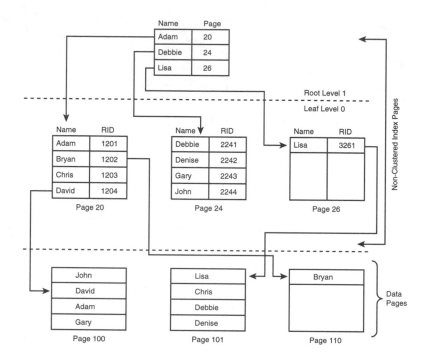

You can have up to 249 nonclustered indexes on a table; although you would *never* want to create anywhere near 249 indexes on a single table. A large number of indexes on a single table affects the performance of other operations, such as UPDATE, DELETE, and INSERT. An index cannot exceed 900 bytes in width or 16 columns. Again, you would *never* want an index that is 900 bytes in width. Remember to use narrow-width indexes to maximize the number of index keys on a data page. This improves performance by requiring less disk I/O to scan the index. In previous versions of SQL Server, we recommended that you try not to exceed 4 columns when creating indexes. However, with SQL Server 7.0, this rule is no longer true. Microsoft has made many significant improvements in index management, memory use, and disk I/O. Keep in mind that indexes with smaller key sizes will outperform indexes with larger key sizes instead of concerning yourself with the number of columns in the index. A table can have both clustered and nonclustered indexes. Because you are allowed to have only a single clustered index on a table, you can meet your other indexing needs with nonclustered indexes. Try not to over-index; in many cases, a clustered index and two to six nonclustered indexes is more than sufficient (except in data warehouse situations).

DATA MODIFICATION AND INDEX PERFORMANCE CONSIDERATIONS

It is widely known that an index can help speed data retrievals; from time to time, you may hear someone say that indexes slow down other operations, such as inserts, updates, and deletes, which is true. It has been mentioned that B-Tree data structures are, for the most part, *self-maintaining data structures*. This means that as rows are added, deleted, or updated, the indexes also are updated to reflect the changes requiring extra I/O to update the index pages.

SQL Server 7.0 has many performance improvements to greatly reduce the disk I/O required to maintain indexes. One new feature worth noting is that non-clustered indexes no longer have to be updated when a clustered index page splits. What is an index page split? Remember, data added to a clustered index is inserted into the correct physical and logical order in the table, and other rows can be moved up or down, depending on where the data is placed, causing additional disk I/O to maintain the index. Over time, as a page grows, a new record might be added that requires the page to be split because the page is full. Thus, records are moved to a new page. In previous versions of SQL Server, the nonclustered index also had to be updated to reflect the rows on the new page. This disk I/O has been totally eliminated from SQL Server 7.0 by using the `clustered index key value` for non-clustered indexes for tables with a clustered index instead of the physical page number. Page splits still occur in SQL Server 7.0 and can affect performance in other ways. For additional information, see the FAQ for this chapter on why `Fill Factor` is important.

In general, you should not worry about the time required to maintain indexes during inserts, deletes, and updates. Be aware that extra time is required to update the indexes during data modification and that performance can become an issue if you over-index a table. On tables that are frequently modified, try to restrict the tables to a clustered index and no more than three or four nonclustered indexes. Tables involved in heavy transaction processing should be restricted to from zero to three indexes. If you find the need to index beyond these numbers, run some benchmark tests to check for performance degradation. Don't forget to use the Index Tuning wizard to help you make your index selections.

22

UNDERSTANDING INDEXES

HOW TO CREATE INDEXES

You can create an index using the new SQL Server 7.0 Index Wizard.

> **NOTE**
>
> You cannot create an index on the following data types:
>   bit
>   text
>   image
> Indexes cannot be created on a view.

Using the SQL Enterprise Manager, select a server and then click the Wizards icon from the toolbar. The Wizard Selection dialog box appears. Expand the Database options by clicking the + sign. Then follow these steps to create an index (the following example uses the pubs database):

1. Select the Create Index Wizard from the Wizard Selection dialog box. The Create Index Wizard Welcome dialog box appears (see Figure 22.8).

FIGURE 22.8

The Create Index Wizard Welcome dialog box.

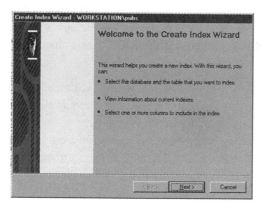

2. Click the Next button. The Database and Table Selection dialog box appears (see Figure 22.9). Using the combo boxes, select the database and the table to which you want to add the index. Click the Next button.

FIGURE 22.9

The Create Index Wizard Database and Table Selection dialog box.

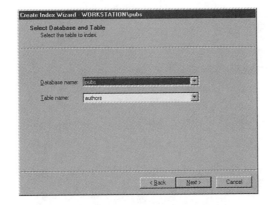

3. If indexes already exist on the table, you will see the Current Index Information dialog box shown in Figure 22.10.

FIGURE 22.10

The Create Index Wizard Current Index Information dialog box.

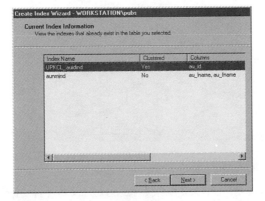

If no indexes exist, the wizard skips this step and goes to step 4.

4. Check the columns you want to include in your index. The Index Wizard enables you to select only columns that have valid index data types. Notice in Figure 22.11, the red x for the table column contract, which consists of an invalid index data type.

After you select the column(s) for your index, click the Next button. The Index Option dialog box appears (see Figure 22.12).

22

UNDERSTANDING INDEXES

FIGURE 22.11

The Create Index Wizard Column Selection dialog box.

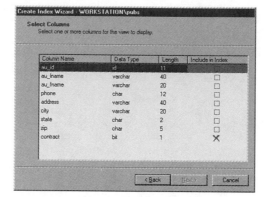

FIGURE 22.12

The Create Index Wizard Index Option dialog box.

5. The Index Option dialog box options are as follows:

- **The Clustered check box:** When the Clustered check box is selected, a clustered index with the selected columns is created on the table. If a clustered index already exists on the table, this option is not available. Remember that you can have only one clustered index per table. When this option is not selected, a nonclustered index is created.

- **The Unique Keys check box:** The Unique option creates an index that enforces uniqueness on the indexed column(s). Use the Unique Keys option when uniqueness is an attribute of the data (for example, the primary key of the table).

CAUTION

If you try to create a unique index on a column with duplicate data, the index creation will fail. You must remove the duplicate data entries to build the index.

- **The Fill Factor field:** The Fill Factor specifies how densely packed you want your index and data pages when creating an index. The default is 0, which leaves room on the nonleaf pages with the leaf pages 100 percent full. A high Fill Factor value increases performance for queries because the index pages are packed, reducing the number of index levels (that is, the number of pages to read when traversing an index). The tradeoff is the increase in time when performing such as INSERT and UPDATE statements caused by page splitting. Use high Fill Factor values for static tables or tables that are not modified frequently. Specify a low Fill Factor value to spread data over more pages. A low Fill Factor value is good for tables involved with many UPDATE and INSERT transactions because the chance of a page split occurring is reduced due to the initial number of rows per page being reduced, thus leaving more empty space on the data page for additional records. The penalty for a low Fill Factor is a decrease in query performance because the number of index levels is increased, requiring more data pages to be read when querying the table. *Note:* The default value of 0 is a special case and is not considered a low Fill Factor value because the leaf pages are filled to 100 percent capacity and some space is left on the index pages). The default Fill Factor value used by your SQL Server can be configured using sp_configure or the Enterprise Manager.

> **NOTE**
>
> The Fill Factor value is not maintained by SQL Server after index creation; it is maintained only when the index is built.

After you select the options you want for the index, click the Next button. The Index Completion dialog box appears (see Figure 22.13).

6. Enter a name for the index in the Index Name text box. Use a meaningful naming convention for indexes and stick with it. For example you can prefix indexes with *cidx* for a clustered index and *idx* for a nonclustered index. If the index is on the primary key table, add *pk*. If the index is a foreign key, add *fk*. Then use the column names to remind yourself which columns make up the index. For example, a clustered index on the primary key column on the authors table, au_id, in the pubs database, the index would be named cidx_pk_au_id. The maximum number of characters you can use for an index is 30. Use the Move Up or Move Down buttons to change the order of the columns in the index. When you are done, click the Finish button to build the index. A dialog box is displayed telling you of the success or failure of your index creation.

When an index is created, a row is placed in the sysindexes database system table.

FIGURE 22.13

*The Create Index
Wizard Index
Completion
dialog box.*

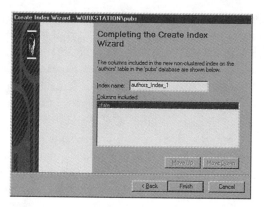

The Transact-SQL statement used to create an index is the CREATE INDEX command,
which has the following syntax:

```
CREATE [UNIQUE] [CLUSTERED ¦ NONCLUSTERED] INDEX index_name
ON table_name (column_name [, column_name]...)
[WITH [PAD_INDEX,][[,]FILLFACTOR = x][[,]
IGNORE_DUP_KEY][[,]DROP_EXISTING][[,]STATISTICS_NORECOMPUTE]]
[ON filegroup]
```

Some of the CREATE INDEX options were discussed in the section of this chapter covering
the Create Index Wizard Index Options dialog box (see Figure 22.12). The remaining
options are as follows:

- PAD_INDEX—The PAD_INDEX option specifies the amount of space to leave open on
  each interior node. By default, the number of items is never less than two on an
  interior page. The PAD_INDEX option works in conjunction with the FILLFACTOR
  option and uses the FILLFACTOR percentage.

- IGNORE_DUP_KEY—The IGNORE_DUP_KEY option does not enable you to create a
  unique index with duplicate values, but if an attempt is made to insert a duplicate
  row, the duplicate row is ignored and an informational message is displayed. If the
  INSERT or UPDATE is part of a transaction, the transaction continues instead of
  rolling back on a duplicate key error. This option exists in SQL Server 7.0 for
  backward compatibility and is only supported for INSERT statements.

- `DROP_EXISTING`—This option is for clustered indexes only and affects the nonclustered indexes on the table. When `DROP_EXISTING` is used on an index creation statement, the clustered index is dropped and rebuilt. The nonclustered indexes are modified only after the index is re-created. Without this option, the nonclustered indexes would also be updated when the clustered index is dropped.

- `STATISTICS_NORECOMPUTE`—The `STATISTICS_NORECOMPUTE` option turns off auto updating of the index statistical information requiring you to perform an `UPDATE STATISTICS` command manually.

> **NOTE**
>
> SQL Server 7.0 provides another method to create indexes called *constraints*. A constraint is added to a table during the table creation and can be used to maintain referential integrity. The `primary key` constraint places a unique index, clustered or nonclustered, on the columns defined as the `primary key`. You cannot drop a constraint index with the SQL Enterprise Manager (using the Manage Index dialog box). To remove a constraint, you must use the `ALTER TABLE` command. Here's the good news if you use SQL Server 7.0: You can use the DBCC `DBREINDEX` statement to dynamically rebuild indexes without having to drop and re-create the index or constraint.

OTHER INDEX OPERATIONS

Following is a quick review of other index operations you can perform using Transact-SQL and/or the Enterprise Manager.

Viewing Indexes on Tables in a Database

In SQL Server 7.0 you can view all the tables in a database, as well as the existing indexes on the tables, the number of rows in the tables, and the amount of disk space being used by each table and index using the Enterprise Manager. To view the table and index information perform the following:

1. From the Enterprise Manager, select the database you want to view the information in by clicking the database in the databases folder (for the following steps the Northwind sample database is used). Database information is loaded into the left frame of the Enterprise Manager.

2. Select the Table and Indexes tab (hyperlink) located in the left frame. The Table and Indexes tab is displayed, shown in Figure 22.14.

FIGURE 22.14

*The Database
Information
Tables and
Indexes dialog
box.*

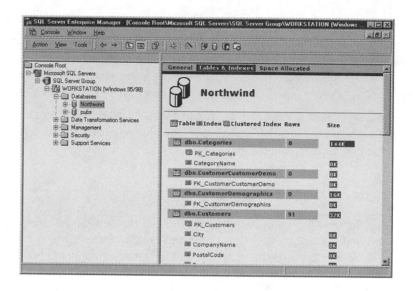

The Table and Indexes tab displays all the tables and indexes associated with the tables in the selected database, as well as the amount of disk space being used by the table and indexes, and the total number of rows for each table. You can use the Transact SQL commands `sp_help_index` and `sp_statistics` to view index information for an associated table.

Renaming, Adding, or Deleting an Index

This section covers how to add, remove, and rename an index by using the Enterprise Manager. Before examining how to perform these tasks with the Enterprise Manager, here are the Transact-SQL statements to delete (remove) an index and rename an index. To remove an index with Transact-SQL, use the Transact-SQL command `DROP INDEX`, which has the following format:

```
DROP INDEX [owner.]table_name.index_name
[, [owner.]table_name.index_name...]
```

To rename an index with Transact-SQL, use the SQL Server system stored procedure `sp_rename`, which has the following syntax:

```
sp_rename objname, newname [, COLUMN ¦ INDEX ]
```

To use the Enterprise Manager to perform index adding, renaming, or deleting, perform the following (note that the following uses the Northwind database):

1. Select the database from the databases folder in the Enterprise Manager.

2. Collapse the database to view the database objects by clicking the + sign located to the left of the database name.

3. Select the Diagrams icon under the selected database.

4. Select a database diagram in the left frame of the Enterprise Manager by double-clicking a diagram (in this example, Relationships is used). The Edit Diagram dialog box is displayed. If one does not exist, add a database diagram by performing a right-mouse click and clicking Add.

5. Select the table where you want to add, delete, or rename an index with a single mouse-click in the Edit Diagram dialog box.

6. Right mouse-click the selected table and select Properties. The Tables Properties dialog box appears.

7. Click the Indexes/Keys tab on the Table Properties dialog box. The Indexes/Keys tab, shown in Figure 22.15, is displayed.

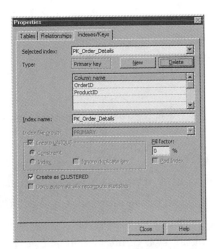

FIGURE 22.15

The Tables Properties Indexes/Keys tab dialog box.

To rename an index, type over the index name displayed in the Index Name text box shown in Figure 22.15.

To delete an index, select the index you want to remove in the Selected Index combo box, and click the Delete button as shown in Figure 22.15.

To add a new index, click the New button shown in Figure 22.15. Add the columns that make up the index in the Column Name grid. Give the index a name by entering the name in the Index name text box. Select the filegroup to place the index using the Index Filegroup combo box. You can then set the fill factor, unique property, clustered index, create as an index or constraint, and check to not automatically updates statistics by

22

UNDERSTANDING
INDEXES

checking appropriate check boxes or radio buttons. Click the Close button shown in Figure 22.15 to save the index.

SUGGESTED INDEX STRATEGIES

Index selection is based on the design of the tables and the queries that are executed against the tables. Before you create indexes, make sure that the indexed columns are part of a query or are being placed on the table for other reasons, such as preventing duplicate data. The following sections suggest some indexing strategies.

What to Index

The following list shows criteria you can use to help determine which columns will make good indexes:

- Columns used in table joins
- Columns used in range queries
- Columns used in order by queries
- Columns used in group by queries
- Columns used in aggregate functions

What Not to Index

The following list shows cases in which columns or indexes should not be used or should be used sparingly:

- Tables with a small number of rows
- Columns with poor selectivity (that is, with a wide range of values)
- Columns that are very large in width (try to limit indexes to columns < 25 bytes in size)
- Tables with heavy transaction loads (lots of inserts and deletes) but very few decision-support operations
- Columns not used in queries

Clustered or Nonclustered Index

As you know, you can have only one clustered index per table. Following are some situations in which a clustered index works well:

- Columns used in range queries
- Columns used in order by or group by queries

- Columns used in table joins

- Queries returning large result sets

Nonclustered indexes work well in the following situations:

- Columns used in aggregate functions

- Foreign keys

- Queries returning small result sets

- When using the DBCC DBREINDEX statement to dynamically rebuild non-clustered indexes, the requested index can be rebuilt without rebuilding all the other indexes on a table. When a clustered index is rebuilt, all the non-clustered indexes are also rebuilt. (Note: with DBCC DBREINDEX you don't have to drop and re-create the index or constraint)

- Information frequently accessed by a specific column in table joins or order by or group by queries

- Primary keys that are sequential surrogate keys (identity columns, sequence numbers)

LETTING SQL SERVER HELP WITH INDEX SELECTION

One of the goals of the SQL Server team was to make SQL Server an easy tool for maintaining and using databases. Index selection has always been a problem because of the knowledge required to tune a query. In addition, one must know how and when to override the query optimizer. SQL Server 7.0 provides several tools to help the DBA take the guesswork out of index creation. The most effective tool is the SQL Server Index Tuning Wizard. The SQL Server Index Tuning Wizard analyzes real workloads captured by the SQL Server profiler. The SQL Server Index Tuning Wizard tests the various SQL statements found in the profiler workload and creates what if indexes. The wizard then checks the what if indexes with the Query Processor to determine the cost of the index. The wizard then makes the best index recommendations based on the workload. The suggested indexes can be created immediately or scheduled. Like all SQL Server wizards, the Index Tuning Wizard is simple to use and can be found under the Enterprise Manager's Wizards dialog box.

Capturing a SQL Server profiler workload is discussed in detail in Chapter 19, "Monitoring SQL Server." The real power of the Index Tuning Wizard from a DBA standpoint is that you do not need to know anything about the application, how the application is used, or the data structure of the database. The SQL Server profiler captures the

SQL statements being performed during actual workloads for the Index Tuning Wizard to analyze—enabling the DBA to do an expert index-tuning job quickly. An important point to make is that to get the most from the tuning wizard, you should capture actual workloads.

If you want suggestions on individual SQL statements as you execute them in the Microsoft Query Analyzer tool, you can enter a SQL statement and then use the SQL Server 7.0's index tuning capabilities to make a suggestion about indexes. Let's walk through a quick example. From the Enterprise Manager, perform the following:

1. From the menu, select Tools and SQL Server Query Analyzer, and the SQL Server Query Analyzer dialog box displays.

2. Using the databases combo box, select the Northwind database.

3. Enter the following SQL command in the Query Analyzer:
```
Select ShipName
from orders
Where  ShippedDate > '01/01/1990' and  ShippedDate < '01/01/1999'
```

4. From the Query Analyzer menu, select Query, and the Perform Index Analysis option. SQL Server will begin to analyze the query to determine whether an index can improve the performance. If it is determined that an index can benefit the execution of the SQL statement, the Query Analyzer Index Analysis dialog box, shown in Figure 22.16, is displayed. Click the Accept button to create the suggested index.

FIGURE 22.16

The Query Analyzer Index Analysis.

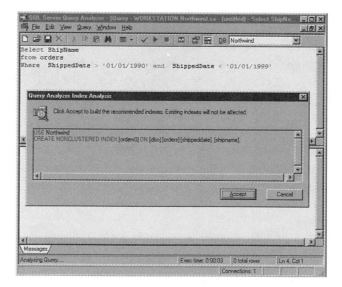

INDEX FAQ

The following section contains several frequently asked questions about and answers about indexes.

Q. How can I view the index selectivity (density) of an indexed column?

A. The index selectivity can be viewed by using the Transact-SQL statement DBCC SHOW_STATISTICS. DBCC SHOW_STATISTICS displays the average key length of an index, the index density, and the distribution steps.

Q. What are composite indexes?

A. Composite indexes are indexes created with two or more columns (The maximum number of columns for an index is 16.) SQL Server 7.0 keeps distribution page and histogram statistics on the columns that make up the index. Try not to get carried away by creating composite indexes with a large number of columns. (I try to keep them under four columns). Too many columns affect performance and make the index key large, increasing the size of the index and requiring you to scan more data pages to read the index keys.

Q. Can SQL Server use more than one index in a single query?

A. Prior to SQL Server 7.0, the query optimizer could use only one index when querying the information. In SQL Server 7.0, the query optimizer can use multiple indexes to retrieve the information.

Q. What is index covering?

A. Index covering is a term used to explain a situation in which all the columns returned by a query and all the columns in the WHERE clause are the key columns in a single nonclustered index (that is, a composite index). SQL Server does not have to read the data pages to satisfy the query; instead, it returns the values on the leaf page of the index, which can boost speed significantly on tables where the table row size is much larger than the index key size. Keep in mind that over-indexing a table can hurt data modification performance.

Q. Can SQL Server use index covering with indexes that are not composite indexes?

A. Prior to SQL Server 7.0, the query optimizer could use only composite indexes for index covering, but SQL Server 7.0 can now use single column indexes to cover a query! The query optimizer can use multiple indexes to satisfy a query by building a hash table to reduce the disk I/O; this is called index intersection. Index intersection provides the same benefits as a covered index. This is an outstanding new feature since the main problem of composite indexes with index covering is having to create composite indexes that covered various query scenarios. Now by creating several single column indexes on columns that are frequently returned, joined, or filtered, you can get the benefits of covered queries via index intersection. Again keep in mind that over indexing a table can hurt data modification performance.

Q. Can users access a table while an index is being created?

A. The table on which the index is being created is locked during index creation. Creating indexes on very large tables or creating clustered indexes (which might reorder the data pages) can take some time to complete. You cannot access the table until the index creation is complete. Try to create clustered indexes and very large nonclustered indexes during nonpeak hours.

Q. What is the best way to drop and re-create an index?

A. The fastest way to drop and re-create a clustered or nonclustered index with SQL Server 7.0 is to use the DBCC REINDEX command.

Q. Do I still have to perform an UPDATE STATISTICS with SQL Server 7.0?

A. SQL Server 7.0 will automatically update statistical information for you as a background task that can be disabled. If you disable this feature, you will need to manually issue the UPDATE STATISTICS command. If you have the auto update statistics feature enabled, you may still want to execute the UPDATE STATISTICS command after importing or updating large amounts of information.

Q. Why are the Index FillFactor and PAD_INDEX options important?

A. FillFactor and PAD_INDEX are important for several reasons. For example, you can use them to maintain contiguous disk space. When SQL Server creates an index using FillFactor and PAD_INDEX, the space allocated for the indexes are contiguous disk space. So when a user queries against the index, sequential disk I/O is being used to traverse the index B-Tree. Over time, as index pages split, the new pages added as a result of the split are no longer contiguous, thus resulting in non-sequential reads (which are slower). The real trick is trying to determine the right combination of FillFactor and PAD_INDEX that will put as many index keys on a page while leaving enough room to avoid page splits. Tables that rarely change can use a FillFactor of 100 to completely fill the page and maximize query time. However, if you add a record to a table with full index pages, you immediately get a page split.

Q. How do I keep distribution statistics on a non-indexed column (or columns)?

A. Use the Create Statistics command to create statistics (histogram and density information) on a column or set of columns without creating an index (this also counts as one of the 249 allowed non-clustered indexes).

Q. Should I always index a table?

A. You should not index tables that have very few rows in them. When a table consists of only a few data pages, it may be faster for SQL Server to perform a table scan rather than walk through an index.

Q. What is the best advice I can give someone on indexes?

A. Try to keep the index key values small. This provides you with lots of rows per data page, which reduces disk I/O. For tables with clustered indexes, it is important to choose small key values because the clustered index key value is stored as the row identifier of non-clustered indexes.

SUMMARY

It is important that you understand the basic ideas behind SQL Server indexes. In the next chapter, you build on the basic concepts of this chapter and learn about the Query Processor. If you understand indexes, the Query Processor and the tools SQL Server provides to help you select the proper indexes; you will be able to provide valuable support to developers. Following are some important points to remember about SQL Server indexes:

- SQL Server maintains indexes with a B-Tree structure.
- In a clustered index, the leaf contains the actual data pages of the table, and the data is physically stored in the logical order of the index.
- The SQL Server query optimizer can use more than one index to resolve a query.
- SQL Server 7.0 can maintain distribution statistics on non-indexed columns.
- SQL Server 7.0 can automatically update statistics for indexes.
- Composite indexes are indexes created with two or more columns.
- Use the Index Tuning Wizard to help you select the proper indexes for you databases.
- Select indexes carefully.

QUERY OPTIMIZATION

by Orryn Sledge

IN THIS CHAPTER

Query optimization involves understanding SQL Server's optimizer, knowledge of query optimization tools, and proper indexing techniques. With this knowledge you can write queries that run faster, build better indexes, and resolve performance problems.

SQL SERVER 6.5 TO 7.0 QUICK REFERENCE

The following is a quick reference to the changes that occurred between SQL Server version 6.5 and 7.0:

What's New

- Graphical Showplan   It's back and significantly improved! Versions 4.2 and 6.0 had a graphical showplan and version 6.5 lacked a graphical showplan. Version 7.0 includes a graphical showplan that provides detailed information as to how SQL Server will execute the query.

- SET SHOWPLAN_TEXT   This statement is a non-graphical showplan that replaces SET SHOWPLAN, which was found in previous versions of SQL Server.

- SET SHOWPLAN_ALL   This statement is also a non-graphical showplan that provides more detail than the SET SHOWPLAN_TEXT statement.

- Auto-update statistics   SQL Server 7.0 automatically updates and maintains index statistics. This reduces the risk of statistics becoming stale. In previous versions, if statistics were stale, meaning that the statistics did not accurately reflect the underlying data, the query optimizer would make incorrect decisions as to the usefulness of available indexes. Previous versions of SQL Server required that UPDATE STATISTICS be run on a frequent basis to prevent stale statistics.

- Index Tuning Wizard   Version 7.0 includes an Index Tuning Wizard that analyzes a query, makes index recommendations, and implements the index if the user approves the recommendation. Even the most experienced SQL Server DBAs will find this tool useful.

- Multi-index support   Queries now utilize multiple indexes per table. Previous versions were limited to using one index per table per query.

- Parallel query execution   On SMP machines, SQL Server 7.0 will automatically run a query or a portion of the query, in parallel, on multiple processors. The degree in which SQL Server runs a query in parallel is based on the server's workload. SQL Server will automatically adjust the degree of parallelism on a continuous basis. On non-SMP machines, SQL Server does not utilize parallel query execution.

- New join strategies   SQL Server 7.0 utilizes hash and merge join strategies, in addition to the nested-loop strategy found in previous versions. These new join strategies are designed to improve query performance.

- Improved data warehouse support   The query optimizer has been improved to work with data warehouse schemas such as the star and snowflake schema.

- Other query optimizer improvements   A query can reference up to 256 tables, whereas previous versions were limited to 16 tables. Additionally, the restriction that a query could not generate more than 16 internal work tables has been removed in version 7.0.

What's Gone

- SET SHOWPLAN   This command has been replaced with SET SHOWPLAN_TEXT and SET SHOWPLAN_ALL.

WHAT'S A QUERY OPTIMIZER?

A query optimizer is a process that generates the "optimal" execution path for a query. The optimal execution path is the path that offers the best performance. Before the query is run, the optimizer assigns a cost based on CPU and disk I/O usage for different execution paths. The optimizer then uses the least expensive execution path to process the query. See Figure 23.1 for examples of execution paths.

23

QUERY
OPTIMIZATION

FIGURE 23.1

Examples of execution paths.

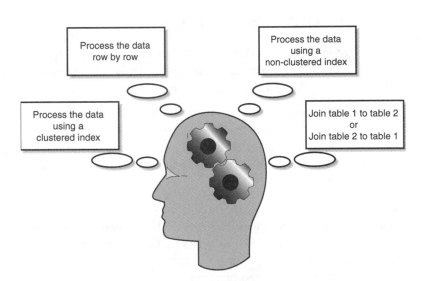

The advantage of the query optimizer is that it relieves users from the tedious process of having to decide how their SQL statements should be constructed to use indexes and in what order the data should be accessed. The query optimizer enables users to build SQL statements that *automatically* take advantage of indexes and *automatically* determine the optimal order to process table joins.

> **NOTE**
>
> SQL Server 7.0 uses an intelligent cost-based optimizer that has been significantly redesigned. In previous editions of this book I stated that a DBA "should not be misled by the word intelligent and that I have yet to meet a query optimizer that is more intelligent than a good DBA."
>
> The changes Microsoft has made to the query optimizer in SQL Server version 7.0 are causing me to eat some of my own words! The optimizer employees techniques such as automatic statistic gathering, enhanced execution strategies, and multi-index operations. These techniques reduce the amount of time spent tuning a query.
>
> However, I still feel that there is no way the query optimizer can ever understand all the nuances and intricacies of your query and your data. I recommend that you try to understand how the optimizer works and how you can finesse it into delivering better performance.

WHAT ARE STATISTICS?

Whenever you create an index, SQL Server creates a set of statistics about the data contained within the index. The query optimizer uses these statistics to determine whether it should use the index to help process the query.

SQL Server 7.0 automatically maintains statistic information. This is a great feature! Previous versions of SQL Server required that the UPDATE STATISTICS command be run on a frequent basis. In previous versions, if the UDPATE STATISTICS command was not frequently run, statistics could become stale. In turn, this would cause the optimizer to ignore useful indexes.

With version 7.0, the query optimizer automatically detects that statistics are out of date and automatically regenerates the statistics. This eliminates the problem with the optimizer ignoring useful indexes. As if this isn't amazing enough, statistic generation occurs almost instantly (on average 1 second)! This amazing feat is accomplished through a data-sampling algorithm.

By default, auto-update statistics is automatically turned on for all tables in version 7.0. Should you need to modify or view this setting use the `sp_autostats` system procedure. This command also displays when the statistics were last updated. The following is the syntax:

```
sp_autostats [@tblname =] 'table_name'
[, [@flagc =] 'stats_flag']
[, [@indname =] 'index_name']
```

Sample query:

```
sp_autostats authors
```

The following is sample output:

```
Global statistics settings for [pubs]:
  Automatic update statistics: ON
  Automatic create statistics: ON

Settings for table [authors]

Index Name                           AUTOSTATS Last Updated
------------------------------------ --------- ----------------------------
authors.UPKCL_auidind                ON        1998-10-29 23:26:09.497
authors.aunmind                      ON        1998-10-29 23:26:09.557
authors.WA_Sys_au_id_07020F21        ON        1998-10-29 23:26:36.573
authors.WA_Sys_au_lname_07020F21     ON        1998-10-29 23:26:36.593
authors.WA_Sys_au_fname_07020F21     ON        1998-10-29 23:26:36.593
authors.WA_Sys_phone_07020F21        ON        1998-10-29 23:26:36.603
authors.WA_Sys_address_07020F21      ON        1998-10-29 23:26:36.603
authors.WA_Sys_city_07020F21         ON        1998-10-29 23:26:36.603
authors.WA_Sys_state_07020F21        ON        1998-10-29 23:26:36.633
authors.WA_Sys_zip_07020F21          ON        1998-10-29 23:26:36.643
```

For those hardcore DBAs, use the `DBCC SHOW_STATISTICS` command to probe deep into the statistics gathered by SQL Server. The following is the syntax:

```
DBCC SHOW_STATISTICS (table_name,
 index_name or collection)
```

Sample query:

```
dbcc show_statistics(authors,aunmind)
```

The following is sample output:

```
Statistics for INDEX 'aunmind'.
Updated              Rows  Rows Sampled Steps  Density        Average key
length
-------------------- ----- ------------ ------ -------------- -------------
-----
Jun 29 1998 11:26PM  23    23           23     3.9697543E-2   22.173912
```

```
(1 row(s) affected)

All density              Columns
------------------------ -------------------
4.5454547E-2             au_lname
4.3478262E-2             au_lname, au_fname

(2 row(s) affected)

Steps
----------------------------------------
Bennet
Blotchet-Halls
Carson
DeFrance
del Castillo
Dull
Green
Greene
Gringlesby
Hunter
Karsen
Locksley
MacFeather
McBadden
O'Leary
Panteley
Ringer
Ringer
Smith
Straight
Stringer
White
Yokomoto

(23 row(s) affected)
```

BASIC QUERY OPTIMIZATION SUGGESTIONS

The following list of suggestions concentrates on the basics of query optimization. It is best to start with the basics when trying to improve query performance. Quite often, a minor modification to a query yields a substantial gain in performance.

- **Target queries that run slowly and frequently.** By simply adding an index, you can often see a dramatic improvement in query performance.

- **Understand your data.** To use optimization tricks, you must understand your query and how it relates to your data. Otherwise, your lack of knowledge may hamper your ability to effectively rewrite a query.

- **Record statistics about the existing query.** Before you begin to optimize a query, record a showplan (see "The Showplan Tool," later in this chapter, for more information) and I/O statistics. This provides you with a benchmark against which you can measure the success of your revisions.

- **Start with the basics.** Look for the obvious when you start to optimize a query. Do useful indexes exist? Are triggers being executed when the query is run? Does the query reference a view? Does the query use nonsearch arguments?

- **Understand the output from a showplan.** It is important to understand what is relevant and what is not when evaluating a showplan.

- **Throw conventional wisdom out the window.** Sometimes, you have to break the rules to optimize a query. Your ability to extract maximum query performance is a mix between art and science. What works on one query may not work on another query. Therefore, you occasionally have to go against conventional wisdom to maximize performance.

TOOLS TO HELP OPTIMIZE A QUERY

The following tools can be used to help optimize a query:

- Index Tuning Wizard
- SQL Server Profiler
- Showplan
- Statistics I/O
- Stats Time tool

Index Tuning Wizard

The Index Tuning Wizard analyzes a query and makes index recommendations. (See Chapter 22, "Understanding Indexes," for more information.) It's like having a DBA on your staff that never sleeps and never asks for a raise!

New and experienced DBAs should look at the Index Tuning Wizard. Overall, the Index Tuning Wizard does a good job of recommending indexes. However, the wizard should be used as a starting point for query optimization and not the ending point. The wizard is not always 100 percent correct. For example, it will occasionally make a mistake by not recommending an index or by recommending a sub-optimal index.

To use the Index Tuning Wizard, enter a Transact-SQL statement in the Query dialog box. From the Query menu, select the Perform Index Analysis menu option. After the query is analyzed, the index recommendations are displayed in the Query Analyzer Index

Analysis dialog box (see Figure 23.2). Click the Accept button to apply the index. If the analyzer decided that additional indexes were not necessary, the `No indexes were recommended` message will appear in the Results portion of the SQL Server Query Analyzer dialog box.

FIGURE 23.2

Index recommen-dations.

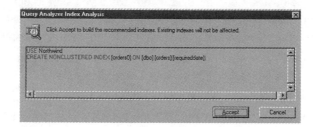

Consider the following query that is run from the NORTHWINDS database:

```
select *
from orders
where RequiredDate = '05/18/1998'
```

If you look at the showplan and statistic I/O before using the Index Tuning Wizard, you can establish a benchmark to see if the recommendation by the Index Tuning Wizard is correct.

SHOWPLAN output:

```
StmtText
- - - - - - - - - - - - - - - - - - - - - - - - - - - - - - - - - - - - - - - - - - - - - - - - - - - - - - - - - - - - - -
  ¦--Clustered Index Scan
     (OBJECT:([Northwind].[dbo].[Orders].[PK_Orders]),
      WHERE:([Orders].[RequiredDate]=May 18 1998 12:00AM))
```

STATISTICS I/O output:

```
Table 'Orders'. Scan count 1, logical reads 22,
  physical reads 0, read-ahead reads 0.
```

The following is the index recommended and implemented by the Index Tuning Wizard:

```
USE Northwind
CREATE NONCLUSTERED INDEX [orders0]
  ON [dbo].[orders]([requireddate])
```

Next, look at the showplan and statistic I/O after using the Index Tuning Wizard. The following is the revised SHOWPLAN output after implementing the index recommendation:

```
StmtText
- - - - - - - - - - - - - - - - - - - - - - - - - - - - - - - - - - - - - - - - - - - - - - - - - - - - - - - - - - - - - - - - -
```

```
¦--Bookmark Lookup(BOOKMARK:([Bmk1000]),
    OBJECT:([Northwind].[dbo].[Orders]))
    ¦--Index Seek(OBJECT:([Northwind].[dbo].[Orders].[orders0]),
        SEEK:([Orders].[RequiredDate]=May 18 1998 12:00AM) ORDERED)
```

Revised STATISTICS I/O output:

```
Table 'Orders'. Scan count 1, logical reads 8,
  physical reads 2, read-ahead reads 0.
```

If you compare the SHOWPLAN output, you will notice that the query optimizer has utilized the new index that was created by the Index Tuning Wizard. If you compare the SHOWPLAN I/O output, you will notice that the number of logical reads (the number of pages read from the data cache) dropped significantly. It went from 23 logical reads to 8 logical reads. If the orders table had thousands of records, you would have noticed a huge decrease in the time required to run the query. As you can see, the Index Tuning Wizard is pretty darn smart!

> **TIP**
>
> I recommend running the Index Tuning Wizard several times against the same query until the No indexes were suggested message appears. This is especially important when optimizing a query that contains multiple tables. Failure to do so may cause the wizard to skip tables, and thus be unable to recommend other useful indexes.

23

QUERY
OPTIMIZATION

> **NOTE**
>
> When a new index is added to a table, there is additional overhead required to process data modification queries because the index page must be updated in addition to the data page. This will increase index page I/O. I recommend performing a balancing act when adding indexes. In an environment where transaction throughput is important (especially INSERT operations), I advise against an index-everything strategy. In a data-warehouse environment, where the majority of activity is SELECT type of operations, increasing the number of indexes on a table probably doesn't hurt anything.

SQL Server Profiler

The SQL Server Profiler is a great tool for finding slow running queries and bottlenecks. (See Chapter 19, "Monitoring SQL Server," for more information on SQL Server

Profiler.) For example, you can run a trace that captures all SQL Server query activity. This information can be loaded into the Index Tuning Wizard. The Index Tuning Wizard can analyze the trace information and suggest the appropriate indexes.

The following is a detailed example of using SQL Server Profiler in conjunction with the Index Tuning Wizard.

Perform the following steps to create sample data:

1. Start the Query Analyzer by double clicking the Query Analyzer icon in the Microsoft SQL Server program group. The Connect to SQL Server dialog box appears.

2. From the Connect to SQL Server dialog box enter the necessary connection information and click the OK button to connect to SQL Server. The SQL Server Query Analyzer dialog box appears.

3. From the SQL Server Query Analyzer dialog box enter the following syntax (see Figure 23.3). This syntax creates a table and populates it with data from the mas-ter..sysmessages table. Note: the INSERT statement in this example is executed four times; this was necessary to create a large recordset to work with.

```
use pubs
go
create table sample_table
(error int not null,
severity smallint not null,
dlevel smallint not null)
go
declare @nLoopCounter int
select @nLoopCounter = 1
while @nLoopCounter <=4
 begin
  insert into sample_table
   select error, severity,dlevel
   from master..sysmessages
  select @nLoopCounter = @nLoopCounter + 1
 end
go
```

4. Execute the previous statement.

Perform the following steps to start the trace:

1. Start the SQL Server Profiler by double-clicking the Profiler icon in the Microsoft SQL Server program group. The SQL Server Profiler dialog box appears.

2. From the File menu, select the New menu option. From the New menu option, select the Trace menu option. The Trace Properties dialog box appears.

FIGURE 23.3

Sample data.

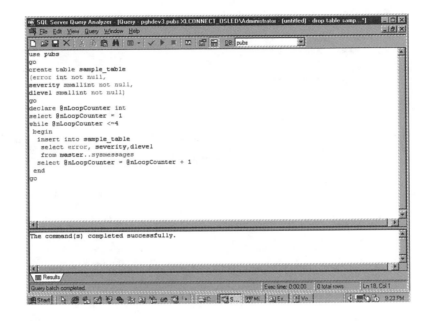

3. At the Trace Properties dialog box, enter the following information: trace name, trace type, server name, and capture settings (see Figure 23.4). For this example, the output is captured to a file.

4. Click the OK button to begin the trace.

FIGURE 23.4

Trace properties.

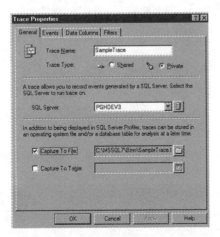

Perform the following steps to create sample trace data:

1. Switch back to the SQL Server Query Analyzer.

2. From the SQL Server Query Analyzer dialog box enter the following query (see Figure 23.5).

```
select *
from sample_table
where error = 102
```

3. Execute the previous statement.

FIGURE 23.5

Sample query.

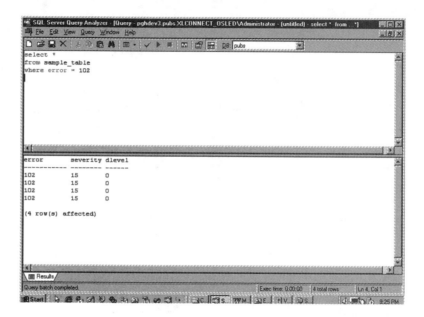

Perform the following steps to stop the trace:

1. Switch back to the SQL Server Profiler.

2. From the File menu, select the Stop Traces menu option. The Stop Selected Traces dialog box appears. Click the OK button to stop the trace.

Perform the following steps to run the Index Tuning Wizard:

1. From the Tools menu of the SQL Server Profiler, select the Index Tuning Wizard menu option. The Index Tuning Wizard dialog box appears (see Figure 23.6). Click the Next button to continue. The Select Server and Database screen appears.

2. From the Select Server and Database screen of the Index Tuning Wizard, enter the following information: server, database, and the optimization type (see Figure 23.7). Click the Next button to continue. The Identify Workload screen appears.

FIGURE 23.6

Index Tuning Wizard.

FIGURE 23.7

Select Server and Database screen.

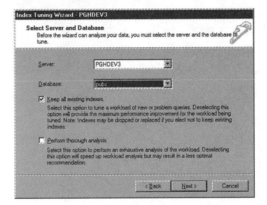

23

3. From the Identify Workload screen of the Index Tuning Wizard, select the workload type. For this example, select the I have a saved workload file radio button (see Figure 23.8). Click the Next button to continue. The Specify Workload screen appears.

4. From the Specify Workload screen of the Index Tuning Wizard, select the Workload source. For this example, select the My Workload file radio button and specify the workload source (see Figure 23.9). Click the Next button to continue. The Select Tables to Tune screen appears.

FIGURE 23.8

Identify Workload screen.

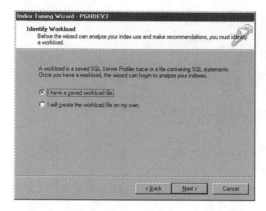

FIGURE 23.9

Specify Workload screen.

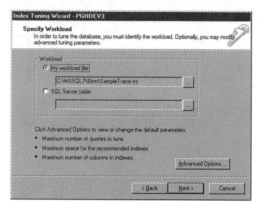

5. From the Select Tables to Tune screen of the Index Tuning Wizard, select the Tables to tune. For this example, you can leave use the default option of tuning all tables (see Figure 23.10). Click the Next button to continue. The Index Recommendations screen appears.

FIGURE 23.10

Select Tables screen.

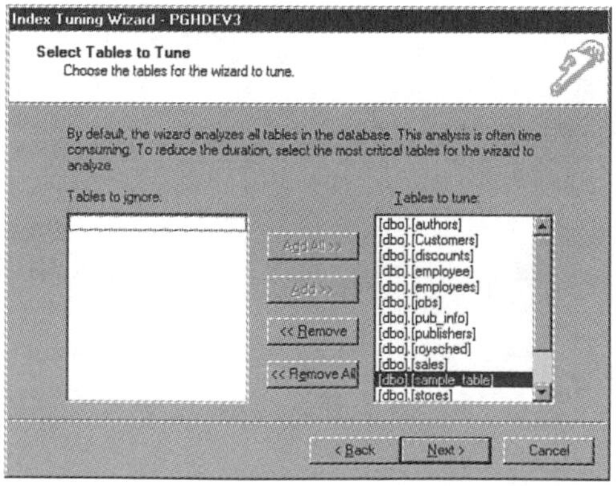

6. From the Index Recommendations screen of the Index Tuning Wizard, you can approve or reject the index suggestions (see Figure 23.11). Click the Next button to continue. The Schedule Index Update Job screen appears.

FIGURE 23.11

Index recommen-dations.

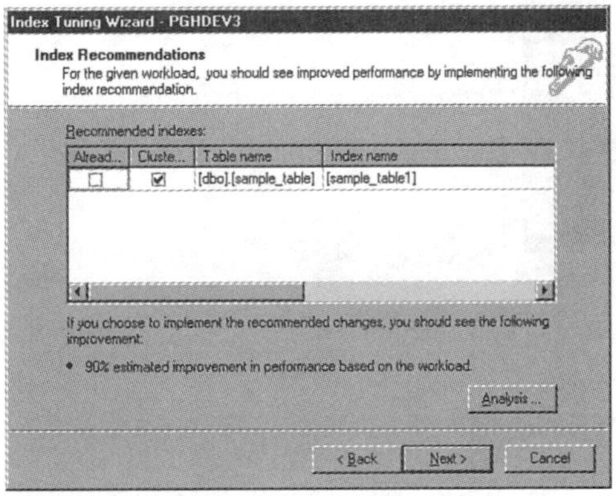

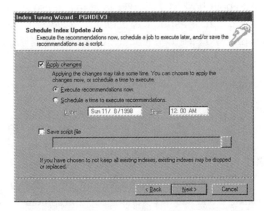

7. From the Schedule Index Update Job screen of the Index Tuning Wizard, select the appropriate method to implement the indexes. For this example, the Execute recommendations now option is selected (see Figure 23.12). This option tells the wizard to immediately create the recommended indexes. Click the Next button to continue. The Completing the Index Tuning Wizard screen appears.

FIGURE 23.12

Schedule Index Update Job screen.

8. From the Completing the Index Tuning Wizard screen of the Index Tuning Wizard, click the Finish button to implement the recommendations (see Figure 23.13). After the wizard implements the indexes, a message box appears notifying you that the indexes have been successfully implemented.

FIGURE 23.13

Completing the Index Tuning Wizard screen.

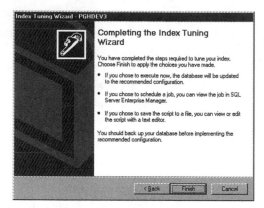

Showplan

A *showplan* provides insight about how SQL Server is going to process a SQL statement. Although version 7.0's showplan information has been made easier to understand, its output is still somewhat cryptic and based on technical jargon. Yet, if you know how to interpret its cryptic output, it can be useful for tuning queries.

The following are the different types of showplans.

- Graphical Showplan
- Text-Based Showplan

Graphical Showplan

The graphical showplan is back! Version 6.5 did not have a graphical showplan component, whereas versions 6.0 and 4.2 did. Version 7.0's graphical showplan sports a completely new interface that is simpler to read.

To generate a graphical showplan, open the Query Analyzer. Enter a Transact-SQL statement in the Query dialog box. From the Query menu, select the Display Estimated Execution Plan menu option.

The graphical showplan appears in the SQL Execution Plan portion of the Query dialog box (see Figure 23.14).

FIGURE 23.14

Graphical show-plan.

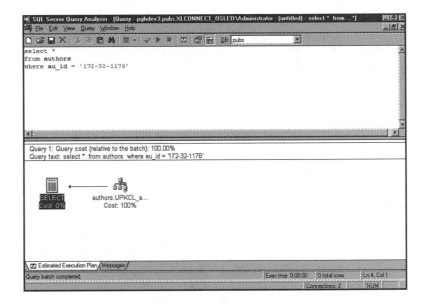

> **TIP**
>
> The graphical showplan window has several great right-mouse click features. For example, right-click a showplan icon and you can manage indexes, create/update statistics, and create missing statistics. Right-click the background of the graphical showplan window and you can adjust the zoom factor.

Text-Based Showplan

An alternative to the graphical showplan is the text-based showplan. The text-based showplan is useful if you need to email someone the query plan or if you prefer to work in a text based environment.

There are two types of text-based showplans: SET SHOWPLAN_TEXT and SET SHOWPLAN_ALL. SET SHOWPLAN_ALL is the more detailed version. To execute a text-based showplan, enter SET SHOWPLAN_TEXT or SET SHOWPLAN_ALL in a query window and execute a query.

The following is the syntax for text-based showplans:

```
SET SHOWPLAN_TEXT {ON | OFF}
SET SHOWPLAN_ALL {ON | OFF}
```

The following is an example of SET SHOWPLAN_TEXT:

Sample query:

```
SET SHOWPLAN_TEXT ON
go
select * from authors
where au_id = '267-41-2394'
go
```

Sample Output:

```
StmtText
- - - - - - - - - - - - - - - - - - - - - - - - - - - - - - - - - - - - - - - - - - - - - - - - - -
select * from authors
where au_id = '267-41-2394'

(1 row(s) affected)

StmtText
- - - - - - - - - - - - - - - - - - - - - - - - - - - - - - - - - - - - - - - - - - - - - - - - - - - -
  ¦--Clustered Index Seek
    (OBJECT:([pubs].[dbo].[authors].[UPKCL_auidind]),
      SEEK:([authors].[au_id]=[@1]) ORDERED)
```

Statistics I/O

Statistics I/O is useful in determining the amount of I/O that will occur to process a query. The less I/O you have, the faster your query will run. When tuning queries, try to minimize the amount of I/O used by the query. SQL Server uses I/O statistics to help determine the optimal query execution path.

Statistics I/O provides four types of I/O measurements: *scan count*, *logical reads*, *physical reads*, and *read-ahead reads*. The following list explains the four types of I/O measurements:

- *scan count* is the number of scans required to process the query.
- *logical reads* is the number of pages accessed in cache to process the query.
- *physical reads* is the number of pages accessed from disk to process the query.
- *read-ahead reads* is the number of pages loaded into cache to process the query.

> **NOTE**
>
> Each time a query is run, the data used to process the query may become loaded into the data cache. This can reduce the number of physical reads required to process the query when it is run again. You can detect whether the

data is loaded into the data cache by monitoring the logical reads and physical reads for a query. If physical reads is less than logical reads, some or all of the data was in the data cache.

To generate statistics I/O, enter a Transact-SQL statement in the Query dialog box. From the Query menu, select the Current Connection Options menu option. Select the Show stats I/O option from the Query Flags page of the Query Options dialog box (see Figure 23.15).

FIGURE 23.15
Setting the Show Stats I/O query option.

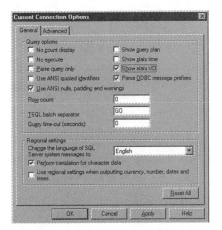

After you execute your query, the output from the statistics I/O appears in the results window (see Figure 23.16).

NOTE

We gained the graphical showplan in 7.0, but we lost the graphical statistics I/O feature! Previous versions displayed in nice graph form with statistics I/O information. Hey Microsoft, maybe we could have the graphical statistics I/O feature back in version 8.0?

FIGURE 23.16

Statistics I/O.

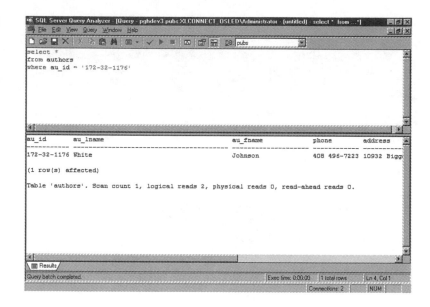

Stats Time Tool

The Stats Time tool displays the time required by SQL Server to parse, compile, and execute a query.

To use the Stats Time option, enter a Transact-SQL statement in the Query dialog box. From the Query menu, select the Current Connection Options menu option. Select the Show stats time option from the Query Flags page of the Query Option dialog box (see Figure 23.17).

FIGURE 23.17

Setting the Show Stats Time query option.

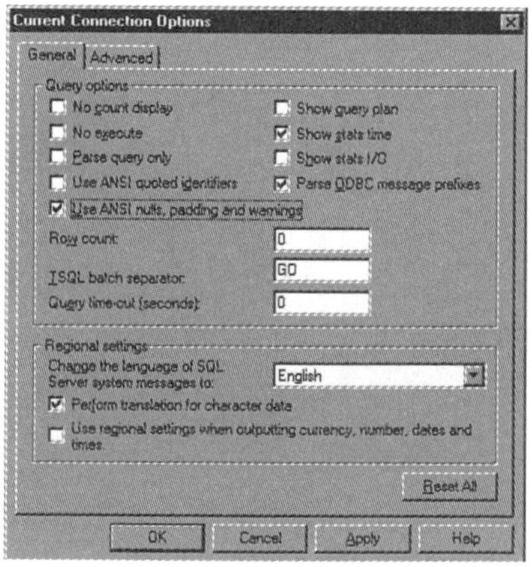

> **TIP**
>
> You may see a performance improvement when moving queries that contain lengthy parse and compile times to stored procedures. This is due to stored procedure being precompiled.

READING SHOWPLANS

The showplan provides insight about how SQL Server is going to process a SQL statement. If you know what to look for in a showplan, the information it provides can be useful for tuning queries.

Those new to SQL Server should not be dismayed by the jargon used in the showplan. For example, the showplan uses words such as STREAM AGGREGATE. This is just a fancy way of saying that the query contains an aggregate function, such as AVG(), COUNT(), MAX(), MIN(), or SUM(). After you get past the lingo used by the showplan, you will find it a useful tool for optimizing queries.

Instead of looking at every possible output from the showplan, look for table scans in the showplan on tables that contain a large number of records (note: it is okay to have a table scan on a table that contains a small number of records). Generally, a query containing a WHERE clause and generating a table scan is a good query to optimize. The table scan is probably slowing down your query because each row in the table is processed, which can lead to unnecessary I/O. To avoid a table scan, try to build a useful index that matches the WHERE clause.

The following example shows the difference in showplans for a retrieval based on a table scan and a retrieval that uses an index. The first listing shows the showplan for a table without an index:

```
Table:
CREATE TABLE sales
          (sales_id int not null,
          descr char(50) null)
Primary Key: sales_id (for this example assume
               that the primary key has not been created)
Indexes: None
Row Count: 1,000,000
Query:
SELECT * FROM sales
          WHERE sales_id = 450
Showplan:
  |--Table Scan(customer..sales, WHERE:(sales.sales_id=[@1]))
```

Now consider the inefficiencies involved with a table scan. The user wants only one row returned from the table, but the server had to process *every row* in the table (see Figure 23.18).

FIGURE 23.18

A table scan on a 1,000,000-row table.

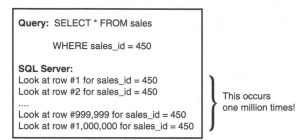

Query: SELECT * FROM sales

　　　　WHERE sales_id = 450

SQL Server:
Look at row #1 for sales_id = 450
Look at row #2 for sales_id = 450
....
Look at row #999,999 for sales_id = 450
Look at row #1,000,000 for sales_id = 450

This occurs
one million times!

To prevent the table scan in this example, create a clustered index on the column sales_id. By creating the index, the optimizer can generate a showplan that directly accesses the data without having to look at each row of data (see Figure 23.19). This will significantly improve performance. The following is the showplan with the clustered index.

```
Index:
CREATE UNIQUE CLUSTERED INDEX sales_cdx ON sales(sales_id)
Showplan:
  ¦--Clustered Index Seek(customer..sales.sales_cdx,
      SEEK:(sales.sales_id=[@1]) ORDERED)
```

FIGURE 23.19

Using a clustered index to find data on a 1,000,000-row table.

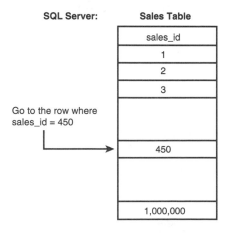

Query: SELECT * FROM sales

　　　　WHERE sales_id = 450

SQL Server:　　　**Sales Table**

sales_id
1
2
3
450
1,000,000

Go to the row where
sales_id = 450

A DISCUSSION ABOUT COMPOSITE INDEXES

A composite index is an index made up of more than one column. The rules regarding composite index optimization sometimes cause confusion. The source of the confusion stems from when SQL Server can take advantage of the index and when it cannot use the index.

Following is the structure of a table that is used for this discussion:

```
/* Table */
CREATE TABLE table1
        (col1 int not null,
         col2 int not null,
         col3 int not null,
         description char(50) null)
/* Implementation of the index */
create index col1_col2_col3_idx
  on table1(col1,col2,col3)
Number of rows:
1000
```

When working with a large table, the optimizer takes advantage of the composite index when one of the following is true:

- All columns in the index are referenced in the WHERE clause and contain useful search arguments.

- The first column in the index is referenced in the WHERE clause with a useful search argument.

For example, the following queries can take advantage of the composite index:

```
SELECT *
        FROM table1
        WHERE col1 = 100
        and col2 = 250
        and col3 = 179

SELECT *
        FROM table1
        WHERE col1 = 100
        and col2 = 250

SELECT *
        FROM table1
        WHERE col1 = 100

SELECT *
        FROM table1
        WHERE col1 = 100
        and col3 = 250
```

continues

The following queries cannot take advantage of the composite index:

```
SELECT *
        FROM table1
        WHERE col2 = 100
        and col3 = 250
SELECT *
        FROM table1
        WHERE col2 = 100
SELECT *
        FROM table1
        WHERE col3 = 100
```

OVERRIDING THE OPTIMIZER

Use the following features to override the optimizer:

- Index hints
- The `SET FORCEPLAN ON` command

Index Hints

By using an index hint, you can force the optimizer to use an index or force it to not choose an index. You usually want to let the optimizer determine how to process the query. However, you may find it beneficial to override the optimizer if you find that it is not taking advantage of useful indexes. Following is the syntax used to override the optimizer:

```
SELECT ...
FROM [table_name] (optimizer_hint)
```

In this syntax, *optimizer_hint* has the following format:

```
(INDEX(index_name|index_id}))
```

In this format, *index_name* is any valid name of an existing index on the table and *index_id* is the corresponding index id.

The following is an example of forcing the optimizer to use a particular index:

```
select * from customer (INDEX(customer_last_idx))
where last_name like 'jacks%'
order by last_name
```

> **TIP**
>
> I recommend using index hints with prudence. Only in cases where SQL Server is choosing a less-than-optimal execution plan should the optimizer be overridden.
>
> For example, sometimes queries that contain wildcards generate table scans. When testing version 7.0, I discovered that the following query was running slowly on my sample database, which has over 100,000 customer records.
>
> ```
> Sample query:
> select * from customer
> where last_name like 'jacks%'
> order by last_name
> ```
>
> I was surprised to see that a table scan was generated because the following index existed:
>
> ```
> create index customer_last_idx on customer(last_name)
> ```
>
> I added an index hint and the query ran significantly faster. The following is the query with the index hint:
>
> ```
> select * from customer (INDEX(customer_last_idx))
> where last_name like 'jacks%'
> order by last_name
> ```
>
> The previous index hint reduced the number of logical scans by 300 percent, which shows that even the query optimizer can occasionally make mistakes!

The SET FORCEPLAN ON Command

The SET FORCEPLAN ON command forces the optimizer to join tables based on the order specified in the FROM clause. Normally, you want to let the optimizer determine the order in which to join tables; however, if you think that the optimizer is selecting an inefficient join order, you can use SET FORCEPLAN ON to force the join order.

When forcing SQL Server to use a predefined join order, you usually want the table with the fewest number of qualifying rows to come first in the FROM clause (or the table with the least amount of I/O, if you are dealing with a very wide or a very narrow table). The table with the second lowest number of qualifying rows should be next in the FROM clause, and so on.

> **CAUTION**
>
> Use the SET FORCEPLAN ON option as a last resort. You usually want to let the optimizer determine the order in which to process tables.

The following example shows how SET FORCEPLAN ON can impact query optimization:

```
SET FORCEPLAN ON
select *
from  titleauthor , authors
where titleauthor.au_id = authors.au_id
SET FORCEPLAN OFF
```

The following is showplan output with SET FORCEPLAN ON:

```
¦--Nested Loops(Inner Join)
     ¦--Clustered Index Scan
         (OBJECT:([pubs].[dbo].[titleauthor].[UPKCL_taind]))
     ¦--Clustered Index Seek
         (OBJECT:([pubs].[dbo].[authors].[UPKCL_auidind]),
             SEEK:([authors].[au_id]=[titleauthor].[au_id]) ORDERED)
```

Notice that, with SET FORCEPLAN ON, the optimizer processes the titleauthor table before processing the authors table.

If FORCEPLAN is not utilized, the query optimizer generates the following syntax:

```
¦--Nested Loops(Inner Join)
     ¦--Clustered Index Scan
         (OBJECT:([pubs].[dbo].[authors].[UPKCL_auidind]))
     ¦--Clustered Index Seek
         (OBJECT:([pubs].[dbo].[titleauthor].[UPKCL_taind]),
             SEEK:([titleauthor].[au_id]=[authors].[au_id]) ORDERED)
```

TIP

Whenever you use SET FORCEPLAN ON, be sure that you turn it off by issuing SET FORCEPLAN OFF. The feature remains in effect for your current connection until the connection is broken or until it is explicitly turned off.

OTHER TUNING TRICKS

Whenever you try to optimize a query, you should be on the lookout for obstructions that can lead to poor performance. The following sections discuss common causes of poor query performance.

Are You Trying to Tune an UPDATE, DELETE, or INSERT Query?

If you are trying to tune an UPDATE, DELETE, or INSERT query, does the table have a trigger? The query may be okay, but the trigger may need improvement. An easy way to determine whether the trigger is the bottleneck is to drop the trigger and rerun the query.

If query performance improves, you should tune the trigger.

Does the Query Reference a View?

If the query references a view, you should test the view to determine whether it is optimized. An easy way to test whether the view is optimized is to run a showplan on the view.

Are the Datatypes Mismatched?

If you are joining on columns of different datatypes, the optimizer may not be able to use useful indexes. Instead, it may have to choose a table scan to process the query, as in the following example:

```
Table:
CREATE TABLE table1
(col1 char(10) not null)
Index: CREATE INDEX col1_idx ON table1(col1)
Row Count: 1000
Table:
CREATE TABLE table2
(col1 integer not null)
Index: CREATE INDEX col1_idx ON table2(col1)
Row Count: 1000
Query:
SELECT *
FROM table1, table2
WHERE table1.col1 = convert(char(10),table2.col1)
and table1.col1 = '100'
```

This query results in a table scan on `table2` because you are joining a `char(10)` column to an `integer` column with the `convert()` function. Internally, SQL Server must convert these values to process the query, which results in a table scan. To avoid this problem, maintain consistency within your database design.

Does the Query Use a Nonsearch Argument?

Nonsearch arguments force the optimizer to process the query with a table scan. This is because the search value is unknown until runtime.

Following are some common examples of queries that use nonsearch arguments and how to convert them to search arguments that can take advantage of an index:

```
Table:
CREATE TABLE table1
(col1 int not null)
Index: CREATE UNIQUE CLUSTERED INDEX col1_idx ON table1(col1)
Row Count: 1000 rows
```

Following is a nonsearch argument query:

```
select *
from table1
where col1 * 10 = 100
```

Following is a search argument query:

```
select *
from table1
where col1 = 100/10
```

Following is a nonsearch argument query:

```
select *
from table1
where convert(char(8),col1) =  '10'
```

Following is a search argument query:

```
select *
from table1
where col1 =  convert(int,'10')
```

TIP

One way to help reduce the use of a nonsearch argument is to keep the table column on the left side of the equation and to keep the search criteria on the right side of the equation.

QUERY OPTIMIZATION FAQ

Following are some of the common questions asked by DBAs about SQL Server Query Optimization:

Q. Does UPDATE STATISTICS need to be run on a frequent basis?

A. Starting with version 7.0, UPDATE STATISTICS does not need to be run on a frequent basis because the query optimizer automatically notices that statistics are out of date and automatically rebuilds the statistics. This is significantly different from previous versions that required that the UPDATE STATISTICS command run on a frequent basis. In version 7.0, it does not hurt anything to run UPDATE STATISTICS but you may not gain anything. In certain rare occurrences, you may need to run UPDATE STATISTICS if you feel that you are getting a poor query optimization plan or if the data is changing rapidly and you need up-to-the minute statistics.

Q. Is automatic updating of statistics always enabled in 7.0?

A. By default, automatic updating of statistics is always enabled regardless of the database backward compatibility setting (6.0, 6.5, and 7.0). If you need to turn off automatic updating of statistics, use the sp_autostats system procedure.

Q. How can I tell when SQL Server last updated an index's statistics?

A. Use the sp_autostats system procedure. This procedure will tell you the time of the last update and the automatic update setting.

Q. Does a query have to be coded a certain way for it to run in parallel on multiple processors?

A. SQL Server automatically decides when a query will run in parallel. This is unlike other database products that require special tuning and syntax to make a query run in parallel. The only requirement for a parallel query is that the machine must have multiple processors. Queries cannot run in parallel on single processor machines.

SUMMARY

Following are some important notes to remember when working with the query optimizer:

- SQL Server 7.0's query optimizer has been significantly improved from previous versions. New optimization techniques result in faster query response times.

- Query optimization is part science, part luck. What works on one query might not work on another query. Try different techniques until you get the performance you expect.

- Use the Index Tuning Wizard, Showplan, Statistics I/O, Stats Time, and SQL Profiler tools to help tune a query.

- If you want to maximize OLTP performance, do everything you can to prevent a table scan on a large table.

A good DBA knows how the SQL Server optimizer works. This knowledge enables the DBA to turn an agonizingly slow query into a fast query. Consequently, knowledge of the optimizer can keep the DBA from creating needless indexes that are never used by the system. The next chapter discusses multiuser considerations.

23

QUERY
OPTIMIZATION

MULTI-USER CONSIDERATIONS

by Orryn Sledge

IN THIS CHAPTER

How many times have you seen an application that works with a single user but when multiple users access the application, all sorts of performance and data problems occur? When these types of problems arise, it usually is up to the DBA to fix them. You have probably heard that SQL Server is a high-performance database capable of handling 100 or more users. That is a true statement. But to extract maximum performance and data consistency in a multi-user environment, you must understand how SQL Server manages transactions. Otherwise, performance and data consistency will suffer. To help you avoid these problems, the topics discussed in this chapter explain how to design multi-user databases that maximize transaction throughput while maintaining data consistency.

SQL SERVER 6.5 TO 7.0 QUICK REFERENCE

The following is a quick reference to the changes that occurred between SQL Server versions 6.5 and 7.0.

What's New

- Row-level locking: SQL Server 7.0 finally has row-level locking! Actually, SQL Server has row, page, and table locking. The lock manager decides the type of lock to utilize and will automatically escalate and de-escalate locks on an as-needed basis. This type of lock management is designed to improve multi-user access. Row-level locking applies to data pages and index pages. Previous versions of SQL Server only had page-level locking.

- Explicit locking enhancements: The following explicit locking options are available for SELECT, UPDATE, DELETE, and INSERT statements: HOLDLOCK, NOLOCK, PAGLOCK, READCOMMITTED, READPAST, READUNCOMMITTED, REPEATABLEREAD, ROWLOCK, SERIALIZABLE, TABLOCK, TABLOCKX, UPDLOCK. In the previous version of SQL Server, only the SELECT statement supported a subset of the explicit locking options listed above.

- REPEATABLE READ isolation level: Starting with version 7.0, the REPEATABLE READ isolation level is different from the SERIALIZABLE isolation level. In SQL Server 6.x, the REPEATABLE READ isolation level was the same as the SERIALIZABLE isolation level.

> **CAUTION**
>
> If you are migrating a database from 6.5 to 7.0, keep in mind that the REPEATABLE READ isolation level does not protect against phantom values, whereas in 6.5 it did protect against phantom values.

- `sp_indexoption`: This is a new system procedure that can control the granularity of index locking.

- `sp_blockcnt`: This is a new system procedure that returns a count of blocked users.

- User definable lock time-out setting: the `SET LOCK_TIMEOUT` statement can be used to specify (in milliseconds) how long a blocked process will wait before timing out. The default setting is no time-out. The global variable `@@lock_timeout` displays the current lock time-out setting.

What's Replaced

- Automatic management of configuration options: SQL Server 7.0 automatically manages the following configuration options:

  - User connections

  - Locks

  - Open objects

  Previous versions of SQL Server required DBAs to manually configure these options. No longer will you receive error messages that tell you, for example, that the maximum number of connections has been exceeded or that SQL Server has run out of locks.

- The `syslocks` table has been replaced with the `syslockinfo` table. This table tracks locking information. Any scripts that reference `syslocks` must be re-written.

What's Gone

- Insert row-level locking (IRL): IRL was a very short-lived feature; version 6.5 introduced IRL and now it's gone in version 7.0! Version 7.0 incorporates row-level locking for all types of operations (`INSERT`, `DELETE`, `UPDATE`, `SELECT`); therefore IRL is no longer necessary.

- The following configuration options are removed from SQL Server 7.0:

  - LE threshold minimum

  - LE threshold maximum

  - LE threshold percent

LOCKS

SQL Server uses *locks* to maintain data consistency in a multi-user environment. SQL Server automatically handles locking behavior, and starting with SQL Server 7.0, locking automatically escalates and de-escalates on an as-needed basis.

To help understand why locks are important, look at the banking example shown in Figure 24.1. Suppose that you decide to transfer $100 from checking to savings. Your bank decides to run a report that shows your combined balance for checking and savings. What happens if the report is run while the transfer is in progress? Would the report show a balance of $200 or $100?

FIGURE 24.1

How locks maintain data consistency.

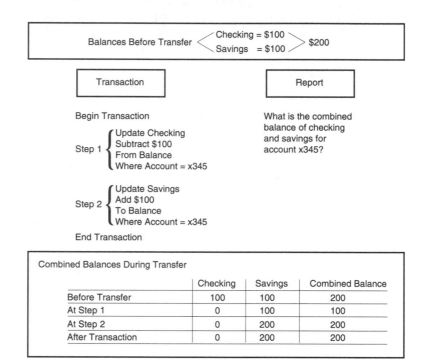

Balances Before Transfer
Checking = $100
Savings = $100
$200

Transaction	Report

Begin Transaction

What is the combined balance of checking and savings for account x345?

Step 1
Update Checking
Subtract $100
From Balance
Where Account = x345

Step 2
Update Savings
Add $100
To Balance
Where Account = x345

End Transaction

Combined Balances During Transfer

	Checking	Savings	Combined Balance
Before Transfer	100	100	200
At Step 1	0	100	100
At Step 2	0	200	200
After Transaction	0	200	200

Balances After Transfer
Checking = $0
Savings = $200
$200

The answer resides in how SQL Server uses locks to maintain data consistency. When the transaction is initiated, SQL Server places a lock on the checking account information and on the savings account information. These locks force other users to wait until the locks are released before they can access the data. This prevents users from reading incomplete or pending changes. Therefore, when the transaction is complete, the report is allowed to access the account data, thus reporting the correct balance of $200.

NOTE

When pending changes can be read by a transaction, it is known as a *dirty read*. SQL Server's default transaction isolation level prevents dirty reads.

Without locks, the report might have shown a balance of $100, which is incorrect. For example, if the report read the data after the $100 was subtracted from checking but before it was added to savings, the report would show a combined balance of $100.

Understanding SQL Server's Locking Behavior

If locks are automatically handled by SQL Server you may wonder, "Why are we having this discussion?" The answer is *blocking* and *deadlocks*. Whenever multiple users try to access or modify the same data, the potential for blocking and deadlocks increases.

By understanding SQL Server's locking behavior, you can decrease the likelihood of blocking and deadlocks.

Following are some of the variables that can impact the frequency of blocking and dead-locks:

- Transaction management
- Query implementation
- Number of records modified or read by a query
- Number of users concurrently accessing the data
- Indexing scheme
- Table design
- Hardware configuration

Blocking

Blocking occurs when a process must wait for another process to complete. The process must wait because the resources it needs are exclusively used by another process. A blocked process resumes operation after the other process releases the resources.

For this example, assume that the bank decides to eliminate the monthly service charge for all existing customers (see Figure 24.2). Therefore, the DBA sets the `service_charge` to $0.00 for all accounts. Not being a good DBA, he runs this transaction during prime hours. This forces transactions 2, 3, and 4 to wait until transaction 1 is complete. The waiting transactions are considered to be *blocked* by transaction 1.

When blocking occurs, it looks like your machine is hung. What has happened is that SQL Server has put your process in a holding queue. The process remains in the queue until it can acquire the resources it needs to complete its tasks.

FIGURE 24.2

A blocking example.

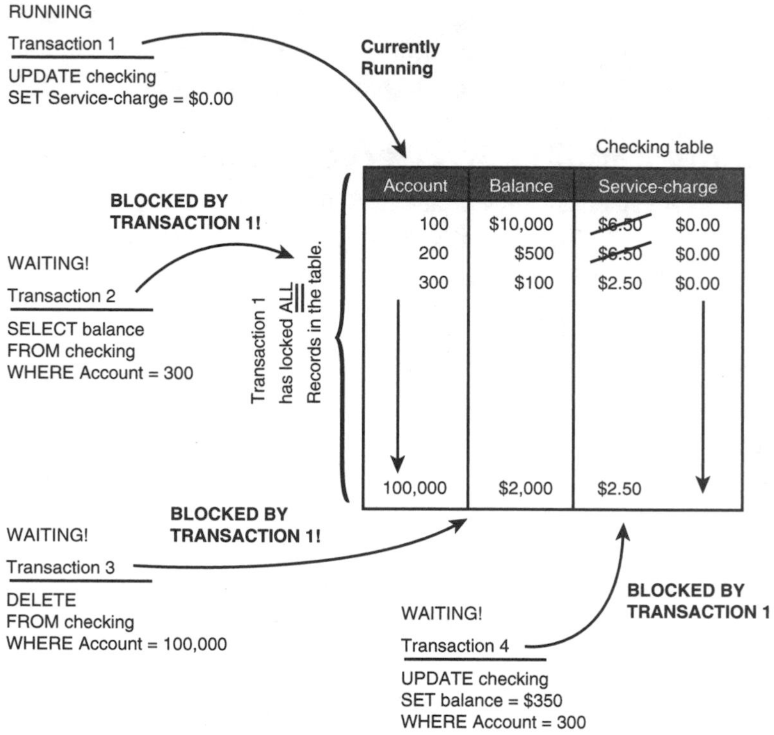

RUNNING

Transaction 1   **Currently Running**

UPDATE checking
SET Service-charge = $0.00

Checking table

Account	Balance	Service-charge	
100	$10,000	~~$6.50~~	$0.00
200	$500	~~$6.50~~	$0.00
300	$100	$2.50	$0.00
100,000	$2,000	$2.50	

BLOCKED BY TRANSACTION 1!

WAITING!

Transaction 2

SELECT balance
FROM checking
WHERE Account = 300

Transaction 1 has locked ALL Records in the table.

BLOCKED BY TRANSACTION 1!

WAITING!

Transaction 3

DELETE
FROM checking
WHERE Account = 100,000

WAITING!

Transaction 4

UPDATE checking
SET balance = $350
WHERE Account = 300

BLOCKED BY TRANSACTION 1

BLOCKING PROBLEMS

I once was thrown into a project that involved converting a mainframe application to SQL Server. Management was eager to convert the application quickly. They did not want any time spent on table design or index strategy. I tried to explain to them that their existing database design could lead to blocking.

The day that application went into production was a prime example of how blocking can impact a system. Whenever certain components of the application were run, the transaction-processing component of the application would halt because of blocking.

The reason the blocking was so severe was because of poor table design and index strategy. The main table used by the application was not properly normalized, thus making it very wide. Very wide tables can substantially slow processing throughput. Additionally, the table lacked any useful indexes. The combination of these factors is a sure-fire way to generate massive blocking.

After management realized what had happened, they were willing to allocate the resources to go back and redesign the table schema and reevaluate the index strategy. After the redesign, the blocking problem ceased, and the application could be used without impacting the transaction processing aspect of the application.

Deadlock

Deadlock occurs when two users have locks on separate objects and each user is trying to lock the other user's objects. SQL Server automatically detects and breaks the deadlock. It terminates the process that has used the least amount of CPU utilization. This enables the other user's transaction to continue processing. The terminated transaction is automatically rolled back and an error code 1205 is issued.

Figure 24.3 shows an example of a deadlock. Assume that transaction 1 and transaction 2 begin at the exact same time. By default, SQL Server automatically places exclusive locks on data that is being updated. This causes transaction 1 to wait for transaction 2 to complete—but transaction 2 has to wait for transaction 1 to complete. This is classic deadlock. To resolve the deadlock, SQL Server automatically terminates one of the transactions.

FIGURE 24.3

An example of deadlock.

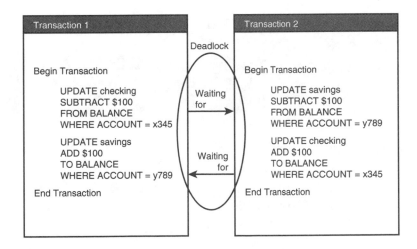

24

Physical Locks

Now that you know why it is important to understand SQL Server's locking behavior, we'll get into the nuts and bolts of locking.

Any transaction that reads or modifies data (SELECT, INSERT, DELETE, UPDATE, CREATE INDEX, and so on) generates some type of lock. The degree of locking is determined by the following two questions:

- Is the data being modified or read?
- How many rows are being accessed or modified?

To answer these questions, you must look at the three levels of physical locks: row, page, and table.

Row Lock

A *row-level lock* is a row of data on a data page or index page. Row-level locking is new in SQL Server 7.0. Previous versions of SQL Server were limited to page-level locking.

Figure 24.4 illustrates row-level locking. The advantage of row-level locking is that it increases data access. The disadvantage of row-level locking is that it increases overhead. Therefore, SQL Server automatically determines when to utilize row-level locking and when it is more efficient to escalate a lock to a page-level lock.

FIGURE 24.4

Row-level locking.

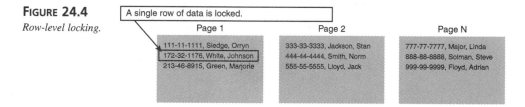

Page Lock

A *page lock* is a lock on an 8KB data page. Whenever feasible, SQL Server attempts to use a page lock rather than a table lock. Page locks are preferred over table locks because they are less likely to block other processes. Figure 24.5 illustrates page-level locking.

Table Lock

A *table lock* occurs when the entire table (data and indexes) is locked. When this happens, SQL Server has detected that it is faster to process the transaction by locking the table rather than incurring the overhead of locking numerous pages. Figure 24.6 illustrates table-level locking.

The drawback of table locking is that it increases the likelihood of blocking. When other transactions try to access or modify information in a locked table, they must wait for the table lock to be released before proceeding.

FIGURE 24.5
Page-level locking.

FIGURE 24.6
Table lock.

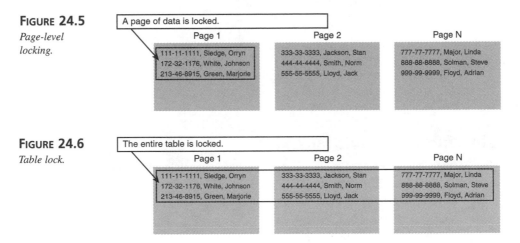

Lock Methods

In addition to managing physical locks, SQL Server's lock manager also manages lock methods. The following are the different lock methods used by SQL Server.

- **Shared.** A *shared* lock is used for read transactions (typically SELECT statements). If a row, page, or table is marked as shared, other transactions can still read the data. A shared lock must be released before an exclusive lock can be acquired. Shared locks are released after the data has been read.

- **Update.** When an UPDATE or DELETE statement is initially processed, SQL Server places update locks on the row, page, or table being read. It then escalates the update locks to exclusive locks before it modifies the data. Only one transaction at a time can receive an update lock. If other transactions are also requesting update locks, the lock manager will make the other transactions wait until the update lock is released.

- **Exclusive.** An *exclusive* lock is used for write transactions (typically INSERT, UPDATE, or DELETE statements). Other transactions must wait for the exclusive lock to be released before they can read or write information.

- **Intent.** An *intent* lock occurs when SQL Server has the intention of acquiring a shared or exclusive resource. SQL Server uses intent locks to keep other transactions from placing exclusive locks on the resource in which it is currently processing. Intent share, intent exclusive, and share with intent exclusive are the three types of intent locks.

- **Schema.** *Schema* locks come in two flavors—schema stability and schema modification. A schema stability lock occurs when SQL Server needs to prevent a table or index from being modified. A schema modification lock occurs when someone is actually modifying the table or index schema.

> **TIP**
>
> Typically, read statements acquire shared locks and data modification statements acquire exclusive locks.

Viewing Locks and Blocking

Now that you know something about locks and blocking, let's talk about how to view them in SQL Server. The following are the different methods used to view locks and blocking. Several of the methods provide overlapping functionality, so choose the method that you are most comfortable with.

- System Procedures
- SQL Server Enterprise Manager
- Performance Monitor
- SQL Server Profiler
- Trace Flags

System Procedures

The system procedures sp_lock and sp_who provide information about locks and blocking. The system procedure sp_lock displays the status of locks for all processes or the information about locks for a particular process.

The following is the syntax for sp_lock.

```
sp_lock [[@spid1 =] 'spid1'] [,[@spid2 =] 'spid2']
```

Use the SQL Server Query Analyzer to run the sp_lock system procedure. The following is sample output from sp_lock.

```
spid    dbid    ObjId          IndId   Type  Resource          Mode        Status
------  ------  -----------    ------  ----  ----------------  ---------   ------
1       1       0              0       DB                      S           GRANT
6       1       0              0       DB                      S           GRANT
7       5       0              0       DB                      S           GRANT
7       5       341576255      1       PAG   1:106             IX          GRANT
7       5       341576255      3       PAG   1:139             IX          GRANT
7       5       341576255      1       PAG   1:137             IX          GRANT
```

7	5	341576255	0	TAB		IX	GRANT
7	5	341576255	2	KEY	(d597a25250d8)	X	GRANT
7	5	341576255	1	KEY	(d597a25250d8)	X	GRANT
..							
8	5	0	0	DB		S	GRANT
8	5	341576255	1	PAG	1:106	IS	GRANT
8	5	341576255	0	TAB		IS	GRANT
8	5	341576255	1	KEY	(d9b61289d4f0)	S	WAIT
9	1	0	0	DB		S	GRANT
9	2	0	0	DB		S	GRANT
9	5	0	0	DB		S	GRANT
9	1	117575457	0	TAB		IS	GRANT

When running sp_lock, I usually look for a status = WAIT. If you see status = WAIT, this is bad in a transaction-oriented environment! This means that a process is waiting for another process to complete. Possible causes are long running queries that are not optimized and poor transaction management.

The system procedure sp_who displays information about users and their processes.

The following is the syntax for sp_who

```
sp_who [[@login_name =] 'login']
```

Use the SQL Server Query Analyzer to run the sp_who system procedure. The following is sample output from sp_who.

```
spid   status     loginame  hostname  blk  dbname cmd
------ ---------- --------- --------  ---  ------ ---
..
7      sleeping   sa        PGHDEV3   0    pubs   AWAITING COMMAND
8      sleeping   sa        PGHDEV3   7    pubs   SELECT
9      runnable   sa        PGHDEV3   0    pubs   DELETE
```

When running sp_who, I usually look at the blk column and the cmd column. If the blk column has a value > 0, it indicates that the process is blocked by the number represented in the blk column. The cmd column displays the command that the process is currently running.

> **NOTE**
>
> Use the DBCC INPUTBUFFER(*spid*) command to gather detail information about a process. For example, sp_who and sp_lock both display process IDs. The process ID returned by either system procedure can be used with DBCC INPUTBUFFER to return detail information about the process, such as the SQL command that is currently running.

NOTE

Two undocumented system procedures in version 7.0 can also be used to diagnose blocking and locking activity. Table 24.1 provides a brief summary of each procedure.

TABLE 24.1 UNDOCUMENTED SYSTEM PROCEDURES

System Procedure	Purpose	Notes
sp_who2	Useful for viewing process and blocking information.	Similar to sp_who, except that it is easier to read and it includes the following additional information: CPUTime, DiskIO, LastBatch, ProgramName.
sp_blockcnt	Returns a count of blocked users.	Useful for quickly determining whether blocking exists.

SQL Server Enterprise Manager

Follow these steps to view locks and blocking from the Enterprise Manager:

1. From the SQL Server Enterprise Manager, click the plus (+) sign next to the server.
2. Click the plus (+) sign next to the Management folder.
3. Click the plus (+) sign next to the Current Activity icon.
4. To view blocking, click the Locks/Process ID icon. The result pane contains a listing of current processes (see Figure 24.7). Processes containing a red exclamation mark indicate the source of the blocking. Processes containing a red square indicate a blocked process.
5. To lock, click the Locks/Object icon. The result pane contains a listing of objects with locks. Left-click an object to view lock information (see Figure 24.8).

FIGURE **24.7**
Locks/process ID information.

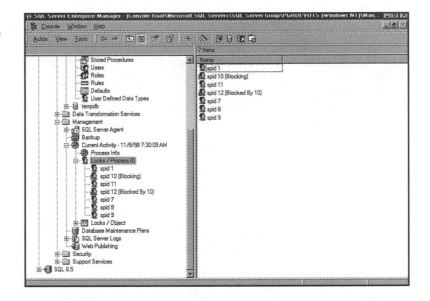

FIGURE **24.8**
Locks/object information.

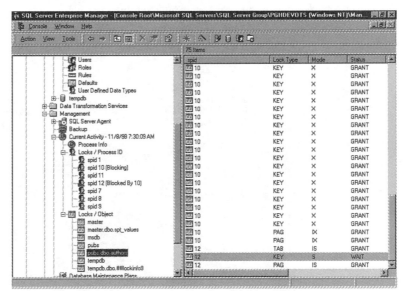

> **NOTE**
>
> I think it is easier to use the system procedures sp_who and sp_lock to diagnose blocking (see the "System Procedures" section for more information), instead of using the Enterprise Manager. This is because when severe blocking occurs, the Enterprise Manager can be slow to respond. Also, the output from the system procedures can be printed and saved to a text file.

Performance Monitor

The Performance Monitor can graphically track lock information. The SQL Server:Locks object and the SQL Server:Memory Manager are useful for graphically tracking locking. The Log feature of the Performance Monitor is useful for logging information over various time intervals. These time intervals can be analyzed for locking activity.

See Figures 24.9 and 24.10 for Performance Monitor Lock Counters, and see Figure 24.11 for a Performance Monitor lock graph sample.

FIGURE 24.9

Performance Monitor SQL Server:Locks object counters.

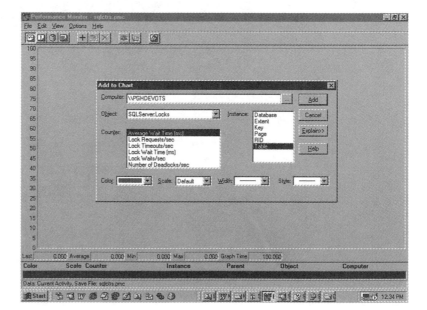

FIGURE 24.10

*Performance
Monitor SQL
Server:Memory
Manager object
counters.*

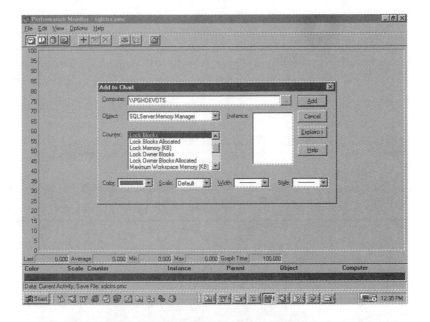

FIGURE 24.11

*Performance
Monitor lock
graph sample.*

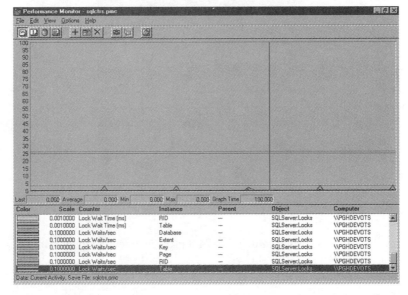

24

MULTI-USER
CONSIDERATIONS

SQL Server Profiler

The SQL Server Profiler can trace a variety of locking details. These details can be stored to a file or table for analysis. A feature of SQL Server Profiler is that the trace can be replayed. This is great for diagnosing and troubleshooting locking issues.

Table 24.2 lists the types of locking events that the SQL Server Profiler can trace.

TABLE 24.2   SQL SERVER LOCKING EVENTS

Event	Event Description
Lock:Deadlock	Tracks deadlocks and related process information.
Lock:Deadlock Chain	Tracks the events that lead to the deadlock.

See Figure 24.12 for SQL Server Profiler Lock events (see Chapter 19, "Monitoring SQL Server," for more information on SQL Server Profiler).

FIGURE 24.12

SQL Server Profiler lock events.

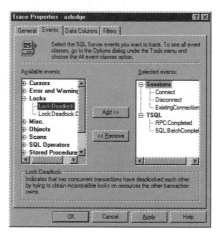

Trace Flags

The trace flags displayed in Table 24.3 provide extended insight into SQL Server's locking behavior and deadlocks.

TABLE 24.3   USEFUL TRACE FLAGS

Trace Flag	Output
1200	Displays process ID and types of locks being requested.
1204	Displays locks in use with a deadlock and the command involved in the deadlock.
1205	Displays information about the commands used during a deadlock.

> **TIP**
>
> The trace flag 1200 can be useful for tracking locking behavior. The easiest way to use the trace flag is to use the DBCC traceon() function. You also must turn on trace flag 3604 to echo trace information to the client workstation, as in the following example:
>
> ```
> DBCC traceon(3604)
> DBCC traceon(1200)
> UPDATE t_1
> SET c_1 = 0
> ```
>
> The following is sample output from DBCC trace flag 1200:
>
> ```
> Process 11 acquiring IX lock on TAB: 5:1861581670 [] result: OK
> Process 11 acquiring IX lock on UNK: 0:297381932:0:d result: OK
> Process 11 acquiring IU lock on PAG: 5:1:229 result: OK
> Process 11 acquiring U lock on RID: 5:1:229:0 result: OK
> Process 11 acquiring IX lock on PAG: 5:1:229 result: OK
> Process 11 acquiring X lock on RID: 5:1:229:0 result: OK
> Process 11 releasing lock reference on RID: 5:1:229:0
> Process 11 releasing lock reference on PAG: 5:1:229
> Process 11 releasing lock reference on RID: 5:1:229:0
> Process 11 releasing lock reference on TAB: 5:1861581670 []
> Process 11 releasing all locks @10EF81EC
> ```

Tips to Help Minimize Locking and Prevent Deadlocks

Try using the tips in the following sections to resolve locking problems. These tips can help minimize locking problems and prevent deadlocks.

Tip 1: Create Indexes for UPDATE/DELETE Statements That Contain WHERE Clauses

Whenever you issue an UPDATE or DELETE statement that does *not* use an index, an exclusive table lock is used to process the transaction. The exclusive table lock may block other transactions.

To reduce the chance of an exclusive table lock, specify a WHERE clause that takes advantage of an existing index. This may enable SQL Server to use row- and page-level locks instead of an exclusive table lock.

Tip 2: Convert a Large INSERT Statement into a Single INSERT Statement Within a Loop

Inserting a large number of rows into a table may result in an exclusive table lock. For example, INSERT INTO table2 SELECT * FROM table1 will result in an exclusive table lock on `table2` that will prevent others from accessing data in `table2`. To avoid this problem, convert the `INSERT` statement into an `INSERT` statement within a loop. For example, the following code opens a cursor and then initiates a loop that fetches the data from `table1` into a variable and then inserts the contents of the variable into `table2`. This approach decreases the likelihood of blocking because it generates locks when the `INSERT` is issued and the lock is immediately released after the `INSERT` is processed. The drawback of this approach is that it runs slower than a batch `INSERT`.

```
declare @col1 varchar(11)
declare sample_cursor cursor
 for select col1 from table1
open sample_cursor
fetch next from sample_cursor into @col1
while @@fetch_status = 0
 begin
 insert into table2 values (@col1)
 fetch next from sample_cursor into @col1
 end
deallocate sample_cursor
```

Tip 3: Avoid Using HOLDLOCK

`HOLDLOCK` is one of the keywords that almost every developer new to SQL Server has tried to use. Quite often, the developer uses `HOLDLOCK` without fully understanding the ramifications behind it.

When `HOLDLOCK` is used with a `SELECT` statement, all shared locks (remember that shared locks are acquired whenever a `SELECT` is issued) remain in effect until the transaction is *complete*. This means additional locking overhead, which degrades performance and increases the likelihood of blocking or deadlocks. When the `HOLDLOCK` command is not used, SQL Server releases the shared locks as soon as possible rather than waiting for the transaction to complete.

What usually happens is that developers use the `HOLDLOCK` command, thinking that they can temporarily prevent other users from reading the same data. What they do not realize is that `HOLDLOCK` only generates shared locks, not exclusive locks. Because the locks are shared, other users can still read the same data values.

Tip 4: Keep Transactions Short

Long-running transactions—especially data modification transactions—increase the likelihood of blocking and deadlocks. Whenever possible, try to keep the length of a transaction to a minimum. Following are suggestions to help decrease the length of a transaction:

- **Break long running transactions into multiple shorter running transactions.** Whenever you can reduce the duration of a lock, you can reduce the possibility of blocking. For this example, assume that table t_2 has 100 records with a sequential ID going from 1 to 100 (the number 100 is used to illustrate this example, a more realistic number would be 100,000 or more records). The following is a long-running transaction:

```
INSERT INTO t_1
SELECT * FROM t_2
```

You can re-write this long-running transaction into two shorter running transactions, reducing the duration of locks in use:

```
INSERT INTO t_1
SELECT * FROM t_2
WHERE t_2.id <= 50
INSERT INTO t_1
SELECT * FROM t_2
WHERE t_2.id > 50
```

- **Minimize nonclustered indexes.** Avoid unnecessary nonclustered indexes. Each index adds more overhead that must be maintained whenever a record is inserted or deleted, or whenever an indexed column is modified. This can decrease throughput.

- **Reduce the number of columns per table.** An INSERT processes faster on a narrow table (a table with few columns) than it can on a wide table (a table with many columns). The reduction of the overall width of a table enables more rows to exist on a page. This means that fewer pages must be accessed to process the transaction, thus shortening transaction times.

Tip 5: Understand Transactions

Two common misunderstandings in using transactions are nested transactions and user interaction within a transaction.

Nested Transactions

Look at the approach taken in Figure 24.13. Do you see any problems with the code?

The problem is with the rollback statement for the inner transaction. If the inner transaction is rolled back, you receive an error message, and both INSERT transactions are automatically rolled back by SQL Server, as in the following error message:

```
The commit transaction request has no corresponding BEGIN TRANSACTION.
```

To avoid the error message, use the SAVE TRANSACTION statement (see Figure 24.14).

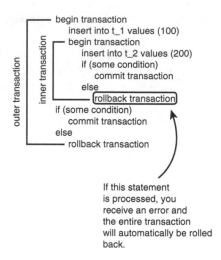

Figure 24.13

A nested transaction: The common (incorrect) approach.

```
        ┌── begin transaction
        │       insert into t_1 values (100)
        │   ┌── begin transaction
outer   │   │       insert into t_2 values (200)
trans-  │inner       if (some condition)
action  │trans           commit transaction
        │   │       else
        │   └──         rollback transaction
        │       if (some condition)
        │           commit transaction
        │       else
        └──     rollback transaction
```

If this statement
is processed, you
receive an error and
the entire transaction
will automatically be rolled
back.

Note

The COMMIT TRANSACTION statement must be issued after the ROLLBACK TRANSACTION INNER_TRANS statement.

Figure 24.14

A nested transaction: The correct approach.

```
        ┌── begin transaction
        │       insert into t_1 values (100)
        │   ┌── begin transaction
        │   │       save transaction inner_trans
outer   │   │       insert into t_2 values (200)
trans-  │inner       if (some condition)
action  │trans           commit transaction inner_trans
        │   │       else
        │   │           begin
        │   │               rollback transaction inner_trans
        │   │               commit transaction
        │   └──     end
        │       if (some condition)
        │           commit transaction
        │       else
        └──     rollback transaction
```

Now look at Figure 24.15. If the outer transaction is rolled back, do you think the inner transaction will also be rolled back? The answer is *yes*. SQL Server always rolls back the inner transaction when the outer transaction is rolled back, even though the inner transaction has been committed. This is how SQL Server handles nested transactions.

FIGURE 24.15

The way in which SQL Server handles nested transactions.

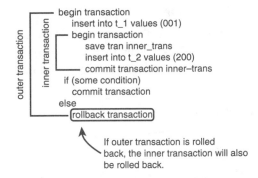

```
        begin transaction
            insert into t_1 values (001)
          begin transaction
              save tran inner_trans
              insert into t_2 values (200)
          commit transaction inner-trans
        if (some condition)
            commit transaction
        else
        rollback transaction
```

If outer transaction is rolled back, the inner transaction will also be rolled back.

> **NOTE**
>
> In my experience as a DBA, the way SQL Server handles nested transactions is often contrary to what developers expect. Developers usually expect the inner transaction to *not* be rolled back because it has been committed. Make sure that your developers understand how SQL Server handles nested transactions.

Whenever you nest a transaction, all locks are held for the duration of the transaction (see Figure 24.16). This means that when the inner transaction is committed, its locks are not released until the outer transaction is committed. Be on the lookout for nested transactions; it increases the likelihood of blocking or deadlocks.

FIGURE 24.16

The way locks are held within a nested transaction.

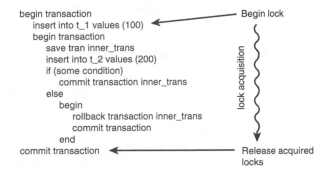

```
begin transaction                                    Begin lock
    insert into t_1 values (100)
    begin transaction
        save tran inner_trans
        insert into t_2 values (200)
    if (some condition)
        commit transaction inner_trans
    else
        begin
            rollback transaction inner_trans
            commit transaction
        end
commit transaction                                   Release acquired
                                                     locks
```

lock acquisition

24

MULTI-USER CONSIDERATIONS

User Interaction Within a Transaction

Keeping a watchful eye on transaction implementation can help ward off blocking. Consider the example in Figure 24.17. This situation virtually guarantees blocking in a multi-user environment. Always avoid user interaction within a transaction.

FIGURE 24.17

User interaction within a transaction.

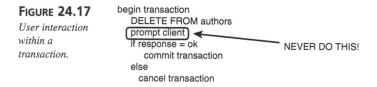

You should re-write the transaction to prompt the user first; based on the user's response, you can then perform the DELETE (see Figure 24.18). Transactions should always be managed in a single batch.

FIGURE 24.18

The transaction rewritten to avoid user interaction.

Tip 6: Run Transactions That Modify Large Amounts of Data During Off-Hours

You should process CREATE CLUSTERED INDEX and mass UPDATE/DELETE/INSERT statements during off-hours. These types of transactions require exclusive table locks and can be resource intensive.

Tip 7: Add More Memory to Your Server

By adding more memory to your server, you increase the amount of data that can remain in cache. This improves transaction performance, which reduces resource contention.

Tip 8: Know How to Safely Increment an id

Most applications require some type of auto-incrementing id to be used as a key field. Before a new record is inserted into the table, the application must get the next available id.

The easiest way to create an auto-incrementing id is to use the identity property. This data type has been optimized for performance and eliminates the need to have a separate table to track the next available id.

If you cannot use the identity property (for example, when you need complete control over the counter values), you can use the following stored procedure to return the next id. Because the update statement is within a transaction, the risk of two users receiving the same id is eliminated.

Sample table that holds the next id value:

```
/* table that contains NEXT ID value */
create table t_1 (id integer not null)
go
/* insert single record to set the SEED value */
insert into t_1 (id) values (0)
go
```

The following stored procedure returns the next id:

```
CREATE PROCEDURE usp_next_id AS
declare @next_id integer
begin transaction
 update t_1
 set id = id + 1
 select @next_id = id from t_1
commit transaction
RETURN @next_id
```

The following is an example of how to use the usp_next_id stored procedure:

```
declare @next_id integer
exec @next_id = usp_next_id
select @next_id
```

Tip 9: Use Cursor Options That Minimize Locking

When using a cursor that provides update or delete capability, use the OPTIMISTIC cursor option instead of the DYNAMIC or SCROLL LOCKS cursor options. The OPTIMISTIC cursor option will not place locks on data when it is read into the cursor (see Chapter 26, "Using Stored Procedures and Cursors," for more information on cursors).

MULTI-USER CONFIGURATION OPTIONS

SQL Server has several configuration options that allow you to tailor locking and other multi-user considerations. These options provide maximum control for multi-user access.

Transaction Isolation Level

With SQL Server, you can configure the transaction isolation level for a connection. A transaction isolation level remains in effect for the life of the connection unless the value is modified or the connection is broken.

To set the transaction isolation level, use the SET TRANSACTION ISOLATION LEVEL command, as in the following syntax. For an explanation of the differences among transaction isolation levels, see Tables 24.4 and 24.5.

```
SET TRANSACTION ISOLATION LEVEL {READ COMMITTED ¦ READ UNCOMMITTED ¦
REPEATABLE READ ¦ SERIALIZABLE}
```

TABLE 24.4   TRANSACTION ISOLATION LEVELS

Setting	Purpose
READ COMMITTED	SQL Server's default transaction isolation level. Prevents dirty reads; nonrepeatable reads may occur with this setting.
READ UNCOMMITTED	Minimizes locking by issuing locks only for UPDATE commands. Using this setting may result in dirty reads, phantom values, and nonrepeatable reads. In terms of performance, this setting is the most efficient option.
REPEATABLE READ	Prevents dirty reads and nonrepeatable reads by locking the data while it is being read. This prevents others from updating the data until the transaction is complete.
SERIALIZABLE	Prevents dirty reads, phantom values, and nonrepeatable reads. In terms of performance, this setting is the least efficient option.

TABLE 24.5   TRANSACTION ISOLATION MATRIX

Isolation Level	Blocking Risk	Prevents Dirty Reads	Prevents Nonrepeatable Reads	Prevents Phantom Reads
READ UNCOMMITTED	lowest	No	No	No
READ COMMITTED*	lower	Yes	No	No
REPEATABLE READ	higher	Yes	Yes	No
SERIALIZABLE	highest	Yes	Yes	Yes

*indicates default isolation level

NOTE

Explicit locking, such as NOLOCK, will override transaction isolation levels. See the section "Explicit Locking" for more information.

You can use the command DBCC USEROPTIONS to display the current transaction isolation level.

TRANSACTION ISOLATION ISSUES AND TIPS

The READ UNCOMMITTED transaction isolation level does not place locks on data when it is being read. This is different from the default transaction isolation level READ COMMITTED, which will place shared locks on data as it is being read. If you need a quick fix to blocking problems, this setting may solve your problems. With this transaction isolation level, locks will only be placed on the data when it is being modified.

Keep in mind that dirty reads, phantom values, and nonrepeatable reads can occur with this isolation level. For some applications, these drawbacks are outweighed by the multi-user access that can be gained by switching to this isolation level.

However, I would only recommend using this isolation level if you are experiencing blocking problems and you have unsuccessfully tried tuning your queries.

The following is the syntax for READ UNCOMMITTED isolation level.

```
SET TRANSACTION ISOLATION LEVEL READ UNCOMMITTED
```

At the other end of the transaction spectrum is the SERIALIZABLE transaction isolation level. This transaction level places range locks on the data until the transaction is complete. This prevents other users from modifying and adding records in the data that is being processed. This increases the likelihood of blocking and increases locking overhead.

Explicit Locking

With SELECT, INSERT, DELETE, and UPDATE statements, you can override SQL Server's default locking behavior. To specify the locking behavior, use the keywords listed in Table 24.6.

> **NOTE**
>
> The ability to explicitly control locking with INSERT, DELETE, and UPDATE statements is new in version 7.0. It is recommended that you do not override the SQL Server's default locking behavior, except when absolutely necessary.

TABLE 24.6 EXPLICIT LOCK SUMMARY

Lock	Purpose	Notes
HOLDLOCK	Forces all locks to be held for the duration of the transaction.	
NOLOCK	Turns off locking. Permits dirty reads.	
PAGLOCK	Forces page locking rather than table locking.	
READCOMMITTED*	Same as setting the transaction isolation level to READ COMMITTED.	
READPAST*	Skips locked rows.	Transaction isolation level must be set to READ COMMITTED (SQL Server's default transaction isolation level). If you execute the same query after the locked rows are unlocked you may receive a different result set.
READUNCOMMITTED*	Same as NOLOCK.	
REPEATABLEREAD*	Same as setting the transaction isolation level to REPEATABLEREAD.	
ROWLOCK*	Uses row locks instead of page or table locks.	
SERIALIZABLE*	Same as HOLDLOCK.	
TABLOCK	Forces table locking rather than page locking and uses a shared lock.	
TABLOCKX	Forces table locking rather than page locking and uses an exclusive lock.	
UPDLOCK	Forces an update lock to be issued rather than a shared lock. This type of lock ensures consistency when you intend to read data and then perform an update based on the values you just read.	

*indicates new feature with version 7.0

The following is the syntax to control explicit locking.

SELECT explicit lock syntax:

```
SELECT select_list
FROM table list WITH [(HOLDLOCK ¦ NOLOCK ¦ PAGLOCK ¦
  READCOMMITTED ¦ READPAST ¦ READUNCOMMITTED ¦
  REPEATABLEREAD ¦ ROWLOCK ¦ SERIALIZABLE ¦
  TABLOCK ¦ TABLOCKX ¦UPDLOCK)]
```

SELECT explicit lock example:

```
SELECT * FROM AUTHORS WITH (ROWLOCK)
  WHERE au_id <= '555-55-5555'
```

INSERT explicit lock syntax:

```
INSERT <table_or_view> (column_list) WITH [(HOLDLOCK ¦ NOLOCK ¦ PAGLOCK ¦
  READCOMMITTED ¦ READPAST ¦ READUNCOMMITTED ¦
   REPEATABLEREAD ¦ ROWLOCK ¦ SERIALIZABLE ¦
   TABLOCK ¦ TABLOCKX ¦UPDLOCK)]
VALUES (values list)
```

INSERT explicit lock example:

```
INSERT authors WITH (ROWLOCK)
  (au_id,au_lname,au_fname,phone,contract)
  VALUES ('111-22-1111','Sledge','Orryn','555-555-5555',0)
```

UPDATE explicit lock syntax:

```
UPDATE <table_or_view> WITH [(HOLDLOCK ¦ NOLOCK ¦ PAGLOCK ¦
  READCOMMITTED ¦ READPAST ¦ READUNCOMMITTED ¦
  REPEATABLEREAD ¦ ROWLOCK ¦ SERIALIZABLE ¦
  TABLOCK ¦ TABLOCKX ¦UPDLOCK)]
SET column = value
```

UPDATE explicit lock example:

```
UPDATE authors WITH (ROWLOCK)
  SET phone = '412-963-0505'
  WHERE au_id = '111-22-1111'
```

DELETE explicit lock example:

```
DELETE <table_or_view> WITH [(HOLDLOCK ¦ NOLOCK ¦ PAGLOCK ¦
  READCOMMITTED ¦ READPAST ¦ READUNCOMMITTED ¦
  REPEATABLEREAD ¦ ROWLOCK ¦ SERIALIZABLE ¦
  TABLOCK ¦ TABLOCKX ¦UPDLOCK)]
```

DELETE explicit lock example:

```
DELETE authors WITH (ROWLOCK)
  WHERE au_id = '111-22-1111'
```

24

MULTI-USER
CONSIDERATIONS

MULTI-USER FAQ

Does the lock manager inspect the number of records in a table when deciding the type of lock to implement?

No, the lock manager utilizes information such as the number of records accessed or modified by the query, the density of the rows per page, and the number of users concurrently accessing the table.

Additionally, the lock manager looks to see whether the table has a primary key. When processing an UPDATE or DELETE statement, the lock manager must utilize a table lock instead of a row- or page-level lock if the table does not contain a primary key.

When should the default transaction isolation not be used?

The default transaction isolation level should be changed when you need to increase multi-user concurrency control or decrease locking. I generally recommend changing the default transaction isolation level (READ COMMITTED) to REPEATABLE READ or SERIALIZABLE only when you need to prevent nonrepeatable reads or phantom reads. Keep in mind that going to REPEATABLE READ or SERIALIZABLE will increase locking and may lead to multi-user access problems. I also recommend changing the default transaction isolation level to READ UNCOMMMITTED only after optimizing your table's indexes. READ UNCOMMMITTED will significantly reduce locking activity; thus potentially improving multi-user access, but it may result in dirty reads.

Does row-level locking eliminate blocking?

No, row-level locking does not eliminate blocking. However, it reduces the likelihood of blocking by locking only a row of information on a data or index page, as opposed to previous versions that locked the entire page.

Is row-level locking always better than page-level locking?

The answer to this question depends on the amount of data being read or modified by a query. Generally speaking, SQL Server will utilize row-level locking when a relatively few number of records are being read or modified. If a substantial number of records are being modified, SQL Server will utilize page or table locking. For example, consider a table that has 1 million records and an UPDATE query that modifies every record in the table. If SQL Server only utilized row-level locking, it would have to make 1 million calls to the lock manager. Obviously, this would not be very efficient. Therefore, SQL Server uses dynamic locking that considers information such as the number of locks required, the number of calls to the lock manager, and other information. For this example, it is more efficient for SQL Server to process the query with a table lock instead of a row or page lock.

SUMMARY

Following are important notes to remember when addressing multi-user issues in SQL Server:

- Locks are used to maintain data consistency in a multi-user environment.

- Excessive locking can lead to blocking.

- Blocking occurs when a process must wait for another process to complete.

- Deadlock occurs when two users have locks on separate objects and each user is trying to lock the other user's objects.

- Use the Enterprise Manager, Performance Monitor, SQL Server Profiler, system procedures (`sp_who`, `sp_lock`), and trace flags to diagnose blocking and locking issues.

- Almost every SQL operation against a table results in some sort of lock.

- Row and page locks are generally preferred to table locks because they are less likely to cause blocking.

- Read statements acquire shared locks; data modification statements acquire exclusive locks.

- Row locks can escalate to page locks, and page locks can escalate to table locks. When this occurs, it is more efficient for SQL Server to process the transaction with the higher level type of lock.

- Always avoid user interaction within a transaction.

24

MULTI-USER CONSIDERATIONS

ADVANCED DBA TOPICS

IN THIS PART

SQL ESSENTIALS

by Anne Yagerline

IN THIS CHAPTER

The SQL primer is an overview of SQL (Structured Query Language), the ANSI-standard relational database language used for managing objects, data and security. This chapter discusses basic SQL statements and commands to get you started accessing and manipulating your data. You learn how to retrieve, add, update, and delete the data in the tables in your database. You also review two ways to create new tables.

All the examples in this chapter query tables in the *pubs* database (*'pubs'*) which comes with SQL Server. Figure 25.1 outlines the structure of the *pubs* tables *authors*, *titleauthor,* and *titles* used in the examples.

FIGURE 25.1

Structure of the authors, titleauthor, and titles tables in the pubs database.

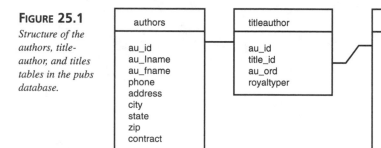

AN OVERVIEW OF BASIC SQL STATEMENTS

The number of different types of SQL statements you can execute is tremendous. Using SQL, you can perform any function from a simple table query to creating tables and stored procedures to assigning user rights. In this primer, you focus on retrieving, updating, and reporting on data from your client application. For this purpose, the most important SQL statements you need to know are SELECT, INSERT, UPDATE, DELETE, CREATE TABLE, and SELECT INTO. A brief description of these commands is shown in Table 25.1.

TABLE 25.1 IMPORTANT SQL STATEMENTS

Command	*Description*
SELECT	Retrieves columns and rows from a table or tables
INSERT	Adds rows to a table
UPDATE	Updates columns in existing rows in a table
DELETE	Deletes rows from a table
CREATE TABLE	Creates a new table based on the specified table schema
SELECT INTO	Creates a new table based on rows and columns output by a SELECT statement

These commands seem simple, but they can be qualified to perform a number of complex functions, as you will see in the following examples.

SELECT

The SELECT statement specifies the columns of data you want to retrieve, where the columns are stored, what criteria the returned data must meet, and the sort order to be applied to the data. A SELECT statement can further group rows of data together and assign retrieval criteria at the group level. The components of the SELECT statement are described in Table 25.2.

TABLE 25.2   COMPONENTS OF AN SQL SELECT STATEMENT

Component	Description
SELECT	Specifies the columns of data to be retrieved
FROM	Specifies the table/s from which to retrieve rows
WHERE	Specifies criteria which returned data must meet
GROUP BY	For aggregate queries, specifies the returned column/s by which the data is to be grouped
HAVING	For aggregate queries, specifies criteria which the aggregate value returned must meet
ORDER BY	Specifies the sort order of the returned rows

A Simple SELECT Statement

The following example queries several columns in the *authors* table:

```
SELECT au_id, au_lname, au_fname, state, zip, contract
FROM authors
```

The results of this simple query (shown in Figure 25.2) reveal that the data in the selected columns was returned for each row that exists in the *authors* table.

Adding the WHERE Clause

Using the same basic SELECT statement, you can narrow down the results by adding a WHERE clause. Suppose you only want to know the names of authors located in the state of California. In the following example, only those records whose *state* column has a value of 'CA' are returned (see Figure 25.3).

```
SELECT au_id, au_lname, au_fname, state, zip, contract
FROM authors
WHERE state = 'CA'
```

25

SQL ESSENTIALS

FIGURE 25.2

The results of a simple SELECT statement.

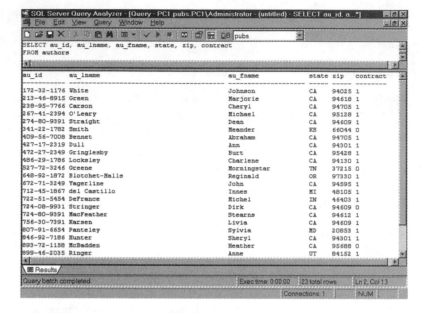

FIGURE 25.3

The results of a simple SELECT statement demonstrating the WHERE clause.

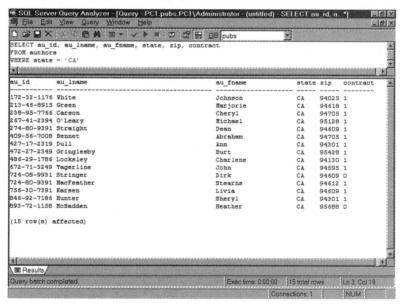

Your WHERE clause can use several columns as criteria for row retrieval. If you wanted only those rows whose *contract* value was zero, you would use a logical AND as in the following example:

```
SELECT au_id, au_lname, au_fname, state, zip, contract
FROM authors
WHERE state = 'CA' AND contract = 0
```

You can also have the query return rows for authors in any state except California. The way to indicate inequality in SQL is to combine a less than and greater than sign (<>).

```
SELECT au_id, au_lname, au_fname, state, zip, contract
FROM authors
WHERE state <> 'CA'
```

The WHERE clause can use different comparison operators for checking field values. Table 25.3 lists and describes these operators.

TABLE 25.3 WHERE CLAUSE COMPARISON OPERATORS

Operator	Description
=	Is equal to
>	Is greater than
<	Is less than
>=	Is greater than or equal to
<=	Is less than or equal to
< >	Is not equal to
IN	Is in a specified list of values or in the results of a specified subquery
BETWEEN…AND	Is between two values
LIKE	Contains the same pattern as a specified string. The pattern being compared is a string that contains one or more wildcard characters. You should refer to SQL Server help for a list of these operators.

In addition to a variety of comparison operators, the columns included in the WHERE clause can be checked using the AND and OR logical operators. If the AND operator is used, both conditions on either side of the AND must be met for a row to be returned. The OR operator requires that at least one of the conditions be met.

Adding the ORDER BY Clause

You can take the simple query one step further and sort the results by author last name (*au_lname*). To do this, add an ORDER BY clause.

```
SELECT au_id, au_lname, au_fname, state, zip, contract
FROM authors
WHERE state = 'CA'
ORDER BY au_lname
```

The resulting rows are returned in ascending alphabetical order by the author's last name as shown in Figure 25.4.

FIGURE 25.4

The results of a simple SELECT *statement demonstrating the* ORDER BY *clause.*

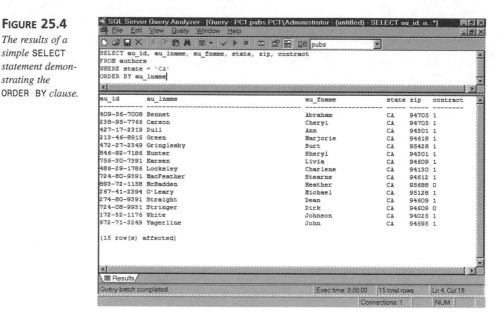

You can also sort the records in a field in descending order using the keyword DESC. Suppose you want to first sort the records in descending order by contract and then in ascending order by author last name. An example is shown in the following SQL statement:

```
SELECT au_id, au_lname, au_fname, state, zip, contract
FROM authors
WHERE state = 'CA'
ORDER BY contract DESC, au_lname
```

> **NOTE**
>
> Microsoft SQL Server offers several sort orders, the default being Dictionary Order, Case-insensitive. The sort order is defined during SQL Server installation and cannot be overridden later.

Using the WHERE Clause to Join Tables

You have seen several ways to use SQL SELECT statements to look at the data in the *authors* table by specifying columns to return, assigning retrieval criteria, and sorting the results. However in the real world, will you only want to look at data from a single table at a time? The answer is most likely no. The data in the *authors* table has relationships with data in other tables in the *pubs* database. For example, what if you wanted to know which titles were written by these authors? The *authors* table alone won't tell you this. You must search the cross-reference table, *titleauthor,* which links *authors* to *titles* by the columns *au_id* and *title_id*. Unfortunately, this isn't enough. Most people don't recognize authors or titles by IDs or codes; they know them by names. Because the names of the authors are located in the table *authors*, the titles are located in the table *titles,* and the relationships between the two are located in *titleauthor*, you need to tie these three tables together in a single SELECT statement. You can do this using the WHERE clause:

```
SELECT authors.au_lname, authors.au_fname, titles.title
FROM authors, titleauthor, titles
WHERE
  authors.au_id = titleauthor.au_id AND
  titleauthor.title_id = titles.title_id
ORDER BY authors.au_lname, authors.au_fname, titles.title
```

The resulting list of authors and their titles is shown in Figure 25.5. Note the way the column names are referenced in this statement. When retrieving data from multiple tables in a single SQL statement, you must preface column names that appear in more than one of the tables in the FROM clause with their associated table names to avoid an ambiguity error.

FIGURE 25.5

The results of a SELECT *statement demonstrating the use of the* WHERE *clause in joining tables.*

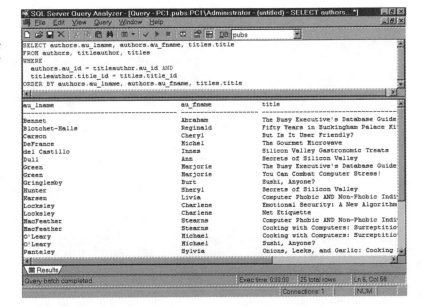

25

SQL ESSENTIALS

Using the Join Operator to Join Tables

Another way to join tables is using the join operator. This is the ANSI standard method for joining tables and uses the following syntax:

```
SELECT column1, column2, column3
FROM table1 join operator table2
ON join criteria
```

The join operator indicates how rows should be returned from the joined tables. The ON clause acts like a WHERE clause, indicating which fields in the joined table should be compared for equality. Table 25.4 describes the different join operators:

TABLE 25.4 TABLE JOIN OPERATORS

Join Operator	Description
CROSS JOIN	Returns each row from the first table joined with each row from the second table resulting in a returned number of rows equal to the product of the two tables' rowcounts.
INNER JOIN	Returns all rows from each table that meet the WHERE clause search criteria and where there is a match on the joined fields in the ON clause.
LEFT [OUTER] JOIN	Returns all rows from the table on the left side of the join that meet the WHERE clause search criteria and only those from the right side of the join where there is a match on the joined fields in the ON clause.
RIGHT [OUTER] JOIN	Returns all rows from the table on the right side of the join thatmeet the WHERE clause search criteria and only those from the left side of the join where there is a match on the joined fields in the ON clause.
FULL [OUTER] JOIN	Returns all rows from each table that meet the WHERE clause search criteria and where there is no match on the joined fields in the ON clause.

Using the join operator, the SQL statement in the previous example would be written as follows:

```
SELECT authors.au_lname, authors.au_fname, titles.title
FROM (authors INNER JOIN titleauthor
    ON authors.au_id = titleauthor.au_id) INNER JOIN titles
    ON titleauthor.title_id = titles.title_id
ORDER BY authors.au_lname, authors.au_fname, titles.title
```

One use for an outer join would be if you wanted a list of all authors and, if they wrote a book, the *title_id* of that book (through an outer join with *titleauthor*). If they did not write a book, you would still be able to see the author's name listed, but the *title_id* would be returned as NULL.

Aggregate Functions in SQL Statements

Aggregate functions return summary values for specified columns or expressions in the form of sum totals, number of records, averages, and so on. The aggregate function may return a single value for all rows represented by the query. If a GROUP BY clause has been added to the SQL statement, such summary values are calculated at each level of grouping. Table 25.5 lists the aggregate functions you can use. Note that the StDev and Var functions are not available in SQL Server.

TABLE 25.5 AGGREGATE FUNCTIONS

Aggregate Function	Description
Avg	Returns the average of all values in the columns by taking their sum and dividing by the count.
Count	Returns the number of non-null values in the specified column or expression. If the expression is an asterisk (for example, count(*)), the result is the number of rows in the query.
Min	Returns the minimum value in the specified column or expression
Max	Returns the maximum value in the specified column or expression
Sum	Returns the sum of values in the specified column or expression.

The following statement illustrates the use of the count function on the entire *titles* table with no grouping.

```
SELECT count(title) 'titles'
FROM titles
```

The result is the total number of title records in the *titles* table as shown in Figure 25.6.

25

FIGURE 25.6

An example of the aggregate count *function on the* titles *table.*

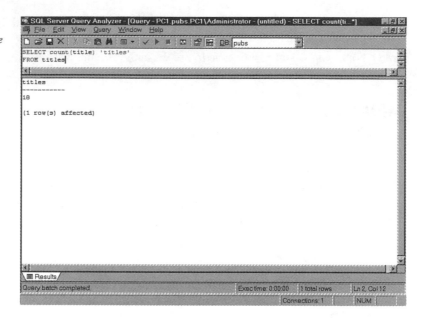

You can use an alias to return a different name for a column or assign a name to a column that returns an expression (and, therefore, has no name). There are three ways to assign an alias to a column:

```
SELECT count(title) AS titles FROM titles
SELECT count(title) 'titles' FROM titles
SELECT 'titles' = count(title) FROM titles
```

Use of the GROUP BY Clause

Suppose you want to group all like rows in the query result by the values of one or more columns. You can group these results by specifying those columns in a GROUP BY clause. If more than one column is specified, the rows are grouped first by the first column and then within those groups by the second column and so on.

In the following example, the GROUP BY clause is combined with an aggregate function to show how that function is applied to the values within each distinct group. Notice that, contrary to the previous example, each group of authors has its own title count, rather than the count being performed on an entire table.

```
SELECT authors.au_lname, authors.au_fname, count(titles.title) 'titles'
FROM authors, titleauthor, titles
WHERE
```

```
   authors.au_id = titleauthor.au_id AND
   titleauthor.title_id = titles.title_id
GROUP BY authors.au_lname, authors.au_fname
```

With the results shown in Figure 25.7, you can determine how many books each author wrote.

FIGURE 25.7

An example of a
GROUP BY *query.*

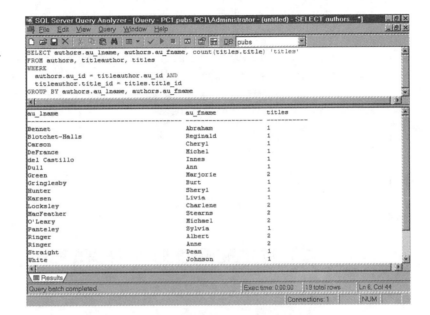

At this point, you are familiar with the use of table names prefacing column names in order to avoid ambiguity in multitable queries. You may also have begun to notice that this can result in lengthy SQL statements. Using a table alias, you can shorten your SQL statement and make it easier to both read and type. As with the previous column alias examples, the table alias is simply the use of a new name to represent the actual table name. Aliases are often used to shorten the SQL statement and to enhance the readability of the WHERE clause, so the table names are usually replaced by an alias of a single character. Look at the preceding SQL example; here aliases replace table names:

```
SELECT a.au_lname, a.au_fname, count(c.title) 'titles'
FROM authors a, titleauthor b, titles c
WHERE
   a.au_id = b.au_id and
   b.title_id = c.title_id
GROUP BY a.au_lname, a.au_fname
```

25

SQL ESSENTIALS

Use of the HAVING Clause

Like the WHERE clause, the HAVING clause is used for specifying criteria for data to be returned in a query. The difference lies in the level at which the criteria is checked. The WHERE clause uses criteria to restrict rows of data returned by a query. The GROUP BY clause then forms the returned rows into groups and calculates any aggregate values. The criteria in the HAVING clause is then used to restrict groups of rows according to the group level data.

In the following example, the HAVING clause is used to return the names of only those authors who have written more than one book.

```
SELECT a.au_lname, a.au_fname, count(c.title) 'titles'
FROM authors a, titleauthor b, titles c
WHERE
  a.au_id = b.au_id and
  b.title_id = c.title_id
GROUP BY a.au_lname, a.au_fname
HAVING count(c.title) > 1
```

Figure 25.8 shows that only those authors with more than one book are returned by the query.

FIGURE 25.8

The use of the HAVING clause.

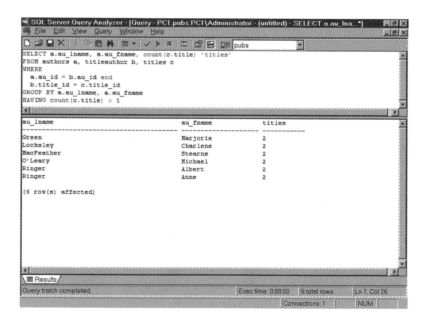

INSERT

The INSERT statement is what you use to add rows of data to a table. The INSERT statement specifies the table to which rows are to be added, the columns in which the data is to be stored, the source of the data being added, and the data itself. The components of the INSERT statement are described in Table 25.6.

TABLE 25.6   COMPONENTS OF AN SQL INSERT STATEMENT

Component	Description
INSERT INTO	Specifies the table to which rows are to be added.
column list	Specifies columns in which to add the data. (It is only necessary to provide a column list when not all of the table's columns are to have data added.) If left blank, the column list can be understood to be every column in the table, in the order in which they appear in the table structure.
VALUES (*value list*)	Specifies the values to be filled in the respective columns in the column list. (For example, the first value in the value list will be assigned to the first column in the column list and so on.)
SELECT	The SELECT statement that returns rows to be added to the table.

Note that either a value list or a SELECT statement (not both) is used to provide the data to be added.

Use of the INSERT Statement with a Value List

This example shows the use of the value list to add a row to the *titles* table, providing values for each column in the table. Note that with a value list, you can insert only a single row into the table.

```
INSERT INTO titles
VALUES
  ('SM1234', 'The Small Business Tax Guide', 'business',
  ➥'1389', 15.99, 3000, 10, 0,
  'Tax guide for owners of small businesses', '1/1/1997')
```

You can also specify which columns to fill in the INSERT clause:

```
INSERT INTO titles (title_id, title)
VALUES ('SM5678', 'The Small Business Marketing Guide')
```

25

A reason for not specifying all values would be that you do not know those values and want any possible default values to be added. Note, however, that if there are no default values for the omitted columns and the structure of the table to which you are adding the row requires that an omitted column be filled, you will get an error.

In the first example shown, you may have noticed that the list of columns in the INSERT clause was omitted. This is the equivalent of listing all columns in the table in the order in which they appear in the table structure. This saves you some typing time. However, it is usually better to include the column list so that if fields are reordered or added to the table at a later date, the SQL statement need not be altered to reflect the structure change.

Use of the INSERT Statement with a SELECT Statement

The following example shows the use of the SELECT statement to add one or more rows of data to the *titles* table. Assume that the *newtitles* table is a temporary working table that holds new title information. From this table you want to add all titles whose processing date is NULL.

```
INSERT INTO titles
( title_id, title, type, pub_id, price, advance, royalty, ytd_sales,
➥notes, pubdate )
SELECT
  title_id, title, type, pub_id, price, advance, royalty, ytd_sales,
➥notes, pubdate
FROM newtitles
WHERE procdate = NULL
```

> **NOTE**
>
> The INSERT INTO...SELECT statement can be interpreted as a two-part query. That is, the SELECT portion of the statement actually is performed by itself as step one of the statement. The resulting set of rows is then given to the INSERT INTO portion of the statement (step two of the statement). For this reason, there is no ambiguity between the identical column lists in these two distinct portions of the SQL statement. Therefore, it is not necessary to preface the column names with the table names to distinguish those in the destination table from those in the source table.

UPDATE

The UPDATE statement is what you use to update column values in existing rows in a table. The UPDATE statement specifies the table to be updated, the columns to update, the new values to assign those columns, and criteria for the rows to updated. Table 25.7 describes the components of an UPDATE statement.

TABLE 25.7 COMPONENTS OF AN SQL UPDATE STATEMENT

Component	Description
UPDATE	Specifies the table to be updated.
SET	Specifies columns to update and the new values to assign to those columns.
FROM	Specifies the tables to include in the UPDATE statement.
WHERE	Specifies the criteria to determine which rows' columns are to be updated.

Setting Columns to a Fixed Value with UPDATE Statement

In some cases, you might want to update columns in a table with a fixed value for every row in the table. For example, assume that you want to update the processing date to January 1, 1997 for each row in the *newtitles* table (see the previous example) which currently has a processing date of NULL:

```
UPDATE newtitles
SET procdate = '1/1/1997'
WHERE procdate = NULL
```

Setting a Column Value Based on Existing Column Values

Suppose you want to increase the price of each book in the *titles* table by 10 percent of the current price. It would be difficult to update the table with fixed values (as in the previous example) because all books need to be updated to different prices; that could take all day. A better way to perform this update is to use the existing price as a base for the updated price. Just as you can assign a fixed value to a column, you can assign the results of an expression as shown in the following statement:

```
UPDATE titles
SET price = price * 1.10
```

25

Therefore, without knowing the value of any of the prices in the *titles* table, you can successfully increase their values by 10 percent in one easy UPDATE statement.

Setting a Column Based on Values in a Joined Table

Now, say you want to update the publisher associated with all titles written by a specific author. The author information is nowhere to be found in the *titles* table. You can only get that information by joining the *titles* table with the *titleauthor* table. To do this, add a FROM clause to the UPDATE statement. This FROM clause works the same way as the FROM clause in a SELECT statement. The UPDATE clause indicates the table to be updated, whereas the FROM clause indicates the source of the data with which to update that table. In the following example, the *pub_id* column is updated to '1389' for all titles associated with *au_id* '998-72-3567':

```
UPDATE titles
SET pub_id = '1389'
FROM titles a, titleauthor b
WHERE
  a.title_id = b.title_id AND
  b.au_id = '998-72-3567'
```

DELETE

The DELETE statement enables you to remove rows from tables. This statement specifies the table from which rows are to be deleted and criteria for the rows to be deleted. Table 25.8 describes the components of a DELETE statement

TABLE 25.8 COMPONENTS OF AN SQL DELETE STATEMENT

Component	Description
DELETE FROM	Specifies the table from which to delete rows.
WHERE	Specifies the criteria that determines which rows are to be deleted.

Using DELETE to Delete All Rows from a Table

To delete all rows from a table, you need only specify the name of the table from which to delete those rows. The following example shows how to delete all rows from the *titles* table:

```
DELETE FROM titles
```

> **NOTE**
>
> SQL Server offers another method for removing all rows from a table called the TRUNCATE TABLE statement. It acts like a DELETE statement without a WHERE clause, with a couple of notable exceptions. The DELETE statement deletes rows from a table one row at a time, logging each deletion as a transaction that can be rolled back. The TRUNCATE TABLE statement, on the other hand, removes entire pages of data from a table and does not log individual row deletions. Rows removed from a table with a TRUNCATE TABLE statement cannot be recovered. The other important note is that delete triggers associated with a table will not be fired when that table is truncated. Why would you use a TRUNCATE TABLE statement? Speed. The TRUNCATE TABLE statement performs the task of removing all rows from a table much faster than a DELETE statement. Just keep in mind that it will always remove all the rows from a table and these rows are *not* recoverable.

Sometimes you will not want to wipe out all the rows in a table. Assume that you want to delete only a specific title from the *titles* table.

Using DELETE to Delete Specific Rows from a Table

To delete specific rows from a table, you add the familiar WHERE clause. As you may expect, only those rows that meet the criteria of the WHERE clause are deleted. The following snippet removes only the title 'Silicon Valley Gastronomic Treats' whose *title_id* is 'MC2222'.

```
DELETE FROM titles
WHERE title_id = 'MC2222'
```

Using a Subquery to Delete Rows Based on Values in a Different Table

Say that the DELETE statement criteria is based on a value in another table. For example, what if you wanted to delete all titles from the *titles* table that do not have an author? Because a title's author information is not stored in the *titles* table, you must search the *titleauthor* table to determine whether any authors exist for that title.

To do this, you need to use a subquery. That is, you use the results of a nested select query as the criteria for the outer delete query. In the following statement, the subquery (shown in parentheses) is a complete SQL statement in and of itself. It returns a resultset of each *title_id* found in the *titleauthors* table. The outer delete query uses this set of *title_ids* as the criteria for rows to be deleted.

25

SQL ESSENTIALS

```
DELETE FROM titles
WHERE title_id NOT IN
( SELECT title_id FROM titleauthor
```

> **NOTE**
>
> Because you can only compare a single column from the outer query to the set of values returned by the nested subquery, your subquery should return only one column. Furthermore, that column's datatype should be compatible with the datatype of the column being compared in the outer query.

CREATE TABLE

The CREATE TABLE statement enables you to create a new table in the database. However, the database should already be established by the DBA. You might wonder why you should have to create a new table from Visual Basic. Sometimes you need to access the data in such a way that a SELECT statement would not effectively produce the desired results. An example might be that the set of data you need must be accessed and processed one row at a time through a cursor. Another example is a resultset that would require table joins so complex that the query takes a very long time to run. In such cases, it is useful to have an empty table structured the way you want the resultset structured so that you can fill in phases by using a cursor or a combination of INSERT and UPDATE statements. Table 25.9 describes the components of a CREATE TABLE statement

TABLE 25.9   COMPONENTS OF A CREATE TABLE STATEMENT

Component	Description
CREATE TABLE	Specifies the table to be created.
column list	Specifies the columns of the new table and their attributes.

Using CREATE TABLE to Create the *authors* Table

To create a new table using the CREATE TABLE statement, specify the table you want to create and the columns that will configure the table. The following statement creates the *authors* table as it is currently structured in the *pubs* database on SQL Server:

```
CREATE TABLE authors
( au_id id NOT NULL ,
  au_lname varchar (40) NOT NULL ,
  au_fname varchar (20) NOT NULL ,
```

```
phone char (12) NOT NULL ,
address varchar (40) NULL ,
city varchar (20) NULL ,
state char (2) NULL ,
zip char (5) NULL ,
contract bit NOT NULL )
```

Table 25.10 lists the possible datatypes you can assign to columns in the CREATE TABLE statement:

TABLE 25.10   CREATE TABLE DATATYPES

Type of Data	Datatypes
binary	binary, varbinary
character	char, varchar
date and time	datetime, smalldatetime
exact numeric	decimal, numeric
approximate numeric	float, real
integer	int, smallint, tinyint
monetary	money, smallmoney
special	bit, timestamp
text and image	text, image

SELECT...INTO

The SELECT...INTO statement is another way you can create a new table. This method differs from the CREATE TABLE method in that the structure of the table to create is not explicitly stated, rather it is determined by the results of a SELECT statement. Table 25.11 lists the components of the SELECT...INTO statement:

TABLE 25.11   COMPONENTS OF A SELECT...INTO STATEMENT

Component	Description
SELECT INTO	Specifies the table to be created.
column list	Specifies the columns of the new table and their attributes.

25

Using SELECT...INTO to Create a New *authortitles* Table

Suppose you want to store the results of a SELECT statement in a table for use later in your application or in a report. The SELECT...INTO statement enables you to do just that. You simply need to add the INTO clause to a standard SELECT statement. In the following example, you use the SELECT statement from an earlier example, which displayed author names and the titles of books that they wrote, to create a new table called *authortitles*:

```
SELECT a.au_lname, a.au_fname, c.title
INTO authortitles
FROM authors a, titleauthor b, titles c
WHERE
  a.au_id = b.au_id and
  b.title_id = c.title_id
ORDER BY a.au_lname, a.au_fname, c.title
```

Now, if you select all rows from the *authortitles* table, you get the same results as you got in the SELECT statement as shown in Figure 25.9.

FIGURE 25.9

The results of using SELECT...INTO *to create the authortitles table.*

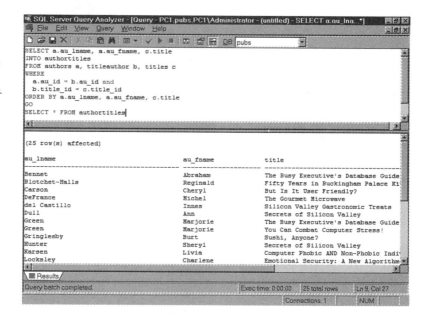

SUMMARY

This chapter provides you with the basic tools for performing the most common SQL commands. You have learned how to retrieve rows in many different formats using the SELECT statement as well as how to add, update, and delete rows in tables using the INSERT, UPDATE, and DELETE statements respectively. You have also learned how to create a new table using either the CREATE TABLE or SELECT...INTO statements. All these statements should get you pretty far, but you may find in your continued development that you require more functionality. You should take the time to try out the commands described here until you feel you have a good understanding of how they work. Then you should research and make use of some of the more advanced features described in SQL Server's online help. You should also become familiar with as many of SQL Server's built-in functions as possible. Such functions enable you to broaden the scope of SQL statements you can create.

25

SQL ESSENTIALS

USING STORED PROCEDURES AND CURSORS

by Orryn Sledge

IN THIS CHAPTER

Does the topic of stored procedures fall into the realm of developers or DBAs? Knowledge of stored procedures is required for DBAs and developers alike. As a DBA, you use stored procedures frequently. Microsoft supplies many stored procedures that you use to perform database and system maintenance. You find that you are frequently required to write your own stored procedures to perform specific DBA tasks for your organization or to help a group of developers solve a complex business problem.

SQL SERVER 6.5 TO 7.0 QUICK REFERENCE

The following is a quick reference to the changes that occurred between SQL Server version 6.5 and 7.0:

What's New

Here is a list of the new features:

Stored Procedures

- Delayed name resolution   Stored procedures in version 7.0 successfully compile when objects that are referenced by the stored procedure do not exist at compilation time. For example, if a stored procedure references a temp table that is created by the calling procedure, the stored procedure successfully compiles. Previous versions of SQL Server required the existence all referenced objects during the compilation process.

- Stored Procedure Wizard   Version 7.0 includes a wizard that helps developers create stored procedures.

- CURSOR OUTPUT parameter   Stored procedures can now return cursors as OUTPUT parameters.

- Names and identifiers can now be a maximum of 128 characters; previously they were limited to 30 characters.

- Maximum of 1,024 parameters per stored procedure. Previous versions of SQL Server were limited to 255 parameters.

- Maximum size of a stored procedure is equal to the batch size (batch size = 128 * Network Packet Size (note: the default network packet size is 4,096)). Previous versions were limited to 65,025 bytes.

- Stored procedures can support up to 32 levels of nesting. Previous versions were limited to 16 levels of nesting.

- ALTER PROCEDURE statement   The ALTER PROCEDURE statement can be used to modify a procedure and preserve the corresponding security of the procedure. To modify a stored procedure in previous versions of SQL Server, the stored procedure had to be dropped, re-created, and the corresponding permissions had to be re-applied.

Cursors

- Local and global cursors   Cursors can now be local or global to a Transact-SQL batch. Previous versions of SQL Server used global cursors. For example, in version 7.0, a stored procedure might contain a cursor named mycursor. This stored procedure can call another stored procedure that also contains a cursor named mycursor. The programs successfully execute if these cursors are declared local to the stored procedures.

- Version 7.0 cursor extension syntax   Version 7.0 includes a new cursor syntax that is similar to ODBC and ADO cursor syntax. The cursor options are similar in name and in functionality.

> **NOTE**
>
> Version 7.0 includes the database option default to local cursor. If the cursor declaration does not include the local or global setting, the cursor defaults to the setting specified by the default to local cursor setting. The default setting in version 7.0 is FALSE. According to SQL Server's documentation, the default setting may change in future versions. Watch out! Be sure to include the local or global keyword when using cursors!

What's Gone

- The sysprocedures table has been removed from SQL Server. In previous versions, the table was used to store a stored procedure's query tree information. Version 7.0 compiles the procedure directly from the syscomments table.

WHAT IS A STORED PROCEDURE?

A *stored procedure* is a series of precompiled SQL statements and control-of-flow language statements. Stored procedures can enhance standard SQL by enabling you to use parameters, make decisions, declare variables, and return information. You can think of a stored procedure as a program or function that is stored as a database object on SQL Server. When a stored procedure is executed, it runs on SQL Server—not on the client issuing the request. A stored procedure can be a simple SQL statement such as this one:

```
Select * from authors
```

A stored procedure can also be a series of complex SQL statements and control-of-flow language statements that apply a complex business rule or task to a series of tables in the database.

> **TIP**
>
> A *trigger* is a special type of stored procedure that automatically executes when certain table data modifications are made (for example, inserts, updates, or deletes). Triggers are used to cascade changes to related tables or to perform complex restrictions that cannot be done with constraints.

STORED PROCEDURE PROS AND CONS

Before further defining a stored procedure, here are some of the pros and cons of using stored procedures:

Stored Procedure Pros:

- Stored procedures enable you to perform complex operations that cannot be performed with straight SQL.

- Stored procedures offer a substantial performance gain over standard SQL statements because the SQL statements in a stored procedure are precompiled. An execution plan is prepared after the stored procedure executes the first time. After the execution plan is created and stored in the procedure cache, subsequent execution of the stored procedure is much faster than equivalent SQL statements.

- Stored procedures can be used as a security mechanism. For example, if you have many tables or views you do not want users to access directly, you can revoke all access to the underlying tables and create a stored procedure granting the users EXECUTE privileges on the stored procedure. The users can then access the tables by executing the stored procedure.

> **TIP**
>
> Using stored procedures as a security mechanism is one way you can prevent users from accidentally modifying a table with an ad-hoc query tool such as MS-Query or Microsoft Access. Grant the users read-only access to the table and then create stored procedures to perform data modifications like UPDATE or DELETE.

Stored Procedure Cons:

- It can be difficult to implement complex logic with a stored procedure. The problem stems from the fact that Transact-SQL does not provide sophisticated programming constructs, such as arrays, or the ability to create user definable functions. Additionally, the Stored Procedure Editor is not like Visual Basic's editor; it's more like Notepad! Likewise, the error messages returned when a syntax error occurs can be difficult to decipher.

- Stored procedures can be difficult to manage. When dealing with development projects or special administrative needs, the number of stored procedures can increase dramatically. Trying to remember what each stored procedure does and what other procedures use the stored procedure can become a problem. SQL Server does not provide any administrative capabilities to ease this task; managing stored procedures requires additional work from you.

TIP

One successful method I have used to keep track of stored procedures is to produce a catalog of stored procedures using a Windows help file. Find a utility that enables you to easily create Windows help files. Create a help file to catalog all your stored procedures. Include the name of the procedure, a description of the procedure, a list and description of procedures, tables, or views that the procedure accesses, and other procedures called. As you add, modify, and delete stored procedures, keep the help file up to date. The help files are easy to distribute and have very good search utilities. However, this approach requires the cooperation of anyone who creates or modifies stored procedures on your system to keep the help file up to date.

HOW TO CREATE A STORED PROCEDURE

To create a stored procedure using SQL Server 7.0, use the Create Procedure statement, which has the following syntax:

```
Create PROCEDURE [owner.]procedure_name [;number][(@parameter1 data_type
➡ [VARYING] [=default] [OUTPUT] [,@parameter2]...
➡[@parameter1024])] [{FOR REPLICATION} ¦
➡{WITH RECOMPILE} [{[WITH]¦[,]}ENCRYPTION]] As SQL Statements
```

> **NOTE**
>
> When you use the Create Procedure statement, you can type the statement Create Procedure as in the following example:
>
> Create Procedure usp_test
>
> Alternatively, you can use the shortcut statement Create Proc as in the following example:
>
> Create Proc usp_test

In this syntax, *procedure name* is the name of the stored procedure. Stored procedure names conform to the standard SQL Server naming conventions. The maximum size of a procedure name is 128 characters. With SQL Server 7.0, you can create a local temporary stored procedure by adding # to the beginning of the procedure name. A local temporary stored procedure can be used only by the connection that created the stored procedure; it is dropped when the connection ends. You can create a global temporary stored procedure by adding ## to the beginning of the stored procedure name. A global temporary stored procedure can be used by all user connections and is dropped at the end of the last session using the procedure. Suggested stored procedure naming conventions are found in Appendix A.

Also in this syntax, *number* is an optional integer that can be used to group stored procedures with the same name so that they can be dropped with a single drop statement. *Parameter* allows parameters to be passed into the stored procedure. Parameters are optional; a stored procedure can have up to 1,024 parameters. The text FOR REPLICATION marks a stored procedure for use only by the replication process.

When the WITH RECOMPILE option is used, the query plan of the stored procedure is not kept in the procedure cache. A new query plan is generated every time the procedure is executed. You cannot use the FOR REPLICATION and WITH RECOMPILE options together.

> **SOLVING THE WITH RECOMPILE MYTH**
>
> The WITH RECOMPILE option is a highly misunderstood option. I have heard things like, "Why would you ever use that? When you use the WITH RECOMPILE option with a stored procedure, you lose the advantage of a compiled query plan. You might as well use straight SQL!" Did you ever think that ignorance is bliss and no wonder your system is slow?

Using Stored Procedures and Cursors

CHAPTER 26

687

26

USING STORED
PROCEDURES AND
CURSORS

When using the `WITH RECOMPILE` statement, you do lose the benefit of a compiled query plan. However, the stored procedure is still faster than straight SQL because the SQL text has already been parsed and a query tree has been constructed. Even more important, in cases when you use the `WITH RECOMPILE` option, you lose the small amount of time it takes to create the query plan as opposed to using an incorrect query plan that may cost minutes or hours.

When do you use the `WITH RECOMPILE` option? When you are passing into a stored procedure parameters that differ greatly in data distribution; these different parameters would cause the query optimizer to create different query plans. Also consider using the `WITH RECOMPILE` option if you pass parameters into a stored procedure and the time to execute the stored procedure is inconsistent. You can force a stored procedure to recompile the next time it is executed by executing the system stored procedure `sp_recompile` on a table or view referenced in the stored procedure.

The `WITH ENCRYPTION` option encrypts the text of the stored procedure in the `syscomments` table so that users cannot query the text of the procedure. Use this option only when necessary.

`SQL Statements` are the SQL statements or control-of-flow language statements that make up the stored procedure.

Now look at some simple examples of creating stored procedures in the `pubs` database. The following example creates a stored procedure called `usp_show_authors` that selects all the columns and rows from the `authors` table:

```
Create Procedure usp_show_authors
as
Select * from authors
```

The next example creates a stored procedure called `usp_Texas_Publisher` that selects all the publisher's names from the `publishers` table using the `WITH ENCRYPTION` option:

```
Create Proc usp_Texas_Publisher WITH ENCRYPTION
as
Select pub_name
From publishers
Where state = 'TX'
```

> **TIP**
>
> Stored procedures are created in the database from which the `Create Procedure` command is executed; the exception is temporary stored procedures, which are created in the `tempdb` database.

Use the Microsoft SQL Server Query Analyzer tool to enter the procedure name and click the green arrow to execute the stored procedure. If the stored procedure is not the first statement, use the `EXECUTE` statement as follows:

```
execute procedure name
```

Here is a shortcut and commonly used format:

```
exec procedure name
```

> **TIP**
>
> Version 7.0 includes a Stored Procedure Wizard that is useful when creating `INSERT`, `DELETE`, or `UPDATE` stored procedures. A nice feature of this wizard is that it automatically creates the necessary variables that are part of most stored procedures.

> **NOTE**
>
> To make your stored procedures easier to read and maintain, add a header to the start of your stored procedure. Following are two examples of headers you can use in your stored procedures.
>
> **Example header style 1:**
>
> ```
> Create Procedure usp_proc_name as
> /******************************************************************************
> ** Name:
> **
> ** Description:
> **
> ** Parameters:
> **
> ** Returns: 0 - Success
> **         -1 - Error
> **
> ** Other Outputs: Populates the table xxxx for Access reports.
> **
> ```

```
** History:
**     Mark A. Spenik KSCS, 6/1/98    Initial Release.
**
*************************************************************************/
```

Example header style 2:

```
Create Procedure usp_proc_name as
/*-----------------------------------------------------------------

Procedure Name

------------------------------------------------------------------
Description:

Called By:

Parameters:

Status Returns:

Other Outputs:

Example: <show an example of calling the stored procedure>
------------------------------------------------------------------
History:
-----------------------------------------------------------------*/
```

HOW TO MODIFY A STORED PROCEDURE

Version 7.0 provides an ALTER PROCEDURE command that enables a developer to modify
the contents of an existing stored procedure. This command will also preserve any
security (EXECUTE permissions) that have been applied to the stored procedure. The following is the ALTER PROCEDURE syntax.

```
Alter PROCEDURE [owner.]procedure_name [;number]
➡[(@parameter1 data_type [=default] [OUTPUT]
➡[,@parameter2]...[@parameter1024])] [{FOR REPLICATION} ¦
{WITH RECOMPILE} [{[WITH]¦[,]}ENCRYPTION]] As SQL Statements
```

See the topic titled "How to Create a Stored Procedure," in this chapter for detailed parameter information.

LIFE IS SIMPLER WITH 7.0!

The new ALTER PROCEDURE command simplifies your life by preserving a stored procedure's security and by avoiding the drop and re-create process. In previous versions, you had to drop and re-create the procedure in order to make modifications. This meant that you had to re-apply the security to the procedure after it was re-created. It was easy to forget to apply the security back to the stored procedure. Even worse, it was easy to forget that you had to export the stored procedure's security prior to dropping the procedure! Fortunately, these issues are things of the past.

CONTROL-OF-FLOW LANGUAGE

Before getting into some of the finer points of stored procedures (like using parameters or returning values), it is important to cover a very important topic: control-of-flow language. Control-of-flow language gives your stored procedures added capabilities not found in standard Transact-SQL. Using control-of-flow language, you can make use of standard programming techniques such as performing loops or conditional processing on variables.

TIP

Want to learn how to write good stored procedures? The first requirement is to learn SQL and the many additional Transact-SQL features. The next step is to become familiar with the different control-of-flow statements and their uses. Learn these fundamentals, and you are on your way to writing good stored procedures.

The following control-of-flow language statements are quickly reviewed in the following sections:

- GOTO label
- BEGIN...END
- IF...ELSE
- WAITFOR
- return
- while

Using Stored Procedures and Cursors

CHAPTER 26

691

26

USING STORED
PROCEDURES AND
CURSORS

- break
- continue

Additionally, the following Transact-SQL extensions are reviewed in the following sections:

- DECLARE statement
- PRINT statement
- RAISERROR

The DECLARE Statement

Using the DECLARE statement, you can create variables using standard SQL Server datatypes. Variables defined with the DECLARE statement *must* begin with the @ symbol. You can declare more than one variable in a DECLARE statement by using commas to separate the variables. The syntax for DECLARE is as follows:

```
Declare @variable1 datatype [,@variable2 datatype ...]
```

The following example creates three variables of different datatypes:

```
Declare @count int, @current_date datetime
Declare @My_Message varchar(255)
```

> **NOTE**
>
> To initialize or set the value of a variable you create with the DECLARE statement, use the keyword SELECT. For example, the following statement sets the value of the variable @count to 100:
>
> ```
> Select @count = 100
> ```
>
> The following example sets the variable @count to the total number of rows in the authors table located in the pubs database:
>
> ```
> Select @count = count(*)
> from pubs..authors
> ```

The GOTO Statement

The GOTO statement performs the same function it performs in many different programming languages like C and Visual Basic. GOTO jumps the execution of the stored procedure to the associated label. The syntax for GOTO is as follows:

```
GOTO label
```

In the following example, the GOTO statement jumps over (skips) the SELECT statement and executes the UPDATE statement:

```
GOTO do_update
SELECT * from authors

do_update:

UPDATE authors
set au_lname = "Spenik"
Where state = 'VA'
```

> **NOTE**
>
> When defining a label, the label name must end in a colon. When using the GOTO statement, refer to the label name but do not include the colon.

The BEGIN...END Statement

BEGIN and END statements are considered block statements because they group a series of SQL statements and control-of-flow language into a single entity. BEGIN and END are often used with IF...ELSE blocks. The syntax for BEGIN and END is as follows:

```
BEGIN
    {SQL Statements | statement block}
END
```

The IF...ELSE Statement

The IF and ELSE statements enable you to check for conditions and execute SQL statements based on a condition. The IF statement checks expressions that return a TRUE or FALSE value (Boolean expressions). If the value returned is TRUE, the block of statements or the single statement that follows the IF statement is executed. If the value returned is FALSE, the optional ELSE statement is executed. The syntax for the IF...ELSE statement is as follows:

```
IF Boolean Expression
  {SQL statement | Statement Block}
[ELSE [Boolean Expression]
  {SQL statement | Statement Block}]
```

Following is an example of IF and IF...ELSE using a single SQL statement and a statement block:

```
If @count = 0
   Select * from authors
else
```

```
   Select * from titles
if @Total != 0
begin
   Select count(*) from authors
   Select count(*) from titles
end
else
begin
   Select * from authors
   Select * from titles
end
```

The WAITFOR Statement

The WAITFOR statement is a delay that allows your stored procedure to wait for a specified time or until a specific time before execution continues. The syntax for the WAITFOR statement is as follows:

```
WAITFOR {DELAY 'time' ¦ TIME 'time'}
```

A WAITFOR statement can delay for up to 24 hours. The TIME and DELAY options use the format hh:mm:ss. The following example causes a delay of 10 seconds:

```
WAITFOR DELAY '00:00:10'
```

The following example waits until 11 a.m.:

```
WAITFOR TIME '11:00:00'
```

The RETURN Statement

The RETURN statement causes a stored procedure to exit and return to the calling procedure or application. The syntax for RETURN is as follows:

```
RETURN [Integer Value]
```

You can return an integer value to the calling routine or application using the following syntax:

```
exec @status = procedure_name
```

The following example consists of two parts. The first part is a stored procedure, called usp_return, which returns an integer to the calling procedure or application. The second part is a stored procedure, called usp_call, which calls the stored procedure usp_return and checks the returned value:

```
Create Procedure usp_return
as
Declare @ret_val int
```

```
Select @ret_val = 0
Return @ret_val
go

Create Procedure usp_call
as
Declare @status int
exec @status = usp_return
if(@status = 0)
   Print "Value returned is zero"
go
```

When writing stored procedures, SQL Server uses the value 0 to indicate success. Negative values indicate that an error has occurred (see Table 26.1 for more information). The return values –1 to –99 are reserved for SQL Server. When you use the RETURN statement, you can return only integer values; if you want to return other datatypes, you must use an output parameter, as described later in this chapter.

The following table lists reserved return values and the corresponding explanation.

TABLE 26.1 RESERVED STORED PROCEDURE RETURN VALUES

Return Value	Explanation
0	Procedure executed successfully
–1	Object missing
–2	Datatype error occurred
–3	Process chosen as deadlock victim
–4	Permission error occurred
–5	Syntax error occurred
–6	Miscellaneous user error occurred
–7	Resource error, such as out of space, occurred
–8	Nonfatal internal problem encountered
–9	System limit reached
–10	Fatal internal inconsistency occurred
–11	Fatal internal inconsistency occurred
–12	Table or index corrupted
–14	Hardware error occurred

Using Stored Procedures and Cursors

CHAPTER 26

695

26

USING STORED
PROCEDURES AND
CURSORS

The WHILE, BREAK, and CONTINUE Statements

The WHILE statement enables you to perform repeating conditional loops for the execution of a SQL statement or a statement block. The BREAK statement causes an exit from the WHILE loop; CONTINUE causes the WHILE loop to restart, skipping any statements that follow the CONTINUE statement. These statements have the following format:

```
WHILE Boolean Expressions
{SQL statement ¦ statement block}
[BREAK ¦ CONTINUE]
```

Examples of these statements can be found in the sample stored procedures shown at the end of this chapter.

The PRINT Statement

The PRINT statement enables you to return a message to the client's message handler. The message can have up to 1024 characters. The PRINT statement has the following syntax:

```
PRINT 'any ASCII text' ¦ @local_variable ¦ @@FUNCTION ¦ string_expr
```

If you print a local or global variable, the variable must be a char or varchar datatype; otherwise, you have to convert the datatype to a char or varchar before printing. Following are some examples using the PRINT statement:

```
Declare @msg varchar(255), @count int
Select @count = 0
Print "Starting the procedure"
While @count < 5
Begin
   Select @count = @count + 1
   Select @msg = "The Value of @count is " + str(@count)
   Print @msg
end
Select @msg = "This about wraps this procedure up."
Select @msg = @msg + " The value of @count is " + str(@count)
Print @msg
```

Listing 26.1 shows the output generated from the preceding PRINT statements, executed from the Microsoft SQL Server Query Analyzer tool.

LISTING 26.1 PRINT STATEMENT OUTPUT

```
Starting the procedure
The Value of @count is           1
The Value of @count is           2
```

continues

LISTING 26.1   CONTINUED

```
The Value of @count is           3
The Value of @count is           4
The Value of @count is           5
This about wraps this procedure up. The value of @count is        5
```

TIP

Use PRINT statements in your stored procedures during testing to help debug the stored procedure. Use the PRINT statement like a trace statement to print out particular locations or values in the procedure.

The RAISERROR Statement

The RAISERROR statement sets an SQL Server system flag to signify that an error has occurred and sends back an error message to the client connection. The syntax for RAISERROR is as follows:

```
RAISERROR ({message_id ¦ message_str}, severity, state [,arg1[,arg2]])
➥ [WITH (LOG or NOWAIT or SETERROR)]
```

Use the WITH LOG option to write the error message to the SQL Server error log and the Windows NT event log.

Comments

Comments in a stored procedure follow the C programming language standard or ANSI style comments. Comments begin with a /* and end with a */. Everything between the /* and the */ is considered part of the comment. Comments that begin with -- are ANSI standard comments. Use a lot of comments to make your stored procedures easy to read and maintain. Following are some examples of comments:

```
/* This is a one line comment */
/* This
   Comment
   Spans
   Several lines */
/*
** This is a comment - I think the added ** makes it easier to read.
*/
--This is an ANSI style comment.
```

Using Stored Procedures and Cursors

CHAPTER 26

697

26

USING STORED
PROCEDURES AND
CURSORS

PARAMETERS USED WITH STORED PROCEDURES

Parameters enable you to write flexible stored procedures by executing the SQL statements with values that are determined at runtime (not at compile time) and that can be changed at every execution. Parameters follow the same naming conventions as standard stored procedure variables. (They must begin with @.) Parameters can be input parameters or output parameters.

Input Parameters

Input parameters are used to pass values into a stored procedure. Input parameters have the following syntax:

```
Create proc Procedure_name @parm1 datatype, @paramN datatype
```

The following example defines three input parameters of different datatypes:

```
Create procedure usp_input @temp_name varchar(30), @total int,
➥ @current_date datetime
```

You can pass the values into a stored procedure in several ways. The standard way to pass the values is as follows:

```
exec usp_input 'Spenik & Sledge', 1000, '03/25/96'
```

When you use the preceding calling form, you must pass the values in the same order as they are declared in the stored procedure. Instead of passing in values, you can also pass in other variables (of the same datatype) as follows:

```
exec usp_input @authors_name, @new_total, @my_date
```

Another way to pass parameters is by using the parameter name. When using the parameter name, you can pass the parameters in any order—but if you use the name for one parameter, you must use the parameter name for all parameters that follow. The following is a valid example of using parameter names:

```
exec usp_input @total = 1000, @temp_name = 'Spenik & Sledge',
➥ @current_date = '03/25/96'
```

The following example is *not* valid because after you start using a parameter name, all the parameters that follow must also include the name:

```
exec usp_input 'Spenik & Sledge', @total = 1000, '03/25/96'
```

Input parameters can also have default values. To assign a default value to an input parameter, use the following syntax:

```
@parameter_name datatype = default_value
```

For example

```
create proc usp_param @p1 int, @p2 int = 3, @p3 int
```

If the procedure is called without a parameter (as in the following example), the default value is used:

```
exec usp_param @p1=5, @p3=100
```

To use an input parameter in a stored procedure, reference the variable name (just like any other variable). The following example checks the value of the parameter; if the parameter is less than 0, a message is printed:

```
create procedure usp_test @p1 int
as
   if @p1 < 0
      print "The value is less than zero"
```

> **TIP**
>
> Input parameters are null unless a non-null value is passed to the procedure or the procedure explicitly sets the parameter. If you are using stored procedures to INSERT data and the data is based on input parameters, verify that the parameters are not null.
>
> Additionally, you can use the DEFAULT clause for a stored procedure parameter to explicitly set a value if a value is not passed to the procedure. This is useful when you have a stored procedure that has numerous input parameters and the parameters may or may not be set by the calling routine.

Output Parameters

Output parameters are used to return values into a variable to a calling stored procedure or application. The syntax to declare an output parameter is as follows:

```
Create procedure procedure_name @parameter_name datatype OUTput
```

The following example declares an output parameter called @p1:

```
create procedure usp_test @p1 int OUT
```

To call a procedure with an output parameter, you must declare a variable to hold the returned value. (The variable does not have to have the same name as the output parameter used in the create procedure statement.) Use the keyword out (output) as follows:

```
exec usp_test @v1 out
```

Using Stored Procedures and Cursors

CHAPTER 26

699

26

USING STORED
PROCEDURES AND
CURSORS

After the procedure executes, you can then use the value in the output parameter (in this example, @v1) for further processing. You can also use the parameter name with output parameters, as follows:

```
exec usp_test @p1 = @v1 out
```

The following example multiplies an input parameter by 2 and returns the string version of the result in an output parameter:

```
Create Procedure usp_Double_Value @old_value int, @new_value varchar(20)
OUT
as
Declare @temp_value int
Select @temp_value = @old_value * 2
Select @new_value = convert(varchar(20), @temp_value)
```

The following example uses the procedure usp_Double_Value and prints out the results:

```
Declare @start_value int, @computed_value varchar(20)
Declare @msg varchar(50)

Select @start_value = 20
exec usp_Double_Value @start_value, @computed_value OUT
Select @msg = "The computed value is " + @computed_value
Print @msg
```

Listing 26.2 shows the output generated from the preceding routine when executed from the Microsoft SQL Server Query Analyzer tool.

LISTING 26.2 PRINT STATEMENT OUTPUT

```
(1 row(s) affected)

(1 row(s) affected)

The computed value is 40
```

COMMONLY USED GLOBAL VARIABLES

SQL Server provides several global variables you can use when writing stored procedures. A *global variable* is distinguished from a standard variable by the @@ that precedes the name. Following is a list of some of the commonly used global variables:

- @@ERROR is probably the most commonly used global variable. @@ERROR is used to check the error status of a statement executed by SQL Server. @@ERROR contains a 0 if the statement executed correctly. (Note: @@ERROR is kept by connection; the value of @@ERROR for your connection is not changed by other users' statements.)

- `@@FETCH_STATUS` is used to check the status of a cursor's fetch command and is discussed in detail in the section, "What Is a Cursor?," later in this chapter. (`@@FETCH_STATUS` is also kept per connection.)

- `@@IDENTITY` holds the value of the last successful identity value inserted. (`@@IDENTITY` is kept per connection.)

- `@@ROWCOUNT` holds the value for the number of rows affected by the last SQL statement. (`@@ROWCOUNT` is kept per connection.)

- `@@SERVERNAME` specifies the name of the local SQL Server.

- `@@TRANCOUNT` is the number of current active transactions for the current user.

- `@@VERSION` contains the version number of SQL Server.

HOW TO DEBUG A STORED PROCEDURE

SQL Server 7.0 does not ship with a stored procedure debugger. However, debugging can be accomplished by using alternate methods. The following are the alternative methods.

- Transact-SQL Debugging
- Other Debugging Tools

Transact-SQL Debugging

The following are some Transact-SQL statements that are useful for debugging stored procedures.

- `PRINT` statement   The `PRINT` statement is useful to display the contents of string variables. Keep in mind that the `PRINT` statement cannot display any variable that is not a string. It can also be used to determine, whether a certain line of code is executed (see the topic titled "The `PRINT` Statement," in this chapter for more information).

- `SELECT` statement   The `SELECT` statement is also useful to display the contents of memory variables. A `SELECT` statement can display any type of memory variable, regardless of its datatype. The following is an example of the `SELECT` statement displaying the contents of a memory variable.

```
declare @myvar integer
select @myvar = 100
select @myvar
```

Listing 26.3 shows the output generated from the preceding routine when executed from the Microsoft SQL Server Query Analyzer tool.

LISTING 26.3   SELECT STATEMENT OUTPUT

```
- - - - - - - - - - -
100

(1 row(s) affected)
```

Other Debugging Tools

In addition to Transact-SQL, you can also use the following tools to debug stored procedures.

- SQL Server Debugger   This product ships with Microsoft Visual C++ 5.0 Enterprise Edition and Microsoft Visual Basic 5.0 Enterprise Edition. The debugging environment is similar to Microsoft's Visual Basic debugger, in that it enables you to set breakpoints and display the contents of a variable.

- ODBC tracing   When calling stored procedures from an ODBC client, it is often useful to view the parameters that the client is passing to the stored procedure. You can use the trace feature in ODBC to store SQL calls to a text file. To activate ODBC tracing, open Control Panel, select ODBC-32, select the Tracing tab, and click Start Tracing Now. Keep in mind that ODBC tracing may slow your application and may generate a large text file.

- SQL Server Profiler   This product traces SQL activity. Again, this can be useful when you are trying to trace the parameters that are passed to a stored procedure. See Chapter 19, "Monitoring SQL Server," for more information on SQL Server Profiler.

USING THE EXECUTE COMMAND TO EXECUTE STRING VARIABLES

You can use the EXECUTE statement to generate dynamic SQL statements and execute them all at runtime. When creating dynamic SQL, remember that you must have the proper access to all the objects you plan to use in the dynamic SQL statement. You are limited to generating dynamic SQL statements that do not exceed the maximum size of a char, varchar, or text datatypes.

On the performance side, keep in mind that dynamic SQL is parsed and compiled at the time the EXECUTE statement is issued. You can also use the INSERT INTO command and the EXECUTE statement to populate a local database table with information from a remote server using a remote stored procedure.

WHAT IS A CURSOR?

A *cursor* is a SQL result set that enables you to perform row-oriented operations on the result set. (This differs from standard SQL result sets, which return all the rows in the result set.) This means that you can process data row by row. With SQL Server's cursors, you can navigate forward and backward through the result set. You can really exploit the power of cursors when you combine them with the EXEC command and a string variable substitution.

Cursors can be used in the following locations:

- In a control-of-flow batch
- Within a stored procedure
- Within a trigger

CREATING A CURSOR

Every cursor must have at least four components. The four key components *must* follow this order:

1. DECLARE the cursor.
2. OPEN the cursor.
3. FETCH from the cursor.
4. CLOSE or DEALLOCATE the cursor.

Step 1: DECLARE the Cursor

The DECLARE statement contains the user-defined name used to reference the result set, as well as the SQL SELECT statement that generates the result set. Think of the DECLARE statement as a temporary table that contains a pointer to your actual data source.

DECLARE Cursor Syntax

The following is the SQL-92 cursor syntax.

```
DECLARE cursor_name [INSENSITIVE] [SCROLL] CURSOR
FOR select_statement
[FOR {READ ONLY ¦ UPDATE [OF column_list]}]
```

The following is the version 7.0 cursor extension syntax. This syntax is similar to the cursor syntax supported by ODBC and ADO.

```
DECLARE cursor_name CURSOR
[LOCAL ¦ GLOBAL]
[FORWARD_ONLY ¦ SCROLL]
```

```
[STATIC ¦ KEYSET ¦ FAST_FORWARD ¦ DYNAMIC]
[READ_ONLY ¦ SCROLL_LOCKS ¦ OPTIMISTIC]
FOR select_statement
[FOR {READ ONLY ¦ UPDATE [OF column_list]}]
```

The following is the SQL-92 syntax explanation.

cursor_name	The cursor name.
INSENSITIVE	Specifies that changes in your data source will not be reflected in the cursor. Updates are not allowed to a cursor when this option is specified.
SCROLL	Allows the following FETCH commands to be used: PRIOR, FIRST, LAST, ABSOLUTE *n*, and RELATIVE *n*.
select_statement	An SQL SELECT statement. The following SQL commands force a cursor to be declared as INSEN-SITIVE: DISTINCT, UNION, GROUP BY, and/or HAVING.
READ ONLY	Prohibits updates from occurring against the cursor.
UPDATE [OF *column_list*]	Allows updates to be performed against the cursor. The optional clause [OF *column_list*] specifies which columns in the cursor can be updated.

The following is the version 7.0 cursor extension syntax explanation.

FORWARD_ONLY	Specifies that cursor navigation only supports the FETCH NEXT command. Use this option to minimize cursor resources and locks.
STATIC	Specifies that the cursor does not allow modifications and that changes to base tables will not be reflected in the cursor. Use this option when the cursor will be read-only and you want to minimize cursor resources and locks.
KEYSET	Specifies that the cursor members and the cursor order is fixed. Only the keys to base tables used by cursor are maintained by the cursor. (*Note*: a KEY-SET cursor reverts to a STATIC cursor if the base table(s) do not contain unique indexes or primary keys.)
DYNAMIC	Specifies that changes to base tables are reflected within the cursor. Use this option to maximize data consistency. However, this option requires substantial cursor resources when compared to the KEYSET or STATIC or cursor types.

FAST_FORWARD	Designates a FORWARD_ONLY, READ_ONLY cursor. This option has been optimized for performance.
SCROLL_LOCKS	Specifies that locks are placed on the data used in the cursor result set. The locks occur when the data is read into the cursor. This option ensures that UDPATES or DELETES to a cursor always succeed because the data is locked by the cursor. This option should probably be avoided when data concurrency is a priority.
OPTIMISTIC	Specifies that the cursor is not in place and locks on the data when it is read into the cursor. UDPATES or DELETES to a cursor may fail if the underlying cursor data has changed after it was read into the cursor. This option should be used when data concurrency is priority.

> **NOTE**
>
> You cannot mix the SQL-92 cursor syntax and version 7.0 cursor extension syntax. Also, the version 7.0 cursor extension syntax is not backward compatible with previous versions of SQL Server, whereas the SQL-92 is backward compatible with SQL Server 6.x.

Example 1: Standard Cursor

```
declare pub_crsr cursor
for
select pub_id,pub_name
from publishers
```

Example 2: Read-Only Cursor

```
declare pub_crsr cursor
for
select pub_id,pub_name
from publishers
FOR READ ONLY
```

Example 3: Cursor That Allows Updates

```
declare pub_crsr cursor
for
select pub_id,pub_name
from publishers
FOR UPDATE
```

Step 2: OPEN the Cursor

After you declare a cursor, you must open it. The OPEN statement should immediately follow the DECLARE statement.

OPEN Cursor Syntax

```
OPEN [GLOBAL] cursor_name
```

    cursor_name   The name of cursor to open.

Example

```
OPEN pub_crsr
```

Step 3: FETCH from the Cursor

After the cursor has been opened, you can retrieve information from the result set on a row-by-row basis. SQL Server provides forward-scrolling cursors *and* backward-scrolling cursors.

FETCH Syntax

```
FETCH [[NEXT ¦ PRIOR ¦ FIRST ¦ LAST ¦ ABSOLUTE n ¦ RELATIVE n] FROM]
➥[GLOBAL] cursor_name
[INTO @variable_name1, @variable_name2, ...]
```

NEXT	Retrieves the next row
PRIOR	Retrieves the preceding row
FIRST	Retrieves the first row
LAST	Retrieves the last row
ABSOLUTE *n*	Retrieves a row based on the absolute position within the result set
RELATIVE *n*	Retrieves a row based on the relative position within the result set

---

TIP

Use negative numbers to move backward within a result set when using the ABSOLUTE and RELATIVE arguments. When you use ABSOLUTE, the rows are counted backward from the last row in the recordset. When you use RELATIVE, the rows are counted backward from the current position in the recordset.

cursor_name	The name of cursor.
INTO @*variable_name1*, @*variable_name2*, and so on	Copies the contents of a column into a variable.

Example 1: Return the Next Row in the Result Set

```
fetch next from pub_crsr
```

Example 2: Return the 5th Row in the Result Set

```
fetch absolute 5 from pub_crsr
```

Example 3: Copy the Contents of the Next Row into Host Variables

```
fetch next from pub_crsr into @pub_id,@pub_name
```

Step 4: CLOSE or DEALLOCATE the Cursor

After you finish processing the cursor, you must CLOSE or DEALLOCATE the cursor. The CLOSE statement closes the cursor but does not release the data structures used by the cursor. Use this statement if you plan to reopen the cursor for subsequent use. The DEALLOCATE statement closes the cursor and releases the data structures used by the cursor.

> **TIP**
>
> Always CLOSE or DEALLOCATE a cursor as soon as processing is complete. Cursors consume resources, such as locks, memory, and so on. If these resources are not released, performance and multi-user problems may arise.

CLOSE and DEALLOCATE Syntax

```
CLOSE [GLOBAL] cursor_name
DEALLOCATE [GLOBAL] cursor_name
cursor_name    The cursor name.
```

Example 1: Close a Cursor

```
CLOSE pub_crsr
```

Example 2: Deallocate a Cursor

```
DEALLOCATE pub_crsr
```

Positional UPDATE and DELETE

In addition to being able to retrieve data from a cursor, you can perform positional updates and deletes against the data contained in the cursor. When a modification is made to a cursor, that modification automatically cascades to the cursor's data source.

Syntax

```
UPDATE table_name
SET column_name1 = {expression1 ¦ NULL ¦ (select_statement)}
[, column_name2 = {expression2 ¦ NULL ¦ (select_statement)}...]
WHERE CURRENT OF cursor_name

DELETE FROM table_name
WHERE CURRENT OF cursor_name
```

table_name	The name of the table to UPDATE or DELETE.
column_name	The name of column to UPDATE.
cursor_name	The cursor name.

Example 1: Update the `pub_name` Column in the `publishers` Table

This update is based on the current row position in the cursor:

```
UPDATE publishers
SET pub_name = 'XYZ publisher'
WHERE CURRENT OF pub_crsr
```

Example 2: Delete a Row in the `publishers` Table

This delete is based on the current row position in the cursor:

```
DELETE FROM publishers
WHERE CURRENT OF pub_crsr
```

Global Variables

The following two global variables can be used to monitor the status of a cursor: @@fetch_status and @@cursor_rows.

The @@@@fetch_status variable displays the status of a last FETCH command. Following are the possible values for @@fetch_status:

0	Successful fetch
–1	The fetch failed or the fetch caused the cursor to go beyond the result set.
–2	The fetch row is missing from the data set.

The following is an example of `@@fetch_status`:

```
while @@fetch_status = 0
   ...do some processing@@
```

The `@@cursor_rows` variable displays the number of rows in the cursor set. Use this variable *after* the cursor has been opened. Following are the possible values for `@@cursor_rows`:

-n	Cursor is currently being loaded with data. The number returned indicates the number of rows currently in the key result set; however, the number continues to increase as SQL Server processes the SELECT statement (this is known as *asynchronous processing*).
n	Number of rows in the result set.
0	No matching rows in the result set.
-1	Indicates that the cursor is dynamic and that the number of records is unknown.

PUTTING IT ALL TOGETHER

Now that you know something about cursor statements, positional updates, and global variables, the following cursor examples show you how all these components fit together.

Example 1: Loop Through a Table

The following example shows how the different components of a cursor (DECLARE, OPEN, FETCH, and DEALLOCATE) are used to loop through the `publishers` table. The `@@fetch_status` global variable is referenced each time a FETCH is performed. After the record pointer reaches the end of the result set, the `@@fetch_status` variable are equal to –1. This prevents the code inside the `while @@fetch_status = 0` section from being executed.

```
/* suppress counts from being displayed */
SET NOCOUNT ON

/* declare a cursor that will contain the pub_id, pub_name columns */
/* from the publishers table */
declare pub_crsr cursor
for
select pub_id,pub_name
from publishers

/* open the cursor */
open pub_crsr
```

Using Stored Procedures and Cursors

CHAPTER 26

709

26

USING STORED
PROCEDURES AND
CURSORS

```
/* get the first row from the cursor */
fetch next from pub_crsr

/* loop through the rows in the cursor */
while @@fetch_status = 0
begin
  /* get next row */
  fetch next from pub_crsr
end

/* close the cursor */
deallocate pub_crsr
```

And the output appears as

```
pub_id   pub_name

0736    New Moon Books
0877    Binnet & Hardley
1389    Algodata Infosystems
1622    Five Lakes Publishing
1756    Ramona Publishers
9901    GGG&G
9952    Scootney Books
9999    Lucerne Publishing
```

Example 2: Display Object Names and Object Types

The following example displays object names and types for all user-defined objects in
the pubs database. It uses two variables (@name and @type) and conditional logic to determine object type.

```
/* suppress counts from being displayed */
SET NOCOUNT ON

/* declare variables */
declare @name sysname
declare @type char(2)

/* declare a cursor that will contain a list of object */
/* names and object types */
declare object_list cursor
for
select name, type
from sysobjects
where type <> 'S'
order by type

/* open the cursor */
open object_list
```

```
/* get the first row from the cursor */
fetch next from object_list into @name,@type

/* loop through the rows in the cursor */
while @@fetch_status = 0
begin
  /* determine object type */
  if @type = 'C'
    select '(CHECK constraint) ' + @name
  if @type = 'D'
    select '(Default or DEFAULT constraint) ' + @name
  if @type = 'F'
    select '(FOREIGN KEY constraint) ' + @name
  if @type = 'K'
    select '(PRIMARY KEY or UNIQUE constraint) ' + @name
  if @type = 'L'
    select '(Log) ' + @name
  if @type = 'P'
    select '(Stored procedure) ' + @name
  if @type = 'R'
    select '(Rule) ' + @name
  if @type = 'RF'
    select '(Stored procedure for replication) ' + @name
  if @type = 'TR'
    select '(Trigger) ' + @name
  if @type = 'U'
    select '(User table) ' + @name
  if @type = 'V'
    select '(View) ' + @name
  if @type = 'X'
    select '(Extended stored procedure) ' + @name

  /* get next table name */
  fetch next from object_list into @name,@type
end

/* close the cursor */
deallocate object_list
```

And the output appears as

```
name               type
(CHECK constraint) CK__authors__au_id__02DC7882
(CHECK constraint) CK__authors__zip__04C4C0F4
(CHECK constraint) CK__jobs__max_lvl__2719D8F8
(CHECK constraint) CK__jobs__min_lvl__2625B4BF
(CHECK constraint) CK__publisher__pub_i__089551D8
(CHECK constraint) CK_emp_id
(Default or DEFAULT constraint) DF__authors__phone__03D09CBB
(Default or DEFAULT constraint) DF__employee__hire_d__30A34332
(Default or DEFAULT constraint) DF__employee__job_id__2BDE8E15
```

```
(Default or DEFAULT constraint) DF__employee__job_lv__2DC6D687
(Default or DEFAULT constraint) DF__employee__pub_id__2EBAFAC0
(Default or DEFAULT constraint) DF__jobs__job_desc__25319086
(Default or DEFAULT constraint) DF__publisher__count__09897611
(Default or DEFAULT constraint) DF__titles__pubdate__0F424F67
(Default or DEFAULT constraint) DF__titles__type__0D5A06F5
(FOREIGN KEY constraint) FK__discounts__stor___2160FFA2
(FOREIGN KEY constraint) FK__employee__job_id__2CD2B24E
(FOREIGN KEY constraint) FK__employee__pub_id__2FAF1EF9
(FOREIGN KEY constraint) FK__pub_info__pub_id__3567F84F
(FOREIGN KEY constraint) FK__roysched__title___1E8492F7
(FOREIGN KEY constraint) FK__sales__stor_id__1AB40213
(FOREIGN KEY constraint) FK__sales__title_id__1BA8264C
(FOREIGN KEY constraint) FK__titleauth__au_id__1312E04B
(FOREIGN KEY constraint) FK__titleauth__title__14070484
(FOREIGN KEY constraint) FK__titles__pub_id__0E4E2B2E
(PRIMARY KEY or UNIQUE constraint) PK__jobs__job_id__243D6C4D
(PRIMARY KEY or UNIQUE constraint) PK_emp_id
(PRIMARY KEY or UNIQUE constraint) UPK_storeid
(PRIMARY KEY or UNIQUE constraint) UPKCL_auidind
(PRIMARY KEY or UNIQUE constraint) UPKCL_pubind
(PRIMARY KEY or UNIQUE constraint) UPKCL_pubinfo
(PRIMARY KEY or UNIQUE constraint) UPKCL_sales
(PRIMARY KEY or UNIQUE constraint) UPKCL_taind
(PRIMARY KEY or UNIQUE constraint) UPKCL_titleidind
(Stored procedure) byroyalty
(Stored procedure) reptq1
(Stored procedure) reptq2
(Stored procedure) reptq3
(Trigger) employee_insupd
(User table) authors
(User table) discounts
(User table) employee
(User table) jobs
(User table) pub_info
(User table) publishers
(User table) roysched
(User table) sales
(User table) stores
(User table) titleauthor
(User table) titles
(View) titleview
```

Example 3: Delete Data from Various Tables in a Database

The following example combines the EXEC command with a cursor to automatically DELETE the data in all tables that begin with word 'SAMPLE'.

```
/* set database */
use pubs
go
```

```
/* create sample tables and data */
CREATE TABLE sample1 (id int, descr varchar(10))
insert into sample1 values (1,'one')
insert into sample1 values (1,'two')

CREATE TABLE sample2 (id int, descr varchar(10))
insert into sample2 values (3,'three')
insert into sample2 values (4,'four')


/* declare variables */
declare @table_name sysname

/* declare a cursor that will contain a list of table */
/* names to be deleted. */
/* NOTE: this example deletes data from tables */
/* that begin with the word SAMPLE. */

declare delete_cursor cursor
for select a.name
from sysobjects a
where a.type = 'U' and a.name LIKE 'sample%'
order by a.name

/* open the cursor */
open delete_cursor

/* get the first row from the cursor */
fetch next from delete_cursor into @table_name

/* loop through the rows in the cursor */
while @@fetch_status = 0
  begin
    /* issue DELETE command */
    EXEC ("DELETE " + @table_name)

    /* get next table name */
    fetch next from delete_cursor into @table_name
  end

/* close the cursor */
deallocate delete_cursor
```

Example 4: Positional Update

The following example looks at each row in the publishers table. If the pub_id column is equal to '1389', the pub_name column is updated to 'XYZ publisher'.

```
/* suppress counts from being displayed */
SET NOCOUNT ON
```

Using Stored Procedures and Cursors

CHAPTER 26

713

26

USING STORED
PROCEDURES AND
CURSORS

```
/* declare variables */
declare @pub_id char(4),@pub_name varchar(40)

/* declare a cursor that will contain the pub_id, pub_name columns */
/* from the publishers table */
/* NOTE: for UPDATE clause allows position updates */
declare pub_crsr cursor
for
select pub_id,pub_name
from publishers
for UPDATE OF pub_id,pub_name

/* open the cursor */
open pub_crsr

/* get the first row from the cursor */
fetch next from pub_crsr into @pub_id, @pub_name

/* loop through the rows in the cursor */
while @@fetch_status = 0
begin
  if @pub_id = '1389'
    update publishers
    set pub_name = 'XYZ publisher'
    where current of pub_crsr

  /* get next row */
  fetch next from pub_crsr into @pub_id, @pub_name
end

/* close the cursor */
deallocate pub_crsr
```

Example 5: Batch Run

The following stored procedure and cursor example enables you to schedule a single stored procedure with the SQL Server scheduler that in turn executes any stored procedures in a table of batch procedures. This example was used for an organization that performed many different types of batch processing using nightly stored procedures. The stored procedures were required to run in a certain order, and the addition of new procedures was a common occurrence. Instead of constantly scheduling the procedures, this example creates a single table, Batch_Procedures, which holds the names of the stored procedures to execute during the nightly batch run. It then creates a stored procedure called usp_Batch_Run that executes each procedure in the Batch_Procedures table.

> **NOTE**
>
> The current limitations to this stored procedure (which you can easily modify) are as follows:
>
> - usp_Batch_Run can execute only stored procedures in the same database as usp_Batch_Run. This limitation exists because the system table sysobjects is checked, as a security measure, to validate that the name in the Batch_Procedures table is an existing stored procedure.
> - usp_Batch_Run does not support stored procedures with parameters.

The batch processing consists of one support table, one report table, and a stored procedure. The table schema for Batch_Procedures is as follows:

```
CREATE TABLE Batch_Procedures (
   priority int,
   procedure_name varchar (20),
   description varchar (255)
 )
CREATE  UNIQUE  CLUSTERED  INDEX cidx_priority ON Batch_Procedures
    ( priority )
```

For example, if you have a stored procedure named usp_rollups that is the first procedure to execute in the batch, you would add the procedure to the table Batch_Procedures as follows:

```
INSERT Batch_Procedures
Values(0,"usp_rollups","First procedure of the batch")
```

The stored procedure usp_Batch_Run opens a cursor on the Batch_Procedures table and executes each procedure in the Batch_Procedures table. The syntax for the Batch_Run procedure is as follows:

```
CREATE PROCEDURE usp_Batch_Run AS
/*-------------------------------------------------------------

usp_Batch_Run

-------------------------------------------------------------
Description: Executes all the stored procedures that are
             stored in the table Batch_Procedures. Results
             from the batch run is stored in the table
             Batch_Results.  This procedure is schedule to run
             via the task scheduler.

Parameters: None.
```

```
Status Returns: None.

Example: usp_Batch_Run
------------------------------------------------------------------
History:
Mark Spenik, SAMS - DBA Survival Guide - 2nd Edition
Sept 30, 1998
2nd Release.
----------------------------------------------------------------*/
Declare @status int, @procedure_name varchar(20)
Declare @priority int, @description varchar(255), @id int
Declare @IsProc int

/*
** Declare a cursor to retrieve each stored procedure listed
** in the Batch_Procedures table.
*/

declare batch_run_crsr cursor
For Select procedure_name,priority,description
from Batch_Procedures
Order By priority

/*
** Clear out the results table from the previous nights run.
*/
truncate table Batch_Results

/*
** Open the cursor to begin running the batch stored procedures.
*/
Open batch_run_crsr
if @@error != 0
   goto Batch_Error

/*
** Get the first Row
*/
fetch next from batch_run_crsr
into @procedure_name, @priority, @description

While (@@fetch_status = 0) And (@@error = 0)
begin

   /*
   ** Make sure it's a stored procedure
   */
   select @IsProc = count(*)
   from sysobjects
   where id = object_id(@procedure_name)
   and type = 'P'
```

```
if @IsProc > 0
begin
    /*
    ** First log the starting time in the batch results table.
    */
    Insert Batch_Results
    Values(getdate(), NULL, @procedure_name, @description, NULL)

    /*
    ** Save identity value for the update.
    */
    Select @id = @@identity

    /*
    ** Execute the Stored Procedure
    */
    Execute @status = @procedure_name

    /*
    ** Update the results table.
    */
    UPDATE Batch_Results
        set end_time = getdate(),            status = @status
    Where id = @id
END /* If IsProc > 0 */
/*
** Get the next procedure.
*/
fetch next from batch_run_crsr
into @procedure_name, @priority, @description

end /* While */

close batch_run_crsr
deallocate batch_run_crsr
return 0

/*
** Simple Error Exit
*/
Batch_Error:
RAISERROR ('Error executing stored procedure usp_Batch_Run',16,-1) return
-100
```

The table Batch_Results is truncated every time the stored procedure usp_Batch_Run is executed. The Batch_Results table is used to log the status of the procedures that are executed during the stored procedure usp_Batch_Run. You can enhance the procedure by selecting all the rows from the Batch_Results table and use email to notify users of the status of the batch run. The table schema for the Batch_Results table is as follows:

```
CREATE TABLE Batch_Results (
   id int IDENTITY,
   start_time datetime,
   end_time datetime NULL,
   proc_name varchar (20)  NULL,
   msg varchar (  255 )  NULL,
   status int NULL
)
CREATE  UNIQUE  CLUSTERED  INDEX cidx_Id ON Batch_Results
   ( id )
```

STORED PROCEDURE AND CURSOR FAQ

Following are some of the common questions asked by DBAs about SQL Server stored procedures and cursors:

Q. Do stored procedures really run faster than sending SQL statements directly to SQL Server?

A. Yes, stored procedures run faster because they are precompiled, cached, and generate less network traffic.

Q. When should I use stored procedures?

A. Whenever you want to maximize performance and consolidate SQL code into a single program. Examples of stored procedure include INSERT, DELETE, and UPDATE stored procedures and reporting stored procedures.

Q. When should I not use stored procedures?

A. Stored procedures probably should not be used for ad-hoc querying because the parameters and the data being returned are often decided at runtime. Stored procedures work best when a predefined result set is being returned.

Q. How many call levels can a stored procedure perform?

A. Stored procedures support up to 32 levels of procedure nesting, meaning that a stored procedure can call another stored procedure, which in turn can call another, until the maximum nesting level of 32 is reached. To determine the current level of nesting, use the global variable @@nestlevel.

Q. Can I create temporary table inside a stored procedure?

A. You can create temporary tables and indexes on the temporary tables using a stored procedure. All temporary tables are created in the temporary database regardless of where the stored procedure executes. Any local temporary table created in a stored procedure is removed when the procedure exits.

Q. Can I create a temporary table in a stored procedure and reference the temporary table from another stored procedure?

A. If you create a temporary table in a stored procedure and call another stored procedure, the procedure called can use the temporary table created by the calling procedure.

Q. Can I create a temporary table inside a stored procedure, drop it, and create another temporary table with the same name?

A. You cannot create a temporary table in a stored procedure, drop it, and then try to create another temporary table with the same name.

Q. What commands cannot be executed from within a stored procedure?

A. You cannot perform the following SQL statements within a stored procedure: CREATE VIEW, CREATE DEFAULT, CREATE RULE, CREATE TRIGGER, and CREATE PROCEDURE.

Q. How can I remove a stored procedure?

A. To remove a stored procedure, use the DROP Procedure command.

Q. How can I rename a stored procedure?

A. To rename a stored procedure, use the system stored procedure sp_rename.

Q. When are stored procedures automatically recompiled by SQL Server?

A. Stored procedures are recompiled when a table is dropped and re-created, when all query plans in the cache are in use, when the procedure is executed with the WITH RECOMPILE option, when an index is dropped, when the procedure is no longer in the procedure cache, or when the procedure is dropped and re-created.

Q. Should I use exact datatypes when creating memory variables within a stored procedure?

A. To decrease the overhead of data conversion when using input parameters within a stored procedure on a WHERE clause, make sure that the datatype of the input parameter matches the column datatype. The exception to this rule is a char datatype column with N characters that allows NULL values. SQL Server treats this as a VARCHAR.

Q. What is a remote stored procedure?

A. A remote stored procedure is a stored procedure that is executed on another SQL Server from your local SQL Server.

Q. Can users access tables within a stored procedure when they do not have permissions to the tables referenced within the stored procedure?

A. A user can execute a stored procedure that accesses tables, views, or other stored procedures to which the user does not have access. The owner of the stored procedure needs the proper access rights to objects used in the procedure. The stored

Using Stored Procedures and Cursors

CHAPTER 26

719

26

USING STORED
PROCEDURES AND
CURSORS

procedure owner then grants to other users the only command permission a stored procedure has: EXECUTE.

Q. How can I time how long a stored procedure takes to execute?

A. To time the stored procedure and display the start and end times in hh:mm:ss:ms format, use the functions getdate() and convert as follows:

```
select convert(varchar(20), getdate(), 14) 'Start Time'
exec Procedure_name
select convert(varchar(20), getdate(), 14) 'End Time'
```

For a stored procedure that returns several rows of data, you can use the following timing routine, which displays both the start and end times at the end of the stored procedure:

```
declare @startmsg varchar(40)
declare @endmsg varchar(40)

select @startmsg = 'Start Time: ' + convert(varchar(20), getdate(),
14)
/* Execute stored procedure */
exec Procedure_name
select @endmsg = 'End Time:   ' + convert(varchar(20), getdate(), 14)


print @startmsg
print @endmsg
```

Q. How can I troubleshoot complex SQL statements within a stored procedure?

A. Use the Microsoft SQL Server Query Analyzer tool and break the stored procedure into parts, testing each part of the stored procedure and validating the results of each part. For example, you can determine whether your WHERE clause is correct is to change the SQL statement into SELECT count(*). You can quickly run the complex SQL statement and determine by the row count whether the WHERE clause is correct. The following example shows how to replace an UPDATE statement with SELECT count(*) to validate the WHERE clause. Here's the original code fragment:

```
UPDATE table_a
Set my_name = table_b.old_name
FROM table_a, table_b
WHERE table_a.id = table_b.id
AND table_a.birth_date IN (Select *
                            From table_c)
```

To test the WHERE clause, change the UPDATE statement to SELECT count(*) as follows:

```
Select count(*)
FROM table_a, table_b
WHERE table_a.id = table_b.id
AND table_a.birth_date IN (Select *
                            From table_c)
```

Q. How can I subtract a date within a stored procedure?

A. To subtract a date, use the `dateadd()` function with a negative number. The following example subtracts 10 days from the current day's date:

```
select dateadd(day,-10,getdate())
```

Q. How can I determine the size of a stored procedure?

A. To determine the size of a stored procedure, you can use `DBCC MEMUSAGE`. This command displays the size of the 20 largest objects in the procedure cache.

Q. How can I display the error messages associated with an error number?

A. Use the `master..sysmessages` table. The following stored procedure takes an error number as an input parameter and returns the severity and the description of the error number from the `sysmessages` table. (Blanks are returned for error numbers that do not exist in `sysmessages`.)

```
create procedure usp_Show_Error_Message @error_number int
as
Select severity "Error Severity", description "Error Message"
from master..sysmessages
where error = @error_number
```

Q. How can I reduce network traffic when using stored procedures?

A. You can reduce the amount of extraneous information sent back by a stored procedure (for example, the message `N rows affected`) by placing the following statement at the top of your stored procedure:

```
SET NOCOUNT ON
```

When you use the `SET NOCOUNT ON` statement, you limit the amount of extraneous information sent back to the calling process, thus reducing network traffic and increasing performance. The following example, created in the `pubs` database, shows how to use the statement in a stored procedure:

```
Create procedure usp_nocount
as
SET NOCOUNT ON
Select * from authors
```

Q. When should I use a cursor?

A. A cursor should be used when you need to perform row-oriented operations. Whenever possible, use SQL statements instead of cursors to perform an operation because cursors may require server resources such as memory and locks. Additionally, SQL statements usually run faster than cursors. However, certain types of operations cannot be performed using standard SQL statements. When these types of situations arise, use cursors.

Using Stored Procedures and Cursors

CHAPTER 26

721

26

USING STORED
PROCEDURES AND
CURSORS

Q. Should I use CLOSE or DEALLOCATE when I am done using a cursor?

A. If you are not planning on re-using the cursor you should use DEALLOCATE. This command releases all server resources used by the cursor. If you plan to re-use the cursor, use CLOSE. When you are done with the cursor, use DEALLOCATE.

SUMMARY

As a DBA, it is important that you understand how you can use stored procedures and cursors to simplify your daily and weekly routines. If you understand what you can and cannot do with stored procedures and cursors, you can be of great benefit to your organization. Following are some important points to remember about SQL Server stored procedures:

- A stored procedure is a series of precompiled SQL statements and control-of-flow language statements.
- Stored procedures are stored on SQL Server and execute on SQL Server.
- A remote stored procedure is a stored procedure that is executed on another SQL Server from your local SQL Server.
- Stored procedures can have input and output parameters.
- The only user command permission that can be granted or revoked for a stored procedure is the EXECUTE permission.
- When creating stored procedures, use lots of comments and headers to simplify future maintenance.

Following are some important points to remember about cursors:

- Use a cursor to perform row-oriented operations on a set of data.
- SQL Server's cursors enable you to navigate forward and backward through a result set.
- Use the EXEC command inside a cursor to construct SQL statements at runtime.

USING SQL-DMO (DISTRIBUTED MANAGEMENT OBJECTS)

by Mark Spenik

IN THIS CHAPTER

Have you ever felt that Microsoft left out a utility or some graphical display that you thought would really make your life easier? With SQL Server 7.0, you might be able to write that utility yourself! "How?" You ask. The answer is an exciting feature added first to SQL Server 6.0 and extended with SQL Server 7.0—SQL-DMO!

SQL-DMO stands for SQL Distributed Management Objects. SQL-DMO is based on Microsoft's Component Object Model (COM) and supports OLE automation. OLE stands for Object Linking and Embedding, but in the past few years has come to stand for so much more. A few years ago, Microsoft and several integrated system vendors created open specifications for application intercommunication called OLE. The OLE specifications defined more than applications communicating with one another; they also specified how applications can expose parts of their functionality as objects to be used by other applications. OLE became part of ActiveX, which is now all part of COM.

The benefits of COM include the ability of application developers to create applications that use parts of other applications to further enhance their own applications. For example, you can create an application that uses the charting capabilities of Microsoft Excel or you can include Microsoft's Word spell checker into a text editor application.

What does all this have to do with SQL Server and database administration? Through SQL-DMO, SQL Server exposes several objects, methods, and properties that can be easily controlled programmatically to perform database administrative tasks. Microsoft calls the objects SQL-DMO (SQL Distributed Management Objects). Using SQL-DMO, you can easily create applications, stored procedures or Web pages that perform many DBA tasks for you!

> **NOTE**
>
> This chapter almost seems out of place in a book on DBA survival. However, it introduces a technology that truly empowers the DBA, enabling the DBA to create his or her own powerful database utilities. Even if you think this chapter seems too much like a programming chapter, hang in there! The explanations in this chapter are geared toward DBAs, not programmers. Even if you don't know how to program, you will at least understand what *can* be done, and you may be able to have someone program your utility for you!

Before going into more detail, here is a quick review of some OLE terminology:

- **Container/controller/client application**: An application that can create and manage OLE objects. Visual Basic is an example of a container application.

- **Server/object application**: An application that creates OLE objects. SQL Server is an object application.

- **OLE automation**: OLE automation is a standard that enables applications to expose their objects and methods so that other applications can use them.

- **Object**: Defining an object is a bit difficult. If the OLE definition of an object is used, the discussion gets into many other aspects of OLE, which are covered in detail in other Sams books but that confuse the topic of this book. This chapter uses a simpler definition: *An object represents some sort of data with properties and methods.* In SQL Server terms, for example, a database is an object, and a stored procedure is an object. Figure 27.1 shows the case of a database object.

  The object has attributes. (In OLE terminology, attributes are called *properties.*) In Figure 27.1, some of the properties of a database object are listed: Name, CreateDate, Size, and Status are all examples of properties of the database object.

  The Name property for the database shown in Figure 27.1 is pubs. A property tells you something about the object. You can read properties, and in some cases, you can set properties.

  Objects also have methods. A method is an action the object performs. Examples of the database objects methods are shown in Figure 27.1. The CheckIdentityValues method, for example, can be used on the database object. If you invoked the CheckIdentityValues method of the database object named pubs, what do you think would happen? If you said, "check identity columns on the tables in the pubs database," you are correct.

FIGURE 27.1

An example of a database object.

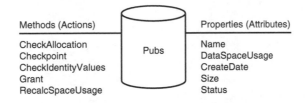

Methods (Actions)		Properties (Attributes)
CheckAllocation		Name
Checkpoint	Pubs	DataSpaceUsage
CheckIdentityValues		CreateDate
Grant		Size
RecalcSpaceUsage		Status

- **Collections**: A collection is an object that consists of items that can be referred to as a group (see Figure 27.2).

  In Figure 27.2, there are several standard SQL Server databases: master, pubs, model, and tempdb. If you group all the databases shown into one large group called databases, you have a collection.

  Collections enable you to easily perform tasks on each item in the collection. To perform a DBCC CHECKDB command on every database on your SQL Server, for example, you can use the collection object to get each database on the server and invoke a method that performs that DBA task.

FIGURE 27.2

An example of a collection object.

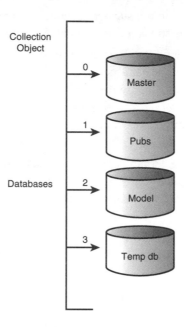

SQL SERVER 6.5 TO 7.0 QUICK REFERENCE

The following is a quick summary of the changes that occurred between SQL Server version 6.5 and 7.0:

What's New

Many new objects have been added due to the overhaul of SQL Server. Check the SQL-DMO object model references with SQL Server 7.0.

What's Been Renamed

The object library has been changed from SQLOLE to SQLDMO.

What's Gone

Again because SQL Server underwent a major overhaul, several objects, such as devices, are missing. See the SQL-DMO object model.

SQL SERVER'S OBJECT MODEL

To use SQL-DMO, you must understand the SQL Server object model. The *object model* is the hierarchy of exposed SQL Server objects you can use programmatically.

You follow the object model as you would a file directory tree. For example, the top level of the object model is the Application object.

> **NOTE**
>
> It is standard practice when creating OLE object models from a standalone application to include an Application object.

To use other objects, follow the tree to the next level to find the objects you will use, for example the SQL Server object. Object models also contain objects that are dependent upon other objects. To use a dependent object, you must first have the parent object of the dependant object. For example, getting an instance of a database object requires getting a SQL Server object first. The database object is said to be *dependent upon* the SQL Server object; that is, you must have a SQL Server object before you can use the database object.

WHY USE SQL-DMO?

What benefits can you get from learning to use SQL-DMO? The real gain is that you can easily create custom solutions for your database administration environment, allowing you more free time to perform other tasks. For example, you can create a user wizard that performs a series of tasks, such as adding the user to every database based on the user's group.

Using SQL-DMO, you can create applications that you normally have to perform manually. Currently, you can automate many tasks you perform regularly by using stored procedures. The advantage SQL-DMO has over stored procedures for performing administrative task is simplicity. By using collection objects, you can easily perform DBCC commands on every database on the server, using only a few lines of code. Many Transact-SQL commands have been simplified. The DBCC command and the many different DBCC options become methods of different objects.

Another advantage SQL-DMO has over stored procedures is that you can use true programming languages that have more powerful programming features than Transact-SQL. Additionally, you can easily integrate your applications into other desktop applications (such as word processors or spreadsheets) to enhance your customized database administration applications. Following is brief list of some of the many administrative tasks you can perform. (This is a *brief* list; SQL-DMO enables you to perform almost any system administrative task.)

- Back up/restore a database
- Generate scripts
- Perform Replication Operations
- Perform DBCC commands such as `CheckTable`, `CheckCatalog`, and so on
- Grant and revoke privileges
- Add alerts
- Perform BCP
- Transfer data from one server to another
- Manage users

CREATING APPLICATIONS WITH SQL-DMO

You can use SQL-DMO using Transact-SQL, in Active Server Pages or build entire applications around SQL-DMO. To build a SQL-DMO application or component requires a 32-bit programming language that can create OLE controller applications. Tools such as Microsoft Visual C++, Borland Delphi, or Microsoft Excel for Windows NT with 32-bit VBA (Visual Basic for Applications) can easily be used. The examples and code samples shown in this chapter are based on Microsoft Visual Basic 6.0. The choice of Visual Basic is easy because it is the most popular and rapid application-development tool available. The core language of Visual Basic 6.0 is VBA and can be found in the Windows 95/98 releases of Access, Project, and Excel.

The remainder of the chapter focuses on using SQL-DMO objects to perform a variety of database administration tasks using Visual Basic.

Using Visual Basic

TIP

If you are not familiar with Visual Basic, pick up a beginner's book and learn the Visual Basic basics. After you know the basics, you can use the suggestions and examples in this chapter effectively to create your own applications. The following discussion of Visual Basic is brief and is given primarily for those who are not familiar with Visual Basic so that they can understand SQL-DMO.

Following is a brief introduction to Visual Basic to help you understand the terminology used later when creating an application that takes advantage of SQL-DMO. The main screen of Visual Basic 6.0 is shown in Figure 27.3.

FIGURE 27.3

Visual Basic 6.0.

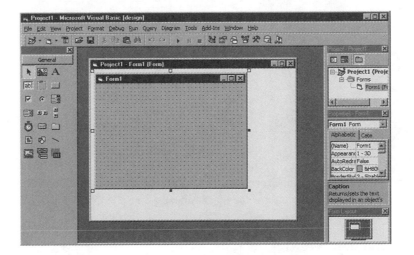

Creating Visual Basic applications consists of creating forms, adding controls to the forms using the toolbar, and adding code to modules and forms that make up the application. The forms and code modules that make up a Visual Basic application are called a *project* and can be found in the project window shown in Figure 27.3. The next sections step you through some Visual Basic rudiments you will need later to create your own SQL-DMO applications or to enhance the application provided on the CD with this book (the DBA Assistant).

Adding a Control to a Form and Setting Properties

A Visual Basic *control* is similar to a SQL-DMO object in that both have properties and methods. Understanding the properties and methods used with a Visual Basic control can help you better understand the concepts of SQL-DMO objects and properties. To add a control to a form, perform the following steps:

1. Click the icon on the toolbar of the control you want to add to the form. Common controls used on the toolbar are shown in Figure 27.4.

2. Place the mouse cursor on the form; while holding the left mouse button, drag the mouse down. Visual Basic begins to draw a control on the form.

3. Release the left mouse button. You have added a control to the form.

FIGURE 27.4

The Visual Basic toolbar.

4. To set properties (such as color, name, height, width, and so on) for the control or the form, click the form or control to make it the active object and press F4. The Properties window for the object appears (see Figure 27.5).

FIGURE 27.5

The Visual Basic form Properties window.

5. To change a property, select the property field and enter a new value. For example, if you want to change the name of the control, edit the Name property.

Declaring a SQL-DMO Object in Visual Basic

To use a SQL-DMO object, you must first declare the object in your code. With Visual Basic, you can use the generic object type, which can hold any type of OLE object, or you can declare an object of a specific SQL-DMO object type by using the type library. To create a variable using a generic object, use the following syntax:

```
Dim Variable_Name As Object
```

To create a specific SQL-DMO, use the following syntax:

```
Dim Variable_Name As SQLDMO.SQL_DMO_OBJECT
```

In this syntax, `SQL_DMO_OBJECT` is the specific SQL-DMO object (such as `SQLServer`, `Database`, `Table`, and so on). For example, to define a SQL-DMO SQL Server object using the type library, enter the following:

```
Dim MySqlServer As SQLDMO.SQLServer
```

> **TIP**
>
> Declare SQL-DMO variables using the type library and declaring specific SQL Server objects rather than using the generic object. Using specific objects is faster and enables Visual Basic to perform *early binding* (checking that you are using proper objects and methods) during compilation rather than at runtime.

Creating a SQL-DMO Object with Visual Basic

After you declare a variable to be an SQL-DMO object, you must create the object before you can use the methods and properties of the object.

> **NOTE**
>
> Creating an object is also referred to as *getting an instance* of the object.

You can create the object with either the keyword `New` or the function `CreateObject`. Following is an example that uses the `New` keyword when declaring a variable:

```
Dim MySqlServer As New SQLDMO.SQLServer
```

You also can use the `New` keyword in code, as follows:

```
Set MySqlServer = New SQLDMO.SQLServer
```

The `CreateObject` function has the following syntax:

```
CreateObject("application_name.object_type")
```

The following code creates a new SQL Server SQL-DMO object with `CreateObject`:

```
Set MySqlServer = CreateObject("SQLDMO.SQLServer")
```

After you create an object, you can use the objects, properties, and methods to perform DBA tasks.

Releasing Objects

Just as important as creating an object is releasing the object when you are finished with it. Objects in Visual Basic are released when they go out of scope. If the object is declared in a procedure, the object is released when the procedure completes. If the object is declared in a form, the object is released when the form unloads. Global objects are not released until the application closes.

It is always good Visual Basic coding practice to release your objects in code when you are finished with them by using the keyword Nothing. The following code, for example, releases a SQL-DMO table object called MyTable:

```
Set MyTable = Nothing
```

Required SQL-DMO Files

To create SQL-DMO objects using Visual Basic, you must have the following files, which are included with the 32-bit versions of SQL Server client utilities for Windows NT and Windows 95. You can find the following files in the SQL Server 7.0 home directory (C:\MSSQL7) in the directory \BINN:

SQLDMO.HLP	SQL-DMO help files, including object hierarchy
SQL Server 3.70 or later ODBC Files	SQL-DMO uses ODBC to connect to the server
SQLDMO.XXX	Localized resource file, the extension will vary
SQLDMO70.DLL	In process SQL-DMO server

> **NOTE**
>
> SQL-DMO is available only in 32-bit Windows environments (Windows NT and Windows 9x).

SQL-DMO Checklist

You can use the following checklist when creating SQL-DMO applications. Use this first checklist to ensure that you have the proper files and utilities required to use SQL-DMO:

❑ Have Windows NT or Windows 9x.

❑ Have installed a 32-bit OLE automation controller (Visual Basic).

❑ ODBC 3.70 or greater SQL Server driver (ships with SQL Server 7.0).

❑ Install the proper SQL-DMO files from the 32-bit SQL Server Client utilities.

The following checklist includes the steps required to create SQL-DMO objects from Visual Basic:

❑ 1. Include the SQL-DMO type library in the Visual Basic environment by adding `Microsoft SQLDMO Object Library` to the Visual Basic references.

❑ 2. Declare a SQL-DMO `SQLServer` object.

❑ 3. Create the `SQLServer` object.

❑ 4. Connect the `SQLServer` object to SQL Server.

❑ 5. Use the SQLServer objects, properties, and methods, and declare and create any other required SQL-DMO objects to accomplish your required DBA task.

❑ 6. Release SQL-DMO objects using the keyword `Nothing` when you are done using them.

❑ 7. Disconnect the `SQLServer` object.

❑ 8. Release the `SQLServer` object.

ENHANCING THE SQL SERVER DBA ASSISTANT

Now comes the real value. As you probably know by now, examples that use SQL-DMO are hard to find. SQL Server ships with a few SQL-DMO samples that are poorly documented. The overall SQL-DMO documentation contains very few descriptive examples but concentrates on describing the objects and methods.

On the CD-ROM included with this book is a Visual Basic project titled `samsdba.vbp`, which is the Visual Basic project file and contains all the source code for the application SQL Server DBA Assistant. The source code is included as a foundation that you can modify and enhance to meet your own needs. The following sections discuss the most important parts of the SQL Server DBA Assistant.

NOTE

The source code for the application is included on the CD-ROM that accompanies this book. The following sections concentrate on the code that uses SQL-DMO, not the Visual Basic code that does not deal with SQL-DMO. The Visual Basic code is well documented so that you can use the code and form to easily add your own functionality to the project.

27

USING
SQL-DMO

What's in the SQL Server DBA Assistant?

Before getting started on developing the SQL Server DBA application, you must decide what type of functionality you are going to put in the application. First, because the purpose of the utility is for actual DBA work and learning, you should create an application that uses several different SQL-DMO objects.

What is missing from Microsoft SQL Server 7.0? Graphical maintenance of tables as well as graphical BCP.

To fix this oversight, the SQL Server DBA Assistant enables you to perform table maintenance on several different databases using the SQL-DMO `database` object and the `table` object. Following is a list of the functionalities of the SQL Server DBA Assistant:

- Lists all the databases in a combo box for selection
- Performs table maintenance on selected tables
- Performs BCP export on selected tables

Connecting to SQL Server

> **NOTE**
>
> This chapter skips a few steps here that are Visual Basic related, such as creating a new project called `samsdba` and adding controls to the logon form.

Assuming that you have all the proper files and have added the Microsoft `SQLDMO` Object Library references to Visual Basic, it is now time to declare a SQL Server object and connect to SQL Server. For logon purposes, use the form shown in Figure 27.6 (`frmLogon`).

FIGURE 27.6

The SQL Server DBA Assistant Logon form.

Using your checklist for creating a SQL-DMO application, perform Step 2: declare a SQL-DMO object, as follows in the Visual Basic module `global.bas`:

Public MySqlServer As SQLDMO.SQLServer 'Global SQL Server Object

The next step is to create a SQL Server object. The code to create a SQL Server object is located in the Visual Basic module sqlserv7.bas in the procedure main. The code for the main procedure is shown in Listing 27.1.

LISTING 27.1 PROCEDURE main: CREATING A SQL SERVER OBJECT

```
Public Sub main()
'SAMS -MicroSoft SQL Server DBA Survival Guide
'
'Main - The procedure main creates a OLE SQL Server Object
'         and then pompts the user to enter the correct SQL Server
'         name.  If the user properly connects to the SQL Server
'         the main form of the application is shown.
'
'Set up Error handling

On Error GoTo Err_Main

'
'Check if the application is already running
'
If App.PrevInstance > 0 Then
    MsgBox "SQL Server DBA Assistant already running on this machine.", _
                vbCritical, "Already Running"
    End
End If

'
'Create a New SQL Server OLE Object
'
Set MySqlServer = CreateObject("SQLDMO.SQLServer")

connected = False 'Set Global to Not Connected
'
'Set SQL Server Connection Timeout Value
'
MySqlServer.LoginTimeout = 15 'Set for 15 seconds
'
'Display the Logon Screen
'
frmLogon.Show 1
Set frmLogon = Nothing  'Reclaim Object Memory

'If We established a Connection Display the Main form
' Otherwise exit the application
If connected = True Then
```

continues

LISTING 27.1   CONTINUED

```
    frmSplash.Show    'Display Splash Screen
    DoEvents          'Allow time to Paint the Splash Screen
    Load frmMain7     'Load the Main Form
    frmMain7.Show     'Make it Appear
    Unload frmSplash  'Make it disappear
    Set frmSplash = Nothing 'Reclaim Memory
    Exit Sub
End If
'
'Exit - If not Connected
Quit_App:

    If Not (MySqlServer Is Nothing) Then
        'Release SQL Server Object
        Set MySqlServer = Nothing
    End If
    End 'End the program
'
'Error Handler
'
Err_Main:
        '
        'Display Error Message
        MsgBox Err.Description, vbCritical, "Connection Error"
        Resume Next

End Sub
```

The following line creates a SQL-DMO SQL Server object using the function `CreateObject` (as specified in Step 3 of the SQL-DMO checklist):

```
Set MySqlServer = CreateObject("SQLDMO.SQLServer")
```

When this line of code executes, the variable `MySqlServer` contains a SQL Server object.

Before you try to connect to a SQL Server by logging on, you set the login time-out value by setting the SQL Server object property `LoginTimeout`, as follows:

```
MySqlServer.LoginTimeout = 15 'Set for 15 seconds
```

You now are ready to perform Step 4 of the checklist: Establish a connection to SQL Server. The logon form appears (refer to Figure 27.6). A user enters the SQL Server, user name, and password and clicks the Logon button on the form. The code shown in Listing 27.2 executes to establish a connection to the SQL Server.

LISTING 27.2   SQL SERVER CONNECTION

```
Private Sub cmdLogon_Click()

    'Set up the Error Handler
    '
    On Error GoTo Err_Logon
    '
    'Connect to the SQL Server
    '
    If txtServer <> "" Then
        Me.MousePointer = vbHourglass 'Turn Cursor to HourGlass
        '
        'Invoke Connect Method of the SQL Server Object
        '
        MySqlServer.Connect ServerName:=txtServer.Text, _
                        Login:=txtLogon.Text, _
                        Password:=txtPassword.Text
        '
        'Sql Server Connected Correctly - Unload the form
        '
        connected = True            'Set Global Connection Variable
        Me.MousePointer = vbDefault 'Turn Mousepointer back to default
        Unload Me                   'Unload the Logon form
    Else
        MsgBox "You must enter a SQL Server Name to Connect", _
            vbCritical, "Invalid Entry"
    End If
    '
    'Exit the routine - If Not Logged In Try Again
    '
Exit_Logon:

    Exit Sub
    '
' Error handler
    '
Err_Logon:
    Me.MousePointer = vbDefault
    MsgBox "Error Connection to Server. Error: " & Err.Description, _
        vbCritical, "Error Connection"
    Resume Exit_Logon
End Sub
    '
```

The following lines of code establish a connection with SQL Server using the Connection method of the SQL Server object:

```
'
'Invoke Connect Method of the SQL Server Object
'
MySqlServer.Connect ServerName:=txtServer.TEXT, _
                    Login:=txtLogon.TEXT, _
                    Password:=txtPassword.TEXT
```

After you establish a successful connection to SQL Server, you are ready to perform Steps 5 and 6 of the SQL-DMO application checklist: perform various tasks by creating objects, invoking methods, and setting properties.

Filling a Combo Box with Databases

To make the SQL Server DBA Assistant a useful tool during database table maintenance, you add the capability to select a database from a combo box and then read all the non-system tables associated with the database into a Visual Basic List Box control.

To read all the databases on the selected server into a combo box, you use the SQL Server SQL-DMO object and the databases collection. The code shown in Listing 27.3 populates a Visual Basic combo box with all the database names in your SQL Server object collection.

LISTING 27.3   POPULATING A COMBO BOX WITH DATABASE NAMES

```
Dim Db As SQLDMO.Database

    CenterForm frmMain7
    '
    'Fill the Combo Box on the form with the
    'available databases by using the SQL Server databases collection
    '
    For Each Db In MySqlServer.Databases
        '   Make sure the database is not currently being loaded
        '

        If Db.Status <> SQLDMODBStat_Inaccessible Then
            cmbDatabase.AddItem Db.Name
            cmbBCP.AddItem Db.Name
        Else
            MsgBox "Database: """ + Db.Name _
              + " """ is can not be accessed at this time.", _
              vbCritical, "Database Loading"
        End If
    Next
    Set Db = Nothing
```

To populate a list box with the tables in the database, you read the tables collection of the selected database. The code to populate the list box using the selected database is shown in Listing 27.4.

LISTING 27.4 POPULATING A LIST BOX WITH TABLE NAMES USING A DATABASE OBJECT AND THE TABLES COLLECTION

```
Private Sub cmbDatabase_Click()
Dim WorkTable As SQLDMO.Table 'SQL-DMO Table Object

    On Error GoTo Get_Tables_Error
    frmMain7.MousePointer = vbHourglass
    '
    'Database changed - Modify Database Object
    '
    Set WorkDb = Nothing       'Clear the Work Database object
    lstTables.Clear            'Clear tables list box
    lstOperateTables.Clear     'Clear the operate tables list Box

    'Get the currently selected database object
    '
    Set WorkDb = MySqlServer.Databases(cmbDatabase.Text)

    '
    'Fill The list box with the table names using the database
    'tables collection exclude any system tables.
    '
    For Each WorkTable In WorkDb.Tables 'Do For Each table in the database
        If Not (WorkTable.SystemObject) Then
            lstTables.AddItem WorkTable.Name 'Add to the list Box
        End If
    Next WorkTable

Exit_Get_Tables:
    Set WorkTable = Nothing
    frmMain7.MousePointer = vbDefault
    Exit Sub   'Leave the Procedure

'
' Error handler
'
Get_Tables_Error:
    Me.MousePointer = vbDefault
    MsgBox "Error reading tables collection " & Err.Description, _
        vbCritical, "Filling Combo Box Error"
    Resume Exit_Get_Tables

End Sub
```

> **TIP**
>
> You can begin to see that using SQL-DMO is simple after you become familiar with the SQL-DMO object model. Study the model and become familiar with the collections, objects, and the hierarchy.
>
> Getting a list of objects is simple using the Visual Basic FOR EACH - NEXT statement. FOR EACH - NEXT is used to read through all items of an array or collection. Examples of the FOR EACH - NEXT statement can be found in Listings 27.3 and 27.4.

Performing Table Maintenance

After a database has been selected, a database object can easily be created using the selected database name and the SQL Server object, as follows:

```
'Get the currently selected database object
    '
    Set WorkDb = MySqlServer.Databases(cmbDatabase.TEXT)
```

When the line of code executes, you have a SQL-DMO database object for the selected database. If you remember the object model for SQL-DMO, you can easily create a table object using the database object. After the table object has been created, you can perform a variety of table maintenance tasks using the different table methods. Following are some examples of the table object methods and the tasks they perform:

CheckTable	Performs the DBCC CheckTable command.
Grant	Grants table privileges to a list of SQL Server users or groups.
RecalcSpaceUsage	Recalculates the space information for the table.
Script	Generates the Transact-SQL statements to create the table.
UpdateStatistics	Updates the data distribution pages used by the Query Optimizer to make proper index selection.

For the SQL Server DBA Assistant, you can select the tables on which you want to perform a table maintenance operation and then click a button to perform the appropriate action. The code that scans through the list of selected tables and invokes the method is as follows:

```
'Execute Update Statistics command on selected tables
    '
    For X = 0 To lstOperateTables.ListCount - 1
        ProgressBar1.VALUE = X
        Set WorkTable = WorkDb.Tables(lstOperateTables.List(X))
```

```
       '
       'Update Statistics on the Table - using the UpdateStatistics Method
       '
       WorkTable.UpdateStatistics
       'Release the Work Table object
       Set WorkTable = Nothing
   Next X
```

The Table Maintenance page of the SQL Server DBA Assistant dialog box is shown in Figure 27.7.

Listing 27.5 shows the code used behind the Update Statistics button (shown in Figure 27.7).

FIGURE 27.7

The Table Maintenance page of the SQL Server DBA Assistant dialog box.

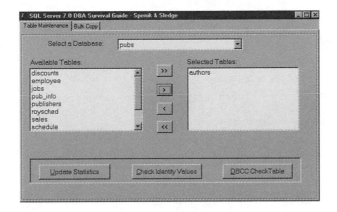

LISTING 27.5 PERFORMING UPDATE STATISTICS ON SELECTED TABLES

```
Private Sub cmdUpdate_Click()
Dim WorkTable As SQLDMO.Table 'SQL-DMO Table Object
Dim X As Integer

    On Error GoTo Up_Stats_Error
    SSPanel1.Enabled = False
    frmMain7.MousePointer = vbHourglass
    '
    'Setup The Progress Bar
    ProgressBar1.Max = lstOperateTables.ListCount
    ProgressBar1.Value = 0
    lblStatus.Caption = "Updating Statistics"
    frmStatus.Visible = True   'Turn On Progress Bar
    DoEvents 'Allow Screen to repaint
    '
```

continues

LISTING 27.5   CONTINUED

```
    StatusBar1.Panels("status").Text = "Updating Statistics - Please
        ➥Wait..."

    'Execute Update Statistics command on selected tables
    '
    For X = 0 To lstOperateTables.ListCount - 1
        ProgressBar1.Value = X
        Set WorkTable = WorkDb.Tables(lstOperateTables.List(X))
        '
        'Update Statistics on the Table - using the UpdateStatistics Method
        '
        WorkTable.UpdateStatistics
        'Release the Work Table object
        Set WorkTable = Nothing
    Next X
    'Cleanup and Exit
Up_Stats_Exit:
    '
    frmStatus.Visible = False
    StatusBar1.Panels("status").Text = ""
    SSPanel1.Enabled = True
    frmMain7.MousePointer = vbDefault
    Exit Sub

' Error handler
'
Up_Stats_Error:
    Me.MousePointer = vbDefault
    MsgBox "Error Updating statistics on table " &
        ➥_lstOperateTables.List(X) _
        & "Error: " & Err.Description, _
        vbCritical, "Update Statistics Error"
    Resume Up_Stats_Exit

End Sub
```

TIP

We have provided you with the following three table maintenance functions already programmed and ready to use. Look on the CD-ROM that accompanies this book; they're with the **SQL Server DBA Assistant**.

- `Update Statistics`
- `Check Identity Values`
- `DBCC CheckTable`

As stated earlier, the purpose of the SQL Server DBA Assistant is to provide you with a foundation from which you can create your own application. If you look behind each of the buttons, you will notice that the code is almost identical except for the methods added. By cutting and pasting the code into new buttons and adding new methods, you can add more functionality. You also can optimize the application by reducing the code behind the buttons by using a shared function or procedure. The list is endless—what are you waiting for?

Performing Table Exports Using Bulk Copy (BCP)

Before SQL Server 7.0, Microsoft had left out a graphical import/export manager for non-SQL Server databases. A graphical BCP utility was in SQL Server 4.21. SQL Server 7.0 of course has the very graphical and powerful DTS services, which perform import/export services to non-SQL Server data sources, but still no graphical BCP. Because the DBA Assistant is all about tools left out of the SQL Enterprise Manager, the ability to perform graphical BCP is very important—especially if you are in environments where the data fed into SQL Server is from mainframe flat files (or vice versa). The SQL Server DBA Assistant provides you with your own graphical BCP tool by adding the ability to export data using the BulkCopy object in the following formats:

- Tab delimited (default)
- Comma delimited
- Native format

The BulkCopy object differs from the objects used so far in these example applications because the BulkCopy object does not depend on other objects. To use a BulkCopy object, you create the BulkCopy object, set the various parameters of the BulkCopy object, and then pass the BulkCopy object as a parameter to a table or view object's ImportData or ExportData method. The BulkCopy object has a single method, Abort, to abort a running BCP; this method must be executed from another thread.

For the SQL Server DBA Assistant, the BulkCopy object is created when the object parameter oBcp is declared using the keyword New as follows:

```
Dim oBCP As New SQLDMO.BulkCopy 'Note BCP object is created here using New
Keyword
```

After the BulkCopy object has been created, the next step is to set the desired properties (such as the import batch size or the number of errors to ignore before halting the bulk copy). Here is an example of setting the BulkCopy objects MaximumErrorsBeforeAbort property:

```
'Max Number of errors before BCP quits
    If IsNumeric(txtMaxErrors.Text) Then
        oBCP.MaximumErrorsBeforeAbort = CInt(txtMaxErrors.Text)
    Else
        'Use Default
        oBCP.MaximumErrorsBeforeAbort = 1
    End If
```

When you set the properties of the `BulkCopy` object to import or export data, you pass the `BulkCopy` object as a parameter to a table or view object's `ImportData` or `ExportData` method. The following example shows the `ExportData` method being used:

```
iNumRows = BCPTable.ExportData(oBCP)
```

The Bulk Copy page of the SQL Server DBA Assistant dialog box is shown in Figure 27.8.

FIGURE 27.8

The Bulk Copy page of the SQL Server DBA Assistant dialog box.

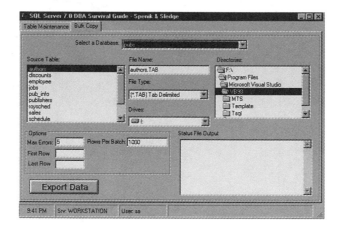

Listing 27.6 shows the code used behind the Export Data button (shown in Figure 27.8).

LISTING 27.6 PERFORMING BCP EXPORT ON SELECTED TABLES

```
Private Sub cmdExportData_Click()
Dim BCPTable As SQLDMO.Table    'SQL-DMO Table Object
Dim oBCP As New SQLDMO.BulkCopy 'Note BCP object is created here using New
                               ➥Keyword
Dim iNumRows As Long            'Stores number of rows returned from BCP
Dim oOutputFile As CFile        'Used for file I/O
Dim sTempBuf As String, sTemp As String 'Temp variables

    'Set up a simple error handler
    On Error GoTo Export_Error
```

```
'Setup display
SSPanel1.Enabled = False
frmMain7.MousePointer = vbHourglass
'
StatusBar1.Panels("status").Text = "Exporting Data - Please Wait..."

'Step 1 - Get a instance of the table object to perform the BCP
'
'Get the table object - to perform the export
'
Set BCPTable = WorkDb.Tables(lstBCPTables.Text)

'Step 2 - Set up the BCP objects properties
'
'        (Note: A instance of the BCP object was created above in DIM
      ➡statement
'                using the keyword New)
'
'Set the BulkCopy input/output file parameter
oBCP.DataFilePath = Dir1.Path & txtFile

'Set the error log and log file parameters
oBCP.LogFilePath = App.Path & "\sams_bcp.log"
oBCP.ErrorFilePath = App.Path & "\sams_err.log"

'
'Do some validation checking and set optional parameters
'
' Batch Size (Not used for exporting - only used in imports
'                added here for your convence - should you modify
'                the program to do imports).
'
If IsNumeric(txtBatchSize.Text) Then
    oBCP.ImportRowsPerBatch = CInt(txtBatchSize.Text)
Else
    'Use Default
    oBCP.ImportRowsPerBatch = 1000
End If

'Max Number of errors before BCP quits
If IsNumeric(txtMaxErrors.Text) Then
    oBCP.MaximumErrorsBeforeAbort = CInt(txtMaxErrors.Text)
Else
    'Use Default
    oBCP.MaximumErrorsBeforeAbort = 1
End If

'First Row to start BCP
If txtFirstRow <> "" Then
```

continues

LISTING 27.6 CONTINUED

```
        If IsNumeric(txtFirstRow.Text) Then
            oBCP.FirstRow = CInt(txtFirstRow.Text)
        End If
    End If
End If

'Last Row to end BCP
If txtLastRow <> "" Then
    If IsNumeric(txtLastRow.Text) Then
        oBCP.LastRow = CInt(txtLastRow.Text)
    End If
End If

'Set the output type for the BCP- based on combo box
sTemp = cmbType.Text

Select Case sTemp
    Case "(*.CSV) Comma Delimited"
        oBCP.DataFileType = SQLDMODataFile_CommaDelimitedChar

    Case "(*.TAB) Tab Delimited"
        oBCP.DataFileType = SQLDMODataFile_TabDelimitedChar

    Case "(*.DAT) Native"
        oBCP.DataFileType = SQLDMODataFile_NativeFormat

End Select

'Step 3 - Export the Data
'
'Here is the part you have been waiting for -
'Pass the BCP object to the table ExportData method and
'away it goes!
'
iNumRows = BCPTable.ExportData(oBCP)

'The output results are written to a file.
'Create a file object to read the contents
'of the file and display the output file results in the status text
➥box.
'
Set oOutputFile = New CFile
oOutputFile.FileName = oBCP.LogFilePath
oOutputFile.IOMode = "INPUT"
oOutputFile.IOType = "SEQUENTIAL"
oOutputFile.OpenFile
If oOutputFile.Status = 1 Then
    oOutputFile.ReadAll sTempBuf
    If sTempBuf <> "" Then
        txtStatus.Text = sTempBuf
```

```
        Else
            txtStatus.Text = Str(iNumRows) & " rows exported."
        End If
    Else
        txtStatus = "Error reading BCP output file."
    End If
    oOutputFile.CloseFile

    'Report the number of rows exported
    MsgBox Str(iNumRows) & " rows exported.", vbInformation, "Bulk Copy"

    'Cleanup and Exit
Export_Exit:
    '
    Set oBCP = Nothing
    Set BCPTable = Nothing
    Set oOutputFile = Nothing
    frmStatus.Visible = False
    StatusBar1.Panels("status").Text = ""
    SSPanel1.Enabled = True
    frmMain7.MousePointer = vbDefault
    Exit Sub

Export_Error:
    MsgBox Err.Description
    Resume Export_Exit

End Sub
```

> **NOTE**
>
> The BCP code provided does not import data, but you can modify the code to add this feature. The value of the `BulkCopy` object property `ImportRowsPerBatch` is set and is included in the export data code—even though it is not used during BCP export—in case you want to modify the code to import data. The log and error files created when performing BCP default to the DBA Assistant application directory (that is, the directory where the DBA Assistant is executing) with the filenames `sams_bcp.log` and `sams_bcp.err`.

USING SQL-DMO WITH STORED PROCEDURES

Not comfortable with Visual Basic but you're pretty good with Transact SQL? Have you ever been writing a stored procedure and wanted to perform some administrative task during the procedure like backing up a database or exporting a table? For those of you that answered yes to any of the previous questions, Microsoft has created a set of stored procedures that enable you to invoke COM based objects that support OLE automation (that is SQL-DMO) within a stored procedure. You can use SQL-DMO via Transact-SQL or you can write your own OLE automation servers using your Windows tool of choice (for example, Visual Basic) to create components that can be invoked through Transact-SQL. Creating your own components enables you to perform complex operations that may be difficult or impossible using Transact-SQL. OLE automation also enables you to use existing business objects that other Windows or COM based applications may already be using. The following stored procedures enable you to write Transact-SQL batches and stored procedures that act as OLE automation clients and can create and control OLE automation servers:

- sp_OACreate
- sp_OAGetErrorInfo
- sp_OAMethod
- sp_OAGetProperty
- sp_OASetProperty
- sp_OAStop
- sp_OADestroy

OLE Automation Procedures

Before looking at an example of using SQL-DMO using Transact-SQL, take a look at each OLE automation stored procedure.

sp_OACreate

sp_OACreate creates an instance of an OLE automation object. Think of it as the Visual Basic equivalent to CreateObject. The syntax is as follows:

```
sp_OACreate 'ProgramID'|'classid', object_token OUTPUT [,process_context]
```

where *ProgramID* has the form OLEComponentName.Class, *classid* is the class identifier of the OLE object which has the form nnnnnnnn-nnnn-nnnn-nnnn-nnnnnnnnnnnn, *object_token* is the returned object token of type Transact-SQL type int and *process_context,* an optional parameter, specifies whether the object runs in the server process, out of process, or supports either. The procedure also returns a status. If the status returned is not 0, an error has occurred.

For example, the following Transact-SQL creates a SQL Server SQL-DMO object:

```
Declare @oSQL int
Declare @status int
@status = sp_OACreate 'SQLDMO.SQLServer',@oSQL OUT
```

Sp_OAGetErrorInfo

When invoking the Transact-SQL OLE automation stored procedures, use sp_OAGetErrorInfo to retrieve error status from the previous sp_OA call. The error status is reset each time an OLE automation stored procedure is called, except for sp_OAGetErrorInfo. The syntax is as follows:

```
sp_OAGetErrorInfo [object_token[,source OUTPUT[,description OUTPUT
➥[,help_file OUTPUT [,help_id]]]]]
```

The syntax breaks down as follows: *object_token* is the object token of a previously created OLE automation object; source is a char or varchar variable to return the source of the error; description is a char or varchar character that returns a description of the error; help_file is a char or varchar variable that returns the help file for the OLE automation object; and help_id, which must be a data type of int, is the help file context id for the OLE automation object.

For example, the following Transact-SQL creates checks for an error using sp_OAGetErrorInfo:

```
If @status <> 0
Begin
exec sp_OAGetErrorInfo @oSQL,@source OUT, @ErrorDescription OUT
end
```

> **NOTE**
>
> In the example code just listed, OUT is a permissible Transact-SQL shortcut for OUTPUT.

sp_OAMethod

To invoke a method on an OLE automation object, use sp_OAMethod. The syntax for sp_OAMethod is as follows:

```
sp_OAMethod object_token, method_name, [,return_value OUTPUT,
➥[,@parametername=]parameter [OUTPUT] [...n]]]
```

In this case, *object_token* is the object token of a previously created OLE automation object; *method_name* is the method to invoke; *return_value* is the value returned from the method; *@parametername* is used to specify a named parameter; *parameter* is a local variable, and *OUTPUT* is required if a value is returned from the method.

sp_OAGetProperty

sp_OAGetProperty retrieves the property value of an OLE automation object. sp_OAGetProperty has the following syntax:

```
sp_OAGetProperty @object_token, property_name [,property_value
OUTPUT][,index...]
```

Here, *object_token* is the object token of a previously created OLE automation object; *property_name* is the name of the property to retrieve; property_value is the variable to return the property value to, and index is an index parameter used by some OLE object properties.

If you do not specify a local variable (such as property_value parameter) to return the property, the value is returned in a resultset that consists of a single column/single row array. Multidimensional arrays and OLE objects can also be returned. The following is an example of getting the path where a BCP log file is to be written:

```
Declare @property_return varchar(255)
exec @status = sp_OAGetProperty @oBCP, 'LogFilePath', @property_return OUT
```

sp_OASetProperty

To set a property on an OLE automation object, use the stored procedure sp_OASetProperty, which has the following syntax:

```
sp_OASetProperty @object_token, property_name new_value [,index...]
```

In this case, *object_token* is the object token of a previously created OLE automation object; *property_name* is the name of the property to retrieve; new_value is the value to set the property, and index is an index parameter used by some OLE object properties.

The following is an example of setting the path where a BCP log file is to be written:

```
Declare @property_return varchar(255)
exec @status = sp_OASetProperty @oBCP, 'LogFilePath', "C:\BCP\LOG\bcp.log"
```

sp_OAStop

The first time sp_OACreate is invoked on a SQL Server, the OLE Automation Environment is started up on that SQL Server and shared by all clients using OLE automation via the OLE automation stored procedures. To stop the environment, use the stored procedure sp_OAStop, which has the following syntax:

```
sp_OAStop
```

This will stop the shared environment and cause errors in any clients that were using OLE Automation via the OLE automation stored procedures at the time of the shutdown.

The next time sp_OACreate is invoked, the environment will restart. It is not necessary to shut down the OLE automation environment because it is shut down when SQL Server is halted.

sp_OADestroy

sp_OADestroy destroys the created OLE object (for example removes the object reference and frees up memory). The syntax is as follows:

```
sp_OADestroy object_token
```

In this case, *object_token* is the object token of a previously created OLE automation object.

> **NOTE**
>
> It is a good programming practice to call sp_OADestroy to clean up and remove any OLE objects you use that are not necessary. SQL Server automatically destroys any objects you use at the end of the Transact-SQL batch.

Transact-SQL Example

The following example is a stored procedure that uses SQL-DMO and the OLE automation stored procedures to perform a bulk copy operation. This example is included because it can be used to solve a common real-world scenario. The (typical) real-world scenario is a stored procedure that is summarizing or rolling up data. After the summarization or rollup is completed, the information is to be exported to a flat file. One of the problems you encounter in this problem is how to know that the stored procedure has successfully summarized or rolled up the information so that you can perform the BCP. The second problem then becomes how to invoke the BCP. The most elegant solution is to use SQL-DMO, which enables you to perform the BCP operation from within a Transact-SQL batch, which solves both of your problems.

The code, shown in Listing 27.7, is well documented and self-explanatory. Read the comments and code to quickly see how easy it is to use SQL-DMO and the OLE automation stored procedures! The following Transact-SQL script is located on the CD that ships with the book in a file called TSQLBCP.sql.

LISTING 27.7   PERFORMING BCP EXPORT ON SELECTED TABLE USING TRANSACT-SQL

```
CREATE          PROCEDURE usp_BCP_Table_Out @tablename varchar(30),
@outpath varchar(255)
 AS

/*
** This stored procedure is an example of using SQL DMO to
** export a table out.
*/

/* Declare Variables used */
Declare @oSQL int, @oBCP int  /* Used to store object tokens */
Declare @status int /* Used to check error status */
Declare @source varchar(255), @description varchar(255)
/* Error information output parameters */
Declare @iNumRows int     /* Number of Rows Exported */
Declare @temp varchar(255) /* Temp area to construct SQL-DMO statement */
Declare @db_name varchar(30) /* database name */
/*
** Create the SQL Server object
*/
exec @status = sp_OACreate 'SQLDMO.SQLServer', @oSQL OUT

if @status <> 0
begin
   exec @status = sp_OAGetErrorInfo @oSQL,@source,@description
   Select  @source "Source of Error", @description "Error Description"
   return
end

/*
** Log on to the SQL Server
*/
exec @status = sp_OAMethod @oSQL, "Connect", NULL, "(local)", "sa"

if @status <> 0
begin
   exec @status = sp_OAGetErrorInfo @oSQL,@source,@description
   Select  @source "Source of Error", @description "Error Description"
   return
end

/*
** Create the BCP object
*/
exec @status = sp_OACreate 'SQLDMO.BulkCopy', @oBCP OUT

if @status <> 0
begin
   exec @status = sp_OAGetErrorInfo @oBCP,@source,@description
```

```
    Select  @source "Source of Error", @description "Error Description"
    return
end

/*
** Set some BCP Properties
*/

/*
** Path to export file to - use path passed in as a parameter
*/
exec @status = sp_OASetProperty @oBCP, 'DataFilePath',@outpath
if @status <> 0
begin
    exec @status = sp_OAGetErrorInfo @oBCP,@source,@description
    Select  @source "Source of Error", @description "Error Description"
    return
end

/*
**Path to create error and log file
*/
exec @status = sp_OASetProperty @oBCP, 'ErrorFilePath',"C:\bcperror.txt"

if @status <> 0
begin
    exec @status = sp_OAGetErrorInfo @oBCP,@source,@description
    Select  @source "Source of Error", @description "Error Description"
    return
end

exec @status = sp_OASetProperty @oBCP, 'LogFilePath',"C:\bcplog.txt"

if @status <> 0
begin
    exec @status = sp_OAGetErrorInfo @oBCP,@source,@description
    Select  @source "Source of Error", @description "Error Description"
    return
end

/*
** Now Let's create the string - to export the table.
** We will use the SQL Server object databases collection and the
** datbase table collection to invoke the table ExportData method.
**
** Note: this stored procedure uses the name of the current
** database by using the DB_Name function.
*/
```

continues

27

LISTING 27.7   CONTINUED

```
Select @db_name = DB_NAME()

/*
** Build SQL_DMO string
*/
Select @temp = 'Databases(' + '"' + @db_name + '"' + ').Tables('
Select @temp = @temp + '"' + @tablename + '"' + ').ExportData'

/*
** Now execute the string using SQL Server Dynamic SQL features
*/
exec @status = sp_OAMethod @oSQL,@temp,@iNumRows OUT,@oBCP

if @status <> 0
begin
   exec @status = sp_OAGetErrorInfo @oSQL,@source,@description
   Select  @source "Source of Error", @description "Error Description"
   return
end

Select @iNumRows "Number of rows exported"

/*
** Clean up and destroy the OLE objects
*/
exec @status = sp_OADestroy @oBCP
if @status <> 0
begin
   exec @status = sp_OAGetErrorInfo @oBCP,@source,@description
   Select  @source "Source of Error", @description "Error Description"

end
exec @status = sp_OADestroy @oSQL
if @status <> 0
begin
   exec @status = sp_OAGetErrorInfo @oSQL,@source,@description
   Select  @source "Source of Error", @description "Error Description"
end
```

SQL-DMO FAQ

Following are some frequently asked questions about SQL-DMO and the COM object stored procedures:

Q. Can I Create Internet SQL-DMO applications?

   A. SQL-DMO is a COM-based interface, so you can create Web-based applications with Web servers that support COM, such as Microsoft's Internet Information

Server's Active Server Pages. To help get you started, we include a small Web-based Active Server Page example that enables you to log on to your SQL Server via the Internet and view the status of scheduled tasks.

Q. I'm having a hard time finding examples of SQL-DMO. Any suggestions?

A. SQL-DMO is one of SQL Server's hidden features. It appears that developers and DBAs have been slow to look into SQL-DMO and use it to their advantage. However, SQL-DMO's usefulness is starting to be noticed. Several NT and developer's magazines have run articles on SQL-DMO. You can also check Microsoft's Web site for SQL-DMO examples as well as performing a Web search on SQL-DMO.

Q. Can I use other COM objects in my stored procedures besides SQL-DMO?

A. Sure, the COM object stored procedures work with any COM-based object that can be created using ActiveX (OLE) automation. The component needs to be properly registered on the SQL Server you want to create the object.

SUMMARY

For the non-Visual Basic DBAs in the crowd, I hope the explanations and code examples in this chapter were easy to follow and that they motivated you to learn Visual Basic.

If you are unfamiliar with Visual Basic but quite comfortable with Transact-SQL, the BCP example of using the OLE automation procedures and SQL-DMO provides you with an example you can learn from and use in your existing applications.

Using SQL-DMO, you can create powerful DBA tools that can be used to simplify your job!

SQL SERVER 7.0 AND THE INTERNET

by Kari A. Fernandez

IN THIS CHAPTER

The use of the Web to provide business solutions has exploded over the past several years and Web users have begun demanding more from those of us who provide information. Clients want up-to-date information fast. Companies can distribute data to the Web in several ways. Critical data can be stored on a Web page or in a database. You can edit static Web pages with new information using HTML-editing tools, such as Microsoft's FrontPage, or create a database-driven solution. A data-centric solution in SQL Server provides you with the ability to create a Web page once and automate its updates.

NOTE

Strictly defined, the Internet is a network of networks. Any two computers connected together is a network and any two networks connected is an internet. Today, virtually all computers can be networked together creating what we consider the Internet, or the World Wide Web. In this chapter, I refer to a Web site to imply an Internet, intranet, or extranet site. I refer to a person who accesses a Web site as a Web user or a client. I refer to Web site content as Web pages, HTML (Hypertext Markup Language) pages, or pages.

If you decide to automate your HTML page updates, your challenge is to implement a solution that allows you to publish HTML pages to your Web site with data presented in a scalable and manageable way. In addition, clients must be able to browse the pages quickly.

Speed in browsing is of course a combination of the ability of the PC requesting the Web page, the speed of the connection to the Web server, and the size of the page. Your Web page generated by the Web Assistant is created with SQL Server data so no further trips to SQL Server are required: there are no more impediments to speed. In other words, the client doesn't have to connect to SQL Server to ask for data: the results of a query have already been provided in a pregenerated static page.

TIP

Graphics slow the load time of an HTML page. Always include the height and width attributes when using the HTML Image tag. The browser will then lay out the page before the images fully load. If you also use the HTML Image tag's Alternate attribute, you can specify an alternate name for the image so the user can see what is loading.

Scalability is primarily achieved through the non-interactive queries you create and whose schedule you control. Manageability is provided through the Microsoft Management Console.

> **TIP**
>
> When designing your HTML page, keep the total download size in mind. Make sure your total page size doesn't exceed 50KB. Some software, such as FrontPage 98, includes utilities that estimate the download time of HTML pages.

Figure 28.1 shows SQL Server 7.0's model for Web-based client access to its databases. As you can see, from the Web browser, the client can request an HTML page from the Web server. In turn, the HTML page has been previously published from the SQL Server via a schedule and format stipulated by you when you ran the Web Assistant Wizard.

FIGURE 28.1

SQL Server 7.0 and the Web.

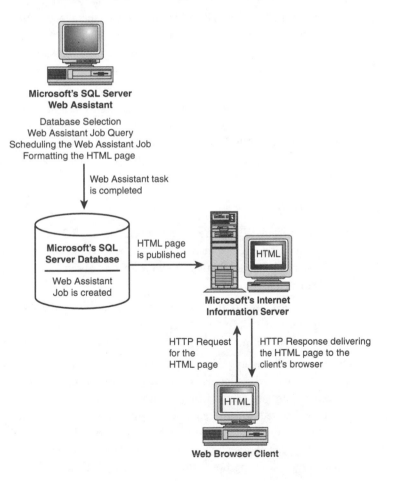

Microsoft's SQL Server
Web Assistant

Database Selection
Web Assistant Job Query
Scheduling the Web Assistant Job
Formatting the HTML page

Web Assistant task
is completed

Microsoft's SQL
Server Database

Web Assistant
Job is created

HTML page
is published

Microsoft's Internet
Information Server

HTTP Request
for the
HTML page

HTTP Response delivering
the HTML page to the
client's browser

Web Browser Client

SQL SERVER 6.5 TO 7.0 QUICK REFERENCE

The following is a quick reference to the changes between SQL Server version 6.5 and 7.0:

What's New

- From the Web Publishing results pane, you can

    Create a new Web Assistant job

    Execute a Web Assistant job

    Delete a Web Assistant job

    View the properties of a Web Assistant job

- When using the Web Assistant Wizard, you can specify the number of rows from your result set that are displayed on each Web page. Any successive pages are linked with NEXT and PREVIOUS URLs and have the same name as the Web page plus the number 1 to the (total number of records returned/number of records per page).

- Scheduled Web Assistant jobs can be managed through the Microsoft Management Console's (MMC) SQL Server Agent node. You now have the ability to create a new Web Assistant job, or start, stop, disable, get a history for, refresh, generate Transact-SQL scripts for, delete or edit the properties for an existing Web Assistant job.

What's Gone

- The Web Assistant Wizard no longer appears in the SQL Server 7.0 program group. However, there are many places in the MMC where you can initiate the Web Assistant Wizard. See the following section about starting the Web Assistant Wizard for details!

- SQL Server 7.0 supports multiple triggers. When using the Web Assistant Wizard and specifying to update the HMTL page when the data changes, if there is more than one trigger on the table, no screen appears to alter the trigger.

In this chapter, you'll see how SQL Server 7.0's implementation of database-driven HTML pages is provided by the use of the all-encompassing Web Assistant Wizard. The Web Assistant Wizard provides an easy-to-use user interface for several SQL Server system and extended stored procedures. The wizard enables you to create queries that run against the SQL Server 7.0 database to push data to your Web site in the form of static HTML pages. You can choose how often the Web client sees the changes in the SQL Server 7.0 data by specifying how often the HTML pages are updated.

You will also see that SQL Server 7.0's Web Assistant is truly a well-rounded tool in that it makes the management of existing Web Assistant jobs easy by organizing them in one place. SQL Server 7.0's Enterprise Manager organizes the Web Assistant jobs in the Web Publishing results pane. SQL Server 7.0 accomplishes this by storing attributes of the Web Assistant job in the `mswebtasks` table in SQL Server's MSDB database. In this way, Enterprise Manager can easily display the jobs, with the name you've specified, in the results pane.

Use the SQL Server Agent if you need to edit existing Web Assistant jobs that are scheduled to run once, or at certain intervals to update the Web page. If the Web page is updated when the SQL Server data changes, update the table's trigger directly.

SQL SERVER 7.0 WEB PUBLISHING

SQL Server 7.0 Web Publishing is automatically installed with Microsoft's SQL Server 7.0. Included with Web Publishing is the SQL Server 7.0 Web Assistant Wizard, which gives you easy access to your Web site. Knowledge of Web technologies is not necessary, although some knowledge of Transact-SQL helps. As shown in Figure 28.2, it also affords you the ability to manage existing Web Assistant Jobs easily.

FIGURE 28.2

The SQL Server 7.0 Web Assistant.

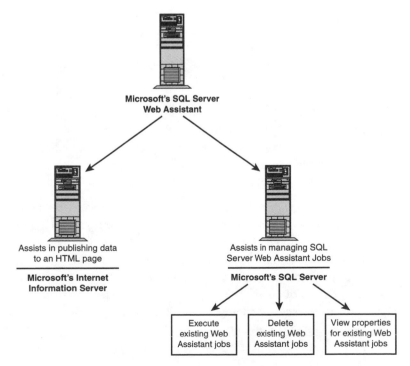

Microsoft's SQL Server
Web Assistant

Assists in publishing data
to an HTML page

**Microsoft's Internet
Information Server**

Assists in managing SQL
Server Web Assistant Jobs

Microsoft's SQL Server

Execute existing Web Assistant jobs

Delete existing Web Assistant jobs

View properties for existing Web Assistant jobs

28

SQL SERVER 7.0 AND THE INTERNET

Using the Web Assistant

After opening the Microsoft Management Console (MMC), you can expand the scope pane's console tree to find the Management node. Under this node, you will find Web Publishing (see Figure 28.3). By right-clicking the Web Publishing node, you can start the Web Assistant Wizard by choosing to create a new Web Assistant job.

FIGURE 28.3

SQL Server 7.0 Web publishing in the Management node of MMC.

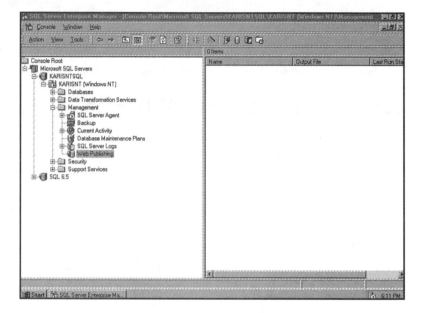

The Web Assistant Wizard steps you through the process that creates a Web Assistant job. This wizard incorporates powerful scheduling options that will push data from a SQL Server 7.0 database to a standard HTML page, or a predefined template file. You can decide what data is published, how often it's published, where it's published, and how it looks when it's published.

HTML pages are generated by using Transact-SQL queries, stored procedures, and extended stored procedures. You can generate an HTML page on a one-time basis, as a regularly scheduled SQL Server 7.0 task, or as a result of a trigger whenever applicable data changes. If you don't have a predefined template file, the Web Assistant will create the HTML page for you after a few simple formatting questions. You can decide to return all or some of the rows from your query, as well as how many rows per page. Optionally, if you specify a template file, any directory, network, FTP, or HTTP path that is accessible from the SQL Server 7.0 can be used.

Web Assistant Jobs

Double-click Web Publishing in the Management node to list all of the Web Assistant jobs in the results pane including jobs that incorporate scheduled tasks managed by SQL Server Agent and jobs that incorporate table triggers. You can view properties of the Web Assistant job by right-clicking and choosing properties (see Figure 28.4).

FIGURE 28.4

The SQL Server 7.0 Web Assistant Job Properties screen.

28

SQL SERVER 7.0 AND THE INTERNET

Using the Web Assistant Wizard to Publish an HTML Page

You may be asking, "Where did the Web Assistant Wizard go?" It is not gone; it is better! Follow the steps later in this section to create and automatically update an HTML page you specify!

But first, because the Web Assistant is an interface for SQL Server 7.0's system procedure sp_makewebtask, the name and description of the arguments will be described as each step is discussed.

This code is included to help you interpret the Web Assistant Job parameters after you create the Web task. If what you want to accomplish exceeds the capability of the wizard, you can create or edit the scripts yourself.

```
sp_makewebtask {[@outputfile =] 'outputfile'} [, [@query =] 'query']
          [, [@fixedfont =] fixedfont] [, [@bold =] bold] [, [@italic =]
          ➥italic]
    [, [@colheaders =] colheaders] [, [@lastupdated =] lastupdated]
    [, [@HTMLHeader =] HTMLHeader] [, [@username =] username]
    [, [@dbname =] dbname] [, [@templatefile =] 'templatefile']
    [, [@webpagetitle =] 'webpagetitle'] [, [@resultstitle =]
          ➥'resultstitle']
```

```
[[, [@URL =] 'URL', [@reftext =] 'reftext']
¦ [, [@table_urls =] table_urls, [@url_query =] 'url_query']]
[, [@whentype =] whentype] [, [@targetdate =] targetdate]
[, [@targettime =] targettime] [, [@dayflags =] dayflags]
[, [@numunits =] numunits] [, [@unittype =] unittype]
[, [@procname =] procname ] [, [@maketask =] maketask]
[, [@rowcnt =] rowcnt] [, [@tabborder =] tabborder]
[, [@singlerow =] singlerow] [, [@blobfmt =] blobfmt]
[, [@nrowsperpage =] n] [, [@datachg =] table_column_list]
```

> **TIP**
>
> Before using SQL Server 7.0's Web Assistant Wizard, make sure that all of the SQL Server 7.0 databases, tables, stored procedures, and template files that you want to reference have been created. Additionally, all Windows 95 Web Assistant users must have SQL Server user accounts in the database used.

1. Start SQL Server 7.0's Web Assistant Wizard

From the Microsoft Management Console (MMC), start the Web Assistant Wizard (refer to Figure 28.3):

- Choose the Tools toolbar option and from the submenu, select Wizards. All of the wizards available in SQL Server are displayed by category. You will find the Web Assistant Wizard under the Management category.

- Choose the Wand icon in MMC's toolbar to display all the available wizards by category. You will find the Web Assistant Wizard under the Management category.

- With Web Publishing highlighted, choose the New icon in MMC's toolbar.

- Right-click the Web Publishing node or any existing Web Assistant job. Choose New Web Assistant Job and the Web Assistant Wizard begins

2. Select the Database

After the introductory screen (see Figure 28.5), select the database that contains the data that you want to publish to an HTML page (see Figure 28.6).

FIGURE 28.5

The Web Assistant introductory screen.

FIGURE 28.6

Selecting a database with the SQL Server 7.0 Web Assistant.

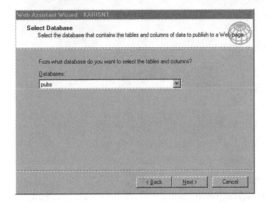

- @dbname is a varchar and can be 1 to 30 characters in length and defaults to the name of the current database.

3. Start the New Web Assistant Job

After selecting the database, you start a new Web Assistant job (see Figure 28.7). Specify the name of the Web Assistant job and how the result set that is published to the HTML page will be generated.

- @procname is a unique nvarchar and can be of 1 to 128 characters in length and defaults to the name of the database and 'Web Page'. Anything over 128 characters is truncated. This name is assigned to the following:

    Stored procedures created in the database specified by the Web Assistant user (if you choose data from tables and columns or data from a SQL statement).

    SQL Server Agent jobs created when a scheduled task is used to update the HTML page.

    Web Assistant jobs shown in the results pane.

- @query is text with no default. This argument specifies the query to be run. If you choose data from tables and columns or data from a SQL statement, the Web Assistant builds the Transact-SQL for you. If you specify a stored procedure, an execute statement is built, including any parameters that are required for the stored procedure.

FIGURE 28.7

Starting a new Web Assistant Job dialog box.

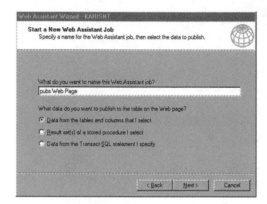

To build the query, you may choose from the following options:

- **Data from the Tables and Columns that I Select:** Selecting this option leads you through two additional screens. The first screen (see Figure 28.8) asks you to select the table and columns you want to publish. The next screen (see Figure 28.9) asks you to select the rows you want to publish. The default option is to select all of the rows of data from the table. However, you can also select columns with certain criteria, or write the Transact-SQL statement yourself. With this option, you can only work with one table or view.

FIGURE 28.8

Selecting a table and one or all of its columns to use as the data source for the HTML page with the Web Assistant.

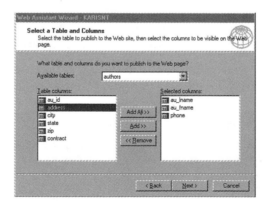

FIGURE **28.9**

Selecting the rows from the table to be displayed on the HTML page with the Web Assistant.

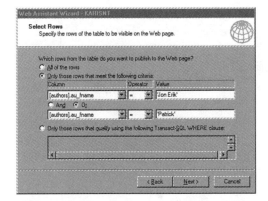

- **Result set(s) of a Stored Procedure I Select:** This option enables you to publish data based on the information returned from a stored procedure. Choose the stored procedure (see Figure 28.10) and if there are parameters necessary, the Web Assistant leads you through one additional screen (see Figure 28.11) where you specify the values for the parameter(s). With this option, multiple SELECT statements in the stored procedure result in multiple HTML tables being displayed in the output file.

FIGURE **28.10**

Selecting the stored procedure to use as the data source for the HTML page with the Web Assistant.

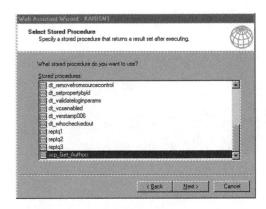

FIGURE 28.11

*Specifying a
stored procedure's
argument(s) with
the Web Assistant.*

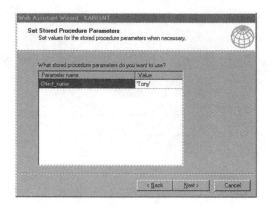

- **Data from the SQL Statement I Specify:** This option enables you to manually
  enter a Transact-SQL statement as the data source for your HTML page (see
  Figure 28.12). Any valid SELECT statement can be used with the following clauses:
  FROM, WHERE, GROUP BY, HAVING, ORDER BY. With this option, multiple SELECT statements result in multiple tables being displayed in the output file.

FIGURE 28.12

*Entering the
Transact-SQL
statement to use
as the data source
for the HTML
page with the Web
Assistant.*

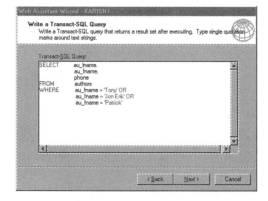

4. Schedule the Web Assistant Job

This option (see Figure 28.13) enables you to specify how often the Web page is
updated. You can also choose whether to generate the HTML page just now, now and
later, or just later. If you choose to generate the HTML page later, the page is created, but
no data is published to the page.

> **CAUTION**
>
> The SQL Server Agent must be running when a Web Assistant job is scheduled
> to run periodically. Otherwise, generation of the HTML page will not occur.

- @whentype is a `tinyint` and can have values of 1 to 10. The default setting is 1.

Table 28.1 shows the @whentype arguments and values.

TABLE 28.1 @WHENTYPE ARGUMENT VALUES OF THE SYSTEM PROCEDURE sp_makewebtask

When the Web Task Is Run	HTML Page Initially Created and Never Updated	HTML Page Not Initially Created and Updated Periodically	HTML Page Initially Created and Updated Periodically
After the completion of the Web Assistant Wizard.	1		
On demand		5	9
Only once, on a specified date, at a specified time.		2	6
When SQL Server 7.0 data changes.			10
On a specified day of the week.		3	7
Every week, day, hour, or minute, as specified.		4	8

- **Only Once When I Complete the Wizard:** If you choose this option (@whentype=1), the Web task will be created, executed immediately, and deleted immediately after its execution.

- **On Demand:** This option specifies that the HTML page is created only upon request. So, the system procedure for creating the HTML page (sp_makewebtask) is created without automatic scheduling. If you choose not to generate an initial HTML page, you must later run the sp_runwebtask system procedure to create and update the HTML page (@whentype=5); otherwise, an HTML will initially be created (@whentype=9). The Web task will run only when a developer executes the sp_runwebtask system procedure and it will only be deleted when a developer executes the sp_dropwebtask system procedure.

FIGURE 28.13

*Scheduling the
Web Assistant job.*

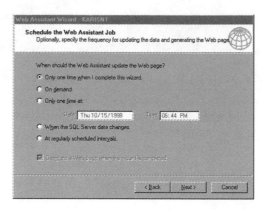

CAUTION

When running under Windows 95, an on-demand Web task can be run by only
the Web task owner or the system administrator (SA).

- **Only Once, at the Following Time:** The system procedure for creating the HTML
  page (sp_makewebtask)is created immediately and execution of the Web task is
  performed as the date and time specify. If you chose not to generate an initial
  HTML page (@whentype=2) no page is created until the targeted date and time,
  otherwise an HTML page will initially be created (@whentype=6) and re-created at
  the targeted date and time. This Web task will be deleted automatically when the
  targeted date and time has passed.

  @targetdate is required and defaults to the current date.

  @targettime is optional and defaults to 12:00 a.m.

- **When the SQL Server 7.0 Data Changes:** The system procedure for creating the
  HTML page (sp_makewebtask) is created immediately and execution of the Web
  task is performed immediately and whenever the data in the table changes
  (@whentype=10). When the data changes, either the INSERT, UPDATE, or DELETE triggers are fired, which in turn runs the sp_runwebtask system procedure, which
  updates the HTML page. This option leads you through an additional screen (see
  Figure 28.14) that asks you which tables and columns (one to all) you want to
  monitor for changes.

FIGURE 28.14

Specifying the tables and column(s) to monitor for changes with the Web Assistant.

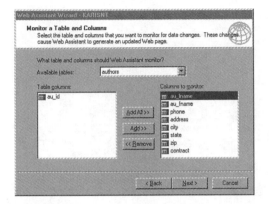

> **CAUTION**
>
> If there are preexisting triggers on the table, the reference to the sp_runwebtask system procedure is added to the end of the trigger if the trigger was not created with WITH ENCRYPTION and the COLUMN field specification in this parameter is ignored. If there is a previously existing trigger on the table created with the WITH ENCRYPTION option, sp_makewebtask system procedure reference fails.

- @datachg is a required text parameter when @whentype = 10. Its value is the table and optional column names that trigger the re-creation of the HTML page when the data changes.

- **At Regularly Scheduled Intervals:** The system procedure for creating the HTML page (sp_makewebtask) is created immediately and execution of the Web task is performed periodically beginning when the date and time specify. This Web task will not be deleted automatically but runs until it is deleted with the sp_dropwebtask system procedure. This option leads you through an additional screen (see Figure 28.15) that asks you when you want the page created. You can specify that the page be created periodically or on certain days of the week. You can also specify the start day and time of the HTML page creation.

- **Periodically:** You can specify that the HTML page is updated every week, day, hour, or minute (@unittype) at intervals (@numunits) you determine (@whentype = 4 or 8).

  - @numunits is a varchar whose values can have a length from 1 to 255 and will default to 1.

  - @unittype is a tinyint and will default to 1. A unit is either hours, days, weeks, or minutes. The values are defined in Table 28.2.

FIGURE 28.15

Scheduling the HTML page update interval with the Web Assistant.

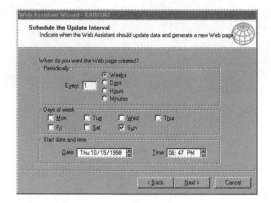

TABLE 28.2   THE @unittype ARGUMENT VALUES FOR THE sp_makewebtask PROCEDURE

Unit	Value
Weeks (default)	1
Days	2
Hours	3
Minutes	4

- **Days of the Week:** You can specify that the HTML page is updated only on certain days of the week (@whentype = 3 or 7).
  - @dayflags is a tinyint that specifies which days to update the HTML page. To specify certain days, use the Table 28.3 and add the values together. For example to specify Tuesday and Thursday, use @dayflags = 20.

TABLE 28.3   THE @dayflags ARGUMENT VALUES OF THE SYSTEM PROCEDURE sp_makewebtask

Day of Week	Value
Sunday (default)	1
Monday	2
Tuesday	4
Wednesday	8
Thursday	16
Friday	32
Saturday	64

5. Publish the Web Page

This option (see Figure 28.16) enables you to specify a file name for the HTML page created. You can specify a physical directory, network directory, and the HTTP or FTP path accessible from SQL Server 7.0.

- @outputfile   is a varchar and can have a length from 1 to 255 with a default of WebPage1.htm. This is the location of the generated HTML page on the computer running SQL Server 7.0.

FIGURE **28.16**

Publishing the HTML page with the Web Assistant.

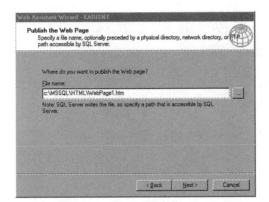

TIP

The SQL Server 7.0 account must have privileges to write the generated HTML document to the specified location.

6. Format the Web Page

This option (see Figure 28.17) enables you to ask the Web Assistant to help you format an HTML page, or specify that you are using a template file. Using a template file gives you greater flexibility in the appearance of the HTML page. For example, stylesheets and additional graphics can be used on the HTML page to improve its appearance. The advanced HTML example at the end of the chapter uses a template file.

If you choose to specify a template file, the following argument is used and Steps 7, 8, and 9 will be skipped:

- @templatefile   is a varchar and can have a length from 1 to 255 with no default. This is the location of the template file used to generate the HTML page. The template file is used instead of HTML-type arguments that would have been found in the `sp_makewebtask` system procedure. Specifically, if a template file is used, the following arguments are ignored: `@bold`, `@Colheaders`, `@fixfont`, `@HTMLHeader`, `@italic`, `@URL`, `lastupdated`, `@reftext`, `@singlerow`, `@tabborder`, `@table_urls`, `@url_query`, and `@webpagetitle`. An example of the use of a template file is found later in this chapter.

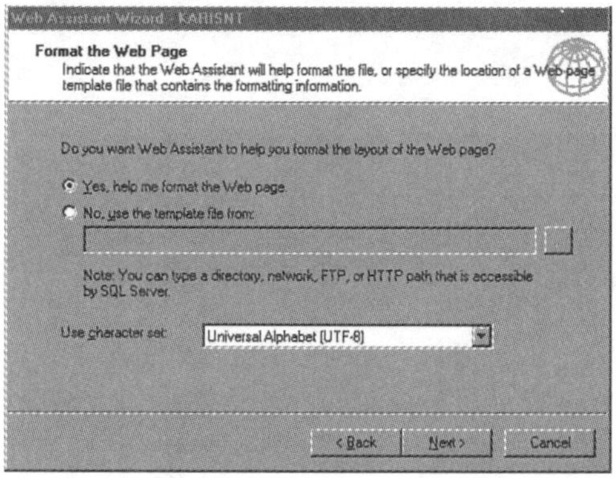

FIGURE 28.17

Formatting the HTML page with the Web Assistant.

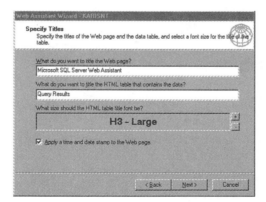

7. Specify Titles

This option (see Figure 28.18) is used when you've asked the Web Assistant for help formatting an HTML page. It enables you to enter the title of the HTML page, the header for the HTML table on the page, and specify the page size, as well as whether there is a time and date stamp on the HTML page.

FIGURE 28.18

Specifying titles for the HTML page with the Web Assistant.

- `@webpagetitle` is a `varchar` and can have a length from 1 to 255 with a default of `Microsoft's SQL Server 7.0 Web Assistant`. This is the title displayed on the HTML page.

> **TIP**
>
> For a blank title, you can enter two spaces for the title. Another way you can change the title of the HTML page is to delete anything between the <TITLE></TITLE> HTML tags in the HTML page after it's created.

- @resultstitle   is a varchar and can have a length from 1 to 255 with a default of Query Results. This is the title displayed above the results table on the HTML page.
- @HTMLHeader   is a tinyint and can have values of 1 to 6 with a default of 3. This is the font of the header row in the results table. The values are defined in Table 28.4.

TABLE 28.4   @HTMLHeader ARGUMENT VALUES FOR THE sp_makewebtask SYSTEM PROCEDURE

Value	HTML Tag
1	H1
2	H2
3 (default)	H3
4	H4
5	H5
6	H6

- @lastupdated   is a tinyint and can have values of 1 or 0 with a default of 1. This argument specifies whether the HTML page will display a Last Updated: timestamp indicating the last updated date and time. The timestamp appears one line before the results table in the HTML page. The arguments are defined in Table 28.5.

TABLE 28.5   @lastupdated ARGUMENT VALUES FOR sp_makewebtask SYSTEM PROCEDURE

Value	Definition
0	No timestamp
1 (default)	The last updated date and time

8. Format a Table

This option (see Figure 28.19) is used when you've asked the Web Assistant for help formatting an HTML page. It enables you to indicate how you want your results table to appear on the HTML page. You can choose to display the column names in the header row or display only the data. You also can determine whether to put borders on the results table and specify whether the font is fixed or proportional, and bold or italic.

FIGURE 28.19

Formatting an HTML table with the Web Assistant.

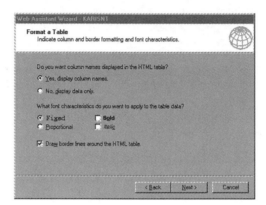

- @colheader is a tinyint and can have values of 1 or 0 with a default of 1 (display column names). This argument specifies whether the HTML page will display an HTML table column header row that shows the SQL table column name.

- @fixedfont is a tinyint and can have values of 1 or 0 with a default of 1 (fixed font). This argument specifies whether the HTML results table uses a default font that's a fixed or proportional font.

- @bold is a tinyint and can have values of 1 or 0 with a default of 0 (nonbold font). This argument specifies whether the HTML results table will use a default font that's bold or nonbold.

- @italic is a tinyint and can have values of 1 or 0 with a default of 0 (nonitalic font). This argument specifies whether the HTML results table will use a default font that's italic or nonitalic.

- @tabborder is a tinyint and can have values of 1 or 0 with a default of 0 (with a table border). This argument specifies whether the HTML results table will have a border.

9. Add Hyperlinks to the Web Page

This option (see Figure 28.20) is used when you've asked the Web Assistant for help formatting an HTML page. It enables you to indicate whether you'd like to add some hyperlinks, a Hypertext Transfer Protocol (HTTP) address of another HTML page or

Web site, to your HTML page. You can specify one hyperlink to be displayed on your HTML page or type in a Transact-SQL statement to query a table where you've stored hyperlinks.

FIGURE 28.20
*Adding hyperlinks
to the HTML page
with the Web
Assistant.*

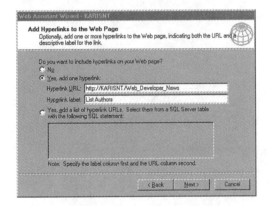

- `@URL` is a varchar and can have a length from 1 to 255 with no default. This argument specifies the destination of the hyperlink.

- `@reftext` is a varchar and can have a length from 1 to 255 with no default. This argument specifies the label for the hyperlink.

> **NOTE**
>
> If `@URL` is specified, you must also enter a label for the hyperlink. Additionally, if `@URL` is specified, `@table_urls` and `@url_query` must not be specified.

- `@table_urls` is a tinyint and can have values of 1 or 0 and has a default of 0. This argument specifies whether the hyperlink(s) displayed on the HTML page are derived from a SELECT statement executed on a SQL Server 7.0 table.

- `@url_query` is a varchar and can have a length from 1 to 255 with no default. This argument contains the SELECT statement to create the hyperlink's destination and its label. This argument must return a result set containing two columns. The first column is the address of a hyperlink, and the second column describes the hyperlink.

> **NOTE**
>
> If @table_urls = 1, then @url_query must be specified. Also, if @table_urls = 1, @URL and @reftext must not be specified.

10. Limit Rows

This option (see Figure 28.21) enables you to indicate whether you want to limit the total number of rows returned by SQL Server 7.0. You also specify how those rows will be displayed (as one row per page or multiple rows per page).

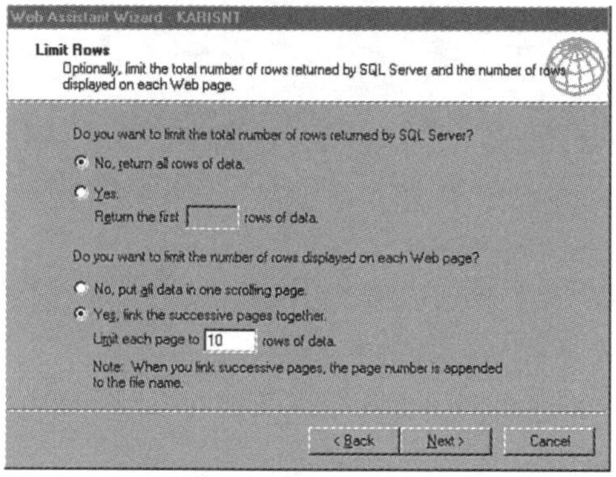

FIGURE 28.21

Limiting the number of rows in the result set and how the rows are displayed with the Web Assistant.

- @rowcnt is an integer with a default of 0 (all rows). This specifies the maximum number of rows to be returned from SQL Server 7.0.

- @singlerow is a tinyint and can have a value of 1 or 0 and has a default of 0 (all data on one scrolling page). With a value of 0, the result set is displayed on one page, in one HTML table. With a value of 1, a new HTML page will be generated for every qualifying row in the result set. Successive HTML pages are generated with a number appended to the specified output filename. When @singlerow = 1, @nrowsperpage must not be specified.

- @nrowsperpage is an int with a default of 0. With a value of 0, all results are displayed on one scrolling page. Otherwise, this argument specifies that the result set should be displayed in multiple pages of n rows on each one. The successive pages will be linked with NEXT and PREVIOUS URLs.

11. Completing the Web Assistant Wizard

This display (see Figure 28.22) shows some general information about the Web task created for you as a result of the Web Assistant Wizard. It shows you the location and name of the output file, the query that generates the output file, the database the query will be run against, and the location and name of the template file, if one was specified.

You can also choose to write the Transact-SQL statement to a file for reference. This statement shows the execution of the sp_makewebtask system procedure and its arguments' values.

Figure 28.22

Completing the Web Assistant Wizard.

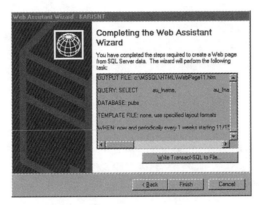

That's all there is to it (see Figure 28.23)! For a more in-depth look at how it all works behind the scenes, continue to the next section.

Figure 28.23

Finishing the Web Assistant Wizard.

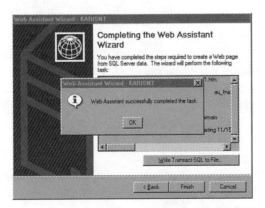

A Behind the Scenes Look at Using the Web Assistant Wizard to Publish Data to a Web Page

The SQL Server 7.0 Web Assistant provides a tremendous amount of automation through a graphical interface that's simple to use. However, to fully implement a Web-based solution with SQL Server 7.0, you must understand how the Web Assistant automatically creates the HTML page. Here's a list and display (see Figure 28.24) of the components used by SQL Server 7.0's Web Assistant.

- Stored procedures
- SQL Server agent
- Triggers
- Web Assistant jobs
- System procedures
- HTML page

Stored Procedures

When you start a new Web Assistant job (refer to Figure 28.6), if you choose to publish data from tables, or if you enter a Transact-SQL statement, the Web Assistant creates a stored procedure in the database you specify.

The stored procedure name is derived from the `@procname` argument to SQL Server 7.0's `sp_makewebtask` system procedure.

Otherwise, the stored procedure you specified will be used.

SQL Server Agent

If you choose to schedule the Web Assistant job once or at regular intervals (refer to Figure 28.12), the SQL Server Web Assistant adds a Web task as a job for the SQL Server Agent to manage. All Web tasks are categorized as Web Assistant in Job Categories in SQL Server Agent jobs. When the scheduled task is run, `sp_runwebtask` is executed. For more in-depth information about managing SQL Server Agent jobs, see Chapter 7, "Enterprise Management Processes," on scheduling tasks.

Triggers

Triggers are created on the tables you specify when you choose to schedule the Web Assistant job when the SQL Server 7.0 data changes (refer to Figure 28.12). The SQL Server Web Assistant creates INSERT, UPDATE, and DELETE triggers on the table and columns you have specified to monitor. When the data changes, the Web task is executed (generating a new HTML page) and the data is updated in one transaction.

FIGURE **28.24**

How the Web Assistant Wizard works.

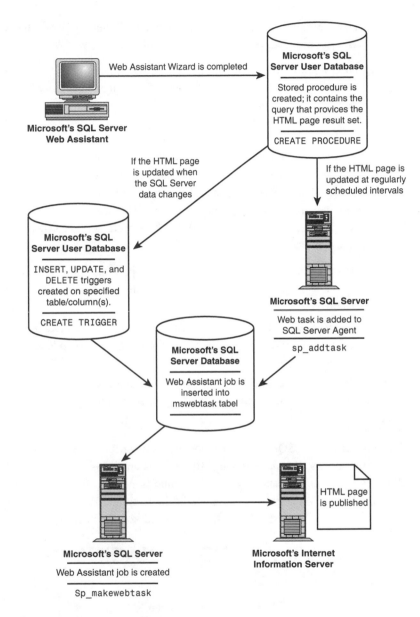

Web Assistant Jobs

A Web Assistant job is created every time you use the Web Assistant Wizard. There are two types of jobs listed in the Web Assistant Jobs' results pane. The first type of job is managed by SQL Server Agent; it updates the HTML page at regularly scheduled intervals. The second kind of job is managed by triggers on the SQL Server 7.0 table, and it updates the HTML page whenever the data changes. What happens when each event occurs is the same: the associated Web task is run.

In either case, a record is inserted in the mswebtasks table in SQL Server's MSDB table. The Web Assistant job name is derived from the @procname argument to the sp_makewebtask system procedure.

System Procedures

There are three SQL Server 7.0 system procedures used to manage Web Assistant jobs. The SQL Server Web Assistant Wizard executes sp_makewebtask and always produces an HTML page. This HTML page could display data immediately, or later (refer to Figure 28.12) depending on how you checked the Do Not Generate an Initial HTML Page option. Subsequent updates to the HTML page are achieved by executing sp_runwebtask.

- sp_makewebtask   creates the Web task that produces an HTML page containing a result set based on a specified stored procedure (created by the user or the Web Assistant Wizard).

- sp_runwebtask   executes a previously defined Web task and generates the HTML page. The task to run is identified by the output filename, by the procedure name, or by both parameters.

- sp_deletewebtask   deletes a previously defined Web task. The task to be deleted is identified by the output filename, by the procedure name, or by both parameters.

HTML Page

The output from the SQL Server Web Assistant Wizard is an HTML page that can be viewed in a user's Web browser. This file is static and doesn't require any further queries of the SQL Server 7.0 data. If you need to modify the HTML page layout after the Web Assistant Wizard has created it, simply edit the template file if one was used, or re-run the Web Assistant Wizard if the wizard formatted your HTML page.

SQL SERVER 7.0 AND MANAGING WEB ASSISTANT JOBS

By right-clicking the Web Assistant job, you can

- Create a new Web Assistant job
- Execute an existing Web Assistant job
- From the Web Publishing results pane, you can delete an existing Web Assistant job

- From the Web Publishing results pane, you can view the properties for an existing Web Assistant job. You can see the job's name, the database, the output filename and location, the Web page title, the character set used, and the command that selects the data to be included on the HTML page.

Remember, choosing to create your HTML page only once (at a specific time) or at regularly scheduled intervals, creates a scheduled task in SQL Server Agent.

Therefore, if you need to manage any aspect of a scheduled task created by the Web Assistant Wizard, you need to use the functionality of SQL Server Agent. From SQL Server Agent, you have the ability to create a new Web Assistant job, or start, stop, disable, get a history for, refresh, generate Transact-SQL scripts for, and delete or edit the properties for an existing Web Assistant job. For more in depth information about managing SQL Server Agent jobs, see Chapter 7 on scheduling tasks.

Conversely, choosing to create your HTML page when the SQL Server data changes creates INSERT, UPDATE, and DELETE triggers on the table you selected. Therefore, if you need to manage any aspect of a trigger created by the Web Assistant Wizard, select Manage Triggers from the Tasks menu option after right-clicking the table you selected in the Web Assistant Wizard.

ADVANCED TEMPLATE FILE EXAMPLE

As was suggested previously when reviewing the steps of publishing an HTML page with SQL Server 7.0's Web Assistant Wizard, you can also specify a template file to use as a building block for the final HTML page. In other words, rather than publish directly to an HTML page that the SQL Server Web Assistant formats (with some direction from you), you can create a template file to be used as a model or shell for the HTML page.

This is useful because although the SQL Server Web Assistant Wizard gives you several formatting options for your HTML page, often you'll want more control over the way the HTML page appears. You might have a standard company user interface that you need to incorporate, such as a stylesheet or specific graphics you might be required to use on some pages. You might also want to try to spice up some of your Web pages with Dynamic HTML. Therefore, if you want the output of your Web Assistant job to be in anything other than an HTML table, you should use a template.

The example (see Figure 28.25) shows a Web application that can be used by Web developers to share information on standards they should be using when developing Web applications for their company. It's an intranet application, which is designed not to constrain creativity, but to ensure that Web developers create consistent Web pages (in format, flow, functionality, and look and feel), within the confines of the standards created.

28

SQL SERVER 7.0 AND THE INTERNET

As shown, references that could be created include the documentation on user-interface standards. These standards could include such things as a list of stylesheets and their properties, a list of fonts and their attributes and when they should be used, or a list of common graphics and how they should be used. Developer's standards could include standards for Web page headers, the order the page is built, standards for the use of VBScript, JavaScript, Java applets, CGI script, DHTML and so on. Internal Software Support could list the software supported by your Operations department and contact numbers, or a list of software that the Web developers recommend for use as development tools and a description of their best use. Technical articles can be used as a way for Web developers to share information such as a great solution to a problem that might benefit others! If a Web developer has published a Javascript function to the common library of functions, this is a great place to announce and describe it. This section could also be used to give a heads up to other developers about upcoming events or technologies. Developer's resources could list developers and their area of expertise along with their contact information. So, if you needed help on a complex SQL Server stored procedure or help calling a Javascript function in an HTML page, you would know who to call. Libraries could be used to document the contents of a Web library directory that stores common functions that all Web developers can use. It could list the functions, examples of usage syntax, any input and output parameters, and a general description of the function.

A Web application is a great place to store this documentation, which should be a living document that Web developers change as time passes.

FIGURE 28.25

Example of the use of a template to generate an HTML page.

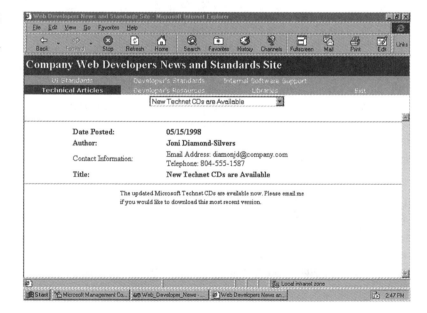

The example shown in Figure 28.25 uses a template file to create a selection list shown in the middle of the Web browser screen. This application is built with two framesets. The first frameset builds the top two rows. When you press a navigation choice, the bottom frameset, which consists of two rows, is built. In this case, the Technical Articles choice was selected. The first row of the bottom frameset shows a selection list and is the HTML page generated from the SQL Server 7.0 Web Assistant Wizard in which the template file was specified. The selection list shows a list of technical articles the Web developers have published. The list is derived from a table of technical articles that stores the article id, article title, the article's author, the date the article was posted, and the article itself.

This discussion refers to the example of running the Web Assistant Wizard shown previously and highlights what you might do differently. The first difference is that in this case, the dev_articles table was chosen (see Figure 28.6). Then Data from the tables and columns was selected (see Figure 28.7). For the columns that are visible on the Web page (see Figure 28.8), two table columns were chosen: the article id key field, and the article title. You could choose to return all of the rows as seen in this example (see Figure 28.9), but again you could restrict what is shown on the HTML page by entering your own criteria or choosing a stored procedure.

For the schedule of the Web Assistant job (refer to Figure 28.13), the HTML page will be generated every time the data changes, so that whenever a Web developer posts an article, a new page is generated. This forces UPDATE, DELETE, and INSERT triggers to be created on the dev_articles table. This example shows that all of the table's columns will be monitored (refer to Figure 28.14). Because, in this case, the SQL Server and Web server are physically located together, a file directory path was specified to indicate where to publish the page (refer to Figure 28.16). If they are not located together, you can type any network, FTP, or HTTP path accessible from SQL Server. Another solution is to store the Web pages and template files in a file directory on the SQL Server and to create a virtual reference to this directory on the Web server. That way you can use the virtual reference in your Web site to access the pages. In this case, your Web server needs to have access to the SQL Server network file directory.

When formatting the Web page (refer to Figure 28.17), a template file was indicated. Again, a file directory path was specified to indicate where to get the template file. For this example, Figures 28.18, 28.19, and 28.20 were skipped. As in the first example, the rows returnedor displayed on the HTML page can be limited. In this example, all rows are returned and all data is placed on one scrolling page.

28

SQL SERVER 7.0 AND THE INTERNET

For your information, Listing 28.1 shows the Web task executed by SQL Server 7.0.

LISTING 28.1   TRANSACT-SQL THAT CREATES THE WEB TASK

```
EXECUTE sp_makewebtask
@outputfile = 'C:\InetPub\wwwroot\Web_Developer_News\
➥content\articles\Article_Tech_Choices.htm',
@query='SELECT article_ID, title FROM Dev_Articles',
@templatefile=
'C:\InetPub\wwwroot\Web_Developer_News\ Templates\Article_template.tpl',
@dbname='Web_Developer_News',
@whentype=10,
@datachg='TABLE=Dev_Articles COLUMN=article_ID,title',

@procname=''Web_Developer_News Web Page'
```

Listing 28.2 shows the code for the template file used to generate the HTML page.

LISTING 28.2   ARTICLES LISTING TEMPLATE FILE

```
'**********************************************************************
'     PROGRAMMER:      Kari Fernandez
'     PAGE NAME:       Article_Template.tpl
'     SITE NAME:       Web Developer's News and Standards Site
'     DESCRIPTION:     Template that builds a drop-down
'                      box of Articles submitted by
'                      Web Developers.
'
'     INPUT Parameters:
'     Name            Description
'----------------------------------------------------------------------
'     OUTPUT Parameters:
'       Name          Description
'----------------------------------------------------------------------
'
'     SPECIAL CONSIDERATIONS:          None
'
'     PROCESSING RESTRICTIONS:         None
'
'     PREREQUISTITES:                  None
'
'     INITIATED:
'
'     Modification:
'       Date          Programmer      Description
'       --------      ----------      --------
'       05/1998 (KAF)                 Original Implementation
'
```

```
' *********************************************************************
</comment>
<HEAD>
<TITLE>Web Developers and Standards Combo Box Template</TITLE>
<SCRIPT LANGUAGE="JAVASCRIPT">
<!--
function BuildURL(s)
{
//  This function allows the user to select a record in the combo box
//  which triggers an http request to fill the bottom frame of the
//  frameset.

    strSelection = s[s.selectedIndex].value ;
    strURL = "Articles_Tech_About.asp?Record=" + strSelection;

    parent.Content.location.href = strURL;
}
-->
</SCRIPT>
</HEAD>
<BODY>
<TABLE WIDTH = "100%">
<TR>
 <TD ALIGN = "CENTER" VALIGN ="BOTTOM">
  <FORM name = "Articles">
     <select name="Category" ONCLICK="BuildURL(this)">
     <%begindetail%>
         <option value=<%insert_data_here%>><%insert_data_here%></option>
       <%enddetail%>
     </select>
  </FORM>
 </TD>
</TR>
</TABLE>
</BODY>
</HTML>
```

28

SQL SERVER 7.0 AND THE INTERNET

The template file shown in Listing 28.2 shows the standard commented header that my company uses. You will see the Javascript function that builds the hyperlink (URL, Uniform Resource Locator), that is used when the client chooses an option from the selection list. The body of the template file consists of the selection list (HTML SELECT tag) with the click event associated with it. As you can see, to loop through the records returned by SQL Server 7.0, you should use the <%begindetail%> <%enddetail%> syntax. To display the data, use the <%insert_data_here%> syntax. When using this syntax, the columns must be returned in the same order they're displayed. In this example, the article id key field and then the article title are returned. In this way, the value of the key field can be placed in the value attribute of the selection list's option. The article id is passed to my Active Server Page (ASP) file so that the correct record from the dev_articles table can be retrieved when displaying the content of the article on the ASP page.

Listing 28.3 shows the HTML page generated by SQL Server 7.0 using the template file.

LISTING 28.3   ARTICLES LISTING HTML PAGE

```
<HTML>
<comment>
'**********************************************************************
'     PROGRAMMER:        Kari Fernandez
'     PAGE NAME:         Article_Template.tpl
'     SITE NAME:         Web Developer's News and Standards Site.
'     DESCRIPTION:       Template that builds a drop-down
'                        box of Articles submitted by
'                        Web Developers.
'
'     INPUT Parameters:
'      Name                      Description
'-------------------------------------------------------------------
'     OUTPUT Parameters:
'      Name                      Description
'-------------------------------------------------------------------
'
'     SPECIAL CONSIDERATIONS:  None
'
'     PROCESSING RESTRICTIONS: None
'
'     PREREQUISTITES:          None
'
'     INITIATED:
'
'     Modification:
'      Date     Programmer      Description
'      ------   ----------      -----------
'      05/1998  (KAF)           Original Implementation
'
'**********************************************************************
</comment>
<HEAD>
<TITLE>Web Developers and Standards Combo Box Template</TITLE>
<SCRIPT LANGUAGE="JAVASCRIPT">
<!--
function BuildURL(s)
{
//  This function allows the user to select a record in the combo box
//  which triggers an http request to fill the bottom frame of the
//  frameset.
```

```
      strSelection = s[s.selectedIndex].value ;
      strURL = "Articles_Tech_About.asp?Record=" + strSelection;

      parent.Content.location.href = strURL;
}
-->
</SCRIPT>
</HEAD>
<BODY>
<TABLE WIDTH = "100%">
<TR>
 <TD ALIGN = "CENTER" VALIGN ="BOTTOM">
  <FORM name = "Articles">

     <select name="Category" ONCLICK="BuildURL(this)">

          <option value=1>New Technet CDs are Available</option>

          <option value=2>ADO versus RDO:  This developer's review</option>

          <option value=4>What's ahead with SQL Server 7.0</option>

          <option value=5>Check this hyperlink for new software
➥patch</option>

          <option value=6>Registry settings for script timeout
➥periods</option>

          <option value=7>ADO and Connection Pooling</option>

          <option value=8>SQL Server and ActiveX Data Objects</option>

     </select>
  </FORM>
 </TD>
</TR>
</TABLE>
</BODY>
</HTML>
```

In Listing 28.3, everything is the same as the template file, with one exception. Now you can see the actual values of the data returned by SQL Server 7.0. Now the value attributes of the selection list options consist of the article id, and the options displayed are the article titles. When the user clicks a selection list option, the Javascript function BuildURL is called. The BuildURL function builds a URL. This URL consists of an ASP page and one query string parameter (Record). Using the JavaScript object model, the location to place the ASP file can be specified. In this example, the ASP page is to be placed in the Content frame of the bottom frameset. To see an example of the article content displayed in the Content frame, see Figure 28.25. It shows the date the article was posted, the author, the author's contact information, and the title and content of the article.

Listing 28.4 shows the ASP file code that shows the content of the article. As you can see, a SQL Server stored procedure is called; the article id is then passed to the stored procedure to find the unique record and its content.

LISTING 28.4 ASP PAGE THAT SHOWS THE ARTICLE'S CONTENT

```
<%@ LANGUAGE="VBSCRIPT" %>
<!--#include FILE="../../includes/adovbs.inc"-->
<%
'*********************************************************************
'     PROGRAMMER:         Kari Fernandez
'     PAGE NAME:          Articles_Tech_About.asp
'     SITE NAME:          Web Developer's News and Standards Site.
'     DESCRIPTION:        Page that shows the content of the web
'                         developer's technical article.
'
'     INPUT Parameters:
'      Name                    Description
'-------------------------------------------------------------------
'     OUTPUT Parameters:
'      Name                    Description
'-------------------------------------------------------------------
'
'     SPECIAL CONSIDERATIONS:  None
'
'     PROCESSING RESTRICTIONS: None
'
'     PREREQUISTITES:          None
'
'     INITIATED:
'
'     Modification:
'      Date     Programmer    Description
'      ------   ----------    ----------
'      05/1998  (KAF)         Original Implementation
'
'*********************************************************************
%>
<HTML>
<HEAD>
<META NAME="GENERATOR" Content="Microsoft Visual InterDev 1.0">
<META HTTP-EQUIV="Content-Type" content="text/html; charset=iso-8859-1">
<TITLE>Web Developers and Standards - Technical Article</TITLE>
</HEAD>
```

```
<BODY>

<%

'********************************************************************
'Using ADO, use the Connection, Command and Recordset objects and call
'  a stored procedure with input and/or output parameters
'********************************************************************

     'Create the connection object
     Set connRecord = Server.CreateObject("ADODB.Connection")

     'Store the connection string to a local variable
     strDSN = Session("Dev_ConnectionString")
     strDSN = strDSN & "UID=" & Session("Dev_RuntimeUserName") & ";"
     strDSN= strDSN & "PWD=" & Session("Dev_RuntimePassword")

     'Open the connection
     connRecord.ConnectionTimeout = Session("Dev_ConnectionTimeout")
     connRecord.ConnectionString = strDSN
     connRecord.Open

     'Create a ADO Command Object
     Set cmdGetRecord = Server.CreateObject("ADODB.Command")

     'Set the Active Connection
     cmdGetRecord.ActiveConnection = connRecord

'********************************************************************
'Set up the Calling Stored Procedure SQL using ODBC syntax for the
'call and parameters.
'********************************************************************

     cmdGetRecord.CommandText = "{call usp_Get_Tech_Article(?)}"

     cmdGetRecord.CommandType = adCmdText
     cmdGetRecord.CommandTimeout = Session("Dev_CommandTimeout")

'Name each parameter and the direction with the following syntax
     cmdGetRecord.Parameters.Append cmdGetRecord.CreateParameter _
          ("ArticleID", adInteger, adParamInput, 4)

     'Set the Input Values
     cmdGetRecord.Parameters("ArticleID") = Request("Record")

     'Create a ADO Recordset Object
     Set rstMain = Server.CreateObject("ADODB.Recordset")

     rstMain.Open cmdGetRecord, , 1, 1
```

continues

LISTING 28.4   CONTINUED

```
'If an error was received on open, then allow the application
'to continue

On Error Resume Next

If Err Then
  Session("Message") = "Error retrieving the record: "
  Session("Messasge") = Session("Message") & Err.Description
  On Error Goto 0
Else
  If (NOT(rstMain.BOF) And NOT(rstMain.EOF)) Then%>
 <HR>
   <TABLE WIDTH = "75%" topmargin = "0" Align = "Center">
   <TR>
   <TD WIDTH = "25%"><FONT FACE="Times New Roman, Arial"
     SIZE="3"><STRONG>Date Posted:</STRONG></FONT></TD>
   <TD WIDTH = "50%"><FONT FACE="Times New Roman, Arial"
     SIZE="3"><STRONG>
       <%Response.Write rstMain("dateposted")%></STRONG></FONT>
   </TD>
   </TR>
   <TR>
   <TD WIDTH = "25%"><FONT FACE="Times New Roman, Arial"
     SIZE="3"><STRONG>Author:</STRONG></FONT>
   </TD>
   <TD WIDTH = "50%"><FONT FACE="Times New Roman, Arial"
     SIZE="3"><STRONG>
       <%Response.Write rstMain("author")%></STRONG></FONT>
   </TD>
   </TR>
   <TR>
   <TD WIDTH = "25%"><FONT FACE="Times New Roman, Arial"
    SIZE="3"></STRONG>Contact Information:</FONT></STRONG>
   </TD>
   <TD WIDTH = "50%"><FONT FACE="Times New Roman, Arial"
     SIZE="3">Email Address:
       <%Response.Write rstMain("email")%></FONT><BR>
     <FONT FACE="Times New Roman, Arial" SIZE="3">
           Telephone:
       <%Response.Write rstMain("phone")%></FONT>
   </TD>
   </TR>
   <TR>
   <TD WIDTH = "25%"><FONT FACE="Times New Roman, Arial"
       SIZE="3"><STRONG>Title:</STRONG></FONT>
   </TD>
   <TD WIDTH = "50%"><FONT FACE="Times New Roman, Arial"
         SIZE="3"><STRONG>
```

```
          <%Response.Write rstMain("title")%></STRONG></FONT>
        </TD>
        </TR>
        </TABLE>
        <HR>
        <TABLE WIDTH = "50%" topmargin = "0" ALIGN = "Center">
        <TR>
        <TD><FONT FACE="Times New Roman, Arial" SIZE="2">
          <%Response.Write rstMain("content")%></FONT>
        </TD>
        </TR>
        </TABLE>

      <%Else%>

        <FONT FACE = "Times New Roman, Arial" Size = "3"><STRONG>
          No record was returned...</STRONG></FONT>
        <%End If%>


    <%End If%>
</BODY>
</HTML>
```

For your information, Listing 28.5 is the SQL Server stored procedure used by the ASP page.

LISTING 28.5   SQL SERVER 7.0 STORED PROCEDURE USED BY ASP PAGE

```
/********************************************************************/
/*                                                                  */
/*  Description:   Gets the Article with the                        */
/*                 matching record number                           */
/*  Name:          usp_Get_Tech_Article                             */
/*                                                                  */
/*                                                                  */
/*  Called By:     Articles_Tech_About.asp                          */
/*                                                                  */
/*------------------------------------------------------------------*/
/*  Tips:                                                            */
/*                                                                  */
/*------------------------------------------------------------------*/
/*  History:                                                        */
/*------------------------------------------------------------------*/
/*  5/98  (KAF)    Initial Implementation                           */
/*------------------------------------------------------------------*/
/********************************************************************/
CREATE PROCEDURE usp_Get_Tech_Article
```

continues

LISTING 28.5 CONTINUED

```
@Record int

AS

SELECT  CONVERT(varchar(12), A.Dateposted, 101) AS Dateposted,
        A.Title,
        A.Content,
        B.fname + ' ' + B.lname AS author,
        B.Phone,
        B.Email
FROM    Dev_Articles A, Dev_Authors B
WHERE   A.Article_ID = @Record AND
        A.Author_ID *= B.Author_ID
```

SQL SERVER AND THE WEB FAQ

The following section lists some commonly asked questions and answers about SQL Server 7.0 and the Web.

Q. What type of permissions does the SQL Server Web Assistant user need to have to create a Web Assistant Job?

A. The Web Assistant user must have SELECT permissions on the table columns specified in the query, CREATE PROCEDURE permissions in the database in which the query will run. The account in which SQL Server is running must have CREATE FILE account permissions.

Q. What should I enter as the path for the HTML page created by the Web Assistant Wizard?

A. You can enter a local directory on the SQL Server or alternatively, you can enter any location that is accessible to the SQL Server via HTTP (Hypertext Transport Protocol), FTP (File Transport Protocol), or a UNC (Uniform Naming Convention) path.

Q. How do I know if my Web Assistant jobs are running properly?

A. If you created a Web Assistant job that is run periodically, at a certain time, SQL Server Agent is managing that task. Open SQL Server Agent; select your Web Assistant job, and specify an email operator to receive emails on success or failure of that Web Assistant job.

Q. Are any errors captured for my Web Assistant jobs?

A. You can view the error log in the SQL Server Enterprise Manager.

SUMMARY

Use of SQL Server 7.0's Web Assistant provides the novice and expert Web Assistant user with an easy way of publishing data to the Web. You can be an expert SQL Server user with not much experience with the Web, or vice versa, and fair equally well when using this tool. SQL Server Web Assistant also saves the day by organizing all of your Web Assistant jobs in one place. From one place, you can now manage every aspect of the Web Assistant jobs you create.

AUTOMATING MAINTENANCE AND ADMINISTRATION TASKS

IN THIS PART

DEVELOPING A SQL SERVER MAINTENANCE PLAN

by Orryn Sledge

IN THIS CHAPTER

Developing a SQL Server maintenance plan is a proactive approach that can help minimize system downtime. SQL Server 7.0 has greatly simplified database maintenance; however, I still like to compare SQL Server to a car. Both require preventive maintenance and periodic tune-ups. To help you keep SQL Server motoring along, this chapter discusses the types of maintenance that should be performed by a DBA.

SQL SERVER 6.5 TO 7.0 QUICK REFERENCE

The following is a quick reference to the changes that occurred between SQL Server version 6.5 and 7.0:

What's New

- **Self-administrating database engine:** Version 7.0 is significantly better than previous versions in automatically administering and adjusting engine parameters. Parameters, such as lock management, memory management, user connections, tempdb sizing, database sizing, and log sizing are automatically managed by SQL Server. (Note: the autogrow setting must be on for databases and logs to automatically resize on-the-fly.) These changes simplify, but do not eliminate, the need for maintenance.

- **Auto-update statistics:** SQL Server 7.0 will automatically maintain an index's statistics. With previous versions of SQL Server, the UPDATE STATISTICS command had to be run on a frequent basis to keep statistics up-to-date.

What's Gone

- **Devices:** Version 7.0 has eliminated devices and replaced them with operating system data and log files. This change simplifies maintenance. Previous versions required maintenance tasks, such as size management and manually recording device allocation information.

- **User connection setting:** Version 7.0 does not have the maximum user connection setting that was found in previous versions. This eliminates the need to monitor and adjust the user connection setting.

- **DBCC CHECKDB no longer necessary:** SQL Server 7.0 has built-in database error detection and a substantially improved database structure. This eliminates the need to run DBCC CHECKDB on a frequent basis. With previous versions of SQL Server, it was generally recommended that DBCC CHECKDB be run before performing a database backup.

AREAS OF MAINTENANCE

As a DBA, you should be concerned with four broad areas of maintenance:

- SQL Server maintenance
- Database maintenance
- Table/object maintenance
- Job maintenance
- Windows NT maintenance

SQL Server Maintenance

The following list summarizes the types of maintenance that should be performed at the SQL Server database engine level:

- Monitor error logs
- Record configuration information
- Manage logins

Monitor Error Logs

As a DBA you should frequently review SQL Server's error log. When you review the error log, look for messages that do not appear under normal circumstances. Unfortunately, the error log contains more than error messages. It also contains statements about the status of events, copyright information, and so on. This means that you have to know what to look for when you scan the error log. A good starting point is to look for the following keywords:

- `error`
- `failed`
- `table corrupt`
- `level 16`
- `level 17`
- `level 21`
- `Severity: 16`
- `Severity: 17`
- `Severity: 21`

> **NOTE**
>
> You can view the SQL Server's error log from the SQL Server Enterprise Manager or from a text editor.
>
> To view the SQL Server error log from the SQL Server Enterprise Manager, select a server from the server group, click the plus (+) sign next to the server that contains the SQL Server error logs, click the plus (+) sign next to the Management folder, click the plus (+) sign next to the SQL Server Logs icon. From the Result pane, double-click an error log to view its contents (see Figure 29.1).
>
> To view the current error log with a text editor, open the file `c:\mssql7\log\errorlog`. You also can view the last six versions of the error log by opening the corresponding file (`errorlog.1`, `errorlog.2`, and so on).

FIGURE 29.1

SQL Server Error Log Result pane.

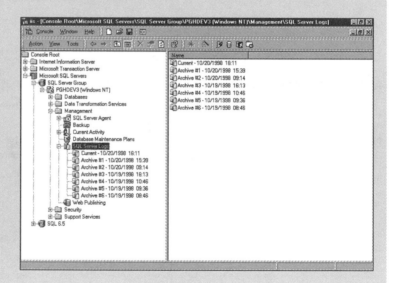

The following listing shows a sample error log. Items in bold indicate errors a DBA may want to investigate:

```
1998-10-20 15:40:12.82 kernel   Microsoft SQL Server  7.00 - 7.00.571
(Intel X86)
        Sep 13 1998 02:20:00
        Copyright  1988-1998 Microsoft Corporation
        Standard Edition on Windows NT 4.0 (Build 1381: Service Pack 3)

        1998-10-20 15:40:12.83 kernel   Copyright  1988-1997 Microsoft
        Corporation.
```

```
1998-10-20 15:40:12.83 kernel    All rights reserved.
1998-10-20 15:40:12.83 kernel    Logging SQL Server messages in file
                                     'C:\MSSQL7\log\ERRORLOG'.
1998-10-20 15:40:12.85 kernel    initconfig: Number of user connections
                                     limited to 32767.
1998-10-20 15:40:12.85 kernel    SQL Server is starting at priority class
                                     'normal'(1 CPU detected).
1998-10-20 15:40:13.04 kernel    User Mode Scheduler configured for
                                     thread processing
1998-10-20 15:40:14.24 server    Directory Size: 5377
1998-10-20 15:40:14.29 spid1     Using dynamic lock allocation. [2500] Lock
                                     Blocks, [5000] Lock Owner Blocks
1998-10-20 15:40:14.29 kernel    Attempting to initialize Distributed
                                     Transaction Coordinator.
1998-10-20 15:40:15.15 spid1     Failed to obtain
                                 TransactionDispenserInterface:
                                     XACT_E_TMNOTAVAILABLE
1998-10-20 15:40:15.18 spid1     Starting up database 'master'.
1998-10-20 15:40:15.18 spid1     Opening file C:\MSSQL7\data\master.mdf.
1998-10-20 15:40:15.25 spid1     Opening file C:\MSSQL7\data\mastlog.ldf.
1998-10-20 15:40:15.45 spid1     Loading SQL Server's  Unicode collation.
1998-10-20 15:40:15.52 spid1     Loading SQL Server's  non-Unicode sort
                                     order and character set.
1998-10-20 15:40:15.87 spid1     7 transactions rolled forward in database
                                     'master' (1).
1998-10-20 15:40:15.89 spid1     0 transactions rolled back in database
                                     'master' (1).
1998-10-20 15:40:16.11 spid1     Starting up database 'model'.
1998-10-20 15:40:16.11 spid1     Opening file C:\MSSQL7\DATA\model.mdf.
1998-10-20 15:40:16.22 spid1     Opening file c:\mssql7\data\modellog.ldf.
1998-10-20 15:40:16.49 spid1     Clearing tempdb database.
1998-10-20 15:40:16.69 spid1     Creating file C:\MSSQL7\DATA\TEMPDB.MDF.
1998-10-20 15:40:18.59 spid1     Closing file C:\MSSQL7\DATA\TEMPDB.MDF.
1998-10-20 15:40:18.59 spid1     Creating file C:\MSSQL7\DATA\TEMPLOG.LDF.
1998-10-20 15:40:18.60 spid1     Closing file C:\MSSQL7\DATA\TEMPLOG.LDF.
1998-10-20 15:40:18.62 spid1     Opening file C:\MSSQL7\DATA\TEMPDB.MDF.
1998-10-20 15:40:18.98 spid1     Opening file C:\MSSQL7\DATA\TEMPLOG.LDF.
1998-10-20 15:40:21.93 spid1     Closing file C:\MSSQL7\DATA\TEMPDB.MDF.
1998-10-20 15:40:21.93 spid1     Closing file C:\MSSQL7\DATA\TEMPLOG.LDF.
1998-10-20 15:40:21.94 spid1     Starting up database 'tempdb'.
1998-10-20 15:40:21.94 spid1     Opening file C:\MSSQL7\DATA\TEMPDB.MDF.
1998-10-20 15:40:22.15 spid1     Opening file C:\MSSQL7\DATA\TEMPLOG.LDF.
1998-10-20 15:40:22.60 spid1     Server name is 'PGHDEV3'.
1998-10-20 15:40:22.61 kernel    Using 'SQLEVN70.DLL' version '7.00.571'.
1998-10-20 15:40:22.61 kernel    Using 'OPENDS60.DLL' version
                                     '7.00.00.0571'.
1998-10-20 15:40:22.61 ods       Using 'SSNMPN70.DLL' version '7.0.571' to
                                     listen on '\\.\pipe\sql\query'.
1998-10-20 15:40:22.62 ods       Using 'SSMSSO70.DLL' version '7.0.571' to
                                     listen on '1433'.
```

```
1998-10-20 15:40:22.63 ods        Using 'SSMSRP70.DLL' version '7.0.571' to
                                   listen on 'PGHDEV3'.
1998-10-20 15:40:22.68 spid6      Starting up database 'msdb'.
1998-10-20 15:40:22.68 spid6      Opening file C:\MSSQL7\DATA\msdbdata.mdf.
1998-10-20 15:40:22.68 spid7      Starting up database 'pubs'.
1998-10-20 15:40:22.68 spid7      Opening file C:\MSSQL7\DATA\pubs.mdf.
1998-10-20 15:40:22.68 spid8      Starting up database 'Northwind'.
1998-10-20 15:40:22.69 spid8      Opening file C:\MSSQL7\DATA\northwnd.mdf.
1998-10-20 15:40:22.69 spid9      Starting up database 'SkillSet'.
1998-10-20 15:40:22.69 spid9      Opening file
                                   C:\MSSQL7\data\SkillSet_Data.MDF.
1998-10-20 15:40:23.22 spid9      Opening file
                                   C:\MSSQL7\data\SkillSet_Log.LDF.
1998-10-20 15:40:23.24 spid6      Opening file c:\mssql7\DATA\msdblog.ldf.
1998-10-20 15:40:23.27 spid7      Opening file c:\mssql7\DATA\pubs_log.ldf.
1998-10-20 15:40:23.28 spid8      Opening file C:\MSSQL7\DATA\northwnd.ldf.
1998-10-20 15:40:25.29 spid7      Starting up database 'customer'.
1998-10-20 15:40:25.29 spid7      Opening file
                                   C:\MSSQL7\data\customer_Data.MDF.
1998-10-20 15:40:25.52 spid9      Starting up database 'Sales'.
1998-10-20 15:40:25.52 spid9      Opening file c:\mssql7\data\SPri1dat.mdf.
1998-10-20 15:40:25.53 kernel     udopen: Operating system error 2(The
                                   system cannot find the file specified.)
                                   during the creation/opening of physical
                                   device c:\mssql7\data\SPri1dat.mdf.
1998-10-20 15:40:25.66 kernel     FCB::Open failed: Could not open device
                                   c:\mssql7\data\SPri1dat.mdf for
                                   virtual device number (VDN) 1.
1998-10-20 15:40:25.85 spid9      Device activation error. The physical file
                                   name 'c:\mssql7\data\SPri1dat.mdf' may be
                                   incorrect.
1998-10-20 15:40:26.00 spid7      Opening file
                                   C:\MSSQL7\data\customer_Log.LDF.
1998-10-20 15:40:30.27 spid1      Recovery complete.
1998-10-20 15:40:30.27 spid1      SQL Server's Unicode collation is:
1998-10-20 15:40:30.27 spid1             'English' (ID = 1033).
1998-10-20 15:40:30.27 spid1             comparison style = 196609.
1998-10-20 15:40:30.27 spid1      SQL Server's non-Unicode sort order is:
1998-10-20 15:40:30.27 spid1             'nocase_iso' (ID = 52).
1998-10-20 15:40:30.27 spid1      SQL Server's non-Unicode character set is:
1998-10-20 15:40:30.27 spid1             'iso_1' (ID = 1).
1998-10-20 15:40:30.34 kernel     Warning: override, autoexec procedures
                                   skipped.
1998-10-20 15:41:09.87 spid7      Using 'xpstar.dll' version '1998.09.12' to
                                   execute extended stored procedure
                                   'xp_regread'.
```

> **TIP**
>
> Use the Windows NT FINDSTR.EXE utility to search for text patterns in the
> error logs. (For the UNIX folks, FINDSTR.EXE is NT's equivalent of GREP.) This
> utility can help automate the process of scanning the log for errors. The fol-
> lowing example shows how to scan the error log for the keyword `error`.
>
> ```
> C:\mssql7\log>findstr /i /n /c:"error" errorlog
> ```
>
> The following is sample output:
>
> ```
> C:\mssql7\log>findstr /i /n /c:"error" errorlog
> 8:1998-10-20 15:40:12.83 kernel   Logging SQL Server messages in file
>                                    'C:\MSSQL7\log\ERRORLOG'.
> 60:1998-10-20 15:40:25.53 kernel  udopen: Operating system
>                                    error 2(The system cannot find
>                                    the file specified.) during the ¦
>                                    creation/opening of physical
>                                    device c:\mssql7\data\SPri1dat.mdf.
> 62:1998-10-20 15:40:25.85 spid9   Device activation error.
>                                    The physical file name
>                                    'c:\mssql7\data\SPri1dat.mdf'
>                                    may be incorrect.
>
>
> 34:95/09/16 11:24:20.42 ods       Error : 17903, Severity: 18, State: 1
> 36:95/09/16 11:24:20.43 ods       Error : 17951, Severity: 18, State: 1
> 53:95/09/16 11:24:35.53 ods       Error : 17903, Severity: 18, State: 1
> 55:95/09/16 11:24:35.54 ods       Error : 17951, Severity: 18, State: 1
> ```

Record Configuration Information

When you are unable to start SQL Server, server configuration information can help
Microsoft's technical support group get you back up and running.

Use the system procedure `sp_configure` to generate a list of configuration information,
as in the following example:

```
exec sp_configure
```

Following is the output:

```
name                            minimum    maximum      config_value run_value
------------------------------- ---------- ------------ ------------ ---------
affinity mask                   0          2147483647   0            0
allow updates                   0          1            0            0
cost threshold for parallelism  0          32767        5            5
cursor threshold                -1         2147483647   -1           -1
default language                0          9999         0            0
```

29

default sortorder id	0	255	52	52
extended memory size (MB)	0	2147483647	0	0
fill factor (%)	0	100	0	0
index create memory (KB)	704	1600000	0	0
language in cache	3	100	3	3
language neutral full-text	0	1	0	0
lightweight pooling	0	1	0	0
locks	5000	2147483647	0	0
max async IO	1	255	32	32
max degree of parallelism	0	32	0	0
max server memory (MB)	4	2147483647	2147483647	2147483647
max text repl size (B)	0	2147483647	65536	65536
max worker threads	10	1024	255	255
media retention	0	365	0	0
min memory per query (KB)	512	2147483647	1024	1024
min server memory (MB)	0	2147483647	0	0
nested triggers	0	1	1	1
network packet size (B)	512	65535	4096	4096
open objects	0	2147483647	0	0
priority boost	0	1	0	0
query governor cost limit	0	2147483647	0	0
query wait (s)	-1	2147483647	-1	-1
recovery interval (min)	0	32767	0	0
remote access	0	1	1	1
remote login timeout (s)	0	2147483647	5	5
remote proc trans	0	1	0	0
remote query timeout (s)	0	2147483647	0	0
resource timeout (s)	5	2147483647	10	10
scan for startup procs	0	1	0	0
set working set size	0	1	0	0
show advanced options	0	1	1	1
spin counter	1	2147483647	10000	0
time slice (ms)	50	1000	100	100
Unicode comparison style	0	2147483647	196609	196609
Unicode locale id	0	2147483647	1033	1033
user connections	0	32767	0	0
user options	0	4095	0	0

Manage Logins

As a DBA, you should periodically review who has access to SQL Server. In large organizations, people frequently change jobs. This means that you may have several SQL Server accounts that are not actively being used. You should deactivate these accounts to prevent unauthorized access to SQL Server. If you are using NT Authentication, you can force password aging and password minimum lengths through Windows NT security.

Use the SQL Server Agent to schedule a job that automatically runs `sp_configure`. When you create the job step, you can capture the output from `sp_configure` to a text file.

To save the output from a job step, select the Advanced tab from the Job Step Properties dialog box and enter an output path and filename. I also recommend using the Append to File feature, found on the Advanced tab of the Job Step Properties dialog box, so that a history of configuration settings can be logged (see Figure 29.2).

FIGURE 29.2

Advanced tab, Job Step properties.

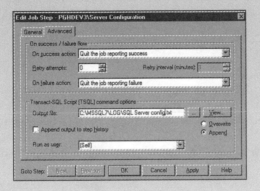

Database Maintenance

The following list summarizes the types of maintenance that should be performed at the database level:

- Back up database and transaction log
- Test your backup strategy
- Audit database access

Several of the tasks discussed in this chapter can be automated through the Database Maintenance Plan Wizard included with SQL Server 7.0. For more information about the Database Maintenance Wizard, see Chapter 30, "Automating Database Administration Tasks."

29

DEVELOPING A
SQL SERVER
MAINTENANCE
PLAN

Back Up Database and Transaction Log

To ensure database recovery, it is essential to frequently back up the database and transaction log. Devise a backup strategy that meets your needs and then periodically review this strategy to ensure that it satisfies your backup requirements (see Chapter 10, "Backup and Restore," for more information).

Test Your Backup/Recovery Strategy

Many DBAs back up SQL Server on a frequent basis, but only the good DBAs actually test their backup strategy by simulating database recovery. You should frequently test the integrity of your backups by actually performing a database recovery (see Chapter 10 for more information). Try to cover all the scenarios: dead server, lost drives, corrupted database, and so on. Do not put yourself in the position of having to be the one to tell the CEO that your backup strategy didn't work.

> **TIP**
>
> An easy way to validate your backup strategy is to create a database with a different name. For example, if I wanted to test my backup/restoration strategy for the pubs database, I would back up the pubs database, create a pubs2 database (or some other database name), and restore the pubs backup to pubs2. If the restoration is successful, I have validated my backup strategy.

Audit Database Access

You should periodically perform a review of who has access to your production databases and what type of rights they possess. Doing so can prevent unauthorized access to production data.

Table/Object Maintenance

The following list summarizes the types of maintenance that should be performed at the table/object level:

- Monitor the record count
- Audit object permissions

Monitor Record Count

In a transaction-oriented environment, it may be necessary to establish a limit on the number of records that should exist in your tables. When the limit is exceeded, the records should be archived from the table. Doing so can ensure a consistent performance level.

Audit Object Permissions

Periodically review the types of permissions (SELECT, INSERT, UPDATE, DELETE, and EXECUTE) that each user has to your production data. Doing so can help prevent security violations.

Job Maintenance

Regularly scheduled jobs should be reviewed for success or failure. Quite often jobs are created and implemented, but never monitored. Do not wait until it is too late to find out that your backup job did not successfully run! The following are items of maintenance and review for jobs. (See Chapter 30 for more information about jobs.)

- **Job status:** Monitor the success or failure of each job.
- **Schedule:** Review the schedule and frequency of the job. Schedules often need to be modified due to changing business needs.
- **Duration:** Review the time it takes to run the job. Load balancing and tuning may be required for jobs that are taking too long to run.
- **Output:** Review the output from the job.

> ### TIP
>
> SQL Server Agent logs errors to the file `c:\mssql7\log\sqlagent.out`.
>
> To view the SQL Server Agent error log from the SQL Server Enterprise Manager, select a server from the server group, click the plus (+) sign next to the server that contains the SQL Server Agent error logs, click the plus (+) sign next to the Management folder, right-click the SQL Server Agent icon, and from the right-click menu select the Display Error Log option. The SQL Server Agent Error Log window appears. From this window, view the contents of the SQL Server Agent error log (see Figure 29.3).
>
> This file can also be viewed with a text editor. You also can view the last nine versions of the SQL Server Agent log by opening the corresponding file (`sqlagent.1`, `sqlagent.2`, and so on).

FIGURE 29.3

SQL Server Agent Error Log.

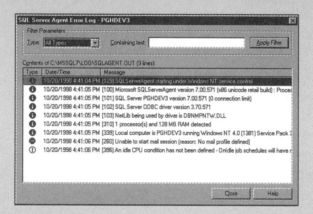

Windows NT Maintenance

The following list summarizes the types of maintenance that should be performed at the Windows NT level:

- Monitor the Windows NT event log
- Back up the Registry
- Keep the emergency repair disk current
- Run disk defragmentation utilities
- Monitor available disk space
- Monitor CPU and memory usage

Monitor the Windows NT Event Log

When it comes to monitoring the event log, you should look for two types of errors: *system errors* and *application errors*.

System errors are hardware and operating system specific. Examples include network errors, hardware problems, and driver errors.

Application errors are those errors associated with the application as well as certain types of SQL Server errors. Examples include connection errors, abnormal termination errors, and database failure errors.

Back Up the Registry

The Registry is vital to the Windows NT operating system. It stores operating system details, hardware information, software information, and user account information. If the Registry is damaged, you may be able to restore it from a backup.

To back up the Registry, use the tape backup software provided with Windows NT or use REGBACK.EXE (REGBACK.EXE is part of the Windows NT resource kit).

Keep the Emergency Repair Disk Current

Whenever hardware and software configurations change, you should update the Emergency Repair disk. Use RDISK.EXE to keep your Emergency Repair disk current.

Run Disk Defragmentation Utilities

You should periodically run disk defragmentation utilities on your server's hard disks. A high degree of hard disk fragmentation can lead to decreased hard disk performance. With version 4.0 of Windows NT, an NTFS drive must be checked with a third-party product. A FAT drive can be checked with SCANDISK.EXE.

> **TIP**
>
> You can download a 30-day version of Diskeeper's NTFS defragmentation product at http://www.alsos.com/PRODUCTS/demo_diskeeper.html.

Monitor Available Disk Space

It's a good idea to have at least 50 percent of the server's hard disk space not in use. This leaves enough free space for database and log growth, database dumps, DTS imports/exports, BCP imports/exports, script generation, and so on.

29

DEVELOPING A
SQL SERVER
MAINTENANCE
PLAN

Monitor CPU and Memory Usage

The easiest way to monitor CPU and memory usage is to use the Performance Monitor (for more information on using the Performance Monitor, refer to Chapter 19, "Monitoring SQL Server"). If you see sustained spikes in CPU usage, it may be time to upgrade your CPU or redistribute the workload. Also, keep an eye on memory usage and the number of free bytes. Insufficient memory leads to a high number of page faults, which degrades performance.

MAINTENANCE CHECKLIST

Here's a checklist of items for maintenance.

Frequency of Execution	*Task*
Daily	
❏	Monitor error logs
❏	Back up database and transaction log
❏	Monitor jobs
❏	Monitor the Windows NT event log
❏	Monitor CPU and memory usage
Weekly	
❏	Monitor available disk space
Monthly	
❏	Test your backup strategy
❏	Monitor record count
❏	Manage logins
❏	Audit database access
❏	Audit object permissions
As Needed	
❏	Back up the Registry
❏	Keep the Emergency Repair disk current
❏	Run disk defragmentation utilities

MAINTENANCE FAQ

Following are some of the common questions asked by DBAs about SQL Server maintenance:

Q. Does the UPDATE STATISTICS command need to be run on a frequent basis, now that version 7.0 has an auto-update statistics feature?

A. No, the UPDATE STATISTICS command does not need to be run on a frequent basis. SQL Server 7.0 automatically manages index statistics. If statistics are out-of-date, SQL Server will detect the problem and automatically update the statistics.

Q. Does DBCC CHECKDB still need to run in version 7.0?

A. According to Microsoft, DBCC CHECKDB does not need to be run on a frequent basis. If you want to be overly cautious, it does not hurt anything to continue to run CHECKDB. The drawback of running CHECKDB is that object creation and modification statements (for example, adding a new column to an existing table) cannot be processed when CHECKDB is running. CHECKDB places shared locks on the objects in the database. These shared locks force object creation and modification statements to wait until CHECKDB is complete.

SUMMARY

Several types of tasks are required to maintain SQL Server. Many of these tasks can be automated through SQL Server's scheduler and Alert Manager. The next chapter, "Automating Database Administration Tasks," discusses how to automate common DBA tasks.

AUTOMATING DATABASE ADMINISTRATION TASKS

by Orryn Sledge

IN THIS CHAPTER

INTRODUCTION

Virtually every organization can reduce administrative effort by automating common DBA tasks. SQL Server 7.0 provides several tools that can help automate common tasks: Job Scheduler, Alert Manager, and Database Maintenance Plan Wizard. These tools are integrated with SQL Server Agent. Together, these tools and SQL Server Agent can automate common tasks and, when taken to the next level, can provide proactive database management.

SQL SERVER 6.5 TO 7.0 QUICK REFERENCE

The "What's New" and "What's Gone" sections that follow provide a quick reference for those migrating from SQL Server 6.5 to SQL Server 7.0. They summarize the changes found in SQL Server that relate to this chapter.

What's New

- SQL Server Agent is a replacement for SQL Server 6.5's SQLExecutive. SQL Server Agent is a big improvement over SQLExecutive in that the former offers an array of features such as job steps and job dependencies, scheduling options based on CPU utilization and thresholds, and management of multiserver jobs.

- Job steps are new in 7.0. A single job can be defined with multiple steps. Each step represents a task. A job step can be dependent on the success or failure of a task and can take an action such as "go to another step" or "quit."

- Active Scripting means that jobs can be extended through scripts that are written in VBScript, JScript, NT Host Scripting, and other scripting languages.

- Multiserver jobs are jobs that can be built once and run on multiple servers. This feature is great for DBAs! For example, a backup job can be created on one server and automatically run on other servers.

- Integrated SQL Server performance condition alerts mean that any SQL Server Performance Monitor object can be defined as an alert with a threshold. An alert can be automatically triggered if a condition goes above or falls below a predefined threshold. Version 7.0 does not require Performance Monitor to be running; SQL Server 6.x required Performance Monitor to be running.

What's Gone

- SQLExecutive is gone. SQL Server Agent is its replacement.
- SQLALRTR.EXE is also gone. Any Windows NT Performance Monitor alerts should be modified to use SQL Server performance condition alerts.

SQL SERVER AGENT

SQL Server Agent is an easy-to-use and robust task scheduler and alert manager. It includes several useful features, such as history logs and the capability to email or page an operator when an event occurs.

SQL Server Agent has the following components:

- Jobs
- Alerts

Jobs

Jobs are typically used to schedule and automate tasks. SQL Server Agent can automate many types of jobs, including the following:

- Backups—Automatic database backups should be an integral part of everyone's production systems. SQL Server Agent can automatically back up a database at a preset interval. See Chapter 10, "Backup and Restore," for more information on automatically backing up the database.
- Scheduled database maintenance—Database maintenance commands, such as DBCC checkdb, can be scheduled to run during off hours.
- Data warehouse import and export routines—Many companies import data into SQL Server and export data to other non-SQL Server systems within the organization. Jobs that are built using the Data Transformation Service (DTS) and run from the SQL Server Agent are great for automating the transfer of information.

Creating and Managing Jobs

Now that you know the types of jobs that can be automated, here's a simple example that actually schedules a job. For this example, assume that you want to schedule a stored procedure that removes any sales data more than seven days old. In addition, you want the procedure to run on a nightly basis at 3:00 a.m., and you want to be notified by email that the procedure successfully ran.

The following is a sample procedure:

```
CREATE PROCEDURE del_remove_old_data AS
/* remove transactions that are 7 or more days old */
DELETE
FROM sales
WHERE DATEDIFF(dd,ord_date,getdate()) > = 7
```

30

AUTOMATING
DATABASE
ADMINISTRATION
TASKS

NOTE

The SQLServerAgent service must be running for the Job Scheduler to work. To determine whether SQLServerAgent is running, check the SQL Server Agent status indicator in the Task Tray or from the SQL Server Enterprise Manager.

To schedule the del_remove_old_data stored procedure, follow these steps:

1. From the SQL Server Enterprise Manager, click the plus (+) sign next to the server that will execute the job.

2. Click the plus (+) sign next to the Management folder.

3. Click the plus (+) sign next to the SQL Server Agent.

4. Right-click the Jobs icon. From the right mouse menu, select the New Job menu option. The New Job Properties dialog box appears (see Figure 30.1).

FIGURE 30.1

The New Job Properties dialog box.

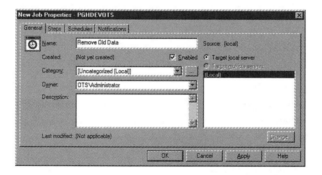

5. From the New Job Properties dialog box, select the General tab. From the General tab, enter a name for the job. Names can be up to 128 characters long. This example uses Remove Old Data for the name.

6. Select the Steps tab. From the Steps tab, click the New button. The New Job Step dialog box appears.

7. From the New Job Step dialog box (see Figure 30.2), enter the following information:

   • Step Name—The name of the step. This example uses Call Delete Procedure for the Step Name.

   • Type—The type of step. This example uses TSQL as the type. The following table describes the purpose of each job type.

Active Script	Runs a script built in Visual Basic Script, Java Script, or other scripting languages. See the "Active Scripting Jobs" section later in the chapter for more information on Active Scripting.
Operating System Command (CmdExec)	Executes a .BAT, .EXE, or .CMD file. Examples include BCP.EXE, ISQL.EXE, and CUSTOM.BAT.
Replication Distributor	Used with replication. Enables you to define replication distribution commands. This type of job is usually managed by SQL Server and is not part of user-defined jobs.
Replication Transaction-Log Reader	Used with replication. Enables you to define replication log reader commands. This type of job is usually managed by SQL Server and is not part of user-defined jobs.
Replication Merge	Used with replication. Enables you to define replication merge commands. This type of job is usually managed by SQL Server and is not part of user-defined jobs.
Replication Snapshot	Used with replication. Enables you to define replication snapshot commands. This type of job is usually managed by SQL Server and is not part of user-defined jobs.
Replication Transact-SQL Script (TSQL)	Executes Transact-SQL statements. Examples include TRUNCATE TABLE authors, UPDATE authors SET au_id = 100, EXEC usp_my_proc, and so on.

- Database—The name of the database. This option is enabled only when the type of task is TSQL. This example uses the pubs database.

30

> **NOTE**
>
> Certain commands are database specific, whereas others can be run from any database. Commands such as INSERT, DELETE, UPDATE, SELECT, and EXECUTE must be run from the corresponding database. Commands such as BACKUP DATABASE, BACKUP LOG, DBCC CHECKDB, and system procedures that reside in the master database (such as sp_addlogin, and sp_configure) can be run from any database.

  • Command—The command to run. This example uses exec del_remove_old_data to run the stored procedure that removes expired sales data.

> **TIP**
>
> Practically anything can be scheduled through the SQL Server Job Scheduler. It isn't just for scheduling backups and DBCC commands. Jobs such as nightly report generation and data summarization are some of the other uses of the Job Scheduler.

FIGURE 30.2

The New Job Step dialog box.

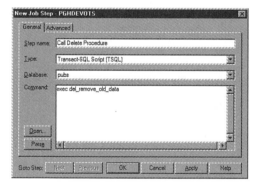

8. Click the Advanced tab to enter additional options. From the Advanced tab (see Figure 30.3), enter the following optional information:

  • On Success Action—This option defines the action to take after the job has successfully run. The following are valid actions for this command: Quit the Job Reporting Success, Quit the Job Reporting Failure, Goto the Next Step. This example uses the Quit the Job Reporting Success option.

NOTE

The On Success Action and the On Failure Action options are important when creating jobs with multiple steps. These options control flow logic. For example, a job may comprise the following four steps: import data from an external system, summarize data, export data to another system, and generate reports. If a step fails to run successfully, the On Failure Action option determines the next action to be taken. For example, if a job fails because the import step failed, the On Failure Action option could be set to Quit the Job Reporting Failure. See the "Job Steps" section later in the chapter for more information.

Table 30.1 contains an explanation of valid job step actions.

TABLE 30.1 STEP ACTIONS

Step Action	Step Explanation
Quit the Job Reporting Success	Terminates the job if the step is successful. This option does not execute any additional steps in the job.
Quit the Job Reporting Failure	Terminates the job if the step fails. This option does not execute any additional steps in the job.
Goto the Next Step	Instructs SQL Server Agent to go to the next step listed in the job. This option is typically used when the job comprises multiple steps that run sequentially.
Goto Step N	Instructs SQL Server Agent to skip to step N.

NOTE

The Goto Step N option is available only if the job contains multiple steps. This option is not visible for single-step jobs.

- Retry Attempts and Retry Interval(minutes)—Sets the number of retries and the retry interval for the step. The default for this option is 0 retry attempts.
- On Failure Action—This option defines the action to take when the job has failed. This example uses the Quit the Job Reporting Failure option. See Table 30.1 for an explanation of Valid On Failure Actions.
- Output File—The filename to log messages.

30

AUTOMATING DATABASE ADMINISTRATION TASKS

> **TIP**
>
> The output file feature of the Advanced tab is great for logging status messages, error messages, or any other type of message that the routine may generate. Additionally, the Append option allows job output to be appended.
>
> The output file feature can also be used for basic reporting. For example, if a job has `select * from authors`, the output from the SQL statement can be written to an output file. This feature is handy for simple reports that need to be run on a regular schedule.

   • Run as User—Specifies the user name to utilize when the step is run.

   Click the OK button to continue. The New Job Properties dialog box re-appears.

9. Select the Schedules tab. From this tab, click the New Schedule button to schedule the job. The New Job Schedule dialog box appears (see Figure 30.3).

FIGURE 30.3

The New Job Step dialog box, Advanced tab.

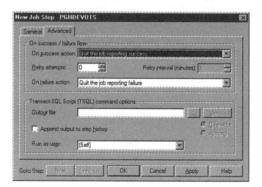

10. From the New Job Schedule dialog box (see Figure 30.4), enter the following information:

   • Name—The name of the schedule. This example uses `Remove Old Data`.

   • Schedule Type—The frequency and scheduling of the job. This example uses the Recurring feature to automatically run the task every day. The Recurring schedule is set in step 10. Table 30.2 contains a listing of schedule types.

FIGURE 30.4

The New Job Schedule dialog box.

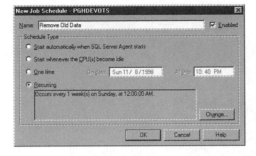

TABLE 30.2   SCHEDULE TYPES

Schedule Type	Explanation	Notes
Start automatically when SQL Server Agent starts	Executes the job when SQL Server Agent is started.	This option is typically not utilized for administrative purposes.
Start whenever the CPU(s) become idle	Executes the job when the CPU is idle.	The option defaults to a sustained CPU usage below 10% and for 600 seconds. This option can be adjusted by going to the Properties dialog box of the SQL Server Agent and selecting the Advanced tab. From the Advanced tab, the Idle parameters can be set.
One Time	Executes the job one time.	This option is useful when a maintenance type of job needs to be run during off-hours. For example, if a table needs a large set of its values updated, you can schedule a one-time job to execute the query. This option is also useful for scheduling long running queries so that the workstation is not held up waiting for the query to finish running.
Recurring	Executes a job on a recurring basis.	This option is typically used for backups and any other type of job that needs to run on a recurring basis

11. Click the Change button from the New Job Schedule dialog box. The Edit Recurring Job Schedule dialog box appears.

12. From the Edit Recurring Job Schedule dialog box (see Figure 30.5), enter the job's schedule.

30

AUTOMATING DATABASE ADMINISTRATION TASKS

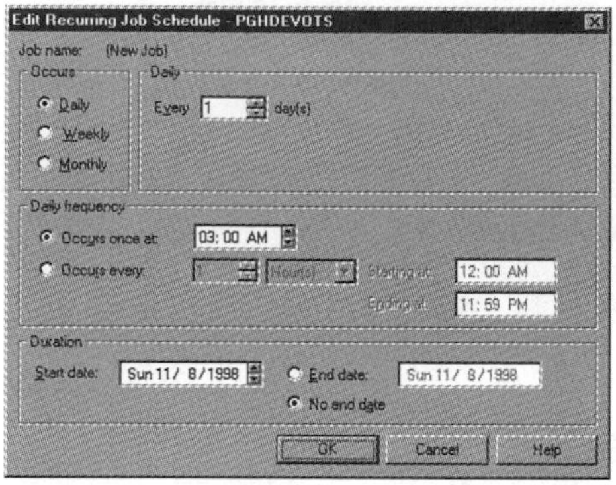

FIGURE 30.5

The Edit Recurring Job Schedule dialog box.

13. Click the OK button to return to the New Job Schedule dialog box.

14. From the New Job Schedule dialog box, click the OK button to return to the Job Properties dialog box.

NOTE

A new feature in SQL Server 7.0 is the capability to define multiple schedules for a single job. For example, a job can be defined to run on Monday at 8:00 p.m. and on Tuesday at 9:00 p.m. To define additional schedules, click the New Schedule button from the Schedules tab in the Job Properties dialog box.

---

15. From the Job Properties dialog box, click the Notifications tab. From the Notifications tab (see Figure 30.6), you can specify the following actions. This example uses an email operator and writes to the Windows NT application event log. It also uses the option when the job completes for email and event log notification. This option will send an email to the operator after the job has run.

- Email operator
- Page operator
- Net send operator
- Write to Windows NT application event log
- Automatically delete job

A FEW TIPS ON EMAIL NOTIFICATION

- To notify an operator by email, SQL Mail must be running and connected to your email service. Use the SQL Mail status indicator in the Enterprise Manager to validate that SQL Mail is successfully running.

- Use the extended stored procedure `xp_sendmail` to test whether your email service is properly configured, as in the following example:

  ```
  xp_sendmail 'recipient_name', 'this is a test'
  ```

- Notifications cannot email query results to an email operator. A notification can email only the following information: job run time, job duration, status, and status messages.

A FEW TIPS ON NET SEND NOTIFICATION

- A net send message can be sent to a computername, username, or messaging name. For more information on the `Net Send` command, type **net help send** at a command prompt.

- The messenger service must be running on Windows NT for a net send notification to work. To determine whether the messenger service is running, open Control Panel, double-click the Services applet, and select the Messenger service. The Status setting displays the condition of the messenger service.

FIGURE 30.6

The Notifications tab in the New Job Properties dialog box.

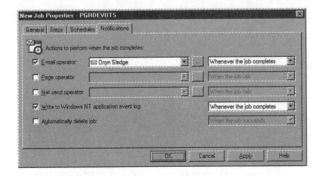

16. Click the OK button to save the job.

After a job has been created, it is a good idea to test the job by manually executing it. Follow these steps to manually execute the job:

1. From the SQL Server Enterprise Manager, click the plus (+) sign next to the server that will execute the job.

2. Click the plus (+) sign next to the Management folder.

3. Click the plus (+) sign next to the SQL Server Agent.

4. Click the Jobs icon. A list of jobs appears in the result pane.

5. Right-click the job that was previously created (this example uses the job Remove Old Data). From the right mouse menu, select the Start Job option. The job starts immediately.

6. Right-click the job. From the right mouse menu, select the Refresh Job option. This step updates the status of the job. (Note: Status information is *not* refreshed automatically.)

7. Review the Last Run Status column in the results pane (see Figure 30.7), to determine whether the job ran successfully. For this example, you also can see that this job was successfully executed by reviewing the email message and the Windows NT event log (see Figures 30.8 and 30.9).

FIGURE 30.7

Last run status.

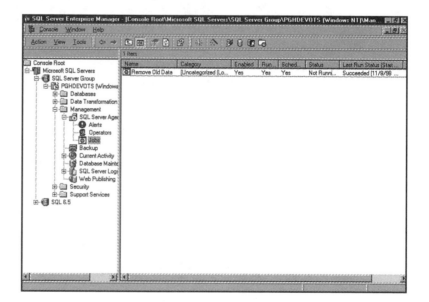

FIGURE 30.8

Email notification.

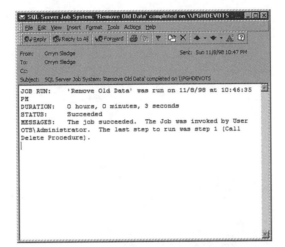

FIGURE 30.9

Event log notification.

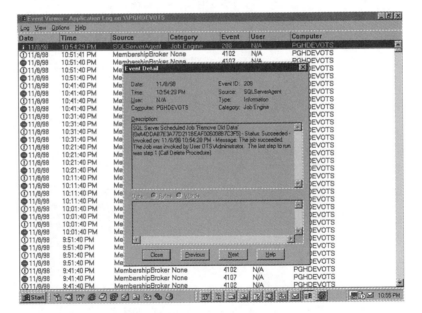

Job Steps

Job steps are new with SQL Server 7.0. Job steps control flow logic such as the following: If job 1 successfully completes, run job 2; otherwise, skip job 2 and run job 3. A more realistic example of job steps is the loading of data into a data warehouse. Figure 30.10 graphically represents the steps involved in loading a data warehouse on a scheduled basis.

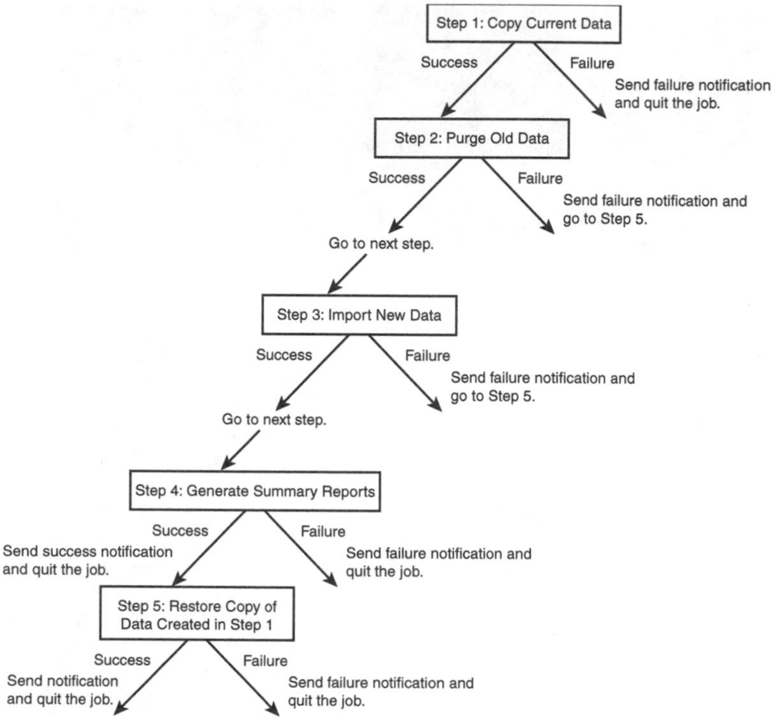

FIGURE 30.10

Job step diagram.

As you can see, a step can be dependent upon the success or failure of another step. If a step fails, a corresponding routine is called to handle failure.

A job step can be defined to take one of the following actions:

- Quit the job
- Go to the next step
- Go to step N

Figure 30.11 provides sample job steps that manage the process defined in Figure 30.10.

See the section "Creating and Managing Jobs" earlier in this chapter for information on implementing job steps.

Active Scripting Jobs

Active Scripting Jobs is new with SQL Server 7.0. This feature allows you to extend a job through scripting. Active scripts can be written in VBScript, JScript, NT Host Scripting, and other scripting languages.

FIGURE 30.11

Sample job steps.

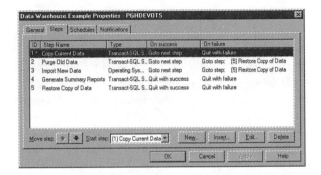

A simple example of an active script job is one that generates a schema for all the tables in the pubs database. The following script generates the tables (this example uses VBScript with SQL DMO; see Chapter 27, "Using SQL-DMO (Distributed Management Objects)," for more information on SQL DMO).

```
Set objServer = CreateObject("SQLDMO.SQLServer")objServer.Connect
➥".","sa"For Each objTable in objServer.Databases("pubs").Tables
➥  objTable.Script, "c:\temp\" & objTable.Name & ".
➥sql"NextobjServer.Disconnect
Set objServer = nothing
```

To schedule an active script, perform the following steps:

1. Follow steps 1 through 4 in the "Creating and Managing Jobs" section. After step 4, the New Job Step dialog box appears.

2. From the New Job Step dialog box (see Figure 30.12), enter the following information:

   - Step Name—The name of the step. This example uses `Generate Table Schema` for the Step Name option.

   - Type—The type of step. This example uses Active Script.

   - Language—The type of language. This example uses Visual Basic Script.

   - Command—The code that is executed.

3. Click the OK button to save the job step.

4. Enter any additional information such as scheduling and notification.

5. Run the job. This will generate the schema scripts to `c:\temp`. Each table will have a corresponding `.sql` file. Figure 30.13 contains an example of the output from this example.

30

AUTOMATING DATABASE ADMINISTRATION TASKS

NOTE

A great feature of active scripting is that it can use objects created in other languages. For example, an object can be created in Visual Basic (or another language that creates ActiveX objects) and implemented in VBScript or JScript.

FIGURE 30.12
Active scripting example.

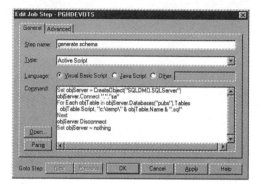

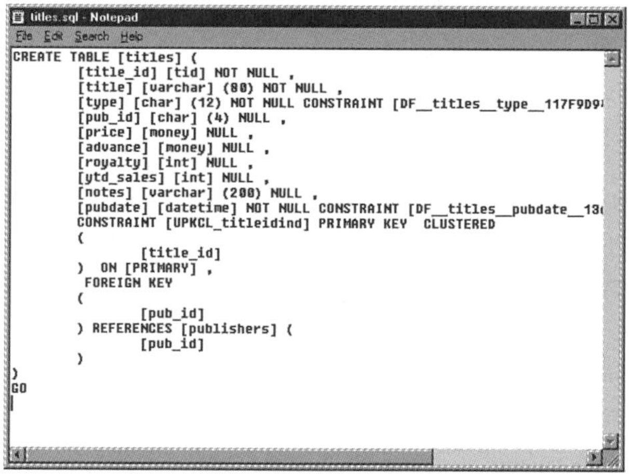

FIGURE 30.13
Sample output from active script example.

Extending Jobs

In the "Creating and Managing Jobs" section, you learned how to schedule a job and how to email an operator when the job is complete. The current section builds on what you learned earlier. For this example, assume that you want to schedule the same job, but you want the email message to contain the number of rows deleted by the stored procedure.

No problem! However, you *do* have to shift the email notification logic to the stored procedure rather than leave it with the Job Scheduler. The Job Scheduler can only send a success or failure email message; the scheduler cannot return the number of rows deleted, updated, and so on.

To send an email message that contains the number of rows deleted, you must make a few modifications to the del_remove_old_data stored procedure. The procedure is enhanced by calling the xp_sendmail extended stored procedure. The xp_sendmail command enables you to email a message that contains the number of rows deleted.

The following stored procedure contains the necessary modifications:

```
CREATE PROCEDURE del_remove_old_data AS
declare @rows_deleted int
declare @e_mail_message varchar(255)

/* remove transactions that are 7 or more days old */
DELETE
FROM transaction_control
WHERE DATEDIFF(dd,transaction_date,getdate()) > = 7

/* store number of rows deleted to a variable */
SELECT @rows_deleted = @@rowcount

/* build message */
SELECT @e_mail_message = 'Numbers of rows removed by del_remove_old_data = ' +
 CONVERT(varchar(20),@rows_deleted)

/* email the results back to the operator */
EXEC master..xp_sendmail 'orryn sledge', @e_mail_message
```

NOTE

Whenever you call an extended stored procedure, you should include the master database in the statement (as in master..xp_sendmail). Otherwise, you must be in the master database to run an extended stored procedure.

FIGURE 30.14

An email message stating the number of rows deleted.

When the Job Scheduler executes the `del_remove_old_data` stored procedure, the number of rows deleted is included in the email message (see Figure 30.14).

Alerts

The *Alert Manager* enables you to define alerts that are executed automatically on the occurrence of an event. When the alert is executed, an operator can be notified by email or pager. An alert also can execute additional jobs, such as calling another Transact-SQL command or calling an external program in the form of .BAT, .EXE, or .CMD file. These features enable a DBA to be more proactive to conditions that require attention.

With the Alert Manager, you can create three types of alerts: event alerts, performance condition alerts, and custom alerts.

Following are examples of event alerts:

- Database out of space
- SQL Server was abnormally terminated
- Database is corrupted
- Table is corrupted

Following are examples of performance condition alerts:

- Transaction log almost full
- Number of merge conflicts exceeds an user-defined threshold

Following are examples of custom alerts:

- Low inventory
- Aborted download

Event Alerts

Now that you have an understanding of the different types of alerts that can be managed, this section runs through a simple example of how to configure the Alert Manager for an event alert. For this example, assume that you want to define an alert that notifies an operator by email when the log file for the pubs database is full.

> **NOTE**
>
> SQLServerAgent must be running for the Alert Manager to work.

To create a sample alert that notifies an operator through email, follow these steps:

1. From the SQL Server Enterprise Manager, click the plus (+) sign next to the server that will execute the job.
2. Click the plus (+) sign next to the Management folder.
3. Click the plus (+) sign next to the SQL Server Agent.
4. Right-click the Alert icon. From the right mouse menu, select the New Alert option. The New Alert Properties dialog box appears.
5. From the New Job Properties dialog box, select the General tab. From the General tab (see Figure 30.15), enter the following information:

FIGURE 30.15
The New Job Properties dialog box—event alert example.

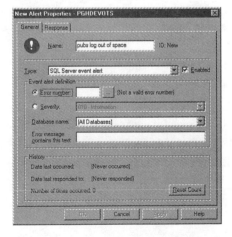

- Name—User-defined alert name. This example uses `pubs log out of space`.

- Type—The type of alert. This example uses SQL Server event alert.

- Event Alert Definition—The error number or severity of the alert. Additionally, a specific database and error message text can be defined.

6. To enable an event alert definition for a specific error number, click the Error Number radio button. Next, click the Manage Error Messages button next to the Error Number field in the Event Alert Definition section of the New Alert Properties dialog box. The Manage SQL Server Messages dialog box appears (see Figure 30.16).

FIGURE 30.16

Manage SQL Server Messages dialog box.

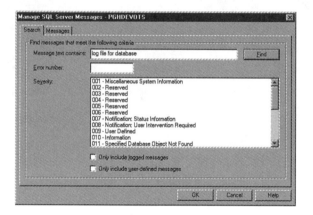

7. From the Manage SQL Server Messages dialog box, you can find, add, delete, and edit error messages. For example, the following message is returned when the `pubs` log is full:

```
Server: Msg 9002, Level 17, State 2
The log file for database 'pubs' is full. Back up the transaction
➡log for the database to free up some log space.
```

To find the corresponding error number for an error message, enter the following in the Message Text Contains section of the dialog box:

`log file for database`

Click the Find button to list all matching error messages (see Figure 30.17).

8. You want to base your alert on error number `9002`. Highlight the row that contains error number `9002` and click the OK button. The New Alert Properties dialog box reappears, showing the selected error number.

FIGURE 30.17

*Finding an error
message.*

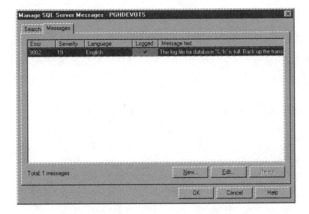

9. Select the Database name. For this example, use the pubs database.

10. From the New Alert Properties dialog box, select the Response tab (see Figure 30.18). From the Response tab, the following information can be entered:

- Execute job

- Operator to notify

- Include alert error text in

- Additional notification message to send to operator

- Delay between responses for a recurring alert

FIGURE 30.18

*The Response tab
in the New Alert
Properties dialog
box.*

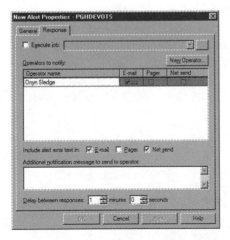

11. Click the OK button to save the new alert.

Congratulations! You just created an alert that notifies an operator when the pubs database is out of space. Figure 30.19 shows the email message the operator receives when the pubs database log is out of space.

FIGURE 30.19

Email notification sent to the operator when the pubs database log is out of space.

Performance Condition Alerts

Any type of alert that can be created in the Performance Monitor can be implemented as a performance condition alert through the Alert Manager. A performance condition alert can be automatically triggered when a condition goes above or falls below a predefined threshold. In turn, the alert can perform an action such as emailing or paging an operator or executing a job. Performance condition alerts are typically used to proactively prevent problems. For example, if a database's transaction log is rapidly filling up, a performance condition alert can notify SQL Server to execute a job such as backing up the transaction log.

To illustrate how performance condition alerts are processed, the following steps build an alert that notifies an operator when the pubs transaction log is more than 70% full. The performance condition alert also backs up the transaction log.

1. From the SQL Server Enterprise Manager, click the plus (+) sign next to the server that will execute the performance condition alert.

2. Click the plus (+) sign next to the Management folder.

3. Click the plus (+) sign next to the SQL Server Agent.

4. Right-click the Alert icon. From the right mouse menu, select the New Alert option. The New Alert Properties dialog box appears.

5. From the New Job Properties dialog box, select the General tab. From the General tab, enter the following information (see Figure 30.20).

> Name: User defined alert name. This example uses `pubs transaction log almost full`.

> Type: The type of alert. This example uses SQL Server performance condition alert.

> Object: The Windows NT Performance Monitor object. This example uses SQLServer:Databases.

> Counter: The Windows NT Performance Monitor counter. This example uses Percent Log Used.

> Instance: The instance of the counter specified. When working with the Percent Log Used counter, the instance is the database log tracked by the counter. This example uses pubs.

> Alert if counter: The threshold for the condition. Alerts can occur if they are below, equal to, or above a specified value. This example uses rises above.

> Value: The threshold limit for the alert. This example uses 70 to specify a value above 70%.

FIGURE 30.20

The New Alert Properties dialog box—performance condition alert example.

6. From the New Alert Properties dialog box, select the Response tab. The purpose of this tab is to specify the action that will take place when the alert is triggered. For this example, we want the following two actions to take place:

   • Execute a job that automatically backs up the transaction log. By backing up the transaction log at the 70% full interval, we increase the amount of free space available to the transaction log.

- Notify an operator by email. When the log is 70% full, an operator will be notified via email that the log exceeded the threshold defined for the alert and that the log was automatically backed up.

From the Response tab, select the Execute Job check box. From the Execute Job pick list, select the (New Job) option. The New Job Properties dialog box appears.

7. From the New Job Properties dialog box, enter the name of the job. This example uses `backup pubs transaction log` (see Figure 30.21). Click the Steps tab.

8. From the Steps tab of the New Job Properties dialog box, click the New button. The New Job Step dialog box appears.

9. From the New Job Step dialog box, enter the following information (see Figure 30.22).

   - Step name: The name of the step. This example uses `backup transaction log`.

   - Type: The step type. This examples uses Transact-SQL Script (TSQL).

   - Database: The name of the database from which the job step is run. This example uses pubs.

   - Command: The command to execute. This example uses the following command to back up the pubs transaction log to a backup file named `c:\mssql7\backup\pubs_log_backup.bak`:

   `backup log pubs to DISK = 'c:\mssql7\backup\pubs_log_backup.bak'`

   Click the OK button. The New Job Properties dialog box reappears.

10. From the New Job Properties dialog box, click the OK button. The New Alert Properties dialog box reappears with the name of the job created in the previous step (see Figure 30.23).

FIGURE 30.21

The General tab on the New Job Properties dialog box.

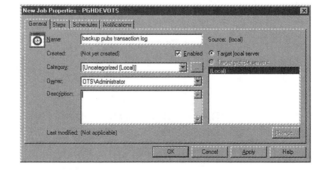

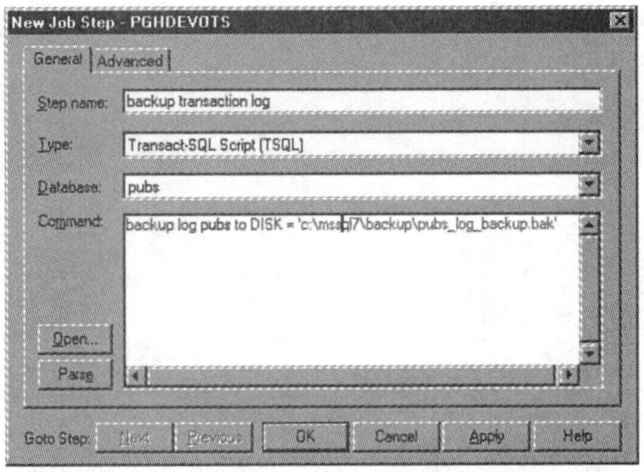

FIGURE 30.22
New Job Step dialog box.

FIGURE 30.23
New Job Properties dialog box—Response tab with job information.

11. To notify an operator by email, click the email checkbox for the name of the operator. For this example, Orryn Sledge is selected to receive email. This step completes the performance condition alert example. Figure 30.24 shows the completed performance condition alert. Figure 30.25 shows the email message an operator would receive when this alert is triggered.

FIGURE 30.24

Completed performance condition alert.

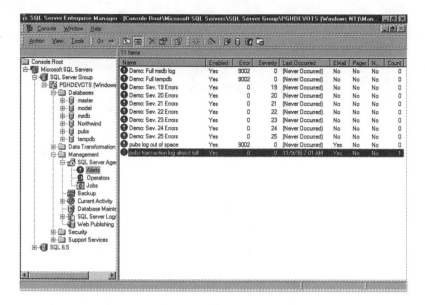

FIGURE 30.25

Sample email message when the alert is triggered.

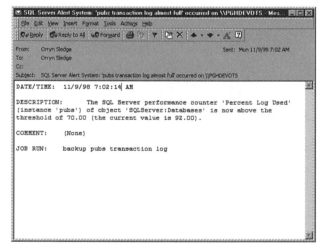

Custom Alerts

In addition to handling SQL Server errors and thresholds, you can use the Alert Manager to alert operators to pre-defined conditions. Suppose that you own a used car dealership and you want to be alerted by email whenever the number of cars on the lot is below 20.

Assume that the number of cars on your lot can be determined by counting the number of records in a table named cars. Also assume that each time a car is sold, it is deleted from the cars table.

The creation of this type of alert consists of two steps:

1. Building the alert notification and define the error number
2. Setting the trigger on the event that executes the error that corresponds to the alert

Step 1: Build the Alert Notification and Define the Error Number

Follow these steps to define a custom error number and message that corresponds to the alert:

1. From the SQL Server Enterprise Manager, click the plus (+) sign next to the server that will execute the job.
2. Click the plus (+) sign next to the Management folder.
3. Click the plus (+) sign next to the SQL Server Agent.
4. Right-click the Alert icon. From the right mouse menu, select the New Alert option. The New Alert Properties dialog box appears.
5. From the New Job Properties dialog box, select the General tab. From the General tab (see Figure 30.26), enter the following information:
   - Name—User-defined alert name. This example uses cars on hand < 20.
   - Type—The type of alert. This example uses SQL Server event alert.

FIGURE 30.26

Custom alert example.

6. Left mouse click the Error Number radio button. Click the Manage Error Messages button next to the Error Number field. The Manage SQL Server Messages dialog box appears.
7. From the Manage SQL Server Messages dialog box, select the Messages tab and click the New button. The New SQL Server Message dialog box appears (see Figure 30.27).

8. From the New SQL Server Message dialog box, enter the following information:

- Error Number—This example uses `50001` for an error number.

- Message Text—This example uses `Car Lot Notification: Inventory is Low. Less than 20 cars on the lot`.

- Always Write to Windows NT Eventlog—Select this option to write the alert to the Windows NT Eventlog; otherwise, the Alert Manager cannot recognize the event.

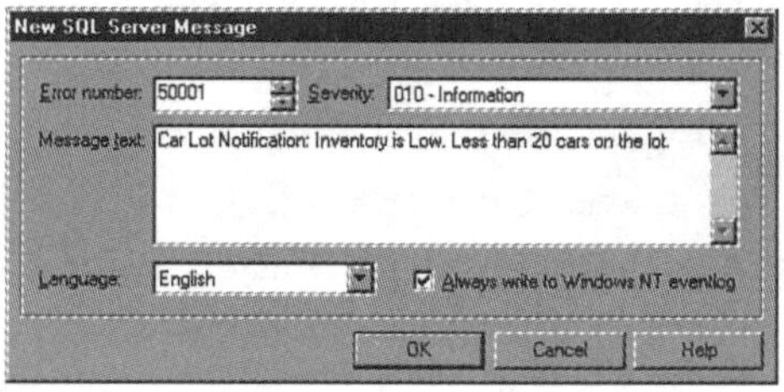

FIGURE 30.27

The New SQL Server Message dialog box.

9. Click the OK button to save the alert. The Manage SQL Server Messages dialog box reappears.

10. From the Manage SQL Server Messages dialog box, click the OK button. The New Alert Properties dialog box reappears with the error number from step 8.

11. Select the Response tab from the New Alert Properties dialog box. From this tab, enter an operator to notify and a notification message (see Figure 30.28).

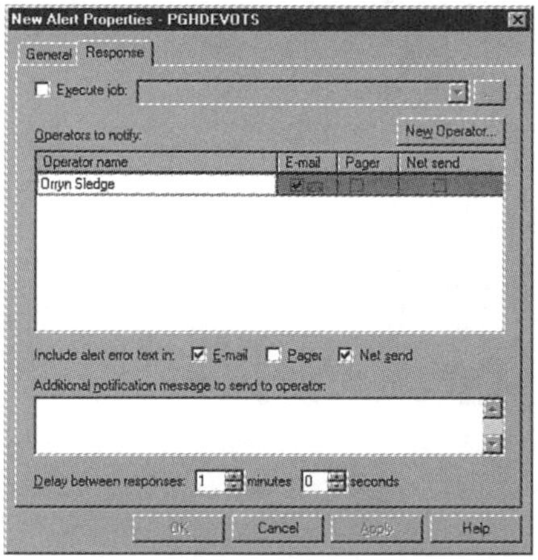

FIGURE 30.28

The Response tab in the New Alert Properties dialog box.

12. Click the OK button to save the alert.

Step 2: Set Up the Event That Executes the Error

Every time a car is sold, assume that it is deleted from the cars table. This arrangement enables you to use a trigger that checks whether the number of cars on hand is below 20. (Remember that triggers are automatically executed when a DELETE, UPDATE, or INSERT event occurs.)

> **NOTE**
>
> The following is the table schema used for this example:
>
> ```
> create table cars
> (car_id int identity primary key,
> car_description varchar(35))
> ```

The following code creates a trigger that automatically issues error number 50001 when fewer than 20 cars are on the lot. In turn, the SQL Server Agent detects error 50001 and automatically sends an email message to the operator.

```
/* DELETE Trigger Example */
CREATE TRIGGER trg_delete_cars ON dbo.cars
FOR DELETE
AS
/* declare variables */
declare @car_count int

/* count the number of cars on hand */
SELECT @car_count = COUNT(*)
FROM cars

/* If quantity is less than < 20 */
/* issue error 50001 (user defined error message).  This will */
/* fire an alert which will notify an operator */
IF @car_count < 20
  BEGIN
    /* RAISERROR parameter explanation: */
    /* 50001 = low inventory message */
    /* 16 = severity level (miscellaneous user error) */
    /* -1 = error state */
    RAISERROR(50001,16,-1)
  END
```

30

AUTOMATING
DATABASE
ADMINISTRATION
TASKS

Now the low inventory alert is automatically executed whenever the number of cars on hand falls below 20. Figure 30.29 shows the email message that an operator receives when this alert is triggered.

FIGURE 30.29

The low inventory email message.

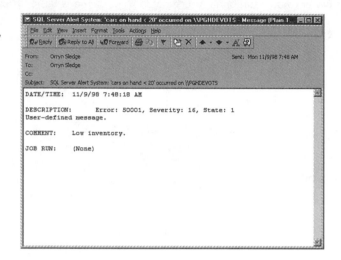

DATABASE MAINTENANCE PLAN WIZARD

The Database Maintenance Plan Wizard automates many of the common jobs a DBA normally performs. Before this wizard was developed, many DBA jobs were script-based. With this wizard, however, you can now graphically automate backups, DBCC commands, and other administrative functions. A nice feature of the Database Maintenance Plan Wizard is that it can email results to an operator.

The following steps explain how to use the Database Maintenance Plan Wizard:

1. From the SQL Server Enterprise Manager, click the Run a Wizard toolbar button. The Select Wizard dialog box appears (see Figure 30.30).

2. From the Select Wizard dialog box, click the plus (+) sign next to the Management topic. Click the Database Maintenance Plan Wizard and click the OK button. The Database Maintenance Plan Wizard appears.

3. From the Database Maintenance Plan Wizard dialog box, click the Next button to continue with this operation. The Select Databases dialog box appears. Select the appropriate database (see Figure 30.31) and click the Next button to continue. The Update Data Optimization Information dialog box appears.

FIGURE 30.30

The Select Wizard dialog box.

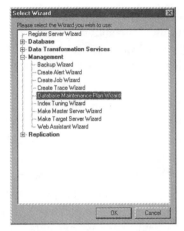

NOTE

Do not forget to include the following system databases when using the Database Maintenance Plan Wizard to automate backups and DBCC jobs: master, model, msdb, and distribution (you do not need to include tempdb in your backup plan). These system databases are actual databases, just as the pubs database or any other database used to store information is a database. It is just as important to back up these databases as it is for any other database.

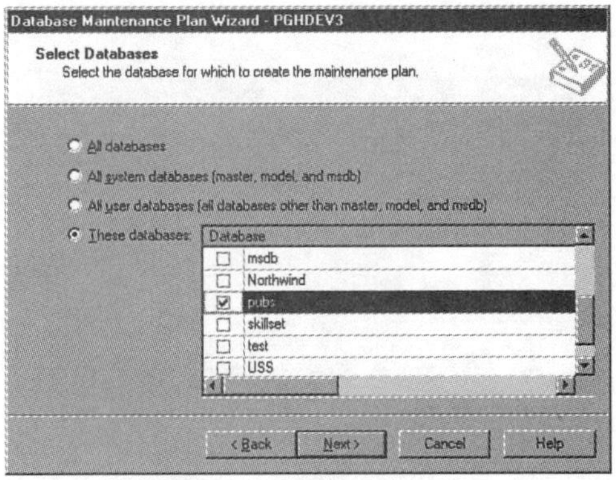

FIGURE 30.31

The Select Databases dialog box.

4. From the Update Data Optimization Information dialog box (see Figure 30.32), select the appropriate responses for the following: Reorganize Data and Index Pages, Update Statistics Used by Query Optimizer, Removed Unused Space from Database Files, and Schedule options. Following are explanations of the Data Optimization options:

   - Reorganize data and index pages—Selecting this option is the equivalent of using the DBCC DBREINDEX command (see Appendix C, "SQL Server Resources," for more information on DBCC DBREINDEX). This option rebuilds all indexes associated with all tables in the selected database (see Chapter 22, "Understanding Indexes," and Chapter 23, "Query Optimization," for more information). Using this option may reduce page splitting and improve data modification performance. Additionally, the Reorganize Pages with the original amount of free space and Change per page percentage to radio buttons control the fill factor level.

   - Update statistics used by the query optimizer—Selecting this option is the equivalent of using the UPDATE STATISTICS command (see Chapters 22 and 23 for more information).

   - Remove unused space from database files—Selecting this will shrink the database files to the specified size. Selecting this option is the equivalent of using the DBCC SHRINKDATABSE command (see Appendix B for more information).

5. Click the Next button to continue. The Run Data Integrity Tests dialog box appears.

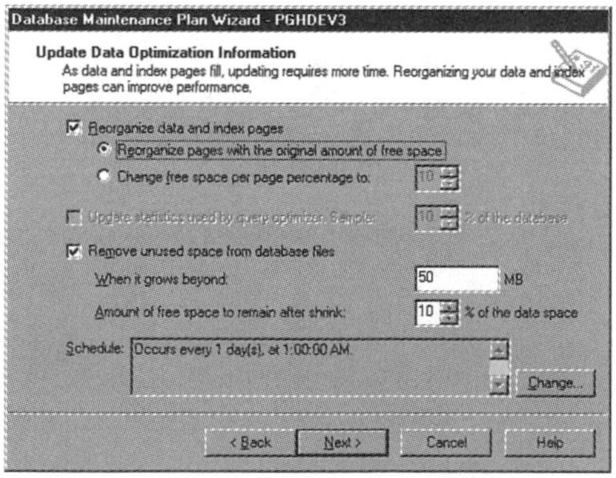

FIGURE 30.32

Update Data Optimization Information dialog box.

6. From the Database Integrity Check dialog box (see Figure 30.33), select the appropriate Check Database Integrity, Perform Tests Before Doing Backups, Schedule options. Explanations of the Data Integrity Check options follow.

- Check Database Integrity—This option checks all data pages and tables in the database for database errors. If the Include Indexes radio button is selected, it is the equivalent of using DBCC CHECKDB (see Appendix B for more information on DBCC CHECKDB). If the Exclude Indexes radio button is selected, it is the equivalent of using DBCC CHECKDB with the NOINDEX option.

- Perform Tests Before Doing Backups—Executes the checks before running the backup.

> **NOTE**
>
> Starting with SQL Server 7.0, the Test Database Integrity option checks text, ntext, and image types. Previous versions of SQL Server required a separate process to check these datatypes.

7. Click the Next button to continue. The Specify the Database Backup Plan dialog box appears.

FIGURE 30.33

Database Integrity Check dialog box.

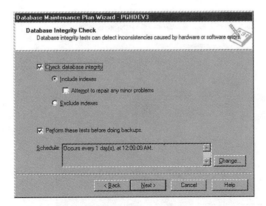

8. From the Specify the Database Backup Plan dialog box (see Figure 30.34), select the appropriate backup and scheduling options. Click the Next button to continue.

If you are storing your backup to disk, the Specify Backup Disk Directory dialog box appears (see Figure 30.35). Enter the appropriate disk backup information and click the Next button. The Specify the Transaction Log Backup Plan dialog box appears.

If you are storing your backup to tape, the Specify the Transaction Log Backup Plan dialog box appears.

> **TIP**
>
> As a general rule, I recommend backing up all databases (don't forget master, msdb, model, and distribution) on a nightly basis. See Chapter 10 for more information.

FIGURE 30.34

The Specify the Database Backup Plan dialog box.

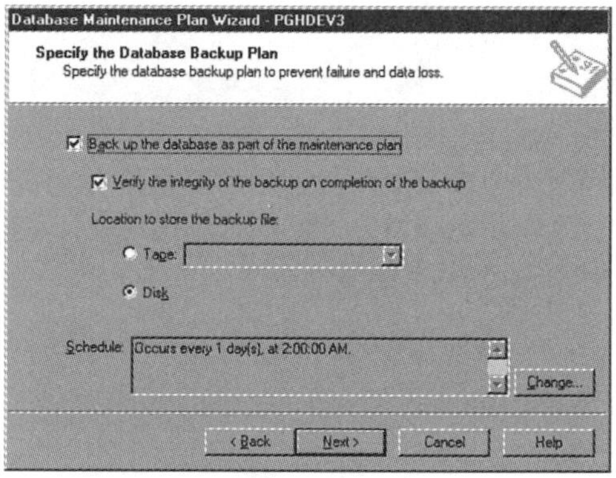

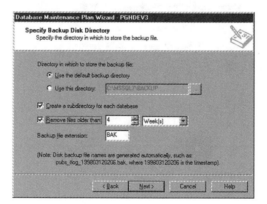

FIGURE 30.35

The Specify Backup Disk Directory dialog box.

9. From the Specify the Transaction Log Backup Plan dialog box (see Figure 30.36), select the appropriate backup and scheduling options. Click the Next button to continue.

   If you are storing your transaction log backup to disk, the Specify Transaction Log Backup Disk Directory dialog box appears (see Figure 30.37). Enter the appropriate disk backup information and click the Next button to continue.

TIP

As a general rule, I recommend backing up the transaction log on a daily basis. I recommend backing up the transaction log more frequently (several times a day) for databases that are subject to constant data modifications. The following databases do not need their transaction log backed up: `master`, `model`, `msdb`, and `distribution`. Additionally, any database that has the database option `truncate log on checkpoint = true` does not need its transaction log backed up. See Chapter 8, "Database Management," and Chapter 10 for more information.

FIGURE 30.36

The Specify the Transaction Log Backup Plan dialog box.

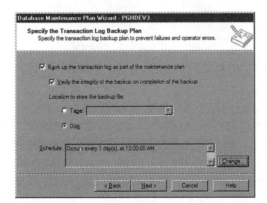

10. From the Reports to Generate dialog box (see Figure 30.38), select the appropriate Write Report to text file, and Email report to operator options. Click the Next button to continue. The Completing the Database Maintenance Plan Wizard dialog box appears.

FIGURE 30.37

The Specify Transaction Log Backup Disk Directory dialog box.

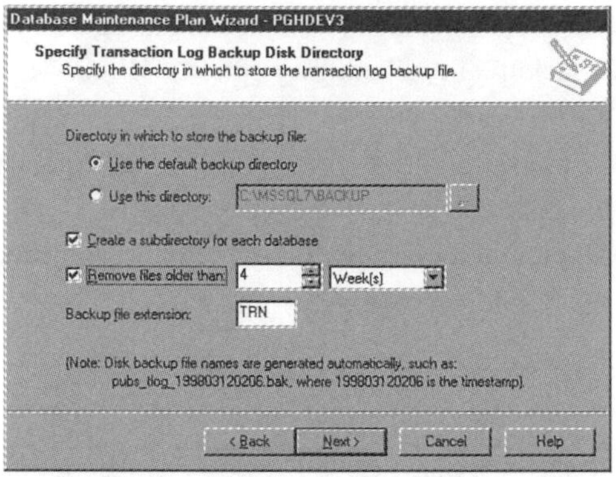

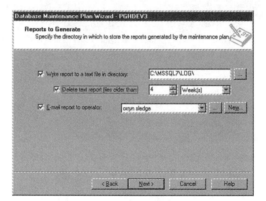

FIGURE 30.38

The Reports to Generate dialog box.

11. From the Maintenance History dialog box (see Figure 30.39), select the appropriate options to record maintenance activities. Click the Next button to continue. The Completing the Database Maintenance Plan Wizard dialog box appears.

12. From the Completing the Database Maintenance Plan Wizard dialog box (see Figure 30.40), review the plan summary information. If the summary information is correct, click the Finish button to complete the job.

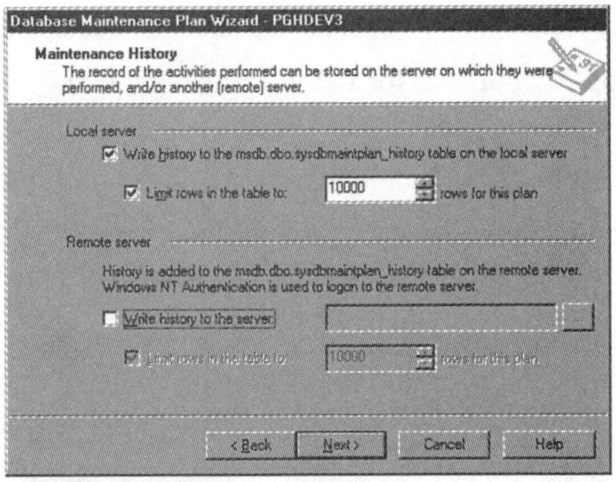

FIGURE 30.39

The Maintenance History dialog box.

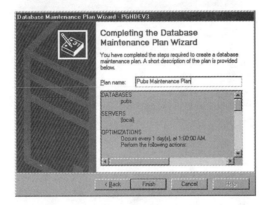

FIGURE 30.40

Completing the Database Maintenance Plan Wizard dialog box.

Congratulations! You have completed the Database Administration Wizard job. If possible, I recommend testing the plan at this point. Doing so helps verify that your backup strategy, email notification, and job components are properly configured. Perform the following steps to run the new plan.

1. From the SQL Server Enterprise Manager, click the plus (+) sign next to the server that will execute the job.

2. Click the plus (+) sign next to the Management folder.

3. Click the plus (+) sign next to the SQL Server Agent.

4. From the expanded SQL Server Agent, click the Jobs icon. The result pane displays a listing of jobs. For this example, the following jobs were created (see Figure 30.41).

   - DB Backup Job for DB Maintenance Plan 'Pubs Maintenance Plán'
   - Integrity Checks Job for DB Maintenance Plan 'Pubs Maintenance Plan'

30

AUTOMATING DATABASE ADMINISTRATION TASKS

- Optimizations Job for DB Maintenance Plan 'Pubs Maintenance Plan'
- Transaction Log Backup Job for DB Maintenance Plan 'Pubs Maintenance Plan'

5. From the right pane, right-click each job in the list. From the right mouse menu, select the Start menu option (see Figure 30.42) to start the job. Note: For this example, run the DB Backup Job before running the Transaction Log Backup Job.

FIGURE 30.41

Listing of jobs.

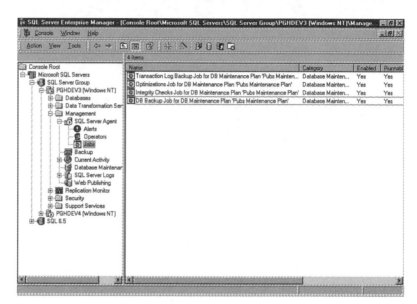

FIGURE 30.42

Starting a job.

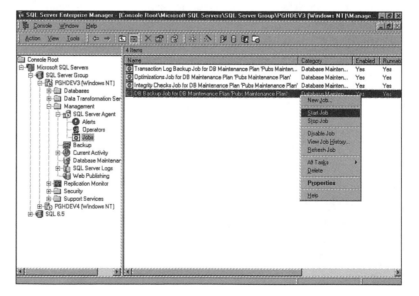

6. Right-click the job to refresh the status information. When the job is complete, check the Last Run Status. If the job successfully executed, the Last Run Status is `Succeeded`.

If you need to modify the job, you can rerun the Database Maintenance Plan Wizard or you can modify the job by double-clicking the job in the right pane.

NOTE

The Database Administrator Wizard uses `sqlmaint.exe` to execute common jobs such as backups, DBCC commands, and so on. In addition, you can run the utility from the command line by typing the following:

`c:\mssql7\binn\sqlmaint.exe`

Here is a listing of the command-line parameters available with `sqlmaint.exe`:

```
sqlmaint
[-?] ¦
  [-S server]
  [-U login_ID [-P password]]
  {
    [ -D database_name ¦ -PlanName name ¦ -PlanID guid ]
    [-Rpt text_file [-DelTxtRpt <time_period>] ]
    [-To operator_name]
    [-HtmlRpt html_file [-DelHtmlRpt <time_period>] ]
    [-RmUnusedSpace threshold_percent free_percent]
    [-CkDB ¦ -CkDBNoIdx]
    [-CkAl ¦ -CkAlNoIdx]
    [-CkTxtAl]
    [-CkCat]
    [-UpdSts]
    [-UpdOptiStats sample_percent]
    [-RebldIdx free_space]
    [-WriteHistory]
    [
      {-BkUpDB [backup_path] ¦ -BkUpLog [backup_path] }
        {-BkUpMedia
          {DISK [ [-DelBkUps <time_period>]
            [-CrBkSubDir ] [ -UseDefDir ]]
          ¦ TAPE
          }
        }
      [-BkUpOnlyIfClean]
      [-VrfyBackup]
    ]
  }
  ]
time_period> ::=
number[minutes ¦ hours ¦ days ¦ weeks ¦ months]
```

30

AUTOMATING DATABASE ADMINISTRATION TASKS FAQ

The following section list some commonly asked questions and answers about SQL Server 7.0 tasks.

Does UPDATE STATISTICS still need to be scheduled on a frequent basis in version 7.0?

No, starting with SQL Server 7.0 UPDATE STATISTICS does not need to be run on a frequent basis. SQL Server 7.0 will automatically update an index's statistics on an as-needed basis.

Does DBCC CHECKDB still need to be scheduled on a frequent basis in version 7.0?

No, Microsoft states that the need to run DBCC CHECKDB on a frequent basis is no longer necessary. If you do decide to run DBCC CHECKDB on a frequent basis, keep in mind that you cannot create or modify tables, stored procedures, and other objects while DBCC CHECKDB is running. Therefore, I recommend running DBCC CHECKDB during the off-hours.

Which database contains job, alert, and operator information?

The database MSDB contains job, alert, and operator information. The following tables store information used by jobs, alerts, and operators: sysjobs, sysjobschedules, sysalerts, and sysoperators.

Are there any commands that the Database Maintenance Plan Wizard does not include that should be part of a scheduled maintenance plan?

Yes, the wizard does not include the DBCC CHECKFILEGROUP command (see Appendix B for more information). This command should be scheduled if the database contains filegroups.

SUMMARY

The following are the key points to keep in mind when you want to automate database administration tasks.

- SQL Server Agent must be running so that alerts and jobs can be processed.
- Use the Job Scheduler to automate common DBA jobs such as backing up a database, backing up a transaction log, running DBCC commands, and importing/exporting data.
- Jobs can contain one or more steps and can have step dependencies.
- Jobs can contain Transact-SQL commands, VBScript, JScript, and scripts built in other languages.
- Jobs can execute external .BAT, .EXE, and .CMD files.
- Use the Alert Manager to automatically notify an operator of problems, such as a database errors or user-defined error messages.
- The Job Scheduler, Alert Manager, and Database Maintenance Plan Wizard can notify an operator through email or a pager.

30

AUTOMATING
DATABASE
ADMINISTRATION
TASKS

DATA WAREHOUSING

PART
IX

IN THIS PART

INTRODUCTION TO DATA WAREHOUSING

by Troy Rackley

IN THIS CHAPTER

You may be asking yourself, "What is a data warehouse, and what does it mean to me?" Well, data warehousing has become one of largest buzzes around the database industry today. Most organizations are either planning or embarking on some sort of data warehousing effort. Because of the large shift of organizations toward the construction of warehouses, it is imperative to the survival of DBAs to understand the concepts and procedures involved with this phenomenon.

This chapter centers on familiarizing you with the current concepts of data warehousing. It will also provide some design issues and architectural considerations for implementing a warehouse solution within your organization.

WHY WAREHOUSE?

Companies are finding that in order to be competitive, in whatever business, they must have easy access to information. Imagine that a sales manager approaches your boss and states that he needs to see the sales totals for a product across a region for the past several quarters to decide whether a certain group should be targeted for a new sales promotion. The executive knows that those doing order-entry are capturing this information. He does not know that you are going to have to do some fancy pretzel-like maneuvers to pull up these sales totals. Over time, you provide him with the report and it ends up being not exactly what he wanted. The executive, now disgusted with the efforts of IT, resorts to having his secretary dump several reports from the mainframe system and selectively pick out bits of the information to be summarized in a spreadsheet. While on the plane back to his territory, the sales manager reads in a popular computing magazine how data warehousing is allowing companies to be more competitive because it gives decision makers access to information to solve problems.

The need for data warehousing stems from the fact that organizations keep their information stored in so many places and that it is difficult to report on all the information available. Because the data is on different systems, it is usually in different formats as well. Consolidation and easy access to data are major themes for warehouses. You must bring all the information together from several sources so that one can learn more about their customers buying habits, suppliers, vendors, and so on.

WHAT IS A DATA WAREHOUSE?

A data warehouse is a centralized storage facility for differing types of data throughout an enterprise. This data is subject oriented, time sensitive, and organized in a way that offers simplified analysis. For example, a data warehouse might contain customer information and sales to these customers over the past five years. It might be derived from several types of disjoint production systems in the enterprise, such as an order-processing system, which resides on a mainframe, or a sales-tracking application housed on an

AS400. Querying these systems for trends might prove to be a difficult task. Data warehousing is the process of collecting, aggregating, storing, and maintaining this information so that executives can use it to make accurate business decisions. Some characteristics and features of data warehousing are as follows:

- Offers one-stop shopping and provides a consolidated store of information from across the enterprise

- Supports data driven decision-making

- Pre-calculated summaries or aggregations offer increased speed

- Offers snapshots of time to better aid business analysis

- Regular schedule of dumps and loads from operational data stores

All these features help differentiate warehouses from typical operational database systems. This leads the warehouse to be separated from these systems and gain its own set of physical requirements. It is common to keep warehouses on separate machines that can be tuned for a lower frequency of users with different querying characteristics. Data warehouses are usually read-only based systems, aside from the periodic loading of current information.

Warehousing is not a trivial task. It involves coercing different groups across the enterprise to work together. The data can be spread across geographical as well as departmental boundaries and differing hardware/software platforms. The data warehousing development team will need a broad range of skills to become a reality. This effort can span many months to many years depending on the needs of the system and the political conflicts that are sure to erupt. The different departments must agree on common information formats such as customer or vendor account numbers. As in most development efforts, it helps to have a strong executive champion to approve budget extensions as the needs of the warehousing project increase.

Decision Support Systems (DSS)

Decision Support Systems (DSS) are applications that provide analysis on the data stored in the warehouse. They can supply trend information that can help business leaders know what customers or products they should concentrate on in the near future. Decision support systems together with data warehouses provide the following benefits:

- Aid management and decision-makers transform raw data into information

- Help management identify key trends

- Help an enterprise foresee predictable events and act in anticipation of those events

- Assist management to understand the big picture and thus reengineer business practices in reaction to what happened

Online Analytical Processing (OLAP)

Online Analytical Processing (OLAP) systems are a type of decision support application. They enable the user to query the data and view it from several perspectives. OLAP applications provide the following:

- Quick canned views of data (common reports).
- Advanced data analysis through pivot tables. Pivot tables are interactive views of data that let you rotate and examine the information from different summary levels, filter for specific data elements, or drill down into detail levels of interest.
- Flexible, easy reporting through ad hoc queries.
- Forecasting, what if analysis, prediction of future outcomes.

Using tools for DSS or OLAP a particular knowledge worker may ask or receive results from the following typical questions:

- Which customers shopped by catalog and waited until the last minute to buy Christmas gifts?
- What was the percentage of customer service calls made during the first few months of a particular phone service installation?
- Which customers supply 80 percent of the revenue? Will these customers fit the profile for the next set of planned sales promotions?
- How many times did a particular customer visit my online store before making a purchase?
- At what point are most users leaving this Web site?

The previous queries are common when doing a type of decision support called segmented profiling. Decision support also enables you to do predictive modeling and predict trends, such as the next big products or which customers might leave. Another technique called data mining involves asking questions that cannot be answered from the data alone, such hidden relationships or patterns.

Data warehousing is entirely about providing easy access to information to support decision making. Supplying this information in a format that is presentable is possibly the most time consuming part of the process. The operational systems that store our vital day-to-day data is usually not simplified enough to help answer these types of questions.

WAREHOUSE DATA VERSUS OPERATIONAL DATA

Operational database systems deal with handling many users and transactions. These are often referred to as online transactional processing systems (or OLTP). Users may be constantly adding, updating, and querying information in these production systems.

Introduction to Data Warehousing

CHAPTER 31

863

31

INTRODUCTION TO
DATA
WAREHOUSING

An example of an OLTP is a typical order entry application. A customer calls a sales representative and orders some products from a catalog. The sales associate can pull up the order entry screen and enter the line items the customer desires. The order is placed, which triggers inventory allocations and so on. This small part of the process has generated many records, and many transactions have taken place. This OLTP system requires transactions to be speedy and inventory levels to be accurate. The sheer volume of these diverse operations and the amount of data that is produced provide a poor environment for decision support.

In contrast, in a typical decision support system, a marketing representative can collect all of the customers that have purchased a particular product from the catalog over the last couple of years and target these customers for a promotion that offers similar products. Because the data warehousing database consists of consolidated information on subjects such as sales, products, or customers, this proves to be a simple task. Additionally, because the operational systems archive information irrelevant to day-to-day operations, the ability for the marketing managers to query on historical events would have been arduous or impossible.

To understand the concept of data warehousing, it is often informative to differentiate it from the common operational systems from which it gains all of its information. Table 31.1 lists some of the differences between OLTP and data warehousing data stores.

TABLE 31.1 OPERATIONAL VERSUS WAREHOUSE DATA

Operational Database	Warehouse Database
Transaction oriented around entities and relationships	Subject oriented around facts and dimensions
Many tables, normalized schema	Fewer tables, denormalized schema
Users adding, updating, and deleting records	Users querying read-only records
Many users accessing records, fewer users reporting	Most users reporting
Transaction/rollback logs used	No transaction/rollback logs needed
Many detail rows	Consolidated, summarized rows
Smaller indexes for speedy updates	Vast indexes for optimized queries
Always currently accurate data, if not, can be updated	Accurate for a specific moment in time

DATA WAREHOUSING COMPONENTS

Figure 31.1 represents the basic design of most data warehousing efforts.

FIGURE 31.1

The data warehousing environment.

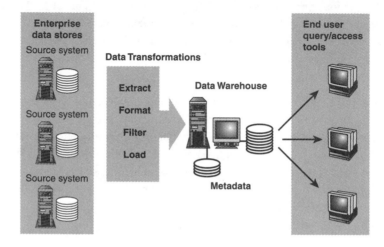

- **Operational data stores:** These are the OLTP systems currently in use by the organization. They might be dispersed throughout the enterprise and provide specialized functionality to different divisions.

- **Data transformations:** The process where data is moved out of the OLTP systems and modified, summarized, or consolidated into a format suitable for the data warehouse. These might involve splitting up a name field into first, last, middle initial or consolidating duplicate customer records from disparate systems into one unified customer account record.

- **Metadata:** The description of the data to be stored in the data warehouse. This might include the source of the original information and the business rules or transformations that were applied when the data was loaded.

- **Data store:** The actual database and server hardware that contains the warehouse. This might consist of one central data warehouse or multiple specialized data marts.

- **End user access/query tools:** These can be third-party query reporting tools or applications built in-house that provide access to the information stored in the data warehouse.

WHAT IS A DATA MART?

A data mart is a repository of data gathered from operational data or other sources that is designed to serve a particular department or functional group. Sound like a warehouse?

Introduction to Data Warehousing

CHAPTER 31

865

31

INTRODUCTION TO
DATA
WAREHOUSING

Yes, but you can think of a mart as being less generic than the typical warehouse. The emphasis of a data mart is on meeting the specific demands of a particular group of knowledge users in terms of analysis, content, presentation, and ease-of-use. The information is stored in the data mart in a format that is familiar to the user's.

A common approach to using data marts is to keep data at a detail level in the data warehouse and summarize this information into the data mart for each functional group or department. Another design method includes building data marts in each departmental unit and merging departmental data into an enterprise-level data store later. Either method offers the benefit of centralizing the information for the end users. Some characteristics of data marts are as follows:

- Data specialized for a particular group of an organization
- Yields quicker return on investment
- Engineered for easy access
- Optimal response from lower volume queries

Because of the simplified and specialized nature of data marts, organizations are turning to data marts as a quick solution to their decision-support needs. Figure 31.2 illustrates how marts and warehouses can coexist in the enterprise.

FIGURE 31.2

Data warehousing with data marts.

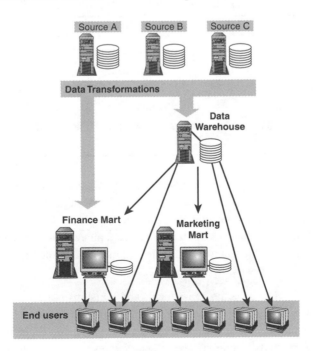

Warehouses Versus Marts

Data warehouses can be viewed as being similar to wholesale warehouse clubs. They contain a large inventory of items; however, they do not seem to specialize in one area in particular. Data marts are like specialized product stores, such as a coffee shop or bakery. They only deal in coffee or baked goods, and they will package it in a format that is familiar and expected for you.

A data mart and a warehouse each tend to imply the existence of the other. It is widely understood that the design of the data mart starts from the requirements of the user. The data warehouse design usually begins from the analysis of currently existing data and how it can be collected to be used later.

A data warehouse is a central aggregation of data. A data mart can be derived from a warehouse, or the warehouse can be derived from the smaller specialized marts. The mart emphasizes ease of access and usability for a particular design purpose. In general, a data warehouse tends to be strategic but often unfinished; a data mart tends to be tactical and aimed at meeting an immediate need. Table 31.2 summarizes some of the key differences between warehouses and marts.

TABLE 31.2 KEY DIFFERENCES BETWEEN DATA MARTS AND DATA WAREHOUSES

Data Warehouse	Data Mart
Enterprise-wide use	Used by department or functional unit
Difficult, more time-consuming to implement	Easier, quicker quick to implement
Larger volume of data	Smaller, more specialized volume of data
Developed using the data currently available	Developed from the users data needs

Data marts are clearly the quick answer to a department's needs. Their lower cost and ease of use allow for quick implementation and an almost instant return on investment (ROI). Often, when a single division's data mart efforts are viewed a success, others will soon follow with implementations of their own. From an enterprise perspective, the existence of several divisional marts may mean the organization is merely a step away from implementing a company-wide solution.

Care must be taken when separate departments and divisions build their own data marts. It is common for many divisional companies to hold differing views of certain business concepts. If, for example, the finance department and marketing department both implement their own data marts, each may keep track of sales but defines them differently.

Later, if someone in marketing needs to gather some information from the finance mart, how will she resolve this difference? A unified vision is necessary even when building data marts from departmental point of view.

TRANSFORMING OPERATIONAL DATA

The key issue with developing data stores of any type is how to change the raw data you have into the information you need. This process is called data transformation. It is rare that the data that exists in the OLTP systems can actually be used to perform complex decision support. Generally, smaller bits of relevant information need to be pulled from a virtual sea of data. A table that consists of 50 or so fields in the operational system may contain 10 columns or less that are useful for this type of business analysis. Data transformations are a set of operations performed on the source data as it is transferred to its destination. Typical transformations include integrating data from several sources into one destination, cleaning up dirty data, mapping different definitions of information to a common model, and performing summarization upon many detail records. Data transformation procedures account for the most time required to implement a warehouse or mart.

Data Integration or Consolidation

Consolidation of data from several sources is a simple but powerful concept. These differing operational sources were never designed to work together. By integrating data elements from each of these sources, you can put together a more robust informative record, maybe the best of both worlds. Consolidation can be as simple as copying the data from the different sources into one destination as is. Alternatively, you might need to massage the data a bit, so that it conforms to a unified model. This type of data consolidation load would create the benefit of having all your data elements in one place for easier query development, thus speeding up response times.

With a warehouse, you can integrate the portions of each system into a common customer table. For example, you can consolidate billing addresses from the financial department's system with the service agreement information from the customer service database and contact data from the sales telemarketing tables.

Another example would be if two systems used a different data type for a similar account number. Account 000125 in system A might be customer 125 in system B. An agreement must be reached as to which format offers the most informative approach to this piece of information; that is the format that should be stored in the warehouse.

Ensuring Data Quality

A key element in gathering and storing data from operational systems is data cleansing or scrubbing. Business processes may dictate to the production users that a particular piece of information follows a particular format; however, in practice there are usually inconsistencies in the data entry. If a name field in a legacy system were to be separated into first name and last name fields in the warehouse, you would encounter many different combinations of first, last, and middle initials strewn throughout the records. There may exist missing fields in the source records, or redundant records all together. Another example of data scrubbing involves specific validation schemes needed to ensure that all account numbers follow a required format.

A great deal of effort should be placed on this aspect of data transformation because it is here that any warehousing project can be perceived as a failure. If users sees that there is an unclean data morsel in data mart, they might begin to question the validity of the other information it contains. User perception can determine whether you end up with a data warehouse or a data outhouse.

Data Mapping and Matching

Legacy systems are famous for embedding numeric values in fields to store hidden information. The priority field in a particular table might be storing values such as 1, 2, and 3. In relational systems these may be implemented as foreign key lookup tables and the true meaning revealed by a simple join operation. However, in flat files and nonrelational databases, the meaning is buried deep within application logic or a programmer's cranium. When this data is transformed to the data warehouse, the numerical values need to be mapped to more meaningful terms, such as a high, medium, and low priority.

A code for an account manager field might contain information regarding her region or territory. Because the warehouse or mart is designed to bring more of this information out in the open, the information tucked deep away in codes should be mapped to descriptive elements such as northeast, or even region number 10. This allows warehousing users or query applications to submit queries such as the following:

```
SELECT sum_profits FROM sales WHERE region = 10
```

instead of

```
SELECT sum_profits FROM sales WHERE SUBSTRING(accmgr_id,1,2) = '10'"
```

This example is simplified. When the data is logically organized within the warehouse, queries like this one become less complex and can offer enhanced results.

Summary

It is common in data warehousing to aggregate data as it is moved from the operational systems to the mart or warehouse. Pre-aggregating the data provides improved performance over applying summarization every time the same query is executed. This also reduces the amount of data that is initially stored.

Often simple aggregation is all that is required, but complex aggregations across several disjointed tables can offer results that are extremely useful in analytical processing.

Extracting, Loading, and Refreshing Data

When you have decided on information to store and the types of transformations needed, you will then be faced with the challenge of loading and periodically refreshing the warehouse. The information in the warehouse represents a slice in time of the operational data. Just how small of a slice is up to you. You might decide to load data into the warehouse on a weekly schedule, or perhaps after a certain closing or posting period during the month. It may be determined that the best time to do such a load is during a low traffic period, say after normal business hours or on weekends.

What rules do you make for extracting data? Do you extract all of the data or just the part that is new or different? The ideal method involves loading only the new information into the warehouse during each interval. This, however, may not prove to be as easy as it sounds for some legacy systems. If the system does not use some form of a transaction log, similar to SQL Server, then more effort will be required to identify the changes made since the last refresh. The time sensitive information (orders, proposals, shipments, and so on) can be retrieved by simple queries specifying a date prior to the last refresh. The static information (customers, suppliers, products, and so on) might be more difficult to probe for changes. You might decide to implement some sort of audit procedure to simplify this, or you might want to simply refresh all of the static tables. This is an example of the tradeoff between having efficient warehousing routines or a shortened warehouse implementation time frame.

Data extraction can involve procedures that run on the existing data sources, such as triggers or scheduled tasks. An example would be a batch job on a legacy system that exports all of the new production orders that have occurred in the last period to a dump file for loading into the warehouse. In this scenario, the data extraction and loading are separate processes. An alternative method might involve the destination data source initiating the refresh and performing the extract and load at the same time. This can be accomplished with the Data Transformation Services (DTS) in SQL Server 7.0. For example, a DTS package could be scheduled to periodically run that imports all of the new production orders that fall into a particular date range. After a warehouse is implemented, the most integral part of its operation are these periodic refresh routines.

Metadata

Data that eventually makes its way into the mart or warehouse could go through any number of transformations listed previously. It could also be from varying systems throughout the enterprise. How do you keep this information regarding transfer of data into the storehouse straight? Just as a normal warehouse keeps an inventory of the items it contains, a data warehouse keeps track of its contents through metadata. Its purpose is to describe the data that is stored in the warehouse, where it has been, what changes have been made to it, and when.

Metadata contains business semantics that explain what a certain column is with friendly names and offer descriptions of what it means to the user. In addition, it describes the data transformations that have been applied to it. This historical log that explains how an item of information was derived is called *data lineage*.

Another purpose for metadata is impact analysis. This determines what data transformations will be broken when schema changes are made to the warehouse database. These informative elements of the data warehousing architecture prove to be invaluable as the needs of the project grow and change over time.

PLANNING THE WAREHOUSE DESIGN

The physical and operational requirements of warehousing solutions between traditional database efforts cause design and maintenance to be quite different. The architecture can be made up of several data marts feeding an enterprise storehouse or a warehouse supplying specialized aggregations for the smaller marts. In either solution, the basic considerations for planning the solution are as follows:

- Gather the key players interested in the warehousing results.
- Evaluate the scope, benefits, and costs of the warehousing effort.
- Determine the intended business use and relationships of data to be loaded.
- Evaluate the enterprise's key facts and subject-oriented dimensions.
- Determine the frequency at which data is to be loaded, extracted filtered, or transformed.
- Provide expectations of the finished warehouse and how it will adapt as business processes change over time.

Introduction to Data Warehousing

CHAPTER 31

871

31

INTRODUCTION TO
DATA
WAREHOUSING

TOP DOWN OR BOTTOM UP?

Which approach should you use when designing the warehouse? Should you start from the top down, designing an enterprise-wide architecture and then construct data stores that conform to that architecture? Or should you implement a bottom-up method, beginning with highly focused and specialized data marts targeted at particular business functions? The key here has to do with deciding whether to address short-term issues of a particular department or to step back and look at the bigger picture of long term benefits.

The bottom-up approach deals with using the smaller, more focused applications of data warehousing, which can simplify the entire process. There are usually smaller data requirements and a limited amount of specialized queries or summarization. The bottom-up approach offers the trade-off of difficulty scaling to the entire organization for a speedier development time. Although this method can return the quickest implementation results, care must be taken to ensure that the tighter focus does not shut the door to later cross-organizational abilities. This approach can be effective because there are usually no political issues regarding data ownership.

For the best long-term results, choose the top-down method. The pitfalls of the bottom-up approach are avoided by determining standardized definitions of business concepts and data requirements up front. The costs, difficulty, and time required are much greater to arrive at this common understanding. Getting business leaders to cooperate without political posturing can also prove to be an arduous task. Usually the biggest questions are, "Who will own the data?" or "Who will cover the costs of development?" What can be gained, however, is a comprehensive resource that is globally accepted throughout the enterprise.

Dimensional Modeling (Stars and Snowflakes)

The traditional entity relationship (ER) model uses a normalized approach to database design. Normalization removes redundancy from the schema to optimize storage. Data warehousing is not so concerned with saving space but providing simplicity from the perspective of the user. A small amount of redundancy is usually acceptable. Dimensional modeling is a more appropriate approach to the warehouse design. It involves designing the schema such that you separate the business into logical events or facts, and a set of corresponding dimensions.

The schema that results is commonly referred to as the star schema. This is because the star schema utilizes few, large, centralized fact tables and many small dimension tables. Figure 31.3 describes an example of a star schema.

FIGURE 31.3

A sample star schema.

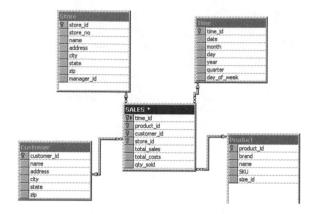

The following is a common query executed against the schema described previously. The results are the customers that bought a particular product in October of 1996.

```
SELECT  c.customer_ID, name, address, sum(qty_sold)
FROM        sales s, time t, product p, customer c
WHERE       month = 10 AND
            year = 1996 AND
            upc_code = 8989764 AND
            s.time_id = t.time_id AND
            s.customer_id = c.customer_id AND
            s.product_id  = p.product_id
GROUP BY    c.customer_id
ORDER BY    c.customer_id(
```

Facts Tables

The central fact table usually consists of business events that can be recorded over time, such as bank transactions, sales, orders, returns, shipments, and Web site visits. They are normally made up of foreign keys to the dimension tables and a set of numerical values. The information stored in the fact tables is usually static because it is historical. The most common example of a fact table in the star schema is for sales.

Dimensions

The dimension tables consist mainly of textual information linked to fact records, such as customer names, product descriptions, suppliers, and vendors. These tables will contain fewer records than the facts tables and are not static. Records in dimension tables may be updated. For example, the customer address might be modified in the source system.

Dimension tables or tables that deal with periods of time are always used in the schema of data warehouses. This is a key element to tracking the time variant information in these types of databases.

There have been several variations upon the classic star pattern. Sometimes a more normalized approach is taken to the dimension tables. It is also common to include aggregations across dimensional hierarchies. The resulting tables are referred to as a snowflake schema or constellation (see Figure 31.4).

FIGURE 31.4

A sample snowflake with aggregations.

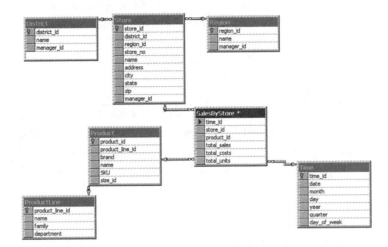

Snowflake schemas of this type offer the best performance when using aggregates such as the sales totaled by store in the previous example. These sales numbers could also be summarized into separate fact tables by region or district. Snowflake schema trades performance for the further complication of maintenance of the warehouse metadata and the transformations required from the source systems.

The dimensional model is a logical technique optimized for queries and reporting. It is the most common model used in current warehousing or mart efforts. It provides simplified paths for end-user features such as drill-downs and roll-ups. You can embed precalculated aggregations in the fact tables. This practice can result in rapid query-response times, which again will directly affect the user.

IMPORTANT DESIGN CONSIDERATIONS

It is generally understood that most first-effort warehouses will fail or not live up to the original expectations. Reasons for failure include lack of adequate corporate sponsorship to neglecting to conform to a unified enterprise model. Whatever the case, there have been several success stories as well. Following is a list of tips that can help you to build a successful warehouse or mart in your organization the first time.

- Start small. The warehousing project is an iterative process. Build for specific applications that will offer immediate return on investment and end-user acceptance such as trend analysis, profit analysis, or expense reduction. This allows you to gain experience and still provide positive results.

- Keep users involved. Do not get the specifications of the project and disappear for several months. The users are the keys to the success for the warehouse. Deliver a prototype a few months into the project. Involve users in the end-user tool selection or construction. Allow the user to test canned queries and validate the data from the transformation efforts. Begin the training of new concepts in data visualization from the very beginning.

- Get to know the data. You will need to know the details of the information stored in the warehouse as well as the source and transformations. Remember garbage in, garbage out? The data in the warehouse is only as good as the data that entered. Try to fix most of your data quality problems in the source systems prior to it making it into your warehouse.

- Always think ahead. Do not build problems for the future by committing to a specialized mart that offers no growth plan or common model. Your system must be flexible to handle success and be open enough to scale to enterprise.

Managing a Data Warehouse or Data Mart

You must realize that the data warehouse will be an evolving project. After you decide to begin one, there will probably be no end in sight. The users will constantly need access to different types of information. Source systems will change, and these changes will disrupt the transformation processes. The success of any system tends to bring forth more users and more new requests, and thus put a larger load on system resources. You must be prepared to handle the following ongoing tasks:

- Backup/Recovery. As with any database, a solution must be reached as to how frequently backups will occur. The data in warehouses can be viewed as less volatile from day to day but not less important. Because the volume of data can grow to enormous sizes, decisions should be made as to when the information is ready for archival.

- Scheduling loads. How frequently should information be captured from the source systems? When should these loads occur?

- Replication. The warehouse might be entirely published. The subscribers may be marts in several departments that gather information from a common source.

- Query performance tuning. Maintaining a warehouse might involve providing canned queries for users or improving response times with schema or index changes.

Introduction to Data Warehousing

CHAPTER 31

875

31

INTRODUCTION TO
DATA
WAREHOUSING

MICROSOFT AND SQL SERVER 7.0 CONTRIBUTIONS TO DATA WAREHOUSING

Microsoft is truly committed to the advancement of data warehousing using its products (see Figure 31.5). It has helped develop a Data Warehousing Framework that describes the integration of technologies (data access, metadata, transformations, end user query, and so on) throughout the cycles of building, managing, and using data warehousing. Microsoft is also providing support in its Office, BackOffice, and Visual Studio product lines for each of the components of the Warehousing Framework. Microsoft has also partnered with other warehousing vendors to form the Data Warehousing Alliance. These vendors came together to cooperate on technologies and protocols that were agreed upon in the Warehousing Framework. This allows for greater interoperability among the various products on the market for data warehousing.

SQL Server 7.0 offers many features that can help in constructing data warehouses. Large database support, query optimizations, and replication add to its usefulness as a solution for a warehouse or mart. Heterogeneous queries allow result sets to be combined across several disjointed OLEDB or ODBC data sources. Other additions include Data Transformation Services (DTS), use of the Repository for metadata storage, the Decision Support Services OLAP tools, and English query tools.

FIGURE 31.5
Microsoft tools for data warehousing.

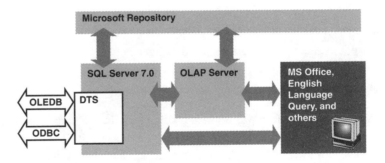

Data Transformation Services

Data Transformation Services is a flexible toolkit built into SQL Server 7.0 that enables you to easily import, export, and transform data from any source to any destination, as long as both support OLE DB. DTS can be thought of as a data pump that enables you to move source records from one place to the next. This is achieved through a simple wizard interface.

DTS provides services for importing and exporting data from a variety of data sources:

- OLE DB data sources Oracle, SQL Server 4.2, 6.5, and others
- ODBC data sources DB2 on MVS, AS400/data, Informix, Microsoft Access, Microsoft Excel, and more
- Text files ASCII, fixed length, or delimited
- Simple transformations using the DTS Wizard approach or complex transformations using the DTS Designer

The DTS framework provides functionality for building robust data warehouses from several heterogeneous operational data stores. It contains tools for setting up regular scheduled data loads as well as validating or transforming the data into the format required by the warehouse.

Repository

The Microsoft repository is an infrastructure for shared metadata. It permits data in the warehouse to be described in a common way. Using the repository, the data requirements can be stored independently of the data it describes and provides access from other components in the warehousing architecture. The repository's data warehousing features include the following:

- Store star schema data models
- Catalog relationships of data elements to source systems
- Record data transformations and data lineage
- Store data extraction and replication rules
- Support for team development

The Microsoft Repository was designed with a generic and open object model, which has garnered support from many tool vendors. This extensive third-party support benefits the organization by enabling a large set of product choices to help with data warehousing development and maintenance.

Decision Support Services

The Microsoft Decision Support Services are tools for bringing the power of OLAP and information in the data warehouse to the masses. It presents the warehousing information in multidimensional cubes that allow for slice and dice data analysis.

The key features and benefits of the Microsoft DSS are as follows:

- Access to any OLE DB compliant data source
- Support for MOLAP (multidimensional online analytical processing), ROLAP (relational OLAP), and HOLAP (a hybrid between the two)
- Bridges the gap between SQL Server and Excel by support for creation of pivot tables
- Allows for mobile or disconnected analysis of information
- Scales from desktop to the enterprise

The OLAP server in DSS multiplies the value of the data stored in the warehouse or mart by providing access and features that enhance decision support. It integrates well with MS BackOffice and Office framework of applications as well as other third party products.

English Language Query Tools

The English query system lets the user submit data requests in plain English. Using a support application, the users map out their schema to English syntax. They are then able to ask or type questions in normal English. SQL statements are generated in the background. This product is designed for ease of use and provides a simpler way for more users to get access to the information stored in the warehouse.

DATA WAREHOUSING FAQ

Below are some common questions DBAs new to data warehousing may encounter.

Q. When should I consider a data warehousing solution?

A. When users are requesting access to large amounts of historical information for reporting purposes, you should strongly consider a warehouse or mart. The user will benefit when the information is organized in an efficient manner for this type of access.

Q. DBAs have always been told that having non-normalized data is bad. Why is it now okay?

A. Normalization in relational databases results in an efficient use of database storage. Data warehousing is not concerned with accomplishing the same storage efficiencies. The main concern is to provide information to the user as fast as possible. Because of this, storing information in a denormalized fashion, including aggregate columns and summarization, provides the best immediate results.

Q. What is the difference between data warehousing and OLAP?

A. These two terms are often used interchangeably. Warehousing is primarily the organization and storage of the data such that it can be analyzed easily. OLAP deals with the particulars of the process on analyzing the data, managing aggregations, and partitioning information into cubes for in-depth visualization.

Q. How often should I load data into my warehouse from my enterprise transaction systems?

A. The answer to this question may depend on the needs of the users and the volume of information that is to be moved. It is common to schedule weekly or monthly dumps from the operational data stores, during periods of low activity (for example, nights or weekends). The longer the gap between loads, the longer processing times for the load when it does run. You will have to weigh the implications of each to come up with an ideal solution for your situation.

Q. How do I get started with data warehousing?

A. Build one! The easiest way to get started with data warehousing is to analyze an existing OLTP database and see what type of trends would be interesting to examine. From there you could model your new schema and load it with some current data. Although this may seem trivial, it is not. Start small and build from there. SQL 7.0 offers excellent tools and technologies for starting any warehousing effort.

SUMMARY

In this chapter, the concepts of data warehousing were covered. A warehouse is a central storage facility for subject-oriented data throughout an organization and data warehousing is the process involved in extracting, storing, and aggregating this information to provide easy access for end users. You learned how warehousing data differs from online transactional systems and how to transform the transactional data from these systems to the warehouse. You were introduced the concept of the data mart as a smaller more specialized warehouse designed to satisfy a particular functional unit. You were also presented with issues related to planning, designing, and maintaining data warehouses in your own organization. Lastly, you were presented the tools and services that Microsoft provides to help in the development of data warehouses.

Warehousing has truly been in the spotlight recently. It appears to be a promising method to help decision-makers sort through the abundance of information their systems have collected. It challenges developers and DBAs to shift the way they have been designing databases for the past several years. The information in this chapter should have shed the light on some of the common warehousing concepts and procedures. This should get you started on the road to providing easy access to information for users in your enterprise.

USING DATA TRANSFORMATION SERVICES (DTS)

by Troy Rackley

IN THIS CHAPTER

Just about everyone who has interacted with SQL Server in the past has had to either import data into or export data out of it. This task has proven to be cumbersome and complex. Bcp, SQL Server's tried-and-true command-line data pump, has probably caused a headache or two for most database administrators (DBAs). Whenever the need arises to import a large amount of information, most people once again look to the help files to figure out how to construct the dreaded format file.

Along comes Data Transformation Services (DTS) in SQL Server 7.0. DTS is a set of tools and interfaces that make it simple to import, export, and transform information from any source to any destination that supports OLE DB. This means that you can load and dump not only SQL Server data, but Oracle, DB2, Informix, text files, or any data source for which you have OLE DB or ODBC drivers. DTS can be thought of as a generic data pump that happens to work with SQL Server very well. Its functionality and robustness are a far cry from the feature set of the limited bcp.

In this chapter we discuss the components that make up the DTS framework and offer some examples of the provided tools.

DTS AND THE DATA WAREHOUSE

Most new database projects follow the same pattern. We are developing this new system to take the place of an older one. We currently have a decade or so of information stored in system A. When we go live with system B, we need to leave all our previously collected information intact. So a fair amount of time is spent designing the database schema and taking into account that we will need to preserve the information as it exists now. A plan usually develops of how we will then extract, transform, move, and finally load this information from System A to System B. The data load is usually done once, and the old machine (whatever it may be) is then turned off and sold for scrap. Because this is usually done only once, the requirements for this conversion process could be less robust: "Just get it there" might be the main idea. Speed and ease of use rarely play a part in the design of a one-time import.

In contrast, data warehousing involves continuously and periodically loading information from one or many heterogeneous data sources. The load should be expected to be efficient and accurate, but not take an extremely large amount of time. It could be as simple as a direct copy of the information, or it could involve complicated validations or summarization. Getting data into a warehouse or smaller data marts usually involves the following steps:

1. Connecting to the external data sources directly
2. Selecting or extracting the desired information

3. Performing any transformations, filling in missing values, aggregating data, and so on

4. Moving the data from the source machine to the destination system

5. Loading the data into the destination tables

DTS provides all these required features, as well as the ability to schedule these operations regularly and share the information about these operations with other tools by storing them in the Microsoft Repository.

DTS AND OLE DB/ODBC

The DTS framework is built solidly around Microsoft's OLE DB, which is a set of APIs that provide a common interface to many types of heterogeneous data sources. In conjunction with OLE DB, DTS can help you communicate with any data source for which you have either an OLE DB or ODBC driver. SQL 7.0 provides native OLE DB drivers for SQL, Oracle, Excel, Access, ASCII text files, and ODBC data sources. ODBC drivers are widely available for most data sources. By integrating OLE DB with ODBC, Microsoft has positioned DTS as an open tool for importing or exporting data across an organization.

If an OLE DB or ODBC driver is not readily available, you can use the SQL 7.0 OLE DB driver for text files, which can usually provide all the needed functionality. Text files still remain one of the most widely used transit mechanisms for data to and from various systems. If you can get your data into a text file, you can usually move it from any database system. Later in this chapter you will see what features are available in DTS that help with managing text file imports and exports.

THE DTS FRAMEWORK

DTS introduces a set of new database objects and tools to help with the movement of information from place to place. Simple wizards provide the typical question-and-answer approach to importing or exporting data. The DTS Designer gives more knowledgeable users the ability to create more complex transformations that utilize many tables and advanced workflow techniques. Along with these two additions to the SQL Enterprise Manager, DTS provides the access to the underlying transformation engine via COM objects. This allows you to build complete import, export, or transformation applications using any Component Object Model (COM) enabled environment such as Visual Basic, a Windows scripting host, or Active Server Pages.

DTS provides the following services:

- The Import and Export Wizards allow you to build simple table imports, exports, or transforms quickly and easily.
- The DTS Designer allows you to build more advanced transformations that incorporate multiple tables and sophisticated workflow operations.
- DTS COM objects are extensible components for integrating DTS functionality into external programs or scripts.

The services provide access to a set of underlying objects that complete the DTS framework. The top-level encompassing object is called a package. Within a DTS package are connections, steps, tasks, and global variables. The DTS Data Pump is the real workhorse of the framework: This is where that the bulk of the information is transferred.

Packages

Packages are self-contained definitions of the tasks that need to be performed as part of a transformation. You can create a package by using any of the three services described in the preceding section. A package can be stored as a file in the operating system, shared in the Microsoft Repository or within the msdb database on the server. You can access the packages that are stored in the latter two places by selecting the Data Transformation Services folder from the Enterprise Manager as illustrated in Figure 32.1.

FIGURE 32.1

The data transformation services.

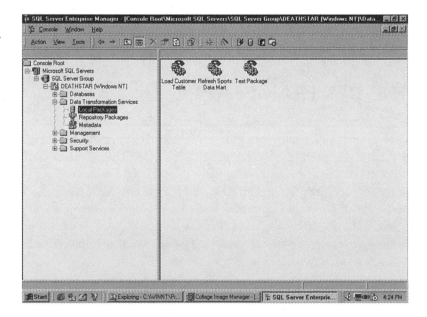

You can execute packages directly from Enterprise Manager, from the command line, or from a script. Security can be assigned on a per-package basis to ensure that only the desired individuals do certain operations.

Each package can contain multiple steps. One step might be to import a product line table. After the successful completion of that step, we might want to import the product table or run some additional SQL scripts to validate the information. If the previous step had failed, we might have wanted to alert the database operator via a simple email message. These operations can be executed conditionally based on pervious steps. These features of the DTS package contribute to robust workflow functionality.

The following DTS package operations are available to you from within the Enterprise Manager:

- Generating new packages using the DTS Wizard
- Creating a new package from scratch using the DTS Designer
- Viewing, editing, and executing packages stored in the local server or the Microsoft Repository
- Loading packages stored in the file system into the DTS Designer

Connections

Connections store the information about the source and destination data stores, either actual database systems or flat files. The connection object contains data such as security credentials, file locations, and data formats. Connections are shared or pooled in order to operate efficiently during the transformation operations.

Tasks

Tasks are the operations that need to be performed within the package. A task can be an ActiveX script, an SQL script, transfer SQL objects, bulk insert, a Win32 executable, data driven query, mail message, or a database transformation. The following are some examples of each:

- *ActiveX scripts*—An example is a script that instantiates an ActiveX server that opens a database and dumps records to a text file for import by another step in the package.
- *SQL scripts*—A simple or complex piece of T-SQL script that, for example, truncates a table prior to the import or performs a backup of the current table before a new import.

- *Transfer SQL Server Objects*—Allows you to copy schema objects such as tables, views, constraints, or indexes from a source server to a destination.

- *Bulk Insert*—The fastest method for importing text files into SQL Server. This speed comes at a price; no data validations or transformations may be performed. This feature is essentially a graphical version of bcp.

- *Win32 executable*—An external process that can be executed as part of the package. This could, for example, run another DTS package.

- *Data Driven Query*—An advanced type of task where each data row needs to be sent to parameterized stored procedures for processing. A data driven query might be used to process incremental updates of a table into data mart.

- *Send Mail*—A mail message to an operator that the weekly load of the customer table executed successfully.

- *Transform*—A set of procedural logic that needs to be performed on each row as it travels from the source to the destination. This can be as simple as a straight copy from source to destination, or it can involve a mapping from the characters M and F to the descriptions Male and Female.

Steps

As mentioned previously, steps provide the simplified workflow functionality of a package. They dictate the order in which the tasks are executed. They separate actual tasks from the flow control between steps. Steps provide the following features:

- They can be executed serially and conditionally based on the results of previous steps.

- They can be executed in parallel to offer optimal performance when loading multiple tables.

- Steps can be given individual priorities that dictate which steps receive more processing power.

The DTS Data Pump

The DTS Data Pump is a COM component that is the real workhorse that performs the movements of the source data to the destination. It provides an extensible, scriptable interface for which complex data validation and transformations can be built. Transformations can incorporate any ActiveX scripting engine, such as VBScript, JScript, or PerlScript. These reusable scripts can combine multiple source columns into a single destination column. The Data Pump scripting facilities can invoke the services of any COM object that supports automation, such as Active Data Objects (ADO).

USING THE DTS WIZARD

DTS supplies two wizards that allow a user to interactively define the tasks for package: the Import Wizard and the Export Wizard. As with the other wizards in SQL 7.0, you access the Import and Export Wizards by selecting Tools and Wizards. Alternatively, you can launch the wizards by right-clicking Data Transformations Packages and selecting New Import or New Export.

> **NOTE**
>
> The Import and Export Wizards are essentially the same, except for some textual elements. You are not restricted to either the source being SQL Server during an export or the destination being SQL Server on the import. Whenever you need to move data from one place to the other, you can select either option, import or export. Throughout the rest of the chapter we refer to both of these wizards as the *DTS Wizard*. See Figure 32.2.

FIGURE 32.2
The DTS Wizard.

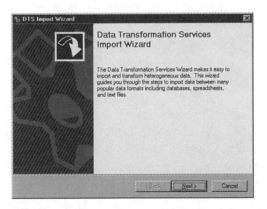

The DTS Wizard essentially helps the user build a package of simple steps based on Data Pump tasks. These tasks move information from any OLE DB or ODBC source to a destination. The number of steps it generates depends on the options that are selected and the number of tables transformed. For example, if the destination table did not previously exist, then a separate SQL script step is created that automatically generates the table. Other subsequent steps actually move the data if the table creation step was a success.

The first phase of the wizard helps you define the connection to the source data. Next, you define the connection the destination data and any transformations that need to take place between the two. Lastly you are able to run the package, save it for later use, and even schedule it to run automatically.

A DTS Wizard Example

The following sections illustrate how to use the DTS Wizard to import a customer table that was previously dumped to text file from a Progress database. Each step of the wizard is described in detail in order for you to understand all the options.

Step 1: Making the Source Connection

When you start the wizard the first item you are prompted for is the data source. This is where the transformation will originate. In this example, we are using a text file on the hard drive. First, select the Text OLE DB provider, and then enter the physical location for the file as seen in Figure 32.3.

FIGURE 32.3

Selecting a data source in the DTS Wizard.

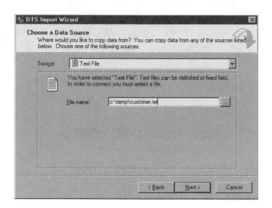

Each OLE DB provider operates differently and contains individual requirements. For example, if you were importing from an Oracle database you would be prompted for a server name, login, and password. Some OLE DB providers support custom settings, in which case you can tweak these options by clicking the button labeled Advanced.

If the data source were a database containing multiple record sources, you would then be prompted to select one. You can choose to copy an entire table or the results of an SQL query, such as queries involving joins of multiple tables. Alternatively, you can choose to build a query using the Query Builder within the wizards. This allows users who are inexperienced with the SQL language to construct queries with familiar drag-and-drop operations.

Step 2: Determining File Format

The next wizard step relates to the text file data source. Here you find options regarding the format of the text file itself. You can select delimited or fixed field lengths. Also, there are options for the file type, record delimiter, and text qualifier. These are common format requirements of data in text files. A preview of the file contents is displayed near the bottom of the wizard to aid in the selection of these options as displayed in Figure 32.4.

FIGURE 32.4

The DTS Wizard file format options.

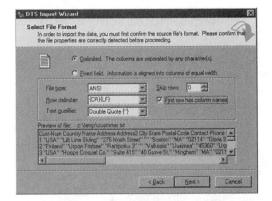

Our text file has the column names on the first row of the file, a carriage-return and line-feeds separating each row, and text columns that are qualified by a double quote. We select these options and move on to the next step.

Step 3: Choosing the Column Delimiter

Step 3 involves options only required for the delimited text file data source. Here, you can select the character that separates columns in the file records. The most common options are provided; an entry field to provide a custom separator is also available. Figure 32.5 displays the column delimiter step.

FIGURE 32.5

Selecting a column delimiter with the DTS Wizard.

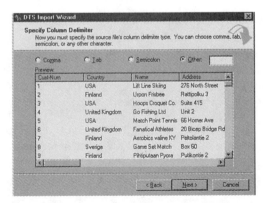

A space character separates text file columns. Because this item is not provided as a common separator, you simply type in a space in the field labeled Other, and the information in the file is then parsed to display the columns, using the delimiter you have chosen.

Step 4: Establishing the Destination Connection

At this wizard step, we are able to define the destination for the transfer. We are importing into SQL Server 7.0, so we choose the SQL Server OLE DB provider. The requirements for this provider are displayed Figure 32.6.

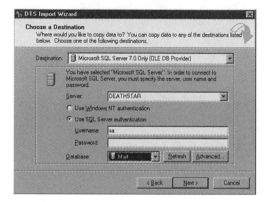

The server, username, and password are required to establish a connection to SQL Server. Also, the wizard needs to know what type of authentication scheme it should use to connect. The wizard needs to read schema information from the destination database, so these parameters are required for the wizard to proceed any further.

After the login credentials have been validated, a list of databases that the username has access to is displayed in the Database combo box. Select the database that will be the destination for your information.

> **TIP**
>
> If your destination database does not currently exist, you need not stop the wizard to create it. From the database drop-down list, select the option <new>. You will then be prompted for a database name and initial sizes for the data and log. The database is then created for you without interrupting the wizard.

The destination for this example is a database that on the local server that is called Mart. It contains a customer table that we will use for this import.

Step 5: Selecting Source and Destination Tables

This step allows you to select the source and the destination tables that receive the data. If the source were a database, such as SQL Server, Oracle, or Access, multiple tables would be listed here and you would select the desired ones to be copied or transformed. However, our source is a text file containing only one table, so this step is easy. The destination for this example is a nearly identical table named `Customer_dim` in the Mart database. This can be seen in Figure 32.7.

FIGURE 32.7

Mapping source to destination tables with the DTS Wizard.

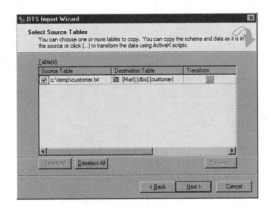

If a simple copy is all that were required, then we could proceed to the next step. But instead of a simple copy, we will perform a slight transformation on this table.

The customer table in our text file has a column for the name of a customer contact. This column is the full name of this person. In our Mart database we want to have the full name split into two separate columns: First Name and Last Name. We will use a small bit of VBScript in a custom transformation to accomplish this.

Each table can have its own transformations applied to it. You will notice a small button to the right of each destination table in the list. This button will launch the Transform dialog box.

Step 6: Column Mappings and Transformations

The Transform dialog box allows you to specify which source columns map to which destination columns. It also allows you to select what operations are done to the destination table prior to the use of the data pump. The following options are supported on the destination table:

- *Create Destination Table*—If this option is selected, you can modify the CREATE TABLE statement to further customize the destination table without leaving the wizard. You can also choose to drop the table if it currently exists. Each of these options creates separate package steps.
- *Delete Rows in Destination Table*—This option generates a package step that truncates the table prior to performing the data pump task.
- *Append Rows to Destination Table*—This option creates no other tasks or steps besides the data pump task. This is the default.

For this example, we will drop the Customer_dim table and re-create it before the load, so the appropriate options are selected, as displayed in Figure 32.8.

FIGURE 32.8

Column mappings in the DTS Wizard.

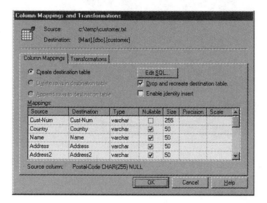

Below these options is a grid showing the default mappings of columns from the source to the destination. It is here that the user can ignore any source columns not required in the destination. Also, valid data conversion can be performed, such as converting a varchar(255) to a varchar(50).

We are planning to do our mappings with some ActiveX script, so we need to take a quick trip over to the Transformation tab to find more options as seen in Figure 32.9.

The default option for the wizard is to copy all mapped columns to the destination. The DTS Wizard generates a transformation script that handles this automatically. If your transformation requires anything outside the realm of a straight copy of data values (as ours does), you need to modify the ActiveX script here. From this page, you select the script engine that you want to use (for example, VBScript). There is also a button for selecting advanced options about how the Data Pump should handle data type conversions.

FIGURE 32.9

Transformations in the DTS Wizard.

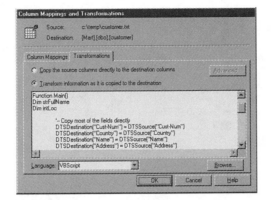

TIP

Scripts may be edited in an external program and then retrieved into this dialog. An editor that provides more features (such as syntax highlighting) is the Microsoft Script Debugger that ships with NT Option Pack 4. More information on the Script Debugger may be found at `http://www.microsoft.com/scripting`.

The script that this example uses is typical of some of the simple operations that can be accomplished with the VBScript language. Listing 32.1 is the script used to transform the Customer table.

LISTING 32.1   CUSTOMER TRANSFORM SCRIPT

```
'*********************************************************************
'   Visual Basic Transformation Script for customer table
'   Perform copy of most fields, and divide Contact name into
'      first name and last name
columns'*********************************************************************
*****

Function Main()
Dim strFullName
Dim intLoc

'-- Copy most of the fields directly
DTSDestination("customer-id") = DTSSource("Cust-Num")
    DTSDestination("Country") = DTSSource("Country")
    DTSDestination("Name") = DTSSource("Name")
    DTSDestination("Address") = DTSSource("Address")
    DTSDestination("Address2") = DTSSource("Address2")
```

continues

LISTING 32.1   CONTINUED

```
    DTSDestination("City") = DTSSource("City")
    DTSDestination("State") = DTSSource("State")
    DTSDestination("Postal-Code") = DTSSource("Postal-Code")
    DTSDestination("Phone") = DTSSource("Phone")
    DTSDestination("Sales-Rep") = DTSSource("Sales-Rep")
    DTSDestination("Credit-Limit") = DTSSource("Credit-Limit")
    DTSDestination("Balance") = DTSSource("Balance")
DTSDestination("Terms") = DTSSource("Terms")
DTSDestination("Discount") = DTSSource("Discount")
    DTSDestination("Comments") = DTSSource("Comments")

    '--  Split ContactName (full) into
    '   first name, last name fields
    strFullName = DTSSource("Contact")
    intLoc = InstrRev(strFullName, " ")
    If intLoc <> 0 Then
    DTSDestination("ContactFName") = Left(strFullName, intLoc)
    DTSDestination("ContactLName") = Mid(strFullName, intLoc + 1)
End If

Main = 1

End Function
```

The source and destination are represented in script as two different collections of data. You can access the elements of the collection with the *collectionName*("*elementName*") syntax. Thus, the City field from the source text file is represented by the term DTSSource("*City*").

The bulk of the script is occupied with straight copies from source fields to the destination columns. It is not until we get down to the Customer Contact name column that any real interesting work is done.

The script in Listing 32.1 first parses the Contact Name field from the right side of the string, looking for a space. Using this location, the following two lines simply extract parts of the string on either side of the space. These two values are then simultaneously stored into the first name (ContactFName) and last name (ContactLName) columns in the destination table. The last line of the script signals to the data pump engine that a successful completion has occurred.

Step 7: Package Actions

On the next wizard page, displayed in Figure 32.10, you can select optional actions related to the current package. You can select to run the package now, and you can also choose to have the wizard publish the destination tables for replication.

FIGURE 32.10

Running, saving, and scheduling transformations with the DTS Wizard.

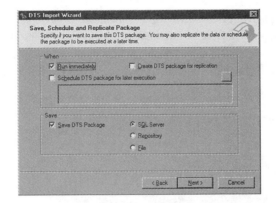

If this is not a one-time import or export, you might want to run it again at another time. To accomplish this, select the option to save the resulting package to SQL Server.

After it is saved, this DTS package can be manually run later or scheduled to run at recurring intervals, similar to any other SQL Agent job. For more information on running and scheduling DTS packages, see the sections "Running Packages" and "Scheduling Packages" later in this chapter.

> **TIP**
>
> It is also convenient to use the wizard to interactively generate the basis of the package. After this is done, you can add more in-depth steps or tasks using the DTS Designer. De-select the Run Task option and select the Save option. After the package is saved, right-click the package and select Design Package. This launches the DTS Designer.

Step 8: Saving a Package

Using this wizard step, you can provide a name, a description, an owner password, and a location for the DTS package. It is always a good idea to be descriptive in your naming of database objects and DTS packages.

The Owner Password field allows you to secure this package. A secure package can only be viewed or modified if this password is provided. Secure packages can also be given an operator password, which enables you to execute the package, but still limits viewing or changing the package steps or tasks to only the owner. If you do not specify a password, the package remains open for any users to view, modify, or execute.

The last section of this page deals with the storage location for this package. You can choose to save the package locally or in the local storage of another SQL Server. The local DTS packages are held in the msdb database. You must choose the appropriate authentication scheme and provide a user name and password for the destination server. Figure 32.11 illustrates this wizard step.

FIGURE 32.11

The Save Package options in the DTS Wizard.

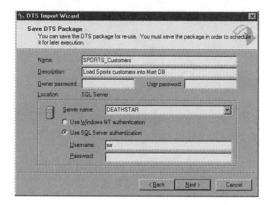

Step 9: Package Execution

A summary of the tasks to be performed is then presented. Pressing the Finish button causes the selected actions to be executed. If you are running the package now, then a screen similar to that in Figure 32.12 is displayed.

FIGURE 32.12

Running the package with the DTS Wizard.

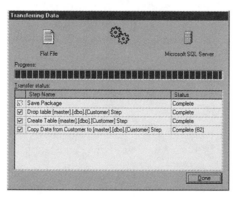

Each package step attempts to execute in a logical order (that is, table creation precedes table loading). As each step completes (or fails), its status is displayed. If a step involving the transfer of data completes successfully, a record count is displayed within the Status column as in the 82 customer records in the example.

If an error occurs during the execution of any step, you can view the error by double-clicking the individual step. Because later steps might be dependent on previous ones, early step failures can halt the execution of the package.

USING THE DTS DESIGNER

The DTS Designer is a graphical workspace for building sophisticated import, export, or transformation operations. Whereas the DTS Wizard is designed to handle most of your simple import or export needs, the DTS Designer picks up where the wizard leaves off by allowing you to define all your own tasks and set precedence constraints on the steps between these tasks.

You arrange source and destination data sources, along with other execution objects, in a fashion similar to a typical flowchart. Arrows connect these objects and form the tasks and steps of the package. These arrows provide the package with directional flow or conditional logic.

The Designer Workspace

Figure 32.13 shows the package we just created, as viewed in the DTS Designer.

FIGURE 32.13
The DTS Designer.

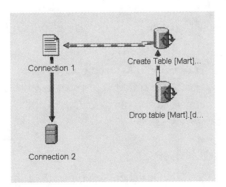

In this example, several objects are visible on the designer workspace:

- *Custom SQL Tasks*—These tasks represent the drop and recreation of the Customer table.
- *Text file icon*—Connection 1 represents the source data file used in this import.
- *Database icon*—Connection 2 represents the destination, a local connection to the Mart database.
- *Dotted arrow*—This is a precedence constraint. The green color of the line and the direction it points indicate that on successful completion of the custom SQL task, the next task can begin.

- *Solid arrow*—The solid line between the two connection objects represents a transformation and movement of data in the direction in which the arrow points.

The environment of the package designer is optimized for quickly producing highly robust DTS applications. To the left sits a tool palette of data source and destination connection objects.

> **NOTE**
>
> The few icons on the toolbox under the data section are not the only types of connections supported by the designer. The complete ranges of OLE DB or ODBC data sources are supported. The most common data types are displayed as quick-connect tool buttons. Each connection type opens a property dialog where you can pick from the entire list of available data sources.

Above the data source/destination palette sits a group of task elements. These elements represent custom tasks for the package:

- *Create Process*—You can launch any external executable, batch file, or script.
- *Execute SQL*—You can enter any T-SQL or execute existing stored procedures.
- *ActiveX Script*—You can launch an ActiveX script using scripting languages such as VBScript or JScript.

The toolbar near the top houses a set of commonly used operations for saving, running, and printing the package, as well as buttons for adding arrows to represent workflow steps and data movement tasks. There are also tools associated with viewing and arranging the objects in the current package.

Creating a Custom Package

When you create a package using the DTS Designer, you typically follow steps similar to those of the DTS Wizard. First you add and configure source and destination data objects.

> **NOTE**
>
> Multiple source connections might point to different heterogeneous data stores within the organization. Sales figures from accounting could exist in an Oracle database, and Web commerce traffic could exist in Internet Information Server log files. This sets the designer apart from the wizard's single source and single destination model. With multiple source objects, the real power of combining data from different parts of the enterprise into a warehousing model becomes more evident.

Next, you define data flows between the connections. After data transformation is defined, you might want to build customized tasks that the package will execute. These might involve running processes before loading new data, or they might validate the information when a transformation completes.

You might also want to define any workflow or precedence constraints on the custom tasks. When the package is complete, you can then decide to run it or save it for later use.

A DTS Designer Example

The example in this section illustrates the use of the DTS Designer to create a package for a data warehouse application. In this example some of the tables of an order handling and invoicing system for a sporting goods company reside in a Microsoft Access database. We will use the DTS Designer to import the information into the Mart database in SQL Server 7.0. The Mart database has been previously built using a star schema model.

Step 1: Adding Connections

You add source and destination connections to the package by dragging and dropping data source objects from the data source palette to the detail pane. After each object is dropped, it launches its Connection Properties dialog, where you define this connection. The connection to the Access database is displayed in Figure 32.14.

FIGURE 32.14

Defining data source connections.

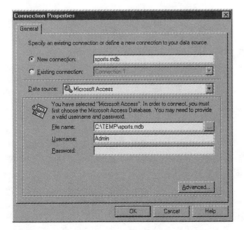

In a similar fashion, you can add an SQL Server connection object that will serve as the destination. In this case, choose the SQL Server 7.0 OLE DB driver, the local server, and the Mart database.

Step 2: Transforming Data

After you have added the source and destination objects, you can define data transformations that occur between the two. To do so, select the data source, and while holding the Shift key, select the data destination object. With both of these objects selected, click the Transform Data toolbar button, which contains a solid black arrow pointing to the right. This produces a solid black line between the source and destination, which represents a data pump task. (See Figure 32.15.)

FIGURE 32.15

Adding a data pump task.

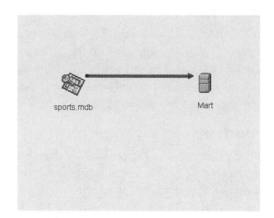

Alternatively, you can add a transformation by selecting the two data sources, right-clicking, and selecting Transform Data from the Workflow menu that pops up. With most of the operations in the designer, you can use either the right-click method or a toolbar button.

> **NOTE**
>
> The last item selected becomes the recipient of the transformed information during a data pump task. Make sure you select your data connections in the correct order. The direction of the arrow indicates the direction of the data flow.

After the direction of a transformation is defined, you need to configure the properties of the Data Pump task. Click the transformation arrow between the two data sources and select the Properties option from the right-click menu. The data pump task information is organized within four tabs: Source, Destination, Transformations, and Advanced.

On the Source tab you can select a set of records from the data source connection. This can be a table, a defined query or view, or a new query that you build. You can type the query into the text window provided, retrieve it from a previously saved script file, or build it graphically.

In this example, we will transfer the dates in the Orders table of the source to the Time dimension of the star schema destination. For this we will use an Access query that selects the different date values that will be used to populate the table:

```
SELECT DISTINCT [order-date],
FROM [ORDER];
```

Next, you need to select a destination table of the transformation. You can choose the desired table name from the drop-down list. If this is to be a new table, you can select Create New, which generates a new table in the destination database. The `time_dim` table in the destination database will receive these records. This has been selected in Figure 32.16.

FIGURE 32.16

Transformation data properties: Choosing a destination table.

The next step is to define the column mappings between the source and destination. Use the dialog shown in Figure 32.17 to select fields from the left list and fields from the right list. If a line is present from the source field to the destination field, then a transformation currently exits. To remove it, select the source field and the destination field from each list and click the delete button. To map a source column to a destination select each field, place the New Transformation drop-down box on the desired type (Copy Column or ActiveX Script), and click the New button.

> **TIP**
>
> You can map one field at a time or map multiple fields at once. In order to produce a transformation script that includes all fields from the left and the right lists, select all fields on either side, un-map them with the Delete button, and re-map them with the New button.

FIGURE 32.17
*Transformation
data properties:
Mapping time
columns.*

You can map fields by using two provided transformation types: an active script transformation or a column copy transformation. The active script transformation allows you to use any operations available to the active scripting technologies. The column copy transformation performs a simple transfer of each field. You can right-click the line between the mapped fields to access the transformation properties.

Next, you can edit the transformation script or retrieve an existing script from the file system. A default script is generated for you that simply copies the source fields to the destination columns. The example in Listing 32.2 uses a couple simple VBScript functions to complete the transformation of the time_dim table.

LISTING 32.2   TIME DIMENSION TRANSFORM SCRIPT

```
'*********************************************************************
'  Visual Basic Transformation Script
'  Copy dates from order table to time dimension
'*********************************************************************

Function Main()
Dim varDate
varDate = DTSSource("order-date")
    DTSDestination("time_id") = varDate
    DTSDestination("month") = DatePart("m", varDate)
DTSDestination("day") = DatePart("d", varDate)
    DTSDestination("year") = DatePart("yyyy", varDate)
    DTSDestination("quarter") = DatePart("q", varDate)
    DTSDestination("dayofweek") = WeekDay(varDate)
    DTSDestination("dayofyear") = DatePart("y", varDate)
    DTSDestination("weekofyear") = DatePart("w", varDate)
    DTSDestination("monthname") = Monthname(DatePart("m", varDate))
    DTSDestination("dayname") = Weekdayname(WeekDay(varDate))
    Main = DTSTransformStat_OK
End Function
```

This transformation script illustrates different uses of the DatePart function to slice and dice the one source field several ways.

Step 3: Adding More Transformations

It is possible to execute many data movement operations from within a single package. Each transformation must be represented graphically in the designer by a solid arrow. You can add more data pump tasks to the two existing data connections by following the same steps above. Alternatively, you can add more data icons and connect them with more data pump task arrows.

Because each connection to the database is expensive, we can share or pool existing connections in the package. To take advantage of connection pooling, you simply add a new data object and instead of creating a new connection, select an existing connection from the list. This increases performance of your package steps by not requiring them to use a new connection to the data source unless absolutely necessary.

The package we are building will load the customer, the item dimensions, and the order fact table. To complete the transformations for this package, we add three additional Microsoft Access objects that use the existing connection to the sports.mdb file. We also add one other Mart object and configure it to use the existing connection to the local Mart database.

This package will reuse the same transformation script presented in Listing 32.1, in the DTS Wizard example. We also add a column copy transformation to load selected fields from the Sports item table into the Mart items dimension. Finally, we add a transformation that loads the Orders fact table from a query based on orders and order lines. These elements can be organized on the detail pane of the designer in a logical fashion similar to that of a flowchart. Figure 32.18 displays the resulting data source objects and associated transformation tasks.

FIGURE 32.18

Adding more connections and transformation tasks to the package.

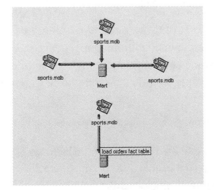

Step 4: Adding Workflow

The transformations that are defined in the current package need to be set to run in a logical order. We do not want the Orders fact table to be loaded until the three dimension table imports have completed successfully. Setting precedence constraints between the tasks will accomplish this.

To add a precedence constraint, select two separate task icons and then select one of the appropriate workflow operations. The precedence choices are on completion, on success, or on failure. In this package, we want three data pump tasks to execute before the orders import takes place. To create this conditional step, we select the destination Mart object of the first set of tasks and then select the source object of the task to be executed last. Next, we click the Workflow menu and choose the On Success precedence option. Figure 32.19 shows the results of adding this workflow step.

FIGURE 32.19

*Adding prece-
dence constraints
to the package.*

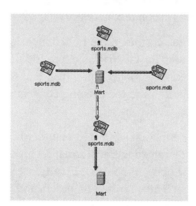

Precedence constraints can be added to set the order of execution on any tasks within the package. The precedence can be unconditional or it can be dependent on the outcome of the previous steps.

You might want to set the order of a set of tasks, but you might not be concerned with whether each one complete. You use the unconditional precedence in these situations. Also, you might need to perform some action when the tasks completes successfully and another action when it fails. An example would be alerting an SQL Server operator with an email message.

Custom Tasks

In addition to data pump tasks, you can also add custom tasks to your package. A custom task might be an SQL script, an external executable, or an ActiveX script. You can set precedence constraints on these types of tasks as well.

To illustrate the use of a custom SQL script task, we have added one to the current package. This task is added by simply dragging a Custom SQL object from the task palette to the detail pane of the designer. After we add the task to the workspace, we can define the properties for this custom, task as Figure 32.20 illustrates.

FIGURE 32.20

Adding custom SQL tasks.

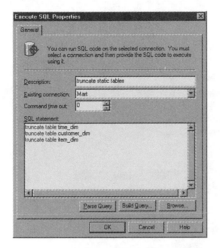

This task merely truncates the Dimension tables before performing any of the import tasks we have already defined. You first select an existing database connection against which this SQL statement will be executed. You can then type in the SQL statement, retrieve it from a file, or build a query interactively.

After this custom task is added, the next step is to define a set of precedence constraints on all the dimension imports. To do this, select the custom SQL task and one of the Access Dimension table source objects. Next, choose the On Success Precedence toolbar button. A green dashed arrow appears. Repeat this for each Dimension table import until the resulting workspace resembles that shown in Figure 32.21.

To run the complete package from the designer, click the Run button on the toolbar. The Run button resembles the play control on a typical home VCR. There are also controls for pausing or stopping the current package that is executing. Figure 32.22 displays the package, after all the steps have been completed successfully.

FIGURE 32.21
Setting steps between custom tasks and data pump tasks.

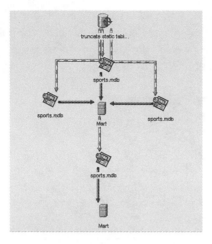

FIGURE 32.22
Running the package.

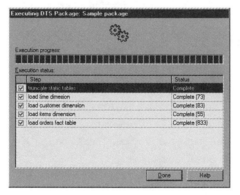

The DTS Designer offers several other operations:

- Saving the package to the file system, the repository, or the local or remote SQL Server database

- Printing the layout of the package steps and tasks

- Setting properties associated with a package, such as the file to log package errors or an execution priority

USING DTS PACKAGES

You can view existing packages from the Data Transformation Services folder of the Enterprise Manager. The DTS packages can be stored in the local msdb database or in the Microsoft Repository.

> **NOTE**
>
> The advantage to storing the packages in the Repository is that objects contained in these packages, such as ActiveX scripts and data transformations, can be accessed from other tools that support the Registry components. Also, by storing DTS packages in the Repository, you can take advantage of data lineage, which helps you keep track of a data element's transformations from the source system to its final destination.

You can view the packages that are contained in these two locations by selecting that icon from the DTS folder in the Enterprise Manager tree. Double-clicking any of these packages opens it in the DTS Designer. You can access other packages stored in the file system by choosing the Open Package task from the DTS folder. If permission to access this package is provided, the DTS Designer loads the package.

Running Packages

You can use the Enterprise Manager to run DTS packages, and you can also run packages with the command-line utility dtsrun. This tool allows you to execute, delete, and overwrite packages that are stored on the local SQL server, in the Repository, or in files. The syntax for the dtsrun utility is

dtsrun /S<*servername*> /U<*user name*> /P<*password*> /N<*package name*>

Figure 32.23 shows an example of using the dtsrun utility on the Customer import package created previously.

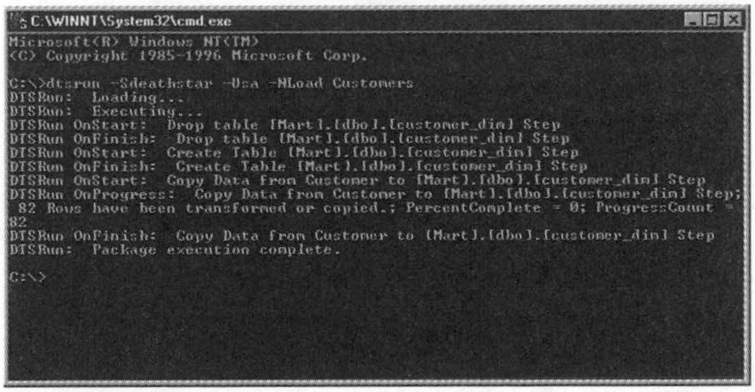

FIGURE 32.23

Using the DTS command-line utility.

Scheduling Packages

You can schedule packages to run at regular intervals from either the DTS Wizard or by manually creating an SQL Agent job. When using the SQL Agent to create a job, you must use the method described in the preceding section for executing the package. Figure 32.24 shows the creation of a `CmdExec` step for a SQL Agent job.

FIGURE 32.24

Creating a scheduled data transformation job.

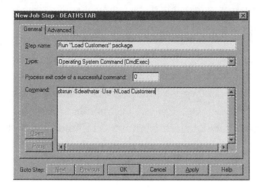

Jobs defined in the SQL Agent can be set to execute on a recurring basis, which allows the data warehousing applications to be constantly updated from the operational sources. To do this, create a new job schedule and click the Change button to set the job to execute at recurring intervals. In Figure 32.25, this job is scheduled to execute every week on Sunday.

FIGURE 32.25

Setting the interval for a recurring scheduled job.

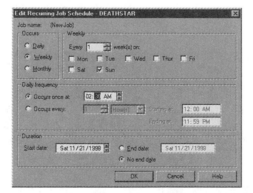

THE DATA TRANSFORMATION SERVICES FAQ

The following section lists some commonly asked questions and answers about SQL Server 7.0 DTS.

Is DTS used only for data warehousing duties?

No, DTS provides functionality for transferring data and schema from various sources to destinations. While this is very important for data warehousing, it is not limited to that. You may use SQL Server DTS tools for any of your data movement chores.

Is DTS only good for importing or exporting data from or to SQL Server?

No. DTS allows you to transfer data to or from any source or destination for which OLE DB or ODBC drivers. This comes in handy when you need to move information between two systems that do not have compatible import/export facilities.

Can I still use bcp to import or export data?

Yes, bcp still exists as the command-line tool. The Bulk Import task from the DTS Designer provides a graphical way to import data at top speed. Also, bcp format files are supported with the Bulk Import task.

Can I execute packages serially, that is, create a package that calls another package?

Yes. You may create a custom task that calls another package with an Execute Process Task. Alternatively, you may run packages together as separate steps of an SQL Server Agent job.

Using the DTS Wizard, can I specify a normalized source to be transferred to multiple destinations?

No. The DTS Wizard will only allow one source and one destination. Using the DTS Designer will allow you to send the data to multiple destinations.

What types of operations can I accomplish in ActiveX scripting during transformations?

Any operations supported by the scripting engines, such as instantiating other components with `CreateObject()`, accessing Active Data Objects (ADO), or calling built-in SQL Server components.

How can I summarize or even skip rows when I am transforming information in a source table to a destination table?

Incorporated into every transformation task is the ability to generate a query of the source data. An extensive Query Designer is provided to graphically construct and validate the query. You could use the query to selectively restrict the output. Alternately, you could write an ActiveX script that conditionally instructs the Data Pump to skip rows based upon some logic that you provide.

In the DTS Designer, the Tasks menu provides an option for Registering Custom Tasks. How are custom tasks generated?

When you reach a point where the particular operation cannot be implemented within the confines of the DTS Designer, you may need a custom task. Custom tasks may be created using the DTS COM interfaces in an external development environment such as Visual Basic, Visual C++, or Visual J++.

SUMMARY

DTS helps SQL Server 7.0 users reach a new level of simplicity. The possibilities are vast and difficult to imagine in the context of one chapter. However, you should now have an understanding of how DTS can make it easy to move information in and out of other data sources (especially SQL Server).

We have shown that the DTS package is a self-contained element that can be cuted, scheduled, and shared. You have seen that the DTS Wizard can help you get up-to-speed quickly by developing packages for simple imports and exports. You have also been introduced to the power of the DTS Designer for complex workflow-oriented transformation application. Also, COM-based interfaces allow you to create highly customized imports, exports, and transformations from other development environments.

By using DTS, an organization can access data that can be distributed in a variety of formats. DTS is built around a strong OLE DB foundation, which lends itself to providing access to a wide variety of database systems. With this newly gained access, knowledgeable workers can gather information for data warehouses and data marts on a regular and timely basis.

INTRODUCTION TO MICROSOFT SQL SERVER OLAP SERVICES

by Kevin Viers

IN THIS CHAPTER

Microsoft SQL Server OnLine Analytical Processing (OLAP) Services is the OLAP database engine that Microsoft ships with SQL Server 7.0. OLAP Services is a feature-rich product in its own right, with the ability to interact with virtually any relational data store. It would be possible to dedicate an entire book to this product, but because it is not the focus of this book, we use this chapter to provide a foundation of knowledge on which you can begin to effectively utilize this product.

WHAT IS OLAP?

The term *OLAP* stands for *OnLine Analytical Processing*. As its name implies, it is a technology centered around the analysis of data. OLAP applications allow users to select, view, and analyze transactional data from a variety of sources, which allows corporations to extract additional value from their traditional On-Line Transaction Processing (OLTP) systems and data warehouses. OLAP is really an extension, or further refinement, of previous genres of applications such as decision support systems (DSSs) and executive information systems (EISs). Those types of applications are intended to provide high-level, summarized information about which decisions can be made and how management can stay informed. OLAP takes that notion and expands it by providing the ability to slice, dice, roll up, and drill down into all your corporate data.

But what really separates OLAP technology from traditional OLTP technology is its ability to provide multidimensional views of transactional data.

UNDERSTANDING MULTIDIMENSIONAL DATA

Before we get too deeply into a discussion about OLAP Services, it is very important that you grasp the concept of multidimensional data and its usefulness as an analytical tool. Most of us, particularly those who are reading this book, are very familiar with relational database systems and the way data is stored and represented in those systems. As shown in Figure 33.1, typical relational database systems provide only a two-dimensional view of data (rows and columns).

This flat representation of transactional data does not lend itself to complex data analysis scenarios that involve looking at quantitative data summarized across many different categories.

A multidimensional database, on the other hand, is capable of providing an *n*-dimensional view of the data. The number of dimensions that can be represented is theoretically unlimited. There are, however, practical storage and performance limitations that keep this number finite.

FIGURE 33.1
*The traditional
relational data
store.*

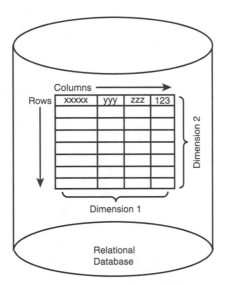

The primary building block in a multidimensional database is called the *cube*. A cube in a multidimensional database consists of a set of dimensions and measures.

> **NOTE**
>
> Don't misunderstand the definition of a cube. We were all taught in school that a cube is a three-dimensional square. Although that may be the geometric definition of a cube, there can be many more than three dimensions in a cube within a multidimensional database.

The *dimensions* of the cube are the categories across which you want to analyze and summarize your data. These dimensions are created from the tables and columns in your relational data store. Typical dimensions in an OLAP multidimensional database are time, geography, and product. Each dimension consists of a set of levels and members that further define the data.

The *measures* of the cube are the quantitative data elements that you want to analyze. Like dimensions, measures are created from the tables and columns in your relational data store. Typical measures in an OLAP multidimensional database are sales, budgets, and costs; however, virtually any quantitative data element can be included as a measure in a multidimensional cube.

Now that you have a basic understanding of multidimensional data, let's take a look at how OLAP Services can be used to create and maintain multidimensional OLAP databases.

THE MICROSOFT SQL SERVER OLAP MANAGER

The OLAP Manager is a snap-in for the Microsoft Management Console (MMC). The MMC will become the standard management console for all of the Microsoft BackOffice suite. The look and feel of this console will become familiar very quickly. As shown in Figure 33.2, the OLAP Manager is a very user-friendly interface with a hierarchical, tree-view representation of the server and all its components in the left pane. You can unlock most of its functionality by highlighting an item in the tree view and right-clicking the mouse.

FIGURE 33.2

The Microsoft OLAP Manager.

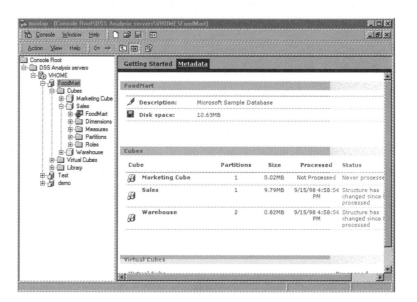

BUILDING AN OLAP DATABASE

The first step in using OLAP Services is to create an OLAP database. In order to bring some real-world value into this discussion, we will use an example throughout the remainder of this chapter. The example will consist of creating a multidimensional OLAP database for the marketing department of a national grocery store chain. The marketing department is concerned about shrinking sales and therefore would like to analyze sales data across a variety of demographic, geographic, and product categories.

To create an OLAP database, highlight the server icon. Right-click to display a shortcut menu. Choose New Database from the shortcut menu. You will see the dialog box shown in Figure 33.3.

FIGURE 33.3

The New Database dialog box.

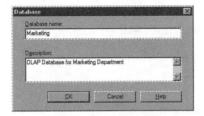

Enter the name of your database and click OK. When you return to the Server Manager, you see your newly created database in the list.

Creating the Data Source

Most OLAP databases do not stand alone as data storage facilities. Rather, they are utilized as a view into your relational transaction-oriented data. Therefore, any OLAP database created in OLAP Services must have a data source that provides the data to populate the dimensions and measures of the cubes.

The data source for your OLAP database can be virtually any relational data store that can expose its data via an OLE DB provider. OLE DB is Microsoft's universal data access object model. As long as your data source can expose itself to an OLE DB provider, you can access that data. SQL Server 7.0 ships with several OLE DB providers, including those for Oracle, Jet, SQL Server, DB2, and OLAP. Many other OLE DB providers are available from various third-party vendors. A discussion of OLE DB is outside the scope of this chapter; however, it is a published standard that is available on Microsoft's Web site.

To create a data source for your OLAP database, expand the database in the Server Manager. Expand the Library folder. Highlight the Data Source folder. Right-click to display a shortcut menu. Choose New Data Source from the shortcut menu. You will see the dialog box shown in Figure 33.4.

Notice that this dialog box looks slightly different from what you may have expected for a data source dialog box. Instead of showing the ODBC data sources, it gives a list of available OLE DB providers. The OLE DB provider must be installed and registered on your server in order to be available in this list. After you choose which OLE DB provider you want to use, click Next. You are then prompted for connection information. Microsoft has built intelligence into this dialog box to change the required connection information based on the OLE DB provider you choose. This is done because each OLE DB provider may require unique connection parameters in order to establish a connection to the data source. For our example, we will use the OLE DB provider for ODBC and the FoodMart ODBC data source.

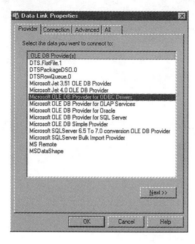

NOTE

Your OLAP database can contain multiple data sources. By using multiple data sources, you can pull data from a variety of transactional or data warehouse systems into one OLAP multidimensional database.

Defining the Dimensions

After you have created an OLAP database, the next step is to define your shared dimensions. A shared dimension is a dimension that is available to any cube in your OLAP database. Remember that the dimensions are categories across which you want to analyze and summarize your data. For our example, you might want to create the following dimensions: store location, customer age, customer gender, product, and time.

To create a new shared dimension, expand the database. Expand the Library folder. Highlight the Shared Dimensions folder. Right-click to display a shortcut menu. Choose New Dimension from the shortcut menu. You can choose to use a wizard or go straight to the editor. For now, let's use the wizard. You will see the dialog box shown in Figure 33.5.

FIGURE 33.5

*The Dimension
Wizard.*

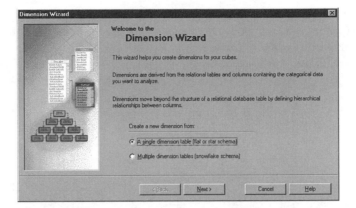

> **NOTE**
>
> Wizards, wizards, everywhere! As I am sure you are aware by now, SQL Server
> 7.0 provides more wizards than ever to walk you through routine tasks. This is
> true in OLAP Services as well. Virtually every operation you may want to per-
> form involves a wizard. Even if you're not a big fan of wizards, you will find
> that the wizards in OLAP Services are useful tools that provide the flexibility
> you need.

The first step in creating your dimension is to choose a dimension table. The *dimension
table* is the table that provides the source data for your dimension. In other words, this
table provides the data about the category for which your dimension is being created.

The wizard asks whether you want to create your dimension from a single table or multiple tables as the source for your dimension. Either option accomplishes the same thing.
You may wonder why you would want multiple tables as the source of your dimension.
The answer really depends on the underlying database schema of your data warehouse. If
your data warehouse uses a snowflake schema, then a dimension table may have many
related tables that describe attributes of the dimension. In this case, you would choose
multiple tables.

To select a dimension table, click Next on the Dimension Wizard dialog box. You will
see the dialog box shown in Figure 33.6.

Expand the desired data source to display a list of available tables. Remember that your
OLAP database can have multiple data sources. You can even create a new data source
from the Dimension Wizard by clicking the New Data Source button. You can also

browse the data that is contained in the dimension table you select. Choose the appropriate table for the dimension you want to create. For our example, we will create a customer location dimension. Click Next.

FIGURE 33.6

The Select Dimension Table dialog box.

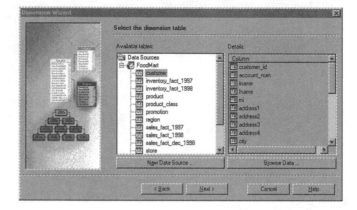

Dimension Levels and Members

After you select a dimension table, the next step in the process is to define the levels and members within your dimension. The dialog box shown in Figure 33.7 is where you define the levels that make up the hierarchy or summarization path of your dimension data.

As shown in Figure 33.7, the Dimension Wizard allows you to create levels within the dimension. To create levels within a dimension, choose the columns from your dimension table that correspond to the levels you want to create, and click the > button. You can use the Move Up and Move Down buttons to organize your levels.

Consider the customer location dimension. This dimension is made up of geographical information about the location of each customer. There is a natural hierarchy within this dimension: Country:State:City. Each point along the hierarchy represents one level.

The levels should be organized from the most summarized to the least summarized data. It is possible that a dimension will only have one level. This is not a problem as long as that one level is the only level of summarization that is needed for your data analysis.

FIGURE 33.7

The Dimension Wizard Select Levels dialog box.

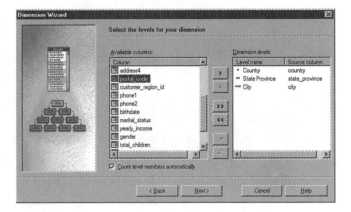

CAUTION

Be careful how you set up your levels. As mentioned previously, the levels must be organized within a dimension from the most summarized to the least summarized data. This implies that each parent level must contain fewer members than the level below it. This maintains an essential one-to-many relationship among the data hierarchy that ensures an accurate drill-down and roll-up. In other words, you would not want the City level above the State level in a dimension hierarchy.

Within each level are members. The members represent the actual data values within the dimensions, and the levels represent the hierarchy. For example, the country level within the customer location dimension may consist of the members USA, Canada, and Mexico. Likewise, the State level may consist of the members Washington, Oregon, and California.

After you have defined your levels and clicked Next, you are done with the Dimension Wizard. At this point, you can provide a name for your dimension and preview the dimension data in the hierarchy that you defined as shown in Figure 33.8.

Click Finish and you will be taken back to the OLAP Manager. You will need to repeat the above steps for each dimension you want to create. You should make sure that you define all the dimensions that you want before you begin creating cubes. The dimensions provide the definition for how users will be able to analyze the data that will be stored in your multidimensional database. In creating your dimensions, you should carefully consider all the ways in which your users may want to analyze the data.

FIGURE 33.8

The Dimension Wizard Finish dialog box.

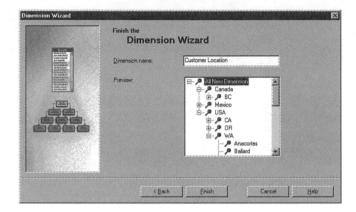

Building the Cube

After you have defined your dimensions, or the categories across which you want to analyze and summarize your data, the next step is to build your cubes. The cube is the basic building block of the multidimensional OLAP database. The cube associates the dimensions you have defined with the quantitative data you want to analyze, such as sales figures or costs.

To create a cube, expand the database and highlight the Cubes folder. Right-click to display a shortcut menu. Choose New Cube from the shortcut menu. You can choose to use the wizard or to go straight to the editor. Let's again use the wizard. You will see the dialog box as shown in Figure 33.9.

FIGURE 33.9

The Cube Wizard dialog box.

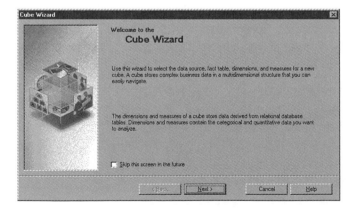

After you click Next, you will be able to assign a fact table to your cube.

The Fact Table

The cube in a multidimensional database serves to associate dimensions with quantitative data. The *fact table* is the table within your relational data store that contains the actual quantitative data you want to analyze. Typical fact data within multidimensional OLAP databases are sales, budgets, and costs.

FIGURE 33.10

The Cube Wizard Select Fact Table dialog box.

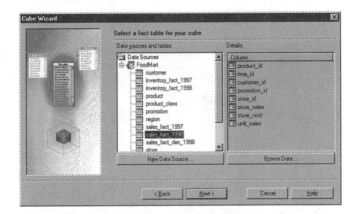

Notice that this dialog box looks exactly like the Dimension Wizard dialog box. Simply expand the desired data source to see a list of available tables and choose the desired fact table.

Typically, the fact table is a table that contains detailed transaction-oriented records, such as sales records. Using our example, you might want to choose the `sales_fact_1998` table as the fact table for your cube because it contains transactional sales data from the organization.

> **NOTE**
>
> Each cube must be based on only one fact table. If more than one table contains data that you want to analyze, you must create a separate cube for each one of those fact tables.

From the dialog box shown in Figure 33.10, click Next to define which data within the fact table you want to analyze. This data is known as the measures of the cube.

33

MICROSOFT SQL
SERVER OLAP
SERVICES

Defining the Measures

The measures represent the columns from the fact table that contain the numeric data you want to analyze.

The Cube Wizard Define Measures dialog box, shown in Figure 33.11, functions in much the same way as the Dimension Wizard Select Levels dialog box. Simply choose the columns you want to analyze and click the > button. Unlike the dimension levels definition, there is no set order or hierarchy to the measures. You can add as many measures to the cube as you want, as long as those columns are present in the fact table.

FIGURE 33.11

The Cube Wizard Define Measures dialog box.

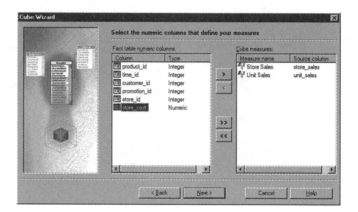

For our example, we want to define a cube that will help us analyze the store sales and unit sales across a variety of dimensions. To do this, we choose the store_sales and unit_sales columns as measures within our cube. The data contained in these two columns in the fact table will be the basis of all the data that is contained in this cube.

CAUTION

The Cube Wizard automatically shows all the numeric columns that are available in the fact table you have chosen. Although a store ID or customer number may be a numeric value, it is probably not a quantitative measure that you want to include in a cube.

From the dialog box shown in Figure 33.11, click Next to define the dimensions you would like to include in your cube.

Adding Dimensions to the Cube

The dimensions provide the categories that are used to analyze the measures of the cube. The dimensions will enable users to drill down or roll up data about store sales and unit sales across any of the dimensions included in your cube. Using the wizard, you can include any of the dimensions that you have previously defined as shared dimensions as shown in Figure 33.12.

FIGURE 33.12

The Cube Wizard Select Dimensions dialog box.

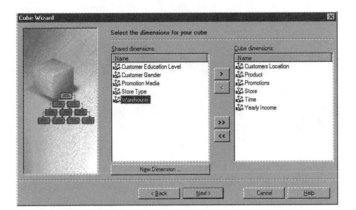

> **NOTE**
>
> The Cube Wizard allows you to include only those dimensions that have been previously defined as shared dimensions. After you have finished using the wizard, however, you are automatically taken to the Cube Editor. From the Cube Editor, you will be able to add additional shared dimensions or create private dimensions that are available only to the cube you are creating.

For our example, we will include the following dimensions in our cube: Customers Location, Store Type, Customer Education Level, Product, and Time. These dimensions apply meaning to the measures. In other words, the user will be able to use this cube to analyze store sales by quarter across each product.

After you have defined your cube dimensions and clicked Next, you are finished with the Cube Wizard. You will see the dialog box shown in Figure 13.13.

This dialog box allows you to provide a name for your cube and will show you a graphical representation of the dimensions and measures that you have defined. For our example, we will call the cube "Marketing Cube." Click Finish to create your cube definition.

33

MICROSOFT SQL
SERVER OLAP
SERVICES

FIGURE 33.13

The Cube Wizard Finish dialog box.

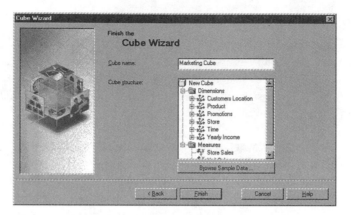

You can repeat the above steps to create as many cubes as you want in your OLAP database. Each cube can have its own set of dimensions and measures. Remember that a cube can only be based on one fact table, so you need a separate cube for each individual fact table that you want to analyze.

At this point, you have seen how to create the dimensions that are used to categorize and summarize your data. You have seen how to create the cube, which defines the relationships between the quantitative data you want to analyze and the dimensions across which you want to analyze that data. However, you have simply created the definition of the cube, or the metadata, within the multidimensional OLAP database.

Before you can actually use the cube, it must be populated with actual data. Populating the cube involves processing all the rows and columns of your dimension tables and fact tables to produce an actual cube of data within the OLAP database. To fully appreciate what happens when the cube is processed and data is stored, we are going to spend some time discussing data storage within an OLAP database.

DATA STORAGE IN AN OLAP DATABASE

Remember that the multidimensional databases created in OLAP Services are all based on underlying source data that resides in other relational data stores. When you process a cube, that source data must be stored in such a way that it can be retrieved by OLAP Services and returned as a resultset to a client application. OLAP Services supports three storage modes:

- Multidimensional OLAP (MOLAP)
- Relational OLAP (ROLAP)
- Hybrid OLAP (HOLAP)

Over the years there has been a heated debate within the OLAP community as to which of these storage methods is the superior way to store data for OLAP purposes. In the following sections, we will discuss each storage method and its implementation in OLAP Services.

MOLAP

The MOLAP storage method involves storing all the detailed cube data within a proprietary multidimensional data store. This means that the relational data stored within the dimension tables and fact tables of the underlying relational data source is written to an optimized multidimensional storage.

In addition to the detailed cube data, all aggregation data is also stored in the multidimensional data store. You are probably asking "What is an aggregation, and why do I care?" We will answer that question shortly, but for now understand that aggregation data must be stored somewhere, and in the MOLAP storage mode, it is stored in the multidimensional data store.

Within OLAP Services, the actual data storage architecture consists of records that are written to 64KB segments. Within each record is a compressed 4-byte to 8-byte key that is a pointer to a set of dimension coordinates within the cube. This storage architecture is optimized for the OLAP Services query processor and offers the best performance of any of the storage modes.

ROLAP

The ROLAP storage method involves storing all the detailed cube data and aggregation data within a relational data store. This means that all the detailed cube data that are found in the dimension tables and fact tables are left alone in their native relational data store. The data are not moved.

When aggregation data is stored, summary tables are created within the relational data store by OLAP Services and populated by using simple INSERT INTO SQL statements. OLAP Services creates all tables and indexes automatically. Remember that this happens only when the aggregation data is stored; the detailed cube data is left alone.

This storage method does not offer the same performance benefits as MOLAP; however, it is an extremely scalable storage mode that allows corporations to leverage existing data storage capabilities.

33

MICROSOFT SQL
SERVER OLAP
SERVICES

HOLAP

The final storage mode supported by OLAP Services is HOLAP. As you might imagine, HOLAP is a combination of MOLAP and ROLAP. This storage method involves storing all the detailed cube data within the relational data store and all the aggregation data within a multidimensional data store. This storage method may provide the best of both worlds: the performance of MOLAP and the scalability of ROLAP.

Now that you have an understanding of the three data storage methods supported by OLAP Services, let's take a look at what is involved in processing the cubes within our OLAP database. The following sections will continue to build on our Marketing Cube example by showing you how to populate the cube with data and optimize its performance within the OLAP database.

OPTIMIZING AN OLAP DATABASE

As mentioned previously, in order to use your OLAP database, you must first process the cubes that are contained within the database. Simply stated, processing the cube populates the cube definition with actual transactional data from your data source. Before you actually populate your cube, however, you need to define certain optimization definitions for your cube. OLAP Services provides two primary mechanisms for optimizing the cubes within OLAP databases:

- Aggregations
- Partitions

Aggregations

Aggregations are summaries of data that are calculated by the OLAP Services and stored in the database along with the transaction level cube data. For example, an aggregation of data would be the total sales data for all stores in the USA for a certain time period. This number must be calculated by summing all the individual sales figures from each member within the store location dimension. This calculation can occur when the cube is processed or when the client application requests the data. By creating an aggregation, the calculation is performed when the cube is processed and the total is stored in the OLAP database.

When a client application requests data from a cube, the OLAP Services first searches all the stored aggregations to determine whether the requested data already exists. If the server finds the requested data, it simply returns that data to the client with no further calculations required. If the requested data does not exist in any stored aggregation, the server must calculate the data on-the-fly. As you can see, there can be significant performance gains when you use aggregations.

There is, however, a downside to aggregations. They take up considerable storage space on your server and they may take significant time to process. When defining the aggregations to use for your cube, it is important to consider the trade-off between performance and storage requirements.

Data Explosion

Beware of data explosion! *Data explosion* is a phenomena of multidimensional databases that indicates that as the number of dimensions in a cube increases, the number of potential aggregations grows exponentially.

Consider a cube with 1 measure and 2 dimensions, each dimension contains 4 levels (for example, a time dimension consisting of years, quarters, months, and weeks; a geography dimension consisting of countries, regions, states and cities; and a measure consisting of sales figures). How many different ways can data be aggregated or summarized across the different levels within this cube? In this example, there are at least 16 potential aggregations or summaries for this cube.

So there are n^x potential aggregations, where n represents the number of levels within a dimension and x represents the number of dimensions in the cube. Based on this formula, a cube with 8 dimensions, each having 4 levels (which is not completely unlikely in a multidimensional OLAP scenario) has 65,536 potential aggregations! Remember that each aggregation must be stored, either in the multidimensional or the relational database. Also keep in mind that each aggregation must be calculated when the cube is processed. As you can see, there are significant implications on both storage space and time required to process a cube when creating aggregations.

Now, let's take a look at how to create and process aggregations for our Marketing Cube within OLAP Services.

Creating Aggregations

To create aggregations for the Marketing Cube, highlight the Marketing Cube within the Cubes folder in the tree-view. Right-click to display a shortcut menu. Choose Design Aggregations. This will launch the Storage Design Wizard as shown in Figure 33.14.

The Storage Design Wizard helps you do two things: choose a storage mode for your cube and aggregation data and design a set of aggregations for your cube.

33

MICROSOFT SQL
SERVER OLAP
SERVICES

FIGURE 33.14

*The Storage
Design Wizard
dialog box.*

Choosing a Storage Mode

The dialog box shown in Figure 33.15 will allow you to determine the storage mode you would like to utilize for the cube. Refer to the section "Data Storage in an OLAP Database" for a complete discussion of the available storage modes and an explanation of each.

FIGURE 33.15

*The Storage
Design Wizard
data storage
dialog box.*

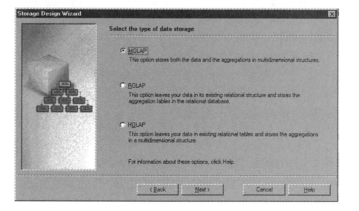

The storage mode determines how OLAP Services stores the aggregation and detailed cube data. You are probably asking "How do I know which data storage mode to use?" This is an important and difficult-to-answer question. The answer depends on your individual situation. However, we'll try to provide some general guidelines.

As mentioned previously, MOLAP storage can provide significant performance advantages over ROLAP and HOLAP. If you have no pressing reasons to use one of the other data storage methods, then you should use MOLAP. The only real drawback to MOLAP storage is that the data storage structure is proprietary to OLAP Services and, therefore, only OLAP clients such as ADO MD and the Pivot Table Service have access to that data.

If you have a tremendous amount of historical data that may not be accessed very frequently, it may make sense to use the ROLAP storage method because ROLAP leverages the existing relational database and leaves the detailed data in its native data store. Keep in mind, however, that every aggregation that is created using the ROLAP storage method results in a new table with indexes in your relational database management system (RDBMS). As mentioned earlier, a cube with 8 dimensions, each with 4 levels, could produce up to 65,536 aggregations. Do you really want to add 65,536 new tables to your database? Probably not. There is a time and place for everything, and ROLAP is no exception.

HOLAP might be an appropriate choice where you have large quantities of detailed data, but your applications need frequent access to that data. HOLAP allows you to take advantage of the scalability of your RDBMS by leaving the detailed data in its native source, but provides some performance improvement by storing aggregation data in MOLAP.

You should not take this decision lightly. Consider all the factors and choose the appropriate storage method for each cube that you are processing. Each cube can have its own storage method. This means that you could store one cube as MOLAP data and another cube as ROLAP. Again, the decision depends on a number of factors that only you, as a DBA, can know.

For our example, we will choose the MOLAP storage mode because we want maximum performance from our cube. Click Next to design the aggregations for your cube.

Designing Aggregations

The dialog box shown in Figure 33.16 allows you to design the aggregations for your cube. What you are actually doing here is telling OLAP Services how many of the potential aggregations to create for your cube. OLAP Services uses sophisticated algorithms to determine which aggregations to create. The only real control you have over this process is to specify the trade-off between disk space and performance.

OLAP Services provides the capability to perform partial preaggregation. This means that you, as a DBA, can determine the appropriate mix between storage space requirements and performance enhancement when creating aggregations.

FIGURE 33.16

The Storage Design Wizard Design Aggregations dialog box.

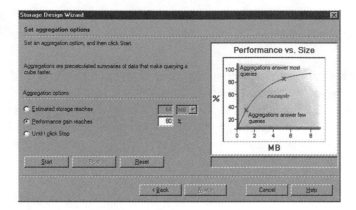

As you can see in Figure 33.16, you have three basic aggregation design options. The options tell OLAP Services to create aggregations until

- Estimated storage reaches *x*MB—Checking this option will cause OLAP Services to create aggregations until it determines that the specified amount of disk space will be utilized.

- Performance gain reaches *x*%—Checking this option will cause OLAP Services to create aggregations until it determines that a specified percentage of performance gain is reached.

- The user clicks Stop—Checking this option will cause OLAP Services to create aggregations until the user clicks Stop.

As is the case with choosing the storage mode, choosing the level of aggregation optimization is really an individual DBA decision that is based on many factors. Microsoft says, however, that 80% performance optimization seems to realize the best disk space versus performance trade-off.

For our example, we will take Microsoft's advice and allow OLAP Services to design aggregations until it determines that we will realize an 80% performance gain. From the dialog box shown in Figure 33.16, click Start. You will notice that the graph on the right-hand side of the dialog box dynamically displays the disk space versus performance gain as the aggregations are designed. After OLAP Services has created the aggregations to satisfy the specified condition, click Next to display the dialog box shown in Figure 33.17.

FIGURE 33.17

The Storage Design Wizard Finish dialog box.

As you can see from this dialog box you have the following choices:

- Process now—Checking this option will cause OLAP Services to process all aggregations when you click Finish. By this, we mean that OLAP Services will perform all data calculations and store the data in the specified data storage mode with the cube.

- Save, but don't process now—Checking this option will allow you to save the aggregation design without actually calculating or storing the data. Remember that you must process these aggregations before the data will be available to the user.

For our example, we want to choose the Process now option and click Finish.

Depending on the level of optimization you have chosen, this process could take a significant amount of time. Also, if you have chosen MOLAP storage, all the detail data must also be written to the multidimensional data store. In any event, OLAP Services displays a detailed status window of all processing. This status shows any database operations that are being performed and indicates either the success or failure of those operations (see Figure 33.18).

FIGURE 33.18

The Storage Design Wizard Process Status dialog box.

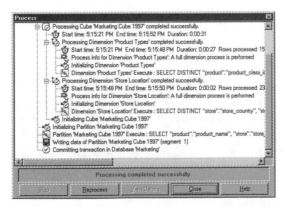

At this point, we have created the OLAP database, defined a cube within that database, designed aggregations to optimize the cube, and processed the data that is stored within the cube. We could actually begin to use our cube now. But before we discuss how to use the cube, a few more optimization issues are worth discussing.

Usage-Based Optimization

After reading the previous sections, you may feel that designing aggregations is a less-than-exact science. You are correct. How do you know what the appropriate level of aggregation is for your cube? More importantly, how can you be sure that the aggregations you wanted were actually created? For example, you may know that your users will frequently request total sales for the Northwest region. In that case, you would like to ensure that an aggregation is created for that scenario.

OLAP Services provides a tool known as *usage-based optimization* to help you more accurately optimize your cube. To utilize this feature, highlight your cube in OLAP Manager. Right-click to display a shortcut menu. Choose Usage-Based Optimization to display the dialog box shown in Figure 33.19.

FIGURE 33.19

The Usage-Based Optimization Wizard dialog box.

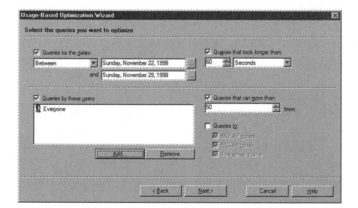

As its name implies, this tool relies on previous cube access to determine which aggregations to design. In other words, you can define how aggregations are created based on actual usage patterns from your client applications. The aggregation design may be based on queries that took too long to execute or queries that were run by certain users.

For example, let's say that John Smith is the president of FoodMart, Inc. He wants to access the overall sales figures across all regions each day. You can use the Usage-Based optimization wizard to indicate that aggregations should be created for all queries executed by John Smith. OLAP Services will then create the appropriate aggregations and store them in the cube.

Over time, you will be able to fine-tune the optimization of your cube based on actual historical user interaction. After the initial guess at performance versus disk space aggregation design, you should always use usage-based optimization.

Usage Analysis

Another tool that will be extremely valuable for any DBA charged with maintaining an OLAP database is the Usage Analysis Wizard. This wizard enables the DBA to print several graphs that give some indication of how the cubes within an OLAP database are being utilized by client applications.

To launch the Usage Analysis Wizard, highlight your cube in OLAP Manager. Right-click to display a shortcut menu. Choose Usage Analysis. The wizard allows you to choose one of the following graphs or tables to determine cube usage.

- Query run-time table—Table showing the run-times of queries executed against the cube ordered from longest to shortest in duration.
- Query frequency—Table showing the frequency of queries executed against the cube, order from the most frequent to the least frequent.
- Active user query—Table showing active users and the queries they have executed against the cube.
- Query response graph—Bar graph showing the response times for all queries executed against the cube.
- Query by hour graph—Bar graph showing queries executed against the cube grouped by hour.
- Query by date graph—Bar graph showing queries executed against the cube grouped by date.

As you can see, this is quite a powerful tool that will enable the DBA to better plan aggregation and optimization strategies.

Partitions

Partitions represent the physical data storage of the cube and aggregation data. The cube is the logical definition of the data. When you create a cube in an OLAP database, OLAP Services automatically creates one partition. After you have created the cube, you can go back and create new partitions. These partitions are used to physically segment the data from your logical cube definition.

The true power of partitions is that each partition can have its own storage mode and its own unique set of aggregations. In this way, one logical cube can be segmented into different physical data stores using a combination of MOLAP, ROLAP, and HOLAP and different aggregation optimizations.

Until now, the Marketing Cube has been based on a single physical MOLAP partition. What if we wanted to have a second physical partition that could store sales data for last year? The following sections will explain how we would do this.

Creating and Using Partitions

To create a new partition, expand the cube and highlight the Partitions folder. Right-click to display a shortcut menu. Choose New Partition from the shortcut menu. You will see the dialog box shown in Figure 33.20.

FIGURE 33.20

The Partition Wizard dialog box.

The first step in creating a new partition is to determine the data source for the partition. Click Next to display the dialog box shown in Figure 33.21.

FIGURE 33.21

The Partition Wizard Specify Data Source dialog box.

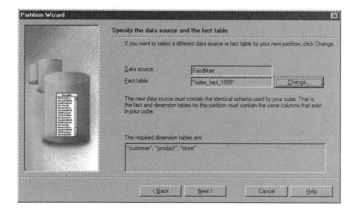

The partition must have a data source. The data source can be the same as the data source of the cube or it can be different. Remember that a cube can be based on only one fact table; therefore, there is only one data source for each cube partition. By creating a new partition with a different data source, you can effectively create a cube with multiple data sources. If you want to choose a different data source for the new partition, click Change.

> **NOTE**
>
> If you are going to base your partition on a different data source than your cube, you need to understand a couple things. First, the new data source must contain copies of the dimension tables for the cube. The wizard points out which tables are required. The dimension tables must be exact copies, including data. You can have a different fact table for your partition, but the new fact table must contain the same fields (not data) as the original fact table.

For our example, we want to create a new partition for our cube that contains sales data from 1997. To do this, we need to change the fact table. From the dialog box shown in Figure 33.21, click the Change button.

FIGURE 33.22

The Choose a Fact Table dialog box.

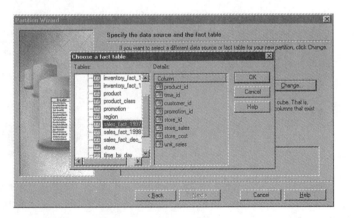

From the dialog box shown in Figure 33.22, we would choose the same data source that our original cube was based on. This time, however, we want to choose a different fact table. Remember that our Marketing cube was based on the sales_facts_1998 table. For the new partition we want to choose the sales_facts_1997 table. The structure of these two tables is identical. This will allow our cube to analyze two sets of sales data across the same dimensions, while keeping the underlying base data physically separated.

The way you create partitions is highly dependent on your individual database situation. For our example, we are creating two partitions for one logical cube. Each partition is based on a different fact table with a different set of data. If the sales data for both 1997 and 1998 had been stored in one fact table, we could still accomplish the same goal by using data slices.

Data Slices

Specifying a data slice enables you to define the segregation of your cube data across partitions using one fact table. For example, let's say that all your sales data is stored in one fact table for many different sales regions. You could specify a data slice that indicates on which partition to physically store cube data for the NorthEast region by specifying a data slice.

Because our example uses two different fact tables, we do not need to create a data slice for our partition, but we will discuss how to create a data slice anyway.

From the dialog box shown in Figure 33.21, click Next to display the Specify Data Slice dialog box.

FIGURE 33.23

The Partition Wizard Specify Data Slice dialog box.

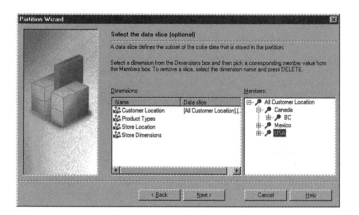

The dialog box shown in Figure 33.23 allows you to specify a data slice for the partition you are creating. To create a data slice, click the dimensions in the left-hand pane of the dialog box. The right-hand pane will then display all the available data members on which you can slice the data. Choose the highest level member for which you want to store data on the partition.

OLAP Services can use the data slice to determine how to physically populate the cube. All data that meets a specified data slice criteria will be stored on the partition that contains that data slice. Additionally, OLAP Services can use the data type to determine where to send user queries. In this way, OLAP Services optimizes the retrieval of data.

Choosing a data slice is optional. After you have chosen a data slice (or decided not to use one) for your partition, click Next to display the dialog box shown in Figure 33.24.

FIGURE 33.24

The Partition Wizard Complete Partitions dialog box.

The dialog box shown in Figure 33.24 allows you to name your partition and to indicate how you want to design the aggregations. Because each partition can maintain its own set of aggregations, you need to decide how you want to process this partition.

This dialog box provides you with the following choices:

- Design aggregations now—Checking this option will launch the Data Storage and Aggregation Design Wizard when you click Finish. Refer to the section "Creating Aggregations" for a detailed description of how to design aggregations.

- Design aggregations later—Checking this option will mean that your partition will not have any aggregations until you create them. You can manually launch the Data Storage and Aggregation Wizard at a later time by highlighting the partition, right-clicking to display the shortcut menu, and choosing Design Aggregations.

- Copy aggregation design—Checking this option will cause your partition to have the exact set of aggregations created as another partition within your cube.

- Process partition when finished—Checking this option will cause OLAP Services to process all aggregation and detail data and store that data in the partition. Remember, just like the cube, each partition must be populated with data before it can be used.

For our example, we want to clone the aggregations based on the original cube partition. We do this because we do not yet see the need to create customized aggregations for the new partition. It is possible that at some point we may determine that the historical sales data is being used differently from the current sales data. We can always run the Usage-Based Optimization Wizard to create a new set of aggregations for our partition. We also

33

MICROSOFT SQL
SERVER OLAP
SERVICES

want to check the option to process the cube when finished. From the dialog box shown in Figure 33.24, click Finish to process the cube.

Congratulations! You have now successfully created a cube based on two different fact tables. The users who access this cube will not know that the underlying sales data for 1997 and 1998 are stored on two physically different partitions. This cube is now ready to be used. This of course brings up an important question: How do you access the cube data? The following sections will discuss some methods for providing access to your cube data.

ACCESSING MULTIDIMENSIONAL DATA

Because this book is written for the DBA, this chapter on OLAP Services focuses on the DBA activities surrounding creating and maintaining OLAP databases. Of course, there wouldn't be much use in creating OLAP databases if you didn't intend to access the data and present it to client applications.

The following sections briefly touch on some of the utilities and technologies that are available to access and utilize the data stored in an OLAP database.

The Cube Browser

You access the Cube Browser from within the OLAP Manager. It can be used to get a quick look at the cube data after your cubes have been created and processed. To access the Cube Browser, highlight the cube and right-click to display a shortcut menu. Choose Browse Data from the shortcut menu.

FIGURE 33.25

The Cube Browser.

As you can see in Figure 33.25, the Cube Browser looks like an Excel pivot table on steroids. You can choose any of the available dimensions and filter data at a high level. You can drag and drop any of the dimensions into the grid. By double-clicking on a dimension within the grid, you can drill down through the levels of the dimension. Data is dynamically updated inside the grid as you manipulate the dimensions.

This Cube Browser is a slick utility that allows you to quickly view the data in the cube.

The Pivot Table Service

Pivot Table Service is packaged with the Microsoft Office 2000 suite of products. The Pivot Table Service shares much of the code base with OLAP Services and is able to provide a client-side cache and a direct interface to Access and Excel. You can also embed Pivot Table Service in a Web browser.

ADO MD

ADO MD stands for ActiveX data objects for multidimensional data. ADO MD extends the functionality of ADO by adding a set of objects to the ADO object model that enables access to multidimensional data. For example, ADO MD includes a cellset object that is the equivalent of a recordset object in ADO.

ADO MD enables client-side application programmers to write applications using Visual Basic, Active Server Pages, Visual C++, and so on that can provide a graphical front end to OLAP Services data.

MDX

MDX stands for multidimensional expressions. MDX is essentially an extension to the SQL syntax that defines a rich syntax for accessing and retrieving data from an OLAP database. MDX is similar in structure to SQL, using many of the same keywords, such as SELECT, FROM, and WHERE.

MDX is an integral part of ADO MD for client-side data access. For example, the ADO MD cellset object must pass a formulated MDX query to the server in order to receive a resultset.

Additionally, many third-party vendors are creating robust front-end OLAP tools specially designed for the OLE DB for OLAP specification. A majority of the OLAP industry has embraced the OLE DB for OLAP specification and it seems that there will be many excited client access alternatives for OLAP analysis in the months ahead.

MANAGING MULTIDIMENSIONAL DATA

Obviously, the transaction-oriented business does not stop once a cube has been created. So far we have discussed the cubes as if they were read-only "snapshot" views of transactional data. Although it is true that OLAP databases are used to perform analysis on historical transactional data, those cubes need to be updated as the underlying transactional data changes.

OLAP Services provides three primary mechanisms for updating the multidimensional data within your cubes:

- Processing the cube
- Merging partitions
- Client write back

The following sections will discuss these topics.

Processing the Cube

As mentioned earlier, in order for a cube to be populated with actual data, it must be processed. Likewise, in order to update data in a cube it must be processed. To update your cube data, highlight the cube in OLAP Manager. Right-click to display a shortcut menu. Choose Process.

FIGURE 33.26

The Process a Cube dialog box.

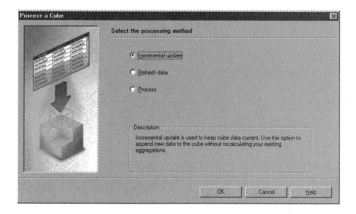

Figure 33.26 shows the dialog box to process a cube with the following options:

- Incremental update—Choose this option to add only changed data to the cube. Existing cube data is left intact and aggregations are re-calculated to add the new data. The incremental update can be performed while users are still connected to the database. Once the update is finished, users have access to the new data.

- Refresh data—Choose this option to clear out all the data in the cube and repopulate. When you choose this option, all aggregations are re-calculated, and the data is stored in the cube based on the original cube definition.

- Process—Choose this option only if the structure of your cube has changed. For example, if you have added or removed a dimension or measure to the cube. This option will completely rebuild the cube based on the current cube definitions. This process is exactly the same as the process you ran when you originally created the cube.

Merging Partitions

OLAP Services enables you to merge data from one partition to another. Why would you want to do this? Let's say that you create a cube to store regional sales information. The cube is created with four partitions, one in each sales region. These partitions are physically distributed but client access is via one logical cube. At the end of the year, you want to combine all the regional sales data into one physical partition located on a central server for faster processing. You can do this by merging the partitions.

To merge partitions, highlight the source or target partition in the OLAP Manager. Right-click to display a shortcut menu. Choose Merge.

33

> **NOTE**
>
> If you intend to merge two partitions at some point in the future, you need to keep some design considerations in mind when originally creating your partitions. In order to merge partitions, they must have the same storage mode (MOLAP, ROLAP, or HOLAP); have identical aggregations; and their fact tables must have identical structures.

Client Write Back

You might wonder whether it is possible for a client to update the data in a cube. After all, the client is the person who is more than likely the most familiar with the data and the one who could spot data that needs to be changed. The answer to this question is Yes, and No.

OLAP Services allows a cube to be write-enabled. When a cube is write-enabled, users can write data back to the cube. The trick is that the data is not actually written to the cube itself or to the underlying source data. Rather, OLAP Services maintains a separate write-back table that stores all the data that is written to the cube. Users are able to browse the write-back data and they are unaware that the data is not stored in the cube.

To write-enable a cube, highlight the cube in the OLAP Manager. Right-click to display a shortcut menu. Choose Write-Enable to display the dialog box shown in Figure 33.27.

FIGURE 33.27

The Write Enable dialog box.

In this dialog box, you can enter the name of a data source and a table where the write-back data will be stored. As far as the user can tell, this data is part of the cube.

Once the cube has been write-enabled, users can actually make changes to the data while they are browsing the cube. These changes are stored in the write-back, but are displayed to the user as if part of the cube.

You can convert this write-back table to a permanent partition at any point as well. Once the write-back table is converted to a partition, the write-back table and all its data are deleted, and the cube once again becomes read-only.

MICROSOFT SQL SERVER 7.0 OLAP SERVICES FAQ

The following section lists some commonly asked questions and answers about SQL Server 7.0 OLAP Services.

When should I consider implementing OLAP technology?

Basically, any business process that requires you to analyze (roll up, drill down, and so on) transactional data across a variety of categories is an excellent application of OLAP technology. Loosely speaking, any time you have created an Excel pivot table, you have started to explore the power of OLAP technology.

What is the difference between relational and multi-dimensional databases?

The primary difference between a relational database and a multidimensional database is semantics. The true differentiation is the manner in which data is represented, and not the underlying technology. Relational databases tend to represent data in a flat, two-dimensional manner, whereas multidimensional databases have the capability to represent data across many dimensions.

It is important to note that the underlying technology between the two kinds of databases does not have to be different. It is possible to create a multidimensional database using SQL Server 7.0. This is a complex task, requiring sophisticated database schemas, such as star schemas, but it can be done. Likewise, it would be possible to create a standard two-dimensional relational database using OLAP Services by creating cubes with only two dimensions.

How do I translate my transactional data into an effective multidimensional database?

In OLAP Services, the multidimensional database is based on a data source; typically this data source is the database that holds your transactional data. In order to create the multidimensional database, you must translate your data. Translating this relational data into an effective multidimensional database requires careful thought and a true understanding of the base data and how your users need to analyze that data.

Basically, the translation involves choosing the appropriate tables and columns within those tables to represent the dimensions and measures of your cube. As is the case with most things, this is often easier said than done. The trick to effectively translating your data is to truly understand the underlying data. In most cases, it is necessary to have many people involved in designing the cubes that make up the multidimensional database.

Can I analyze data that is calculated from my source data such as net profit?

Yes, OLAP Services supports calculated members. A calculated member is essentially a measure that does not have a value explicitly stored in the underlying fact table but whose value can be derived from other values that are explicitly stored in the fact table. Once you have defined a calculated member, it appears as any other measure within the cube and its source is invisible to the user.

33

MICROSOFT SQL SERVER OLAP SERVICES

SUMMARY

As you can see, Microsoft SQL Server OLAP Services is an exciting new technology that will have a significant impact on business application development. It is expected that the OLAP and data warehousing market will be the fastest growing segment of the database market over the next five years. Microsoft is poised to become a major player in this market segment with the introduction of the OLAP Services.

APPENDIXES

PART

X

IN THIS PART

Naming Conventions

by Orryn Sledge

The following are recommended naming conventions for SQL Server.

TABLE A.1   SUGGESTED NAMING CONVENTIONS

Object	Naming Convention	Example
database	(business name)	sales
table	(business name)	customer
constraint		
foreign key constraint	(table name) + _fk	customer_fk
primary key constraint	(table name) + _pk	customer_pk
unique key constraint	(table name) + _uniq	customer_uniq
OR		
foreign key constraint	fk_ + (table name)	fk_customer
primary key constraint	pk_ + (table name)	pk_customer
unique key constraint	uniq_ + (table name)	uniq_customer
index		
clustered	(column_name) + _cdx	customer_id_cdx
nonclustered	(column name) + _idx	customer_id_idx
trigger		
delete	(table name) + _dtr	customer_dtr
insert	(table name) + _itr	customer_itr
update	(table name) + _utr	customer_utr
insert and update	(table name) + _iutr	customer_iutr
OR		
delete	dtr_ + (table name)	dtr_customer
insert	itr_ + (table name)	itr_customer
update	utr_ + (table name)	utr_customer
insert and update	iutr_ + (table name)	iutr_customer
stored procedure (style A)	usp_ + (business name) usp_customer_inquiry (usp stands for user-defined stored procedure)	
stored procedure (style B)	This style combines the action being performed in the stored procedure with a business name. For example, a stored procedure that deletes the customer profile has the name del_customer. If the stored procedure performs multiple business functions, use oth_ + (business name).	

Object	*Naming Convention*	*Example*
DELETE	del_ + (business name)	del_customer
INSERT	ins_ + (business name)	ins_customer
SELECT	sel_ + (business name)	sel_customer
UPDATE	upd_ + (business name)	upd_customer
Other types of actions	oth_ + (business name)	oth_customer
view	(business name) + _view	customer_view

NOTE

To improve readability, I recommend standardizing of lower-, upper-, or mixed case. Personally, I make everything lowercase. Uppercase makes it look like someone is shouting at you!

DBCC Commands

by Orryn Sledge

IN THIS APPENDIX

DBCC stands for *Database Consistency Checker*. However, over the years DBCC has grown to include commands that display configuration information, probe SQL Server's internals, and perform other commands. Therefore, it is recommended that administrators review this appendix for commands that can detect database problems and for commands that provide other types of interesting SQL Server information.

DBCC commands are commonly used to perform the following tasks:

- **Verify database integrity**: It is good idea to periodically run the DBCC CHECKDB command. This command can help isolate database and table problems before they manifest themselves into larger issues.

- **Investigate errors**: Use DBCC to pinpoint the source of errors such as Table Corrupt or Extent not with segment. DBCC commands such as CHECKDB can help you isolate corruption, and starting with version 7.0, the CHECKDB command can repair certain types of corruption.

- **Analyze SQL Server**: Several DBCC commands provide information about transactions, memory usage, and trace flag settings. These commands are often used to help fine-tune SQL Server.

SQL SERVER 6.5 TO 7.0 QUICK REFERENCE

The following is a quick reference to the changes that occurred between SQL Server version 6.5 and 7.0:

What's New

- **Improved DBCC performance:** Performance has been significantly improved for the following DBCC commands: CHECKDB, CHECKTABLE, and CHECKALLOC. I have seen examples where the DBCC performance gain found in 7.0 is amazing. For example, with version 6.5 a 28GB database required 64 hours to run CHECKDB, now the command runs in 1 hour!

- **DBCC CHECKDB:** This command has been revised to check text, ntext, and image data pages. Therefore, you no longer need to use the TEXTALL or TEXTALLOC commands if you are using CHECKDB. This command has also been improved so that it can automatically repair various types of table and index corruption (see the section "CHECKDB" for more information).

- **DBCC commands use fewer server resources:** DBCC commands such as CHECK-DB, CHECKTABLE, and CHECKALLOC can be run while other users are in the system. In previous versions of SQL Server, the database needed to be in single user mode to obtain optimal performance for DBCC commands such as checkdb. Also in previous versions of SQL Server, DBCC commands placed locks on tables that made it difficult for users to query and modify data when these commands were run. Version 7.0 has eliminated these issues due to significant changes in the way that SQL Server stores data.

- **New DBCC commands:** the following are new DBCC commands found in version 7.0: CHECKFILEGROUP, SHRINKDATABASE, and SHRINKFILE.

- **DBCC CHECKIDENT:** The following optional parameters have been added:

  { NORESEED ¦ {RESEED [, *new_reseed_value*] } }

What's Gone

- **DBCC DBREPAIR:** This command is no longer supported. Use the DROP DATABASE command.

- **DBCC SHRINKDB:** This command is no longer supported. Use the DBCC SHRINKDATABASE command.

- **DBCC TEXTALL:** This command is no longer necessary because DBCC CHECKDB includes the TEXTALL functionality. This command is supported for backward compatibility in version 7.0 and may not be supported in future versions of SQL Server.

- **DBCC TEXTALLOC:** This command is no longer necessary because DBCC CHECKTABLE includes the TEXTALLOC functionality. This command is supported for backward compatibility in version 7.0 and may not be supported in future versions of SQL Server.

- **DBCC ROWLOCK:** This command is no longer necessary. Version 7.0 automatically utilizes row-level locking, whereas in version 6.5 this command would enable row-level locking. This command is supported for backward compatibility in version 7.0 and may not be supported in future versions of SQL Server.

- **DBCC DBREINDEX:** The following optional parameters are removed:
  SORTED_DATA ¦ SORTED_DATA_REORG

- **DBCC NEWALLOC:** This command is supported for backward compatibility. Use the CHECKALLOC command.

- **DBCC MEMUSAGE:** This command is no longer supported. Use the Performance Monitor to track memory and cache information.

QUICK REFERENCE

The following is a quick syntax reference for DBCC commands.

Command

```
DBCC CHECKALLOC
( 'database_name'
[, NOINDEX
¦
{ REPAIR_ALLOW_DATA_LOSS
¦ REPAIR_FAST
¦ REPAIR_REBUILD
}]
) [WITH {ALL_ERRORMSGS ¦ NO_INFOMSGS}]

DBCC CHECKCATALOG [(database_name)] [WITH NO_INFOMSGS]

DBCC CHECKTABLE
    (    'table_name'
         [,      NOINDEX
              ¦ index_id
              ¦    {      REPAIR_ALLOW_DATA_LOSS
                      ¦ REPAIR_FAST
                      ¦ REPAIR_REBUILD
              }]
    ) [WITH {ALL_ERRORMSGS ¦ NO_INFOMSGS}]

DBCC CHECKDB
    (    'database_name'
         [,      NOINDEX
              ¦      {      REPAIR_ALLOW_DATA_LOSS
                      ¦ REPAIR_FAST
                      ¦ REPAIR_REBUILD
              }]
    ) [WITH {ALL_ERRORMSGS ¦ NO_INFOMSGS}]

DBCC CHECKFILEGROUP
    (    [{'filegroup' ¦ filegroup_id}] [, NOINDEX]
    ) [WITH {ALL_ERRORMSGS ¦ NO_INFOMSGS}]

DBCC CHECKIDENT [(table_name)] [, { NORESEED ¦ {RESEED
    [,new_reseed_value] } } ] )

DBCC DBREINDEX (['database.owner.table_name' [, index_name
    [, fillfactor ]]])[WITH NO_INFOMSGS]

DBCC dllname (FREE)

DBCC INPUTBUFFER (spid)

DBCC OPENTRAN ({database_name} ¦ {database_id}) [WITH TABLERESULTS]
    [,NO_INFOMSGS]

DBCC OUTPUTBUFFER (spid)

DBCC PERFMON
```

```
DBCC PINTABLE
      (database_id, table_id)

DBCC SHOW_STATISTICS
      (table_name, index_name)

DBCC SHOWCONTIG
      (table_id, [index_id])

DBCC SHRINKDATABASE (database_name [, target_percent]  [, {NOTRUNCATE
      ¦ TRUNCATEONLY} ])

DBCC SHRINKFILE
   (      {file_name ¦ file_id }
             {     [, target_size]
             ¦     [, {EMPTYFILE ¦ NOTRUNCATE ¦ TRUNCATEONLY}]
             }
   )

DBCC SQLPERF (LOGSPACE)

DBCC TRACEOFF (trace# [,...N])

DBCC TRACEON (trace# [,...N])

DBCC TRACESTATUS (trace# [, trace#...])

DBCC UNPINTABLE (database_id, table_id)

DBCC UPDATEUSAGE
   (      {'database_name' ¦ 0}
             [, 'table_name' [, index_id]
             ]
   )   [     WITH [COUNT_ROWS] [, NO_INFOMSGS ]
       ]

DBCC USEROPTIONS
```

TIP

When DBCC performance is a primary concern (especially when working with very large databases), use the NOINDEX argument with the following commands: CHECKALLOC, CHECKTABLE, CHECKDB, and CHECKFILEGROUP. When the NOINDEX argument is specified, only clustered indexes are inspected for errors. All nonclustered indexes are ignored. This option is generally safe to use because damaged indexes can be dropped and re-created without affecting the data within a table.

B

DBCC COMMANDS

READING THE OUTPUT FROM DBCC COMMANDS

DBCC commands often generate a great amount of output. The problem is determining what is relevant within the output. Use the following list as a guide of what to look for in the DBCC output:

- Any message that contains the string *corrupt* (for example, `Table Corrupt`).

- Error messages that range from `2500` to `2599` or `7900` to `7999`. DBCC error messages usually contain these error numbers.

- Messages that contain the string `error`.

TIP

To help reduce the amount of information returned by a DBCC command, use the `WITH NO_INFOMSGS` option. By using this option, DBCC will return only relevant information such as error messages. For example

```
DBCC CHECKDB (pubs) WITH NO_INFOMSGS
```

The following DBCC commands support the `WITH NO_INFOMSGS` option.

- `CHECKALLOC`
- `CHECKCATALOG`
- `CHECKDB`
- `CHECKFILEGROUP`
- `CHECKTABLE`
- `DBREINDEX`
- `OPENTRAN`
- `UPDATEUSAGE`

RESOLVING ERRORS REPORTED BY DBCC

When an error is reported by DBCC, you should immediately investigate it. Unresolved errors can propagate throughout a database, increasing the likelihood of permanent data corruption.

The following items provide a general guideline for investigating and resolving errors reported by DBCC:

- Save and print DBCC output. On very large databases, DBCC commands can sometimes take hours to run. Do not take a chance on forgetting an error message and having to rerun the DBCC command!

- Look up the specific error code in the "Troubleshooting" chapter in the *SQL Server Books Online*. The chapter provides error-specific solutions.

- Shut down and restart the SQL Server. This action flushes out the data cache and may resolve the problem.

- Contact Microsoft Support for additional assistance.

ESSENTIAL DBCC COMMANDS

You should run the DBCC CHECKDB and DBCC CHECKCATALOG commands to detect database and table corruption, along with structure inconsistencies. Additionally, you may want to schedule these commands prior to or immediately after running a backup. Keep in mind that these commands should be run for all databases, excluding pubs and tempdb. This includes your user-defined database and master, model, and msdb.

NOTE

Due to improved data storage and built-in real-time data checks, Microsoft no longer recommends running CHECKDB before or immediately after performing a backup. With previous versions, it was common to schedule CHECKDB to run as part of the backup/database maintenance task.

TIP

The easiest method to automate and schedule CHECKDB and other DBCC commands is to use the Database Maintenance Plan Wizard. Selecting the "Check database integrity" prompt will automatically schedule the CHECKDB command.

B

DBCC COMMANDS

DBCC COMMANDS FOR VERIFICATION

The following DBCC commands are used for verification:

CHECKALLOC

CHECKCATALOG

CHECKDB

CHECKFILEGROUP

CHECKIDENT

CHECKTABLE

DBREINDEX

SHOWCONTIG

UPDATEUSAGE

CHECKALLOC

Syntax

```
DBCC CHECKALLOC
( 'database_name'
[, NOINDEX
|
{ REPAIR_ALLOW_DATA_LOSS
| REPAIR_FAST
| REPAIR_REBUILD
}]
) [WITH {ALL_ERRORMSGS | NO_INFOMSGS}]
```

CHECKALLOC scans the database to ensure that data page allocation is correct. In SQL Server 7.0, CHECKALLOC should be used instead of NEWALLOC. This is ironic, because in version 6.x Microsoft told us to use NEWALLOC instead of CHECKALLOC!

See Table B.1 for an explanation on the REPAIR_ALLOW_DATA_LOSS | REPAIR_FAST | REPAIR_REBUILD options.

> **NOTE**
>
> CHECKALLOC does not need to be run if CHECKDB is run. The functionality provided by CHECKALLOC is encompassed in CHECKDB.

CHECKCATALOG

Syntax

```
DBCC CHECKCATALOG [(database_name)] [WITH NO_INFOMSGS]
```

CHECKCATALOG checks the system tables for consistency by verifying the data and relationship between the syscolumns table and the systypes table. It verifies that each table and view in the sysobjects table has one or more matching records in the syscolumns table.

Use this command to analyze the system tables within a database or when you suspect corruption within the system tables.

Example

```
DBCC CHECKCATALOG (pubs)
```

CHECKDB

Syntax

```
DBCC CHECKDB
    (       'database_name'
         [,        NOINDEX
             ¦     {      REPAIR_ALLOW_DATA_LOSS
                    ¦ REPAIR_FAST
                    ¦ REPAIR_REBUILD
              }]
    ) [WITH {ALL_ERRORMSGS ¦ NO_INFOMSGS}]
```

CHECKDB checks all tables and indexes in a database for pointer and data page errors, that data and index pages are properly linked, that indexes match the proper sort order, and that page offsets and page information is correct. In version 7.0, CHECKDB also checks text, ntext and image pages.

Example

```
DBCC CHECKDB(pubs)
```

Sample Output (output has been abbreviated and is indicated by the "..." symbol)

```
Checking pubs
Checking sysobjects
There are 97 rows in 1 pages for object 'sysobjects'.
Checking sysindexes
There are 48 rows in 1 pages for object 'sysindexes'.
Checking syscolumns
...
```

B

DBCC COMMANDS

```
There are 23 rows in 1 pages for object 'authors'.
Checking publishers
There are 8 rows in 1 pages for object 'publishers'.
Checking titles
...
CHECKDB found 0 allocation errors and 0 consistency errors in database
'pubs'.
```

Example

```
DBCC CHECKDB(pubs) WITH NO_INFOMSGS
```

```
DBCC execution completed. If DBCC printed error messages, contact your
system administrator.
```

NOTE

The following are notes on the CHECKDB command.

Use this command to verify database integrity: CHECKDB validates the integrity of every database object inside a database. CHECKDB is the equivalent of running CHECKALLOC against the database and CHECKTABLE against every table in the database.

Use the NO_INFOMSGS option: CHECKDB can generate a lot of meaningless information. Therefore, I recommend using the NO_INFOMSGS option so that only relevant information is displayed.

Repair option usage: Version 7.0 includes the following repair options listed in Table B.1. **NOTE:** the database must be in single user mode to run the repair options listed below.

TABLE B.1   REPAIR OPTIONS

Repair Option	Explanation
REPAIR_ALLOW_DATA_LOSS	This option will remove corrupt data and will attempt to resolve structural errors. This option includes the functionality found in the REPAIR_REBUILD option. This option may lead to data loss. This option can be part of transaction, which can be rolled back if necessary. The following is an example of this command within a transaction:
	`/* place database in single user mode */` `sp_dboption pubs,'single user',true`

```
                        go
                        begin transaction
                        go
                        dbcc checkdb(pubs, REPAIR_ALLOW_DATA_LOSS)
                        with NO_INFOMSGS
                        go
```

After the CHECKDB command has executed, you can commit the changes or rollback the changes. The following is an example of the commit and rollback logic.

Commit example

```
/* if everything is ok -> commit changes */
commit transaction
```

Rollback example

```
/* if everything is NOT ok -> rollback changes */
rollback transaction
```

The last step is to take the database out of single user mode. The following is an example of taking the database out of single user mode.

```
/* take database out of single user mode */
sp_dboption pubs,'single user',false
go
```

REPAIR_FAST	This option will resolve simple errors such as non-clustered indexes containing extra columns. This option will not lead to data loss.
REPAIR_REBUILD	This option will rebuild all the indexes in the database. Depending on the database size, number of indexes, and number of errors, this can be a time consuming task. This option also includes the functionality found in the REPAIR_FAST option. This option will not lead to data loss.

Ignore row count adjustment messages: You can safely ignore the following messages that are sometimes generated by CHECKDB:

```
The number of data pages in Sysindexes for this table was 9. It has
been corrected to 1.
The number of rows in Sysindexes for this table was 273. It has
been corrected to 16.
```

These messages indicate that SQL Server is performing some internal housekeeping to keep row counts accurate for the sp_spaceused command.

> **CAUTION**
>
> CHECKDB requires shared locks: CHECKDB will place shared locks on all tables and indexes in the database. Therefore tables, indexes, views, stored procedures, defaults, user defined data types, users, roles, or permissions, cannot be created, altered, or dropped while CHECKDB is running. Keep this in mind when you run CHECKDB on a production table! However, users can query and modify data while CHECKDB is running.

CHECKFILEGROUP

Syntax

```
DBCC CHECKFILEGROUP
    (    [{'filegroup' ¦ filegroup_id}] [, NOINDEX]
    ) [WITH {ALL_ERRORMSGS ¦ NO_INFOMSGS}]
```

CHECKFILEGROUP validates the integrity of tables, indexes, and data that resides in a file-group.

> **NOTE**
>
> CHECKFILEGROUP is the same as running CHECKDB, except that the tables, indexes, and data that reside in a filegroup are checked. With CHECKDB, the entire database is checked.

Example

```
/* check all filegroups in the database */
use sales
go
dbcc checkfilegroup
go
```

Sample Output

```
DBCC results for 'Sales'.
DBCC results for 'sysobjects'.
There are 38 rows in 1 pages for object 'sysobjects'.
DBCC results for 'sysindexes'.
There are 29 rows in 1 pages for object 'sysindexes'.
DBCC results for 'syscolumns'.
There are 391 rows in 5 pages for object 'syscolumns'.
DBCC results for 'systypes'.
There are 24 rows in 1 pages for object 'systypes'.
```

```
DBCC results for 'syscomments'.
There are 108 rows in 11 pages for object 'syscomments'.
DBCC results for 'sysfiles1'.
There are 7 rows in 2 pages for object 'sysfiles1'.
DBCC results for 'syspermissions'.
There are 36 rows in 1 pages for object 'syspermissions'.
DBCC results for 'sysusers'.
There are 13 rows in 1 pages for object 'sysusers'.
DBCC results for 'sysdepends'.
There are 181 rows in 1 pages for object 'sysdepends'.
DBCC results for 'sysreferences'.
There are 0 rows in 1 pages for object 'sysreferences'.
DBCC results for 'sysfulltextcatalogs'.
There are 0 rows in 1 pages for object 'sysfulltextcatalogs'.
DBCC results for 'sysfilegroups'.
There are 3 rows in 1 pages for object 'sysfilegroups'.
DBCC results for 'sysallocations'.
There are 1 rows in 1 pages for object 'sysallocations'.
CHECKFILEGROUP found 0 allocation errors and 0 consistency errors in
database 'Sales'.
DBCC execution completed. If DBCC printed error messages, contact your
system administrator.
```

CHECKIDENT

Syntax

```
DBCC CHECKIDENT [(table_name)] [, { NORESEED ¦ {RESEED [,
new_reseed_value] } } ] )
```

The CHECKIDENT command checks the IDENTITY datatype in a table and will repair the identity value if it is incorrect. This command can also be used to modify the identity value. It returns the current identity value and the maximum identity value.

Example

```
DBCC CHECKIDENT(jobs)
```

Sample Output

```
Checking identity information: current identity value '14', current column
value '14'.
```

Example

```
DBCC CHECKIDENT(jobs, RESEED, 1000)
```

Sample Output

```
Checking identity information: current identity value '14', current column
value '1000'.
```

CHECKTABLE

Syntax

```
DBCC CHECKTABLE
    (    'table_name'
            [,      NOINDEX
                ¦ index_id
                ¦    {     REPAIR_ALLOW_DATA_LOSS
                        ¦ REPAIR_FAST
                        ¦ REPAIR_REBUILD
                }]
    ) [WITH {ALL_ERRORMSGS ¦ NO_INFOMSGS}]
```

CHECKTABLE ensures that all pointers are correct, that data and index pages are properly linked, that indexes match the proper sort order, and that page offsets and page information are correct. Run this command when you suspect that a table is corrupt or as part of your periodic maintenance plan.

See Table B.1 for an explanation on the REPAIR_ALLOW_DATA_LOSS ¦ REPAIR_FAST ¦ REPAIR_REBUILD options.

> **NOTE**
>
> CHECKTABLE does not need to be run if CHECKDB is run. The functionality provided by CHECKTABLE is encompassed in CHECKDB.

Example

```
DBCC CHECKTABLE(titles)
```

Sample Output

```
Checking titles
There are 18 rows in 1 pages for object 'titles'.
DBCC execution completed. If DBCC printed error messages, see your System
Administrator.
```

DBREINDEX

Syntax

```
DBCC DBREINDEX (['database.owner.table_name' [, index_name
[, fillfactor ]]])
[WITH NO_INFOMSGS]
```

The DBREINDEX command rebuilds a table's indexes. This command is often used when a PRIMARY KEY or UNIQUE constraint needs to be rebuilt. The advantage of using this command instead of the CREATE INDEX command is that you do not have to specify the table and index information to rebuild the constraint.

Example (rebuilds all indexes for the titleauthor table)

```
DBCC DBREINDEX (titleauthor,"")
```

Example (rebuilds a particular index for the titleauthor table)

```
DBCC DBREINDEX (titleauthor,"auidind")
```

SHOWCONTIG

Syntax

```
DBCC SHOWCONTIG (table_id, [index_id])
```

SHOWCONTIG determines the amount of table fragmentation. A high degree of fragmentation can lead to poor query performance because more data pages must be read by SQL Server to process a query.

Fragmentation occurs when modification statements (DELETE, INSERT, and UPDATE) are performed on a table. A table subject to many modification statements is more likely to become fragmented than a table that is seldom modified.

To determine the degree of fragmentation, inspect the Scan Density information. A Scan Density value less than 100% indicates that some fragmentation exists. Tables that generate low values such as a Scan Density <= 90% will benefit from defragmentation.

To defragment a table, drop and re-create the table's clustered index *or* use DBCC DBREINDEX *or* use BCP to copy out the data, drop the table, re-create the table, and use BCP again to copy in the data.

TIP

Use the object_id() function to determine a table's ID.

Example

```
/* get table id */
use pubs
go
SELECT object_id('authors')
-----------
117575457
/* run DBCC command */
DBCC SHOWCONTIG(117575457)
```

B

Sample Output

```
DBCC SHOWCONTIG scanning 'authors' table...
Table: 'authors' (117575457); index ID: 1, database ID: 5
TABLE level scan performed.
- Pages Scanned................................: 1
- Extents Scanned..............................: 1
- Extent Switches..............................: 0
- Avg. Pages per Extent.........................: 1.0
- Scan Density [Best Count:Actual Count].......: 100.00% [1:1]
- Logical Scan Fragmentation ...................: 0.00%
- Extent Scan Fragmentation ....................: 0.00%
- Avg. Bytes Free per Page.....................: 6008.0
- Avg. Page Density (full).....................: 25.77%
```

UPDATEUSAGE

```
DBCC UPDATEUSAGE ({'database_name'¦ 0} [, 'table_name' [, index_id]])
[WITH
[NO_INFOMSGS]
[[,] COUNT_ROWS]
```

When an index is dropped from a table, sp_spaceused may inaccurately report space utilization. Use the UPDATEUSAGE command to correct the inaccuracy.

> **NOTE**
>
> Generally speaking, DBCC UPDATEUSAGE is only necessary when you question the information being returned from sp_spaceused. To validate if information is correct from sp_spacused, perform a SELECT COUNT(*) FROM table_name on the table used by the sp_spaceused command. You should run DBCC UPDATEUSAGE if SELECT COUNT(*) FROM table_name returns a different row count than the row count returned by sp_spaceused.
>
> Dropping and re-creating the table will also resolve any inaccuracies.

Example (update a single table)

```
dbcc updateusage ('pubs','employee')
```

Sample Output

```
use pubs
go
DBCC UPDATEUSAGE: sysindexes row updated for table 'employee' (index ID 1):
        USED pages: Changed from (4) to (5) pages.
        RSVD pages: Changed from (4) to (5) pages.
```

Example (update all tables in a database)

```
dbcc updateusage ('pubs')
```

Sample Output

```
DBCC UPDATEUSAGE: sysindexes row updated for table 'syscolumns' (index ID 2):
        USED pages: Changed from (2) to (8) pages.
        RSVD pages: Changed from (2) to (8) pages.
DBCC UPDATEUSAGE: sysindexes row updated for table 'authors' (index ID 1):
        USED pages: Changed from (6) to (5) pages.
        RSVD pages: Changed from (6) to (5) pages.
DBCC UPDATEUSAGE: sysindexes row updated for table 'publishers' (index ID 1):
        USED pages: Changed from (4) to (3) pages.
        RSVD pages: Changed from (4) to (3) pages.
DBCC UPDATEUSAGE: sysindexes row updated for table 'titles' (index ID 1):
        USED pages: Changed from (6) to (5) pages.
        RSVD pages: Changed from (6) to (5) pages.
DBCC UPDATEUSAGE: sysindexes row updated for table 'titleauthor' (index ID 1):
        USED pages: Changed from (8) to (7) pages.
        RSVD pages: Changed from (8) to (7) pages.
DBCC UPDATEUSAGE: sysindexes row updated for table 'stores' (index ID 1):
        USED pages: Changed from (4) to (3) pages.
        RSVD pages: Changed from (4) to (3) pages.
DBCC UPDATEUSAGE: sysindexes row updated for table 'sales' (index ID 1):
        USED pages: Changed from (6) to (5) pages.
        RSVD pages: Changed from (6) to (5) pages.
DBCC UPDATEUSAGE: sysindexes row updated for table 'roysched' (index ID 0):
        DATA pages: Changed from (1) to (2) pages.
DBCC UPDATEUSAGE: sysindexes row updated for table 'discounts' (index ID 0):
        DATA pages: Changed from (1) to (2) pages.
DBCC UPDATEUSAGE: sysindexes row updated for table 'jobs' (index ID 1):
        USED pages: Changed from (4) to (3) pages.
        RSVD pages: Changed from (4) to (3) pages.
DBCC UPDATEUSAGE: sysindexes row updated for table 'pub_info' (index ID 1):
        USED pages: Changed from (4) to (3) pages.
        RSVD pages: Changed from (4) to (3) pages.
DBCC UPDATEUSAGE: sysindexes row updated for table 'dtproperties' (index ID 1):
        USED pages: Changed from (4) to (3) pages.
        RSVD pages: Changed from (4) to (3) pages.
```

B

DBCC COMMANDS

DBCC COMMANDS TO RETURN PROCESS INFORMATION

The following two DBCC commands return process information.

Syntax

```
DBCC INPUTBUFFER (spid)
```

```
DBCC OUTPUTBUFFER (spid)
```

The INPUTBUFFER and OUTPUTBUFFER commands enable a DBA to monitor process activity. The INPUTBUFFER command displays the command last executed by a process; the OUTPUTBUFFER command displays the corresponding result. Unfortunately, the information returned from the OUTPUTBUFFER command can be difficult to understand because it is displayed in hexadecimal and ASCII text.

> **NOTE**
>
> The INPUTBUFFER command returns the first 255 characters of syntax. If you need additional information beyond 255 characters, use the SQL Server Profiler.

> **TIP**
>
> Use the system procedure sp_who to determine the spid of a process.
>
> Use the INPUTBUFFER command to diagnose blocking and resource utilization problems. When performance begins to suffer, look for data modification queries that do not contain WHERE clauses or SELECT queries that perform table scans on large tables.

Example

```
DBCC INPUTBUFFER(11)
```

Sample Output

```
EventType      Parameters EventInfo
-------------- ---------- ----------------------
Language Event 0          select * from authors
```

DBCC COMMANDS TO RETURN PERFORMANCE MONITOR STATISTICS

The following two DBCC commands return Performance Monitor statistics.

Syntax

```
DBCC PERFMON
```

```
DBCC SQLPERF (LOGSPACE)
```

The PERFMON command provides various statistics such as general performance, I/O statistics, and read-ahead statistics. When the SQLPERF command is used with LOGSPACE parameter, a listing of database log statistics will be displayed.

Example

```
DBCC PERFMON
```

Sample Output

```
Statistic                        Value
-----------------------------    -----------------------
Reads Outstanding                0.0
Writes Outstanding               0.0

(2 row(s) affected)

Statistic                        Value
-----------------------------    -----------------------
Cache Hit Ratio                  99.992455
Cache Flushes                    0.0
Free Page Scan (Avg)             0.0
Free Page Scan (Max)             0.0
Min Free Buffers                 331.0
Cache Size                       4362.0
Free Buffers                     46.0

(7 row(s) affected)

Statistic                        Value
-----------------------------    -----------------------
Network Reads                    16992.0
Network Writes                   12644.0
Command Queue Length             0.0
Max Command Queue Length         0.0
Worker Threads                   0.0
Max Worker Threads               0.0
Network Threads                  0.0
Max Network Threads              0.0
```

B

DBCC COMMANDS

```
(8 row(s) affected)

Statistic                        Value
-------------------------------  ------------------------
RA Pages Found in Cache          0.0
RA Pages Placed in Cache         0.0
RA Physical IO                   0.0
Used Slots                       0.0
```

Example

```
DBCC SQLPERF(LOGSPACE)
```

Sample Output

```
Database Name           Log Size (MB)          Log Space Used (%)          Status
--------------------    --------------------   ------------------------    ------
distribution            3.7421875              23.68215                         0
board                   4.9921875              14.152973                        0
sales                   1.9921875              18.995098                        0
pubs                    2.4921875              18.064262                        0
msdb                    1.9921875              42.965687                        0
tempdb                  1.9921875              33.740139                        0
model                   1.0                    33.513779                        0
master                  3.9921875              24.143835                        0
```

TRACE FLAG COMMANDS

The following commands are used to turn on and off trace flags and to check the status of a trace flag.

Syntax

```
DBCC TRACEOFF (trace# [,...N])

DBCC TRACEON (trace# [,...N])

DBCC TRACESTATUS (trace# [, trace#...])
```

> **TIP**
>
> The trace flag 1200 can be useful for tracking locking behavior. You must also turn on trace flag 3604 to echo trace information to the client workstation (see SQL Server's Books Online for a complete list of trace flags).

Example

```
use pubs
go
DBCC traceon(3604)
DBCC traceon(1200)
UPDATE authors
SET au_lname = 'smith'
WHERE au_id = '172-32-1176'
go
/* turn trace flags off */
DBCC traceoff(3604)
DBCC traceoff(1200)
go
```

Sample Output from DBCC Trace Flag 1200

```
DBCC execution completed. If DBCC printed error messages, contact your
system administrator.
Process 10 acquiring S lock on  DB: 1  result: OK
Process 10 acquiring S lock on KEY: 1:36:1 (924d4009008e) result: OK
Process 10 releasing lock on KEY: 1:36:1 (924d4009008e)
Process 10 acquiring S lock on KEY: 1:36:1 (924d4009008e) result: OK
Process 10 releasing lock on KEY: 1:36:1 (924d4009008e)
Process 10 acquiring S lock on KEY: 1:36:1 (e4120d0900e0) result: OK
Process 10 releasing lock on KEY: 1:36:1 (e4120d0900e0)
DBCC execution completed. If DBCC printed error messages, contact your
system administrator.
Process 10 releasing all locks @10ADEABC

Process 10 acquiring IX lock on TAB: 5:117575457 [] result: OK
Process 10 acquiring IX lock on UNK: 16454:858993459:1071854387:d result:
OK
Process 10 acquiring IU lock on PAG: 5:1:96 result: OK
Process 10 acquiring U lock on KEY: 5:117575457:1 (0afe9ce59186) result:
OK
Process 10 acquiring IX lock on PAG: 5:1:96 result: OK
Process 10 acquiring X lock on KEY: 5:117575457:1 (0afe9ce59186) result:
OK
Process 10 releasing lock reference on KEY: 5:117575457:1 (0afe9ce59186)
Process 10 acquiring X lock on KEY: 5:117575457:2 (dba93ee7e0d7) result:
OK
Process 10 releasing lock reference on KEY: 5:117575457:1 (0afe9ce59186)
Process 10 acquiring IX lock on PAG: 5:1:123 result: OK
Process 10 acquiring IX lock on PAG: 5:1:123 result: OK
Process 10 acquiring IIn-Null lock on KEY: 5:117575457:2 (d5968ed3b619)
result: OK
Process 10 acquiring X lock on KEY: 5:117575457:2 (f8ac17e7faf7) result:
OK
Process 10 releasing lock reference on KEY: 5:117575457:2 (dba93ee7e0d7)
Process 10 releasing lock reference on KEY: 5:117575457:2 (f8ac17e7faf7)
Process 10 releasing lock reference on PAG: 5:1:96
Process 10 releasing lock reference on TAB: 5:117575457 []
Process 10 releasing all locks @10ADEABC
```

B

DBCC COMMANDS

DATA CACHE COMMANDS

The PINTABLE command forces a table to remain in cache until it is removed from the cache with the UNPINTABLE command. You should be careful when pinning a table in the cache. By keeping a table constantly in the cache, you can improve data access performance. However, a large table can dominate the data cache. This could reduce the amount of data held in cache for other tables, thus hindering performance.

Syntax

```
DBCC PINTABLE (database_id, table_id)

DBCC UNPINTABLE (database_id, table_id)
```

Example

```
use pubs
```

> **NOTE**
>
> Tables that are forced into cache via the PINTABLE command will remain in cache after SQL Server is restarted. Use the UNPINTABLE command to remove the table from cache.

```
go
declare @id integer
select @id = object_id('authors')
/* 5 = pubs database */
DBCC PINTABLE (5,@id)
go
```

Sample Output

```
WARNING: Pinning tables should be carefully considered. If a pinned table
is larger or grows larger than the available data cache, the server may
need to be restarted and the table unpinned.
```

```
DBCC execution completed. If DBCC printed error messages, see your System
Administrator.
```

TRANSACTION COMMANDS

Use the OPENTRAN command for information about transactions.

Syntax

```
DBCC OPENTRAN ({database_name} ¦ {database_id}) [WITH TABLERESULTS]
[,NO_INFOMSGS]
```

The OPENTRAN command reports the oldest open transaction. An open transaction can stem from an aborted transaction, a runaway transaction, or poor transaction management. If necessary, you can terminate the offending transaction by issuing the KILL command with the process ID returned from the OPENTRAN command.

Example

```
DBCC OPENTRAN(pubs)
```

> **TIP**
>
> Long-running transactions can lead to contention for resources, which can lead to blocking. Use OPENTRAN to detect open transactions. If necessary, use the KILL command to cancel the transaction.

Sample Output

```
Transaction information for database 'pubs'.

Oldest active transaction:
    SPID (server process ID) : 10
    UID (user ID) : 1
    Name           : user_transaction
    LSN            : (7:202:1)
    Start time     : Oct 18 1998  2:42:34:480PM
```

OTHER DBCC COMMANDS

The following sections cover some of the other types of DBCC commands.

SHOW_STATISTICS

Syntax

```
DBCC SHOW_STATISTICS (table_name, index_name)
```

SHOW_STATISTICS displays index distribution information.

Example

```
use pubs
go
```

B

```
DBCC SHOW_STATISTICS ('authors','aunmind')
go
```

Sample Output

```
Statistics for INDEX 'aunmind'.
Updated                  Rows   Rows Sampled Steps  Density      Average key length
------------------------ -----  ------------ -----  -----------  ------------------
Sep 13 1998  3:16AM  23    23             23     3.9697543E-2 34.956524

(1 row(s) affected)

All density             Columns
----------------------  -------------------------------------------------
4.7258981E-2            au_lname
4.3478262E-2            au_lname, au_fname

(2 row(s) affected)

Steps
---------------------------------------
Bennet
Blotchet-Halls
Carson
DeFrance
del Castillo
Dull
Green
Greene
Gringlesby
Hunter
Karsen
Locksley
MacFeather
McBadden
O'Leary
Panteley
Ringer
Ringer
Smith
Straight
Stringer
White
Yokomoto

(23 row(s) affected)
```

SHRINKDATABASE

Syntax

```
DBCC SHRINKDATABASE (database_name [, target_percent]
  [, {NOTRUNCATE ¦ TRUNCATEONLY} ]  )
```

SHRINKDATABASE reduces the physical size of the database. A database can be reduced to a certain percentage of its current size by specifying a *target_percent* value (for example 80 will reduce the database by 20 percent of its current size). If a *target_percent* is not specified, the database will be reduced to the smallest size possible for the database. A database cannot be shrunk beyond the amount of storage space required to store data and other types of information.

> **NOTE**
>
> A database cannot be shrunk beyond the size specified for the model database.

Example

```
DBCC SHRINKDATABASE (sales)
```

Sample Output

```
DBCC execution completed. If DBCC printed error messages, see your System
Administrator.
```

SHRINKFILE

Syntax

```
DBCC SHRINKFILE
    (    {file_name ¦ file_id }
        {    [, target_size]
         ¦    [, {EMPTYFILE ¦ NOTRUNCATE ¦ TRUNCATEONLY}]
        }
    )
```

SHRINKFILE reduces the physical size of data file. A data file can be reduced to a certain size by specifying a *target_size* value. If a *target_size* is not specified, the data file will be reduced to the smallest size possible for the data file. A data file cannot be shrunk beyond the amount of storage space required to store data and other types of information.

Example

```
use pubs
go
```

B

DBCC
COMMANDS

```
/* shrink log file */
dbcc shrinkfile(pubs_log)
go
```

Sample Output

DbId	FileId	CurrentSize	MinimumSize	UsedPages	EstimatedPages
5	2	96	63	96	56

USEROPTIONS

Syntax

```
DBCC USEROPTIONS
```

The USEROPTIONS command displays the status of SET commands for the current session.

Example

```
DBCC USEROPTIONS
```

Sample Output

Set Option	Value
textsize	64512
language	us_english
dateformat	mdy
datefirst	7
ansi_null_dflt_on	SET
ansi_warnings	SET
ansi_padding	SET
ansi_nulls	SET

DBCC *dllname* (FREE)

Syntax

```
DBCC dllname (FREE)
```

This command removes a DLL (dynamic link library) from memory.

Example

```
DBCC mydll (FREE)
```

SQL Server Resources

by Orryn Sledge

Tables C.1 and C.2 contain listings of popular SQL Server Web sites and newsgroups.

TABLE C.1   SQL SERVER WEB SITES

Web Site	Web Site Name	Notes
`http://www.inquiry.com/ techtips/thesqlpro/`	Ask the SQL Server Pro!	Provides answers to frequently asked questions and allows users to post new questions.
`http://www.acedb.com/ pghssug/`	Pittsburgh SQL Server User Group	Provides tips and links to other SQL Server Web sites.
`http://www.winntmag.com/ sql/index.html`	WIN NT Magazine SQL FAQ	Contains a forum and articles on SQL Server.
`http://home.gvi.net/ ~spyder/sqlserver.html`	Spider SQL Server Links	Contains a listing of links to SQL Server sites.
`http://www.swynk.com`	Swynk BackOffice Resource	SQL Server FAQ and comprehensive information on other BackOffice products.
`http://www.pinpub.com/ sqlpro/home.htm`	SQL Server Professional Magazine	Online listing of the SQL Server Professional Magazine.
`http://www.bhs.com/ ntwebsites`	Beverly Hills NT Resource Center	Lots of information on NT and BackOffice.
`http://www.sqlserver.com`	SQL Server Online	Contains articles, reviews, tips, and more.
`http://www.microsoft.com/ sql`	Microsoft's SQL Server Web site	This is listed just in case you forgot the location! :)

TABLE C.2   SQL SERVER NEWSGROUPS SITES

SQL Server Newsgroups*
`news://msnews.microsoft.com/microsoft.public.sqlserver.server`
`news://msnews.microsoft.com/microsoft.public.sqlserver.connect`
`news://msnews.microsoft.com/microsoft.public.sqlserver.odbc`
`news://msnews.microsoft.com/microsoft.public.sqlserver.programming`
`news://msnews.microsoft.com/microsoft.public.sqlserver.replication`
`news://msnews.microsoft.com/microsoft.public.sqlserver.datawarehouse`
`news://msnews.microsoft.com/microsoft.public.sqlserver.clients`

*Note the newsgroups listed above can be accessed through the following link:
http://backoffice.microsoft.com/bbs/

What's on the CD-ROM

by Mark Spenik

IN THIS APPENDIX

The following applications have been included on the CD-ROM that accompanies this book to help you with your database administration tasks:

- The SQL Server DBA Assistant
- SQL Scripts

THE SQL SERVER DBA ASSISTANT

The SQL Server DBA Assistant is an application written in 32-bit Visual Basic 6.0. Using the SQL Server Assistant, you can perform the following tasks:

- Populate a combo box with database names
- Allow exporting of data using graphical BCP
- Perform table maintenance functions, including recompiling references, updating statistics, checking identity column values, and using the DBCC CheckTable command

The SQL Server DBA Assistant source code is included on the CD-ROM so that you can make your own modifications and enhancements to the application.

> **NOTE**
>
> The code in the application is discussed in detail in Chapter 27, "Using SQL-DMO (Distributed Management Objects)."

Following are the prerequisites for using the SQL Server DBA Assistant:

- You must be running Windows NT 4.0 or Windows 95/98
- You must have the following files (included with the SQL Server Client Utilities Installation):

SQLDMO.HLP   SQL-DMO help files, including object hierarchy

SQLDMO.DLL   In-process SQL-DMO server

SQLDMO.rll   Local resource file (Note: extension varies)

Installing SQL Server DBA Assistant

To install the SQL Server DBA Assistant, run the executable SETUP.EXE file included on the CD-ROM.

Using SQL Server DBA Assistant

Follow these steps to use the SQL Server DBA Assistant:

1. To start the SQL Server DBA Assistant, run the executable (SAMSDBA.EXE). The Logon dialog box appears (see Figure D.1).

FIGURE D.1

The SQL Server DBA Assistant Logon dialog box.

2. Enter the name of the SQL Server to which you want to log on.

3. Enter the login ID and the password and then click the Logon button. An attempt is made to connect to the specified SQL Server. If the logon is successful, a splash screen appears, followed by the SQL Server DBA dialog box with the Table Maintenance tab.

   To perform table maintenance, click the Table Maintenance tab (see Figure D.2).

FIGURE D.2

The Table Maintenance tab in the SQL Server DBA Assistant dialog box.

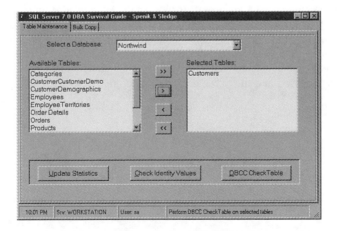

4. Select a database from the combo box. To select a table, click the table name in the left list box. To move a table from the Available Tables list box to the Selected Tables list box, click the > button. Click the < button to move the selected table from the Selected Tables list box to the Available Tables list box. Click the >> or << button to move all the tables.

5. To perform table maintenance, click the appropriate command button. The selected function is performed on all the selected tables. Any error messages or results returned from SQL Server are displayed.

6. To export data, click the Bulk Copy tab (see Figure D.3).

FIGURE D.3

The Bulk Copy tab in the SQL Server DBA Assistant dialog box.

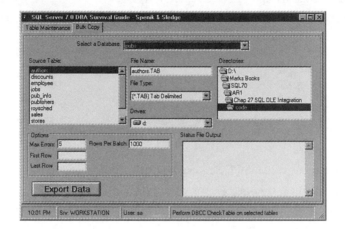

7. Select a database from the Select a Database combo box.

8. Select the table you want to export data from using the Source Table list box.

9. Select the file export file format from the File Type drop-down list box and specify the name of the file to which you want to export the data. (Use the Directories pane to specify the path as necessary.)

10. Click the Export Data button to export the data to the specified file. The selected table is exported and the process is complete.

INDEX

Query response graph, 933
Query run-time table, 933
query wait configuration
  parameter, 529, 536, 551
Question Builder object
  model, 405
Quit the Job Reporting
  Failure step action, 821
Quit the Job Reporting
  Success step action, 821
quitting
  cursors, 706
  Distributed Transaction
    Coordinator (MSDTC), 55,
    59
  Microsoft Search, 55, 59
  SQL Server, 55, 59, 121, 126,
    144, 294
  SQL Server Agent, 55, 59
  traces, 608
Quoted Identifier option, 195

R

RA cache hit limit configura-
  tion options, 530
RA cache miss limit configu-
  ration options, 530
RA delay configuration
  options, 530
RA pre-fetches configuration
  options, 530
RA slots per thread configu-
  ration options, 530
RA worker threads configu-
  ration options, 530
RA. *See* Asynchronous Read
  Ahead
RAID. *See* Redundant Array
  of Inexpensive Disks
RAISERROR statement,
  359-360, 696
RAS connections, replicating
  via, 491
RDBMS. *See* Relational
  Database Management
  System
re-creating
  indexes, 594
  publications with scripts, 489

READ COMMITTED transac-
  tion isolation level,
  650-651, 654
READ ONLY cursor, 704
Read Only option, 188
READ ONLY statement, 703
read statements, 636
READ UNCOMMITTED trans-
  action isolation level,
  650-651, 654
read-ahead logic, 503
read-ahead reads measure-
  ment, 614
read-only cursors, syntax, 704
reading
  output, Database Consistency
    Checker (DBCC) commands,
    956
  showplans, 617-620
  transaction logs, 211
  values, log files, 518
reads, 630, 651
reattaching database files,
  289
Rebuild Master Database
  Utility, 287-288
rebuilding
  indexes, DBREINDEX state-
    ment, 587
  master databases, 287-296
  Registry entries, 139
RecalcSpaceUsage method,
  740
receiving email, 386-387
recompiling stored proce-
  dures, 718
Reconfigure command, 536
recording configuration information, 805-807
records
  inspecting, lock manager, 654
  monitoring number of, 809
records. *See* rows
recovery
  creating plans, 424
  data, database administrator's
    role, 29
  databases, 261, 278-296
  files, 261
  testing strategies, 808
RECOVERY command, 301
Recovery Completion State
  Frame option, 286

recovery conn timeout configuration options, 530
recovery flags configuration
  options, 530
recovery interval configuration parameter, 536, 551
Recursive Triggers option,
  189
reducing
  database size, 198
  log size, 198
  network traffic, stored proce-
    dures, 720
  time
    creating clustered indexes,
    325
    restore, 283
redundancy, 558, 871
Redundant Array of
  Inexpensive Disks (RAID)
  benefits of, 86
  described, 184-186
  disk striping, 502
REFERENCE statement, 72
reference tables, 477
referencing
  linked servers, 392-393
  views, queries, 623
referential integrity, enforcing triggers, 72
Refresh data option, 941
refreshing
  data, 869-870
  tables, snapshot replication,
    465
registering
  data sources as subscribing
    servers, 435-436
  servers, SQL Server Enterprise
    Manager, 146-149
Registry
  backing up, 811
  editing, 56-57
  entries, rebuilding, 139
  keys, SQL Server 7.0, 57
  viewing, 56-57
regrebld, 139
REINDEX command, 594
Relational Database
  Management System
  (RDBMS), 10, 17-20
relational databases, 877,
  943

X-Z

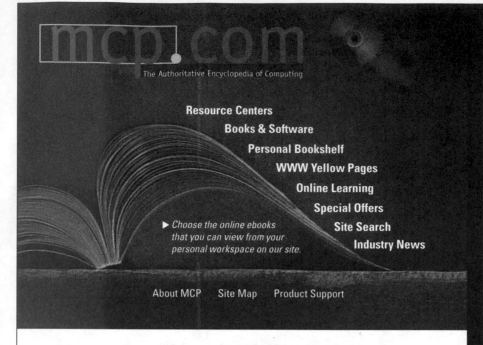

Microsoft® SQL Server 7.0

DBA SURVIVAL GUIDE

Roger Jennings Database Workshop: Microsoft Transaction Server 2.0
Steven Gray and Rick Lievano
ISBN: 0-672-31130-5
$39.99 USA / $57.95 CAN

Other Titles

Microsoft SQL Server 7.0 Unleashed
Greg Mable, et al.
ISBN: 0-672-31227-1
$49.99 USA / $71.95 CAN

Microsoft SQL Server 7.0 Programming Unleashed
John Papa, et al.
ISBN: 0-672-31293-X
$49.99 USA / $71.95 CAN

Building Enterprise Solutions with Visual Studio 6
G.A. Sullivan
ISBN: 0-672-31489-4
$49.99 USA / $71.95 CAN

Microsoft Exchange Server 5 Unleashed
Greg Todd, et al.
ISBN: 0-672-31034-1
$59.99 USA / $85.95 CAN

Windows NT 4 Server Unleashed
Jason Garms
ISBN: 0-672-31249-2
$49.99 USA / $71.95 CAN

Visual Basic 6 Unleashed
Rob Thayer, et al.
ISBN: 0-672-31309-X
$39.99 USA / $57.95 CAN

Programming Windows 98/NT
Viktor Toth
ISBN: 0-672-31353-7
$49.99 USA / $71.95 CAN

Roger Jennings' Database Developer's Guide with Visual Basic 6
Roger Jennings
ISBN: 0-672-31063-5
$59.99 USA / $85.95 CAN

Windows NT Troubleshooting and Configuration
Robert Reinstein, et al.
ISBN: 0-672-30941-6
$59.99 USA / $85.95 CAN

SAMS

www.samspublishing.com

All prices are subject to change.

WHAT'S ON THE CD-ROM

WHAT'S ON THE DISC

The companion CD-ROM contains many useful third-party software, plus two applications provided by the authors.

WINDOWS 95 INSTALLATION INSTRUCTIONS

1. Insert the CD-ROM disc into your CD-ROM drive.
2. From the Windows 95 desktop, double-click the My Computer icon.
3. Double-click the icon representing your CD-ROM drive.
4. Double-click the icon titled DBASETUP.EXE to run the installation program.
5. Installation creates a program group named "DBA Survival Guide." This group will contain icons to browse the CD-ROM.

> **NOTE**
>
> If Windows 95 is installed on your computer, and you have the AutoPlay feature enabled, the SETUP.EXE program starts automatically whenever you insert the disc into your CD-ROM drive.

WINDOWS NT INSTALLATION INSTRUCTIONS

1. Insert the CD-ROM disc into your CD-ROM drive.

2. From File Manager or Program Manager, choose Run from the File menu.

3. Type `<drive>\DBASETUP.EXE` and press Enter, where `<drive>` corresponds to the drive letter of your CD-ROM. For example, if your CD-ROM is drive D:, type `D:\DBASETUP.EXE` and press Enter.

4. Installation creates a program group named "DBA Survival Guide." This group will contain icons to browse the CD-ROM.

LICENSING AGREEMENT

By opening this package, you are agreeing to be bound by the following agreement:

Some of the software included with this product may be copyrighted, in which case all rights are reserved by the respective copyright holder. You are licensed to use software copyrighted by the Publisher and its licensors on a single computer. You may copy and/or modify the software as needed to facilitate your use of it on a single computer. Making copies of the software for any other purpose is a violation of the United States copyright laws.

This software is sold as is without warranty of any kind, either expressed or implied, including but not limited to the implied warranties of merchantability and fitness for a particular purpose. Neither the publisher nor its dealers or distributors assumes any liability for any alleged or actual damages arising from the use of this program. (Some states do not allow for the exclusion of implied warranties, so the exclusion may not apply to you.)